# MANIFEST DESTINY

## A STUDY OF NATIONALIST EXPANSIONISM IN AMERICAN HISTORY



AMS PRESS
NEW YORK

Professor Albert K. Weinberg was born in Baltimore, Maryland, and studied at The Johns Hopkins University. He was Professor of American History at Johns Hopkins until his retirement several years ago.

THE WALTER HINES PAGE SCHOOL OF INTERNATIONAL RELATIONS
THE JOHNS HOPKINS UNIVERSITY

# MANIFEST DESTINY

## A STUDY OF NATIONALIST EXPANSIONISM IN AMERICAN HISTORY

ALBERT K. WEINBERG
*Fellow of the Page School
and Lecturer in Political Science
in The Johns Hopkins University*



BALTIMORE
THE JOHNS HOPKINS PRESS
1935

**Library of Congress Cataloging in Publication Data**

Weinberg, Albert Katz.
Manifest destiny.

Reprint of the 1935 ed. published by the Johns Hopkins Press, Baltimore.
Includes bibliographical references.
1. United States—Territorial expansion.
2. Political science—United States—History.
I. Title.
E179.5.W45 1979 327'.11'0973 75-41293
ISBN 0-404-14706-2

First AMS edition published in 1979.

Reprinted from the edition of 1935, Baltimore, from an original in the collections of the University of Chicago Library. [Trim size of the original has been slightly altered in this edition. Original trim size: 13.4 × 20.3 cm. Text area of the original has been maintained.]

MANUFACTURED
IN THE UNITED STATES OF AMERICA

To

MY WIFE

## PREFACE

The writer takes pleasure in acknowledging the assistance which he has received in the preparation of this work. He is greatly indebted to Professor Arthur O. Lovejoy, of The Johns Hopkins University, not merely for criticism of his manuscript but also for past instruction which largely stimulated this application of methods of ideological analysis to political attitudes. He is also deeply in debt to Professor Kent Roberts Greenfield and Associate Professor William Stull Holt, of the Department of History, The Johns Hopkins University, for abundant encouragement, advice, and criticism. Mr. James Bunyan has given generously of his time and knowledge in editing the manuscript. The writer's wife has been an indispensable helper in all stages of the work.

Valuable assistance was received from members of the Page School of International Relations, including Professor Frederick Sherwood Dunn, Professor Gilbert Chinard, and Dr. Ernest B. Price. It is only fair to state, however, that this assistance was directed toward the more effective development of the writer's own ideas rather than toward the presentation of views common to the members of an institution. A study having to do with highly controversial issues of political history and morals demands treatment from an individual point of view; thus the errors or prejudices which may be in the following pages are the author's own. This book owes its existence fundamentally to the fact that the Page School not merely permits such individualism in research but apparently encourages investigators who wander somewhat from the most beaten tracks of study in order to attempt — what is as intriguing as it is precarious — exploration of the complex motives of international behavior.

Albert K. Weinberg

# FOREWORD

The most tantalizing problems faced by students of international relations are those which revolve around the question of motivation in national action. The rôle of ideas and attitudes in determining the behavior of nations is an obtrusive factor in every international situation, yet in the present state of our knowledge this factor is shrouded in obscurity. The importance of the subject has long been recognized, but effective methods of analysis and tools of inquiry for dealing with it have not been adequately developed. The result has been that we have tended either to slight the subject or else to approach it primarily from a moral viewpoint, without, however, subjecting to careful critical analysis the logical basis of our moral judgments.

Consider, for example, the pervasive phenomenon called nationalism. We seek to " explain " the course of international events in terms of this complex pattern of ideas, feelings, dogmas, emotional drives, moral attitudes and what not, yet our explanations are often mere verbal cloaks to cover up our lack of comprehension of the elements involved. Thus to attribute the action of a nation or people in a specific situation to the " spirit of nationalism " may temporarily satisfy our desire for a causal explanation, but in reality it does little more than give a name to a complex set of variables that remain as far removed from our understanding as before. Much the same thing may be said in regard to our explanations of events in terms of " imperialism," " militarism," " isolationism " and other characteristic ideologies that appear as determinants of national action.

To this important problem of the ideological factor in international behavior, Dr. Weinberg now makes a striking contribution. The ideology of expansionism, which he has selected as the subject of his inquiry, is one that throws into peculiarly strong relief the operation of moral ideas in relation to national action. He has subjected to a new and fertile type of analysis the various manifestations of this ideology that have appeared in the course of the growth of the United States from an infant republic occupying the seaboard of a little-known continent to a vast world power with oversea possessions. The history of the moral justifications that have accompanied this development is an illuminating study of the evolution of American nationalism. At the same time it gives us insight into the general problem of the growth of ideologies and their relation to national action, and adds to our understanding of the behavior of men as members of a political body. It likewise reveals the extensive confusion of ideas and of moral values that often lies at the basis of national conduct.

As the period of American expansion recedes in time and takes on perspective, it stands revealed as an amazing phase of our national development. The mere physical extent of the territory acquired is impressive enough, but the really astonishing thing is the range of ideas and moral doctrines that have been advanced in justification of this extension of the national domain at the expense of other—and usually weaker—peoples. Each phase of this movement has developed its own set of doctrines that have caused territorial aggrandizement to appear either as the inevitable working of Providence or as the dictate of the highest international morality. While the development of each of these doctrines makes a fascinating story in itself, the cumulative force of the whole is far more than the sum of its parts taken separately. One is struck with the constantly recurring tendency to see the pursuit of national self-interest as a manifestation of international altruism. One likewise finds many revealing parallels between the doctrines associated with past American expansion and those which we now condemn as morally indefensible when advanced by other nations in justification of their own steps toward territorial enlargement.

Dr. Weinberg does well to caution against the easy cynicism that is apt to follow upon superficial observation of the close connection between national self-interest and moral ideology. There is little ground for the dogmatic generalization that, because of this association, the ideological justification for expansion is necessarily hypocritical or insincere. The evidence points rather in the other direction. While such justification may, to a later observer, appear as mere rationalization of action readily accounted for in terms of self-interest, the moral problem is complicated by the fact that such rationalization is often clearly unconscious. As Dr. Weinberg points out, the real problem lies rather in the peculiarly inverted character of international morality which causes altruism to appear in the form, not of self-sacrifice, but of self-aggrandizement.

It becomes clear that the moral issues involved in the question of national expansion are far more complex than has been commonly supposed. This is illustrated by what happens to the simple idea of growth when carried over from the individual to the national sphere. In itself, the idea of growth is assuredly not morally reprehensible; on the contrary we customarily look upon it with high favor, as an essential attribute of life itself. But in circumstances where the growth of one individual or unit can be carried out only at the expense of other individuals or units, the moral issue becomes highly complex. Such is the case in the international community, where the habitable portions of the earth's surface have already been preempted, with no interstices between the units. Here the growth of one member of the community almost inevitably means the enforced contraction of another. Under such circumstances, our customary moral attitudes become highly dubious guides to national policy.

Again, to the extent that nationalism means the submersion of the selfish strivings of the individual in favor of the collective effort to advance the good of the national community as a whole, it may receive ready moral approval as an essential condition for social cohesion. Yet to the extent that this collective striving seeks external fulfilment at the expense of other communities, it may in fact be a socially disruptive force of great power.

These are but samples of the many moral problems that issue from the urge toward national expansion in the community of nations as it is at present constituted. Thinking by analogy from the plane of individual conduct to that of international action is almost certain to lead to error. Those who have criticized on moral grounds the expansionist activities of nations have not, as a rule, taken any greater pains to examine the logical basis of their judgments than have those who have argued in favor of expansion. Indeed, one of the significant results of the present study is the revelation that, while the ideology of the expansionists has often defeated itself through stark logical inconsistency, the reasoning of the anti-imperialists has not fared much better. Critical appraisal of expansionist activities, if it is to be effective, must proceed on the basis of a very much more acute analysis of the moral values involved than has heretofore been thought necessary.

Only those who have been closely associated with the author during the conduct of his investigation can know the immense amount of painstaking labor that has gone into the amassing of his material and into the equally arduous task of selection, arrangement and composition. The Page School is happy to have a part in presenting this study to the public, and hopes that it will point the way to many similar inquiries into the ideologies that have accompanied national action in international relations.

FREDERICK S. DUNN

THE WALTER HINES PAGE SCHOOL
OF INTERNATIONAL RELATIONS

# CONTENTS

# INTRODUCTION

> To understand in the best sense, it is necessary not only to recognize the interests of a nation, but to enter as well into its feelings; tracing them where possible to the historic origin which once occasioned, and may still account for them. Such understanding is essential to just appreciation. The sentiment of a people is the most energetic element in national action. Even when material interests are the original exciting cause, it is the sentiment to which they give rise, the moral tone which emotion takes, that constitutes the greater force. Whatever individual rulers may do, masses of men are aroused to effective action—other than spasmodic—only by the sense of wrong done, or of right to be vindicated. For this reason governments are careful to obtain for their contentions an aspect of right which will keep their people at their backs.
>
> ALFRED THAYER MAHAN, *The Interest of America in International Conditions,* pp. 167-68.

> Well, then, the books are something like our books, only the words go the wrong way . . .
>
> LEWIS CARROLL, *Through the Looking-Glass,* pp. 8-9.

"This great pressure of a people moving always to new frontiers, in search of new lands, new power, the full freedom of a virgin world, has ruled our course and formed our policies like a Fate."[1] In this day, when America's foreign policies are or seem to us those of the "good neighbor," it may appear strange that the foregoing words of Woodrow Wilson are applicable to American history from its beginning until a relatively recent past. It may seem even more strange that one purpose of an expansionism often imperialistic was to make "every foot of this land . . . the home of free, self-governed people,"[2] as Wilson also said. And it may well appear passing strange that an expansion movement so bound up with spontaneous human will was viewed as "plain destiny"[3]—words used by Wilson in 1902 as a variant of a traditional phrase. "Manifest destiny," the once honored expansionist slogan, expressed a dogma of supreme self-assurance and ambition—that America's incorporation of all adjacent lands was the virtually inevitable fulfilment of a moral mission delegated to the nation by Providence itself.

Through such works as the present these attitudes of a partially estranged past may find comprehension if not appreciation. This is not a diplomatic history of American expansion but a study in the history of American "expansionism," the inner springs of which the diplomatic history can consider only briefly. American expansionism is viewed here as an "ism" or ideology, exemplified but by no means exhausted by the ideas of manifest destiny. The ideology of American expansion is its motley body of justificatory doctrines. It comprises metaphysical dogmas of a providential mission and quasi-scientific "laws" of national development, conceptions of national right and ideals of social duty, legal rationalizations and appeals to "the higher law," aims of extending freedom and designs of extending benevolent absolutism. The intensive study of the nature and history of this ideology demands an extreme selectiveness which should not be confused with simplification of expansionist motivation. Taking the liberties necessary to an analytic history of ideas, this work considers separately the leading expansionist doctrines in the order in which successive annexationist movements brought each into focus, and with special reference to the issue or period in which it figured as chief, even if by no means sole, ideological determinant.

Though history requires no justification beyond its intrinsic interest, it can be pointed out that such an historical enterprise bears upon present and enduring problems in the interpretation of nationalist attitudes. In one aspect it is a study in the genealogy of American nationalism, the inheritor of both the expansionist's virtues and faults. It is also an investigation of historical specimens of expansionist ideas still entertained today by nations whose ambitions the United States now finds morally incomprehensible. But the history of expansionist ideology is perhaps of chief interest in its exemplification of the ideas which enable governments right, wrong, or indifferent, to "keep their people at their backs." In the rationalizations of the expansionist one best gains insight into that queerly functioning entity which is the despair of the social philosopher and yet his only hope — the moral consciousness of man as citizen.

To be sure, Admiral Mahan's thesis that moral sentiment profoundly influences national behavior may at first thought seem ironical to those who hold that certain national policies tend to be morally questionable if not unquestionably immoral. Far from accepting Mahan's view, some of the first students of imperialism explained it in a manner which reflected their indignation at its injustices and exploitations. For example, J. A. Hobson wrote in 1902:

> Imperialism is a depraved choice of national life, imposed by self-seeking interests which appeal to the lusts of quantitative acquisitiveness and of forceful domination surviving in a nation from early centuries of animal struggle for existence.[4]

Today, however, most investigators of national behavior recognize that, as Montesquieu long ago observed in answering Hobbes, the desire for dominion is highly complex — too complex to be explained in language of moral indignation. One element in expansionism appears to be the moral factor — a desire either for what Adam Smith calls praiseworthiness or merely for freedom from blame. It is or should be a truism that moral ideology influences not merely individual experience, but also, largely by virtue of the mechanism which Mr. Clutton-Brock describes as the pooling of self-esteem,[5] social experience. Expansion is no exception to the thesis of Dr. Albert Shaw that "the power and persistence of ideas lie at the base of all historical movements."[6] Indeed, it is moral self-assurance which largely explains the expansionist's very delinquencies. The great influence which some investigators attribute to moral ideology is reflected in Professor Reeves's generalization about American expansion:

> No one fact, either economic, or social, or even political, can account for it. Perhaps a national idealism—call it manifest destiny or what you will—has had more to do with this expansion movement than anything else.[7]

Even Professor Beard, disposed toward a realistic recognition of the force of self-interest, admits with respect not only to expansionism but to national policy in general that moral obligation, "whether viewed as a covering ideology or as an independent political philosophy . . . constitutes a psychological force in determining the course of external relations." [8]

As yet, however, one hears much more of the effect of the nationalist's moral ideology than of its nature. In no adequate degree, as Dr. Beard recognizes,[9] has a systematic and historically documented study been made of either the logical content of this ideology or its meaning in relation to the total pattern of motivation. The fact that such a study requires a special technique is only one of the causes of the neglect in which it still lies. At its base lie an oversimplified conception of the nature of international morality and a resultant failure to see the curious problem that it presents.

This oversimplification appears in two types. One is illustrated by the postulate of Edmund Burke that the principles of true politics are but those of individual morals enlarged. Such a view, a derivation from early jurists of the natural law school, was expressed by Olphe-Galliard more sharply when he said that "in the formulation of the moral law no distinction has been established between the private individual and the citizen, between the individual and the sum of individuals who compose the nation; and the law of love, enunciated by Christ, applies to peoples just as to individuals." [10] The other view, as old at least as Machiavelli, is that international morality is not and should not be identical with individual morality but is antithetic to it in idealizing self-aggrandizement, or at least what Treitschke calls "self-maintenance." It was this theory which prompted Cavour's frank remark: "If we did for ourselves what we do for our country, what rascals we should all be."

These two theories, while antithetic in conclusion, are alike in reducing international morality to a principle which, whether it be egoism or altruism, is familiar in individual experience. But the truth seems to be that, among the general run of men, even if not among Machiavellis or consistent Christians, international morality is as different from anything in individual experience as is the world portrayed by that most profoundly mad of books, *Through the Looking-Glass.*

Do we not all suspect, indeed, that Carroll had somewhat in mind the actual phenomena of nationalism in writing of the proud Red Queen, the chivalrous but awkward White Knight, the queer Messengers with "Anglo-Saxon attitudes," Humpty Dumpty's definition of glory as "a nice knockdown argument," and the furious combat of Tweedledum and Tweedledee over an old rattle. At any rate, the difference between individual and international morality is like nothing so much as the difference between Alice's every-day world and the world discovered when she penetrated the looking-glass. What was the salient characteristic which distinguished Looking-Glass House from the every-day world? It was, we all remember, that while the familiar objects and concepts of the every-day world were existent in this fanciful house, they all behaved in a way which is the delightful inverse of the logic of the real world. To some degree the precocious Alice had anticipated this when, with the inverting effect of the looking-glass in mind, she prophesied that though the books would be something like our books their words would go the wrong way. Nevertheless it was with constant wonderment that she found this inversion consistently carried out in the behavior and conversation of all the living characters — even to Tweedledee's amazing instance of what he pleased to call logic.

Now in the romantic world of nationalism the books of morality are something like those of individual morality in that they have approximately the same major premises. At least since national policy came to depend on democratic support, the premises of national morality have consisted predominantly of rights and ideals which are determined negatively or positively by the concept of international good. But the really important point in morality is less the general premise than the specific conclusion drawn from it. In individual morality, imperfect as is its common application, premises lead most often to a conclusion dictating self-restraint or even self-sacrifice; as Professor Hocking has said in *The Spirit of World Politics*, individual morality is differentiated by such subordination of self-interest to principle as "means in effect some sort or degree of self-sacrifice."[11] But in international morality these premises ordinarily go the wrong way: they lead not to the conclusion of self-sacrifice but to the conclusion of self-aggrandizement.

*Mirabile dictu*, the altruism of international morality leads to an aggrandizement which usually requires the contraction of some other party. The inverted character of international morality is most striking in the ideology supporting territorial expansion. It is just as true that national policies in general, though showing various degrees of prudent moderation, tend to be self-aggrandizing in some sense. This is not to say as does Ludwig Gumplowicz that "egotism is the only directive of the actions of states and peoples." [12] Rather is it to say that moral ideology as directive is altruistic in premise and selfish in conclusion. Lewis Carroll does not tell what ideology caused the Red Queen to say to the bewildered Alice: "I don't know what you mean by *your* way; all the ways about here belong to *me*." But if this queen was a typical nationalist, her moral justification of this pretentious claim was certainly the fulfilment of the Red Queen's Burden or some other lofty ideal commended by a Kipling poet laureate.

Let us not be infected by the spirit of our fantastic analogue to the point of exaggeration. The foregoing is no more than the least false generalization which is possible in a sphere where no generalization can be true. May this admission of the impossibility of generalization serve as a footnote to every future expression such as "*the* nationalist," "*the* expansionist," "*the* American" — rhetorical liberties which indicate only the tentative conception of predominant or common types and not a belief in the empirical reality of hypostasizations.

But the tendency to base the way of national self-interest on the premise of international altruism is sufficiently common to form perhaps the most obtrusive aspect of international morality. Its commonness explains the fact that there have been the two conflicting theories of international morality; for one of them is correct with respect to the nationalist's ordinary premises and the other with respect to his usual conclusions. However, the theory which reconciles these conflicting impressions is also one which increases the oddness of international morality to the point of a paradox. For from the viewpoint of individual morality, the self-aggrandizing nationalist appears to pursue his objective by following the paradoxical advice of the Rose of Looking-Glass House — to go away from it.

Comprehension of the nationalist's inversion of moral method is the more difficult because of two considerations. The first is that, whereas Alice actually reached the Red Queen by following the Rose's strange direction, the nationalist arrives very seldom at his professed social ideals. His moral failures prompted Joseph Chamberlain to define imperialism as an impotence to maintain good political relationships. On the other hand, the nationalist does arrive very frequently at the goal of self-interest. But the second source of perplexity is the apparent impossibility of concluding in the light of average human nature that the ordinary nationalist is intent upon self-interest alone. The very charge that "the bright cloak of *Intellectual Imperialism* serves to cover the sordid calculations of Economic Imperialism"[13] testifies to a public conscience from which such calculations require concealment. Even the "sincerity in folly" of our rulers was admitted by the ordinarily cynical Fisher Ames.[14]

To understand this inverted ideology one can do nothing else than enter into the wonderland of nationalism for laborious but entertaining exploration. In immediate experience, indeed, this land is seldom entered without the partial logical paralysis of the dreamer. But in history there is a greater possibility of attaining dispassionate objectivity. Moreover, it is history which, despite what Carroll's Mouse tells us of its fearful dryness, shows nationalist ideology in relation to the very human factors which determine it.

The explanation of nationalist ideology necessitates attention not only to moral principles but also to the factors causing a strange refraction as principles pass to the medium beyond the looking-glass. National experience contains peculiar factors which, through their effect upon the nationalist's minor premises, are capable of making the conclusions of his moral syllogism as extraordinary as Humpty Dumpty's perversions of language. It contains interests requiring a peculiar instrumental logic, sentiments intense enough to destroy moral objectivity, national traditions encouraging conformity rather than independent thinking, and loose habits of thought permitting easy self-deception. The peculiar feature perhaps most illuminative of international morality is a nationalist philosophy that, in contrast with the equalitarian assumptions of individual moral experience, involves the same illusion of royalty or preeminence which made Alice and her fellow creatures of the Looking-Glass House behave with perverse individualism. This is the philosophy of manifest destiny — in essence the doctrine that one nation has a preeminent social worth, a distinctively lofty mission, and consequently unique rights in the application of moral principles.

The historian's approach to moral doctrines is, of course, different from that of the abstract moralist. The historian is not given to the passing of moral judgment, involving a conflict of ultimate values which is perhaps as indecisive as the conflict between Tweedledum and Tweedledee. On the other hand, he can attempt the more fruitful task of internal criticism and inquire concerning the consistency or inconsistency of one doctrine with another, of premise with conclusion, and of assumed fact with discoverable fact. This type of examination, wherein the expansionist is judged in the light of his own rather than someone else's values, may well reveal that his most forceful critic is expansionist ideology itself.

American history is an excellent laboratory for the study of expansionist ideology, but not because its expansionism calls for sharper moral criticism than does that of other countries. On the contrary, it is excellent because — aside from other reasons, such as the ingenuousness and loquacity of democracy — the expansion of the United States was of a character which can be viewed with minimal moralistic prepossession. In the pages of its history there is relatively little of the tragedy which, though it induces reformist emotion, interferes with correct interpretation of human motives. Although Filipinos and Haitians can well deny that " the shadow of a sigh " never " trembles " through the story, it is perhaps the most cheerful record of such perilous ambitions that one can find. The capital executions have been only occasional and the deliberate orders " Off with his head " rarer still. In any event, the entire land-hungry assemblage disappeared eventually from the national scene just as Alice's banqueters flew off into air. The traditional demands for " ali the ways " on the continent, or for any lesser aggrandizement, seem as far removed from our present reality as does the comedy of a dream. Whether through the assumed special Providence or merely undeserved good luck, destiny seems to have eventuated not badly.

Without its tragic mask the nationalist spirit may seem a manifestation of the romanticism which turns to a looking-glass world to find all the meanings of life reflected in perspective more alluring than the stale, flat, and unprofitable routine of individual experience. For the nationalist, though not without his elements of reasonableness, takes for his very object of devotion the transcendental fiction which he calls the nation. The full enjoyment of this fiction demands not merely the grandiose delusions of manifest destiny but the still more delusory postulate that morals and the wish-fulfilments of nationalism usually converge. Thus the tragedy into which the nationalist spirit so frequently leads is apparently no part of its purpose or foresight. Tragedy comes to the nationalist because the setting of *his* kingdom of fantastic ideas is unfortunately the world of reality.

# CHAPTER I

## NATURAL RIGHT

The century of the American Revolution witnessed in various lands the growth of nationalism from instinct to idea. The same century saw the first indications of the development of nationalism from idea to fervid prepossession.[1] Before the end of the eighteenth century this development had initiated in nationalism itself a revolution which marked its history with ironical inconsistency. The aim typical of nationalism as fervid prepossession was the very antithesis of the original idea of nationalism.

Nationalism as idea had confined its claims to limits which do not transgress the rights of any alien people. But nationalism as fervid prepossession betrayed this innocuous ideal by adopting an end which, because of the means required for its realization in a world limited in terrestrial space, is seldom compatible with respect for alien rights. This end was territorial expansion, a national aggrandizement which tends to lessen international amity and peace. While the attachment to territorial extensiveness was perhaps "as old as human society,"[2] expansionism derived from nationalism a potent stimulation which enhanced its emotional drive. The very peoples who had drunk most deeply of the new humanitarian nationalism succumbed most readily to the expansionist intoxication which led into the age of imperialism.

One instance of this perversion of an idea was offered by revolutionary Frenchmen, who became "oppressors in their turn" when they veered from Rousseau and the abjuration of conquest to Bonaparte. Another example, no less striking, though less unhappy in its results, was presented by the United States of America. Its appealing declaration of independence was immediately followed by a war not merely for independence but for the extension of power as well. America's affirmation of equality and the foundation of government on consent was mocked in less than three decades by the extension of its rule over an alien people without their consent.

This strange and yet world-wide transmutation of anti-imperialistic nationalism into nationalist expansionism deserves and has evoked the consideration of those hopeful of making somewhat intelligible the body of human inconsistencies which is called history. Its causation was so complex that it has perhaps not even yet been adequately considered in all its aspects. Moreover, there are some whose explanations betray the same emotional bias which was in large measure responsible for the curiosities of the development of nationalism. Thus Mazzini's derivation of French imperialism from the desire for glory,[3] and no less Dr. Channing's interpretation of American expansionism as a restless cupidity,[4] are over-simplifications reflecting vexation at the apparent fall of nationalism from an ethereal plane of humanitarianism. It was not merely self-interest which caused nationalism to become expansionistic. Moral ideology, which made of nationalism a fervid prepossession, also enabled the nationalist to pursue expansion without a sense of heresy to his original ideal. For expansion was so rationalized that it seemed at the outset a right, and soon, long before the famous phrase itself was coined, a manifest destiny. Moral ideology was the partner of self-interest in the intimate alliance of which expansionism was the offspring.

The strangest fact about this incongruous union has to do with the nature of original expansionist philosophy. It was derived from the same method of thought, the same conception of human rights, which was used and popularized by the original nationalist. So protean are ideas that it is a wise father who can know his own intellectual offspring. The expansionism which an anti-imperialistic nationalist would have regarded as some profligate's monster child was in reality the nationalist's child — perhaps illegitimate, perhaps unfortunately reared, but still his very own.

The central figure of this tragedy or comedy of errors is the idea of natural right. Broadly defined, the historic concept of natural right is that of a right which "Nature," regarded as a divinely supported system of "natural law" inclusive of moral truths, bestows prior to or independently of political society. The honorable genealogy of this idea can be traced back at least as far as the Greek conception of those things which are right "by nature," that is, inherently, and can be recognized by every rational being to be so.[5] Stoicism and Roman law subsequently conceived of "natural rights" as being among the truths inherent in natural law, the rational system of the physical and moral universe; still later, Christianity harmonized these ideas of paganism with its own theology by regarding natural law as the expression of the eternal reason of God. Successive schools of politico-legal thought used the concept of natural right to justify rights of property, civil liberties, and, with the rise of democratic thought, rights of popular sovereignty. Philosophers of the eighteenth century, seeking freedom from all the shackles of past "prejudices," brought the concept of natural right into the center of political thought by selecting, of all things, this time-worn notion as their instrument of emancipation. And in the eighteenth century natural right did figure as the opening wedge for at least one new political claim — the momentous pretension later to be called nationalism.

The nucleus of nationalism is the thesis that homogeneous populations have the right to form independent political associations. This doctrine was on the one hand a justification of the existing states resting upon popular will; on the other hand, however, it justified separation from existing states on the part of peoples desirous of independence. The revolutionary movements of the eighteenth century were in some measure inspired by, and later in turn inspired, this innovating philosophy of nationalism. It is true that probably the majority of eighteenth-century philosophers were led by their humanitarian cosmopolitanism to disdain local engrossments and provincial exclusiveness. But others, no less devoted to humanity at large, espoused the claims of the peoples who had not achieved independence, and gave to nationalism its first systematic presentations. They included thinkers as diverse as the culturally nationalistic Herder, the democratic Rousseau, the Tory Bolingbroke, and the liberal physiocrats. But virtually all based their doctrine of nationalism on one or both of two principles respecting natural right.[6] The first principle affirmed the natural right of groups to determine upon and organize the desired form of government. The second asserted that nationalities were the most natural agencies for promoting not only the rights of particular groups but also, by virtue of the social contributions of each nationality, the rights of mankind in general.

Such principles arose in part as a challenge to the Machiavellian morality which had long held that the welfare of the state was its highest law, that expansion was necessary to state welfare, and that the dismemberment of states was "a normal resource of diplomacy."[7] Reacting against the dynastic wars which such notions were still causing, publicists and jurists of the eighteenth century maintained that "individuals of one nationality should have a high regard for the interests and sentiments of individuals of other nationalities."[8] This seemed dictated by both phases of the philosophy underlying original nationalism. On the one hand, conquest was condemned as an infraction of every people's natural right to self-determination. Rousseau declared that conquest had no other basis than the law of the strongest, that is, no moral basis at all.[9] From a similar point of view Holbach, in his *La politique naturelle,* affirmed "the madness of conquests" to be far from sane politics.[10] The aristocratic Bolingbroke[11] was at one with liberal physiocrats such as Dr. Richard Price[12] and Major John Cartwright[13] in believing that the universal law of reason, the source of natural rights, required a foreign policy of peace and amity with other nations. The Swiss jurists Vattel[14] and Burlamaqui[15] (popular among Americans) forbade aggressive expansion as contrary to the law of nature on which they founded the equal rights of sovereign nations. On the other hand, anti-imperialism was also deduced from the nationalist's assumption that a diversity of homogeneous states was most favorable for advancing the rights and welfare of humanity. Thus Herder regarded the indiscriminate enlargement of states as "unnatural" because it meant "the wild mixing of all kinds of people," a destruction of the ethnic homogeneity making possible distinctive cultural contributions.[16] A prejudice against expansion as well as against imperialism was thus the original consequence of the nationalist's philosophy of natural right.

Such were the European winds of doctrine which blew fresh and strong in the century ascribing perfectibility to men and states. They carried across the wide Atlantic and there first helped to set a new ship of state into motion. These doctrines, however, were destined to move it in an unexpected direction and to produce a curiosity of intellectual history — the adoption of the idea of natural right as the moral rationale of America's expansionism.

Perhaps it was prophetic of such a development that America's spirited people had always tended to stress the rights of natural law more forcibly than its duties. The conception of natural right was first used by New England clergymen in behalf of rights of ecclesiastical independency. It descended from their pulpits into the arena of public discussion about 1760 when Americans became concerned with issues of their political rights under Great Britain. As parliamentary assertion of taxing power provoked irritation and then resistance, colonial leaders well-read in the English literature of natural law opposed the actions of Parliament not only with legal considerations but with the argument from the law of nature. Thus James Otis maintained that by " the law of God and nature " Americans were entitled to all rights of their fellow subjects in Great Britain, not excluding consent to taxation.[17] The American interpretation of natural law and natural right is exemplified by the following citation from Alexander Hamilton's pamphlet of 1775 on America's " right " to legislative autonomy:

> Good and wise men, in all ages, . . . have supposed, that the Deity, from the relations we stand in to Himself, and to each other, has constituted an eternal and immutable law, which is indispensably obligatory upon all mankind, prior to any human institution whatever.
>
> This is what is called the law of nature, 'which, being coeval with mankind, and dictated by God himself, is, of course, superior in obligations to any other. It is binding over all the globe, in all countries, and at all times. No human laws are of any validity, if contrary to this; and such of them as are valid, derive all their authority, mediately, or immediately, from this original.'—Blackstone.
>
> Upon this law depend the natural rights of mankind: the Supreme

> Being gave existence to man, together with the means of preserving and beautifying that existence. He endowed him with rational faculties, by the help of which to discern and pursue such things as were consistent with his duty and interest; and invested him with an inviolable right to personal liberty and personal safety.[18]

One sees in this beautiful simplification of truth the derivation of natural rights from an eternal, universal, and supremely binding natural law, dictated by God. One sees the further postulate that human reason intuits natural rights, examples of which are liberty and personal safety. But what one does not see — and thereby hangs a tale — is the precise nature of the rights which Hamilton mentions without definition. What does he mean by liberty, a concept which changed in meaning from the Greeks to Montesquieu? One can infer only that he included under it all the political liberties then desired by Americans as British citizens.

But it was not long before the natural right to liberty meant much more. When Great Britain's coercive acts had driven Americans to open resistance, the still bolder Thomas Paine penned as common sense the proposition: "A government of our own is our natural right." [19] The reasoning by which the implication of liberty was enlarged to sanction the self-determination of a group appears in the Declaration of Independence. It proclaimed that men free and equal instituted government and consented to its powers in order to protect the inalienable natural rights with which their Creator had endowed them. This premise permitted the deduction that when governments become destructive of natural rights there arises the right of revolution. Accordingly, Americans resolved to "assume among the powers of the earth, the separate and equal station to which the Laws of Nature and of Nature's God entitle them."

As the reference to "Nature's God" indicates, the philosopher of natural right was sufficiently confident of his intuition of divine purposes to present his moral judgments and expectations as indubitable dogmas of truth and destiny. The American thus had faith not only in the justice but also in the inevitability of independence. Even Paine, priding himself on possessing as little superstition as any man living, believed that Providence would not give up to military destruction a people striving for a liberty so obviously right that its denial seemed to him an atheism against nature.[20] "The cause of Liberty must be under the protection of Heaven," declared Richard Henry Lee, "because the Creator surely wills the happiness of his Creatures . . ."[21] Holding the same mystical view, John Adams wrote solemnly on the day after the declaration of independence: "It is the will of Heaven that the two countries should be sundered forever."[22] Thus the first doctrine which reflected the nationalistic theology of "manifest destiny" was that of God's decree of independence.

This doctrine was quickly followed by one which, according to Robert Michels, is essential to every people as their *Daseinsberechtigung*[23] — the doctrine of a national mission. This doctrine, which was to have so great and enduring an effect on subsequent American nationalism, was itself very largely the product of various past attitudes. Among these determinants were the religious idealism of the Mayflower Covenant, pride such as the poet Freneau's in "The Rising Glory" of America's free empire,[24] and faith such as John Adams's in the design of Providence to utilize the settlement of America for the "illumination" and "emancipation" of all mankind.[25] But the mission attributed to the new nation derived its specific form from the idea of natural right. The fundamental premise of the mission idea was that, as John Jay said in 1777, Americans were the first people favored by Providence with the opportunity of choosing rationally their forms of government and thus of constructing them upon respect for the "great and equal rights of human nature."[26] While this assumption perhaps oversimplified history if not theology, it gave a specious basis to the conception of Americans that in the order of Providence they were the special champions of the rights of all men. America's cause seemed, as the humanitarian Paine said, "the cause of all mankind."[27] Providence itself, Franklin proudly asserted, had called America to a post of honor in the struggle for the dignity and happiness of human nature.[28]

The humanitarian mission imposed by Providence seemed to

be twofold. On the one hand, America was given the appointment to preserve and perfect democracy, the application of the doctrine of natural rights to government. Fulfilment of this high task would enable America to figure immediately (in the words of Franklin) as an " asylum for those who love liberty." [29] The development of democracy would also make it possible, as Nathan Fiske proclaimed, for " liberty " eventually to " extend " its " benign influence to savage, enslaved, and benighted nations," and thus to reign universally.[30]

The second phase of the idea of a national mission concerned international ideals and involved a strong anti-imperialism. The exalted visionaries who felt themselves " citizens of the world " envisaged America as setting the example of an international policy such as had been dreamed of by the humanitarian nationalist philosophers of Europe. This policy excluded such conquest as Great Britain was attempting in her war against America. Conquest, Paine wrote in 1780, gave only a right originally founded in wrong and therefore not " right within itself." [31] Forgetting that European philosophers such as Locke [32] had helped to inspire Americans with an aversion to conquest, Timothy Dwight contemptuously relegated conquest to Europe:

> To conquest and slaughter let Europe aspire;
> Whelm nations in blood, and wrap cities in fire;
> Thy heroes the rights of mankind shall defend . . . [33]

These lines were written by a chaplain, but he condemned conquest no more strongly than did the soldier poet, Colonel David Humphreys. His poem of the Revolution, *The Happiness of America,* contrasted the past empires, built upon conquest, and the new empire, built on " freedom's base " and dedicated to " humanity's extended cause." [34] A similar thought is found in the somewhat later poem, *The Vision of Columbus,*[35] whose author, Joel Barlow, related the principle of nationality to natural law.[36] At one with the poets on this issue were many of the clergy, whose view appears in Dr. Samuel Cooper's oration of 1780 before the Governor and Legislature of Massachusetts. He proclaimed that " conquest is not . . . the aim of these rising States." They had before them an object more truly honorable — the fulfilment of a divine calling to "make a large portion of this globe a seat of knowledge and liberty." [37] Speaking with greater authority than the philosophers, poets, or clergymen, John Jay, president of the Continental Congress, informed the French envoy that America's constitution was "inconsistent with the passion for conquest." [38]

However, the passion for conquest or expansion is apparently little restrained by its inconsistency with theoretical pronunciamentos. The practice of Americans is illustrative of the observation of a modern Frenchman that practice, by its very nature, distorts idea. Between ideology and conduct there existed in this instance an inconsistency even greater than that which the complexities of experience usually make inevitable.

The discussions and pamphlet literature of the Revolution showed "a conception of the ability of the Americans not only to take territory by the sword, but to hold and govern it under a colonial status." [39] Still more did Revolutionary practice show this conception, for both its military strategy and its diplomacy were considerably determined by expansionism. Almost the first campaign, the Arnold-Montgomery expedition to Canada, indicated a purpose of territorial aggrandizement. In February of 1776 John Adams wrote to James Warren, with no great exaggeration: "The Unanimous Voice of the Continent is Canada must be ours; Quebec must be taken." [40] In the following month the "Plan of Treaties" adopted by the Continental Congress provided for an understanding with France that the United States remain in possession of all the continental or adjacent island territories which might be wrested from Great Britain. The actual French treaty of 1778 carried out this program for America's scope of possible conquest, save that France was permitted conquests in the West Indies. Even after military reverses discouraged active enterprises of invasion, "the hope of ultimately acquiring not only Canada, but also Nova Scotia, and even Florida, long persisted." [41] In the latter years of the Revolution, attention came to be focussed on the western country between the Alleghanies and the Mississippi, to which America's legal claim was so shady that even some of the

French allies ridiculed it.[42] The desire for the winning of the West underlay the dashing expedition of George Rogers Clark. In the congressional discussion of terms of peace, the small-territory party under the influence of France's diplomatic representative was finally defeated by the expansionist group on the issue of the western boundary. In his peace negotiations with Great Britain Franklin even put in a request for unconquered Canada.

Alarmed by such projects, French diplomats and even the friendly Abbé Raynal sought to dissuade the infant nation from disappointing their hopes. But that this expansionism was merely aggressive ambition is not a conclusion sustained by an examination of the typical utterances of its champions. It is true that land-hunger had long been evident in the projects of large land speculators and the incursions of American pioneers upon adjacent lands of the Indians or the French; moreover, it is not to be denied that an element in the enthusiasm of Western frontier sections for the Revolution was avidity for lands not accessible under British administration. On the other hand, Americans in general, agreeing with Thomas Paine that their dominion was already a world,[43] did not attach importance to increase of domain for its own sake.

Most Revolutionary Americans ascribed importance to territorial aggrandizement only as a means to an invaluable end — security. Land was related to security by virtue of the fact that lesser or greater extent of domain would respectively permit or remove the adjacency to the thirteen States of a dangerous neighbor. The idea of removing a formidable neighbor by expansion had been suggested originally by colonial difficulties with France; even before the American expansionism of the French and Indian War the realistic Rev. Jonathan Mayhew urged conquest of the territory of the French Papists who were "spreading desolation thro' the land." [44] After the British had in turn become objects of fear, Samuel Adams, writing in April of 1776 with independence in view, expressed to Dr. Cooper the then common opinion that "our Safety" very much depended upon our success in Canada.[45] The attacks on Canadian posts in the first phase of hostilities had the purpose of preventing

Great Britain from using Canada as a base for attack. But what of the persistence of designs of conquest even after the course of the war entered American borders and made more important the defense of American soil itself? The motive in this instance was still security, conceived not so much in relation to the present as to the future. "So long as Great Britain shall have Canada, Nova Scotia, and the Floridas, or any of them," wrote John Adams in 1778, "so long will Great Britain be the enemy of the United States, let her disguise it as much as she will." [46] In the congressional discussions of peace terms, according to the French envoy Luzerne, the chief argument for extended boundaries was the necessity of keeping dangerous neighbors at a distance.[47] Franklin, unable to foresee that the "unguarded" northern border would eventually be a matter of national pride, implied the objective of security in asking for Canada from the British peace commissioner. Through all the utterances of the expansionists runs the same prepossession, a veritable phobia.

But the desire for security does not in itself account for the sense of right with which expansionists asserted or implied a rather extraordinary pretension, that the complete assurance of their future security was paramount to another nation's legal possessions. To explain this it is also necessary to bring into view the idea of natural rights, which by reason of its vague and general character could easily provide an apologetic for national self-interest. Thomas Paine had written that one who takes nature for his guide is not easily beaten out of his argument.[48] That this observation is correct is largely due to the fact that natural law is a guide-post which points in different directions and permits a convenient diversity of arguments. Thus, though the natural right to liberty did not lend itself to expansionism, Hamilton had mentioned in connection with this right another which did. This was the natural right that seemed to be its complement — the natural right to "safety" or security. Its exponent may consider it as modest as the right to liberty but the concept of security is logically flexible to a degree permitting much more sweeping political demands. What conditions constitute security? What practical measures are allowable in the pursuit of security? The failure of the natural right philosophy to provide definite and restrictive answers makes the right of security preeminently serviceable in the justification of expansion.

At the very outset Revolutionary expansionism exemplified the ease of overcoming moral difficulties by reference to the right to security. Security, as has been seen, meant to Americans at first protection against Great Britain's imminent thrust from Canada; self-defense thus demanded seizure of Canada as Great Britain's base of attack. But this measure meant invasion of the territory of presumably friendly Canadians — an unprovoked injury which called forth protest even from certain Americans. Nevertheless the Continental Congress defended the invasion by saying that " the great law of self-preservation " dictated what had been done.[49] This " great law of self-preservation " was later ascribed supreme authority in James Wilson's essay deducing the law of nations from natural law.[50] It was the apparent assumption of this initial expansionism that as the first law of nature self-preservation knows no restraint.

In the later expansionism of the Revolution the idea of a right to security passed into a further stage of development. After the war entered American territory invasion of Canada was a deviation from the most pressing present needs; it was dictated only by the desire for security in the future. However, the argument of natural right seemed applicable also to security in the broader sense. An instance of this broadened conception of the natural right to security is in a letter of Samuel Adams in 1778. After expressing his hope that America would acquire Canada, Nova Scotia and Florida, he went on to say:

> We shall never be upon a solid Footing till Britain cedes to us what Nature designs we should have, or till we wrest it from her.[51]

Apparently generous " Nature " designed the peaceful or forcible acquisition of this territory precisely because it was essential to " a solid footing," that is, to future safety. Although the claim under natural right had thus advanced beyond obvious self-preservation, it was in accord with the theory of eighteenth-century jurists of the natural law school that conquest in a just war is a right incident to war. The article on conquest in the *Encyclopédie* based just conquest on "*la loi de la nature, qui fait que tout tend à la conservation des espèces.*" [52]

Discussion of peace brought a third expansionist doctrine of natural right. It was concerned not with the right of conquest but with the territorial demands proper in the settlement of war. Again we may quote Samuel Adams. After mentioning the great and permanent protection which possession of Canada and Nova Scotia would give to the fisheries, he discussed the objections of anti-expansionists:

> But these, say some, are not Parts of the United States, and what Right should *we* have to claim them? The Cession of those Territories would prevent any Views of Britain to disturb our Peace in future and cut off a Source of corrupt British Influence which issuing from them, might diffuse Mischiefe and Poison thro the States.[53]

Doubtless it was the same idea of a right to security, divinely ordained, which prompted James Lovell, in a letter to Horatio Gates in 1779, to introduce God into the issue of American expansion. In avowing his desire for Nova Scotia he referred with irritation to the men "who think a stark naked Acknowledgem't of the 13 United States under territorial Limits which Britain will not dispute is all that we are warranted to *demand*." In demanding territory essential to the secure enjoyment of the fisheries, we Americans would only be asking "what the Deity intended for us." [54]

Among the few preserved extracts from the congressional debates on boundaries is a speech by John Witherspoon which touches on the right to security in connection with America's claim to the western country. After noting the general doubt of America's legal claim, he spoke as follows:

> But if arguments drawn from old Charters . . . should be found to have no weight with the mediating powers and other powers in Europe . . . would any Gentleman wish to preclude our ministers from using an argument which would have weight, an argument drawn from general security, the force of which had been admitted in former treaties, and would be admitted by every disinterested power of Europe. . . . This nation was known to be settled along the Coasts to a certain extent; if any European country was admitted to establish colonies or

settlements behind them, what security could they have for the enjoyment of peace? What a source of future wars! [55]

Here one encounters the most extreme pretension thus far asserted as a right in the Revolution — that just settlement of a war demands a nation's curtailing its unconquered land in deference to the security of another. To be sure, a colonial precedent for this pretension was Franklin's insistence in 1760 that France cede Canada, at the conclusion of its war with Great Britain, in satisfaction of the "right" of the colonies to security.[56] Doubtless it was the same conception which encouraged Franklin to ask in 1782 that Canada be ceded to avoid "the Occasions of fresh Quarrel and Mischief." [57]

Thus even the sparsity of the available documents does not conceal evidence of the rapid propulsion of Revolutionary expansionism by the idea of natural right. There is a consideration, however, which makes it impossible to hold that the propulsion has as yet gone very far. It is the fact that expansionism was not the advocacy of a permanent or indiscriminate policy of aggrandizement but merely of the attainment in an unsought war of safeguards against future wars.

After the peace treaty of 1783, generally satisfactory because of its cession of territory extending to the Mississippi, expansionism quickly subsided. One of the major objections to the Constitution alleged that the large domain of the thirteen States made greater political unification inadvisable. This objection harked back to Montesquieu's admonition against extensive territory for republican governments, and also represented a reversion to the anti-expansionist interpretation of natural rights. As is made clear in Rousseau's theory of direct democratic government, the democrat's objection to extensive territory assumed the impossibility of safeguarding natural rights except in small states.

Despite the absence of evidence the Spanish statesman Aranda predicted from a priori cynicism that the new nation, born a pigmy, would grow into a colossus menacing to its erstwhile benefactors.[58] If he happened to be correct, it was primarily because his own government pursued from the beginning a course which Americans considered a violation of their rights. Although the southern boundary between the two countries remained unadjusted until 1795, the issue with Spain was not primarily one of land, but of the use of a river. The United States did not fear the adjacency of this decaying European power, but it did resent Spain's withholding the free navigation of the Mississippi to the Gulf from the Americans inhabiting its upper banks. The acquisition of this right had been sought during the Revolution, but the peace of 1783 brought no settlement of the issue. When negotiations were resumed after the Revolution, Spain was found to be still unwilling to grant Americans navigation through her territorial waters. On the other hand, the Americans in the rapidly thickening western settlements of the United States now urgently demanded the use of the Mississippi as the only practicable highway for shipping their surplus produce to its eastern markets. The whole nation became sensible of a stake in the issue as it appeared that the loyalty of the West to the Union might depend upon acquiring the right of navigation essential to its economic prosperity. Thus, despite the initial disinterestedness of certain Eastern States, the attainment of the right of navigation became soon after the treaty of peace a major aim of American diplomacy.

In this issue Americans found useful the same non-legal philosophy on which they had based their declaration of independence. To be sure, they did argue for the free navigation of the Mississippi on legal grounds also. But the legal argument that the United States derived from Great Britain a right of navigation was highly dubious; and despite Grotius's justification of innocent passage, Hall's careful discussion of the question, as well as that of most other jurists, denies the American contention that free navigation of alien territorial waters by inhabitants of the upper banks is a claim valid in international law.[59] Perhaps a subconscious suspicion of the weakness of their legal case caused Americans to lay primary emphasis on the argument of natural right. The declaration of 1788 of the insistent Convention of Kentucky spoke first of "the natural right of the inhabitants of this country to navigate the Mississippi" and only secondarily of treaty rights. The natural right was based on the necessity of free navigation to the agricultural development of a fair, rich soil the neglect of which would be "inconsistent with the immense designs of the Deity." [60] This preachment, beneath its aesthetic and religious ornamentation, represented an enlargement of the traditional right of property; the right now embraced all privileges essential to the development of property. Marbois, French statesman and historian, thought such an argument typical of men "still surrounded by the vestiges of a primitive state, where every individual thinks that he has a right to whatever he considers necessary for his preservation and well-being." [61] But it was not only the crude frontiersman who used this argument. The cultivated Jefferson also believed no sentiment to be written in deeper characters on the heart of man than that "the Ocean is free to all men, and the Rivers to all their inhabitants." [62]

Although Jefferson's thesis may seem appealing in the abstract, the very philosophy of natural right to which Jefferson appealed provided a refutation of the American claim in this instance. For it was maintained by the natural law jurists generally that, since "no right can be founded on an injury," [63] passage through territorial waters could be refused when the sovereign power deemed such passage injurious to itself. Spain considered exclusive regulation of commerce on the Mississippi essential to the prevention of smuggling through New Orleans, as well as to vital political interests. Jefferson himself came to realize the importance of exclusive use of territorial waters after the United States acquired the lower part of the Mississippi. In response to a suggestion that he exchange Louisiana for the apparently more valuable Floridas, he declared that he would be averse to such an exchange because "it would let Spain into the Mississippi on the principle of natural right, we have always urged." [64] Later the United States maintained in theory a claim to exclusive control of its rivers, although this policy did not prevent its request in the 'twenties for the navigation of the St. Lawrence on the ground of natural right. Spain, notwithstanding the legal justification of its original exclusiveness, decided in the late 'eighties to permit navigation upon payment of toll. But even after the issue became less serious Americans continued to demand free navigation on the ground of natural right.

This claim to free navigation was the beginning of a new growth of expansionism. The idea of natural right is apparently like a pebble which, however diminutive, on being cast into the water sets up ripples in remarkably increasing scope. The first stage in the enlargement of the American claim was the demand for the use of a port at the mouth of the Mississippi. In 1784 Madison, a firm believer that "Nature" had given to Americans the navigation of the Mississippi,[65] wrote to Jefferson that the use of the shores near the Gulf was essential to the exercise of the right of navigation.[66] As Secretary of State, Jefferson in 1790 formulated this unusual claim to territorial privileges in connection with the proposition that "the right to use a thing, comprehends a right to the means necessary to its use." [67] With respect to necessary means he a week later went still farther on the swift tide of the argument of natural right. Seeing an auspicious opportunity in Spain's involvement in the Nootka Sound dispute with England, he wrote to America's envoy in Madrid as follows:

> You will observe, we state in general the necessity, not only of our having a port near the mouth of the river (without which we could make no use of the navigation at all) but of its being so well separated from the territories of Spain and her jurisdiction, as not to engender daily disputes and broils between us. . . . Hence the necessity of a well-defined separation. Nature has decided what shall be the geography of that in the end, whatever it might be in the beginning, by cutting off from the adjacent countries of Florida and Louisiana, and enclosing between two of its channels, a long and narrow slip of land, called the Island of New Orleans. The idea of ceding this could not be hazarded to Spain, in the first step. . . . Reason and events, however, may, by little and little, familiarize them to it. That we have a right to some spot as an entrepôt for our commerce, may be at once affirmed.[68]

Here for the first time official statement is given to the idea that America's rights comprise the sovereign possession of a port — preferably New Orleans — as inherent in the natural right of navigation. The Government created in 1789 had taken with moral assurance the first step on the path of expansionism.

But the advance of the United States on this path seemed halted in 1795, when Spain, embarrassed by the perils of her foreign relations, ceded not only the free navigation of the Mississippi but also the use of New Orleans as an *entrepôt.* It is true that Jefferson, John Adams, Hamilton, and others envisaged the eventual gravitation to the Union of the new territories to which American pioneers wandered. It is also true that land-hungry frontiersmen of the South and Southwest were tempted to filibustering as they eyed the attractive Spanish lands. But neither the people as a whole nor the Government had adopted expansion as a deliberate program. On the contrary, there were heard voices such as that of the Reverend Cyprian Strong, who, even in a fourth of July oration, declared in 1799 that "the enlargement of territory can never be the object of pursuit, if our desires are kept within the limits of moderation." [69] Jefferson himself, despite his previous expansionism, said in his inaugural address of 1801 that America possessed "a chosen country, with room enough for our descendants to the thousandth and thousandth generation." [70]

But the optimistic Jefferson could not foresee events which destiny was even then preparing. These events shattered American complacency to the extent of producing, as Jefferson said, "more uneasy sensations through the body of the nation" than any felt since the Revolution.[71] The first apprehension, arising shortly after the turn of the century, was that Spain had ceded Louisiana and perhaps the Floridas as well to the most formidable power of Europe, Napoleonic France. On the heels of this fear, which proved correct with respect to Louisiana, came another shock — the Spanish Intendant's suspension of the right of deposit at New Orleans. The act seemed a presage of the policy of France as the possessor of New Orleans.

Despite the Spanish envoy's assurance that the suspension was an error, the hot-headed throughout the land clamored for immediate seizure of points on the lower Mississippi. Jefferson, however, sought to maintain the nation's tranquillity. More to quiet the imprudent than with any real hope, he despatched

Monroe to Paris to attempt the purchase of New Orleans and as much as possible of the Floridas. His plan in the event of Monroe's failure differed from that of Federalists like Ross only in tempering belligerence with discretion. To Livingston he wrote of his resolution to " marry " the nation to the British fleet, and, after this marriage of convenience, to attack France at the first favorable moment.[72]

It is true that " peace alone " [73] — the attainment of a security compatible with pacifism — prompted the projects which Professor Chinard paradoxically calls " Protective Imperialism." [74] But this consideration in itself scarcely explains the moral confidence with which the expansionists contemplated aggression under such circumstances. Spain's cession of Louisiana and France's acceptance were both within legal right. Moreover, it was pointed out truly by Du Pont de Nemours, surprised at his friend Jefferson's perturbation and threats, that France had no hostile intention toward the United States and would doubtless be no less sympathetic than Spain to America's claims.[75] Why did Jefferson consider hostilities to be as inevitable as the " laws of nature " [76] when nothing in the situation deviated from the ordinary course of international relations?

The explanation lay largely in the peculiar notion about natural law which Jefferson had revealed to Dr. Mitchell just before the Louisiana crisis:

> Nor is it in physics alone that we shall be found to differ from the other hemisphere. I strongly suspect that our geographical peculiarities may call for a different code of natural law to govern relations with other nations from that which the conditions of Europe have given rise to there.[77]

To virtually all save the unorthodox Montesquieu, natural law had heretofore signified law which was everywhere uniform. Jefferson's paradoxical conception of a different code of natural law was either *naïveté* or philosophical genius. It was perhaps sage in applying Montesquieu's correlation of law with geography to a country isolated by the ocean and situated on a virgin continent. On the other hand, Jefferson was perhaps not so sage in overlooking the practical difficulties in this curious project of a geographically bifurcated law of nations. In any event Jefferson's trend of thought was indeed " dangerous." [78] Its danger to Europe was shortly to be manifested in the ideology which American expansionists expressed in the Louisiana issue. For in the name of natural law they put forth propositions which went far beyond not only the European code of natural law but even the sufficiently liberal past claims of Americans.

The first of the new propositions concerned the use of the Mississippi. The question was no longer regarded as merely that of the natural right of navigation, although this " undoubted right from nature " [79] remained a premise. Senator Ross derived from it the right not merely to the possession of a port but to the entire mouth of the Mississippi. In defending his resolution affirming the right to territorial security for the right of navigation, Ross said:

> This evident right was one, the security of which ought not to be precarious: it was indispensable that the enjoyment of it should be placed beyond all doubt. He declared it therefore to be his firm and mature opinion, that so important a right would never be secure, while the mouth of the Mississippi was exclusively in the hands of the Spaniards. . . . From the very position of our country, from its geographical shape, from motives of complete independence, the command of the navigation of the river ought to be in our hands.[80]

A House committee report went still further by advocating the purchase or conquest of both New Orleans and the Floridas. The right to the coastal territory was deduced from the fact that it seemed as if " nature had intended for our own benefit " the rivers emptying into the Gulf after running almost exclusively within our own boundaries.[81] The conception of a right of innocent use had thus grown to that of an absolute right of possession.

A second argument was the natural right to security. By virtue of America's possession of this right, Spain was held not to possess the right of disposing of her territory without consulting the United States. Senator Ross pointed out that giving us new and powerful neighbors would " change our present security into hazard and uncertainty." [82] Senator Gouverneur Morris, concurring in this view, made what must have seemed to European jurists an amazing generalization:

> No nation has a right to give to another a dangerous neighbor without her consent.[83]

Rufus King, envoy to Great Britain, affirmed the converse of this proposition in communications to Lord Hawkesbury and the American envoy Livingston. Not only legal considerations but also " the duty we owe to ourselves and posterity " gave America the right, he declared, to exclude France forever from the country east of the Mississippi.[84] For French occupation of this country could not " be satisfactorily reconciled with a just regard to the rights and security of those powers between which this portion of America is divided and by which the same is at present possessed." [85] Americans had thus travelled far from the relatively moderate request for security in the territorial settlement terminating a war. They had come to the affirmation of a right to control in the interest of security even the territorial transactions of other powers in peace.

Though the natural rights to free navigation and to security occupied the focus of attention, there is evidence that a third natural right, much more comprehensive than the first two, was now for the first time seen by some in relation to expansion. It was that American discovery, the right to the pursuit of happiness. A writer in the *New-York Evening Post* affirmed its expansionist implications boldly and joyfully:

> It belongs *of right* to the United States to regulate the future destiny of *North America.* The country is *ours*; ours is the right to its rivers and to all the sources of future opulence, power and happiness, which lay scattered at our feet; and we shall be the scorn and derision of the world if we suffer them to be wrested from us by the intrigues of France.[86]

The excitation of nationalism in this issue had thus given rise to the sporadic intimation of a later diffuse and explicit ambition — nothing less than to exercise dominion over the North American continent.

Capping the rights formulated as objectives was still another right — that of taking all the measures necessary to attain these objectives. The nature of these measures had been prophesied in 1787 by a belligerent statement in the *American Museum* that " the laws of nature, superior to the narrow policy of any sovereign court," must speedily turn the Western claimants of America's commercial rights into "a host of myrmidons." [87] Now a valiant philosopher, writing in the *New-York Evening Post,* explained why the laws of nature justified the exercise of force on the part of the entire nation:

In vain would nature give us a right not to suffer injustice; in vain would it oblige others to be just with respect to us, if we could not lawfully make use of force when they refused to discharge their duty. The just would be at the mercy of fraud and injustice, and all their rights would soon become useless. In vain does nature prescribe to nations, as well as to individuals, the care of their self-preservation, and of advancing their own perfection and happiness, if it does not give the right to preserve themselves from everything that can render this care ineffectual. We have then in general the right of doing whatever is necessary to the discharge of our duties. Every nation, as well as every man, has therefore a *right* not to suffer any other to obstruct its preservation, its perfection and happiness, that is, to preserve itself from all injuries. It is this right of self-preservation from all injury, which is called the *right of security.*[88]

One might suppose that only an irresponsible exponent of natural law would assert the natural right of injuring another nation before it has displayed any hostile intent. But the resolutions offered by Senator Ross and favored by many Federalists called for seizure of points on the lower Mississippi as a pledge for our rights. Jefferson believed no less that by "a law of nature" the quarrels of neighborhood would sooner or later compel aggressive appropriation of the one place whose possessor, *ipso facto,* must be "our natural and habitual enemy." [89] Thus the doctrine which at first justified conquest merely in an unsought war had finally become a doctrine of aggression — at best a doctrine of self-defensive aggression.

The questionable ideology of this issue is veiled now by the turn of events which obviated the necessity of action upon it. Napoleon, first announcing the momentous decision in his bath, decided in view of a shift in his international plans upon the sale of Louisiana to the United States. As Professor Channing writes, the Louisiana Purchase "came in the nick of time to save Jefferson from violating the code of international ethics." [90]

We have seen, however, that Jefferson and the other expansionists had their own code — one which had evolved from the very concept of natural law upon which contemporary jurists based the law of nations. Although Americans carried the right of security to a degree which infringed upon the legal rights of others — that is, to a degree to which the juristic philosophers of natural right never intended that it should go — they had not yet carried it to a point which violated a right of others as fundamental as that which they sought for themselves. The case had always been one of the security of the United States against a European nation's mere maintenance or extension of power.

But the Louisiana Purchase, which gained for the nation its desired security, had a sequel which placed Americans in a more embarrassing position than any of the past with respect to the ethics of natural right. After France had acceded to American desires, there still remained one problem — that of the attitude of the native inhabitants of the land which was to be transferred. Although the Louisianians had long been the pawns of European politics, many of them chose this last change of sovereignty as an occasion for displaying a perversity which created difficulty for the United States. For some strange reason they conceived that Spanish sovereignty, despite its political absolutism, was more congenial to their easy-going Gallo-Hispanic civilization than the authority of the republican but officious Americans. As the day for taking possession of New Orleans drew near, it appeared possible that its citizens might resist this incursion of strange and unchosen sovereigns. The course adopted by the peace-loving but realistic Jefferson was the despatch of troops to the scene. This precaution prevented martial conflict but it was apparently in logical conflict with the American principle that government rests on the consent of the governed. What moral argument could justify this first recourse of champions of natural right to imperialism?

Jefferson himself did not append to his decision to send troops any comment which reflected his awareness of the moral issue; the case was for him, as it would also have been for any European statesman, not one to be viewed academically. Although Americans in general were silent because of ignorance of the facts, one document of the time does give an engaging exhibition of an intellectual skill in vaulting the issue of imperialism with the aid of democratic "Nature." This is an address which was circulated, apparently by officials of Mississippi, among the disaffected inhabitants of New Orleans in order to reconcile them to the approaching American occupation. The pith of this ingenious appeal is as follows:

> Nature designed the inhabitants of Mississippi and those of New Orleans to be one single people. It is your peculiar happiness that nature's decrees are fulfilled under the auspices of a philosopher who prefers justice to conquest, whose glory it is to make man free and not a slave, and who delights in benevolence instead of splendor. Yet although he is careful of your happiness, he will not permit you to destroy it by obstructing our rights. . . .
>
> Would you . . . try vainly to prevent New Orleans from fulfilling its destiny? [91]

The foregoing contains two doctrines, the more important of which is left implicit because it is the less pleasant. It is the doctrine that by the destiny manifest in geography America's natural right to territory essential to its security must override the right of self-determination claimed by its inhabitants. Here for the first time the idea that "our rights" must not be destroyed leads to the destruction of that cornerstone of the nationalist's natural right philosophy, the universal right to political liberty. By the time of the subjugation of the Filipinos this imperialistic idea had become commonplace, and Dr. Talcott Williams illustrated imperialist ethics by reference to the subordination of the political liberty of inhabitants at the mouth of the Mississippi to the general welfare of the larger geographical unity.[92] But Americans of 1803 were too close to 1776 to feel comfortable in imperialism. Thus the address contains also another doctrine, supplying the imperialistic thesis with a sugar coating. This is the conception that Louisianians would find their true liberty in the acceptance of Jefferson's benevolent rule. The philosopher who fulfilled nature's decrees was of the same opinion, as is shown by Jefferson's declaration that Louisiana offered "a wide spread for the blessings of freedom and equal laws." [93] Though this view of the matter may have been quite correct, the method by which liberty was extended to Louisianians was in undeniable conflict with Jefferson's original generalization that the governed have the natural right to consent to government, whether for better or for worse.

Although the possibility of difficulty with the inhabitants of New Orleans escaped general attention, a later issue became a matter of national discussion and compelled the expansionists to engage in new casuistical dexterity. This issue was the provision of government for the inhabitants of the new territory. The Administration proposed a form of government which, though not designed as permanent, carried out in a strange way for the time being Jefferson's professed intention of spreading free government. It gave to the Louisianians neither a state nor even a territorial government, but one in which they had no representation. American anti-imperialists called it a "complete despotism," [94] an infringement upon rights given "by nature." [95] Petitioners claiming to represent the people of Louisiana asserted in 1804 that they were not too ignorant of their natural rights to perceive that the government was "inconsistent with every principle of civil liberty." [96]

The Americans who approved the absolutistic government were no longer disposed to consider the issue of self-government from the viewpoint of natural right. Their approach to the question purported to be realistically utilitarian. Thus Representative Eustis spoke in a congressional debate as follows:

> I am one of those who believe that the principles of liberty can not suddenly be ingrafted on a people accustomed to a regimen of a directly opposite hue. The approach of such a people to liberty must be gradual. I believe them at present totally unqualified to exercise it.[97]

This conservative Federalist had now a strange intellectual bedfellow, the equalitarian Jefferson. The latter wrote that "our new fellow citizens are as yet as incapable of self-government as children," and that those Americans were mistaken who could not bring themselves to "suspend" the principles of self-government for an instant.[98] Even the once radical Thomas Paine answered the remonstrance of the Louisianians by saying that he agreed with its principles of liberty abstractly, but not with granting political powers before understanding of principles.[99] This was to tell the disappointed Louisianians that they did not understand what they were talking about. In fact, the views of the imperialists themselves are perhaps more reasonable in the abstract than in their application; for Louisianians, even if far from mature in political capacity, seemed to many Americans as well as to themselves to be qualified at least for partial self-government.

But did the American's traditional philosophy of natural rights permit in any case this reasonableness of the imperialist? Jefferson's declaration that all men are created equal — in view of which a historian of Louisiana condemns Jefferson for inconsistency in this issue[100] — did not, indeed, explicitly specify Lincoln's plausible deduction that *all* men *remain* so in respect of political rights. But the omission, though significant of vague thinking, is one which American imperialists have probably used for more than it is worth. On another occasion the author of the Declaration of Independence was less ambiguous. "Every man and every body of men on earth," Jefferson wrote, "possesses the right of self-government" — a right which men "receive with their being from the hand of nature."[101] As late as 1816 Jefferson wrote that nothing was "unchangeable" but "the inherent and inalienable rights of men." Yet his own intelligently inconsistent development showed that, however unchangeable natural rights may be as essences, the heart of man wherein they are "legible" did change in its conception of one of them. Americans of 1803 had not, to be sure, arrived at the thoroughgoing imperialism which John Burgess expressed in 1890: "The Teutonic nations can never regard the exercise of political power as a right of man."[102] But the early expansionists did deviate from Jefferson's nationally advantageous generalizations by temporary denial of political power to those incapable in American eyes of exercising it advantageously — for American as well as Louisianian self-interest. Truly, as John Figgis observes, the main practical implication of the doctrine of natural right is "the relativity of all political dogma."[103]

It is a curious fact, however, that even the qualification of the previous generalization about political equality was susceptible of justification by the natural right doctrine from one point of view. What chiefly underlay the imperialism of Americans was not their conviction of the political incompetence of the Louisianians but the fact that their exercise of the right of self-government would have conflicted with a natural right of Americans. This fact was evident when Representative Eustis affirmed that the absolutistic government of Louisianians was needed to prevent "acts subversive of their relations to the United States" and "to secure the rights of the United States." [104] The nature of the principal American right in question was indicated when he declared that the Administration's plan of government would give more "security" [105] than one of liberal character. From beginning to end, then, American imperialism in this period was directed by the philosophy of the natural right to security. Subordinating to their own right to security another people's right to liberty and equality, Americans apparently considered that no natural right of another was inalienable upon one occasion — that on which it conflicted with the always inalienable rights of Americans themselves.

In one aspect the entire development toward expansionism by way of natural right appears now as the growth of a willingness to attain national rights at the expense of the rights of other peoples. Such a violation of alien rights was doubtless not intended by the American when he first sentimentalized over the natural rights of mankind; he probably believed as does a contemporary jurist that "rights in their essence do not conflict." [106] But the truth is, of course, that political experience demands dealing with rights not as essences but as specific conflicting claims. After the American philosopher of natural right became a practical statesman his action came to accord with the principle which Carnot enunciated for Revolutionary France in 1793: namely, that since the law of nature sanctions the right to security, "every political operation which the welfare of the State demands is lawful," irrespective of its injury to the rights of others.[107] When he eventually overrode another people's right to liberty, the American statesman laid himself open to the charge of violating a cardinal principle of the philosophy of natural right. This principle was stated by Jefferson as follows: " No man has a natural right to commit aggression on the equal rights of another . . ." [108]

The explanation of this curious development was to a large extent supplied by the shrewd psychology which Americans of this very period elaborated in their moments of greatest realism. Reference is not made to the traitorous Wilkinson's observation to the Spanish that he who disavows self-interest as his motive lies. It is rather to the more complex psychology of man which is exemplified by the less cynical postulate of the *Federalist*:

> As long as the connection subsists between his reason and his self-love, his opinions and his passions will have a reciprocal influence on each other; and the former will be objects to which the latter will attach themselves.[109]

To the foregoing may be added John Adams's observations in his essay on " self-delusion," which he called " the spurious offspring of self-love " and the parent of the greatest part of human misdeeds.[110] This eighteenth-century psychology, conceding sincerity to ideology but assuming its unconscious determination by self-interest, will prove far more helpful than modern psychoanalysis in our studies. It explains in large part the almost invariably advantageous conclusions of national morals even in considerations about the rights of mankind.

However, there remains the further problem of determining the logical characteristic which enabled the interpretations of natural right to take the mold demanded by self-interest. One notes first of all that such a philosophy supplied no objective criterion for estimating the relative weight of conflicting rights. Thus the contestant could not only act as his own partial judge but had it open to him to believe that the right which he attained was superior to the alien right which he violated. This consideration, however, merely raises another question — the nature of the ideology which permitted the American always to see his own nation's rights as outweighing those of another. To answer this teasing question we must now bring into view a doctrine which was not systematically considered heretofore because its influence upon American expansionism was implicit rather than explicit. The idea was touched upon, however, in noting that the American's sense of championing the rights of mankind gave rise to a belief in his nation's manifest destiny or providential mission in behalf of all peoples.

As the dogma of America's social mission first presented itself, it was not in patent conflict with that equalitarianism which caused a Herder, one who considered national pride " the most harmful disease in history," [111] to affirm that " no nationality has been solely designated by God as the chosen people of the earth." [112] In its original form the idea of America's mission was in accord with the cultural nationalist's supposition that every people is assigned the making of a social contribution reflecting its distinctive genius. But the logical composition of ideas may contain elements which, as the ideas enter into chemical reaction with more emotional factors, cause them to undergo precisely the transformations which their original propounders would most abhor.

Thus the doctrine of America's mission developed rather quickly into the dogma of special delegation, just as, through teachings which Fichte foreshadowed in his " Addresses " of 1807, this proud dogma eventually became current among the people of Herder. Given the preeminent value attached to democracy, it was natural that the mission of the champions of human rights should also come to seem preeminent. This ideological development received momentum from successive achievements or victories that had the aspect of providential dispensations — success in the Revolution, the foundation of the Federal Union, the adoption of America's principles by Revolutionary France. It was perhaps the patriotic clergy who first propagated the idea of an " American Israel," the phrase forming the keynote of the distinguished Ezra Stiles's sermon of 1783, " The United States Elevated to Glory and Honor." [113] In 1785 Jefferson proposed that the seal of the United States should represent the children of Israel led by a pillar of light [114] — a suggestion supporting a biographer's observation that he was convinced that " the American people was a chosen people, that they have been gifted with superior wisdom and strength." [115] In 1796 John Cushing stated explicitly what had merely been Jefferson's implication — that God's dispensations to America reminded of those to Israel.[116] The theological poet Timothy Dwight revealed still more frankly his Hebraic nationalism when he in 1787 referred to Americans as "this chosen race." [117] This dogma of the chosen people has its roots in national egoism but it flowers into a consciousness of moral potentiality. Its moral phase is revealed in Jefferson's reference of 1801 to America as "the world's best hope." [118] His inaugural address of 1805 resurrected in morally rationalized form the Puritan's Calvinistic dogma of God's elect — the conception that "God led our forefathers, as Israel of old." [119]

This idea of a special mission would disrupt not merely the psychological equalitarianism of the original philosophy of natural right but also its ethical equalitarianism, that is, the doctrine that all are entitled to the same rights in equal degree. For the people believing itself a supreme contributor to the needs of all other peoples will conclude — and the conclusion is quite logical if one grants the premise — that the rights essential to its existence or healthful development are weighted with the rights of all mankind. Thus John Adams, observing in 1787 that the new republic was "destined" to spread over the entire northern part of this quarter of the globe, reflected joyfully that America's expansion would be "a great point gained in favor of the rights of mankind." [120] Such an attitude would presumably be still more influential when any foreign nation acquired a point of vantage from which it could "invade the shrine where sacred lies . . . the well-earned prize." [121] When France was about to occupy Louisiana, its alleged right, together with that of the Louisianians, seemed outweighed by the American right welded in the flame before the ark of the covenant. This right was formulated by one aggressive expansionist as follows:

> We have a right to the possession. The interests of the human race demand from us exertion of this right.[122]

To be sure, France had felt similarly as it took the course which Edmund Burke, outraged at the "havoc," blamed upon "the pretended rights of man"; havoc or blessing, this course of thought tends to be the way of all highly self-conscious nationalism. Its method of fulfilling an assumed destiny to establish the rights of mankind is to violate these rights.

The alchemy which transmuted natural right from a doctrine of democratic nationalism into a doctrine of imperialism was thus the very idea of manifest destiny which the doctrine of natural right created. But manifest destiny was such a creature as Frankenstein fashioned. Gaining control over the doctrine of natural right, it in effect changed the impartial law of nature into the unique code favorable to the rights of one nation. In the end natural right was not a right universal, moderate, and innocuous, but a right special, exorbitant, and potentially aggressive. To be sure, the transmutation was so largely unconscious that from the viewpoint of formal definition the doctrine of natural right continued to bear its original features. But from the viewpoint of application it had the change of bulk which comes with elephantiasis.

What were the ulterior consequences of this pathological hypertrophy of the idea? One was that the later use of the phrase exhibited a pretentiousness which from the viewpoint of its original meaning bordered upon madness. In the 'fifties an expansionist, only half-ironical, deduced from the premise that Americans were the elect of the world "a natural right on the part of our race, to possess the earth," and especially Cuba.[123] As late as the centennial year of the Louisiana Purchase an expansionist organ asserted America's "natural right and manifest destiny to control of the Pacific," the ocean to which Louisiana had paved the way.[124] But a still more noteworthy development was the fact that as a concept of America's expansionism "natural right" experienced in the course of the nineteenth century a rather steady decline.

The chief cause of this decline was not a positivistic disillusionment such as caused Bentham to call natural right "simple nonsense." It was apparently, as the foregoing examples indicate, the increasingly conscious acceptance of the doctrine of rights conferred by manifest destiny, that is, the conception that special rights were bestowed by Providence upon its elect. Although this doctrine of manifest destiny had emerged from the belief in America's championship of natural rights, the maturation of the idea of special rights scarcely allowed of the continued life of the idea of universal and equal rights. Thus the doctrine of natural right met an unnatural demise through an absorbing growth from its own logical tissue.

This fate may seem the more pathetic because the doctrine of natural right performed in its day rather remarkable and memorable service. It contributed to the ideals of new nationality, to the nation's growing needs, and finally to ideals and needs simultaneously by the very fact that it obscured the conflict between original principles and entrance upon the path of empire.

# CHAPTER II

## GEOGRAPHICAL PREDESTINATION

Despite the doubling of America's territorial domain the accession of Louisiana was not followed by a subsidence of expansionism. While Monroe was writing to Secretary of State Madison that the acquisition secured " everything which is essential to the sovereignty of our Country, to the peace, prosperity, & happiness of our people," [1] word was already *en route* from Madison ordering Monroe to attempt to purchase the Floridas. The government which would once have been happy with New Orleans pursued the Floridas with a kind of " passion " [2] for nearly two decades. Simultaneously Americans entertained so many territorial ambitions that they seemed to the French Consul-General De Beaujour to tend to " nothing less than to devour the whole of North America." [3]

Appetite had grown with the eating. Yet the moral idea was still needed, no less as spice than as postprandial sedative. To be sure, the traditional doctrine of natural right was no longer *à propos*; the political necessity which it made a condition of valid expansionism no longer existed. But a change in exegetical method enabled the new expansion movement to retain nature as its divinity and yet to derive from her cult sanctions more liberal.

Instead of reading the law of nature primarily from the heart of man expansionists took to reading it principally from the configuration of the earth. This was not to disassociate nature from reason but rather to assume that reasonable dictates for politics were written in the territorial foundation of national life. The expansionists added to the idea of the natural boundary a metaphysical dogma which converted it into the theory that may be called geographical predestination. They quaintly held that nature or the natural order of things destined natural boundaries for nations in general and the United States, the nation of special destiny, in particular.

The importance of geographical conceptions in early American expansionism is a matter of common historical knowledge. Thus the foremost student of the acquisition of Florida has noted the idea that Florida "physiographically belonged to the United States." [4] Again, in his *Recollections*, C. J. Ingersoll describes the ideal of early American expansionism as "an empire of natural territories, boundaries, and circumadjacent waters, comprehending one and the same nation, by configuration exclusively vicinal." [5] Such formulations, however, leave unanswered the question why the natural boundary was generally conceived by Americans to be far in advance of the boundary that they already had.

This mystery of American history is the greater because in European history the principle of the natural boundary had figured chiefly, at least in theory, as a doctrine of restraint. Grotius gives numerous quaint examples of such a use of the principle in ancient history, among them being Pliny's observation that "barriers . . . were destined for the separation of states." [6] To Grotius and other jurists of the natural law school it seemed that nothing "is more suitable for separating . . . states than a boundary which is not easily crossed." [7] In modern European history the doctrine of the natural boundary was employed by anti-imperialists as an argument against dynastic expansionism. Herder pointed out how significantly nature had "separated nationalities . . . by woods and mountains, seas and deserts," [8] and Rousseau inferred from such features that "nature herself has decided with regard to the number and greatness of the nations." [9] While the principle of natural frontiers influenced the expansionism of the French Revolution, as well as that of Richelieu and Louis XIV previously, it can be blamed only for the initial and relatively moderate phase of Revolutionary expansionism. Even as a doctrine of expansion the natural boundary had seemed to permit territorial extension only within strictly defined limits. And if natural frontiers are not possessed by a nation at the outset their acquisition would not seem to require ordinarily a long journey.

Because of such considerations certain contemporary Europeans criticized American expansionism as a violation of the doctrine of the natural boundary. Thus Vicente Folch, Governor of West Florida, wrote that in its intoxication with the acquisition of Louisiana the Government of the United States had "abandoned all idea as to natural boundaries." [10] In 1814 a similar opinion was expressed by De Beaujour's English translator and by Félix de Beaujour himself in his *Sketch of the United States of North America.* "Since the Americans have acquired Louisiana," the latter wrote, "they appear to be unable to bear any barriers round them." [11]

Yet it was precisely natural boundaries which even the most ambitious Americans seemed to themselves to be seeking. The explanation of this paradox lies in a history which places in sharp relief the attitudes and logical ambiguities giving the concept of the natural boundary a flexibility defiant of all limits save those of desire.

At the very outset American history exhibited a tendency toward the formation of a conceptual association between the natural boundary and expansion. The idea of the natural boundary made its début in the history of American expansion in connection with the issue of the western boundary of the Confederation. The committee appointed by the Continental Congress to explicate Jay's peace instructions asserted that "the river Mississippi will be a more natural, more distinguishable, and more precise boundary than any other that can be drawn eastward of it." [12] This appeal to the principle of the natural boundary was supplementary to a legal claim to the trans-Alleghany country by virtue of old charters. The charters needed supplementation, for they were as ambiguous as the legal delimitations of most domains in the new continent. As later words of Edward Everett suggested, [13] the absence in America of the rigid, well-established legal divisions of Europe created an unconventional attitude which from the very start invested the principle of the natural boundary with an importance new in political history.

The issue of the western boundary showed not only the importance which Americans attached to the natural boundary but also their tendency to apply geographical criteria different from those of Europeans. Just as French and Spanish statesmen doubted America's legal claim to extend to the Mississippi, so they evidently doubted its pretension that the most natural boundary would be this river. In 1789 Talleyrand referred to the Alleghanies as " the limits which nature seems to have traced " for the Americans.[14] Since a river is not a barrier, as the historian Turner points out with reference to the Mississippi,[15] it is probably true that a mountain is superior to it as natural boundary. But Americans chose the farther of two natural boundaries instead of the better. This fact is explicable not only by the desire for navigation of the Mississippi but also by an enduring determinant of the American attitude toward frontiers — the wish to have spacious territory as a natural protection against neighbors.

From being ancillary to a legal claim the doctrine of the natural boundary passed after the peace of 1783 into a more pretentious rôle. Here it figured as an expansionist argument supporting the acquisition of territory essential to the security of a " natural right " to free navigation through the portion of the Mississippi river still possessed by Spain. In 1787 a Captain Sullivan, reflecting the attitude of the Western pioneers, inveighed against the " unnatural boundaries " which obstructed " free passage into the ocean." [16] A few years later Secretary of State Jefferson affirmed that " Nature " had decided the political geography of the mouth of the Mississippi by detaching New Orleans from Florida and Louisiana as a port which might serve for America's commerce.[17] However, it was not until 1802, when the reported cession of Louisiana and Florida to France seemed to menace not merely America's use of the Mississippi but also its strategic security, that the doctrine of the natural boundary was applied by Americans to this issue widely and emphatically.

In this issue the desired boundary seemed to be indicated not only by geography but also, as in the expansionist ideology of the French Revolution, by all the criteria of the current natural law philosophy. The *New-York Evening Post* declared that Florida and New Orleans were within " the limits which appear to be assigned to us by nature and by reason." [18] Senator Jackson associated geographical nature with its Divine Author:

"God and nature have destined New Orleans and the Floridas to belong to this great and rising empire."[19] The most striking characteristic of the doctrine of the natural boundary was its association with the conception of rights arising from political necessity. Senator Gouverneur Morris, having declared that the possession of Florida and New Orleans by another would be fatal to the United States, affirmed these territories to be "a natural and necessary part of our empire."[20] It was the idea of the natural as the politically necessary boundary which differentiated the early form of the geographical doctrine from that which it was generally to assume later. To John Burgess in the 'nineties "geographic unity" was a principle which in and of itself justified the resort to force in expansion.[21] But even the militant expansionists of the Mississippi issue did not conceive a claim to the natural boundary as valid except in conjunction with the political necessities establishing a claim by natural right.

However, the doctrine of the natural boundary soon became disassociated from the principle of the natural right to a political necessity. After the United States acquired Louisiana there was no longer any question either of the immediate security of the United States or of the use of the Mississippi. Yet the pursuit of the Floridas continued. And one of the reasons for the continuance was the new idea that geographical predestination existed independently of political necessity. Sufficient necessity lay in the consideration that, as Governor Claiborne said, "nature has decreed the union of Florida with the United States."[22]

But why was nature supposed to decree this union after it had already filled America's cup of good fortune to overflowing? According to Americans, nature still had good reasons. Secretary of State Madison's first letter of instructions to Monroe after news of the Louisiana treaty reveals one of them:

> These colonies, separated from her other territories on this continent by New Orleans, the Mississippi, and the whole of Western Louisiana, are now of less value to her than ever; whilst to the United States they retain the peculiar importance derived from their position, and their relations to us through the navigable rivers, running from the United States into the Gulf of Mexico. . . . The Spanish Government must

understand, in fact, that the United States can never consider the amicable relations between Spain and them as definitively and permanently secured, without an arrangement on this subject, which will substitute the manifest indications of nature for the artificial and inconvenient state of things now existing.[23]

Madison's words reveal the idea that nature destined not merely boundaries satisfying vital necessities but also — at least for the privileged United States — boundaries serving convenience. Madison judged the issue in the light of the consideration that location made Florida useless to Spain but a convenience both to the commerce and to the security of the United States. The same idea was expressed in a later editorial of *Niles' Register* as follows:

The Floridas may be considered as naturally belonging to the United States—or, in other words, as rightfully to be possessed by the power holding the adjacent countries of Georgia, Alabama, and Mississippi; for they are *without value* to any other . . . [24]

It was not merely America's practical convenience that nature allegedly considered in its geographical predestinations. After the acquisition of Louisiana opened up vaster horizons of national greatness the expansionist came to conceive that nature also destined far-flung boundaries for the sake of America's glory. As Fisher Ames observed, when the Mississippi ceased to be a confining boundary the imagination of Americans almost rushed into space like a comet to bound the glory of America by the stars.[25] Thus Joseph Chandler declared in a fourth of July oration of 1804 that Louisiana was only " the commencement of our anticipating hopes " and envisaged the day when " our boundaries shall be those which Nature has formed for a great, powerful, and free State." [26] The very grandeur which nature had written into the American scene suggested to the *Journal of the Times* that America would become a still grander nation.[27] It was in the years following the Louisiana Purchase, as Félix de Beaujour rather scornfully noted, that Americans came to " measure their future grandeur by the extent of their vast territory." [28]

Nevertheless, neither a sense of convenience nor the desire

for glory could in itself have caused Florida or any other territory to seem within America's natural boundary. Such factors exert influence only as they exist in conjunction with the belief that in the configuration of the earth itself there are "manifest indications of nature" which make deprivation of a territory geographically "artificial." The geographical conceptions are not only necessary to the assumption of a natural boundary but have the intrinsic aesthetic appeal attested by Henry Clay's observation that Florida was desired because "it fills a space in our imagination." [29] It now becomes necessary to determine the purely geographical criterion on the basis of which Florida seemed to give America, as Representative Anderson said, a "complete natural boundary." [30]

A geographical principle was suggested by Senator Jackson when he said with reference to Florida that the natural boundaries of the South were the Atlantic, the Gulf, and the Mississippi.[31] According to this view, Americans had a right to a water boundary to the south as well as to the east and west. Such a thesis, which may be called the doctrine of the natural barrier, assumes that a state should have as boundary a topographical feature serving as a barrier or natural line of separation. The authority Sir Thomas Holdich states that "boundaries must be barriers"; [32] indeed, it is the most common view that the natural barrier is the sole true criterion of the natural boundary.

However, a second argument in the Florida issue was concerned not with the natural barrier but with another geographical consideration. It was suggested by Gouverneur Morris's assertion that Florida is "joined to us by the hand of the Almighty," [33] and also by the observation of the New Orleans *Gazette* that Florida is a natural "appendage" of the United States.[34] The evident consideration here is contiguity, or more generally stated, propinquity. Dr. Quincy Wright's article on "Territorial Propinquity" points out that the doctrine has not infrequently been used in the claim to unoccupied and politically undefined territory.[35] But in the present case propinquity was held to give the adjacent state a better claim to territory than that possessed even by its distant sovereign.

Still a third geographical principle was implied by Madison's reference to the relations formed between Florida and the United States by common rivers. According to a previously cited report of a House committee, the fact that these rivers ran almost exclusively within American limits gave the impression that by nature they were "intended for our own benefit." This conception that lands are connected by common rivers falls under a doctrine which may be called the principle of the territorial nexus. It posits the geographical unity of two adjacent regions on the ground of some common feature which appears as a nexus between them. In the words of C. J. Ingersoll, writing of American geography, "rivers of inexhaustible affluence, and far-interior lakes" constitute "national ligaments." [36]

All these considerations were reflected in the following typical press comment on the treaty of 1819 ceding Florida to the United States:

> Any man, the least acquainted with the geography of our country, must have seen that the Floridas would certainly pass into the possession of the United States. They as naturally belong to us as the county of Cornwall does to England.[37]

In point of fact the geography of the country was effective only because it facilitated the pressure of American pioneers and statesmen upon weak Spain. Yet the notion that Florida naturally belonged to the United States added moral force to expansionism; for it was the common dogma that, as Joel Barlow said, "as long as we follow nature, in politics as well as morals, we are sure to be in the right." [38]

Yet we observe that nature's behests were interpreted not uniformly but by three distinct principles, a plurality making the following of nature somewhat complicated. Common to all principles, indeed, was the conception that the natural boundary was that which encloses a geographical unity. But the three ways of conceiving geographical unity were radically different. Unity was posited on the grounds of propinquity, enclosure by the same natural barrier, or a common territorial feature such as a river.

The pragmatic effect of this triple character of the criterion of the natural boundary was all to the advantage of expansionism. For although in the Florida issue the three principles were used in conjunction, there was nothing to prevent them from being used independently. There were thus three distinct ways whereby the expansionist could claim as natural the boundary which appeared desirable in the light of necessity, convenience, glory, or merely geographical symmetry.

In preparing to consider other applications of the doctrine of the natural boundary we are conscious of a question which was suggested by the Florida issue but could not be answered by the data of this issue alone. Is each of the geographical criteria applied with consistency or with divergences of meaning which make the indications of nature more manifold than manifest? The answer lies in a comparative analysis which will traverse a range of justificatory ideas as great as the extent of territorial ambitions.

The first territorial issue after Monroe's early attempt to acquire Florida arose when the United States claimed Texas as part of Louisiana, the boundaries of which had been defined by the treaty of sale unintelligibly. It was the contention of the American commissioners in 1805 that Texas went with Louisiana in consequence of the French discovery of the Mississippi and the adjacent coast:

> . . . when any European nation takes possession of any extensive sea coast, that possession is understood as extending into the interior country, to the sources of the rivers emptying within that coast, to all their branches, and the country they cover . . . [39]

This broad proposition, as the jurist Lindley points out, is now considered erroneous; a nation discovering a seacoast has only a contingent title to a reasonable amount of inland territory which, as Bluntschli says, forms an "*ensemble naturel*" with the coast.[40] But the argument of the American commissioners had another foundation — geographical predestination as indicated by the territorial nexus:

> Nature seems to have destined a range of territory so described for the same society, to have connected its several parts together by the ties of a common interest, and to have detached them from others.[41]

This belief caused Benton in 1820 to hurl an imprecation at the American statesmen who, yielding Texas to Spain, subjected part of the "magnificent valley of the Mississippi" to "dismemberment."[42] In the 'forties, when independent Texas offered to restore itself to the United States, Robert J. Walker like other expansionists affirmed refusal of this offer to be an impious dissolution of what God made one when he "planned down the whole valley, including Texas, and united every atom of soil and every drop of water of the mighty whole."[43] The practical logic in the expansionist metaphysics was reflected in Representative Chappell's assertion that nature had designed an economic interdependence between the grain-growing country of the upper Mississippi and the southern territory around the Gulf.[44] This postulate corresponds to Fichte's theory that natural boundaries are those which create economic self-sufficiency.

But the interpretation of the territorial nexus in the Texas issue was in conflict with the interpretation of the same principle in the West Florida question. Although it was maintained in both instances that territories were brought by a common river into a geographical unity, the question of the proper owner of this unity received conflicting answers. In the West Florida issue it was held by Americans that the country containing the greater part of the river had a right to the seacoast at its outlet. In the Texas issue it was held that the country possessing the seacoast had a right to the inland territory through which the river flows. Thus, apart from the difference in legal considerations, the argument of natural boundary advanced in the Texas issue would have lost for the United States its case for the possession of West Florida. But by virtue of its ambiguity the principle of the territorial nexus permitted the two conflicting arguments to have the one common merit of establishing the claim of the United States.

The next issue of expansion showed the principle of the territorial nexus in an aspect which illustrates even more strikingly its convenient flexibility. The issue in question had to do with northern territory and arose in connection with the War of 1812. It has been plausibly argued by Professor Pratt that this war, long explained by reference to impressment and commercial restrictions, was caused fundamentally by the desire of Western States for the annexation of Canada.[45] This desire, according to Professor Pratt, was rooted in the determination of Westerners to terminate the supposed activity of British agents in fomenting Indian attacks upon America's Western settlements. Although this motive was probably predominant, one must not overlook the factor recognized by Professor Anderson — the desire for territory essential to the completion of our "natural boundary." [46] A natural boundary to the north was desired by Northwestern States because it would secure the St. Lawrence as an outlet to the ocean for their commerce.

The geographical self-justification of many expansionists was precisely the principle which presented a river as a territorial nexus. Representative Johnson, after declaring that the map would prove the importance of acquiring Canada, proved its propriety with both geography and theology:

> The waters of the St. Lawrence and the Mississippi interlock in a number of places, and the great Disposer of Human Events intended those two rivers should belong to the same people.[47]

In the same session Representative Harper revealed the pragmatic consideration which the "Disposer of Human Events" allegedly had in mind — the fact that with Canada annexed to the United States the St. Lawrence and the Lakes would become "a great outlet . . . at our command for our convenience and future security." He thereupon affirmed a thesis of geographical predestination which embraced Florida as well as Canada:

> To me, sir, it appears that the Author of Nature has marked our limits in the south, by the Gulf of Mexico; and on the north, by the regions of eternal frost.[48]

A writer in the *Boston Patriot* of 1812 felt certain that "the God of nature" had given the navigation of the St. Lawrence to the American inhabitants of the adjoining country; but his warning that these Americans would join Canada if the United States did not obtain the right of navigation showed that the expansionist argument could be used in reverse.[49] In 1813 the expansionist version of predestination was heard from Representative Emott: "These two great rivers seem to have been intended by Providence for an inland navigation from North to South . . ." [50]

To the original identification of the territorial nexus with one river expansionists have added the broader conception that a nexus is formed by two rivers the branches of which interlock. The second version is as different from the first as two rivers are from one. It seems, however, an equally justifiable deduction from the same general principle which was implied by the first version. The principle of the territorial nexus initiates a line of thought which is as difficult as water to stop.

Thus there was a third deduction from the principle of the territorial nexus, more far-reaching than either of those preceding. It was also connected with the War of 1812 in so far as this was an attempt to assert America's interpretation of maritime law in the Atlantic. In 1806 Jefferson had justified a claim to American supremacy in the North Atlantic upon an interesting geographical ground:

> We begin to broach the idea that we consider the whole gulph Stream as of our waters, in which hostilities and cruising are to be frowned on for the present, and prohibited so soon as either consent or force will permit us.[51]

This curious claim was apparently based upon the view that the Gulf Stream is an extension of the Mississippi; thus it was a claim to an oceanic sphere of influence by virtue of a nexus consisting not only of a river but also of an extensive stream of the sea. It is probable that a similar conception reinforced the ambition presented in the congressional debates on the naval bill of 1812 — "mastery in the American seas, particularly as far as the Gulf Stream." [52] Representative Widgery affirmed that the limits of American jurisdiction "on the Southeast should be the Gulf Stream, a line drawn by the god of nature." [53] These early expansionists had outdone those who in the 'fifties believed it "destiny" that the Gulf of Mexico become "mare nostrum." [54]

Just as the principle of the territorial nexus reaches its

farthest point of development, the course of events takes one to a second of the three principles of the natural boundary. This doctrine was the foundation of Representative Trimble's impassioned protest against the renunciation of Texas in the Spanish treaty of 1819. The treaty was denounced by Trimble because " our barriers are surrendered — bartered away." Our barriers to the south and southwest, according to Trimble, were the Rio Grande and the mountain ranges which marked the limits of Texas. We have to do here, then, with the principle of the natural barrier. The philosophy of the natural barrier received from Trimble grandiloquent statement:

> The Father of the Universe, in his peculiar providence, had given natural boundaries to every continent and kingdom—permanent, physical, imperishable barriers, to every nation, to shield it from invasion. Man, in his mad career of glory, his thirst for dominion, had rejected as useless the great and permanent boundaries of nature, and sought out ideal, perishable limits of his own creation. . . . It is physical barriers alone that check encroachment, and give repose to feeble nations. . . .
>
> The great Engineer of the Universe has fixed the natural limits of our country, and man cannot change them; that at least is above the treaty-making power. To that boundary we shall go; ' peaceably if we can, forcibly if we must '; beyond it, all to us is worthless; we would not have it as a gift; not if Spain would give a dowry with it; that would lay the foundation of perpetual collisions; the other would exclude them so far as human wisdom can avert the danger.[55]

The principle of the natural barrier is thus concerned not with the unifying territorial features but with those which clearly and securely separate peoples. But here as in the principle of the territorial nexus there is the assumption that an indisputable natural boundary is destined for all eternity.

Trimble's belief that Americans would take nothing but the Rio Grande as the southern boundary was not, however, confirmed by events. The treaty renouncing Texas was ratified and Texas did not become a serious issue until the 'forties. Then, however, there were some who believed as did Representative Ingersoll that not the Rio Grande but the immense deserts between the Rio Grande and the Nueces rivers formed " the natural boundaries between the anglo-Saxon and the Mauritanian races." [56] Most expansionists, indeed, harked back to Trimble and thought the Rio Grande "the boundary prescribed by nature." [57] Yet this view was to be superseded after the Rio Grande became the legal boundary. Minister Gadsden, believing a river inadequate as a barrier, urged Mexico in the 'fifties to anticipate the inexorable by selling to the United States the six northern provinces above the Sierra Madre mountains, thereby securing "a natural Territorial boundary, imposing in its Mountain and Desert outlines." [58] But when Mexico defied destiny he accepted the thinner strip in the Gadsden Treaty, which gave no natural boundary at all. In the following decade Senator Nye would have solved the whole problem of barrier by incorporating all Mexico in the interest of "the symmetry of this republic." [59] Such were the variations which lasted even into the twentieth century, when the *Independent*, in an editorial entitled "A Scientific Border," came forth with the relatively modest proposal of a boundary taking in the full length of the Colorado River.[60] But as early as 1804 Joseph Chandler outdid all these expansionists by anticipating the southernmost ambition of American history.[61] It was the Isthmus of Panama, where, Thomas Green was to assert after the canal project had arisen, a permanent barrier would be formed by the union of the two great oceans of the world.[62]

Let us see whether there was any greater agreement with respect to America's western boundary. After the Spanish treaty ceding Spain's western claims it was the great range of the Rockies, a boundary which a recent historian has declared to be "more natural than any reached since or likely to be reached in any period of subsequent expansion." [63] In the discussion of the Oregon issue in 1823 Representative Tracy did admit that there "nature has fixed limits for our nation; she has kindly interposed as our Western barrier, mountains almost inaccessible, whose base she has skirted with irreclaimable limits of sand." [64] Senator Benton, likewise seeing there the limiting hand of nature, would have placed upon the highest peak of the Rockies the immovable statue of the great god Terminus.[65]

However, Representative Baylies rose in 1823 to present a very different conception of the *ultima Thule:*

If we reach the Rocky Mountains, we should be unwise did we not pass that narrow space which separates the mountains from the ocean, to secure advantages far greater than the existing advantages of all the country between the Mississippi and the mountains. Gentlemen are talking of natural boundaries. Sir, our natural boundary is the Pacific Ocean. The swelling tide of our population must and will roll on until that mighty ocean interposes its waters, and limits our territorial empire.[66]

Baylies's prediction was in accord with Joshua Pilcher's observation with reference to the Rockies — that the man " must know but little of the American people, who supposes that they can be stopped by any thing in the shape of mountains, deserts, seas, or rivers." [67] It was in conformity with Ratzel's generalization that " young countries know no exclusion from the sea," [68] and with an American geographer's thesis that " the ocean is the only absolute boundary." [69] It was in the spirit of the Roman conceit: " Our empire is bounded by the ocean, our glory by the stars." And it was prophetic of the actual course of events.

However, there remains the problem of explaining these and other divergences with regard to that " limiting hand of nature " which was supposed to be so obvious. Do the disagreements result merely from varying estimations of the value of topographical features as barriers? The difficulty with this explanation is the frequency of the phenomenon noted by Robert Winthrop in a classic *reductio ad absurdum* of geographical predestination:

It is not a little amusing to observe what different views are taken as to the indications of ' the hand of nature ' and the pointings of ' the finger of God,' by the same gentleman, under different circumstances and upon different subjects. In one quarter of the compass they can descry the hand of nature in a level desert and a second-rate river, beckoning us impatiently to march up to them. But when they turn their eyes to another part of the horizon, the loftiest mountains in the universe are quite lost upon their gaze. There is no hand of nature there. The configuration of the earth has no longer any significance. The Rocky Mountains are mere molehills. Our destiny is onward.[70]

The true explanation of these geo-theological inconsistencies lay probably in the differences in the value of the lands beyond the topographical features in question. When the land seemed undesirable, the nationalist considered some topographical feature an effectual barrier to it; but when the land beyond appeared desirable he did not feel that it was cut off by any barrier whatsoever. An editorial of the *Nashville Republican* in 1829 was amusingly ingenuous in determining the natural boundary by the value of lands beyond. After asserting that the Rio Grande was apparently " designated by the hand of Heaven, as a boundary between two great nations of dissimilar pursuits," the editorial proceeded to say:

> Another reason why this river seems to be marked out for a boundary is this:—On this side of the Rio Grande, the country is seasonable, fertile, and every way desirable to the people of the United States. On the other side the lands are unproductive, crops cannot be matured without irrigation; in short they are entirely calculated for a lazy, pastoral, mining people like the Mexicans.[71]

But the Rio Grande did not seem a natural boundary after Americans developed a desire for Mexican mines; nor did even the mountains beyond appear a proper line of separation from the Spanish-American race after Americans conceived a desire for the control of an Isthmian route.

With such considerations in view we may return to the explanation of the divergences of theory about the western boundary. It is well known that in the 'twenties the majority of Americans did not consider Oregon as a territory which was valuable in its natural resources or in any other respect. But Baylies, having greater imagination in commercial matters than most of his contemporaries, avowedly realized that " with two oceans, washing our shores," that is, with control of ports opening up the possibility of Far Eastern trade, " the commercial wealth of the world is ours." It was doubtless because he envisaged " the greatness, the grandeur and the power that await us " as possessors of the western shore, that he could not conceive of the Rockies as a true barrier on the west.[72]

Others saw a different advantage in possessing Oregon — the strategic advantage of excluding Europe from a country adjacent to the United States. The rub was, however, that Great Britain held claims to the Northwestern Coast which conflicted with those of the United States. Now the principle of the natural barrier did not in itself establish the superiority of America's claim to that of Great Britain, the sovereign of the country to the north. To understand the American's assumption that his country's claim was superior, it is necessary at this point to turn to a third principle of the natural boundary, utilized in the diplomatic correspondence of the United States with Great Britain.

Upon no American did the importance of excluding Europe from Oregon impress itself more strongly than upon Secretary of State John Quincy Adams. But Adams in his office of state had to note, even if not to admit as valid, the British and Russian claims which conflicted with those of the United States on the Northwestern Coast. This conflict, giving rise to Adams's formulation of his non-colonization principle, was adjudged by him in America's favor not merely upon legal grounds but also upon the ground of geographical predestination. In a despatch of 1823 to the American Minister to Great Britain, Adams penned the famous words containing this geographical dogma:

> It is not imaginable that, in the present condition of the world, *any* European nation should entertain the project of settling a *colony* on the Northwestern Coast of America; that the United States should form establishments there, with views of absolute territorial right and inland commerce, is not only to be expected, but is pointed out by the finger of nature . . . [73]

It is easy to determine that " the finger of nature," an expression curiously poetic for a diplomatic despatch, referred to the principle of propinquity. Minister Rush, presenting the content of the despatch to his British colleague orally, translated Adams's phrase into the proposition that the settlement of Americans on the Northwestern Coast was " naturally to be expected as proximate to their own possessions and falling under their immediate jurisdiction." [74] Adams himself in another despatch of 1823 suggested this meaning. He wrote to Minister Middleton that the Northwestern Coast was of greater importance to the United States because " it is but the continuity of their possessions from the Atlantic to the Pacific

Ocean." [75] Again in his "Confidential Memoir" of September, 1821, on the same issue, he maintained that the coast was most important to the United States by virtue of the "bordering position" of the United States to one part of that coast.[76] It is to be noted that the principle of propinquity had developed somewhat since the time of its use by Madison in the Florida issue; for whereas no natural barrier intervened between the United States and Florida, the Rockies might well have seemed a decisive separation of the United States from Oregon.

The most flagrant weakness in Adams's use of the doctrine of propinquity was his inconsistency in not recognizing that Great Britain could apply the same doctrine to the portion of the coast adjacent to its American possessions. However, there was a consideration which always seemed to Americans a sufficient answer to such a charge of inconsistency. This consideration, used notably by Edward Everett's despatch of 1852 on the tripartite Cuban convention, was that Europe had no right to consider a mere colony, remote from its vital interests, as establishing propinquity in America. Just as Everett refused to concede that the burdensome colony of Jamaica gave Great Britain a vital interest in Cuba, so Adams was doubtless unwilling to admit that Britain's sovereignty over American territory north of the forty-ninth parallel gave a geographical claim to any portion of the Northwestern Coast. Adams was the less disposed to make such a concession since he doubted, as we shall shortly see, even the geographical propriety of Europe's permanent retention of any colony in North America.

On the other hand, the United States appeared to Adams to derive from propinquity territorial rights which went far beyond Oregon. Even before his use of the principle of propinquity in the Oregon correspondence of 1823, Adams had employed it in claims still more ambitious. In a despatch of 1818 on the Oregon issue, he had stated for Great Britain's enlightenment:

> If the United States leave her in undisturbed enjoyment of all her holds upon Europe, Asia, and Africa, with all her actual possessions in this hemisphere, we may very fairly expect that she will not think it consistent either with a wise or a friendly policy, to watch with eyes of jealousy and alarm every possibility of extension to our natural dominion in North America . . . [77]

This was really to say that, in return for American generosity in leaving British possessions undisturbed, America's extension anywhere in North America was to be regarded as natural.

An episode in the following year showed that Adams had a still more pretentious view of America's territorial rights. It was too bold to receive statement in a diplomatic document, but it could be stated *en famille.* Mention in a Cabinet meeting that Europe considered America ambitious elicited from Adams a bland expression of unconcern. What really concerned him was the possibility that Europe underestimated America's valid ambition:

> . . . the world shall be familiarized with the idea of considering our proper dominion to be the continent of North America. From the time when we became an independent people it was as much a law of nature that this should become our pretension as that the Mississippi should flow to the sea. Spain had possessions upon our southern and Great Britain upon our northern border. It was impossible that centuries should elapse without finding them annexed to the United States; not that any spirit of encroachment or ambition on our part renders it necessary, but because it is a physical, moral, and political absurdity that such fragments of territory, with sovereigns at fifteen hundred miles beyond sea, worthless and burdensome to their owners, should exist permanently contiguous to a great, powerful, enterprising, and rapidly-growing nation. Most of the Spanish territory which had been in our neighborhood had already become our own by the most unexceptionable of all acquisitions—fair purchase for a valuable consideration. This rendered it still more unavoidable that the remainder of the continent should ultimately be ours. But it is very lately that we have distinctly seen this ourselves; very lately that we have avowed the pretension of extending to the South Sea; and until Europe shall find it a settled geographical element that the United States and North America are identical, any effort on our part to reason the world out of a belief that we are ambitious will have no other effect than to convince them that we add to our ambition hypocrisy.[78]

Here, then, Europe is denied even its existing territorial possessions in North America. However, America's claim to the continent derives allegedly not from ambition but merely from the recognition of a destiny rooted in the earth, a law of nature assigning fragments of adjacent territory to the proximate power rather than the distant. By such projection of their ambitions upon laws of nature Americans were very frequently to attain self-assurance in pursuing lands with the greatest energy if not aggressiveness.

Yet the geographical logic of continental dominion had possessed from America's beginning an intrinsic persuasiveness. In a poem of the Revolution Jonathan Mitchel Sewall wrote imaginative lines which were quoted with wearisome frequency throughout the history of American expansion:

> No pent-up Utica contracts your powers,
> But the whole boundless continent is yours! [79]

Again, in 1786 Judge Campbell of Franklin posed the rhetorical question: "Is not the continent of America one day to become one consolidated government of United States?" [80] Joseph Chandler's already cited oration of 1804 ascribed the same continental boundaries to nature's designs, more manifest after the purchase of Louisiana.[81] The expansionist movement preceding the War of 1812 gave rise to popular appeals such as that of a writer in the Nashville *Clarion:* ". . . where is it written in the book of fate that the American republic shall not stretch her limits from the capes of the Chesapeake to Nootka sound, from the isthmus of Panama to Hudson bay?" [82] It was in the second decade of the nineteenth century, as Professor Pratt [83] points out and as the words of Adams attest, that the idea of manifest destiny in its continental version first became rather general. The destiny of continental dominion did not, however, become a firmly established article of the national creed until the decade of the 'forties, when John L. O'Sullivan, in the editorial containing the first widely noted use of the phrase "manifest destiny," asserted that "the God of nature" had marked Oregon and all other continental territory for our own.[84] Adams's reference to contiguity indicated that the principle of propinquity was the main determinant of the conception of the continent as a geographical *ensemble.* But another important determinant was the idea that the continent was "boundless" in the sense that all natural barriers save the ocean had no finality for Americans, no capacity to restrain their powers.

If propinquity be interpreted with this latitude why not acquire a still larger geographical unity — the Western Hemisphere? Inasmuch as the two continents were not separated by a natural barrier but joined by an isthmus, the logical conclusion of the principle of propinquity was not Panama but Cape Horn. The failure of most American expansionists to go the entire length was probably due to an illogical element of weariness, together with the fear that extension of a principle to its logical conclusion might seem an *extensio ad absurdum.*

However, the principle of propinquity is carried to its conclusion by one American pretension, a claim to what might be called a " hemisphere of interest." This pretension is of course the Monroe Doctrine, which because of a geographico-political principle of security excludes Europe from either interference or further colonization in the Western Hemisphere. The influence of geographical reasoning upon " the doctrine of the two spheres," of which the Monroe Doctrine is only the most important expression, is suggested by observations of Americans in many issues and periods. Thomas Paine's reference to America's distance from Great Britain as a " strong and natural proof " of independence,[85] together with Washington's allusion to " our detached and distant situation " [86] and to the improvement of the advantages which " nature has given us," [87] evidence the geographical element in the ideals of both independence and isolation. Hamilton's assertion that its " situation " prompted the United States to aim at " an ascendant in the system of American affairs " marks the beginning of the conception of hemispheric hegemony as a consequence of isolation.[88] Gouverneur Morris's observation that the waves of an immense sea would carry out the edict of Time and Fate against European intrusion into Louisiana reflects the conception of a destiny protecting American isolation.[89] John Quincy Adams's assertion that the finger of nature pointed out only America's colonization on the Northwestern Coast suggests the relation between geographical predestination and the non-colonization principle of the Monroe Doctrine, for which Adams appears primarily responsible. A geographical interpretation was subsequently given to the Monroe Doctrine very frequently. Thus

Representative Stanton asserted in the Oregon debate of 1846 that Monroe's doctrine was identical with the following principle:

> The law which makes the ocean a barrier to instantaneous commerce between nations—the law of nature, which has separated continents by interposing vast abysses, forbids that nations on one continent shall have rights on another by implication, extension, contiguity, or by any other invisible, intangible, metaphysical principle whatever.[90]

One may note incidentally that the same geographical principle was asserted even before Monroe's pronouncement in the Manifesto of the Provisional Board of the Mexican Government. After citing various instances of the fact that "Nature has marked out the territories of nations" by natural boundaries, the Manifesto affirmed: "Policy must necessarily conform to the order of nature; and as it would be monstrous to put in the same space the contrary elements of fire and water, it is equally so to unite in one province people who are distinct and distant, especially if that difference and distance extend to the extremity of the two worlds."[91] The common indication of such observations is that the American doctrine of the separation of the two hemispheres tends to be suggested or reinforced by a geographical rationale combining the principle of propinquity and the principle of the natural barrier. It is the former principle, however, which is preponderant in the special doctrine of the hegemony of the United States in the Western Hemisphere. The conception here is that "geographical proximity," as Olney said, makes the countries of the Americas allies whose political integrity the United States must defend against Europe.[92]

But such geographical reasoning is a sword which cuts in two ways. It interdicts not merely Europe's territorial extension in another hemisphere but also America's expansion anywhere off the mainland. For the distant wandering of the principle of propinquity must finally be ended by the idea that, as Lord Curzon says, "of all Natural Frontiers the sea is the most uncompromising, the least alterable, and the most effective."[93] Because the sea had seemed "inviolate" there had been little intimation, as late as 1820, that American expansionists would wish to depart from the continent. Thus Representative Rhea, when warned in 1811 that the creation of Orleans Territory might be a precedent for taking the West Indies, responded that he would not become interested in the West Indian islands unless " it would please the Almighty Maker of worlds to move the foundations of the West India islands and place them close alongside of the United States." [94]

However, there arose later a different attitude toward a West Indian island even though its foundations were unchanged. Cuba hove into the American's horizon shortly after 1820 because of the threat of European or Latin-American seizure during the Spanish-American revolutions. The crisis having increased the realization of the strategic importance of Cuba to American coasts and commerce, Secretary of State John Quincy Adams not merely opposed the transfer of Cuba but predicted its future annexation by the United States. Of chief interest here is the fact that he justified the acquisition of Cuba by a theory of geographical predestination.

Strangely, the geographical theory turns out to be the very principle of propinquity which might seem to forbid departure from the continent. In a despatch of 1823 to America's Minister to Spain, Adams supported a prediction of annexation by the following geographical consideration:

> These islands from their local position are natural appendages to the North American continent; and one of them, Cuba, almost in sight of our shores, from a multitude of considerations has become an object of transcendent importance to the political and commercial interests of our Union.[95]

The contemporary observation of Alexander Everett, American Minister to Spain, attests the general influence of the doctrine of the appendage:

> It has always appeared to me, and such I believe is the general opinion in the United States, that this island forms properly an appendage of the Floridas.[96]

Various geographical ideas combined to produce this conception of Cuba as a natural appendage of the United States. The most obvious is the notion of virtual contiguity which was suggested by the circumstance that Cuba is "almost in sight of our shores." Another is the realization that Cuba is more adjacent to the United States than to any other continental state. This consideration appears in Secretary of State Clay's comment of 1825 upon Mexican and Colombian designs on Cuba: ". . . if that Island is to be made a dependence of any one of the American States, it is impossible not to allow that the law of its position proclaims that it should be attached to the United States." [97] Finally there is the geographical reasoning of President Monroe in his letter of 1823 to Jefferson in favor of the acquisition of Cuba: "I consider Cape Florida, & Cuba, as forming the mouth of the Mississippi . . ." [98] These ingenious considerations are to be understood in part in the light of the fact that their rationalizations of the "natural appendage" aim to conceal the conflict of this version of propinquity with the doctrine of the natural barrier.

But can even the cleverest logic overcome the force of the bare geographical fact that the "natural appendage" is after all an island, beyond the great barrier of the sea? That Cuba is not really an appendage of the United States would be the quick conclusion of any one trying to swim to the island. To be sure, in 1859 Seward tried to bridge the gap logically by asserting that "every rock and every grain of sand in that island were drifted and washed out from American soil by the floods of the Mississippi, and the other estuaries of the Gulf of Mexico." [99] But such a geological origin might just as well be interpreted to mean that nature designed the separation of Cuba from the United States. Nor can one ascribe decisive authority to Adams's dictum in the Oregon dispute that both international and natural law consider adjacent islands as appendages to continents.[100] For in the Lobos Islands controversy, when America's self-interest demanded the antithetic position, the equally learned Daniel Webster argued with equal dogmatism that even an island distant only a few miles from the mainland could not be claimed on the ground of proximity.[101]

One can only say that, although the principle of the natural barrier is violated by the first departure from the continent, the departure urged by propinquity in the case of Cuba was comparatively slight and was not intended to form a general principle. American statesmen of the 'twenties considered Cuba as a "*ne plus ultra*" in the ocean.[102] But could it remain a *ne plus ultra* after the principle of propinquity was freed of the fettering conception that the sea is ever a barrier?

The true logical tendencies of these geographical principles can only be seen in the extended perspective of history. We may glance briefly at the later course of the doctrine of propinquity to see how strangely far the tide of desire was to propel it. To be sure, in the 'forties the expansionist was modestly content with the North American continent; his geographical claim to Oregon and Mexican territory seemed to him superior to Europe's by virtue of "the principle of contiguity, free from the intervening barriers of formidable oceans."[103] Stephen Douglas declared in 1844: "I do not want to go beyond the great ocean—beyond those boundaries which the God of nature has marked out."[104] In the subsequent decade, however, Douglas and most other expansionists did desire to go beyond the great ocean to acquire Cuba, which seemed to form part, as the Washington *Daily Union* held, of America's strategic "natural boundaries."[105] And if Cuba be a natural appendage, was it unnatural for expansionists of the 'sixties to contemplate the strategically desirable annexation of the Dominican Republic as well? Governor Pownall said in 1780 that whether the West Indies were naturally parts of the North American continent was a question for curious speculation.[106] In 1869 Representative Woodward and others concluded definitely that these islands were "a part of the American continent" and "naturally belong to us."[107] The extension of America's interest in West Indian Islands had been effected by the Civil War, which demonstrated the usefulness of naval stations in this maritime area. In two more decades the strategic interest in "natural outposts" had shifted with the growth of oversea commerce to the Pacific. Of the Hawaiian Islands, the crossroads of the Pacific, Admiral Belknap wrote in 1893: "Indeed, it would seem that nature had established that group to be ultimately occupied as an outpost, as it were, of the great Republic on its western border, and that the time had now come for the fulfilment of such a design." [108] The doctrine of propinquity is reflected still more clearly in the statement of Representative Henry that "we want them because they are more contiguous to our territory than to that of any other nation." [109] To be sure, there were some like Representative Clark who objected to the proposed annexation as a departure from the continental bounds which "Nature" had set for the Republic.[110] But Senator Chandler affirmed the acquisition of Hawaii to be a continental policy on the ground that nature had made the islands a part of the defense system of the continent.[111] Apparently there is nothing either near or far but thinking makes it so.

Although Hawaii was two thousand miles from the American continent its acquisition did not conflict with Jefferson's principle of "a meridian of partition through the ocean." [112] But once Hawaii had been annexed the imperialists found it easy to extend the principle of propinquity past the oceanic meridian to the Philippines. "We are stretching out our hands," wrote ex-Minister Denby, "for what nature meant should be ours." [113] One conception which underlay this interpretation of nature's design was that of the propinquity of the Philippines to Hawaii. A second was the notion, expressed in the *New York Recorder*, that because of greater adjacency to the United States than to Europe "the outlying islands in the two oceans belong not to the European but to the American system." [114] Kimpen, the German historian of American expansion, affirms amusingly but not very convincingly that another geographical justification of America's colonial policy was the theory that the Philippines are a part of the American western half of the earth according to Pope Alexander's ancient bull of division.[115] No less ingenious was the response of Senator Beveridge to the objection that the Philippines are not contiguous: "Our navy will make them contiguous!" [116]

After the Philippines were annexed some could view as natural even America's participation in the territorial division of China. Thus the *Boston Herald*, demanding America's share in any partition by the powers, implicitly appealed to the doctrine of propinquity in the words: "The Philippine Islands is our stepping-stone to China." [117] Unrepresentative as was such a view, there is no doubt that the conception of the ocean as a barrier had disappeared as completely from expansionist philosophy as had the old clipper from transportation. Whitelaw Reid, whose newspaper in 1889 thought Samoa "intended by nature to be an Australian rather than an American dependency," [118] held at the time of acquiring Samoan Tutuila that the ocean "unites you with the whole boundless, mysterious Orient." [119] Similarly Beveridge proclaimed that "the ocean does not separate us from the lands of our duty and desire" but "joins us." [120] Americans had learned the imaginative feat of British imperialists, of a Harrington who thought that "the growth of Oceana gives law to the sea," [121] and of a Coleridge who affirmed that "God seems to hold out his finger to us over the sea." [122] Development of the principle of propinquity had changed the ocean from natural barrier to territorial nexus.

In the last years of the nineteenth century some expansionists took to speaking semi-humorously of "the manifest destiny of the English race and the Yankee nation to inherit the earth." [123] In fact, the doctrine of propinquity had gone so far that there was no longer a geographical reason for its ever stopping. When the principle of propinquity traverses the ocean it has passed the last possible natural barrier. There looms then the possibility noted by Ugarte in commenting upon Marcy's geographical claim to Cuba: "It is clear that this view of strategic dependence and of the inevitable results of proximity might lead, little by little, to the conquest of a world." [124]

Fortunately for the world, weariness imposes a check which geographical logic does not. Thus shortly after the turn of the century America's doctrine of propinquity retreated from world-wide conquest and concentrated upon North America. But now the thesis of the expansionist or of the interventionist that "propinquity creates special political relations" [125] was open to the charge of inconsistency. When an expansionist member of the National Conference on Foreign Relations declared all the European island colonies of the adjacent Caribbean to be "naturally and strategically a part of the United States," [126] Mr. Moorfield Storey countered as follows:

Let us not say that proximity to the coast of America dictates the destiny of these islands, while proximity to the coast of Asia does not interfere with our claim to the Philippines.[127]

In carrying America's sovereignty to the Philippines the doctrine of propinquity had committed logical suicide in the manner of the legendary serpent which grew until it swallowed its own tail. For by going past mid-sea this doctrine had lost the right to fulfil its original purpose — establishment of the superiority of America's adjacent territorial claim to that of some oversea power like Spain. As sovereign of the Philippines the United States itself was in another hemisphere, one in which Japan was soon to assert a claim to hegemony on the ground of the principle of propinquity which the West had taught her. Although the Monroe Doctrine continued in effect, Americans could no longer consistently support it, as did Olney, with the proposition that " three thousand miles of intervening ocean make any permanent political union between an European and an American state unnatural and inexpedient." [128]

Not merely the doctrine of propinquity but the entire American philosophy of the natural boundary had apparently met with logical catastrophe. This is not to deny von Engeln's thesis that " place contributes the essential and significant basis of all human association," [129] or its corollary that, as Lord Curzon says, " frontiers are indeed the razor's edge on which hang suspended the modern issues of war or peace, of life or death to nations." [130] It is not even to deny that, as Miss E. C. Semple has written, " every forward step in American expansion meant a more scientific boundary." [131] But the characteristic assumption of the American doctrine of geographical predestination was not the expediency of constantly advancing boundaries but the assumption that there was a natural terminus to advancement. Strange as it may seem, the geographical doctrine was meant to be a doctrine of " limits "; [132] its basic premise was that reason apprehended in each quarter of the compass a natural boundary which (to quote Benton) would be " everlasting " because even posterity would clearly see it as such.[133] It was precisely this theory that the natural boundary is eternally obvious which the history of American expansion disproved. Not only posterity but other expansionists of the same period did not see Benton's western boundary as final; nor did he himself see it as such several decades later when Americans came to want Oregon. Both to the west and to the south the geographically justified terminus of one expansion movement became the point of departure for a subsequent one. The doctrine of the natural boundary was refuted in that what purported to be a doctrine of universally binding limits was applied by expansionists who could not agree upon limits.

The egregious failure of the doctrine to limit expansion is no longer difficult to understand. To stop the march of empire would doubtless have proved too much for any philosophical principle; for each advance of the frontier solved one set of problems only to create another, satisfied one desire only to stimulate a new one. But the "natural boundary," a concept discovered in general history to be possessed of "the most diverse meanings,"[134] was a poorer barrier than almost any other because of its lack of any logical rigidity. So flexible were its three versions that in any territorial issue a logical twist could make one of the three open the way to the conception of a natural boundary. It is no wonder that Robert Winthrop observed that "the finger of God never points in a direction contrary to the extension of the glory of the republic."[135] Between desire and geographical criterion there was no more conflict than between the wind and a weathercock.

On the contrary, the doctrine of geographical predestination created a force greater than could have been exerted by desire unassisted. For the very fact that each advance was believed at the time to be final aroused in desire greater insistence. The hand of nature seemed to beckon to a terminus just beyond the horizon, to a boundary which demanded all effort because it would bring permanent rest. It really beckoned to an ever-retreating mirage, the indefinite pursuit of which, as Fisher Ames feared when America departed from its first natural boundary, would have been like a quest for the bounds of infinite space.

# CHAPTER III

## THE DESTINED USE OF THE SOIL

The acquisition of satisfactory boundaries in the Spanish treaty of 1819 was followed by a movement aiming not at the extension of national boundaries and yet, paradoxically, at the enlargement of domain. The movement was expansionist in the sense that its purpose was the extension of the domain of States. The Indian was still tenant on vast tracts and enjoyed a degree of political autonomy described by Chief Justice Marshall as that of "domestic dependent nations." [1] Before the third decade of the nineteenth century, it had usually been possible to satisfy recurrent need or fancy for lands through curtailing the Indian holdings by treaties — if such a name can be given to agreements so frequently reeking with alcohol and bribery. But after 1821 certain large Indian tribes of the South, having decided that their concessions had already exceeded reason, announced that they would cede no more land.[2] The resultant prospect of permanent *imperia in imperio* was so repugnant to Southern States that from 1820 to 1840 the acquisition of Indian lands overshadowed every question of national boundaries and was even viewed with the emotion and ideology of expansionism.

Jefferson had written in 1786 that "it may be taken for a certainty that not a foot of land will ever be taken from the Indians without their own consent." [3] In spirit if not in letter, the action of Americans of the Jacksonian period belied this optimistic prediction. Three Southern States passed bills declaring Indian laws void and in effect making all organized Indian society impracticable. Of these States, Georgia prepared for forcible dispossession — a course in which it received moral support from President Andrew Jackson, himself no lover of Indians. The climax of this course of imperialism was the passage by Congress of the Indian Removal Bill of 1830. Although providing nominally only the administrative machinery for Indian removal by treaties, it was actually designed, as everyone recognized, to facilitate the plans of the Southern States willing to exercise constraint. By the end of the next decade, virtually all Indian tribes east of the Mississippi had taken their virtually enforced departure as "the victims of our destiny." [4] The episode was typical of a phase of American history which has been described even by an American Secretary of the Interior as "in great part a record of broken treaties, of unjust wars, and of cruel spoliation." [5]

Many contemporaries condemned the coercive policy as violative of the Indian's plain legal rights. Condemnation of the so-called "Century of Dishonor" has become even more general now that the completion of expropriation leaves no further temptation. This moral condemnation has directed itself upon motive as well as deed with the effect of influencing the interpretation of the former. It is generally believed that the motives of Indian policy were, if not profoundly villainous, at least not illustrative of the rôle of moral ideology in politics.

But an expansionist society "never admits that it is doing violence to its moral instincts" [6] and is least disposed to do so when this violence is condemned by others. Thus in a congressional debate of 1830 an advocate of Indian removal contended with apparent sincerity that he had "advanced no principle inconsistent with the most rigid morality." [7] So little, indeed, had the principles advanced appeared immoral to their exponents that the ultimate authority for them was ascribed to God. The principles centered in a philosophy of the use of the soil. The white race seemed to Senator Benton to have a superior right to land because they "used it according to the intentions of the CREATOR." [8] The theory that a use of the soil was ordained by God or morality figured not only in the entire history of Indian relations but also in all issues in which Americans found themselves desiring soil occupied by an "inferior" race.

What were the intentions attributed to the Creator with respect to the soil, and why did they seem to favor only one group of his creatures? Here, as in most questions of theology, there was unfortunately a confusing variety of answers. The history of the idea in question may not illuminate the intentions of the Creator, but it will at least show the logical methods whereby American and other expansionists, irrespective of their own varying intentions regarding territory, have found it possible to expropriate aboriginal peoples with constant self-assurance.

The self-assurance of those favoring expropriation was the greater because the basis of their justificatory doctrine, as Senator Benton's words attest, was religious in character. The doctrine was derived from the American Puritans, who were sure of the Creator's intentions with regard to everything. Though the Puritans were probably not the first interlopers in the New World to justify their trespass by theology, they were the first to leave a record of their ideology for the edification of posterity. Thus John Winthrop of Massachusetts, in his *Conclusions for the Plantation in New England*, wrote as follows:

> The whole earth is the lords Garden & he hath given it to the sonnes of men, w^th^ a generall Condicõn, Gen: l. 28. Increase & multiply, replenish the earth & subdue it, w^ch^ was againe renewed to Noah, the end is Double morall & naturall that man might injoy the fruites of the earth & god might have his due glory from the creature, why then should we stand hear striveing for places of habitation . . . and in ye mean tyme suffer a whole Continent, as fruitfull & convenient for the use of man to lie waste w^th^out any improvement.

To this conception there did, indeed, present itself one objection, namely, that the American continent was already the property of certain of "the sonnes of men." But this objection did not seem to Winthrop to be based upon a true conception of property, which he defined from the point of view of the agriculturist:

> That w^ch^ lies common & hath never been replenished or subdued is free to any that will possesse and improve it, for god hath given to the sonnes of men a double right to the earth, there is a naturall right & a Civil right . . . And for the Natives in New England they inclose noe land neither have any settled habitation nor any tame cattle to improve the land by, & soe have noe other but a naturall right

to those countries Soe as if wee leave them sufficient for their use wee may lawfully take the rest, there being more than enough for them & us.[9]

While for the most part their practice was more considerate than their theory, the settlers of Massachusetts did at times follow the frugal method suggested by biblical precedent: They " seized and settled " Indian lands " because they were not waving with fields of yellow corn duly fenced in with square-cut hawthorne." In 1633 the biblical principle was used in the decision of the general court to the effect that " what lands any of the Indians have possessed and improved, by subduing the same, they have just right unto, according to that in Genesis, ch. i. 28, and ch. ix. I." [10] What this primarily meant was that " the Indians having only a natural right to so much land as they had or could improve . . . the rest of the country lay open to any that could and would improve it." [11]

Such a principle imperilled the Indian's land tenure almost as greatly as did the Papal Bull of Alexander VI, dividing the New World between two Christian nations in presumable accordance with the scriptural decree that the meek shall inherit the earth. To be sure, the idea of most later Americans that North American Indians did not practice agriculture is as much in conflict with the records as is the opinion of Governor Pownall that the white race had been land-workers from the beginning.[12] It is true, however, that Indians gained their subsistence chiefly by the use of the soil in the manner for which the hunter Esau had set the precedent, followed also by Anglo-Saxon huntsmen for purposes of sport. The Indians differed from the whites in their religious philosophy of the use of the soil. The philosophy of the former was revealed by a Pawnee chief who, according to James Buchanan, addressed the President in 1822 as follows:

The Great Spirit made us all—he made my skin red, and yours white; he placed us on this earth and intended that we should live differently from each other.

He made the whites to cultivate the earth, and feed on domestic animals; but he made us, red skins, to rove through the uncultivated woods and plains; to feed on wild animals and to dress with their skins. He also intended that we should go to war—to take scalps—*steal horses from* and triumph over our enemies—cultivate peace at home, and promote the happiness of each other.[13]

But this liberal theory of the intentions of the Great Spirit was largely blasphemous in the eyes of those who were certain that the Creator demands uniformity in the morals and habits of his children. To be sure, as Irving's ironical Diedrich Knickerbocker points out in speaking of "the right by cultivation," the savages could have pleaded that "they drew all the benefits from the land which their simple wants required . . . and that as Heaven merely designed the earth to form the abode, and satisfy the wants of man, so long as those purposes were answered, the will of Heaven was accomplished." But Knickerbocker gives the Puritan counter-argument that "this only proves how undeserving they were of the blessings around them — they were so much the more savages, for not having more wants." Knickerbocker concludes that the newcomers "were but taking possession of what, according to the aforesaid doctrine, was their own property — therefore, in opposing them, the savages were invading their just rights, infringing the immutable laws of Nature, and counteracting the will of Heaven."[14]

After this pious indictment the heathen Indian's case for his land could rest on only one possibility — that the scriptural passage on which it purported to rest had been misinterpreted. It did indeed seem to Roger Williams that, though the Scriptures command the tilling of the earth, they contain no statement whatever that the agriculturist has the right to expropriate those who do not till it.[15] But exegetical uncertainty did not trouble either the Puritan advocates of dispossession or many of their descendants. The religious argument passed down to later generations; it was said by John Quincy Adams, notwithstanding Henry Clay's laughter, to be "the best argument we had."[16]

But for the edification of those who considered references to God's word as "canting," there came into currency in the eighteenth century another type of doctrine, which, while not divorced from religious philosophy, addressed its appeal primarily to "natural reason." This argument for dispossession developed as jurists of the natural law school based the criteria of sovereignty over new lands upon the utilitarian values suggested by the crowded conditions of the Old World. During the American Revolution, as the traveller Johann David Schöpf noted, discussion of the future disposition of Indians' lands was marked by many expressions of the idea exemplified by the following words from the *United States Magazine* of 1779:

> The law of nature, where the law of revelation is not known, sufficiently enjoins on every man that he contract his claim of soil to equal bounds, and pursue that manner of life which is most consistent with the general population of the earth, and the encrease of happiness to mankind.[17]

Pasturage and hunting, the writer proceeded to explain, required too much soil and did not develop civilization; therefore property claims based upon a nomadic mode of life were not justified by natural law. The law of revelation was also adduced, but was blended with the moral argument through the conception that pasturage and hunting were abhorrent to God because they were incompatible with his design that the soil be used in the interest of civilization. Having discredited the Indian in the eyes of both God and nature, the writer proposed to restrict him to land which he actually cultivated. In 1782 Hugh Brackenridge affirmed that "extermination" would be a more useful fate for "the animals vulgarly called Indians," who, not having made "a better use of the land," had no natural right to it.[18] Benjamin Franklin's *Autobiography* suggested humorously that rum was "the appointed means" of fulfilling "the design of Providence to extirpate these savages in order to make room for the cultivators of the earth."[19]

An eighteenth-century exponent of natural law who greatly influenced American thought in the Indian issue was the Swiss jurist Vattel. The following passage from his treatise on the law of nations became classic:

> There is another celebrated question, to which the discovery of the New World has principally given rise. It is asked, if a nation may lawfully take possession of a part of a vast country, in which there

> are found none but erratic nations, incapable, by the smallness of their numbers, to people the whole. We have already observed in establishing the obligation to cultivate the earth, that these nations cannot exclusively appropriate to themselves more land than they have occasion for, and which they are unable to settle and cultivate. Their removing their habitations through these immense nations cannot be taken for a true and legal possession; and the people of Europe, too closely pent up, finding land of which these nations are in no particular want, and of which they make no actual and constant use, may lawfully possess it and establish colonies there. We have already said that the earth belongs to the human race in general, and was designed to furnish it with subsistence. . . . People have not, then, deviated from the views of nature, in confining the Indians within narrow limits.[20]

To advance the property rights of Europeans Vattel propounded a doctrine of world ownership which is, curiously enough, tantamount to a kind of international communism. An earlier statement of the same doctrine is found in Sir Thomas More's account of the international morality of the communistic society of Utopia.[21] Another precedent is offered by one with as great a prejudice in favor of ordinary property rights as Melanchthon. To justify the expropriation of the Catholic ecclesiastics he was obliged to affirm that those making bad use of their property had no right to it.[22]

Unlike both primitive Christians and modern Communists, bourgeois Protestants could not espouse Vattel's doctrine with much appearance of consistency. For it is somewhat at variance with their institution of private property and their conception of an unqualified right to property. A similar inconsistency was noted in Americans by Lincoln when he said that "the love of property and a consciousness of right and wrong have conflicting places in our organization."[23] In relations with a different race this love of property welcomes reasons for denying to others the property rights claimed by the white race for itself.

It is noteworthy, however, that the American expansionists did not even conform to Vattel's prescriptions. For Vattel makes the right of expropriation contingent upon being "too closely pent up"; he declares that those unable to cultivate all their land have no right to expand. The American people, as no one denied, had at the time an extent of territory which was beyond their own capacity to cultivate. This consideration, though it must have occurred to the advocates of Indian dispossession, did not seem to trouble them. John Quincy Adams presented a consideration which perhaps represents the typical counter-argument. Defending America's Indian policy against British animadversions after the War of 1812, he argued that American population was growing at so rapid a rate that permanent Indian barriers would deprive *future* generations of their means of subsistence.[24] But this argument, as was noted by William Wirt,[25] is valid only upon the assumption that the right to provide for posterity does not belong to the red race even when the white race needs no lands for those living. In sum, the utilitarian criterion does not square with the actual circumstances under which Americans applied it.

As if to remedy the logical defect, there arose a type of argument which employed not the criterion of need but a kind of aesthetic consideration. This new ground for the dispossession of Indians first came into prominence during the westward movement of the second decade of the nineteenth century. Its use was facilitated by the fact that, however prosaic the motives of individual pioneers, the abstract conception of the westward tide lent itself to poetic idealization. When this movement broke through the barriers of Indian territory, Governor Harrison of Indiana justified dispossession of the aboriginals as the conquest of the wilderness by civilization. He asked the rhetorical question:

> Is one of the fairest portions of the globe to remain in a state of nature, the haunt of a few wretched savages, when it seems destined by the Creator to give support to a large population and to be the seat of civilization, of science, and of true religion?[26]

The thesis implicit in the foregoing is not that the population is pressed for lands. Rather is it Chevalier de Chastellux's idea that "all that multiplies men in the nation, and harvests on the surface of the earth, is good in itself, is good above all things."[27] The same apologetic was employed by Representative Strother in a congressional debate of 1819 on the Seminole War:

Sir . . . the Western frontier is that portion of the world where civilization is making the most rapid and extensive conquest of the wilderness, carrying in its train the Christian religion and all the social virtues. It is the point where the race is most progressive; establish but the principle, that the God of nature has limited your march in that direction—that the Indian is lord paramount of that wide domain, around which justice and religion have drawn a circle which you dare not pass—the progress of mankind is arrested and you condemn one of the most beautiful and fertile tracts of the earth to perpetual sterility as the hunting ground of a few savages.[28]

This argument for dispossession thus justified the extension of the agriculturist's civilization by the principle that, irrespective of whether Indian lands are immediately needed, the more there is of a good thing the better. Such an argument can scarcely be attacked in the abstract. It is to be noted, however, that pressing into unneeded Indian lands resulted in neglect or careless treatment of the vast fertile land which the pioneers left behind them — in other words, in injury to the very value which Indian dispossession was supposed to forward. Moreover, the unnecessary haste of the march of the pioneers caused Tecumseh and others to offer the organized resistance which made the soil a battle-ground rather than the seat of agricultural development.

A little later came abundant new territory without any war; for the Spanish treaty of 1819 ceded to the United States not only Florida but all Spanish territory as far west as the Rockies. In view of this acquisition of territory the settlement and development of which would require generations, it may appear that the aboriginals might have been left in at least temporary possession of the country which they preserved in its pristine beauty. Actually the acquisition of vast new territory was followed by the first organized movement to remove all Indians from the country east of the Mississippi. The impetus to this movement came not from the Western pioneers but from Eastern States. It did not arise because of any need of lands; the Governor of Georgia and a Georgian Congressman boasted that the State possessed an abundance of cheap land already.[29] The movement arose because of the desire of Southern States to remove interruptions to their jurisdiction, the avidity of many individuals for cheap but valuable lands, and the belief of many in the North as well as in the South that the Indians would be better off in a region where they were spared the evil influences of adjacent white civilization.

Those interested primarily in the welfare of the aboriginals held as did President Monroe that removal should take place only by consent of the Indians themselves. Abstention from coercion seemed plain legal justice. From its very beginning the Government's Indian policy, quite distinct from the policy of the pioneer, had recognized the Indian's legal right of possession. Secretary of War Knox had written to the like-minded President Washington:

> The Indians being the prior occupants, possess the right of the soil. It cannot be taken from them unless by their free consent, or by the right of conquest in case of a just war.[30]

Even had there been no such original right, both European nations and the United States conferred legal right on the Indian through the general practice of entering into treaties of purchase when they wished to acquire Indian lands. Some of the Indian treaties with the United States, like those of the Cherokee nation, contained a guarantee of the remaining lands. The legal status of Indian lands, clear enough from the Government's practice, was definitely stated by Chief Justice Marshall of the United States Supreme Court in 1823. In the case *Johnson* v. *McIntosh*, Marshall upheld the Indian's right of possession in the following words:

> It has never been contended that the Indian title amounted to nothing. Their right of *possession* has never been questioned. The claim of Government extends to the *complete ultimate title,* charged with the *right* of possession, and to the exclusive power of acquiring that right.[31] [Italics mine.]

In other words the Indian's tenure had the one qualification that land could be ceded only to the Government; it was, however (to quote from a later decision of Marshall), the source of an "unquestioned right to the lands they occupy until that right shall be extinguished by a voluntary cession to our Government."[32]

The difficulty of the 'twenties was that the Cherokees and other Indian tribes now exercised their admitted right of refusing to cede their land to the Government. The Georgians, who in 1802 had gained the promise of the Federal Government to extinguish when possible the Cherokee title, were particularly perturbed when the Georgian Cherokees in 1827 set up the framework of a permanent government modelled after that of the United States. Georgia and other Southern States were resolved to prevent permanent or even temporary autonomy. The elements of their project were three: passage of restrictive State laws to make the Indians thoroughly uncomfortable; passage by Congress of a bill providing the Government's financial and administrative assistance in exchanging present Indian holdings for Government lands in the West; and if necessary the use of force to secure removal. But how could the necessary sympathy of the nation be gained in this first attempt to make Indian removal a systematic governmental policy?

In the face of the legal difficulties, one possible course for the advocate of Indian removal was to appeal to "a higher law," as did a writer of 1820 in the *North American Review*. Though admitting that in the abstract the rightful proprietors of the soil were its original incumbents, he went on to observe that the legal right to property rests upon a frail foundation even among civilized nations, who without scruple take away each other's lands in war. But from the standpoint of natural morals, the right of property ought to be even more frail when claimed by those who "held hunting and fishing be a more proper mode of existence than tilling and pasturage." This casuist concluded that to resist the providential movement carrying the Indian away was to preserve barbarity at the expense of industry and thrift.[33]

The Southerners who advocated coercive removal were doubtless appreciative of such reasoning. But it seemed better to them to emphasize before Congress and the nation a more conventional type of argument. They therefore elaborated a legal doctrine which denied the Indian's right of possession and declared the aboriginal to be no more than a "tenant at will."[34]

This disregard of Marshall's ruling reflected the influence of the doctrine of State sovereignty, which long detracted from the prestige of Supreme Court decisions. To be sure, the legal view of the Southerners was presented, no less than Marshall's, as an objective interpretation of the legal doctrine of the past. But in reality their legal interpretation afforded one of the most striking instances in legal history of the extent to which subjective factors can distort history and logic.

To affirm that temporary occupancy was the only privilege bestowed on Indians from the beginning was apparently to fly in the face of all the treaties with Indian peoples. A treaty of purchase would not seem to be legally necessary if the purchaser is dealing only with a tenant at will. But Governor Gilmer of Georgia explained away the treaties in words which relate the legal issue to religious dogma:

> Treaties were expedients by which ignorant, intractable, and savage people were induced without bloodshed to yield up what civilized peoples had a right to possess by virtue of that command of the Creator delivered to man upon his formation—be fruitful, multiply, and replenish the earth, and subdue it.[35]

The report of a House committee of the Twenty-first Congress stated similarly that the practice of buying Indian titles was but the humanitarian substitute for the sword in arriving at the actual enjoyment of claims derived from discovery and "sanctioned by the natural superiority allowed to the claims of civilized communities over those of savage tribes."[36]

What historical evidence was adduced in support of this view that treaties were signed with the tongue in the cheek? There existed no documentary evidence except a few colonial laws, disposing arbitrarily of uncultivated Indian lands. But the occasional expropriations by individual colonies do not outweigh the evidence noted by Marshall as characteristic of governmental policies. Explicit assertions of ownership being so few, a legal claim to Indian lands had to be inferred from the European's religio-ethical theory of property. The early discoverers and settlers were said by a House report of 1830 to have based their claim upon the scriptural injunction to till the earth.[37] Reference was also made to the theory of property entertained by philosophers of natural law such as Locke. Thus Representative Wilde declared that all property was "founded on utility," and that land became individually owned only as labor was incorporated with it.[38] But the advocates of dispossession made no mention of the numerous eighteenth-century writers on natural law who had affirmed the natural right of the Indian to his lands.[39] Nor did these Southerners recognize like Chancellor Kent that even if the white agriculturist had a natural right to Indian lands originally, the Indian acquired rights under subsequent circumstances:

> As far as Indian rights and territories were defined and acknowledged by the whites by treaty, there was no question in the case, for the whites were bound by the moral and national obligations of contract and good faith.[40]

The weakness of legal reasoning is often explicable by the fact that a moral conviction makes legal accuracy appear relatively unimportant. Thus it seems that those committing flagrant legal errors in this instance were influenced fundamentally by the three moral arguments for dispossession which had been inherited from the past. Despite the inconsistencies between them, they were all now seen as pointing to the supersession of the huntsman by the agriculturist. The biblical argument of the Puritans was used by Representative Wayne of Georgia in his declaration that the decree which denied the Indian's right to be lord of his uncultivated domain was "the Almighty's command to his creatures to till the earth." [41] Despite the Southerner's notorious waste of land in cotton cultivation, the ultilitarian argument of natural law was stated by Representative Wilde of Georgia:

> And if it were possible to perpetuate the race of Indians, what would be the consequence? Why, that a hundred or a thousand fold the number of white men would not be born, because the Indians would roam over and possess, without enjoying, the land which must afford the future whites subsistence.[42]

Lewis Cass, in an article on Indian removal in the *North American Review* of 1830, used the argument stressing the intrinsic value of extending civilization:

> There can be no doubt . . . that the Creator intended the earth should be reclaimed from a state of nature and cultivated; that the human race should spread over it, procuring from it the means of comfortable subsistence, and of increase and improvement.[43]

All three arguments, together with historical experience, underlay the theory of manifest destiny stated by Wilde:

> Jacob will forever obtain the inheritance of Esau. We cannot alter the laws of Providence, as we read them in the experience of the ages.[44]

The triune ethico-religious argument was presented by many with all the dogmatism of the Lord's elect who consider the earth their garden. The self-assurance, however, was rather strange. For at one point the factual foundation of the argument was so weak as to jeopardize the entire logical edifice erected during centuries of American-Indian relations. The moral philosophy of dispossession had been founded and developed in a time when the Indians were huntsmen. The great majority of them, indeed, still roamed in the chase. But one of the tribes, the very tribe upon which the controversy of the 'twenties centered, had turned to agriculture as though with a perverse intention of confounding the race desirous of their removal! This was the Cherokee nation of Georgia.

The whole difficulty with the Cherokees, Calhoun observed in a Cabinet meeting, arose from their progress in civilization.[45] The American commissioners sent to urge removal upon them learned this fact to their consternation. The Cherokees, who had not only farms but printing-presses, schools, and churches, gave as the ground of their refusal to remove to the wilderness the fact that they had "unequivocally determined never again to pursue the chase as heretofore." [46] Consternation increased when their leaders showed greater dialectic skill than the emissaries of civilization. The commissioners, pointing out that the Cherokees had more land in proportion to their population than the Georgians, argued that the Heavenly Creator had not intended such great inequality between his white and red children.[47] The Cherokee leaders maliciously responded that, though they did not know the intentions of the Creator, they wondered why, if such was his intention, "the laws of civilized and enlightened nations allow a man to monopolize more land than he can cultivate, to the exclusion of others." [48]

The surprisingly changed complexion which the Indian issue assumed in this situation was described by ex-President Madison in a letter to William Wirt:

> The plea with the best aspect for dispossessing Indians of the lands on which they have lived, is that by not incorporating their labour, and associating fixed improvements with the soil, they have not appropriated it to themselves, nor made the destined use of its capacity for increasing the number and the enjoyments of the human race. But this plea, whatever original force be allowed it, is here repelled by the fact that the Indians are making the very use of that capacity which the plea requires . . . [49]

The embarrassment of the situation was increased by the fact that even so ardent an advocate of Indian dispossession as John Quincy Adams had previously conceded that cultivated Indian lands would always be respected.[50]

It may seem that, despite the extraordinary talent of *homo sapiens* in justifying his desires by his reason, there must certainly be some few issues in which moral reason is so strongly against him that elementary logical integrity will force him to relinquish his desire, or at least to admit that the gratification of it is without moral justification. Doubtless even the history of expansionism contains such instances; but, contrary to natural expectation, we have not at this point come upon one of them.

The logic of the Georgians in this issue rather supported Benjamin Franklin's generalization: "So convenient a thing it is to be a reasonable creature, since it enables one to find or to make a reason for everything one has a mind to do." As was observed by the amazed William Wirt, the legal defender of the Cherokees, there appeared "the new and strange ground" that the Cherokees "had no right to alter their condition and to become husbandmen." [51] The strange new position may be seen in part in the following lines from a message of Governor Troup to the Georgia Assembly:

> . . . with regard to the territory of Georgia . . . this right of use can only be construed to mean, what in all the treaties it did mean, the

right of use for hunting. When, therefore, the United States, by changing the mode of life of the aboriginals upon the soil of Georgia, changed essentially this right, and caused her lands to be separately appropriated for the purpose of tillage, and gave every encouragement to fixed habits of agriculture, they violated the treaties in their letter and spirit, and did wrong to Georgia.[52]

The foregoing denies, if not the general right of the Cherokees to become husbandmen, at least their legal right to become such within Georgia's boundaries.

Now this position might seem to be in flagrant conflict with the traditional dogma that the soil was destined to be tilled. But the Georgians were quite equal to arguing that there was no conflict at all. In Governor Troup's exposition of "the destiny which is fixed and unchangeable" it was made clear that, though the Georgian soil was destined to be tilled, it was destined to be tilled by the white man and not by the Indian![53]

There was more than this to call forth William Wirt's hopeless exclamation over "the omnipotent sophistry of interest and passion."[54] Justifying the dismissal of a tribe with agricultural aspirations to a soil considered fit generally only for hunting, the Georgians argued somewhat to the effect that the soil was not destined to be tilled by Indians at all. It seemed to them evident from Indian character and habits that it was not the Indian's destiny to cultivate the soil. The advocates of dispossession denied the accuracy of the generally accepted reports ascribing to the Cherokees considerable social progress. They maintained, as in the House report which favored removal, that not more than one-tenth of the population, a portion largely half-breed, was above the condition of the savage.[55] It was admitted, however, that this estimate was not based upon statistical study. Such a claim, unsupported by any evidence other than hearsay, can scarcely outweigh the evidence to the contrary which was partially admitted by Governor Troup when he attacked Cherokee agriculturists. And while some sentimentalists doubtless exaggerated the civilization of this Indian people, the very admissions of Federal commissioners indicate that the sentimentalists were less far from the truth than the Georgians.[56]

But the advocates of dispossession refused to see what they did not wish to see. Therefore, they could maintain a quasi-scientific thesis asserting that (to quote a Georgian Congressman) "the laws of nature have fixed an insuperable barrier between the moral condition of the savage and the Christian."[57] To Representative Graham of North Carolina it seemed that one might as well expect the red man to change the color of his skin as his habits and pursuits.[58] The memorial of the General Assembly of Georgia on the removal of the Cherokees maintained that "a dispersed and wandering people are not in a condition to become the object of the benefits of civilization," whereas their removal would "give to these sons of nature a wilderness congenial to their feelings and appropriate to their wants."[59] Senator King of Georgia not only shared this view but showed the enthusiasm of a Rousseau over the Indian's return to nature:

> It had been urged as a reason why they should remove, that in the woods they would lose their civilization, and become wild. He had seen sufficient to convince him, that the wild Indian of the woods had more nobleness of character than the half-civilized Indian, who, for the most part, contract the vices of the lower class of whites, and become drunken and thievish, and were as unfit for the duties appertaining to civilized life, as they were for that courage and enterprise which distinguished the true Indian.[60]

Passage of the Indian Removal Bill signified abandonment of the hope and ideal of civilization through proximity, cherished by well-disposed individuals like Thomas Jefferson and Jedediah Morse. The hope was abandoned just as the Cherokees gave earnest of its approaching realization. But even the subjection of the Indians to adverse conditions did not prevent, as the Indian *Handbook* of the Bureau of Ethnology testifies, their ultimate adaptation to the occupations of civilization. Of interest is the intelligent comment which the doctrine of the Indian's inevitable extinction evoked in the Cherokee paper, the *New Echota Phoenix*:

> Those who assert this doctrine, seem to act towards these unfortunate people in a consistent manner, either in neglecting them entirely, or endeavoring to hasten the period of their extinction. For our part,

we dare not scrutinize the designs of God's providence towards the Cherokees.[61]

The removal of all Indians in the 'thirties — under conditions of hardship described lugubriously in a recent work of Grant Foreman [62] — removed the destiny of this race from the American's view. It was not so with the doctrine of territorial utilization itself. "Manifestly," writes J. G. Wise in his *The Red Man in the New World Drama,* "such a people could not have dealt with a subordinate race . . . without an enduring effect upon their moral point of view." [63] The doctrine of territorial utilization was destined not only to figure in many later issues but to undergo an often curious development. Tending always to enlarge its pretensions, it may seem in its later history to confirm the observation of R. H. Tawney that the children of the mind are like the children of the body: "Once born they grow by a law of their own being."

The first stage in the natural growth of the doctrine was its extension to territorial issues other than those involving Indians. This stage quickly arrived with the Oregon issue of the 'forties, involving a territorial dispute between the United States and Great Britain. It was argued by John Quincy Adams and other expansionists that the right of Americans to the territory was greater than that of Englishmen because the former alone could utilize the country in accordance with the scriptural injunction to till the earth.[64] But the allegation that the British desired Oregon only for hunting furs was as gratuitous as the former generalization about the occupational limitations of Indians.

The next territorial issue was of a different character and brought the principle of utilization into a new phase of development. It concerned the land of the Mexicans, who were tillers of the soil but did not till it efficiently or in more than relatively small part. California was claimed on the ground of the capacity of Americans to develop it more fully; after the outbreak of the Mexican War the territorial claim was enlarged until it embraced all of Mexico. The report of the New York State Democratic Convention of January, 1848, advocated annexation on the ground of a familiar philosophy:

> We would hold it, not for our use, but for the use of man . . . Labor was the consecrated means of man's subsistence when he was created. To replenish the earth and subdue it, was his ordained mission and destiny.[65]

About the same time, Sam Houston observed with his delightful ingenuousness that Americans had always cheated Indians, and that since Mexicans are no better than Indians "I see no reason why we should not go on the same course, now, and take their land."[66] In the following decade Caleb Cushing, affirming annexation of Mexico to be destiny, asked the rhetorical question: "Is not the occupation of any portion of the earth by those competent to hold and till it, a providential law of national life?"[67] The answer was given by Representative Cox in a general "law of annexation": "That no nation has the right to hold soil, virgin and rich, yet unproducing . . ."[68] According to the *United States Democratic Review* of 1858, "no race but our own can either cultivate or rule the western hemisphere."[69] The principle of cultivation, at first applied only to Indians, had been developed by expansionists to a generality contesting the land tenure of all other peoples of the continent.

But the expansionism of the 'fifties introduced still another important stage in the growth of the doctrine. Mexico was desired in this decade less for its agricultural resources than for the reason stated by an expansionist article in the *United States Review* of 1853:

> The painful scarcity of silver which at present afflicts the entire trading and agricultural community, can only be removed, as the scarcity of gold was removed, by the application of American enterprise to the mines of Mexico. Silver coin will never be abundant in the United States, until the boundary of the South includes the mineral fields of Central Mexico, now occupied by a people who have no knowledge, or no appreciation of their value.

The writer then justified the claim to silver lands with the doctrine originated by the agriculturist:

> The time is not far distant, when the enterprise of the South will direct itself upon those regions, which belong to it . . . by the well-founded and legitimate rights of industry and intelligence; . . . the

same that confirms the title of every free people to the soil upon which they stand.[70]

The same philosophy was affirmed by an editorial on Mexico in the *New York Herald*[71] in 1858, and was intimated in President Buchanan's annual message of 1859 calling for intervention.[72]

It is even more interesting to observe the changed aspect of the doctrine when the 'seventies brought Indian lands again into focus. Encroachment renewed itself despite the fact that the new home in the West had been guaranteed to the Indians perpetually; indeed, the barriers of Indian Territory were broken through in five years and were never after effective. The contract seemed void when the original assumption that the Middle West was "the Great American Desert" was discovered in the westward movement of the 'forties to be a myth. The finding of unsuspected agricultural resources in the West was followed several decades later by the discovery of rich mineral resources upon Indian reservations. In the 'seventies, for example, gold and silver were found upon the lands of the Colorado Ute Indians. A bill was thereupon introduced in Congress to purchase their reservation and assign them lands in severalty. In the debate of 1880 dispossession of the "thriftless" Indian — he had once been sent to the West to indulge his idleness — was proclaimed to be manifest destiny.[73] Representative Belford urged the passage of the bill in the following words:

> You give the sanction of the Government to the act of the miner in taking up a claim . . . and you apprise the Indian that he can no longer stand as a breakwater against the constantly swelling tide of civilization. . . . It settles for all time the doctrine which has received illustrations in the past that an idle and thriftless race of savages cannot be permitted to guard the treasure vaults of the nation which hold our gold and silver, but that they shall always be open, to the end that the prospector and miner may enter in and by enriching himself enrich the nation and bless the world by the results of his toil.[74]

There arises the curious question whether this principle of dispossession is consistent with the earlier ground that "the whole earth is destined to feed its inhabitants." [75] It may seem at first that to demand another's land for the sake of its precious minerals represents a more grasping spirit than does demanding it for the sake of its grain. So, apparently, thought the Georgians who desired Cherokee lands in the 'twenties; for though gold had been discovered also on these lands, they preferred to base their moral case not upon mining but upon agriculture. Yet after all, gold and silver are not only convertible into food and other necessities, but may aid more in the economic organization of the world's nutrition than does any addition to the extent of arable space. This fact would naturally impress itself less strongly in the agricultural society of the 'twenties than in the later period when the industrial economy was becoming predominant. Considering his economic context, one must concede that Belford was not departing from the spirit of Vattel's agricultural doctrine when he demanded Indian lands which would "bless the world" with gold and silver.

But once the simple agricultural criterion is replaced by a broader one, where will the expansionist stop? The question increases one's interest in following the history of the doctrine further. It was assured of a continuance in history when expansionists of the 'nineties were prompted by America's great industrial development to seek tropical lands as sources of raw materials. John W. Burgess, in his treatise of 1890 on political science, foreshadowed one theory of these expansionists when he denied the moral or legal right of a few thousand savages to reserve for hunting-grounds the lands capable of sustaining millions of civilized men.[76] Whereas this thesis was traditional, the incorporation and conquest of the Philippines were attended by the broadening of the traditional doctrine to meet new circumstances. One new element in the situation was the fact that the Filipino could scarcely be accused of not tilling his soil to the best of his capacity. And this fact worried certain earnest persons who would have been quite prepared to dispossess Indian huntsmen. For example, a letter to the *Outlook* argued as follows:

The wresting of the North American continent from its aboriginal possessors, and its transference from a vast game preserve into the granary of the world, seems legitimate, as may in time the culture of cabbage in your Central Park, or the passing of the vast uncultivated estates of the Old World to those entitled to them under the divine right of hunger. But the soil in the Philippines, as in China, is occupied and tilled by their native population. The Anglo-Saxon farmer has no moral right there.[77]

Yet the fact that the Filipinos tilled their soil did not prevent ethical expansionists like Lyman Abbott [78] from recalling the moral principle of Indian dispossession as a precedent for expansion in this case. The writer in the *Outlook* failed to recognize that this principle had been enlarged to accord not only with a scientific agriculture but also with an industrial economy. Ex-Senator Peffer wrote that "God must have intended that savage life and customs should yield to higher standards of living, or he would have made the earth many times larger." [79] Captain Mahan related higher standards of living to natural right:

> Thus the claim of an indigenous population to retain indefinitely control of territory depends not upon a natural right, but upon political fitness, shown in the political work of governing, administering, and developing, in such manner as to insure the natural right of the world at large that resources should not be left idle, but be utilized for the general good.[80]

Here, then, is a blanket reference which apparently takes in all "resources"— rubber and hemp as well as cabbages.

The Filipinos cultivated cabbages but not the resources needed by an industrialized society. The imperialists envisaged in the Philippines the economic revolution described by Assistant Secretary of the Treasury Vanderlip:

> They see great development companies formed to cultivate tobacco and sugar by modern methods, others formed to test the richness of the unknown mineral deposits, and still others to develop transportation or to reap the treasures of the forest.[81]

Rubber, for example, was a forest product vastly more necessary to the economic scheme of the world than was the increased production of any edible; from this point of view, rubber bore more vitally upon "the divine right of hunger." The offense of tropical people now lay precisely in the fact that in drawing only their food from the soil they neglected the raw materials of industry. It is thus a curiosity of the history of ideas that the same doctrine originated by the agriculturist to dispossess the huntsman was used ultimately by the industrialist to dispossess the agriculturist. But the jest is entirely on the darker races, the victims of the doctrine first as huntsmen and then as agriculturists.

In the latter instance, however, the doctrine had a consequence different from that in the first. Restrictive action against the Filipinos was not so much seizure of land as deprivation of independence. For there was no desire to send the Anglo-Saxon farmer to a tropical land where life would be inconvenient and unpleasant for him. The new idea, expounded by Kidd in his influential work of 1898 entitled *The Control of the Tropics*, was that the white man should supervise the exploitation of the tropics from his own land, thus making physical labor the colored and not the white man's burden.

Though left to occupy its land, the colored race was threatened by the new doctrine more seriously than ever before in the political sense. For Kidd and others made the principle of political interference much more far-reaching than had Mahan's formula. It would seem from Mahan's principle that some tropical peoples — those who develop their natural resources sufficiently — are to be left in political independence. But in the light of certain assumptions regarding the effect of tropical climate, the question as to what tropical peoples develop their resources adequately may evoke the answer that virtually none can do so. This answer was given by Kidd when he assailed the belief that "the colored races left to themselves possess the qualities necessary to the development of the rich resources of the lands they have inherited." The colored races of the debilitating tropics were and would remain at a childish stage of human evolution. The only solution from the viewpoint of world economic welfare seemed to Kidd that the tropics in general "be administered from the temperate regions." [82] The premise that all tropical peoples are under an eternal doom of economic incapacity may well seem to be of a more sweeping character than scientific caution would justify. But by 1900, as the works on imperialism by both Reinsch [83] and Hobson [84] attest, Kidd's thesis had become the foremost moral plea of imperialist powers. The doctrine applied at first solely to Indians had been extended to all races of color in the tropics.

Yet Americans as well as other imperialists were to develop that doctrine still more in their apparent eagerness to inherit the earth. Its non-agricultural as well as agricultural version was enlarged to apply not merely to the dark races, but also to peoples who, though largely white in population, were considered inferior in civilization and economic efficiency. Thus America's perturbed relations with disorderly Mexico gave rise to an expansionist ideology largely confirming the contemporary observation of the *New Republic*: " . . . in popular political philosophy the sole valid title of a nation to natural riches is the title of use." [85] Interest in annexation was mainly confined to the northern area, to which, Arthur Richard Hinton wrote in the *Independent* in 1914, " Mexico has given . . . no development." [86] Senator Ashurst, presenting his resolution of 1919 for the purchase of Lower California, affirmed that America could change this wilderness into a garden rich with fruits for civilization.[87] More numerous than the expansionists were those who favored intervention — the method most convenient for economic imperialists. Their ideology was also characterized by the conception that, as William Ledyard Rodgers wrote in 1927, since " Mexico has products that the world looks to her to provide " she " can not go on making the world wait." [88]

But in the twentieth century the doctrine of territorial utilization has been used chiefly by Americans like Roland Usher [89] and John Carter,[90] who advocate frankly peaceful economic penetration. Economic penetration is called financial imperialism when, as during the Taft period of Dollar Diplomacy, it involves governmental control or influence in connection with international investment. " It is desirable," wrote a distinguished American banker as he recalled our Indian policy, " that these investments by the advanced countries shall be made, . . . that the waste places shall be developed, and that the production of those things which minister to the comfort and well-being of mankind shall be increased." Should this commercial extension be obstructed, it is to be borne in mind that " the right to occupy a portion of the earth's surface is . . .

qualified by a proper consideration for the general welfare." [91] But inasmuch as the loans of international bankers flow largely into enterprises that do not directly increase the productivity of the soil, that is, into public works, improvement of transportation facilities, and the refinancing of public debt, the doctrine of territorial utilization takes on in financial imperialism an extension. It is broadened to a form which advocates the investment of foreign capital, protected by such external political supervision as may be necessary, not merely for the cultivation of natural resources but for all economic activities within the domain of backward countries. Here the expansion of the doctrine finally stops; for any further expansion is apparently impossible.

But just as the doctrine reached its full growth, conditions in the world underwent a change which embarrassed its entire traditional logic. Malthus's prophecy to the contrary notwithstanding, world economy has expanded to the point of disastrous overproduction in all fields; as someone has said, we are stripped bare by the curse of plenty. A doctrine which developed amid fears of underproduction should now, it would seem, be radically amended—at least for the duration of the depression. Unless it is only the perversity of phantasy which prompts us, its amended form should proclaim that Providence has destined virgin soil *not* to be cultivated. However, the ambitions of nations are so little determined by rational economic logic that the anachronistic principle may not be amended at all.

The immediate future of this doctrine in American foreign policy is made unpromising by the morality of our era of abundance, represented by ex-President Hoover's indictment of "economic or other domination of other peoples." [92] Future Indian policy is foreshadowed by Indian Commissioner Collier's recent proposal whereby agricultural overproduction—the unexpected retribution for the past policy of excessive dispossession — is relieved by giving submarginal lands to Indian wards.[93] But in the world in general, if one may judge by the attitude of the Japanese toward Manchuria and of some Englishmen toward the African-owned lands recently found to be rich in gold, it is likely that the doctrine justifying the seizure of Naboth's property will continue to be put periodically to good or bad use.

If the doctrine lives on it will be in part because there is a kernel of truth in it. The bewildering variety of the versions that this concept has assumed does not discredit its essence, which is, as Walter Weyl says of the imperialist economic argument, always the same — "the resources of the world must be unlocked." [94] Such a formulation is not essentially different from Vattel's doctrine that the earth must be cultivated because it belongs to the human race in general for its subsistence. In all its forms the doctrine might be designated as "the principle of beneficent territorial utilization." This utilitarian principle may seem to have a logical force far stronger than the ordinary counter-arguments of an emotional anti-imperialism, so often distinguished more by moral earnestness than logical coherence. For it is an application to international relations of an imposing and scarcely debatable law of the supremacy of the general good.

Since the general good has its economic aspect the imperialist is not troubled by the allegation that in supporting economic profit his doctrine is sordid. "Sordid, indeed!" exclaimed Senator Lodge in answer to such an allegation, as he proceeded to observe that the Philippine policy would increase the wages and employment of millions in both the United States and the Orient.[95] A twentieth-century expansionist who believed in this country's duty to redeem the waste places in both Americas would "acknowledge no fault requiring apology or subterfuge in advocating for the United States the fullest measure of commercial expansion." [96] It is his assumption of an international benefit in commercial expansion which saves the imperialist from any moral perturbation over the national or even individual profit in economic exploitation.

However, the imperialist must also face the objection that economic expansionism conflicts with self-determination. The conflict is indeed sharp, but the anti-imperialist errs greatly in hoping that the imperialist will feel disturbed by the fact. For it seems romantic folly to the imperialist that the desire of benighted peoples to govern or misgovern themselves should be allowed to prevent the development of resources necessary to world welfare. Like Admiral Mahan he denies an "inalienable right in any community to control the use of a region when it does so to the detriment of the world at large."[97] Philosophical imperialism, as Dr. Powers declares, is "the assertion of world ownership over local tenancy at will."[98] Such a philosophy is as threatening to the backward peoples logically as is the imperialist's weapon of force physically.

Yet this principle, however formidable to the backward races, is also the one logical weapon formidable to the imperialist. It is like some boomerang which though thrown at the opponent causes fatality in an unexpected quarter. One has only to extend the imperialist's own logic a little farther to make it return and pierce the intellectual armor of the imperialist himself.

The weak point in that armor is the assumption that his country's economically motivated expansion operates to the fullest advantage of international society. This is true only in so far as the methods of imperialistic exploitation extend to the world at large its needed and proper share of economic products. But no consideration receives so much emphasis from students of the economics of exploitation as the failure of most imperialist enterprises to result in this equitable division. Thus, it is the thesis of C. K. Leith's essay "Exploitation and Progress" that the exploitation of the world's mineral resources shows "the conflict of two powerful opposing forces — on the one hand, world demand for raw materials, which knows no national boundaries and which is forcing coöperation in order that demand may be sufficiently satisfied; on the other, the nationalistic force directed towards partitioning resources for national gain or security."[99] Similar testimony is offered by Carlton Hayes's indictment of the economic policy of integral nationalism for penalization of the foreigner in every sphere.[100] That imperialist expansion does not serve the common good is also the conclusion of von Engeln in his geographico-economic study, *Inheriting the Earth*.[101] It is arguable, indeed, that the expansion of the great powers is not opposed to the common good when national interest is adjusted to world interest by compromise. But despite the recent theoretical introduction of the mandate system it seems that, as Mr. Leith observes, there has ordinarily been little or no actual application on the part of imperialist powers of those basic principles which "compromise legitimate national aspirations with insistent world pressure." [102]

The pathetic logical suicide overtaking the imperialist through a doctrine cutting in two ways is now clear. The imperialist's weapon is a principle demanding that he subordinate to world interest not merely the claims of the backward people but also the pretensions of his own country. The expansionist is unwittingly using a principle which gives a *coup de grâce* to his country's self-interested expansion.

Moreover, the principle of the paramountcy of international society prescribes a consideration for the welfare of the colored aboriginal, a part of international society even though its "forgotten man." Vattel himself apparently recognized this fact when he approved of "moderation" on the part of civilized peoples in their relations with Indians.[103] The doctrine of Vattel would permit the expropriation of backward peoples only when their lands are actually and immediately needed for world advantage, not merely for land-hunger. It is also clear that Vattel's doctrine permits infliction of no greater injury upon the aboriginal people than is necessary to world interest, not merely to the pioneer's inordinate haste. "It is perfectly possible," a critic of America's Indian policy has truly written, "to meet all the needs of the growing race in the best and most practical way, and yet to preserve to the individual of the weaker race his rights and opportunities." [104]

The inconsistency between the doctrine of beneficent territorial utilization and its largely unbeneficent practice is probably significant of another inconsistency between ideology and motive. The ideology of expropriation is internationalism; its ordinary motive appears in the light of behavior to be nationalism. Stated from a different point of view, the discrepancy is between the nationalist's pretension to interest in the use of territory and his fundamental interest in its possession. It is because of the possessive instinct and not the plough that the soil is destined for the race using the cannon rather than the bow and arrow.

## CHAPTER IV

### EXTENSION OF THE AREA OF FREEDOM

In the "roaring 'forties," a decade thus designated because the spirit of American life rose into high and turbulent flame, there was welded an association of two ideals which gave a new integration to the American's consciousness of national destiny. One of the two ideals was territorial expansion. After several decades of relative quiescence, expansionism was rekindled by the issues of Texas and Oregon and was fanned to white heat by the oratory of Democrats in the presidential election of 1844. For the first time the wish of numerous Americans fathered the thought that their eventual possession of no less a domain than the entire North American continent was "manifest destiny" — a phrase which now passed into the national vocabulary.

The central implication of "manifest destiny" in the 'forties, however, was less a matter of the scope of expansion than of its purpose. The conception of expansion as a destiny meant primarily that it was a means to the fulfilment of a certain social ideal the preservation and perfection of which was America's providential mission or destiny. This ideal, conceived as "the last best revelation of human thought," was democracy — a theory of mass sovereignty but in a more important aspect a complex of individualistic values which, despite Fisher Ames's observation that America was too democratic for liberty,[1] Americans most frequently summarized by the inspiring word "freedom." It was because of the association of expansion and freedom in a means-end relationship that expansion now came to seem most manifestly a destiny.

While the championship of the rights of man appeared from the beginning of national life to be America's special destiny, expansion had not seemed in general to be a necessary element in this preeminent national purpose. It is true that expansionists of the Revolution and the War of 1812 tendered "liberty"[2] to the "oppressed" Canadians, and that Jefferson once included not only Canada but Cuba and Florida as well in America's "empire for liberty."[3] Yet in all these instances, as foregoing evidence has suggested, the extension of democracy was probably neither a primary motive of any expansionists nor even a secondary motive of many of them. It was not until the 'forties that the popular ideology of expansionism centered in democracy. The new importance of this ideal to the expansionist was shown by the words which rang through the land as his slogan, "extension of the area of freedom."

It was because of its infusion with this ideal that American expansionism of the middle 'forties became possessed, as Professor Adams says in his valuable essay on "Manifest Destiny," of a "spiritual exaltation" in contemplation of the assumed superiority of American institutions. A recognition of the rôle played by idealistic American nationalism in this expansion movement has led to an explanation which is very different from that of most early American historians. Writers close to the passions of the Civil War attributed expansionism to "the glut of our slaveholders,"[4] the desire of the Southern States to extend the system of slavery. More objective contemporary historians believe that the intensity and extensity of expansionism, while due partly to sectional interests, were caused primarily by nationalistic attitudes resting not merely upon practical interests but also upon the "emotion" of "manifest destiny"[5] and its correlate, the "idealism"[6] of the spirit of democracy.

However, it is as yet more common to refer to democracy as an explanation of American expansionism than to attempt an explanation of expansionist democratic idealism itself. The zeal for extending the area of freedom raises several interesting and important problems. Why is it that, despite the fact that neither expansionism nor the attachment to democracy was new, the two did not come into fusion before? What were the historical circumstances which overcame the previous estrangement of these pieties? Most important of all, what was the true meaning of the ideal described vaguely as extension of the area of freedom?

The point of the last question is made sharper by the fact that the most usual connotation of such words as "extension of the area of freedom" does not make sense in the light of the historical context. The phrase was used primarily by those who urged the annexation of Texas. But Texas already had a a republican government, as was pointed out by anti-expansionists attacking the slogan. Thus Representative McIlvain asked "how, if freedom mean republican liberty, can its area be extended by the union of the two governments?" [7] Perplexed by the same question, Representative Marsh characterized "extension of the area of freedom" as "an argument addressed to the ear and not the understanding — a mere jingle of words without meaning, or, if significant, false in the only sense which the words will fairly bear." [8]

Unfortunately the matter cannot be so quickly dismissed. The popular slogan is often vapid, but in this case it did have a meaningful content. Only, it was very different from the significance which contemporary anti-expansionists and even later historians attached to the shibboleth. To understand its rather surprising implication, it will be necessary to turn first to the historical background of the expansionist ideal in order to survey briefly the previous development of the relationship between the ideas of democracy and expansion.

When Representative Severance urged in the 'forties that Americans "rather extend the 'area of freedom' by . . . our bright and shining example as a pattern republic," [9] he was reverting to the conception which had been held by the founders of the nation. Originally "the extension of the area of freedom" signified extension of freedom regardless of political connection. Moreover the chief method chosen for extending freedom was the purely passive one of radiating democratic influence through impressive example. Thus Joel Barlow said in 1787 that "the example of political wisdom and felicity, here to be displayed, will excite emulation throughout the kingdoms of the earth, and meliorate the condition of the human race." [10] Thomas Jefferson spoke of America as "a standing monument and example" which would "ameliorate the condition of man over a great portion of the globe." [11] Jefferson also suggested another non-expansionist method of extending freedom. It was the pioneer migration covering even the Western

Coast "with free and independent Americans, unconnected with us but by the ties of blood and interest, and employing like us the rights of self-government."[12] It is clear from many such utterances that Americans at first perceived no necessary logical relationship between the extension of democracy and the extension of America's boundaries.

Why did early Americans see no logical nexus between the two ideals which were firmly associated by their descendants? One reason for the original disassociation of democracy and expansion was the internationalist orientation of many of the founders of the Republic. Early idealists, as the nationalistic Gouverneur Morris complained, had a *penchant* for referring to themselves as "citizens of the world."[13] Associated with this internationalism was a devotion to democracy for its own sake. If only the offshoots of the American Republic blossomed into freedom, the retention of political connection seemed to Jefferson "not very important to the happiness of either part."[14]

Yet it is doubtful whether these magnanimous attitudes account fundamentally for the non-expansionist character of early democratic philosophy. Indifference to the national label of expansive democracy may be explicable basically by the aspect in which expansion of territory presented itself from the viewpoint of self-interest. It did not seem originally that wide extent of territory was needful to the American democracy. Its original domain appeared, Thomas Paine said, as a world; as late as 1801 Jefferson thought that it would suffice unto the thousandth generation. But in addition to those who thought territorial expansion unnecessary there were many who believed it dangerous to democracy. Thus a large group attached to State sovereignty opposed the Constitution on the ground, largely derived from the theory of Montesquieu, that the existing domain even of the thirteen States was too large for one national government. The authors of the *Federalist* countered by distinguishing between a pure democracy and a representative republic and by assuming the greater immunity of the large republic to faction. Even they, however, had reference not to expansion but only to the amalgamation of the thirteen States.

After adjusting themselves to the new Federal Union the small-territory party took renewed alarm from the proposal to purchase the "vast new world" of Louisiana. A republican government, declared Fisher Ames on this occasion, could not be practicable, honest, or free, if applied to the government of a third of God's earth.[15] The anti-expansionist arguments in this and the later issue of Orleans Territory reveal clearly the ideas which made democracy and expansion seem incompatible. The chief objection to expansion was that it would cause, sooner or later, the very destruction of a republican government. The reasons for this view were set forth by Representative Griswold:

> The vast and unmanageable extent which the accession of Louisiana will give to the United States; the consequent dispersion of our population; and the destruction of that balance which it is so important to maintain between the Eastern and Western States, threatens, at no very distant day, the subversion of our Union.[16]

Eight years later Josiah Quincy, opposing the incorporation of Orleans Territory, asserted similarly that the bill contained "a principle incompatible with the liberties and safety of my country," and if passed would be "a death-blow to the Constitution." [17]

A second objection, felt by some more keenly than the first, was that expansion endangered the rights and liberties of the individual States. This objection was offered in the Louisiana discussion, and again in Josiah Quincy's speech opposing the creation of Orleans Territory. Quincy avowed frankly that his first public love was the Commonwealth of Massachusetts, whereas his love of the Union was merely devotion to a safeguard of the prosperity and security of his State. He opposed expansion because it introduced a new power to overbalance the political weight of any one State. He decried as an "effective despotism" that condition of things in which the original States must lose their political control to the new States, which, taking advantage of a conflict of interests, would throw themselves into the scale most conformable to their purposes.[18]

A third type of criticism alleged the danger of expansion to the liberties of individual citizens. Representative Griswold opposed the Louisiana Purchase because of fear that "additional territory might overbalance the existing territory, and thereby the rights of the present citizens of the United States be swallowed up and lost." [19] Certain Americans, like Josiah Quincy, not merely feared to throw their "rights and liberties" into "hotch-pot" with those of an alien race.[20] They even feared, as Senator White declared in the Louisiana debate, that their own citizens who roved so far from the capital would lose their affection for the center and develop antagonistic interests.[21] Both fears motivated John Randolph's words of 1813:

> We are the first people that ever acquired provinces . . . not for us to govern, but that they might *govern us*—that we might be ruled to our ruin by people bound to us by no common tie of interest or sentiment.[22]

Thus the original failure to relate democracy and expansion was due not merely to altruism, but also, and perhaps primarily, to egoistic fear for the liberties of the American nation, States, and individual citizens. A general tendency to associate democracy and expansion could not possibly develop before these fears had disappeared.

The years following America's first territorial acquisition did in fact witness the gradual dissipation of one after another of the anti-expansionist's apprehensions. The first to pass was the morbid notion that the Union itself could be destroyed through plethora of territory. Louisiana was scarcely incorporated before it seemed an increment of natural growth rather than of elephantiasis. In his oration of 1804 on the acquisition, Dr. David Ramsay taunted those who had prophesied that the Constitution would never answer for a large territory.[23] Jefferson's inaugural address of 1805 reminded those once fearful of Louisiana that "the larger our association the less will it be shaken by local passions." [24]

The fear that extended territory would prove injurious to the liberties of the individual States also quickly evaporated. By 1822 President Monroe could say with an expectation of general approbation:

> The expansion of our Union over a vast territory can not operate unfavorably to the States individually. . . . With governments sepa-

rate, vigorous, and efficient for all local purposes, their distance from each other can have no injurious effect upon their respective interests.[25]

State anti-expansionism was lessened not only by the defeat of the particularists in the War of 1812 but also by the rise of the political theory which Monroe's words intimated. The years following the War of 1812 witnessed the increasing popularity of the view that the United States Government was based upon a distinctive principle of federation dividing power between State and Federal Government in a manner safe and efficacious for both. The encouraging implication of this theory for expansion was stated by Edward Everett in an address of 1824:

. . . by the wise and happy partition of powers between the national and state governments, in virtue of which the national government is relieved from all the odium of internal administration, and the state governments are spared the conflicts of foreign politics, all bounds seem removed from the possible extension of our country, but the geographical limits of the continent. Instead of growing cumbrous, as it increases in size, there never was a moment, since the first settlement in Virginia, when the political system of America moved with so firm and bold a step, as at the present day.[26]

The fear that the inhabitants of the distant sections would subvert the liberties of their eastern fellow citizens also proved unfounded. The Eastern States learned that their western kinsmen were not only the strongest of Unionists but also the most democratic of the democrats. One may again turn to an address by Everett, who, though of the same State as the particularist Josiah Quincy, spoke in 1829 to citizens of Tennessee with utmost friendliness. After prophesying that the sceptre of political power would depart from Judah, the East, to the multiplying States of the West, he said:

We look forward to that event without alarm, as in the order of the natural growth of this great Republic. We have a firm faith that our interests are mutually consistent; that if you prosper, we shall prosper; if you suffer, we shall suffer; . . . and that our children's welfare, honor, and prosperity will not suffer in the preponderance, which, in the next generation, the west must possess in the balance of the country.[27]

Not only did Everett trust the West but he regarded westward migration as the " *principle* of our institutions " going forth to take possession of the land.[28]

By the decade of the 'thirties there had disappeared every apprehension of incompatibility between the principle of democracy and America's existing domain; the course of this decade was to witness the beginnings of the belief in the compatibility of democracy and future increased domain. One factor in this development was a growing confidence in the flexibility of the federative principle. Thus a writer in the *Democratic Review* of 1838 affirmed that " the peculiar characteristic of our system . . . is, that it may, if its theory is maintained pure in practice, be extended, with equal safety and efficiency, over any indefinite number of millions of population and territory." [29] Favorable contemplation of indefinite future expansion was also induced by the fact that the self-consciousness and spiritual inflammability of Jacksonian equalitarianism brought to most intense fervor, not only the appreciation of democracy, but also the belief that, as Jackson's Farewell Message asserted, Providence had chosen Americans as " the guardians of freedom to preserve it for the benefit of the human race." [30] So grandiose a status seemed to some to demand as its symbol a grandiosity of territorial extent. Thus an essay in the *Democratic Review* of 1838, depicting America as " The Great Nation of Futurity," not only foreshadowed its editor's later coinage of the phrase " manifest destiny " but also exemplified the incipient transition of the idea of manifest destiny from its non-expansionist to its expansionist form:

> The far-reaching, the boundless future will be the era of American greatness. In its magnificent domain of space and time, the nation of many nations is *destined to manifest* [italics mine] to mankind the excellence of divine principles; to establish on earth the noblest temple ever dedicated to the worship of the Most High—the Sacred and the True. Its floor shall be a hemisphere—its roof the firmament of the star-studded heavens, and its congregation an Union of many Republics, comprising hundreds of happy millions, calling, owning no man master, but governed by God's natural and moral law of equality, the law of brotherhood—of 'peace and good will amongst men' [31]

While the conception of the United States as embracing an entire hemisphere outdid even the ambition of the 'forties, the very ambitiousness of the vision indicates the relegation of its fulfilment to the distant future. With respect to the present, the 'thirties were not a decade of active expansionism. Like others the *Democratic Review* was cool toward the vague possibility of annexation raised by the Canadian revolts.[32] The definite proffers of annexation by Texas after its successful rebellion were successively rebuffed, despite the recognition by Senator Niles and other Americans that "destiny had established intimate political connexion between the United States and Texas."[33] In some measure the apathy regarding immediate expansion was due to the persistence of the sedentary ideal of radiating freedom by example — an ideal expressed by a writer in the *North American Review* of 1832 when he affirmed that "we can wait the peaceful progress of our own principles."[34] But this attitude is an inadequate explanation of the fact that Americans rejected an opportunity to render greatly needed assistance in the progress of their democratic principles. Such assistance was refused the Texans when they appealed for annexation after falling into deplorable difficulties. The reserve of Americans toward their former compatriots was caused not only by the fear of difficulty over annexation with both Mexico and American abolitionists, but also by the absence of any belief in the urgent need for expansion. The speeches of Jackson as president exude the complacency and sense of self-sufficiency of this decade. Especially noteworthy is his confident observation concerning an issue always highly determinative of the attitude toward expansion: "You have no longer any cause to fear danger from abroad . . ."[35]

One finally comes to the task of explaining the sudden rise in the 'forties of the ideal of extending the area of freedom by expansion. Is it conceivable that, after having been cold to the sufferings of the Texans for seven years, Americans quite spontaneously developed an overwhelming desire to enfold them with their protective democracy? Such a conception is the more difficult because the expansionists themselves made no pretension to undiluted altruism. On the other hand, only a priori cynicism would suppose that the democratic ideology was merely a hypocritical grace whereby the American appeased conscience before indulging the land-hunger of this decade. An examination of the circumstances and ideas attending the inception of the expansionist movement reveals that a definite international development, suddenly placing new problems in the center of the American's political horizon, was the factor which brought into play the spirit of democracy as well as other motives of expansionism.

The development was the emergence of that " danger from abroad " which Jackson had declared to be absent in the 'thirties. " In Texas, in California, and in Oregon," as Professor Perkins writes with reference to the years following 1841, " the ambition or the intrigue of European nations seemed to the dominant political generation of Americans to threaten fundamental American interests." [36] British and French attempts to establish sovereignty or political influence in adjacent countries appeared to threaten not merely economic and strategic interests but also the security of democracy. The expansionism of the 'forties arose as a defensive effort to forestall the encroachment of Europe in North America. So too, as one can see in the most numerous utterances, the conception of an " extension of the area of freedom " became general as an ideal of preventing absolutistic Europe from lessening the area open to American democracy; extension of the area of " freedom " was the defiant answer to extension of the area of " absolutism."

The European scare started with Texas and at least as early as 1843. In the early months of that year President Tyler was brought by information about British influence in Texas to the fear which was reflected in the reference of his annual message to " interference on the part of stronger and more powerful nations." [37] In 1843, also, Andrew Jackson wrote his famous letter on Texas to Aaron V. Brown, in which, amid warnings of British intrigue, he coined a famous phrase by advocacy of " extending the area of freedom." [38] The year 1844, which witnessed the negotiation of Tyler's unratified treaty of annexation, saw also the publication of Jackson's letter, and the popularization of his felicitous phrase. Although many Southerners wished for annexation primarily to forestall British abolitionist efforts, they also used, without sense of inconsistency, the democratic argument of Andrew Jackson. Texas, Senator Lewis of Alabama wrote to his constituents, was the "great Heritage of Freedom," to be held "in defiance of that power which has well-nigh enslaved the world." [39] The New Orleans *Jeffersonian Republican* represented press economico-ethical sentiment in arguing that unless American supremacy were extended to the Rio Del Norte a few years would suffice for the establishment of an influence near us "highly dangerous to our prosperity, and inimical to the spread of Republican institutions." [40] The discussions of annexation in the congressional debates gave rise to numerous similar observations, and the passage by the Senate of the resolution for annexation of Texas was acclaimed by the New Orleans *Picayune* as "the triumph of republican energy over royal finesse; as the triumph of free minds over the diplomacy of foreign task-master." [41] President Polk's message announcing the acceptance of annexation by Texas gave prominent place to an attack upon the attempted application of the European doctrine of the balance of power to America — an application which he attributed to hostility to "the expansion of free principles." [42]

No less frequently did the ideal of defending democracy figure in the Oregon issue, in which the claims of the United States were again pitted against those of Great Britain. This question seemed to Senator Dickinson to be "a question between two great systems; between monarchy and republicanism." [43] The annexation of Oregon, Representative Sawyer declared, would rid the continent of British power and thereby "hand down to posterity, pure and unadulterated, that freedom we received from the fathers of the Revolution." [44] For it seemed, as Representative Levin said, that the spirit of republicanism "permits not the contaminating proximity of monarchies upon the soil that we have consecrated to the rights of man." [45] Such an attitude toward the Oregon issue also occasioned Senator Allen's resolution affirming that European political interference or colonization upon this hemisphere would be "dangerous to the liberties of the people of America." [46]

With justification Americans also feared the British lion in the wilderness of California. The Whig *American Review* spoke typically in accusing Great Britain of seeking sovereignty over California in order to interpose a barrier to the general growth of the American Union and thereby to "the progress of republican liberty, by which she believes her own institutions and the position of the family of European sovereigns, to be seriously menaced."[47] Such interposition, it declared, was dangerous to the self-preservation of the United States and therefore unallowable. Secretary of State Buchanan's despatch of 1845 to Consul Larkin, indicating the favorable view which a petition of the colonists for annexation would receive, spoke of Great Britain's designs as conflicting with the desire of the colonists for republican institutions.[48] The *New York Herald,* calling likewise for protection of free institutions, wished to annex the whole of Mexico instead of merely California.[49] Stephen Douglas hoped to check absolutism by annexing Canada. Representative Cary stated his constituents' broader doctrine:

> Their doctrine was, that this continent was intended by Providence as a vast theatre on which to work out the grand experiment of Republican government, under the auspices of the Anglo-Saxon race. If the worn-out and corrupt monarchies of the Old World had colonies here; let them be kept within the narrowest limits, consistent with justice and the faith of treaties. Let all which remains be preserved for the growth and spread of the free principles of American democracy.[50]

However, the toleration of existent European colonies seemed to still bolder spirits to be contrary to the true purpose of Providence. In the July number of the *Democratic Review* of 1845 an article on the Texas question affirmed nothing less than continental dominion to be America's "manifest destiny." The historic phrase, as the researches of Professor Pratt indicate, seems to have been used for the first time in this article. The article is attributed by Professor Pratt[51] on the ground of internal evidence to John L. O'Sullivan, editor of the *Democratic Review* and the *New York Morning News,* later Minister to Portugal, who was called by John St. Tammany rather fulsomely "one of the ablest writers and most accomplished scholars and gentlemen of the times."[52] The passage using the later famous phrase is as follows:

Why, were other reasons wanting, in favor of now elevating this question of the reception of Texas into the Union, out of the lower region of our past party dissensions, up to its proper level of a high and broad nationality, it surely is to be found, found abundantly, in the manner in which other nations have undertaken to intrude themselves into it, between us and the proper parties to the case, in a spirit of hostile interference against us, for the avowed object of thwarting our policy and hampering our power, limiting our greatness and checking the fulfilment of our manifest destiny to overspread the continent allotted by Providence for the free development of our yearly multiplying millions.[53]

European encroachment must thus be thanked for making manifest the destiny of continental dominion. With truth Professor Rippy remarks that "manifest destiny never pointed to the acquisition of a region so unmistakably as when undemocratic, conservative Europe revealed an inclination to interfere or to absorb."[54] What was not manifest to Americans was the vicious circle which their defensive expansion created; for Europe's inclination to interfere in North America was caused chiefly by fear of the growing economic and political ambition of the United States.

The view that European interference in America menaced American democracy apparently rested on three principal grounds. The first was the belief that whatever threatened American security was a danger to the political principle which the nation embodied. The second was the supposition that, irrespective of strategic menace, European absolutism would "pollute" American democracy by its very contiguity. The third and perhaps most influential of all was the recognition that adjacent European power threatened the extension of American democracy — an ideal which was made more precious by this very menace.

European adjacency doubtless entailed commercial and political disadvantages, but the foregoing assumptions may seem great exaggerations in respect to danger to the life of the Republic or its democratic institutions. Though the fear expressed was doubtless sincere — for the fears of nations seldom develop in strict accord with logic — there was much more to the question than the fear of the European menace. Considerations which were logically independent — however much the European menace acted as a catalytic agent in their generation — also caused Americans of the 'forties to believe that expansion was essential to the life or healthful development of American democracy.

Whereas it had once been feared that the existence of the Union was jeopardized by expansion, it was now apprehended that the Union might be imperilled by failure to expand through annexing Texas. The Southern States held Texas to be necessary to their economic prosperity, the security of their "peculiar institution," and their maintenance of a balance of political power with the North. It therefore seemed to many that, as Robert J. Walker wrote in his widely read letter on Texas, the defeat of annexation by the North might lead to a union of the South and Southwest with Texas.[55] Ground for this fear was given by certain statements of some Southerners, such as the observation by Senator Lewis of Alabama that if the treaty were rejected he would consider the Union at an end.[56] The fact that the Union seemed synonymous with republicanism created a logical link between solicitude for the Union and zeal for the extension of freedom. Thus Senator Merrick, who warned his colleagues that the failure of annexation would endanger sectional tranquillity, affirmed that the success of annexation would mean the formation of a more perfect union and the securing of the blessings of liberty to ourselves and our posterity.[57] It seemed similarly to Thomas W. Gilmer that "our union has no danger to apprehend from those who believe that its genius is expansive and progressive, but from those who think that the limits of the United States are already too large and the principles of 1776 too old-fashioned for this fastidious age." [58] In fact it is difficult to know which side endangered the Union more. For the threats of Northern abolitionists to dissolve the Union in the event of annexation were just as numerous as those of the Southern expansionists with reference to its failure.

A second line of argument gives the impression that to many the chief consideration was not the Union but the individual State. For, just as the traditional argument regarding the effect of expansion on the Union was inverted, so was also the traditional argument regarding the State. It was the original fear of New England particularists that expansion would be prejudicial to States' rights. After the War of 1812, as already stated, this fear was destroyed by a theory of the distribution of powers according to which the needful powers of the State need not be prejudiced by expansion. In the 'forties this theory was developed by circumstances into the view that expansion was not only not injurious to the individual States but was in fact essential to the preservation of their liberties.

The general logic of this view was stated briefly by Representative Belser of Alabama, during the Texas debate, in the words: "Extension . . . was the antagonistical principle of centralization."[59] In amplification of this view one may quote from Representative Duncan's speech on the Oregon bill:

> There is a strong and constant tendency towards consolidation of power toward the centre of federal government; and that tendency has been favored by a party in this country, who desired at first that our federal government should possess unlimited powers. . . .
>
> To oppose that constant tendency to federal consolidation, I know no better plan than to multiply States; and the farther from the centre of federal influence and attraction, the greater is our security.[60]

From this point of view, extension of the area of freedom meant increase of the security of American States against a curious enemy, their own federal government.

Whereas Representative Duncan was an Ohioan, the theory which he expressed was espoused more frequently by Americans of the Southern slave-holding States. The theory came to the fore at this time principally because of the bearing of the annexation of Texas upon the economic and political interests of the South. Opposition to the annexation desired by these interests was attributed by Southerners both to inimical abolitionists and to advocates of a federal authority overriding States' rights. Thus an advocate of the annexation of Texas in the *Southern Quarterly Review* of 1844 attributed such wicked opposition to those using the epithets "general," "national," and "American" to derogate from rights guaranteed to the States by the Constitution.[61] Representative Rhett of South

Carolina called for annexation as a means of defeating those antagonistic to the rights of Southern States. Having declared that the South must be permitted to participate in the nation's expansion, he added:

> Every census has added to the power of the non-slaveholding States, and diminished that of the South. We are growing weaker, and they stronger, every day. I ask you, is it the spirit of the constitution to strengthen the strong against the weak? What are all its checks and balances of power, but to protect the weak and restrain the strong? The very object of a constitution, in all free governments, is to restrain power. . . . If this measure, therefore, will tend to strengthen the weaker interest in the Union it will be moving in strict accordance with the whole spirit of the constitution.[62]

It was thus true that, as anti-expansionists charged, "we were to extend the area of freedom by enlarging the boundary of slavery."[63] But it was not true that, as anti-expansionists also charged, the phrase about extending freedom was used merely to cover up the design of extending slavery. The strange truth of the matter is that the extension of slavery, which virtually no Southern expansionist denied to be one of his motives, did not seem to the slaveholder incompatible with the ideal of diffusing democracy. The harmonization of the two purposes is explained in part by the Southerner's belief that religious and natural law made the negro a necessary exception to the principle of political equality. But it is also explained by the fact that the extension of slavery appeared essential to States' liberties. In this view the Southerner overlooked the consideration that slavery seemed to abolitionist sections an equal infringement of their right to a union based on universal individual liberty.

North and South saw with one eye, however, on one topic — the liberty of the American (white) individual. Here again, as though some Hegelian metaphysical dialectic of antitheses were at work, one meets the inversion of a traditional argument. Anti-expansionists had maintained originally that the political untrustworthiness of a remote pioneer population made extended territory dangerous to individual liberties. Now, with particular view to the very pioneers who were once feared, expansionists declared that territorial extension was essential to the fullest liberty of the individual.

The idea of individualism perhaps did more than anything else to cement the association between democracy and expansion. For the sturdiest element in democracy was its valuation of individualism — the thesis of the individual's right not only to exemption from undue interference by government but also to the most abundant opportunity for self-development. Those entirely misread its spirit who believe that the enthusiasm for democracy was merely enthusiasm over a form of government as such. Fundamentally, indeed, the Jeffersonian American rather disliked government; though recognizing the necessity of giving some power to the State, he at least verged on anarchism in his belief that "the best government is that which governs least." Whereas individualism in its negative phase meant restraint from undue interference with individual rights, in its positive phase it signified that "care of human life and happiness" which Jefferson called the only legitimate object of government.[64]

Although both individualism and the pioneer spirit had prevailed from the beginning, it was not until the 'forties that the enterprise of the pioneer seemed the most perfect expression of American individualism. The coming of the pioneer movement to self-consciousness in this decade was due to various factors: the popular interest aroused by the accelerating trek to Oregon and the Southwest; the fact that the pioneer movement now became involved with territorial issues of national concern; and above all, perhaps, the general land-hunger which caused the pioneer to seem now not a deviation from but the very expression of Americanism. It was in the fervent appreciation of the pioneer movement that there were forged all the links uniting individualism and expansionism.

Among such links was the conception of the economic value of expansion to the individual. Expansion, later to be depicted by anti-imperialists as a means to economic exploitation and slavery, was seen in this period as a means to economic liberty. Economic freedom had become as important as political freedom to the philosophy of democracy, which, giving full recognition to the Platonic truth that before one can live well one must live, was unhesitant about attaching an almost moral valuation to even the material values of land-ownership. Land, as Professor Fish has pointed out, seemed to the American of the 'forties the very key to happiness.[65] The demand for abundant territory in the name of economic liberty is exemplified by the words of Representative Duncan in support of the Oregon Bill:

> First, to extend our population we require the possession of Oregon. I have before remarked that personal liberty is incompatible with a crowded population. . . .
>
> By whatever means the lands and wealth of a country fall into the hands of a few individuals, it establishes a feudal system as oppressive and destructive of the liberties of the people as if it were established by conquest, and equally enslaves the people. . . . The inability of the weak, the humble, and the non-assuming, to contend with the overbearing, the cunning, and the grasping monopolist makes it necessary, to the equality of circumstances and personal liberty, that the advantages of territory should constantly be kept open to all who wish to embrace it.[66]

The foregoing is unimpeachable in logic so far as concerns the privileges of homestead. It is not clear, however, that the enlargement of individual agrarian opportunities required further national expansion. The anti-expansionist maintained correctly that the Republic already "had an ample area for hundred millions of human beings," [67] with vast regions as yet scarcely explored. Indeed the boast of the average American was like that of Mr. Bovan in *Martin Chuzzlewit*: "We have a vast territory, and not — as yet — too many people on it."

The rub lay precisely in the "as yet." Just as in the issue of Indian lands, the expansionist took his main position on the ground of need of territory for posterity. In calculating the territorial needs of posterity Americans used the rate of population growth which had been maintained as late as the census of 1840 — approximately a doubling of population every twenty-five years. According to the typical estimate of John L. O'Sullivan, a century from 1845 would see an American population of approximately three hundred millions.[68] These calculations were a favorite occupation of American nationalists, who agreed with the biblical writer that in the multitude of the people is the king's honor — or more correctly the honor of democracy, to which they actually attributed American fecundity. It seemed, then, a duty to the hasty American to provide territory for a future population even before the need arose. Referring to reproductive capacity as the American multiplication table, Representative Kennedy asked how room would be found for posterity without the acquisition of Oregon.[69] Representative Belser, prophesying the three hundred millions of a century thence, declared confinement of the area of freedom an impossibility.[70] Presentiment of this "stupendous" growth of population seemed to John L. O'Sullivan the fundamental cause of the popular movement toward territorial extension.[71]

But today, nine decades after O'Sullivan's prophecy of three hundred million in a century, America's population is still not much more than a third of that estimate. The gross miscalculation arose from an erroneous statistical method. As an anti-expansionist writer pointed out in 1849, expansionists overlooked the consideration that as a people become denser they mutliply more slowly.[72] The unusual growth-rate of American population was ascribed in Alison's work of 1840 on *Principles of Population* to the continual influx of immigrants to better their fortunes on the unappropriated lands of the West.[73] With the settlement of surplus land immigration and likewise the rapid growth of population would subside. The true cure for the overgrowth of population was thus to cease expanding. But instead of adopting this disagreeable cure, the American nationalist proposed to continue expanding. Thus he was laying the basis for the very superfluity of population which he cited as the justification of expansion.

But reasoning in regard to needs of population was not responsible fundamentally for the association of expansion and individual liberty. The pioneer was not rational as he rushed from the abundant fertile land at hand to stake his claim on land more distant. He was impelled onward, if the contemporary interpretation does not over-romanticize him, by some fever in the blood, some spirit of adventure. So, too, the philosopher of the pioneer movement was thinking of liberty in a sense broader than the freedom to satisfy economic needs. He was envisaging a liberty for the pioneer impulse as such, an impulse of adventure and self-expression. This impulse seemed good in and of itself as an essential element in the energetic spirit produced by free institutions. It was the fact that it gave scope for the satisfaction of such an impulse which primarily caused expansion to be related to individual liberty.

Observations illustrative of this association received at times a naïvely naturalistic expression, as in the words of Major Davezac at the New Jersey Democratic State Convention of 1844:

> Land enough—land enough! Make way, I say, for the young American Buffalo—he has not yet got land enough; he wants more land as his cool shelter in summer—he wants more land for his beautiful pasture grounds. I tell you, we will give him Oregon for his summer shade, and the region of Texas as his winter pasture. (Applause.) Like all of his race, he wants salt, too. Well, he shall have the use of two oceans—the mighty Pacific and turbulent Atlantic shall be his . . . He shall not stop his career until he slakes his thirst in the frozen ocean. (Cheers.)[74]

So far was Representative McClernand from shame of such cravings that he called the American impulse of expansion "glorious" and "divine." He thought it "a new impulse called into action by free institutions operating upon the restless and daring spirit of the Anglo-Saxon blood."[75] Similarly, Representative Ficklin apotheosized the unmercenary, exploratory spirit which sent Americans to distant Oregon:

> This wild spirit of adventure gives nerve and energy to the mental and physical man, and prompts its possessor to deeds of peril and of danger, from which the tame and timorous would shrink with horror; it expands the heart, and unfetters its joys, its hopes, its aspirations; it lends a new charm to life, a new spring to human energies and desires, and wakens in the breast a kindred feeling with that which animated our first parents in the garden of Eden.[76]

"Wide shall our own free race increase,"[77] wrote an American poet who was quoted by a congressional expansionist. But what limits would this free race, irresistible to others, set for itself? Even the least grandiose conceptions assumed that under "the influence of free institutions" the pioneer movement would cover "everything in the shape of land not already occupied by comparatively large numbers from some foreign nation." [78] This embraced at least Texas, California, and Oregon. But there was a much broader vision which was confessed by many expansionists and was in the subliminal expectation of nearly all. It was identical with that which De Tocqueville, his dazzled imagination following the course of the deluge of pioneers, expressed in the 'thirties:

> At a period which may be said to be near,—for we are speaking of the life of a nation,—the Anglo-Americans alone will cover the immense space contained between the polar regions and the tropics, extending from the coasts of the Atlantic to those of the Pacific Ocean.[79]

If the detached foreigner could believe that "the continent which they inhabit is their dominion," [80] would not the same belief suggest itself the more readily to self-confident Americans? The literature of the time is replete with the expression of that belief. The toast at a political banquet urged the march of the "Spirit of Democratic progression" until "*the whole unbounded continent is ours.*" [81] In an article of 1844 on "The Texas Question" a writer in the *Democratic Review* declared that the increase and diffusiveness of America's population, occupying all territory until checked by great natural barriers, would at no distant day cover "every habitable square inch of the continent." [82] Continental dominion was predicted by John L. O'Sullivan in the light of both natural law and providential design:

> Texas has been absorbed into the Union in the inevitable fulfilment of the general law which is rolling our population westward; the connexion of which with that ratio of growth in population which is destined within a hundred years to swell our numbers to the enormous population of *two hundred and fifty millions* (if not more), is too evident to leave us in doubt of the manifest design of Providence in regard to the occupation of this continent.[83]

Jefferson and other imaginative early Americans also foresaw a time when "our rapid multiplication will . . . cover the whole northern, if not the southern continent." [84] But whereas Jefferson did not care about the political tie, expansionists of the 'forties insisted upon it as essential to the realization of freedom. They held that seekers for economic and social liberty must be followed by a government solicitous for their political liberty. Thus Representative Bowlin, describing the progress of the pioneer race, declared that the Government should follow them with the laws and instructions which they love and cherish, and thereby also add strength and permanent glory to the Republic.[85] So too, Senator Linn, champion of the Oregon settlers, proclaimed that the irresistible advance of American population should march "with every public right in the lead." [86] The association between the ideal of the free pioneer and that of the extension of the political area of freedom appears in the lines of a contemporary poet who said that the increase of our "free race" would extend widely the elastic chain

> That binds in everlasting peace
> State after State — a mighty train.[87]

"We are the pioneers of the continent," proclaimed an expansionist editorial in the organ of the author of the phrase "manifest destiny." [88] It is in the light of this pioneer ideal that one must interpret not only the immediate territorial ambitions but even the dream of eventual continental dominion. This future empire, like the immediate annexation of Texas, was not to be achieved through the military conquest which imperialists of 1898 were to conduct in the name of liberty. The continental republic was rather to be the natural consummation of what O'Sullivan called the "destiny to overspread the whole North American continent with an immense democratic population." [89] To paraphrase Walt Whitman, the expansionist proposed to "make the continent indissoluble" [90] by filling it with the spreading but politically cohesive American race.

Freedom for the American nation; freedom for the American State; freedom for the American individual: such, then, were the principal elements in the fundamentally egoistic program of extending the area of freedom. One sees finally why the anti-expansionists talked beside the mark when they pointed out that Texas was already republican. The freedom sought by expansionists was a distinctively American freedom which went far beyond nominal republicanism. The area in question was the domain in which American pioneers might freely spread themselves and all their institutions. The extension of the area of freedom could thus be only the expansion of the United States. Freedom, in sum, had become nationalized.

It is an exaggeration, indeed, to suppose that international philanthropy was entirely absent from the expansionist ideal. However, even its elements of altruism, as analysis will show, were restricted in a manner which can be explained only by the nationalistic orientation of the ideal.

Thus the altruistic phase of democratic expansionism had as one presupposition an egoistic disparagement of the capacity of other peoples to help themselves. This disparagement reflected in some measure, to be sure, the disillusionment which experience had brought to the original hope of extending freedom by mere example. Most of the New World peoples who had followed the example of the American Revolution fell shortly into ways of political disorder which seemed to an American of 1838 to "depress the hopes of those who desire to see civil liberty established throughout the world." [91] Most depression came from those of whom most had been hoped, the Texans. As though they had lost the talent for democracy in losing contact with their native soil, these former Americans exhibited a political and social confusion prompting one American editor's description of Texas as a "Quasi Republic." [92] Despite previous belief in the triumph of democracy through man's "eternal principle of progress," [93] Americans now saw reason to believe that not every Tom, Dick and Harry among nations had the genius for democracy. The disappointment to undue impatience caused the pendulum to swing to a pessimism as extreme as the former optimism.

Abandonment of the hope of teaching democracy by remote example led to acceptance of the alternative pedagogical method, that of taking other peoples into "the district school of democracy." Of course, the Texans strongly resented any patronizing attitude; a prominent Texan diplomat believed that the annexation of Texas was "coupled with the paramount security of Republican institutions in the United States." [94] But Representative Dean and other expansionists regarded it as "philanthropy" to extend to Texans America's blessing of civil, political, and religious liberty.[95] America's expansion seemed even more essential to the liberation of peoples non-American in blood; and Dean saw annexation as a means of releasing from their "shackles" every nation on the continent.[96] While only Canada was subjected to a monarchy, all these republican nations were in shackles in so far as they had not attained American or true freedom.

Above all, the oppressed of Europe, a section of the world in which the American had almost lost hope, were supposed to see in the United States their only refuge. Still far removed from the "one-hundred-per-cent Americanism" of the twentieth-century immigration policy, Americans of the 'forties felt toward their gracious country as did Bryant:

> There's freedom at thy gates and rest
> For Earth's down-trodden and opprest,
> A shelter for the hunted head,
> For the starved laborer toil and bread.[97]

Benjamin Franklin's still vital conception of America as "an asylum for those who love liberty" [98] easily became an argument for expansion. Thus Representative Duncan proclaimed: "If ours is to be the home of the oppressed, we must extend our territory in latitude and longitude to the demand of the millions who are to follow us, as well of our own posterity as those who are invited to our peaceful shores to partake in our republican institutions." [99] There were those who, disregarding De Tocqueville's observation that the movement toward equality was world-wide, believed as did Governor Brown that "in the order of Providence, America might become the last asylum of liberty to the human family," [100] and must therefore lay its foundations deep and wide for the innumerable refugees of later ages. Similarly Representative Stone, advocating the annexation of Texas and an ocean-bound republic, affirmed that "Providence intended this western hemisphere to be an asylum for the oppressed." [101] Representative Belser related the salvation in freedom to biblical conceptions:

> Long may our country prove itself the asylum of the oppressed. Let its institutions and its people be extended far and wide, and when the waters of despotism shall have inundated other portions of the globe, and the votary of liberty be compelled to betake himself to his ark, let this government be the Ararat on which it shall rest.[102]

Thus the American expansionist's nationalism was so little exclusive that it offered refuge to all the devotees of freedom in a world elsewhere threatened with a rising deluge of despotism.

None the less the typical expansionist's altruism was not only conditioned by but distinctly secondary to his interest in his own people. That expansionist altruism was influenced by nationaism is clear from the fact that the expansionist became concerned about other peoples only as he conceived of them as in some sense American. There was never a period (reference is made to the years of the 'forties preceding the European revolutionary movements of 1848) when the average American was less interested in world developments not bearing directly upon his own hemisphere. But even in viewing his own hemisphere the American was interested primarily in those sections inhabited altogether or largely by pioneers from the United States. The Texan was a kind of *alter ego,* described affectionately as "bone of our bone, and flesh of our flesh." [103] All three of the immediate territorial interests of the United States — Texas, Oregon, and California — were, or promised to be, settled by Americans. The adjacent Latin peoples were recipients of consideration not so much for their own sake as because they inhabited the American continent, which "the God of nature" had designed for "liberty." [104] The fundamental consideration was that no despotism should "pollute" the soil adjacent to that of the pure American democracy.

The secondary character of the expansionist's altruism is evidenced partly by the fact that most of his encomia of freedom stressed liberty for the American himself. It is also indicated by the concentration of the expansionist's interest not upon territories whose inhabitants stood in greatest need of freedom, but upon territories whose inhabitants, being entirely or largely former Americans, could most advantageously be assimilated to the Union. Aside from Texas, Oregon, and California — territories where Americans had already set their stakes — the American expansionist was willing to postpone annexation until the pioneer's Americanization of the continent had succeeded, as one expansionist said, in "irrigating it for the growth and predominance of liberty."[105] Further instances of the American's long-dominant revulsion from amalgamation with supposedly inferior peoples will be given in a subsequent chapter concerned with the ideal of regenerative expansionism.

Thus, those entirely miss the spirit of the ideal of extending the area of freedom who see it as altogether or primarily an attachment to international philanthropy. Very shortly, indeed, the altruistic form of the democratic ideal was to be developed by the issue of amalgamation raised in the Mexican War. But before the Mexican War democratic expansionism was primarily a concern for the freedom of Americans themselves; the concern for others was such as overflows even from a Nietzschean's euphoria. Precisely because the idealism of the expansionist of this period was rooted in egoism, it had a sincerity and an intensity which later expansionists probably never fully attained in their somewhat forced altruism.

An interesting problem is raised by the contrast between the American's version of extending freedom and the altruistic form which prevailed among French Revolutionists, absolutistic Pan-Slavs, and most other peoples in the history of nationalism. Why did extension of freedom mean to the American of the middle 'forties less the liberation of other peoples than the aggrandizement of his own freedom — and territory?

The reasons are interesting even if not in all cases edifying. Undoubtedly one explanation was the American's healthy-minded egoism, a matter of instinct rather than of logic. Another was the fact that the American philosophy of individualism blessed egoism in its affirmation of a natural right to the pursuit of happiness. Still another factor lay in the circumstance that the annexation of the willing Texans involved no obvious transgression (Mexico to the contrary notwithstanding) upon alien rights, and thus did not cause the uneasy conscience for which professions of international altruism are so often a compensation. But none of these reasons touches on what is probably the basic ideological explanation — the influence exerted upon the American's democratic thought by his philosophy of manifest destiny.

To understand this influence one must begin by recognizing that the egoism of the American's philosophy of the destiny of democracy did not exclude a love of democracy for its own sake. When the American spoke of extending the area of freedom he had in mind not only greater freedom for Americans but also greater freedom by means of Americans. This impersonal element in the American's attachment to the cause of freedom is abundantly illustrated in the expansionist literature. The *New York Morning News,* affirming that the great experiment of democracy required nothing less than the continent, saw the end of this experiment as "the free development of humanity to the best and highest results it may be capable of working out for itself." [106] The vision which caused the American expansionist's heart to leap was described by Representative Cathcart as that of "State after State coming into this great temple of freedom, and burning their incense upon an altar consecrated to the enjoyment of civil and religious liberty." [107] The migrations which would extend American territory would also, Representative Tibbatts declared, "extend the principles of civil liberty, for they march *pari passu* with the migrations of the Anglo-Saxon race." [108]

This very attachment to freedom was one element underlying the American expansionist's self-engrossment. For in his devotion to the ideal he cast about for the best instrument to realize it and found — himself. The philosophy of American nationalism developed a belief incongruous with the equalitarianism of democracy — the belief that, however equal men might be at birth, Americans had become subsequently a super-people.

The American had never been a sufferer from self-depreciation. But the 'forties witnessed the full flowering of national self-esteem in consequence of the undeniable promise in American life, of intensified democratic self-consciousness, of heightened nationalism, and of the partial stupidity of national adolescence. It was in this period that an Iowa newspaper urged ironically that America repudiate its debts to Europe on the ground that Europe was sufficiently recompensed by having assisted the spread of American civilization! [109] National boasting was reconciled with civilization by one American orator's explanation: " It is not good taste in individuals to indulge in boasting; but a nation is allowed to assume an elevated tone." In an editorial of the *United States Journal* of 1845 one finds an observation in a very elevated tone:

> It is a truth, which every man may see, if he will but look,—that all the channels of communication,—public and private, through the school-room, the pulpit, and the press,—are engrossed and occupied with *this one idea,* which all these forces are combined to disseminate:—that we the American people, are the most independent, intelligent, moral and happy people on the face of the earth.[110]

The foregoing words are not those of a satirist but of one who admitted the truth of the proposition. It was no matter that the very same page of his editorial reported the failure of Pittsburg female operatives in their strike for a ten-hour working day!

But in the national self-complacency of the " fabulous 'forties " there was the redeeming quality of moral ambition. The *United States Journal* entitled its editorial " Forward Forward " and called from drowsy satisfaction to meliorative effort. Walt Whitman, who wrote that " we are the most beautiful to ourselves and in ourselves," also exclaimed: " I will make the most splendid race the sun ever shone upon." [111] While these words are from a later decade, in the 'forties he gave prose expression to the same ideal:

> And it is from such materials—from the democracy with its manly heart and its lion strength, spurning the ligatures wherewith drivellers would bind it—that we are to expect the great FUTURE of this western world! a scope involving such unparalleled human happiness and rational freedom, to such unnumbered myriads, that the heart of a true

*man* leaps with a mighty joy only to think of it! God works out his greatest results by such means; and while each popinjay priest of the mummery of the past is babbling his alarm, the youthful Genius of the people passes swiftly over era after era of change and improvement, and races of human beings erewhile down in gloom or bondage rise gradually toward that majestic development which the good God doubtless loves to witness.[112]

These swelling periods exemplify the modern version of the chosen people, which Whitman's compatriots, on six days of the week even if not the seventh, made the chief tenet of their religious philosophy as well as of their nationalism. This thesis differed from the Hebraic in that " a kingdom of priests and a holy nation " was ordained to preserve, not the law of man's duty to God, but the law of man's duty to man — democracy. In his anthropocentric theology, in which God himself served chiefly as a Providence watchful for mankind and human values, the American approached perilously close to changing the traditional dogma, that man exists *ad majorem gloriam Dei,* into the heresy that God exists *ad majorem gloriam hominis.* And Providence had entrusted the fullest achievement of the moral glory of man to the best of human material, the mighty American democracy. It is small wonder that the American like the ancient Hebrew was self-engrossed. The " chosen people " is indifferent to the heathen because it believes that the best material for the creation of its ideal is itself.

Enshrined in expansionism, then, was this dogma of the special mission. Moral idealism divested of all intent of sacrilege the half-belief that God, who walked with Noah, rode with the American pioneer in his journeys over the continent. Even theological literature was scarcely more abundant in references to Providence than was the literature of expansionism. For it seemed that especially in expanding our territory, as a poet wrote upon the prospect of annexing Texas, " we do but follow out our destiny, as did the ancient Israelite." [113] The expansionist conception of destiny was essentially ethical in its assumption that " Providence had given to the American people a great and important mission . . . to spread the blessings of Christian liberty." [114] It was ambitiously ethical in its further assumption that " Providence " had a " design in extending our free institutions as far and as wide as the American continent." [115] But the primary providential end was no more the elevation of the Latin-American heathen than was the elevation of the adjacent Philistines the end of the Israelite's journey to the Promised Land. The end in view was, as stated by John L. O'Sullivan in his first passage on manifest destiny, "the free development of our yearly multiplying millions." But in a second reference to manifest destiny he implied the moral significance of this free development of Americans. Americans were destined to develop themselves as subjects in "the great experiment of liberty and federated self-government entrusted to us." [116]

Such was the credo which encouraged American expansionists to conceive that the free rather than the meek would inherit the earth. Its logic harmonized Calvinistic pride and equalitarianism. Still greater was its service in permitting the harmonization of the American's two deepest impulses — the expansionism oriented toward the good earth, and the democratic idealism oriented toward "Fair freedom's star." Believing like the Crusader that "God wills it," the expansionist had the joyful illusion of hitching his pioneer wagon to a star.

There is, of course, the quite different question whether territorial expansion was objectively essential to freedom — the American's or any one else's. The expansionist's cosmology, refreshing as it was, perhaps seemed to offer little convincing evidence that the star of democracy would not have shone as brightly in the world's firmament even with less nationalist heat in man for the addition of stars to the flag.

# CHAPTER V

## THE TRUE TITLE

In his message announcing Texan acceptance of annexation, President Polk also made recommendations raising to the plane of immediate national policy the territorial aspiration popularly coupled with Texas — the annexation of Oregon. Common to the two issues was the element of British opposition, the defeat of which was urged by Polk in the second issue as in the first. However, Great Britain's position in the Oregon issue rested on stronger ground than did its interference in Texas. The obstacle to manifest destiny in Oregon was a European country's legal claim — an impediment which would either give American expansionism pause or force it to enlarge its moral pretensions.

In the case of Texas, Great Britain had intrigued without legal warrant to frustrate the legitimate American ambition of union with an independent country. In the case of Oregon, on the other hand, it presented a long-standing legal claim which the United States itself had recognized to the extent of entering into a temporary convention of joint occupation. The American claim was at best debatable. To be sure, Polk now denied the validity of great Britain's legal position and maintained the American title to all Oregon to be unquestionably clear. Yet his own Secretary of State, attorney for this title in the diplomatic argument with Great Britain, intimated in a Cabinet meeting that north of the forty-ninth parallel America's claim did not bear defense. Perhaps an American historian did not greatly exaggerate when he wrote that no American took the full legal claim seriously.[1] The insistence upon all Oregon might therefore seem a fulfilment of Dr. Channing's lugubrious prediction that expansionism would eventuate in an unwillingness to take international morality seriously.[2]

But what the American attitude in the Oregon issue really showed was that it is possible to take international morality seriously without taking international law quite seriously. Even while the legal claim was perfunctorily argued, it was asserted that, after all, the true criterion of right in this issue was not positive law. A biographer of Stephen Douglas noted the non-legal criterion when he spoke of the latter's belief that, irrespective of the right derived from priority of discovery, America possessed a greater right by virtue of a consideration identified with the theory of manifest destiny.[3] Despite its recent alliance in the Texan issue with legal right, in the Oregon issue expansionism took up arms against legality and in its new independence adopted the bold doctrine that the true title was the title by manifest destiny.

The ironic comment of Robert Winthrop on the new expansionist doctrine was that it suggested a new chapter for the law of nations.[4] In reality, the ideas which stir men profoundly may often be curious but are seldom utterly ridiculous. Nor was this idea by any means "unique," as Polk's biographer suggested.[5] In what follows we shall see the doctrine of the higher title as the species of an ideological genus which, though changing its form as it evolved, pervaded all American history, as doubtless it pervades history in general. Seen in its true historical and logical perspective, it will probably appear not mad at all, but, like most verdicts of legal justice, a compound of error and truth.

Curiously enough, the idea which Robert Winthrop satirized was in direct line of descent from a doctrine first propounded in America among the Puritans led by his distinguished ancestor, Governor John Winthrop of Massachusetts. The doctrine of a title higher than the legal reincarnated the Puritan doctrine of the superiority of divine law to human positive law. This doctrine, as Professor Dunning observes in speaking of the anti-legalist element in Wycliffe, has been common to all the Christian ages.[6] For an inevitable consequence of Christian other-worldliness and political indifferentism was the identification of the supremely binding law with what Justice Holmes once called a "brooding omnipresence in the sky."[7] The American Puritans carried the doctrine of the supremacy of divine law to unusual lengths because of their revolt against the legalism which had interfered with their ecclesiastical independency in England. They believed that the only true law was the law of God and that human law achieved dignity only as it applied divine law. John Winthrop's history of New England cites an official report declaring that should any law have been established otherwise than in accordance with the law of God, "it was an error, and not a law." In other words, such a law was not truly binding.[8]

In the ideology of the American Revolution the superiority ascribed to divine law was also attributed to natural law. For natural law too was conceived as ordained by divine will; it differed from divine law chiefly in being discoverable through natural reason rather than revelation. From natural law were derived the rights of man, which in contrast with purely legal rights were assumed to have a validity prior to and independent of political authority. In the words of Thomas Paine a natural right is "a *right founded in right,*" in the contemplation of which the mind feels no compunction such as is given by a legal right founded in injustice.[9] Prophetic of the very rhetoric of the Oregon issue are words of Alexander Hamilton respecting rights derived from the Author of Nature:

> THE SACRED RIGHTS OF MANKIND ARE NOT TO BE RUMMAGED FOR AMONG OLD PARCHMENTS OR MUSTY RECORDS. THEY ARE WRITTEN, AS WITH A SUNBEAM, IN THE WHOLE VOLUME OF HUMAN NATURE, BY THE HAND OF THE DIVINITY ITSELF; AND CAN NEVER BE ERASED OR OBSCURED BY MORTAL POWER.[10]

Upon these higher rights bestowed by "Nature" and "Nature's God" were based, in the absence of sound legal foundation, America's claims to autonomy and ultimately to complete independence.

However, there was an important difference between the American application of the "higher law" in the eighteenth century and its later use in the Oregon issue. Eighteenth-century Americans contrasted the rights derived from nature with the laws imposed upon subjects by oppressive rulers. On the other hand, these early Americans did not usually place natural law and international law in contrast, as did the expansionists of the Oregon issue. International law escaped disparagement in part because the dispute between America and Great Britain was at first apprehended as one between a sovereign power and subjects rather than between independent nations. But a second reason, of greater interest here, was the original identification of the unwritten law of nations with natural law.

This identification accorded at the time of the American Revolution with contemporary juristic theory. Grotius himself, though distinguishing theoretically between the law of nature and the voluntary law of nations, had in fact been subconsciously influenced by ideas of natural law in determining the practices typical of voluntary law. Subsequently, and especially in the following century, leading international jurists raised the law of nature from a subconscious to a conscious criterion of international law. Thus Vattel considered the law of nature as identical with the "necessary" law of nations and as the moral basis of positive international law. Other jurists, like the Swiss Burlamaqui, popular in eighteenth-century America, made no such dichotomy but expressly identified the entire law of nations with the law of nature. It was this latter theory which appears chiefly to have influenced Americans; thus the jurist James Wilson taught that "the law of nations is only the law of nature judiciously applied to the conduct of states." [11] Obviously, there could be no law higher than the law of nations if the latter was identical with the supreme law of nature.

But a disassociation of the law of nations and the law of nature was gradually to develop among Americans. It began, indeed, even in the period when their theoretical identification was current. For the confusion called by Dr. Dickinson "a failure or refusal to distinguish between the kind of rule of conduct to which the name of law seems best fitted, and the raw materials for such a rule" [12] may be corrected quickly by adverse experience with law. When Americans learned of international practices which went counter to America's case, some of them, adapting their theory to their interest, differentiated between the faulty voluntary law of nations and the ideal law of nature.

An instance is offered by the comments of John Adams upon the Tory argument that nations discovering distant territories are legally justified in subjecting the inhabitants to the laws of the mother country. His first objection to this theory unfavorable to the American cause was that "the practice of free governments alone can be quoted with propriety to show the sense of nations." [13] This proposition, going far beyond the Grotian precedent of confining observation to the practice of "enlightened" nations, was in itself legally surprising. But Adams also asserted a still more radical thesis: "Their practice must be reasonable, just and right, or it will not govern Americans." [14] Thus, despite his previous admission that the law of nations and the law of nature were identical, Adams here implied definitely that even the law of nations as deduced from enlightened practice would not be acceptable to Americans were it not in accord with their own democratic super-enlightenment. In 1779 Richard Henry Lee made a similar observation in connection with America's claim to the free navigation of the Mississippi and the use of the northern fisheries. To be sure, he called these claims "rights" and apparently thought that the law of nations sanctioned them as such. But in referring to the contrary view of some Americans he said: "Nature and reason have given us both, no Attorney quirks can shake titles derived from such sources." [15] In other words, nature and reason gave a title withstanding any adverse consideration of international law. Revolutionary Americans did not wish to rebel against international law, but they were just as unwilling to tolerate any nonsense from it.

The birth and early years of the Federal Government were marked by the conflict of two tendencies: Federalism, with its emphasis upon the sanctity of legal contracts; and the liberal Republicanism whose spokesman, Jefferson, denied the right of any generation to bind legally a subsequent one. But there were two issues which from the earliest time tended to make Americans of both parties think more and more of a moral rather than of a legal source of national rights. The first was the issue of Europe's acquisition of dominion upon this continent. It was very difficult to defend America's opposition to all such aggrandizement solely on legal grounds. Doubtless this fact was responsible for Jefferson's conception of "a different code of natural law" for the international relations of this geographically detached country. Such a conception did not imply a rejection of positive international law but it did assume that positive law was subject to modification in accordance with a geographically conditioned morality. Jefferson's unorthodox idea was popularized among Americans by the enunciation of the Monroe Doctrine. The following question of C. J. Ingersoll in reference to Monroe's principle reflects this development:

> . . . is that doctrine less rational than that interpolation into the law of nations that the European intruder into the mouth of an American river thousands of miles long . . . entitles the sovereign of that intruder to ownership of all the territories it washes, from mouth to source, although where the source may be is totally unknown? [16]

The other issue which encouraged the conception of a "rational" rather than legal criterion was expansion, a policy tending to clash with legal standards. True, the doctrine of natural right which sustained the first expansion movement of American history purported to be derived from the natural law of nations. But it has been seen that the claims put forward in the name of natural right strained the law of nations as greatly as the incorporation of Louisiana strained constitutional law. The doctrine of the natural boundary was not even presented as a legal doctrine, for writers on international law had only asserted its expediency. Indeed, Representative Trimble's exposition of this doctrine in 1820 explicitly contrasted it with a legal claim to territory. Depreciating the legal phase of the Texan issue, he declared: "Title was nothing. Boundary and barriers were everything." [17] The case is similar with the principle of beneficent territorial utilization, introduced by the issue of Indian lands. While some jurists had approved the application of this principle under certain circumstances, none had deemed it valid when it conflicted with specific commitments to the aboriginals. As a previously cited article in the *North American Review* pointed out, the fundamental ground for dispossession was social welfare and not law. These considerations do not mean that early expansionism was, as a rule, consciously anti-legal. But its deeds were often unconsciously antilegal and its philosophy was consciously extra-legal.

Expansionism was to be developed from extra-legalism into anti-legalism by the Oregon issue. At first, indeed, the question of Oregon was not considered from an anti-legal viewpoint; this fact, however, is perhaps explicable in part by the original remoteness of the issue from national interest. Proposing to Great Britain in 1818 the division of the country by extension of the line of the forty-ninth parallel to the Pacific, the American commissioners based America's claim to the Columbia River valley on the discoveries of Captain Gray, the explorations of Lewis and Clark, and the settlement at Astoria. But in 1823, when the United States was eager to establish the non-colonization principle of the Monroe Doctrine, Secretary of State Adams introduced the first non-legal consideration into America's case. It was the metaphysical ground that America's settlement and sovereignty on the Northwestern Coast were pointed out by "the finger of nature"[18] — that is, by nature's principle of "contiguity."[19] The first extra-legal argument thus entered the issue in connection with the attempt to assert the broad claim embodied in the Monroe Doctrine, itself an unconscious appeal to the higher law.

Adams's metaphysical phrase, however, was designed as a mere elaboration of what was supposed, though incorrectly, to be a legal doctrine. This fact became clearer in the renewed negotiations with Great Britain in 1826, when Albert Gallatin urged Adams's principle of contiguity in legal phraseology. He presented as a principle of international law the proposition that "the extent of contiguous territory to which an actual settlement gives a prior right, must depend, in a considerable degree, on the magnitude and population of that settlement, and on the facility with which the vacant adjacent land may, within a short time, be occupied, settled, and cultivated, by such population, as compared with the probability of its being thus occupied and settled from any other quarter."[20] But as the jurist Twiss pointed out, Gallatin was mistaken in assuming that contiguity gives a claim to exclusive right. This assumption seemed to Twiss a disguised appeal to the principle of the *vis major,* an implicit denial of the legal equality of all nations in rights.[21]

From another viewpoint, however, Gallatin was appealing from an orthodox law inconclusive in this issue to a principle which, though not orthodox, seemed not only just but conclusive. His pamphlet of 1846 on the Oregon issue showed his conviction that, with respect to the new continent, the facts of original discovery and settlement were of an inadequate character which did not permit the definitive operation of ordinary legal criteria.[22] It was quite true that, despite Grotius's denial of the skeptical proposition, "to fix by certain Rules Things so uncertain" was impossible. So it came about that at all stages the Oregon issue encouraged Americans to turn to a moral criterion as an escape from the inconclusiveness of the legal method.

Whereas the moral criterion with Adams was the geographical doctrine of contiguity, with Gallatin contiguity began to blend with the doctrine of beneficent territorial utilization. The latter doctrine came into still greater prominence when, as was poetically written in a House report on Oregon in 1839, migration seemed to be flowing westward "with the never-ceasing advance of a rising tide of the sea." [23] After Senator Linn's bill of 1842 to assist the Columbia River settlers had called the Oregon movement to the attention of Americans, Secretary of State Calhoun called it in 1844 to the attention of Great Britain in a passage implying the principle of beneficent utilization:

> Our well-founded claim, grounded on continuity, has greatly strengthened . . . by the rapid advance of our population towards the territory—its great increase, especially in the valley of the Mississippi—as well as the greatly increased facility of passing to the territory by more accessible routes, and the far stronger and rapidly-swelling tide of population that has recently commenced flowing into it.[24]

Though Calhoun's argument that Oregon was " destined to be peopled by us " [25] is philosophical rather than legal, it is clear that Calhoun like Gallatin before him believed or professed to believe that the principle of continuity was a conventional legal argument. Thus far the idea tending toward "the title by manifest destiny" had not developed beyond a belief that America's legal title was, as Robert Greenhow said in his memoir of 1840, "more consistent with the principles of national right, than those of any other Power." [26]

After the presidential campaign of 1844, however, the heterodox idea was to develop further by reason of circumstances which we are now to consider. In this campaign the Democrats, seeing that the South and North were set for expansion in antipodal directions, believed that it would be politically expedient to couple "the reannexation of Texas" with "the reoccupation of Oregon." What was the extent of the territory to which America's title was said to be "clear and unquestionable"? Gallatin's brief of 1818 mentioned only the valley of the Columbia, and John Quincy Adams's despatch of 1823 specified the northern extent of the claim as the fifty-first parallel. But Americans of the 'forties were in no mood to "yield one single inch to the demands and schemes of monarchy" [27] — even though the portion of Oregon in dispute seemed worthless. They claimed up to fifty-four degrees and forty minutes, or the southern limit of Russia's possessions. The legal claim was not presented in a bargaining spirit as heretofore. Though traditionally the United States had been willing to compromise at the forty-ninth parallel, the slogan of the campaign of 1844 was that alliterative challenge, "Fifty-four Forty or Fight."

A fight for fifty-four forty, however, would have had less legal justification than has even the average war. The one thing clear about America's claim to fifty-four forty is that it was, to say the least, questionable. The British pointed out such damaging considerations as the following: that Captain Gray was not commissioned by the United States, and that his voyage had been antedated by those of Captain Cook and other British navigators; that the explorations of Lewis and Clark did not touch on the headwaters of the principal branch of the Columbia River, and took place later than those of the British Mackenzie; that Astoria had not been occupied by Americans as the legal criterion required; that Louisiana extended only as far as the Rockies, and that the associated claim of contiguity had no legal status; and that the United States inherited no exclusive claim from Spain, since by the previous treaty of Nootka Sound Spain had bestowed upon Great Britain an interest in the territory.[28] To be sure, American jurists could point out equally serious flaws in Great Britain's title. But the two titles, though better than that of any third country, were sufficiently bad to make the question eminently one for compromise, as most jurists have since concluded.[29] Even in the 'forties many judicious Americans, including Albert Gallatin, the original advocate of America's claim, pointed out that each country might "recede from its extreme pretensions without impairing national honor." [30]

Despite their excitement over national honor, many of those asserting claim to the entire country could scarcely have been unaffected by the skepticism of the well-informed. It is even possible that the very vehemence of the former was an attempt to suppress a sense of uncertainty. But one who is bent upon something to which his legal right is dubious may adopt an even better way of maintaining his front and self-assurance. The American expansionist exemplified this when, probably with no deliberate design of deception or evasion, but with the same unconsciousness of directive bias which characterizes many a lawyer, he shifted emphasis from positive law to a higher law.

The heterodox tendency at first manifested itself only in a partial anti-legalism. One early expression of it was the proposition that international law required change in some respects in order to adapt it to American standards and in effect to American advantage. Thus in the *Southern Quarterly Review* of July, 1845, a writer on the Oregon question observed that "the international law of discovery is the offspring of an age anterior to that of our first appearance in the family of nations, and that in consequence, this law ought, so far as we are concerned and are to be governed by it, to receive some modification suited to the peculiar nature of our republican institutions." The suggestion was not as queer as it sounds, for it had reference to the apparent fact that the existent law of discovery "excludes republics from the acquisition of anything except by the most solemn act of legislation, while the mere license of a crowned head is to have a signification and authority sufficient to perfect a title to whole regions." The writer proceeded, however, to introduce in a discussion of the principle of contiguity a metaphysical consideration which was apparently held to be as important as the legal doctrine. This consideration was that Oregon formed " a natural part of our domain," and that " nature and nature's God seem to have decreed it as our heritage." [31] In the following month Governor Reynolds of Illinois discriminated the nature-given title more explicitly from the legal title:

> But independent of this right of prior discovery and prior occupation, nature has made it necessary, right, and proper that Oregon should form a part of the United States. Independent of any parchment or paper title, Oregon is bound to compose a part of this confederacy.[32]

A little later one finds in the *New York Morning News* a series of editorials affirming an American and unconventional criterion of title to be not merely independent of but better than the European and orthodox criterion. Thus, on October 13, 1845, an expansionist editorial affirmed that " public sentiment with us repudiates possession without use, and this sentiment is gradually acquiring the force of established public law." The principle which had the force of domestic law was employed by the editorial writer to justify the wanderings of the pioneers to the Rio del Norte and to the Pacific, " the limit which nature has provided." A few weeks later, in an editorial entitled " The Policy of America," the applicability of " European " juristic standards to American expansion was questioned in the light of the American doctrine of territorial utilization:

> Take, for instance, our virtual protest against claims to territory that are not vindicated by use. Is this just or unjust? What lessons or instructions, on such a topic, can we derive from European experience or precedent? None whatsoever. We must inquire and judge for ourselves, on grounds purely American, and which certainly are not elucidated in the elaborate works of the eminent men of past time. Our own belief is that the American idea or impulse, is fit and just, in harmony with the fair and bountiful offers of nature and with the manifest designs of the Creator . . . [33]

In November the *Morning News* applied this " American " idea to the Oregon dispute. Under the caption, " Oregon and War," the writer asserted:

> There is in fact no such thing as title to the wild lands of the new world, except that which actual possession gives. They belong to who-

ever will redeem them from the Indian and the desert, and subjugate them to the use of man. Title by discovery is nothing unless sustained by occupancy, for of what consequence is it, who first sailed along their front on the Pacific, landed in their harbors, or named their localities? None. And such shadowless title is all that Great Britain makes to Oregon.[34]

Was this writer justified in saying that " European " international law did not make the use of territory a condition of valid title? Though his stricture was correct as regards the great body of European practice, it was not well-founded with respect to much of juristic theory. Both Grotius and Pufendorf had in fact maintained that only discovery followed by occupation gave a valid title to territory.[35] Jurists of the eighteenth century, notably Vattel, had gone even farther in defining the extent of territory to which discovery opens a claim. Vattel stated as criterion precisely the principle of utilization which the *Morning News* considered an American innovation. He declared that " the Law of Nations will only recognize the *ownership* and *sovereignty* of a Nation over unoccupied lands when the Nation is in actual occupation of them, when it forms a settlement upon them, or makes actual use of them." [36] The cavilling *Morning News* was evidently uninformed not merely of this theory of international law, but also of an incident in the history of the Oregon dispute. In 1826 the British commissioners took virtually the position of Vattel; on the other hand, the American Gallatin argued that " the right derived from prior discovery and settlement, was not confined to the spot discovered or first settled " but extended in the case of the discovery and settlement of the mouth of a river to the whole country drained by such a river and its several branches.[37] This theory was not utilitarian at all, except in supporting the American legal position.

The *Morning News,* though far enough away from Gallatin's deference to international law, had still not gone beyond entering an exception to one of its principles. Both the editor of this paper and others, however, were soon to be emboldened by the course of events to the point of denying the very jurisdiction of international law. One encouraging development was the Texan acceptance of annexation. It was the apparent confirmation of the growing sense of a national destiny outweighing the legal rights of autocratic Mexico or of any monarchical interloper — the manifest destiny of extending freedom over the entire continent.

A second factor in the ideological development was the crisis in the Oregon issue which became public in December, 1845, with President Polk's account of his actions in this dispute. He had at first offered the traditional compromise to which the acts of his predecessors seemed to commit him. When Pakenham asked for a better compromise, Polk responded by withdrawing his compromise and reasserting America's claim to the entire territory. In his message of December 2, 1845, he recommended to Congress not only the establishment of a territorial government in Oregon but also the giving of notice that the convention of joint occupation would be terminated. Previously all the talk of fighting had little seriousness; it expressed America's fearlessness of the big, bad lion when no one expected any encounter with it. But this rhetorical bravado had forced Polk into a move which, if his declared intention were carried out, might well lead to war.

The prospect of war tends to bring ideas of national right into involvement with theological dogmas offering emotional encouragement. President Polk thus affirmed before his Cabinet the statesman's proper and customary faith in God's support, in which Sir Robert Peel was simultaneously professing equal faith before Parliament. To be sure, Secretary of State Buchanan responded to Polk by expressing doubt that God would assist Americans in a war for the territory north of forty-nine. But Buchanan did not need to be troubled by God's presumable awareness of the weakness of our legal position. For it was about this time that some lay theologian propounded the doctrine which made it clear that Providence was less interested in legal considerations than in the forwarding of this nation's beneficent destiny. Now at last it was unhesitatingly proclaimed that America's true title was the title by manifest destiny — a destiny to possess the entire Oregon country, and the rest of the continent as well for good measure.

It was Representative Robert Winthrop who on January 3, 1846, without identifying the author, first called the attention of Congress and thereby of the American people to this new theologico-legal doctrine. After subjecting other arguments of expansionists to logical criticism, he turned to this new one with irony:

> There is one element in our title, however, which I confess that I have not named, and to which I may not have done entire justice. I mean that new revelation of right which has been designated as *the right of our manifest destiny to spread over this whole continent.* It has been openly avowed in a leading Administration journal that this, after all, is our best and strongest title,—one so clear, so pre-eminent, and so indisputable, that if Great Britain had all our other titles in addition to her own, they would weigh nothing against it. The right of our manifest destiny! There is a right for a new chapter in the law of nations; or rather, in the special laws of our own country; for I suppose the right of a manifest destiny to spread will not be admitted to exist in any nation except the universal Yankee nation! [38]

Winthrop concluded with a request, like that of Francis I when the New World was assigned to two nations, to see the clause in Adam's will bequeathing this exclusive title by manifest destiny.

These vitriolic words did not shrivel the new and strange legal philosophy but caused a quite different reaction. Expansionist Congressmen, following abundant historical precedent relating to terms of opprobrium, thanked their opponents for having taught them the term and inscribed it upon their banner. Representative Baker was the first of the expansionists to "address himself to a point which had excited some sneers; namely, to the doctrine that it was our manifest destiny to come into the ultimate possession of this territory of Oregon." There was such a thing, he insisted, as the manifest destiny of a nation, a providential end foreshadowed by history. He confessed, moreover, that he was not much interested in musty records, voyages of sea captains, and Spanish treaties; for in our manifest destiny we had a higher and better title under the law of nature and of nations.[39] This title seemed in any event to be more interesting, for expansionists throughout the debate dwelt upon it with greater gusto than that given to wearisome technicalities.

It was significant of their spirit that, as one Congressman noted, poetry was all the rage in their speeches. In a poetic mood the idea of manifest destiny was first embraced; to that mood, despite the frequent badness of the poetic prose in which it resulted, the idea ever afterward appealed.

Other anti-expansionists followed Winthrop in ridiculing this "new" and "irresistible" title,[40] which "overrides all titles, and sets at defiance all reasoning."[41] But ridicule frequently owes much of its effectiveness to its distortion rather than its refutation of an opponent's ideas. Let us turn to the actual arguments of the expansionists in order to consider whether what seemed irrationality to some was not in essence a moral reasoning poetically expressed.

We may consider first the editorial which Winthrop probably had in mind in referring to the new title by manifest destiny. Professor Pratt's previously cited article on the origin of the phrase "manifest destiny" submits the plausible hypothesis that the editorial was probably one of the *New York Morning News* of December 27, 1845, under the caption, "The True Title." This hypothesis is supported not merely by Pratt's evidence but also by the fact that, as the foregoing has shown, the *Morning News* had for some time been publishing editorials of an anti-legal trend. According to Pratt, the editorial employing the phase "manifest destiny" was probably written by the editor, John L. O'Sullivan. Although the editorial was unsigned, O'Sullivan on January 5, 1846, published a signed letter in the *Morning News* in which he employed a phrase similar to "manifest destiny" in declaring that Oregon was committed to his country "by clear historical and legal title as well as by *the manifest intentions of Providence* [italics mine]." An article also attributed by Pratt to O'Sullivan had used "manifest destiny" before, this first use being in July, 1845, in his magazine, the *Democratic Review*; but the editorial of the *Morning News* first brought the phrase to national attention. The passage which apparently launched "manifest destiny" is as follows:

And yet after all, unanswerable as is the demonstration of our legal title to Oregon—and the whole of Oregon, if a rood!—we have a still better title than any that can ever be constructed out of all these antiquated materials of old black-letter international law. Away, away with all these cobweb tissues of rights of discovery, exploration, settlement, continuity, etc. To state the truth at once in its neglected simplicity, we are free to say that were the respective cases and arguments of the two parties, as to all these points of history and law, reversed—had England all ours, and we nothing but hers—our claim to Oregon would still be best and strongest. And that claim is by the right of our manifest destiny to overspread and to possess the whole of the continent which Providence has given us for the development of the great experiment of liberty and federated self-government entrusted to us.

O'Sullivan's emphatically expressed ideas resolve themselves into two propositions — one a metaphysical dogma and the other a moral judgment. The metaphysical dogma holds that America's manifest destiny under Providence to democratize the continent confers a title to Oregon which not merely reinforces America's legal title but would of itself outweigh the strongest legal title of a European disputant. But implicit in this assertion is a value-judgment which can be stated without metaphysical terms. It is the judgment that the moral ideal of democracy is more relevant to the justice of the issue than are technical criteria of international law. This judgment might be stated still more generally to the effect that a moral source of right outweighs a purely legal one.

What is curious about the foregoing is not the high valuation of morals but the low valuation of international law. The placing of international law in a virtual opposition to morals is incongruous with the origin of international law. For the first notable attempt to create " black-letter international law " was really, as any student of Grotius knows, an appeal from repellent contemporary practice to the moral principles discoverable in the *enlightened* practice of the ages. And international jurists following Grotius appealed still more directly to the moral criterion when they made the law of nature a criterion superior to all practice.

However, the fact that what started as an attempt to systematize men's common moral judgments ultimately appeared a tissue of cobwebs is understandable. In the first place, practice rather than the ideal law of nature had become the dominant criterion of international jurists. Still more important is the fact that the moral ideas appealing to one age no sooner solidify as international law than change in external circumstances or moral values initiates the gradual disintegration which ends in law seeming a disfiguration of the ideal. It is this fact which lends plausibility to Mr. Bumble's classic contempt of court, "The law is a ass" — an impertinence which, though debatable as a generalization, frequently arouses appreciation in some of the best minds. The appeal of this anti-legalism is exemplified by the words of the humanistic Emerson, who wrote in 1844:

> The law is only a memorandum. . . . The statute stands there to say, yesterday we agreed so and so, but how feel ye this article to-day? Our statute is a currency, which we stamp with our own portrait; it soon becomes unrecognizable, and in process of time will return to the mint.[42]

What made international law appear outworn currency to O'Sullivan was especially the fact that it had been formulated in a time when the destiny of a new western nation to extend democracy could not yet be manifest. To interpose international law against the fulfilment of this high destiny was as stupidly pedantic to O'Sullivan as would have seemed to the Crusaders the legal objections of some Grotius among the Saracens.

O'Sullivan only gave expression to an attitude already half-conscious among the general body of American expansionists. Congressional expansionists, although apparently not acquainted with his editorial itself, no sooner heard of its reference to a title by manifest destiny than they gave to the conception a general meaning similar to that of O'Sullivan. These expansionists also supposed God to be on the side of morals rather than law, and interpreted the title by manifest destiny in a moral sense. Thus Representative Stanton said that destiny does not make the possession of Oregon right but that "it is our destiny because it is right." [43] Moreover, congressional expansionists in numerous instances identified the moral title by manifest destiny with the title by democracy.

Thus Representative Chipman affirmed that this continent, "by manifest destiny, or by Adam's will, or by whatever else they will," was destined to "belong to a free people," this Yankee people the spread of whose institutions "could not be anywhere resisted."[44] Representative Sawyer said that our title to Oregon dated further back than even Adam's will; we "received our rights from high Heaven — from destiny," which willed that on the American continent "the principles of pure republicanism and democracy shall finally prevail."[45] According to Representative Levin, America's "inherent and preexistent right" to exclude European colonization could be based on "the genius of American institutions — on the spirit of republicanism, that permits not the contaminating proximity of monarchies upon the soil that we have consecrated to the rights of man." Moreover, Oregon was assigned to America's manifest destiny by a claim which "subtle diplomacy and international law in vain assail" — the right of the Americans in Oregon to free government and the liberty to choose their own laws without monarchical interference.[46] Representative Cathcart saw the title by manifest destiny in the possibility of peopling the entire continent with one republican family and moulding them all to a common devotion to the altar of civil and religious liberty.[47] From the foregoing it appears that, in any possible dispute on this continent between the United States and a monarchical country — the case of dispute with another democracy is not considered — the title to territory goes to the United States on the score of its democracy. Such a criterion has at least the advantage of simplicity.

The question is complicated, however, by the fact that the expansionists did not stop with the simple democratic criterion. Further examination discloses as another criterion of title the principle of the natural boundary or of geographical predestination. For example, the same Levin who in one place identified the criterion of title with the destiny of democracy affirmed elsewhere that "the natural foundation of all legitimate claims to national territory" was the "principle of contiguity."[48] Similarly Representative Stanton, asserting that he would assume "higher ground" than the legal, referred to this principle of contiguity in denying that a nation on another continent could rightfully extend its possessions to this.[49] Representative Baker identified his faith in manifest destiny with belief in the title established by the doctrine of the natural boundary; according to this, contiguity gives Oregon to the United States whereas a rolling ocean separates it from Great Britain.[50] We may deviate from the congressional debate to note the poetic expression of this doctrine of contiguity in a contemporary number of the *Democratic Review*:

> Why clamor in the question, 'whose the right
> By conquest or discovery?—what eye,
> Briton or Apalachian, had first sight
> Of the great wastes that now disputed lie?'
> The right depends on the propinquity,
> The absolute sympathy of soil and place . . .[51]

Disregarding for the present the question of the accuracy of their application, we now note that, in addition to these two conceptions of the true title, there was a third. It was derived from the natural right to provide for vital national needs such as room for future population and future security. Representative Baker, perhaps unconscious of his multiplication of titles, expounded this consideration most fully:

> Mr. Baker insisted that we had a right to look to the future, and make it a rule for the present; and it was our right and our duty to provide for future generations as well as for ourselves. . . . For his own part, Mr. Baker had not much [sic] on the question of title to musty records and the voyages of old sea captains, or to Spanish treaties, because we had a higher and a better title under the law of nature and of nations; because no other nation might be allowed to interfere with Oregon consistently with our safety. . . . We had a continent before us in which to spread our free principles, our language, our literature, and power; and we had a present right to provide for this future progress. To do so was to secure our safety, in the widest and highest sense; and this our destiny had now become so manifest that it could not fail but by our own folly.[52]

Whereas the foregoing emphasized the natural right to security, in another place Baker touched on the right to provide for future population. Destiny itself, according to him, was identical with the "duty of every statesman to look, not only at what a country is, but to look forward to see what, by the blessing of God, it may become." He affirmed that "England was not to be allowed to . . . hold Oregon because we, the people of the United States, had spread, were spreading and intended to spread, and should spread, and go on to spread." [53] The laughter which followed this repetitious rhetoric did not necessarily indicate that the argument itself was not taken seriously. Thus Representative Kennedy, confessing that the little-read men of the West left to others the establishment of our legal title, addressed himself to the more interesting task of demonstrating our manifest destiny by reference to "the American multiplication table," our remarkable increase in population.[54]

Such was the intellectual fecundity of the expansionist lawyers that the analyst can distinguish also a fourth conception of the title by manifest destiny. Espoused by one of the most legally learned of American statesmen, John Quincy Adams, it was called by an ironical editorial writer of the *Baltimore American* "Title from Scripture." [55] Referring to a biblical passage, Adams declared: "That, sir, in my judgment, is the foundation not only of our title to the territory of Oregon, but the foundation of all human title to all human possessions." [56] As may be imagined, the passage was that in Genesis enjoining man to multiply and to subdue the earth. Just as Adams had advocated dispossessing the Indian huntsman, now he affirmed that America's intention to subdue the earth gave it a right superior to that of Great Britain, which, according to Adams, intended to use the territory only as a hunting-ground in the fur trade.[57] Similarly, Representative Hunter affirmed that if the American people sought Oregon for agricultural settlements, then, "by a most 'manifest destiny' it must be ours." [58] Representative Levin, especially prolific in conceptions of the true title, joined Adams and Hunter on this ground. Excoriating the "wily and defrauding" European diplomats who argued by reference to treaty and discovery, he challenged them to "point to any principle of human nature, any law of God that confers on them a monopoly of God's earth for the aggrandizement of a monarch, while millions of natives of the soil claim it, hold it, cultivate it, as necessary to satisfy their hunger and afford them room for habitation." [59]

The title by democracy had thus procreated three additional titles. Is one to take it that O'Sullivan would have disowned the other three as illegitimate? In the light of the cited part of the editorial on manifest destiny it might seem so. But one should return to this editorial to read farther. The paragraph immediately following that expounding America's title by destiny described this right by reference to a concept logically distinct from democracy:

> It is a right such as that of the tree to the space of air and earth suitable for the full expansion of its principle and destiny of growth—such as that of the stream to the channel required for the still accumulating volume of its flow. It is in our future far more than in our past, or in the past history of Spanish exploration or French colonial rights, that our True Title is to be found. Consider only the wonderful law of growth which has been thus far exhibited in the increase of our population from the commencement of our present system of government—namely, that of *doubling every quarter of a century*. . . . Our present population being 20,000,000, what will it become under the continued operation of this law . . . ?
>
> *Three hundred millions*, within little more than the ordinary term of hale and healthy old age. The duty and the right of providing the necessary accommodation for all this stupendous future of the American destiny . . . in these views . . . resides the title we prefer to dwell upon . . .

This second title, then, is the familiar one resting upon a natural right to the vital necessity. But in a third paragraph O'Sullivan was led by his anticipation of America's huge future population to remark that, whereas in Great Britain's possession Oregon "must always remain worthless for any purpose of human civilization and society," in America's ownership Oregon must fast fill with a population capable of developing a great civilization. This adds the title by beneficent territorial utilization, identical with that emphasized by John Quincy Adams. Finally O'Sullivan added a fourth consideration: "The God of nature and of nations has marked it for our own . . ." [60] We thus come to the title by geographical predestination, that is, by contiguity. The sum of the matter is that O'Sullivan's brief had used the same four criteria which appeared later in the congressional debate.

Now these four conceptions of the title by manifest destiny are none other than the four principles which had dominated the previous development of American expansionist ideology. Whereas previously they had involved generally only an unconscious anti-legalism, in the Oregon issue they stepped forth defiantly as principles of conscious anti-legalism. The doctrine of the true title is thus not a primary element of moral thought but a precipitate from the reaction of a plurality of old moral principles upon the traditional principles of international law.

The fact that the doctrine of the true title resolves itself into four different criteria raises a curious question. Which of the four true titles is, so to speak, the truest title? The expansionist gave no answer. Possibly he did not even know that his brief case contained four titles instead of merely one. Possibly it seemed to him that a title strong by any one of the four claims becomes fourfold strong when all the claims converge. And if they all do converge this belief is correct. But what must be said of his many-sided criterion in view of the possibility that the four different claims of title might not and probably would not converge?

By overbuilding his case the expansionist erected a tower of Babel which collapsed through its excessive height. For, whereas one of the four criteria of the true title might award the disputed territory to one party, a different criterion might give it to the other. The absence of any assumption as to the relative importance of the various criteria makes it logically impossible to adjudicate a case in which their implications conflict.

Furthermore, a conflict of criteria might actually have been present in the Oregon issue the American expansionist to the contrary notwithstanding. By the criterion of democracy America undoubtedly deserved to receive the territory. But the criterion of contiguity was indecisive, Oregon being contiguous to British North America as well as to the United States. Moreover, as the *Baltimore American* pointed out, it was an entirely gratuitous conception that Great Britain never intended to utilize Oregon agriculturally. Finally, it would seem that by the criterion of need for future population Great Britain had a better title than the United States. In the words of the *Baltimore American,* "her surplus population is immense, while we have none, and her necessities demand large territories and wide scope, which our broad republic, for an hundred years, will have no need of."[61] The application of the four criteria of title thus results in a draw between America's title by democracy and Great Britain's by the right to provide for surplus population.

Conflict of criteria and resultant uncertainty are, unfortunately, characteristic of moral judgment. It is true, indeed, that legal judgment is also at a disadvantage in being compelled at times to select from a mass of "undifferentiated, confused, and inconsistent" precedents.[62] But to substitute the moral criterion for the legal is apparently to make confusion many times confounded.

The embarrassment created by this anti-legal doctrine has not yet been considered in full. Just as America's two principal legal claims seemed to the British reciprocally nullifying, so its entire legal case was prejudiced by the simultaneous presentation of an anti-legal argument. Secretary of State Buchanan not only adhered to legal considerations but even pointed out in one place that the traditional legal principles regarding territorial acquisition were necessary to preserve the peace of the world.[63] The anti-expansionist *Baltimore American,* however, applied O'Sullivan's anti-legalism in reverse: "Are the suggestions of cupidity or ambition less corrupt because a man finds them justified in a book and reads in the margin that the immaculate Justinian, or some truckling lawyer of his, hunted it up, or invented it?"[64] The doctrine of O'Sullivan thus cut in two ways in that it discredited America's legal case as well as that of the British.

Yet, of the two titles, the expansionists chose at the end not O'Sullivan's "true title" but the legal. This is to say that they consoled themselves by legal considerations for the conclusion of this issue, Polk's compromise yielding to Great Britain much of what had been so defiantly claimed. This compromise was accepted generally, and even by the once so antinomian O'Sullivan, with surprising legal reasonableness. O'Sullivan's newspaper observed without complaint that the sentiment of the country for the full claim had been shaken by Senator Benton's speech exposing the legal weaknesses of the American position.[65] Did this change in attitude represent a spontaneous alteration of philosophy? It is very improbable that it did. The reason for the favorable view of Polk's compromise was evidently that there had arisen the danger of war with Mexico and thus the necessity of bringing the dispute with England to a settlement. The title by manifest destiny ceased to seem so manifest when insistence upon it became too dangerous.

But the doctrine of the higher title reemerged periodically in subsequent American history. So, too, did the most dogmatic emphasis upon the antithetic concept — the legalism which Charles Cheney Hyde identifies with America's official position.[66] The alternation of the two, surveyed briefly in the following pages, presents a curious historical commentary on the very conception of "the true title."

One notes first that, though Polk's justification of war against Mexico stressed her violation of "solemn treaties," [67] the expansionism of this war was marked by observations like that of Walt Whitman, who claimed Mexican lands by "a law superior to parchments and dry diplomatic rules" [68] — the law of beneficent territorial utilization. Similarly, in the 'fifties there were those who, while blaming Mexico for her failure to maintain legal order, agreed with a writer in the *United States Review* that the United States deserved Mexico's territory by a title superior to the legal title resting on conquest — "the well-founded and legitimate rights of industry and intelligence." [69] Moreover, the very Americans who defended slavery by reference to its legality argued that Spain's possession of the American colony desirable to the South was "a possession by mere strictness of title, and without any reason or equitable consideration," [70] and wished to act upon the notion that "Cuba naturally belongs to us." [71] And while the United States demanded from Spain strict accordance with maritime law, some, like Representative Anderson, affirmed that "no technical impediment " such as the neutrality law should " be thrown in the way of our Americanizing Central America " — our " manifest destiny." [72]

In the 'fifties the question chiefly giving rise to conflicting criteria of the ultimate source of right was the domestic issue of slavery. Just as the Austrian Government has recently subordinated its constitution to a higher " law of nature," [73] so Seward laid down the classic thesis that " there is a higher law than the Constitution," a law which, written on the hearts and consciences of freemen, repudiates compacts condemning territory to slavery.[74] Indeed, some of the New England anti-expansionists who had condemned the title by manifest destiny took the same anti-legal position when it accorded with their moral revulsion from slavery. On the other hand, some of the expansionists who had used O'Sullivan's doctrine were horrified when the same principle was used in behalf of abolition. For the doctrine propounded originally in behalf of America's growth had come to menace its very existence.

Three decades after the Civil War another war was justified by an appeal to the higher law. The Cuban intervention was defended in a Senate committee report by the implication that a humanitarian consideration is superior to a technical.[75] Henry Watterson was more explicitly anti-legal in his justification of the war:

> We are not going to the musty records of title archives to find our warrant for this war. We find it in the law supreme—the law high above the law of titles in lands . . . the law of man, the law of God. We find it in our own inspiration, our own destiny.[76]

But the Spanish-American War gave rise to a succession of inconsistencies on the issue of the true law. After the United States had come to deal with the Philippine insurrection, the Filipino's imitation of America's traditional assertion of a natural right to independence was condemned on the ground that " those people must remain respecting the law." [77] At the same time, there was adopted a quite different view with regard to the constitutional difficulties either in acquiring the islands or in governing them in the manner desired. " The general feeling seems to be," wrote Ernst Freund contemporaneously, " that legal difficulties should not be allowed to stand in the way of the consummation of a policy which for other reasons may seem wise or necessary." [78] The jurist Freund himself conceded that "policy . . . must in the long run be superior to law." [79] Senator Beveridge, speaking of the Anglo-Saxon impulse for imposing positive law on backward peoples, proclaimed inconsistently that "the inherent tendencies of a race are its highest law." [80]

Early issues of the twentieth century brought to view the same capacity for quick shift of attitude. When the Clayton-Bulwer Treaty was presented as an obstacle to America's acquisition of exclusive control over an Isthmian canal, it appeared to Representative Hepburn's House committee that "irrepealable statutes are not tolerated," [81] and to Representative Ryan that "international law is at its best but a flimsy guidance." [82] But when the United States engaged in a dispute with Canada over Alaska's boundary, it seemed to Americans that our legal rights should triumph over Canada's need for a commercial outlet. The alleged manifest destiny of the party with greater need did not seem a valid title when America's legal claim was less questionable than in the Oregon issue.

Similarly, President Roosevelt felt that Colombia deserved severe blame when she delayed in ratifying the Hay-Herran Treaty permitting the United States to construct the Panama Canal. Later, however, he and other Americans viewed the canal issue less formally. The change came when Roosevelt found it advantageous to intervene on the Isthmus in a manner which scarcely bore legal justification. The proposition that "we are certainly justified in morals, and therefore justified in law" [82a] was to be expected from a native antinomian like Roosevelt, who had written of Oregon that "we were the people who could use it best, and we ought to have taken it all." [83] On the other hand, it might have seemed somewhat surprising that the jurist Elihu Root waved aside discussion of technical rules and precedents in order to emphasize that "the thing we have done was just and fair." [84] It might have seemed amazing to conventional minds that Attorney-General Knox cut short President Roosevelt's legal rationalizations with the delightful unconventionality: "Oh, Mr. President, do not let so great an achievement suffer from any taint of legality." [85] But just when a European analyst of American imperialism had decided that one of its dominant characteristics was a "*mépris des formes*" [86] which permitted Americans to escape from any treaty binding them unsatisfactorily, the world heard Roosevelt's exhortations to Latin America in behalf of adherence to legal obligations and constitutional government.

In the same message in which President Roosevelt implicitly indicted the Dominican Republic for failing to pay its debts, he formulated a doctrine of America's international police power which goes far beyond the rights of intervention granted by international law. A consideration underlying this doctrine was doubtless the plausible thesis asserted in the same year by an American philosopher — that a utilitarian rule will, under modern conditions, "require those nations upon whom rests the responsibility of superior power to exercise compulsion and constraint upon independent states for a greater diversity of reasons than has hitherto been generally recognized by international law." [87] From the same point of view it seemed to the *New Republic*, convinced of the beneficence of America's intervention in 1916, that Mexican sovereignty was "not a sacred legal abstraction" but "a living political instrument which must be justified by its fruits." [88] While in the twentieth century the doctrine of the higher law has influenced Americans chiefly in interventionism, it has also figured in occasional reversions to territorial expansionism. G. W. Crichfield advocated annexing parts of South as well as North America on the ground implied in the following rhetorical question: "Shall the immense uncultivated tracts of land remain forever waste . . . because of some technical interpretations of international law . . . ?" [89] But he condemned Latin America on the ground that "the plainest and most elementary precepts of international law are overruled by the decretas of half-breed Dictators." [90]

One impression which emerges from the foregoing is that, as Professor Herbert Kraus has pointed out in his lectures on international morality, peoples are apt to judge other nations by criteria different from those which they apply to themselves.[91] The illegality of others was blamed by Americans notwithstanding the fact that it may have seemed justifiable by the same principle of the higher title employed often by themselves. The other party is judged differently not merely because his moral case is not understood but also because only one's own nation is supposed to have a manifest destiny. The effect of this idea of a special mission upon American attitude toward law is exemplified by Senator Clarke's assertion during the Panama crisis that the doctrines of international law "must be applied and understood rationally, leaving room for legitimate exercise of the aggressive spirit of progress, which is the mission of the American people." [92]

It must be confessed, however, that in recent years the spirit of progress has not seemed to Americans to require "legitimate exercise" of the doctrine of the higher law even by the United States. On the contrary, there are indications that this doctrine has passed into a sharp decline which threatens to bring it into opprobrium. Thus recent American statesmen have been very careful to subsume all American interventions in the Caribbean under legal rubrics, even when the interventions were of a character which seemed to some jurists to place them in the sphere of political expediency rather than law. The directors of American foreign policy have also striven to give American interventions a legal sanction, in some instances through treaties obtained by force. One American Secretary of State implicitly defended the forcibly obtained rights in Haiti by asking defenders of the Versailles Treaty whether imposition voided a treaty.[93] Americans have gone so far in legalism that they permit even the Monroe Doctrine, that preeminent instance of splendidly unconventional statesmanship, to suffer from the taint of legality by being presented as an ordinary application of the legal right of self-preservation. To be sure, such determinations of legality may have been unconsciously influenced by value-judgments as individual as those which Professor Frederick Sherwood Dunn points out as largely determinative of legal criteria in the protection of nationals. Consciously, however, Americans today reject the doctrine of the true title with an intolerance which bespeaks little gratitude for its past services to America.

This recent development of legalism probably rests upon more than a recognition of the social value of legalism. In the first place, anti-imperialists have probably impressed upon the American statesman that they will attack a purely moral defense both for illegality and for hypocrisy, whereas they can attack a careful legal argument only for its alleged disregard of morality. Also, statesmen have become more sophisticated in realizing that the flexible legal doctrine of self-defense can be invoked to justify almost everything that formerly seemed to require the justification of the higher law. Important above all is the fact that America's interests lie now not in further expansion but in the maintenance of a political *status quo* and of the commitments supporting a stable international order.

But the memory of history should warn against too great confidence in the permanence of America's present legalism. It is true, as Dr. Powers wrote in 1900, that "our whole experience has accustomed us to honor dynamic rather than static rights," and that we are constantly reminded of the validity of dynamic rights by the fact that possibly they constitute "our only title to all we possess."[94] How easily America's ordinary legalism may crack under unusual pressure is clearly shown by the moral assurance with which American legislators recently cancelled the legal obligation to pay aliens in gold.

The history surveyed cannot be said to have made clear what the true title is. It must be confessed, however, that there was no great reason to expect such illumination. For one of the most difficult questions of morals arises out of the inevitability of conflict between two basal principles of man's moral experience: positive law, needed to effect the systematic application of men's moral judgments, and these moral judgments themselves, too complex and relative to permit of entirely or permanently satisfactory standardization. The Jeffersonian's prescription of frequent change of law in the light of new standards or conditions would lessen the points of conflict but it could not entirely eliminate them; *summum jus summa injuria* will be an eternally valid formula. With reference to the solution of the conflicts there are two theories. One is that, since positive law was designed in behalf of morals, conflicts between the two are proper occasions for obeying moral intuitions rather than law. Another is that deviations from legality must be avoided because, once the demand for universality in lawful conduct is conspicuously diminished, there is the danger of relapse into the chaotic condition when every man did what was right in his own eyes and wrong in the eyes of those injured. Which of these theories is correct perhaps only Heaven knows. Therefore in private experience the ordinary moral individual compromises between them by restricting his deviations from legality to instances where they seem obviously justified by overwhelming social need.

On the other hand, the nationalist seems to take a dogmatic position in favor either of informal morals or of legality, as either serves his nation's case. In the history surveyed, he always favored the title which was true in the pragmatic sense of leading to the desired land. What requires explanation is not the nationalist's inconsistency but the fact that it tends consistently to his nation's interest.

An all too easy error is that of explaining the change of attitudes quite cynically. The most scornful explanation is the theory of some of the Greek Sophists that the law is defended or attacked with a view only to self-interest. Such an explanation is, however, sophistical. It overlooks the fact that, though Anatole France's epigram "*On croit ce qu'on désire*" may be true, desire ordinarily determines belief unconsciously. Thus the vacillations on the issue of legality may represent sincere judgments that this or that policy is under the circumstances in accord with both self-interest and social good, which will generally seem to coincide as long as each patriot is best acquainted with his own nation's case.

The nationalist's judgments with respect to law are perhaps determined fundamentally by an ideology which remains constant though all else be in permutation. It is that fundamental article of nationalist faith — the manifest equity in the lofty mission of one's own nation. Be it positive law or morals, hook or crook, the true title fulfils the supreme law of this manifest destiny.

# CHAPTER VI

## THE MISSION OF REGENERATION

The pacific expansionist who rejoiced in the bloodless annexation of Texas was shortly mocked by the resultant war with the aggrieved recent owner of that disputed country. The War with Mexico was in turn the cause of a new territorial ambition which, though it resulted merely in the acquisition of New Mexico and Upper California, was directed for a time toward the annexation of all Mexico and fell short of it only through a slight turn of events. This ambition marked a momentous change both in the policy and in the ideal of American expansionism.

The previous policy of expansion was well described by Secretary of State Calhoun as one of " increase by growing and spreading out into unoccupied regions, assimilating all we incorporate." [1] It was, in other words, the policy of annexing territories which, like Texas and Oregon, had been settled by the American pioneers in the course of their overflow into regions unoccupied or sparsely settled. Louisiana and Florida, which at first seem exceptions to this policy, in reality go to prove the rule. The alien population of these territories was too small to present a serious problem of assimilation. But traditional policy excluded the annexation of Mexico because in greater part it was inhabited densely by a people two-thirds of whom were Indian or negroid.

The annexationism of the Mexican War represented a conscious change to a toleration of amalgamation with other breeds. And the fact that not many Mexicans became American by the treaty of 1848 did not prevent the expansion movement from having important ulterior consequences. It set up a trend which pervaded most of subsequent American expansionism and resulted in the 'nineties in tropical annexations which were as distant from original American policy as from American shores.

The change effected in expansionist ideology by the Mexican War was no less sharp than the turn in policy. For the slogan "extension of the area of freedom," used in the Texas and Oregon issues, had meant the extension of republican institutions not to non-American peoples but rather to the American pioneers colonizing adjacent territory. Yet this slogan, as well as "manifest destiny," did presently take on the altruistic connotation which figured through most of the later history of American expansion. Expansionist ideology changed during the strange tutelage of a war from an almost Nietzschean self-realizationism to a quasi-altruism. The moral inspiration of the expansionists during the war was derived from the conception of a religious duty to regenerate the unfortunate people of the enemy country by bringing them into the life-giving shrine of American democracy.

Justin Smith's classic study of the Mexican War touches upon this imponderable in referring to the expansionist's argument that "Providence called upon us to regenerate her [Mexico's] decadent population." [2] Professor Fuller's study of the movement to acquire all Mexico adverts to the same ideal in stating that expansionist sentiment reached the fervor of a "religious revival." [3] But the ideal of regenerative annexation, though frequently noted as a major factor in this expansion movement, has not been analyzed to an extent commensurate with its importance in American history and in international relations in general.

A belief in the possibility and the duty of changing another people's chosen way of life is by no means obviously reasonable or self-explanatory. Indeed, to Albert Gallatin and other contemporary anti-expansionists this belief seemed contrary both to the psychological and to the moral premises of democracy.[4] Moreover, the sudden emergence of extraordinarily altruistic pretensions in national life raises a problem which transcends the sphere of conscious reasoning. It raises in this case the question of the latent factors which so regenerated the American expansionist as to induce his acceptance of a hitherto neglected duty.

It may be asked at the outset whether previous American

history had evidenced so great a benevolence toward " lesser breeds " as to justify attributing the expansionist's aspiration to inherent national sentimentality. Although generalizations about a predominant national type are difficult, the body of evidence before us is strongly suggestive of an answer. One may note first the policy and attitude of the American toward the stranger races in his own house, the negro and the Indian. Did any ardent altruism impel him to the civilization of these wards? Despite the Jeffersons and Jedediah Morses, the only answer approaching generality is negative. The institution of negro slavery rested not merely upon a pessimistic racial theory but also upon an indifference to civilizing the colored race. The governmental policy of civilizing the Indian was carried out, as even the frontier president Andrew Jackson admitted,[5] by driving him ever farther into the wilderness. The Indian Removal Bill of 1830, passed just when the Cherokees were most promising, forswore the entire ideal of bringing the Indian within the fold of civilization.

The fact that negroes and Indians were widely considered to be doomed by nature may prevent the attitude toward them from being the fairest test of the depth of American altruism. Let us look, therefore, at the attitude of Americans toward Spanish-American countries partly white in population. Opposition to the incorporation of Louisiana was based in part upon a revulsion from amalgamation with its inhabitants, whom Fisher Ames described as " savages and adventurers." [6] To be sure, annexation would have uplifted them. But Representative Griswold declared that the government of the United States " was not formed for the purpose of distributing its principles and advantages to foreign nations " but " with the sole view of securing these blessings to ourselves and our posterity." [7] Even the philanthropic Paine said in response to a Louisiana petition for political privileges that the memorial involved a fallacious idea of our moral obligations; though we fought for our own rights, it was not " incumbent upon us to fight the battles of the world for the world's profit." [8] While Jefferson's second inaugural address spoke of civilizing Louisiana Indians, expansionists in general seem to have given little or no weight to the possible benefit of this annexation for the native inhabitants. The same consideration applies to the purchase of Florida, discussed in President Monroe's inaugural address of 1821 without mention of any but its national benefit. Because expansionists were motivated primarily by national self-interest they preferred to acquire lands which were encumbered with few inhabitants.

The egocentrism and exclusiveness of the American expansionist were clearest in the movement of the 'forties to acquire Texas and Oregon. Despite the urgency of land-hunger, the prospect of amalgamation with assumedly inferior peoples spoiled the appetite and caused the ambition of continental dominion to be postponed to a distant future. Thus John Galt pointed out that Americans limited themselves to the policy of annexing vacant lands.[9] O. C. Hartley renounced further ambition until "the whole continent shall have been peopled with men as enlightened in politics, as liberal in spirit, and as capable of enjoying civil liberty, as are the choice of our own citizens."[10] Continental lands occupied by inferior peoples would first have to be fumigated by American pioneers, who would ultimately Americanize the continent. Americanization was admitted by Representative Duncan to be more beneficent for the land than for its inhabitants:

> There seems to be something in our laws and institutions, peculiarly adapted to our Anglo-Saxon-American race, under which they will thrive and prosper, but under which all others wilt and die. Where our laws and free institutions have been extended among the French and Spanish who have been on our continent, they have and are gradually disappearing; not that they move away, but they neither prosper nor multiply, but, on the contrary, dwindle. There is something mysterious about it; and, if accounted for, it can only be done on the principle that though they may be fitted for refined civilization, they are not fitted for liberal and equal laws, and equal institutions.[11]

Spanish-American disappearance might also have been accounted for by the less flattering assumption that Americans themselves, as Frederick Starr asserted in 1914,[12] never mastered the gentle art of assimilation. But the expansionists were not greatly interested in that art since extension of the area of freedom meant primarily the extension of the area in which Americans themselves might freely develop, whether or not the native inhabitants withered.

The original question whether a very philanthropic disposition toward " lesser breeds " was native in the American character can thus be answered with some degree of confidence. Such philanthropy was so little present that a preference for lands without inhabitants was perhaps the fundamental reason for the earlier American policy of limiting expansion to sparsely settled territories. One need not assume, as did Charles Francis Adams in 1898, that the American lacked feeling for the " inferior " races.[13] He merely did not feel tenderly enough to desire political association with them or even to endure it for the sake of teaching the way to political salvation. This attitude was understandable even if morally debatable. One determinant was the judgment that democratic institutions functioned best among a racially homogeneous and generally intelligent population. Another reason was the Nietzschean judgment that it is more important to develop the "most splendid race" than to lift up the inferior. Still another influence was the aristocratic exclusiveness which repels untouchables with a *noli me tangere.* The exclusiveness was not merely that of the aesthete but involved the impatience of the hardy pioneer with the incompetent.

The fact that Mexicans were neighbors did not secure for them a greater sympathy than that felt for other Latin-American peoples. To be sure, there had been a flush of enthusiasm over the Mexican revolution and the attendant prospect that, as Iturbide said, the two republics were " destined to be united in the bonds of the most intimate and cordial fraternity." [14] But when incompetence soon overtook Mexican affairs, Americans felt less fraternal toward Mexico; by contemporary admission, their feeling changed to " comparative indifference." [15] When Santa Anna resorted to cruelty in combating the revolt of the Texans, Americans tended to believe that Mexicans generally were sadistic. Mexico's subsequent failure to pay American financial claims added to the other unfavorable judgments a cordial dislike on the score of injury sustained;

and Mexico's resentment of the annexation of Texas aroused the deepest of all dislike — that of the party whom one has injured. "The United States have borne more insult, abuse, insolence and injury from Mexico," declared the *New Orleans Commercial Bulletin* in 1846, "than one nation ever before endured from another."[16] This typical view overlooked the sense of injury that had been developed in Mexicans by American policies and attitudes which were frequently far from considerate. But Mexicans were equally intolerant in regarding the Yankee as an impossible braggart, and the Southern slaveholders as "the degenerate portion of the English race."[17] These attitudes were regarded by Americans as among the least pardonable faults of their neighbors.

There was no original desire to annex Mexico in order to reform her faults. But there did exist, as the *Democratic Review* affirmed in 1845, "a pretty general conviction" that Mexico "is destined to become an integral portion of these United States at some future period."[18] So far as concerned the present, amalgamation seemed impossible for two reasons. One was the opinion, stated by the *Democratic Review*, that "the Mexican people are unaccustomed to the duties of self-government,"[19] and required for their government a change in our democratic forms which would be "earning the glories . . . of enlarged dominion at too great expense."[20] Another was the disdain for the character of a population which, according to the *Illinois State Register*, was "but little removed above the negro."[21] A supercilious theory of racial inequality had been current in the land of political equalitarianism for years before Count de Gobineau elaborated the thesis. Americans had also anticipated Darwin in a theory of the survival of the fittest. Annexation of Mexico could await the completion of the laws of natural selection whereby, as the *Missouri Reporter* stated, the country would eventually be "absorbed by the Anglo-Saxons, now overspreading the continent."[22]

To the statement that there was no present desire for Mexican territory one must make, however, an exception in the case of California. California was an exception not merely because it was politically and commercially valuable but also because it was sparsely settled by Mexicans, whereas the Anglo-Saxon foot, as the *Democratic Review* noted,[23] was already on its border. The ideology justifying the ambition for California was a development of the ideal of beneficent territorial utilization which had figured in the Indian issue. This ideal, by way of contrast with that of regenerating a people, may be called the ideal of regenerating the land. It is exemplified by the declaration of the *Hartford Times* in 1845 that should war be forced upon the United States heaven itself would call Americans "to redeem from unhallowed hands a *land,* above all others favored of heaven, and hold it for the use of a people who know how to obey heaven's behests." [24] Heaven's behests are, evidently, at times very practical.

The *Times,* however, prophesied correctly when it affirmed that Americans would not undertake an offensive war against Mexico. It is not true that, as an earlier school of American historians maintained, President Polk sought "to obtain by force what the 'manifest destiny' of the United States imperatively required." [25] President Polk desired to obtain California, but by peaceful means. Polk's secret instructions to his envoy Slidell show that despite the bid for Upper California he would have been willing to leave Mexico alone had she only acceded to settlement of the boundary and claims questions. Instead Mexico refused to receive his envoy and thus left no prospect of settling injuries which frequently have seemed legally valid grounds for war. That the desire for California predisposed Polk to the *ultima ratio* of nations is doubtless true. But there is no evidence that this desire would have led him to force if the unsettled injuries and Mexico's belligerent attitude since the annexation of Texas had not made war seem both legally valid and politically necessary. Somewhat the same considerations apply to Americans in general. It is true that as early as the fall of 1845 the evidences of American belligerence were so numerous that the *New York Herald* observed, "The multitude cry aloud for war." [26] But those who demanded war were motivated not merely by expansionism but also by the belief that "a full and thorough chastisement of Mexican arrogance and folly" [27] was the only course left open by Mexico's own attitudes and actions. The fundamental cause of the war was, then, the tension which was created by the annexation of Texas and made critical by the subsequent follies of both countries.

However, the fact that Mexicans shed the first blood caused almost all Americans save the politically prejudiced Whigs to accept President Polk's statement that "war exists . . . by the act of Mexico herself."[28] Consequently American dislike of Mexico was deepened by the outbreak of the war into passionate hostility. Even the formal report of the House Committee on Foreign Affairs spoke of the United States as having been "forced into conflict with a semi-barbarous people."[29] Representative Chipman called Mexico "worse than barbarian" in her disregard of the rights of other nations and her particular animus against peoples with free institutions.[30] In exaggerated degree the contemptuous anger of the time is portrayed in the words which James Russell Lowell put into the mouth of the Yankee soldier:

> Afore I come away from hum I hed a strong persuasion
> Thet Mexicans worn't human beans,—an ourang outang nation,
> A sort o' folks a chap could kill an' never dream on't arter . . .[31]

That others besides the illiterate were vindictive is shown by the words of Walt Whitman: "Yes, Mexico must be thoroughly chastised." He added that America knew how to crush as well as to expand.[32]

Thus, the immediate background of the sentimental ideal of regeneration was marked by as hearty a hostility as the quarrel-ridden arena of international relations has ever seen. It is, of course, an error to expect of national attitudes, which are so largely the product of hasty emotion, the same degree of consistency that might reasonably be looked for in individual attitudes. On the other hand, it seems clear that a complete change in the normal current of national feeling required the intervention of some experience of powerful force.

Americans were in the fiery crucible of war — the very experience capable of causing the most profound and sudden changes in national sentiment. It is in the course of the war, the source of new stimuli and consequently of new dispositions, that we must search for the meaning of the strange metamorphosis of American expansionism.

For some time, indeed, there was no obvious indication that the war was to overcome the inhibition of the past in regard to amalgamation with Latin-American peoples. To be sure, the outbreak of hostilities immediately crystallized the desire for Upper California, and the early conquest of this province was followed by a resolution never to haul down the flag. But the decision to retain California was an expression of conformity to previous expansionist policy rather than of deviation from it. California seemed preeminently satisfactory as a territorial addition for the same reason which made it acceptable before the war — the smallness of its Mexican population. The *Nashville Union*, calling in October of 1846 for California alone as territorial indemnity, affirmed that at present the condition of the Mexican people was not such as to fit them for annexation to a democracy.[33] Lewis Cass, after declaring in a Senate speech of February 10, 1847, that we did not want any " deplorable amalgamation " with the people of Mexico as either subjects or citizens, told what we did want: " All we want is a portion of territory, which they nominally hold, generally uninhabited, or, where inhabited at all, sparsely so, and with a population which would soon recede, or identify itself with ours." [34] In desiring this sparsely inhabited territory expansionists were inspired by the traditional aspiration of regenerating the soil. " Shall this garden of beauty be suffered to lie dormant in its wild and useless luxuriance . . . ? " [35] asked the *Illinois State Register* of California. The *New York Herald* answered when it declared that by " divine right " this territory belonged not to indolent Mexico but to the people who would use it to scatter God's blessings to mankind.[36] On the other hand, most expansionists wasted no sentimentality over the ideal of regenerating the people of the desired land. The inhabitants of Mexico's gorgeous garden seemed to one of them to be " reptiles " who must " either crawl or be crushed."[37] The *Democratic Review*, believing American occupation of new territory the great movement of the age,[38] proclaimed that " the process, which has been gone through at the north, of driving back the

Indians, or annihilating them as a race, has yet to be gone through at the south." [39] With many such observations in view, the *American Review* in 1847 branded the idea of manifest destiny as an expectation that the Spanish-Indian peoples would waste away at the overwhelming advance of Americans.[40]

On the other hand, long before contemplation of departure from previous expansion policy the war set into development some of the ideas which were ultimately to induce that deviation. In the first place, not many months of war had passed before some expansionists, especially the more tender-minded, foreshadowed later ideals by viewing the regeneration of inhabitants as a redeeming incident of the conquest of land. Thus in July, 1846, the humanitarian Walt Whitman based his demand for the retention of California on the ground that America's territorial increase meant "the increase of human happiness and liberty." [41] Rev. Dr. M'Vickar informed soldiers departing for California that they were "our chosen carriers to introduce into less favored lands a higher and purer civilization." [42] An interesting shift occurred in the moral attitude of the originally anti-expansionist and anti-war *New Englander* when it became aware of the advantage to commercial New England of new western territories which "open to us, in a narrower part of the continent, a way to the Pacific Ocean." Second thought convinced this organ that a bad motive was often used by a wise Providence to produce good results: "This war may result in great good to the world — to this country — to Mexico herself — to the cause of learning, good government, and religion." [43] Even the *Illinois State Register*, sponsor at times of vindictive sentiments, observed on one occasion that the war was an opportunity for the prosecution of "our glorious mission" which ought not be left unutilized.[44] There was every moral reason why a mission to regenerate the inhabitants of Upper California should develop into a mission to regenerate all Mexicans.

However, the enlargement of territorial aim was probably due less to philanthropy than to a consideration of national self-interest. It was the principle of demanding territorial indemnity in proportion to the length of the war. This principle was accepted at the outset without awareness of the possibility that circumstances of the war might give it an implication necessitating amalgamation with many Mexicans. For the original demand for Upper California as territorial indemnity was premised by the assumption that the war would be over in a breath. But this expectation, in spite of early victories, was not realized. As the war was dragged out by Mexico's stubborn resistance, the demand for territorial indemnity increased in proportion to the increase in expense, grief over casualties, and indignation at Mexico for refusing to acknowledge defeat. The first increase demanded by public opinion was sparsely inhabited New Mexico, which was conquered in the fall of 1846. By January of 1847, the editor of the *Illinois State Register*,[45] Representatives Tibbatts [46] and Sims,[47] and others expressed the desire for territorial indemnity extending to the Sierra Madre. In this they prefigured the eventual reasoning of the New York *Weekly Herald* that the logical conclusion of the principle of indemnity was the annexation of all Mexico.[48] In the winter and spring of 1847 the victories of the American army not merely fostered the desire for more indemnity but gave rise to talk of temporary occupation of the entire country to guarantee fulfilment of a peace treaty. At least temporary contact with the abhorred Mexicans began to seem inevitable.

Fortunately, expansionists could think of moral compensations. By April, 1847, the *Boston Post* had been brought by the victories of Taylor and Scott to the conviction that the war would " do more for the spread of commercial and political freedom," as well as for the wealth and glory of the United States, than any event since the declaration of American independence.[49] It was consideration of the temporary occupation of all Mexico which prompted the most important development of the regenerative ideal. In the late winter and spring of 1847 such important organs as the *Democratic Review*,[50] the New York *Sun*,[51] and the *New York Herald* considered that the extended presence of the American army would guarantee not merely the collection of due indemnity but also the " regeneration " of the Mexican people. The latter expectation perhaps showed more optimism than the previous history of military occupations warranted. But the *Herald* went so far as to say:

> The universal Yankee nation can regenerate and disenthrall the people of Mexico in a few years; and we believe it is a part of our destiny to civilize that beautiful country and enable its inhabitants to appreciate some of the many advantages and blessings they enjoy.[52]

However, there had been as yet no disposition to permit all Mexicans to enjoy permanently the blessings of the American flag. It was the protraction of the war over the summer of 1847 which first suggested to a few, like the regretful F. W. Byrdsall, that having so far weakened Mexico, "*now* we must take her, in order to keep her from the hands of others." [53] In August there came from an unexpected source a more enthusiastic proposal: the acquisition of all Mexico through the submission of annexation to the free decision — acceptance of such a boon seemed certain — of every Mexican state. This strange expansionist was the editor of the *National Era*, an organ of the abolitionist party which had opposed all territorial aggrandizement on the assumption that it would extend slavery. Like many others the abolitionist editor had discovered that Mexican territory was for the most part not suited to slavery and that annexation would mean an increase in the number of free states. While chiefly concerned with establishing "freedom as the fundamental and unchangeable law of the North American continent," the *National Era* argued that by permitting Mexico to enter the Union the United States would appear as "its greatest benefactor." [54] Here was the beginning of that expansionist "anti-slavery conspiracy" which Professor Fuller indicates in his article refuting the traditional generalization of a "pro-slavery conspiracy." [55]

The fall of 1847 brought two events which developed expansionism even more than did the realization of many that expansion would not extend slavery. The first was the failure which overtook Trist's peace negotiations in consequence of Mexico's unwillingness to accede to the cession of New Mexico and Upper California. This firm stand meant that Mexico was skilled in denying defeat even if not in escaping it. It began to be evident that it would be necessary to bring Mexico to her senses by carrying the American conquest to her capital itself. A few weeks later the brilliant campaign of General Scott had accomplished this very feat. Even the capture of Mexico City, a key to the entire country, did not bring Mexico's capitulation. That country was like an individual combatant who has been brought to his knees but cannot be released for a moment because he still threatens spirited attack. In such a situation what is the course that suggests itself?

Killing another nation is a course which political necessity does sometimes suggest. So drastic a measure had not appealed to Americans, warned by the *Richmond Enquirer* that the most dire result of all wars is termination of another nation's existence.[56] This result had seemed dire to Americans less because of the crime against the god of nationality than because of the necessity of entering into union with an "inferior" people. In the fall of 1847, however, more than a few Americans, including chiefly editors of expansionist newspapers but also eminent figures like Generals Worth, Persifer Smith, and Quitman, first advocated the extinction of Mexico's government as "the only way of making a peace" [57] — that is, a peace with satisfactory territorial indemnity.

In the same period expression was for the first time given rather widely to an inspiring educational hypothesis — that annexation of the surviving wards of the Mexican government would result in their regeneration. It was as though an individual faced with the necessity of a disagreeable marriage formed the noble resolution to remodel the prospective partner after a Pygmalion's desires and ideals. The New York *Weekly Herald* thus admitted that it had looked upon immediate annexation as an evil; but "as we are forced to encounter it," the editor said, "we should grapple with the evil manfully, vigorously, and as becomes a great nation." [58] This meant that the American Secretary of the Treasury and the American army should undertake not only to develop the resources but to "regenerate the natives of that country." [59] The *National Whig* — was it because it supported General Taylor for the presidency? — concurred in the view that the United States should annex

Mexico for the sake of the peace, quiet, and happiness of that land.[60] The correspondent of the St. Louis *Republican* affirmed that annexation was not only the best result for both countries, but was desired by the Mexican wealthy classes themselves.[61] That Europe was not averse to America's expansion was the encouraging word sent to officials by Minister Bancroft, who thus believed it safe as well as philanthropic that we "rescue a large part of Mexico from anarchy." [62]

The most important argument for this enterprise of reform was its evident accordance with the design of Providence. The New York *Sun*, which called for an immediate proclamation of union to end the warfare, could see the "finger of Providence uplifted for the salvation of a people oppressed by tyrants and robbers." [63] The Washington *Daily Union*, also tending toward the idea of annexation, published a letter from a Pennsylvanian who called the war "the religious execution of our country's glorious mission, under the direction of Divine Providence, to civilize and christianize, and raise up from anarchy and degradation a most ignorant, indolent, wicked and unhappy people." Divine Will commanded that the wicked be cut off, but that the well-disposed be "regenerated and protected." [64] Even the *New York Journal of Commerce* sponsored such theology when it published as typical of a growing view at Washington the following noble letter:

> The supreme Ruler of the universe seems to interpose, and aid the energy of man towards benefiting mankind. His interposition . . . seems to me to be identified with the success of our arms. . . . That the redemption of 7,000,000 of souls from all the vices that infest the human race, is the ostensible object of both, appears manifest. . . .
>
> Heretofore I have looked upon our relations with Mexico with comparative indifference, always believing that at a future day the Anglo-Saxon race would spread over the American Continent. I now flatter myself that our authority may be established in my day, and that I may live to see Mexico prosperously raising her head from the dust, under the Government of our laws." [65]

The loftiness of such sentiments does not quite prevent a smile; for the change from "comparative indifference" to an ideal of regenerating the people took place just when it became difficult to regenerate the land without the people.

In the fall of 1847, however, it was still questionable whether religion or any other factor would make the demand for all Mexico dominant. At this time even many expansionists still agreed with the *Democratic Review* that union with the "degraded" Spanish-Mexican race was made impossible by the Anglo-Saxon's very virtues.[66] But by the end of December there had arisen new conditions which placed the possibility of fulfilling the mission in a more promising light.

Almost every newspaper, Calhoun pointed out on December 20 without much exaggeration, was speculating on the annexation of all Mexico.[67] Consequently it soon appeared to leading Democrats that the time had become propitious for expansionist appeals fanning winds of public sentiment that might blow them to victory in the forthcoming elections. In January, 1848, the New York Democratic State Convention and a Democratic mass-meeting at Tammany Hall passed resolutions implicitly advocating annexation. Secretary of State Buchanan, Secretary of the Treasury Walker, Vice-President Dallas, all more or less definitely expressed opinions favorable to incorporation of all Mexico. President Polk was advised by the expansionistic Buchanan to refer to "that destiny which Providence may have in store for both countries."[68] The President's message did speak not only of demanding more than Upper California and New Mexico, but also of the possible necessity of an indefinite military occupation, which might be turned by the logic of events into annexation. Senators Hannegan and Dickinson introduced resolutions favorable to annexation, and according to Senator Niles most of the Democratic Senators were tending in the direction which the resolutions and numerous expansionist speeches urged.[69]

Annexationist sentiment grew in intensity and in extensity as it was nurtured by propaganda, the nationalism of war, the thrill of martial victories calling for consummation, and the temptation lying in opportunity. The expansionist intoxication which Lowell wrongly attributed to rum was, indeed, best reflected in some of the toasts at political banquets. At a banquet attended by the Vice-President and other notables, Senator Dickinson toasted "*a more perfect Union*: embracing the entire North American continent." [70] Those at a supper to Colonel Morgan drank to immediate annexation of Mexico, the Isthmus of Panama as next resting-place, and ultimate continental dominion.[71] In an address at Tammany Hall Sam Houston summoned Americans to their mighty march over the continent which they rightfully regarded as their " birthright "; he observed incidentally that the march would be made more pleasant by the numerous " beautiful señoritas " in Mexico.[72] " Our Destiny higher an' higher kep' mountin' " (in the contemporary words of Lowell) [73] as orators expatiated on " ' manifest destiny ' — the spread of the Anglo-Saxon race — the glory of extending our territory from sea to sea." [74]

In reverting from the motive of avid impulse to that of the ideal, we may again do well to let homely analogy suggest the probable interaction between the two. Whereas previously we compared the American to an individual who is faced with an alliance necessary but attractive from no standpoint, we may now liken him to one who considers the prospective partner's single attraction to be a dowry. What effect would the new interest in this dowry have upon the reformist ideal which at first was only endured? It is at least conceivable that it would result in the ideal being enthusiastically embraced.

Whether the coincidence was casual or significant, it did so happen that, as the land dowry of the Mexican people came to appear more attractive, the mission of regeneration became more widely and impressively manifest. On January 11 the disgusted Senator Reverdy Johnson reported hearing numerous metaphysical doctrines as far-fetched as " that we were constituted missionaries by Heaven, even by fire and by sword and by slaughter, to carry the light of civilization into that benighted land." [75] In the same month, the perturbed *Niles' Register* published an article describing the " Manifest Destiny Doctrines," which, making the expansionist phrase for the first time popular, were being propagated by public journals, returned soldiers, and numerous orators who believed it the duty of the American people to " hurry on to fulfill the manifest destiny " ordained by " ' the purposes of Providence ' in regard to these our next neighbors." The *New-York Evening*

*Post*, which had once declared amalgamation with Mexicans unfortunate, was now quoted to the effect that Providence had decreed against their existing independently alongside us. For evidence of such sentiment among returning soldiers, *Niles' Register* pointed to Commodore Stockton's speech deriving " a duty before God " from " the great mission of liberty committed to our hands." [76] It gave elsewhere citations from Democratic leaders as eminent as Vice-President Dallas, Senator Dickinson, and William B. MacLay, who spoke respectively of our assignment to " the guardianship of a crowded and confederated continent," of our " errand " to the Mexican people of " humanity, civilization and peace," and of " that destiny which contemplates the spread and success of free government over the face of this continent." [77] These and numerous other individuals in tune with destiny presented the mission of regeneration as a ground for an effort or a willingness to acquire all Mexico, a large part of it, or at least a virtual protectorate involving indefinitely a military occupation.

What were the avowed grounds of the belief in the regenerative mission itself? Analysis of the edifying ideology will show that all its theses were reversals of the views current when the American did not consider himself a disagreeable brother's keeper.

The fundamental premise that the Mexicans were in a bad way was not, indeed, new in itself. It was stated, however, in connection with a new explanation and tone of sympathy. In the era of bad feeling it had been usual to place responsibility for Mexico's unfortunate plight upon the Mexican people as a whole. Now it was generously conceded that blame rested really upon Mexico's rulers and that the Mexican people themselves were proper objects of sympathy. Thus Commodore Stockton deplored the fact that " poor, unfortunate, wretched Mexico " was the victim of " misgovernment." [78] Senator Dickinson called the rulers who had hastened Mexico's downfall " rapacious spirits," [79] and the *New-York Evening Post* branded them as "ignorant cowards and profligate ruffians." [80] From the " bad intentions " of such scoundrels, declared Colonel Morgan, Americans " as Christians " were " bound to protect the Mexicans." [81]

Since the malady of the Mexicans now seemed misgovernment, the previous hopelessness with regard to a congenitally "inferior" people could be superseded by the dogma that a change in government would cure and even regenerate the patient. A sampling of expansionist pretensions gives an interesting exhibit of medico-political optimism. The most modest claim was in Senator Cass's observation that annexation would sweep away "the abuses of generations." [82] Senator Dickinson envisaged in place of previous abuses a personal and economic security which would appear to Mexicans the special interposition of providential favor.[83] Protection of property, it seemed to Senator Rusk, would enable Mexico to "develop its mighty resources, and prevent them from being monopolized by a few foreign capitalists, whose interests are in conflict with those of the United States." [84] Senator Henley, however, dwelt upon the fact that "prosperity and happiness would be found" wherever one introduced the more intellectual influences of American life — "the schoolmaster, the minister of the gospel, and a free press." [85] The Protestant minister of the gospel, formerly excluded by religious oppression, appeared to Commodore Stockton essential to the Mexican's eternal as well as mundane happiness.[86] Senator Foote, like most others, summarized all benefits under "liberty," which would be brought to Mexico as a "banner of moral regeneration." [87] It was true, indeed, that liberty in the political sense was out of the question for the Indians, who constituted three-fourths of the Mexican population. But Senator Sevier observed that even this "degraded" race could be made less degraded through American laws, education, and kindness.[88] The *National Era* supported this hope by maintaining that "no race is so degenerate as to be beyond the influences of the agencies which a kind Providence has arranged in these latter days for the redemption of all his children." [89]

At one time even expansionists felt that the redemption of other peoples could be achieved only at the cost of injuring unduly the elect, and was therefore a philanthropy which America ought prudently to eschew. Now, however, it was denied that the incorporation of many Mexicans would have upon the United States an effect which Senator Cass had called in February of 1847 " deplorable." [90] After having said in 1847 that no such evil would come in his day, Senator Cass admitted in 1848 that the acquisition of all Mexico might shortly come, and called in any event for expansion as far as the Sierra Madre.[91] Although he still avowed apprehension of annexing the entire country, he in 1848 emphasized the consideration that the full dose would not be fatal.[92] Similarly the *Democratic Review*, which throughout the entire previous portion of the war had depicted annexation as " a calamity," [93] declared in February of 1848 without the least evidence of embarrassment:

> Whatever danger there may be in blending people of different religions into one nation, where religion is established by law,—or in annexing by conquest, under arbitrary governments, which trample upon the rights of all their subjects, and conquer only to enslave,—a free nation, which shows equal toleration and protection to all religions, and conquers only to bestow freedom, has no such danger to fear.[94]

The article concluded with a call for bold advance as far as our just claims and circumstances might carry. There was little need for encouragement. According to the New Orleans *Daily Picayune*, Americans had " that sort of confidence in the vigor and longevity of the principle of liberty, as to believe it would survive an epidemic conquest embracing in its ravages all Christendom." [95]

The consideration which probably inspired the greatest confidence was the dogma of manifest destiny, of the lofty mission indicated for America by the very course of events. But whereas previously the pacific advance of the pioneers suggested a destiny which used peace as its handmaid, the Mexican War occasioned a reinterpretation of providential plan. The New York *Sun* believed that " Providence had willed the war " to " unite and exalt both nations." [96] Sam Houston cited God's support of the wars of the Israelites in affirming that " the Divine Being has been evidently carrying out the destiny of the American race " to civilize the continent.[97] Representative Stanton interpreted the trend toward victory and annexation as indication of " the great design of Providence in this whole movement." [98] The New York Democratic convention, justifying title by conquest, crushingly asked those hesitant over participating in the movement whether they could "prescribe a better course of duty than that of the God who made us all." [99] The philosophy interpreting war as a divine instrument for social progress was expounded most fully by Senator H. V. Johnson:

> I would not force the adoption of our form of Government upon any people by the sword. But if war is forced upon us, as this has been, and the increase of our territory, and consequently the extension of the area of human liberty and happiness, shall be one of the incidents of such a contest, I believe we should be recreant to our noble mission, if we refused acquiescence in the high purposes of a wise Providence. War has its evils. In all ages it has been the minister of wholesale death and appalling desolation; but however inscrutable to us, it has also been made, by the Allwise Dispenser of events, the instrumentality of accomplishing the great end of human elevation and human happiness. . . . It is in this view, that I subscribe to the doctrine of 'manifest destiny.' [100]

Since virtually all wars seem to be begun by the other party, Johnson's disavowal of aggressive intention imposed on manifest destiny little restriction. However, expansionists believed sincerely — and in this respect they differed from the imperialists of 1898 — that in this unsought war they were not forcing their government on the Mexican people. For the latter seemed to them to "deprecate nothing so much as the withdrawal of our army, and restoration of Mexican authority." [101] They also differed from the later imperialists in not proposing to assign to the incorporated country a permanent status of colonial dependency. For while it was conceded that Mexicans generally were not "at this time fitted for an equal union with us," [102] and that *bien entendu* the Indians would never be, it was held to be a corollary of the very ideal of regeneration that all Mexicans susceptible of political enlightenment should ultimately be placed "upon an equality with native-born citizens." [103]

Yet the expansionism of the Mexican War anticipated the ideology of the white man's burden by accepting the obligation to the darker peoples. Expansionists contemplated not merely the regeneration of the Mexicans but a whole series of civilizing enterprises among the lesser breeds. Ashbel Smith proclaimed that the war was "a part of the mission, of the destiny, allotted to the Anglo-Saxon race," the Americanization of the continent.[104] Senator Dickinson affirmed that "new races are presented for us to civilize, educate and absorb."[105] It seemed to Senator Breese that since our institutions were better calculated than any others to elevate the masses, "it cannot be that it is the decree of heaven that none but the white race shall enjoy them."[106] The expansionists were in the first flush of that "youthful optimism" which, as Carl Schurz said in his essay on "Manifest Destiny," inspired the belief that "this republic, being charged with the mission of bearing the banner of freedom over the whole civilized world, could transform any country, inhabited by any kind of population, into something like itself simply by extending over it the magic charm of its institutions."[107]

The greatest curiosity in connection with this self-confident ideology is not its reversal of America's more conservative traditions, but the fact that after apparent acceptance it was repudiated by actual policy. Accepting a treaty acquiring only New Mexico and California, the United States left the great bulk of the Mexicans outside the Union and unregenerate. The treaty had been procured by an envoy who was out of touch with expansionist sentiment in his country and was himself inclined to be a Jeffersonian anti-imperialist. But since the irrepressible Trist had been repudiated by President Polk before the negotiations of terms of peace, there was the less obligation to accept the treaty when it arrived at the unpsychological moment. From a military point of view the annexation of all Mexico was more in America's power than ever before. In contrast with the Philippine situation, annexation could have been achieved with relatively little opposition from the Mexican people; for although expansionists invariably declare the ordinary people of the desired land to be in favor of its conquerors, it so happened that in this case they were largely right. And despite all the exaggerations of the expansionists, their assumption that annexation of Mexico would make possible great benefactions in a country of great miseries was not fundamentally unreasonable or without a persuasive moral implication.

The miscarriage of international philanthropy must apparently be explained by other considerations than those of moral ideology. Acceptance of the treaty was induced by a practical discretion which suddenly came to seem the better part of valor and even of altruism. Further effort toward expansion would have aroused opposition from both the pro-slavery and the abolition camps, invited sectional dissension, played into the hands of the Whig House, and possibly lost what had already been gained. These considerations, together with the disadvantage of acquiring too great a Mexican population, appealed especially to President Polk. Moreover, the arrival of the treaty as a *fait accompli* suddenly evoked a sharp and general feeling of war-weariness.

What of the moral obligation to the Mexicans who were weary of long oppression? In the discussion of the peace treaty very little was said of this obligation which a few weeks before had seemed so pressing. The New York *Weekly Herald* asserted what previously only anti-expansionists had accepted — that Mexico could be subject to the influence of American principles despite its independent existence.[108] It seems that with the decrease of desire for Mexican land there came a diminution of zest for arduous moral enterprise. It appears also that, just as the presence of temptation had lessened resistance against union with Mexicans, so the removal of temptation revived the resistance, the more particularly as anti-expansionists vehemently warned against embracing this "loathsome dead body." [109] An editorial of the *New York Weekly Evening Post* commended the treaty because the ceded territories of Upper California and New Mexico were "so thinly peopled." [110] Thus, despite all the moral philosophy recently accepted, despite the evident regret of many Mexicans, the mission of regeneration was foregone.

It was foregone, however, only for the time being. By being once handled, the forbidden fruit becomes more tempting thereafter. The ideal which encouraged the plucking of this fruit was destined to make several more entrances and exits in the American historical drama. It appeared and disappeared, as we shall briefly observe, under substantially the same conditions as those of the Mexican War.

The first reappearance came shortly after the ratification of the treaty of peace, which probably brought to many the regret that tends to follow an abstention. These saw an opportunity for partial consolation when Polk placed before Congress in April Yucatan's appeal for protection from marauding Indians. In a number of Senate speeches there was a more or less definite intimation that occupation of Yucatan might eventuate in annexation. Thus Senator Hannegan, chairman of the Committee on Foreign Relations, declared that political motives might lead to permanent occupation.[111] National aggrandizement and fear of European occupation were not, however, the only motives avowed. The note of humanitarian sentiment, relatively subdued since the pedal of expansionism had been inactive, now was loud again. Senator Houston urged the fulfilment of America's lofty mission,[112] which Senator Cass derived from America's providentially assigned position of leadership on this continent.[113] Senator Bagby, whose sympathies at the devastating siege of Matamoras had been avowedly engrossed with the American soldiers, now expressed his humanitarian opinion that manifest destiny should be applied to the miserable and degraded races occupying not only Yucatan but the whole of Mexico.[114]

Such expressions of international philanthropy were cut short when news arrived that Yucatan had settled her own problems. Another opportunity for philanthropy came in August, 1848, when Mexico requested American military assistance in maintaining order. President Polk, however, preferred not to involve his country in such an arduous undertaking. Altruism was seldom heard during the subsequent Whig administration; on the contrary, there was considerable bitterness with Mexico over border irritations and boundary disputes. The subsidence of the ideal of regeneration was coincident with the Government's discouragement of territorial ambitions.

With the election of Franklin Pierce, however, there came a

vigorous resurgence of expansionism; during the rest of the decade, all lands of the continent, but particularly Mexico, were viewed with avid eyes. Mexico was of special interest because of fear of European intervention, desire for control of a canal route, and interest in establishing conditions more favorable to American commerce. Amid these promptings of self-interest American expansionists revived the ideal of regeneration which might have been fulfilled so much more easily in 1848. There was no doubt that the earlier failure to fulfil the mission had resulted in making the condition of "the sick man" worse than ever before. Some, like the editor of the *Washington Union*, coldly proposed that the United States "silently . . . gaze upon the death-struggle of the victim, and when all is over with the poor helpless sinner," allow our armies of industry to undertake "regenerating Mexico by the axe, the hoe and the plough." [115] Others, interested in the people as well as the land, held as did Representative Lane that humanitarianism demanded early annexation.[116] These were convinced, as one observer commented, of "the inherent power of a form of government to regenerate mankind." [117] Despite America's faults and crimes, Gerrit Smith modestly said, the United States was "the mightiest of all the civilizing and renovating agencies." [118] The *United States Democratic Review* went so far as to declare America's regenerative power stronger than death:

> Mexico is in a state of suspended animation. She is in fact dead. She must have resurrection. She must be electrified — restored. This American Republic is strong enough to do anything that requires strength. It is vital enough to inject life even into the dead.[119]

The same confidence in the miraculous capacity of America's vitality suggested to Representative Latham and others that our "proud mission" was to "cultivate, fertilize, regenerate" one country after another until our rule and civilization extended "to the most remote part of this continent and to its neighboring islands." [120]

The Civil War, which brought the mightiest of regenerating powers nearly to dissolution, broke rudely into the dreams of both expansion and continental philanthropy. During the European subjugation of Mexico, Seward's prudent self-restriction to diplomatic protest was not cast aside even when South American countries called upon this advocate of Pan-Americanism to assume leadership in a course of continental opposition. After the Civil War, save for the brief and limited expansionism of the late 'sixties, the desire for Mexican territory was long at low ebb. Territorial manifest destiny, as Professor Rippy has pointed out,[121] was succeeded by economic infiltration. Although in the 'seventies Mexico was as painfully distraught as ever, Americans were reluctant to intervene farther or longer than was necessary to protect the harassed border. The reason was stated by Consul Ulrich in a dispatch to the State Department:

> I would not for a moment be considered . . . as having the least desire to bring about a permanent occupation of Mexico, or any part of it. To do so would, in my opinion, be about equal to ingrafting a cancer on a human body . . .[122]

Yet in the 'nineties there were ingraftments more radical than any considered before. These were the tropical dependencies which seemed necessary to America's commerce, security, and imperial glory. But they seemed essential also to the fulfilment of the mission of regeneration, which in its imperialistic form received the name of the white man's burden. Although it appeared to Charles Francis Adams that the racial antipathy of the American to the Asiatic had been greater than to any other species of the human race,[123] the Asiatic was now presented as " the little brown brother " requiring civilization. But the Philippine insurrection shortly renewed doubts concerning both the advantage and the moral obligation of such difficult amalgamations. As Mark Sullivan has pointed out, American expansionism subsided with the realization that the fundamental American impulse was for colonization and not colonial administration.[124]

In ensuing decades of increasing distaste for such burdens, the mission of regeneration seemed to summon only to temporary intervention in behalf of political and economic order. Appropriately enough, it called most urgently to the country where the United States left a mission unfinished in 1848. As though to punish for this dereliction, Mexico in the second decade of the twentieth century wrought injuries upon American life, property, and self-esteem. Once again the initial reaction was the natural one of indignation and hostility. But once more, too, those recommending a course of radical intervention developed a mood of altruism. They conceived of "our divine mission to clean up Mexico"[125] for the benefit not only of the irritated world but also of the unhappy Mexican people themselves. Thus the Fall Committee report implied "the moral and international duty of lending assistance to the suffering people of Mexico."[126] But when, about the same time, there came the opportunity to do enormous good by accepting a mandate over distant Armenia, "the risks and possible disadvantages outweighed the moral obligation."[127]

Nor was there any general desire to help even the Mexicans by annexing them. Annexation best insured regeneration but it was ruled out by a racial exclusiveness much greater than that existing in 1848. There were, however, Americans who expressed a desire to annex Lower California and Sonora, territories with relatively few inhabitants. Senator Ashhurst, introducing in 1919 a resolution directing the President to negotiate for the purchase of this territory, contributed the last noteworthy version of manifest destiny with respect to Mexican land:

> If it remains in Mexican possession, it will be the same one hundred years from to-day as it is to-day, a dreary, barren waste; whereas American money, American spirit, American enterprise can make it into gardens and farms, and a blessing to civilization.[128]

These words might have been spoken by an expansionist of 1846 in urging the purchase of Upper California. The history of meliorative expansionism ended as it began, not with the regeneration of the people, but with that prudent and well-balanced ideal — the regeneration of the land.

The mission of regenerating peoples has come and gone, a strange interlude. Not merely the sentiment but the ideology of reformist expansionism has become a thing of strangeness. Two recent statements are interesting commentaries on this disappearance of a noble experimentalism. Dr. L. S. Rowe, adverting in a presidential address before the American Political Science Association to American attempts to teach self-government forcibly, spoke as follows:

> While such government has always been characterized by great integrity and great ability in the execution of public works and other technical enterprises, it has always signally failed in preparing the people over which it has had control for the responsibilities incident to the management of their own affairs.[129]

Such words confess a failure of moral hopes which is almost the common lot in national life. Even more pathetic, however, is a repudiation of the premises of a traditional ideal. This repudiation is admitted in Secretary Stimson's words:

> Our former loose optimism has disappeared. We recognize now more adequately the real difficulties of popular government and the danger to that institution of trying to blend into our nation a too rapid influx of citizens having political experiences and traditions entirely different from our own.[130]

But loose optimism regarding others and ourselves did not disappear until something else had disappeared — land-hunger itself. Like Siamese twins, land-hunger and the moral ideal were together in their death as in their birth.

It has appeared that, though the opportunity to do great service was frequent if not constant, the ideal of regenerating another people stirred most Americans only when they felt an impulse to acquire or control its land. Though the entire tale of this correlation provokes a smile, it should not be laid down until one knows in the light of its true meaning whether to smile cynically or tolerantly.

*Felix qui potuit rerum cognoscere causas.* But to most contemporary anti-expansionists it seemed plain that, in the words of Albert Gallatin, "the allegation that the subjugation of Mexico would be the means of enlightening the Mexicans . . . is but the shallow attempt to disguise unbounded cupidity and ambition." [131] And so they cried angrily: "Away with this mawkish morality! with this desecration of religion! with this cant about 'manifest destiny'. . ." [132] Despite this impatience of their opponents, the expansionists did not cease with their moralizing. Even setting aside the likelihood that the charge of hypocrisy indicts ordinary human nature too sensationally, one can scarcely explain as hypocrisy that which obviously had so little chance of making a favorable impression.

That the ideology was designed to " deceive ourselves " was another view, expounded by Charles T. Porter as follows:

> Desire harbored for a moment, invents a thousand plausible excuses for its gratification, until we are convinced that its indulgence is hardly inconsistent with the severest morality. Arrayed in the garments of virtue, vice often dares to appeal even to our sense of duty, and we strive to believe that we should be guilty of wrong in refusing to obey its impulses.[133]

But expansionists perceived in land-hunger no " vice " which required the concealment of their appetite from self-knowledge. Thus Sam Houston, whether because he was unregenerate or because he had the wisdom of nature, testified proudly: " There is not an American on earth but what loves land." [134]

The belief that the moral ideology was in any sense insincere rests probably on a mistaken identification of the sincere or honestly felt ideal with the exclusively motivating ideal. In fact, the ethical ideals entertained most sincerely or honestly are those which, like the reformist aspiration of the Christian ascetic tempted by the beautiful Thaïs, coincide with natural impulses. Thus the American expansionist's interest in land enabled him to feel for its inhabitants a sympathy much deeper than he could possibly have felt without this interest. For the effect of the associated ideal is ordinarily to make the pursuit of self-interest more harmonious, significant, and pleasant. Precisely because it was entertained sincerely, the ideal of regeneration made up to the expansionist for his aversion to taking up company with the inhabitants of the land. In the first place it held in view the possibility that the at present incompatible Mexican might through regeneration be made tolerable. In the second place it substituted for the pleasure of acquiring desirable fellow citizens the pleasure of a glorious enterprise of moral pedagogy.

The real problem does not lie in the fact that the ideal flourishes upon the soil of self-interest but in the fact that it tends not to grow at all without this soil. The individual as such can undertake heroic altruisms — as the Christian saint can even embrace the leper — through no other incentive than sympathy. But the matter is quite different with the nationalist of all climes. Despite sympathy and a willingness for services moderate and convenient, he ordinarily regards the dangerous or even arduous assistance of politically leprous peoples as absurdly sentimental save when such assistance coincides with self-interest and then suddenly appears as a solemn duty. The classic recognition of this unedifying attitude is Washington's assertion that it is absurd to expect from other nations disinterested favors.[135] As the history of America's expansionism shows, Americans have regarded only one thing as more absurd than this expectation — to permit entirely disinterested motives to control their own foreign policy.

The subordination of national altruism to national self-interest is not, however, due merely to the instinctive attitude noted even by the sentimental Rousseau: "One loves what is one's own more than another's." Certain moral judgments, paradoxical as it may seem, are also responsible for it. Vattel long ago observed that the statesman has no moral right to sacrifice the interests of which he is trustee to the impulses of a noble and generous heart. Former Assistant Secretary of State F. Huntington Wilson, stating America's aspirations, pointed out the moral considerations which restrain also the generosity of the ordinary patriot:

> Service to humanity is not mentioned separately because charity begins at home; because it is America's first duty to serve America; because America, as a government, can amply serve humanity in spheres and in ways in which America also serves itself.[136]

One noteworthy element in the foregoing is the recurrent nationalist idea which may be called the doctrine of the incidental dispensation. This doctrine makes it morally possible to dispense with self-sacrificial altruism by emphasizing the benefits to humanity that are incidental to national egoism. Another doctrine of the same writer is the typical nationalist paradox that self-service is the highest philanthropy.

Such judgments are meant to sound very reasonable; yet they cannot be fully understood except by reference to a mystical metaphysics. This is the very philosophy of manifest destiny which suggests to the nationalist the mission of regeneration.

For though this philosophy ascribes to the nation the mission of enhancing the welfare of others, it places preeminent weight upon the welfare of the patriot's own nation as the bearer of the highest values. And from this premise it would quite logically follow that the mission of regenerating others is always contingent upon the possibility of simultaneously enhancing the vitality of the chosen people itself.

The social philosopher, whose idiosyncrasy it is to escape from the nationalistic interpretation of destiny, must view such considerations with a smile tolerant but sad. For he sees that the entanglement of the nationalist's altruism with his patriotism must tend sadly to curtail the social usefulness of the former. This curtailment seems apparent even if one admits that under certain circumstances there is truth in Lord Acton's words: "Inferior races are raised by living in political union with races intellectually superior." [137] The difficulty is that expansionists are likely to select their missions with reference less to the needs of the beneficiaries than to those of the benefactors. Although the poor Mexicans in 1848 largely desired and perhaps needed to enter the Union, they were left to flounder through the ages because American expansionists at the last minute preferred the regeneration of lands to the regeneration of disliked peoples. On the other hand, the Filipinos, who did not desire to enter the Union and might have been helped best by friendly protection, were given the choice of regeneration or death by imperialists intent upon permanent sovereignty. Such are the actions which justify Charles Francis Adams's observation that "divine missions" are things the assumption and fulfilment of which are apt to be at variance.[138]

In what may be the best of all possible worlds, it is true that, as Rev. Dr. M'Vickar pointed out during the Mexican War, "the deep laden barques of self-interest that rush in, are still made to bear His gifts to destitute or savage lands." [139] Yet the barques bearing the gifts of nationalists cannot be trusted to float far without the tide of self-interest, much less to float against it. Thus it will always be till the nationalist spirit is itself regenerated — a miracle which will probably not take place till human nature is regenerated.

# CHAPTER VII

## NATURAL GROWTH

The past territorial growth which American expansionists proudly surveyed at the middle of the nineteenth century had been abnormal in both its speed and its excess of national needs. Yet in one respect it seemed natural even to anti-expansionist Whigs after their arrival in power disposed them to reconciliation with past policy. Past expansion, Secretary of State Everett asserted, had taken place predominantly through reasonable acceptance of opportunities rather than through a "grasping spirit." In the light of this fact it seemed to Everett a "natural growth."

But scarcely had Everett called America's past aggrandizement natural when developments in public opinion and governmental policy portended a less normal future. The Democratic Pierce's accession to the presidency brought into the open the deliberate, ambitious, and rather aggressive expansionism which makes the 'fifties seem the heyday of "spread-eagleism." The deliberateness of its expansionism is reflected in the fact that Pierce's inaugural address was the first in American history to declare territorial aggrandizement an aim of the incoming administration. His successor Buchanan prophesied not only for his own administration but apparently for the entire future: "Expansion is in the future the policy of our country, and only cowards fear and oppose it." [1] Lack of luck rather than of boldness limited the decade's achievement to the thin Mexican strip delivered by Gadsden's treaty of 1853. The Government sought more extensive Mexican territory, Cuba, and Hawaii; a large public clamored for still more, and some, as Representative Boyce said, had "such inordinate stomachs that they are willing to swallow up the entire continent." [2] So great an appetite overcame squeamishness. More than a few wished to acquire the vineyards of neighbors aggressively and a few translated the wish into filibustering. In sum, the expansionists of the 'fifties showed the very configuration of characteristics which Everett had repudiated as a "grasping spirit."

Those possessed of this "evident, hearty, and unappeasable land-hunger" were not only not confounded by denunciations but espoused a moral ideology which might well have confounded Everett. For the same criterion used by Everett to praise the relative self-restraint in America's past was now employed to justify the grasping spirit. Confirming Adam Ferguson's observation that of all words "natural" is the most indeterminate, the idea of natural growth turned apostate and lent itself to the thesis that expansionist prehensility was really a grasping for the nutriment which nature itself designed for the nation's healthy enlargement.

This doctrine rested upon a conception of "nature" which was different from that emphasized in early expansionist ideology. Nature in the present case was the hypostasization not of the natural reason peculiar to the human being but of the organic life represented equally by man, lower animal, and plant. The proposition that expansion was natural growth thus meant in the first place that nature implanted in the healthy nation an instinct which, independently of reason, made territorial expansion as normal a destiny for the young nation as is growth for the young organism. This biological doctrine of manifest destiny resembled most other versions of destiny in associating an ought-implication with a proposition of fact. The doctrine implied in the second place that the expansionism as well as the expansion resulting from this growth-instinct was natural in the sense of being morally normal.

The foregoing formulations are less an explanation than a point of departure for explanation. For although this doctrine of natural growth is a recurrent type of ideology among expansionist peoples, it may seem from the viewpoint of the moralist not natural at all. One may wonder why the expansionist resorted for his moral criterion to that animal kingdom which, as John Stuart Mill in his essay on "Nature" observed, is replete with such acts as seem in man to be bestially immoral. This indiscriminate naturalism was far from Grotius's mind when he judged political associations in the light of the law of nature. Believing man to be "much farther removed from all other animals than the different kinds of animals are from one another," he identified the law of nature with the dictates of that "well-tempered judgement" which constitutes man's uniqueness.[3]

However, one must begin by recognizing that the idea of nature, like a vine twisting with its supporting structure, developed in the divergent directions of the human impulse using it for ornament. Whereas one of its traditional meanings emphasized the unique elements in human nature, another stressed the organic aspect, not only of individual man, but also of the human aggregate termed state. According to the idea that Professor Coker has called the organismic theory of the state, the state is an analogue, a special form, or an ordinary form of organic life. This curious conception, useful to upholders of the unity of the state, passed through a long and variegated evolution which tended more and more toward a biological theory of political morality.

The original form of the organismic theory merely presented the state and the human body as analogous. Thus Plato compared the state to a magnified human being, and Cicero likened the head of the state to the spirit ruling the human body; political thinkers of both the Middle Ages and the early period of national states continued the use of such analogies as Hobbes's Leviathan in justifying unified authority from the viewpoint of either ecclesiastical or secular supremacy. A second stage of development came about when early nineteenth-century idealists, reacting against the conception of the state as mechanism, maintained that as an ethical or functional unity, in which all individuals are interdependent, the state itself was a real even if a unique organism. About the middle of the nineteenth century, the organismic theory culminated in the doctrine that the state as organism was not unique but radically akin to other living organisms; while one form of the doctrine alleged that the state had a psychic life like that of human beings, a more common one affirmed that its structure, function, and evolution were like those of organisms in general. "The development of biological science gave an impetus to theories of the state in which the methods and categories of natural science were applied to the interpretation of political phenomena," [4] and a few found in the state even such organs as stomach, navel, or nose. In America the more moderate type of organismic theory was taught by the distinguished Francis Lieber when he wrote in 1838 that the state "is an organism," that is, a moral unity which originated in and ever rested upon man's social instinct.[5]

The question of the validity of these provocative conceptions, still supported by more than one school of German political thought, will not be discussed until later; in the first place we wish merely to follow their logical development into expansionism. The first noteworthy stage in this evolution is the conception expressed by Emerson to the effect that in nature "all is nascent." [6] The deduction that the state as a species of nature has a characteristic habit of growth is a second stage, represented by thinkers as diverse as early believers in the divine right of kings and the nineteenth-century Bluntschli. It is true that most of these pictured the growth of the state as the increase of its population and resources. But the obvious analogy between physical growth and territorial expansion easily led Machiavelli, Algernon Sidney, and others to a third doctrine — that the necessary growth of the state included extension of boundaries. An American example of this culminating idea is an expansionist article, published in 1848 in the *Democratic Review*, entitled "Growth of States." Herein the proposition that "a State must be always on the increase or the decrease" was deduced from the "truism" of "the law of movement," a phrase which embraced in implication the invisible growing movement of the organic species.[7]

Although partially influenced by these abstract organismic theories, Americans were apparently led to the doctrine of natural growth primarily by the biological suggestiveness in a specific phase of America's national development. This interpretation is supported by the fact that the doctrine first received popular attention about the middle of the 'forties. The time of its emergence was one when Americans not only felt the quickening of an expansionist impulse in themselves but observed evidence or promise of growth in all the elements and particularly the territorial phase of national life.

Edwin de Leon's commencement address of 1845 exemplified the general sense of national growth in portraying America as a young giant on the threshold of a manhood which the Old World could not restrain.[8] About the same time John L. O'Sullivan, launching the phrase "manifest destiny," compared America's predestined title to Oregon to the right of a tree to the space necessary for its growth.[9] He elaborated this idea also by human metaphor:

> In the growth of our national greatness, and the progressive development of that democratic element which is the true principle of its vitality and the true index of its destiny, we seem to have reached a period which, like the marked physical transition in the human frame from the age of childhood to the noble stature and vigor of young manhood, is stamped with distinct features of expansion, change, development.[10]

Despite this conception of growth as a property of democracy, it seems that the expansionist's insistence upon America's destiny of further growth was also the result of his envious observation of the contemporary growth of Old World monarchies. John L. O'Sullivan's *Democratic Review* took note of a British publicist who had affirmed that "growth is now, and must for some time, continue to be the normal state of our existence in the East," that is, until Great Britain reached "the natural limits of the empire" and the impulse of conquest ceased of itself. In a congressional debate on Oregon in 1846, Representative McDowell quoted these words in order to ask:

> In accordance with which doctrine, we (Americans) might well ask: 'What are those *natural limits* of the United States, where the impulse of *annexation* will cease of itself? Is not growth the normal state, also, of the Federal Union?'[11]

Unfortunately America's normal growth clashed in Oregon with the equally normal expansion of Great Britain. There were some Americans to whom "masterly inactivity" seemed advisable; for they believed that "nature, and our own natural growth, are doing everything for us."[12] Thus Representative

Davis urged postponement of all political effort until the " natural progress " of its population toward the limits marked by " Nature " decided the issue in America's favor.[13] Representative Bedinger deduced ultimate success from the consideration that, in the growth-cycle of states, America was in " the vigor of youth " while Great Britain had " passed her prime." [14] A poet in the *Democratic Review*, however, advocated the doctrine of natural growth more belligerently:

> We can not help the matter if we would;
> The race must have expansion—we must grow
> Though every forward footstep be withstood
> And every inch of ground presents its foe . . . [15]

This a priori confidence in growth received apparent confirmation when, considerably before the race needed expansion, the demands of both peaceful diplomacy and war added Texas, Oregon, and a large part of Mexico to the stature of the vigorous youth. The biological principle suggested originally by mystic presentiment now seemed to some to be open to inductive demonstration. Thus, shortly after the settlement of the Mexican War brought us a territorial appetizer, the author of the article " Growth of States " observed that we were swallowing, digesting, and assimilating all Mexico just as an animal eats to grow.[16] It is true that the Whigs, though elected to office in 1848 through the popularity of a military hero, had no intention of following such a jungle diet in their foreign policy. Yet with respect to the past they began to understand, to forgive, and even to take pleasure in the expansion which they had once denounced. Henry Clay declared in 1850 that America's territorial magnitude commanded the respect if not the awe of other powers; [17] Secretary of State Webster forced this magnitude upon Austria's attention in the boastful despatch which won at least the applause of his countrymen.[18] Americans in general, then, entered the 'fifties with the consciousness of recent territorial growth as one of the salient elements of their pride. Their country, however, still seemed in the light of some subjective criterion to be young and in the growth of youth. The first years of the 'fifties witnessed the emergence of the Democratic group which called itself " Young

America" and justified a perilously "progressive" domestic and foreign policy by the doctrine that "you cannot put down what is natural and ought to exist."[19]

It was after the political resurgence of expansionist Democracy in 1852 that the doctrine of natural growth first came into widespread use and influence. That it became popular was doubtless due primarily to the fact that it obscured the unpleasant aspect of the now entirely conscious land-hunger as completely as a Whitmanian epigram denying all evil in the body. But the more immediate cause of this popularity was the formulation of the doctrine of natural growth on December 1, 1852, in one of the most discussed diplomatic documents of the period. Its author, Edward Everett, the Secretary of State succeeding Webster in the Fillmore administration, was curiously a member of the generally anti-expansionist Whig party.

After Everett became Secretary of State it was one of his first duties to answer the proposals of Great Britain and France that the United States join them in a tripartite convention of permanent self-abnegation with respect to the acquisition of Cuba. Here was a *contretemps* for even an anti-expansionist administration. For though the Whig regarded the annexation of Cuba as "fraught with serious peril,"[20] he also saw the political peril to himself in renouncing the island for all eternity at a time when many approved even the filibusterer's efforts to acquire it immediately. Everett steered between Scylla and Charybdis by an answer which at the same time disclaimed any expansionist intention and refused to enter into the convention. Everett gave numerous political reasons but then proceeded to develop at greatest length a reason not political but philosophical or biological. It was "the law of American growth and progress," or in more general terms, an expansive tendency described as being "as organic and vital in the youth of states as individual men."

Reference to this law was preceded by an appreciative survey of the history of American expansion. Because one acquisition followed another with an ease suggesting destiny more than human design, Everett thought it impossible

> . . . for any one who reflects upon the events glanced at in this note to

mistake the law of American growth and progress, or think it can be ultimately arrested by a convention like that proposed.

He further pointed out:

That a convention such as is proposed would be a transitory arrangement, sure to be swept away by the irresistible tide of affairs in a new country, is, to the apprehension of the President, too obvious to require a labored argument. The project rests on principles applicable, if at all, to Europe, where international relations are, in their basis, of great antiquity, slowly modified, for the most part, in the progress of time and events; and not applicable to America, which, but lately a waste, is filling up with intense rapidity, and adjusting on natural principles those territorial relations which, on the first discovery of the continent, were in a good degree fortuitous.[21]

As early as the 'twenties, a decade wherein his discourses were full of appreciation of the pioneer movement, Everett had spoken words which showed how the idea of unfulfilled "destinies" of "growth" gripped his hopeful imagination.[22] It is clear that from the beginning his idea of the inevitability of territorial expansion rested upon a faith in the speedy growth of population. Population was the "irresistible tide" which would overflow into adjacent territory, Americanize it, and eventually bring it peacefully into the Union. This interpretation seems confirmed by Everett's words in an oration of July 4, 1853:

The pioneers are on the way; who can tell how far and fast they will travel? Who, that compares the North America of 1753 . . . with the North America of 1853—with its twenty-two millions of European origin, and its thirty-one States . . . will dare to compute the time-table of our railway progress . . . ?[23]

Again, in a Senate speech of 1853 Everett declared that such geographical extension as was necessary would come about "in the natural progress of things"; meanwhile Americans should have a real, solid, substantial growth by "the simple peaceful increase of our population" as they fulfilled the injunction to be fruitful and multiply.[24] America's law of growth thus seemed to Everett the necessary correlation between the natural increase of population and extension of territory. Everett's conception was much like that which Sir John Seeley put forward when he identified "natural growth" with the "mere normal extension of the English race into other lands." [25] Seeley, however, recognized a fact which Everett overlooked — that in history this colonization by superfluous population has most frequently been distinct from the extension of sovereignty.

From the purely descriptive phase of the doctrine of growth we must pass now to its moral form, the view that natural growth is morally normal. For Everett implicitly espoused in regard to expansion a moral theory. It was the view that natural growth is expansion which takes place not through a grasping spirit but in accordance with the law of growth. Thus in his despatch on the tripartite convention he said approbatively that no word or deed of the President's would ever question Spain's title to Cuba, and in a later letter to Lord John Russell he disclaimed personal desire for Cuba. He told Russell that the purpose of his Cuban note was to dispel the European impression that America's rapid expansion had been due to "a grasping spirit on the part of the Government and its people." He wished to show that "our growth had been a natural growth; that our most important accessions of territory had taken place by great national transactions, to which England, France, and Spain had been parties, and in other cases by the operation of causes which necessarily influence the occupation and settlement of a new country, in strict conformity with the laws of nations and not in violation of it." [26] Such growth, Everett believed, would in the future as in the past arise from the irresistible movement of American population into undeveloped land. Everett's attitude toward territorial aggrandizement was thus paradoxical: he approved natural expansion but not expansionism, the grasping spirit which seeks for expansion.

We may gain greater light upon Everett's method of moral thought by viewing briefly its genealogy. A traditional moral method, as old at least as the fifth century B. C., was the deduction of moral standards from a "Nature" viewed as the objectification of divine reason. The derivation of moral lessons from nature was practiced in subsequent ages by thinkers as separated temporally and temperamentally as Aquinas and Walt Whitman. The former observed with conscious Aristotelianism that "those things which follow nature are best, for in every instance nature operates best." [27] The latter was unconsciously Aristotelian when he held up as model "the politics of Nature." [28] Followers of nature have operated with so many phases of the natural universe that Friedrich Nicolai affirmed the idea of nature to be a Jack-of-all-trades and Professor Lovejoy has distinguished among its uses more than five dozen distinct meanings.

But an aspect of nature in which sermons have been read with particular frequency is animate nature, the antithesis to stone and brook. An early example of the use of organic instinct as a moral criterion is Justinian's dictum that the law of nature is that which nature has taught to all animals, not to the human species alone.[29] In the nineteenth century the popularization of biological science gave rise to a type of moral philosopher who believed that, "man's place in organic nature being determined, it would then be possible to formulate the nature of human good in organic terms, and thus to find standards for judging human behavior which are, so to speak, embedded in the nature of things." [30] Like these optimistic moralists Everett identified the natural with that which conforms to the standards in organic nature. Because growth is the most conspicuous feature of animate nature, national expansion seemed good. But because the growth of nature appears to be undeliberate, expansion seemed good only if coming about through causes almost as independent of human volition as is the growth of the body. Such interpretations merely rationalized, to be sure, the predispositions of Everett's own conservative temperament.

But as we resume our historical narrative we meet a development which was far from confirming Everett's theory of the natural processes of America's future growth. This development, though doubtless highly repugnant to Everett, was unintentionally assisted by him through his doctrine of the law of growth. His note kindled American nationalism in seeming (as the *Southern Quarterly Review* asserted) "the first distinct assertion of our position as the leading power of the western world." [31] More than this, it intensified the very expansionism which Whigs in the last presidential campaign had sought valiantly to lessen. Attention was not paid to Everett's disclaimer of territorial ambition but merely to the fact that he had laid down to foreign governments the law — the irresistible law of America's growth. No other document, Stephen Douglas declared, " ever received such a universal sanction of the American people " as this one showing such keen perception of the " destiny of the nation." [32] It was applauded because the conception of a law of growth seemed to be a new and scientific version of the idea of manifest destiny, that optimistic necessitarianism in which, as Representative Latham said, Americans were then regularly educated.[33] Senator Mallory declared Everett's despatch " the most ' manifest destiny ' document that ever emanated from the State Department." [34] Almost the only unpleasant note in the reception of the document came from Europe. Lord John Russell commented with terse sarcasm on the length and unusual character of the discourse in which Everett had been naïve enough to abandon his philosophic reserve.

But the unkindness of Russell was surely not so perturbing to Everett as was the appreciation of his countrymen. As is frequently the case in the history of ideas, his intellectual child was like the human children who get beyond the control of the parent and take directions which bring him to grief. The perversion of meaning on which most of the appreciation rested became apparent as soon as the Senate discussed the Everett correspondence in the debates on the Clayton-Bulwer Treaty and European colonization in America. Senator Soulé, though meaning to praise Everett for pointing out " the law of progress " in American history, much more probably insulted him in declaring that there was much of filibustering in his note. It seemed to Soulé that when the time came, " neither the surges of the sea, nor her forts, nor her garotes, nor the edicts of her Galianos " would save Cuba for Spain from " our mighty grasp." [35] Senator Mallory interpreted Everett's despatch as indicating the " vigorous march of Young America upon these continents." [36] The acquisition of Cuba would in his opinion soon become a political necessity to this nation;

and though the mighty and peaceful "progress" which Everett had described would eventually bring that country into the American democracy, America must meanwhile regulate her policy by the maxim that heaven helps those who help themselves.[37] Senator Butler believed that when America had been indurated with growth it would not refrain from acquiring any adjacent territory.[38] Senator Cass, thanking Everett for his reproof to an officious European diplomacy, proclaimed that "manifest destiny" made immobility or circumscription of expansion impossible and required America to be "progressive" till her great objects were accomplished.[39] Senator Douglas drew from Everett's law of growth the most radical implication, one provoking a bitter condemnation from the Whig *National Intelligencer*. He envisaged this imperious law of growth as breaking the fetters which any number of treaties might place upon the expansion of the giant Republic. It was folly, therefore, to make treaties pledging abstention from Mexican territory or abnegation of designs upon Central America. Douglas declared that the "laws of progress which have raised us from a mere handful to a mighty nation" would continue to govern America's action and compel it to follow the course of its destiny southward.[40]

The expansionist utterances of the Senate debates were followed by President Pierce's statement in his inaugural address that the policy of his administration would "not be controlled by any timid forebodings of evil from expansion." [41] By this time the conception of America's law of growth had been so much associated with good that the Washington *Union*, reputed Administration organ, interpreted Pierce's prospective expansion policy to its readers by reference to this principle. His inaugural speech was credited with showing "a recognition of the law of our national growth" in that it affirmed "as a great good, and as in no sense a peril or an evil, the unchangeable law and the inevitable tendency of our territorial growth." [42] About the same time an article in the *United States Review* declared without intention of insulting the President that whether Americans' foreign affairs "are directed by a sot or a simpleton they will continue to grow and expand by a law of nature and a decree of Providence."[43]

As the Gadsden Treaty of 1853 acquiring Mexican territory showed, the law of growth from which Everett had deduced the policy of masterly inactivity was subsequently interpreted by most Democrats as implying deliberate expansionist efforts. The explanation of this fact may take its departure from the consideration that certain ideas are combinations of two things —a method of thought and an implication derived by that method. Although the progenitor of such an idea usually overlooks the fact, the method of thought can be used by others to deduce different implications more congenial to their desire. This deflection was particularly easy with a method of thought so flexible as the teleological interpretation of nature.

Whereas Everett had in view the relative effortlessness of natural growth, others could point out that in a different aspect natural growth is not effortless at all. Even if making no deliberate effort to grow, the organism does have an impulse toward those activities upon which healthy growth is largely dependent. Thus it will strive desperately if need be for nourishment. The need of nourishment for natural growth is an implicit theme in the Senate report of 1859 advocating the purchase of Cuba:

> The law of our national existence is growth. We cannot, if we would, disobey it. While we should do nothing to stimulate it unnaturally, we should be careful not to impose upon ourselves a regimen so strict as to prevent its healthful development.[44]

The report went on to observe that the tendency of the age was the expansion of the great powers of the world by " the absorption of weaker powers generally inferior." The international phenomenon corresponding to the process of nourishment was thus taken to be the digestive absorption of other countries.

There was another way of deducing the implication of expansionist effort from the doctrine of natural growth. It was pointed out that the growth of the species depends not merely upon nourishment but also upon the healthful exercise which speeds the circulation and develops the body generally. That nature itself provides the instinct for this exercise seemed evident from the fact that there exists in man and beast a sportiveness, a love of activity for its own sake. Americans, for example, were so abundant in energy that they had not been wearied by the many enterprises of the 'forties but had derived from them increased zest. In 1850 a writer in *De Bow's Review,* predicting the fulfilment of America's manifest destiny in both Americas, observed that over the boundless field before us there brooded a power which "grows every day in energy." [45] In 1852 the expansionist Democratic platform called for a Union affording scope for "the full expansion of the energies and capacity of this great and progressive people." [46] Attorney-General Caleb Cushing, speaking in 1853 from the train of the new President, gave utterance to words which expressed by their own nervous rhythm as well as their logical content the high-strung energy of the age:

> This is now the United States—that colossus of power, that colossus of liberty, that colossus of the spirit of nations . . .
>
> He who is strong, who feels coursing in his veins the blood of maturity and vigor, needs action and must have action. It is the very necessity and condition of existence.[47]

As in the popular song of a more frivolous later age, there was thus the irrepressible urge, "Let's go places and do things!"

Doing things meant above all to the American of the 'fifties the exciting sport of extending the national boundaries. That Cushing himself identified action with expansion is indicated by a later observation in connection with the assertion that Mexico lay in the path of our destiny:

> Can you say to the tide that it ought not to flow, or the rain to fall? I reply, *it must!* And so it is with well-constituted, and, therefore, progressive and expansive nations. They cannot help advancing; it is the condition of their existence.[48]

Similarly, it appeared to the *Western Democratic Review,* political organ in the area where men were most fully men, that "expansion is almost a necessary condition of our existence." [49] Even more forcibly did James K. Paulding, in a letter congratulating Representative Quitman for his support of the filibusterers, express the same idea:

> I say, let the energy and enterprise of the people of the United States have their way, for that they will have whether you let them or not. In their expansion, they are but obeying the law of God and nature.[50]

Postulation of such a law was the main feature of the ideology which (together with less philosophical considerations of national interest and glory) made the 'fifties a decade of recurrent effort and constant declamation in expansionism. Had the restrained Everett's doctrine of natural growth developed into an undiscriminating naturalism? It had indeed developed into something which Everett abominated; yet it had one feature which saved it from being the indiscriminate passion suggested by Hobbes's "perpetual and restless desire of power after power." This feature is shown by the line of the Senate Cuban report which says that we must do nothing to stimulate the principle of growth "unnaturally." Thus, even this expansionism glorifying instinct was somewhat sicklied over by the pale cast of thought, the source of a discrimination between natural and unnatural growth.

However, one subscribing to Adam Ferguson's thesis that all human actions are equally the result of nature may ask how any expansion can be unnatural. Although it is difficult or impossible to give an answer satisfactory to a logician, one can easily imagine the answer which satisfied the expansionists themselves. Like all moralists who use nature as norm, they distinguished between the full content of nature, in which even Aristotle admitted monstrosities, and that part in which they seemed to see intelligent design. The organic norm was identified with nature sober, not with nature drunk. Nature meant that which *phusis* denoted in the Hippocratic medical writings — the *healthy* functioning of an organism. Truly natural growth was therefore normal growth as opposed to elephantiasis. Though Everett's conception that natural growth excluded deliberate expansionism had been rejected, there remained the idea, one implying a degree of free will, that expansionist effort was to be limited to the lines which nature indicated.

Thus unlike the instinctively acting lower species, expansionists sought to formulate and pursue a method of natural expansion. The method of expansion raises logically three issues: the when, the how, and the where. Upon all these issues, it seemed to expansionists, nature offered its guidance in living characters too plain to be misunderstood. An interesting question is whether they all understood nature in the same way.

One may consider first the fundamental question of the time or occasion of expansion. A common answer to this question held that expansion was natural growth when it was dictated by political necessity. Even Everett, though discountenancing expansionist effort generally, admitted that the possibility of an "overruling necessity of self-preservation" forbade permanent renunciation of Cuba.[51] Interpreting "overruling necessity" more liberally than did Everett, expansionists affirmed that we were overruled already. Thus their argument for the acquisition of Cuba was its necessity not only to the Slave States but also to national security. Its acquisition, declared the Senate report which used the doctrine of natural growth, was "a fixed purpose of the United States, a purpose resulting from political and geographical necessities."[52] In the Ostend Manifesto three American diplomats affirmed with physiological metaphor that Cuba was "as necessary to the North American republic as any of its present members," and implied further that its continued possession by Spain might endanger national self-preservation in view of Spain's policy on slavery.[53] A different kind of necessity, however, was implicit in the formulation of the law of growth by Stephen Douglas and others. Like the later Bernhardi, Douglas stressed the healthy nation's need of territory for growing population: "This is a young, vigorous, and growing nation, must obey the law of increase, must multiply, and as fast as we multiply we must expand."[54] One couldn't resist this "law of our existence" if one tried, according to Douglas.[55] A general thesis relating expansion to political necessity was stated in terms of the law of growth by Senator Pugh as follows: "Mr. President, the expansion of our Federal system, as one emergency after another shall require, is the law of our development; it is the sign of our national vitality; the pledge of our national endurance." [56]

Why did it seem that expansion was natural when politically necessary? The answer apparently lies in the conception of growth in nature as purposeful, designed for either the preservation or the healthful development of the species. Expansionists desiring Cuba sometimes followed the authors of the Ostend Manifesto in quoting the ancient adage that self-preservation is the first law of nature. At other times, as in the Senate Cuban report of 1859, they affirmed that Cuba was "necessary to the progressive development of our system." [57] Thus a territorial acquisition was conceived to be as essential to the healthful development of a political system as is the growth of a vital member to that of the individual species.

However, it is very questionable whether there was any political necessity for expansion in the 'fifties. The implication of the Ostend Manifesto that conditions in Cuba menaced the nation's self-preservation was repudiated by Secretary of State Marcy himself. Talk of need of territory for population was even more remote from present realities than it had been in the 'forties. The contrast between America's already vast resources and its luxuriant ambitions gave the anti-expansionist reasonable ground for charging: "Nor are we motivated by any motives of political necessity, but it is said to be our manifest destiny to annex all the territory that is near us and a great deal that is not." [58]

Perhaps those who spoke of necessity were subconsciously influenced by a doctrine which confused political necessity with a kind of biological destiny. In any event others adopted consciously the theory that the law of growth dictated expansionist effort not merely when it was politically necessary but virtually all the time. Such a doctrine was intimated in the Senate Cuban report of 1859. With respect to the expansion of European powers the report generously acknowledged:

> In this they are but obeying the laws of their organization. When they cease to grow they will soon commence that period of decadence which is the fate of all nations as of individual man.[59]

Senator Collamer referred to this passage in denying that the authors of the Ostend Manifesto and President Buchanan really believed the possession of Cuba essential politically to the United States. The necessity to which they alluded was, he declared, that "we must take it, or we commence dying." [60] It is true in any event that just such a notion was expressed or intimated in many documents of the time besides the report cited. A writer in the *United States Democratic Review* of 1859 argued for the acquisition of Cuba as follows:

> We are governed by the laws under which the universe was created; and therefore, in obedience to those laws, we must of necessity move forward in the paths of destiny shaped for us by the great Ruler of the Universe. Activity and progress is the law of heaven and of earth; and in the violation of this law there is danger.[61]

The *New York Herald* specified the danger as it exhorted:

> National glory—national greatness—the spread of political liberty on this continent, must be the thought and action by day, and the throbbing dream by night, of the whole American people, or they will sink into oblivion . . . [62]

Others, however, thought that there was no choice. An expansionist Congressman reached the height of spread-eagleism with the exclamation that it was "no more possible for this country to pause in its career than it is for the free and untrammeled eagle to cease to soar." [63] Frank Soulé in his *Annals of San Francisco* declared it "the fate of America ever to 'go ahead'" even though the "morality of the various steps in the fated pilgrimage . . . may be dubious." [64] The biographer of Governor Quitman of Mississippi defended the latter's filibustering proclivities as follows:

> We proceed upon the theory that the condition of a republic is repose. What an error! That is the normal condition of absolutism. The law of a republic is progress. Its nature is aggressive. It is founded on the conflagration of ancient and polluted things, and it must have play and action on surrounding nations, or, like Saturn, devour its own offspring.[65]

The fear of America's devouring its own offspring probably reflects the apprehension of internal conflict over slavery. The advocates of activity hoped to avert this conflict by deflection of national energies into either expansion or a vigorous foreign policy such as Seward suggested to Lincoln on the very eve of the Civil War. This doctrine of natural growth was thus in part the result of the abnormal political situation which, like a diseased physical condition, made repose painful and perturbing.

However, that this idea of natural growth had also an intrinsic persuasiveness is indicated by the long influence which it has enjoyed in the history of thought. Machiavelli justified territorial expansion by the same idea: "But as all human things are kept in a perpetual movement, and can never remain stable, states naturally either rise or decline, and necessity compels them to many acts to which reason will not influence them . . ."[66] Similarly, Algernon Sidney said that the city like the child must "grow" or "perish."[67] Still later came the observation of Humboldt to which the American, William Greenough, alluded in *The Conquering Republic* as follows: "To this people applies with peculiar force, the observation of Humboldt: 'It is with nations as with nature which knows no pause in progress and development, and attaches her curse on all inaction.'"[68]

Undeniably the aspect of nature to which the believers in perpetual motion referred is as real as that envisaged by those limiting expansion to occasions of political necessity. For though the growth of the species seems purposeful (as the latter maintain), it is accomplished by a physiological activity which, whether external or internal, is unceasing. Each of the two conflicting doctrines regarding the occasion for expansion seems equally in accord with a two-faced nature.

From this logically unsatisfying speculation we turn to the second issue of natural growth, the manner of expansion. Should the acquisition of territory take place by peaceful methods or war? Everett pointed the way to the interpretation of natural growth as peaceful. The United States had enlarged its dimensions, he said, "by the arts of peace and the healthful progress of things."[69] Though this statement scarcely applied to the recent Mexican War, many Democrats professed concurrence with the recommendation in Pierce's inaugural address to expand in "a manner entirely consistent with the strictest observance of national faith." [70] Pierce's inaugural pronouncement was praised by the influential Washington *Daily Union* not only for its recognition of the law of our national growth, but also for its admission that even this law was "strictly subordinate to the paramount obligation of national justice and faith." [71] The *Union* also praised Pierce's annual message of 1853 because it both emphasized the ideal of expansion and identified it with "natural, legitimate, and safe progress." [72] This paper believed that only if "honorable and peaceful" would the acquisition of Cuba be "in manifest harmony with the whole law . . . of American progress." [73] Similarly, the *Richmond Enquirer* observed in 1855 that American expansion had resulted from unchangeable "laws of nature" rather than aggression.[74] So great was the confidence of the *United States Review* in "the laws of Nature" that it believed that the American people, far from requiring spasmodic efforts for the attainment of power, would "conquer North America in their bedchambers." [75] Again, it deduced peaceful policy from the consideration that empires "grow outward like the rings of an oak, by an irresistible expansion and accretion." [76]

What was the biological rationale of this ideal of peaceful expansion? It is suggested by Representative Latham's observation that "the laws of nature . . . are silent and secret, not boisterous and noisy, by fits and starts." [77] It is also revealed by C. J. Ingersoll's contrast between conquest and America's "spontaneous, natural, and tranquil accretions." [78] Still more illuminating are the words of Parke Godwin in a book of 1854:

> Precisely, however, because this tendency to the assimilation of foreign ingredients, or to the putting forth of new members, is an inevitable incident of our growth . . . there is no need that it should be especially fostered or stimulated. It will thrive of itself; it will supply the fuel of its own fires; and all that it requires is only a wise direction. . . . The fruit will fall into our hands when it is ripe, without an officious shaking of the tree. Cuba will be ours, and Canada and Mexico, too—if we want them—in due season, and without the wicked imperative of a war.[79]

In other words, peaceful growth seems natural in that it comes about through gradual and tranquil processes such as those of the growth of the body.

Despite this pacific interpretation of the law of growth, the spirit of the 'fifties was largely that foreshadowed by a writer of 1850 in *De Bow's Review*: "The military spirit of the country . . . is rife for anything . . ." [80] The least frivolous expression of the martial spirit was the proposal to seize Cuba forcibly as a matter of self-preservation. This, the method considered in the Ostend Manifesto, could be justified by a biological ethics which in abstract form might have appealed even to the pacific Everett. If self-preservation be the first law of nature it is equally true that, as one expansionist Congressman ominously proclaimed, "necessity knows no law." [81]

However, the argument of self-preservation was obviously irrelevant to many ambitions which were aired in this decade. There were some, like Representative Cox, who called upon the Government to apply a policy of aggressive intervention in all the lands to the south. But the method chiefly proposed by the advocates of force was exemplified by the *Democratic Review:* though believing that the Government should remain above aggression, it called upon private enterprise to initiate and accomplish aggression through "the exuberance of its strength and its superfluous wealth and spirit." [82]

The decade was actually enlivened by the private encroachment called filibustering. Mexico, Nicaragua, and Cuba all felt the tread of impetuous American filibusterers, bands of ambitious and romantic individuals who, despite the neutrality laws of their country, attempted daringly the overturn of backward tropical governments. William Walker, colorful filibusterer, called "the grey-eyed man of destiny," succeeded for a time in maintaining his revolutionary government in Nicaragua and planned the forcible acquisition of a Central American empire. It was the general though erroneous opinion that Walker contemplated the annexation of Nicaragua to the United States. Although the discrete Government looked askance upon such escapades, more than a few Americans, some of them legislators and governors, viewed with approbation the lawless efforts of their adventurous countrymen, and even urged the suspension of the neutrality laws. A writer who described filibustering as "wars of conquest waged by the strong against the weak, with little or no provocation," thought, as did numerous others, that there was "a 'manifest destiny' . . . in this (so-called) filibustering movement of America" which would spread American civilization through benighted regions.[83]

Although it appeared to President Buchanan that "the natural course" of fulfilling American destiny in Central America was peaceful emigration,[84] filibustering seemed to many to accord with natural laws which had long determined the relations of unequal races. Thus William Walker himself justified his course as follows:

> That which you ignorantly call 'Filibusterism' is not the offspring of hasty passion or ill-regulated desire; it is the fruit of the sure, unerring instincts which act in accordance with laws as old as creation. They are but drivellers who speak of establishing fixed relations between the pure white American race, as it exists in the United States, and the mixed Hispano-Indian race, as it exists in Mexico and Central America, without the employment of force. The history of the world presents no such Utopian vision as that of an inferior race yielding meekly and peacefully to the controlling influence of a superior people.[85]

Accepting this same philosophy of history, Mr. Hofer of Virginia wrote in *De Bow's Review* that Walker was "an involuntary instrument in the hands of an unchangeable fate," which he identified with both natural law and America's manifest destiny.[86] A writer in the *Democratic Review* affirmed the recession or disappearance of the inferior before the superior races to be sanctioned by "analogy."[87] A writer in *De Bow's Review* supposed the sanction of the conquest or even of the extermination of inferior races to be a "natural law" promoting the development of civilization.[88] The biographer of Governor Quitman, legal defender of Walker, supplied the most original justification of conquest when he said that it was essential to the "internal repose" of a people "in the restless period of youth."[89] Even in Congress there were expressions of this philosophy of rugged imperialism. Representative Cox, urging in 1859 a protectorate over Mexico and the acquisition of certain Mexican provinces, formulated the "inevitable" law that "the weaker and disorganized nations must be absorbed by the strong and organized." [90] Houston affirmed the same principle in the Senate in connection with a prophecy of Anglo-Saxon dominion over Central America and even territory beyond.[91]

This grim type of inference from nature dated back at least to Dionysius, who proclaimed "a law of nature common to all, which no time will ever destroy, that the stronger always rule over the weak." [92] In the nineteenth century these ancient words were reincarnated in the historian Mommsen's assertion that a universally valid "law of nature" compelled a superior people to absorb its neighbors who are in intellectual nonage.[93] The organismic political thought of this century was reflected in Adam Müller's assertion that the condition of war was as natural for the state as was that of peace.[94] The study of evolution which Darwin published in 1859 suggested to many — though not to the more cautious Darwin himself — not only that strife is a part of "the natural history of mankind" [95] but also that "the survival of the fittest seems to be the law of nations as well as the law of nature." [96]

The biological rationale of the tough-minded expansionists is epitomized by the American slogan of commercial refinement, "Nature in the raw is seldom mild." That the proposition is true of nature in one aspect can scarcely be denied. For growth, as Dr. Powers was to say in the 'nineties, sooner or later means conflict.[97] Species live and grow amid a violent struggle not only for existence but also for enhanced well-being. The peaceful process of physiological growth receives its nutriment from the spoils of belligerent competition, the severity of which in the realm of human life is increased by the will to power. These considerations mean not that the pacifist interpretation is wrong but merely that the oracle of nature was again equivocal.

There remains, however, the question of the "where" of expansion. In this issue nature as biological process and nature as territory were subject to the easy confusion which one sees even today in the German political speculation calling itself "*Geopolitik*." The idea of the natural boundary thus influenced the statements of the law of growth by both Everett and the Senate Cuban report. The former spoke of the adjustment of political relations on the continent according to natural principles and made it clear that geographically Cuba was an American question. The authors of the Senate report affirmed that as long as America's growth was justified by geographical position no fault was to be found with it. From this viewpoint Seward found fault with Great Britain's deviations from her hemisphere but attributed our own ambitions in America to the prompting of "nature." [98] It seemed quite clear that only Americans could expand naturally in America.

From the practical viewpoint, however, the important question was that of the direction in which America's expansion in her own hemisphere was prompted by nature. One theory harmonized suspiciously with the desire of the South for slavery extension in the tropics. Southern expansionists, however, could support their inclination by the theory of natural law exemplified in the statement of Representative Evans of Texas that history showed a "natural tendency of populations to expand in a southern direction," that is, toward a warmer climate. It seemed to Evans that a demand upon Americans to cease southward expansion was "simply demanding that they should change the constitution of their nature and reverse the everlasting laws of liberty and even of animal life." [99] But Americans of other sections also desired to go southward and affirmed the naturalness of the direction. Thus the annexation of Mexico was called for by the *United States Review* as being in the order of "the regular growth" of the Republic.[100] Similarly it seemed to the *Western Democratic Review* that "in no other direction can the God Terminus so naturally continue his march as toward the capital of Mexico." [101] The law governing the progress of the Anglo-Saxon race appeared to Commodore Stockton to dictate a southern direction by virtue of the fact that the westward march of empire had met resistance from the ocean.[102] Such observations were apparently influenced by the idea that in growth and movement nature takes the line of least resistance.

A different theory of the direction of natural growth commended itself to the Northerners who saw in southward expansion the extension of the abnormality of slavery. They felt that (to quote the *New York Herald*) British North America was "our natural and most necessary complement."[103] One consideration underlying this belief is revealed by Senator Bell's reference to the bodies of water which "nature has formed for a ready and direct communication and navigation for the commerce of the northern territory to the ocean."[104] The idea of natural growth is in this case determined by that doctrine of the natural boundary which conceives inland waters as a territorial nexus. Probably a still more important influence was the conception expressed by Senator Bell when he said that Canadians were bone of our bone, and people whose addition to the Republic would add "strength and vigor to the body-politic."[105] Natural growth seems here to be associated with a homogeneous increment rather than an alien ingraftment. The same thought appeared in Herder's observation that since a nationality was a "plant of nature," the most natural state was "one nationality with one national character."[106]

A divergence prevailed also in the issue of eastward versus westward expansion. Those interested in safeguarding the institution of slavery posited the naturalness of the southeastern extension which would add Cuba to the United States. This adjacent territory, the Ostend Manifesto declared, "belongs naturally" to the American family of States.[107] Desiring to utilize "the natural and least costly routes of trade and increase," even the Northerner John Thrasher held that the question of the acquisition of Cuba "involves the question whether we shall follow the paths of development which nature has provided for us."[108] His underlying idea was apparently that stated by Everett — that the acquisition of Cuba would be "in the natural order of things"[109] because the island was "a natural appendage to our continent."[110] The idea derived from the impression that, growth in nature being continuous, natural empires are those with "limits of continuity."[111]

Yet there were those who looked not to the Atlantic but to the western ocean for America's natural expansion. For more than a few felt a keen interest in Marcy's attempt to annex distant Hawaii, which unlike Cuba could scarcely appear as a natural appendage of the North American continent. And Seward, who in the subsequent decade showed official interest in Hawaii's annexation, related America's progress upon the Pacific no less than that upon the continent to its law of growth. In the Senate debate of 1854 on the mail line to China, he suggested that America's past expansion, which seemed ever to tend toward commerce and influence in the Pacific Ocean, had been shaped not so much by a self-guiding wisdom of our own as by " a law of progress and development impressed upon us by nature herself." [112] The *Illinois State Register* called unequivocally for the annexation of Hawaii as a territory placed by nature within our reach.[113] To a writer on Hawaii in *De Bow's Review* it seemed similarly that America's preponderance in the Pacific was " a natural sequence " of the annexation of California and Oregon.[114] To others it seemed a natural sequence of the broader movement noted by Bishop Berkeley in the poetic line which they endlessly quoted: " Westward the course of empire takes its way." [115] In 1856 E. L. Magoon's curious book entitled *Westward Empire* drew the conclusion that " all healthful expansion and improvement is ' out West ' " from the premise that " by a natural movement, in not one of its great elements has civilization gone eastward an inch since authentic history began." [116] The naturalness of the movement was suggested not merely by an oversimplification of history but perhaps also by the consideration that natural expansion like the growth of nature must continue in the dominant direction of the past. By this ingenious reasoning, which might just as well have justified the annexation of China, advocates of westward expansion controverted the argument that since Hawaii is not a part of the American continents it did not lie within America's natural boundaries.

The sum of the matter is that in every issue of expansion there was a curious disagreement with regard to the implication of nature for policy. More curious than divergences of political motive was the fact that every aspect of nature counselling one course was controverted by some other aspect equally real and suggestive. This indeterminateness in the criteria of natural growth augured poorly for any restraint in expansion.

Ultimately, however, restraint was imposed by a force more potent than moral logic. The Civil War deflected all energies from expansion as Americans fought to avoid national dissolution. Until the very eve of this scission, as Senator Corwin sardonically pointed out, there were those who talked of growth.[117] Despite the pretension of the 'fifties to Herculean vitality, the cancer of the "irrepressible conflict" had grown throughout the decade and infused into the expansionist's enthusiasm the fever of illness. It is an ironical fact that a major cause of the war between the States was nothing other than expansionism. For territorial ambitions raised the issue of the sectional balance of power and thus lent fuel to the mutual fear and distrust. A Spenglerian witness of the resultant catastrophe might have felt that, in the words of *The Decline of the West,* "the expansive tendency is a doom" — "the typical symbol of the passing away." [118]

What was the biological expansionist's belief in regard to the awesome contingency of national death? It might seem that the logic of his own doctrine necessitated the acknowledgment that national decline and death ensue with inexorable determinism upon growth. Precedents for this admission were Rousseau's declaration that dissolution was "the natural and unavoidable tendency of even the best constituted governments" [119] and Ernst von Lasaulx's morbid obsession with the thought that "nations, no less than individuals, must in the course of nature die of age." [120] Among American expansionists, also, the authors of the Senate Cuban report acknowledged at least that "decadence" was the "inevitable fate of all nations as of individual man." But apparently they dated America's decline so far in the future that it gave no more concern than did the eventual day of judgment.

Nor did any of those attached to the Union appear to deduce from the biological doctrine America's actual death. Only to nations of the past, a writer in the *Democratic Review* hoped, could one apply the Persian epitome of the life of nations, "They were born, they were wretched, they died." [121] As for

America, the Venetian's "*Esto perpetua*" could be converted into a dogma of immortality. The ordinary American nationalist would not brook even the complimentary question of the French statesman, "If such is the youth of that republic, what will be its old age?" Senator Cass's answer was: "Sir, it will have no old age."[122] America would forever be "Young America," a Peter Pan refuting the alleged fate of senescence.

The explanation of this superb hopefulness does not lie entirely in the American nationalist's inability to follow even his own logic to an unpleasant conclusion. For just as Jefferson had once supposed America unique in its physics, so the expansionists posited with reference to the United States a unique biology devoid of death. Americans believed with Berkeley that their country was "Time's noblest offspring," a land "where nature guides" in all its virtue.[123] This conception was tantamount to the proposition that America's physical and moral vitality was an unprecedented organic phenomenon. A writer in the *United States Review* confidently affirmed that the United States contained in proportion to numbers "a greater mass of physical strength and activity than is to be found in any other people."[124] In the same magazine a believer in the moral uniqueness of American democracy defended even more exaltedly the conception of America's peculiar historic rôle:

> Unfold the whole scroll of history and show us the nation which, from its cradle to its manhood, has bristled so ceaselessly at every step with the movements of the electric machinery of Divine Providence. Our history was borrowed from none of the stereotyped forms of national life in the elder world. It began alone—it exists alone.[125]

Thus in one respect the doctrine of natural growth reflected not the biological conception of uniformity but the metaphysical idea of one nation's special destiny.

To the optimistic philosopher of manifest destiny, however, even the skeptic might sometimes say, "Almost thou persuadest me." For the Civil War was marvelously survived, the malignant growth of slavery was removed, and health quickly returned. A few years after the war some like Senator Stewart were already urging new annexations on the ground that expansion was as natural an element in the nation's growth as is the enlargement of trunk in the growth of the oak.[126]

About three decades later the desire for oversea expansion had become general and with it the conception that the growth of America's commerce made adherence to continental limits unnatural for any national species of amphibian character. Despite the fact that for three decades America had been healthy without expansion, the Washington *Star* declared that the United States could not be healthy if it now stood still territorially, nations like individuals being confronted always with the alternative of growth or decay.[127] Representative Gibson, portraying America as a growing youth which must take unhealthy exercise if not healthy, added theology to biology in saying that " when God made us a nation, He gave us the right to grow." [128] More influential than theology, however, was the now popularized evolutionism which, with its misinterpreted concepts of race and struggle for existence, was universally " contributing to imperial expansion the force of popular ideas, the justification of accepted conclusions." [129]

Whereas the annexation of Hawaii had seemed natural as early as the 'fifties, the demand of Americans of 1898 for the Philippines repudiated the one criterion of natural growth upon which all expansionists of the 'fifties had agreed. It was the principle of propinquity which made a meridian of partition through the ocean a *ne plus ultra.* American anti-imperialists of 1898, adopting the same criterion, could use the doctrine of natural growth in reverse. Albert Heston Coggins thus maintained that the imperialist " makes the fatal mistake of overlooking Nature's supremest law " — that a nation " must grow just as an individual — just as a plant." [130] Similarly, E. V. Long affirmed that whereas past expansion was " a natural growth " in arising from " the natural spread " of population, aggrandizement through coercion was " an excrescence upon the body politic." [131]

Imperialists, however, believed that the distant expansion of the world power was demanded by America's very entrance upon unconfined manhood. Senator Platt thus held the incorporation of the Philippines to be no exception to the statement that "every expansion of our territory has been in accordance with the irresistible law of growth." [132] Whitelaw Reid maintained that, just as a tree which stops growing is ready for the ax, so a nation which sets limits to its development "has passed the meridian of its course." [133] Before the learned American Academy of Political and Social Science the expansionistic Professor Powers drew from "the well-known biological principle that growth is a necessary consequence of life and . . . without it life cannot possibly persist" a sensational inference. It was that, like every other people, Americans "want the earth, — not consciously as a formulated program, but instinctively." [134]

The biological philosophy of such imperialists represents an abandonment of any attempt at restrictive criteria of natural growth. *All* growth now seemed to many to be natural growth. This is a conclusion which the expansionists of the 'fifties had not accepted but which one of them had at least foreshadowed. It was Stephen Douglas, who had said that "a young nation . . . desires no limits fixed to her greatness, no boundaries to her future growth." [135] The principle that all growth is natural could seem in accord with the fact that youth appropriates all nutriment and exercise to the progress of growth. To the British Seeley it appeared to accord also with the natural phenomenon of "the acorn spreading into the huge oak, that has hundreds of branches and thousands of leaves." His question, "Is there anything necessarily unnatural in the . . . view, that the State is capable of indefinite growth and expansion?" [136] would have been answered by many American as well as British imperialists in the negative.

The doctrine of natural growth reached its full logical development only to sink shortly afterward, in the manner of some matured species, into decline. For when the emotion of expansionism died down at the turn of the century, the doctrine that territorial expansion is natural growth rapidly lost its intellectual appeal. To the extent that the biological norm persisted it took chiefly the more moderate form stated by Captain Mahan in his work of 1900 urging America's expansion of influence and commerce in Asia: namely, that though "growth is a property of healthful life," it does not "necessarily imply increase of size for nations" but only "the right to insure by just means whatever contributes to national progress."[137] To be sure, there were some few who read sympathetically Homer Lea's assertion that the boundaries of political units must always "either expand or shrink."[138] Again, the magazine of the Navy League sponsored Edward Finlay's dictum that, since world empire is "only logical and natural" for a nation, "the proper diet for a nation or State is land."[139] And as late as 1916 the still land-hungry *Independent* asserted that "to say that henceforth the United States shall cease growing seems to us as foolish as it is wicked."[140] But after the purchase of the Virgin Islands had satisfied an apparent strategic necessity the Wilsonian doctrine of ceasing growth was credited more and more with wisdom and virtue. Perhaps the interpretation of nature was affected by the appetite. In any event, after the subsidence of land-hunger territorial growth no longer seemed "natural."

However, the doctrine of natural growth continued in the twentieth century to encourage European imperialists, whose biological notions have doubtless seemed either shocking or incomprehensible to most modern Americans. General Scharnhorst, teacher of German officers, thus appealed for militant nationalism in the words: "Moral forces are never static; they inevitably sink and decay if they stop developing."[141] The outbreak of the World War gave rise to such observations as that of the author of *Deutscher Imperialismus*: "We have but one choice: to grow or to decline."[142] Violation of Belgian neutrality seemed an application of the German Chancellor's previous dictum that "the old truth still remains, that the weak are the prey of the strong."[143] The distinguished Friedrich Meinecke's work of 1924 on the principle of "reason of state" gave quasi-scientific justification to this "old truth" by affirming that an elemental and inexpugnable side of the state is of 'biologic" and therefore egoistic character.[144] The most notorious recent expression of this old conception of German thought is the pseudo-biological militarism of Adolph Hitler's *Mein Kampf,* which proclaims stridently the fundamental necessity for the " laws of nature " stipulating " battle and conflict." [145] This " dog-eat-dog " philosophy is not, of course, confined to any one country but seems rife among all peoples who believe that their country's needs or glories demand further growth. Indeed, Italy's virile dictator goes so far as to say that " every living being that has the will to live must have imperialistic tendencies." [146]

The wide and enduring appeal of biological imperialism is primarily due, however, not to the will to live, but to its sanction of those tougher and less scrupulous qualities without which it is very difficult today to satisfy the will to power. In part, indeed, the appeal of the doctrine of natural growth arises from a confusing characteristic of its logical organization. It consists of both a biological and a moral judgment, and thereby uses " natural law " in both a factual and a normative sense. Each judgment can thus support the other in an unconsciously circuitous reasoning. On the one hand, the doctrine that nations are endowed by nature with a tendency to grow invests expansion with an aspect of moral normality. On the other hand, the belief that expansion is morally normal promotes the view that a wise nature has established a law of national growth. This mutuality of support seems like collaboration between the blind and the dumb in that each element of the doctrine is in itself weak.

The proposition that the state is subject to a law of growth is an error which arises primarily from the assumption that the state is so much akin to individual organisms that " the conclusions of biology must be taken to be those of sociology as well." [147] But the ascription of organic character to the state confuses the purely legal unity of the state and the " real " or physiological unity of the individual organism. The adherents of the organismic theory are effectively criticized in the words of Francis Coker:

> To give meaning to their statement that the State is living, they should have determined the nature and action of the elementary political units in their relations to the genesis and life of the State. . . . A living thing is distinguished from a non-living thing radically through the nature and action of its elementary units in their relation to the genesis, growth, subsistence, and coherent action of the composite

which they constitute. Yet none of the theorists who have maintained that the State is a living organism have demonstrated any such rudimental similarity between the two objects which they thus associate.[148]

The doctrine of natural growth has been founded by others, to be sure, less on the organismic conception of the state than on the theory that its component members can find only in expansion a satisfaction of natural desires and energies. This narrow interpretation of human nature represents the distortion of psychology by psychobiological preconceptions. Expansionists would never have made such an assumption had they learned their lesson from Aristotle, one of the first to deduce political implications from nature. Though he taught that the state was formed in order to satisfy man's desires he also observed that it was not the nature of the good citizen to desire conquest. Though he recognized the need of action in political life he also pointed out that even isolated states may be active, inasmuch as " there may be activity also in the parts; there are many ways in which the members of a state act upon one another." [149] In the 'fifties, Senator Collamer developed this Aristotelian idea in his criticism of the " law of growth ":

> It goes upon the ground that nothing can be gained to the nation; that it can make no progress in national grandeur and greatness and power, unless it steals from its neighbors. I utterly deny that there is any such principle of national growth. A nation may grow in numbers, in wealth, in civilization, may grow for centuries, and never enlarge its territories one inch.[150]

Denial of the law of growth does not in itself, to be sure, invalidate the moral phase of the doctrine; for "*sequere naturam*" expresses not a law but an exhortation. Yet it is true for another reason, as social philosophers have come increasingly to realize, that " a moral politics cannot be based on mere adoration of natural processes." [151] What makes it impossible to follow nature has been shown rather strikingly by the data of this study. The surprising obstacle is nature itself.

For nature is " so full of a number of things " that anyone impartially observant does not know what to follow. What the believer in the doctrine follows is merely that aspect of nature which is selected from many others because it makes him happiest. Thus the criterion of nature was used to support expansionism and anti-expansionism, necessary expansion and unnecessary, peaceful aggrandizement and belligerent, adjacent extension and distant. The variety of deductions confirmed the words of a later biologist, Professor Conklin: "Those who are searching for biological analogies to support almost any preconceived theory in philosophy, are likely to find them."[152] The teleological interpretation of nature leads to all conclusions and therefore to no conclusion. With truth the ancient poet said:

> By naked Nature ne'er was understood
> What's Just and Right.[153]

# CHAPTER VIII

## POLITICAL GRAVITATION

Like a convalescent's impulse to leap from a bed of nearly mortal sickness, a resurgence of expansionism ensued directly upon the close of the Civil War and appeared in many individuals with a vigor greater than any of the past. Henry Adams noted contemporaneously that many expansionists were now sufficiently athletic to envisage as America's goal the acquisition not only of the North American continent but also of all adjacent islands.[1] Some had the great energy to aspire toward a southern boundary at Cape Horn.[2] Indeed, according to the classic anecdote of Fiske, a few Americans toasted their country's ultimate destiny with reference to the Aurora Borealis, the equinox, and other equidistant places as ultimate boundaries.[3] Ambition vaulting the stars might seem the logical culmination of the ever-growing pretensions of Democrats since the 'forties. The fact is, however, that now the foremost votaries of manifest destiny were not Democrats but the very Republicans and ex-Whigs who largely had opposed Democratic expansionism.

These turncoats had once opposed expansion because of their revulsion not only from slavery but also from the Southern expansionist's aggressiveness. The fact that their ambitions became more far-reaching than even those of the slavocracy, who had looked primarily toward the south, laid Republicans open to the charge of having the same aggressiveness. Thus a Democratic Congressman accused his opponents of attempting to wield the magic sword which King Arthur had laid down.[4]

However, the Republican expansionists denied not only any intention but any necessity of using imperialistic weapons. The fulfilment of their broad expansionist ambitions was ascribed to a quite different agency by a doctrine which permitted pacific humanitarians to take up the quest of manifest destiny without any sense of apostasy to their former ideals. This doctrine gave quasi-scientific sanction to the belief that other peoples of North America did not require the dictate of the sword, but in the course of natural law were "all coming" to the Union "as rapidly as we could wish." [5] The basis of this optimism was not the biological doctrine of the 'fifties; for this idea assumed a law of growth which if universal would cause every people to strive against rather than toward the extinction of its independence. With characteristic flexibility expansionists had turned from biology to physics as the science sustaining their hopes.

It was Newton's law of gravitation which seemed to lend its imposing authority to the justification of expansionist expectations and morals. The principle formulated by Newton as a universal law of matter was now extended to the psychically conditioned sphere of politics and enunciated as a law of nations, under the designation, "the law of political gravitation." From this law expansionists made the deduction that adjacent nations within the range of America's attraction would fall to the Union by a process as inevitable as that causing the ripe apple to fall to the earth.

No doctrine in the history of American expansionism was the source of firmer expectations and of more exalted moral sentiments than those which gathered about the principle of political gravitation. At the same time, no doctrine is more curious than this principle which attributes to the experience of nations, composed of human organisms, tendencies of behavior characteristic of inorganic matter. To understand how it could have appealed to some of the greatest figures of America's expansionist movement will require an analysis arduous but not unprofitable. For this very rationalization purporting to be scientific affords us the clearest insight into the nationalist's deviations from scientific ways of thinking — deviations not more curious from the standpoint of empirical method than they are natural in the light of nationalist hopes, egoisms, and moral aspirations.

While not the scion of science, the expansionist's doctrine possessed an old ideological ancestry which anticipated and perhaps partially determined its peculiarities. The oldest of its historical determinants was the tendency of monistic philosophers to conceive physical and mental phenomena as subject to the same laws. This tendency, dating back to early Greek philosophy, experienced an important revival in the rationalism of the eighteenth century. One of the sequels of this revival was the application of Newton's law to the sphere of social behavior. Such an application, by no means original with Americans, was first notably suggested by the French philosophy of the sociological school beginning with Saint-Simon. His apparently utopian ideal of establishing productive association through spiritual sympathy was supported by the hypothesis of a law of social behavior making its fulfilment not merely possible but probable. Believing the moral universe to be governed by the same laws as the physical, he conceived of Newton's law of gravitation as the fundamental force in social behavior and as explanatory of the tendency to social collaboration. Although Saint-Simon eventually admitted the failure of this attempt to introduce physical law into sociology, the atmosphere of his time, as the historian Flint points out, was full of ideas of this kind.[6] Saint-Simon's rival, Fourier, also deduced "the law of passional attraction" — as he called the central principle of social organization — from Newton's law of gravitation. The concept of a law of social attraction was familiarized to Americans by Fourier's disciple, Albert Brisbane, one of whose books was reviewed in 1840 in the prominent Democratic organ of John L. O'Sullivan.[7] In the same decade Emerson penned in his *Journals* words which interpret all the beneficent tendencies of natural human behavior in terms of gravitation:

> Gravitation is Nature's Grand Vizier and prime favorite. . . . In morals, again, Gravity is the *laissez-faire* principle, or Destiny, or Optimism, than which nothing is wiser or stronger.[8]

The traditional tendency to import gravitation into morals or social law was probably of some influence upon those whose hope of world reform lay in gravitational processes abetting America's manifest destiny.

Expansionists were doubtless influenced even more by previous application of the principle of gravitation in the sphere of international relations. In 1750 the French physiocrat Turgot, lecturing on the history of Phoenician colonization, made the following observation:

> Colonies are like fruits, which hold to the tree only until their maturity; when sufficient for themselves, they did that which Carthage afterwards did,—that which some day America will do.[9]

Charles Sumner, in his *Prophetic Voices Concerning America,* quoted these words in connection with a query regarding America's annexation of Canada: "When will the fruit be ripe?"[10] The American's first use of the doctrine of gravitation was not in expansionism, however, but in the justificatory ideology of the American Revolution. How greatly Newtonianism as an apparent synthesis of rationalistic philosophy affected eighteenth-century American political thought has been pointed out by Professor Carl Becker.[11] Thomas Paine's summons to revolution spoke in the Newtonian terminology of the time when it related America's separation from England to the law of the motion of the spheres:

> In no instance hath nature made the satellite larger than its primary planet; and as England and America, with respect to each other, reverse the common order of nature, it is evident that they belong to different systems. England to Europe: America to itself.[12]

This conception that a natural law underlay their revolution was also suggested to Americans by the sympathetic Abbé Raynal, in his soon translated and widely read work of 1780 on the history of European settlements in the West Indies. In one place he warned Englishmen of a decree of nature which they could not change — "that great bodies always give law to smaller ones."[13] In another place, after observing that nature had established laws of equilibrium for the earth as for the heavens, he declared that "by the rule of quantity and of distance, America can belong only to itself."[14] The English historian Seeley exclaimed with reference to this type of metaphor: "When a metaphor comes to be regarded as an argument, what an irresistible argument it always seems!"[15]

However, metaphorical arguments frequently resist each other. The revolutionary doctrine of gravitation is in one aspect antithetic to the expansionist doctrine of gravitation. For it posits the gravitation of a people not to dependence but to independence. Yet in presenting an existent political connection as inherently unstable, the original doctrine of gravitation foreshadowed the central element of the expansionist's doctrine. A kind of gravitation which prevails also in the sphere of ideas was to draw the doctrine from its original plane to a different one by the attraction of changing self-interest.

The transition to the expansionist form of the doctrine was made by some Americans not long after the beginning of national life. Quickly they felt that America had become, as Thomas Pownall said, "a new Primary Planet, which . . . must shift the centre of gravity" in the world of politics.[16] A shift in the center of political gravity seemed to make it likely that Europe's North American colonies, attached only by a fragile stem to the mother country, would eventually fall to the powerful nation to which they were adjacent. Thus in 1805 Secretary of State Madison said to Tourreau in reference to Canada: "When the pear is ripe it will fall of itself." [17] Just before the War of 1812 it seemed similarly to a prophet of destiny in the Nashville *Clarion* that "the Floridas will sink into the Confederation of American States." [18] During the war, Secretary of State Monroe's instructions to his peace commissioners revived the thesis concerning Canada: "That these provinces will be severed from Great Britain at no distant day, by their own career, may fairly be presumed even against her strongest efforts to retain them." [19] The commissioners were to anticipate fate by pressing for Canada in the settlement.

The first American to use notably the phrase "political gravitation" was apparently John Quincy Adams. He propounded the idea in 1819 when he told the Cabinet that Europe's North American colonies were destined to come to the United States by a "law of nature" rather than by aggression.[20] But the phrase "political gravitation" first occurs in his despatch of April 28, 1823, to America's Minister to Spain on the problem raised by the possibility of Cuba's joining in the revolt of other Spanish-American colonies against Spain. In his discussion Adams affirmed that in view of all the natural relations between the two countries eventual annexation seemed "indispensable to the continuance and integrity of the Union itself." He admitted, indeed, that oversea expansion raised numerous and formidable problems. But the determinant of the issue would in any event be the natural law described in the following:

> . . . there are laws of political as well as of physical gravitation; and if an apple severed by the tempest from its native tree cannot choose but fall to the ground, Cuba, forcibly disjoined from its own unnatural connection with Spain, and incapable of self-support, can gravitate only toward the North American Union, which by the same law of nature, cannot cast her off from its bosom.[21]

The impermanence of Cuba's unnatural connection with distant Spain, her incapacity for self-support, her necessary gravitation toward the United States, her necessary reception by the United States — these are the four elements of Adams's idea of political gravitation as applied to Cuba. Politico-geographical considerations perhaps justified judgments of probability which correspond to each of these elements. For example, there was much justification in the impression which the London *Courier* expressed in saying that Cuba was "tottering to its fall." [22] However, Adams stated a judgment of inevitability rather than probability in consequence of his conception of "laws" of political gravitation. A law implies universal occurrence under given conditions. Adams, unable to foresee the interest which later attached to his words, was extremely vague and did not state the general conditions of political gravitation. He had, however, enriched the imagination of Americans even if not their scientific knowledge.

After quiescence during several decades of little expansionist interest, the idea of political gravitation had some revival in the expansion movement of the 'forties. The appeal of the Texans for annexation seemed to many to be evidence that the federation of contiguous states was a natural law. Thus a writer on the Texan issue in the *Democratic Review* of 1844 described annexation in terms of electrical magnetism:

> Suppose a powerful magnet suspended in the air—and near it, within the full force of its attraction, suppose a piece of iron similarly suspended, and free to obey the call of the mysterious metallic sympathy;—while they are thus situated, so long as they are forcibly held asunder by any other sufficient counterbalancing force, their natural instinct toward cohesion may be for the time frustrated; but

the moment that obstacle is removed or relaxed, they rush together—and the result is *Annexation*. That Texas is to be, sooner or later, included in the Union, we have long . . . regarded as an event already indelibly inscribed in the book of future fate and necessity.[23]

After the fulfilment of this prophecy, Representative Levin could more confidently predict the acquisition of all Oregon by virtue of " an eternal law of nature " decreeing that all contiguous territory yield to " the social attraction of gravitation." [24] During the Mexican War some opponents of belligerent expansion dwelt upon the alternative of trusting to " moral and physical laws " to detach at some future date the whole of northern Mexico from Mexico's jurisdiction.[25] After the war, certain Whigs began to intimate the prospect of political gravitation from the north. Thus the annexation of Canada was predicted by a writer in 1849 as the result of " a latent attraction . . . like that which a great and growing orb exercises over a smaller one, heretofore under the influence of another that is now waning." [26] Similarly, Charles Sumner in 1849 wrote to Richard Cobden: " There are natural laws at work which no individual and no parliament can control, and it seems to me that by these Canada is destined to be swept into the wide orbit of her neighbor." [27] But despite such observations as the foregoing, expansionists of the 'forties did not use the doctrine of political gravitation to any great extent. The concept was not altogether congenial to a decade which based its expectations not upon the native desire of other continental peoples for annexation but rather upon the filling of their territories with American pioneers who would eventually smuggle in the apple as did the Texans.

The word " gravitation " first began to be commonly applied to political apples in the 'fifties. It was the emergence of a desire for Cuba which caused congressional expansionists to discover Adams's words and call them to general attention. Senator Toombs affirmed in 1859 — with such force as to become slightly confused in both grammar and metaphor — that " that gravitation of Cuba towards us, of which Mr. Adams spoke, continues, like the gravitation of the earth, gaining accelerated motion every day it moves; and what was gravitating fifty years ago, is now coming with terrific power against that island." [28] Seward likewise asserted that Cuba "gravitates to the United States" but did not agree with Toombs that time and opportunity had already ripened it for acquisition.[29] References to political gravitation in the press included the assertion by the *United States Democratic Review*, presented as a proposition of political science, that Cuba must "succumb to the law of political gravitation and to the power of state absorption, existing naturally in the United States Government." [30] For the most part, however, expansionists of the 'fifties did not associate the natural law of manifest destiny with political gravitation; for they desired to be "coming with terrific power against" Cuba and other territories, not to await patiently their gravitation. A more suitable ideology was the doctrine of natural growth which sanctioned the eating of stolen apples.

Long as the law may have been in operation, it was not until the years following the Civil War that the doctrine of political gravitation came to the height of its influence. Why did it ripen just at this time? The aspect of conditions in surrounding countries was only a secondary cause. The maturing factor with this as with other doctrines of manifest destiny was apparently the fertile soil supplied in America itself by the needs which unconsciously form the nationalist's pragmatic criterion of truth.

One subjective factor was the intense anti-imperialism which characterized certain Republican leaders and many of their followers. Anti-imperialism was evidently a product not only of the same humanitarianism which underlay Republican opposition to slavery but also of war-weariness. Whatever its causes, the effect of this anti-imperialism was to exclude various methods by which expansion is frequently if not ordinarily accomplished. It excluded first and foremost all aggrandizement by war, antipathy to which Henry Adams ranked first among American political traits.[31] "I abhor war, as I detest slavery," Seward had written in connection with the assertion that he would not give one human life for all the continent that remained to be annexed.[32] Notwithstanding the belligerent proposals of Senator Chandler and other Anglophobes for acquiring Canada, the pacifism cherished by Seward was rather general. The anti-imperialism of many went beyond pacifism and included O. A. Brownson's stipulation that annexation must not take place without the free consent of the states annexed.[33] Finally, there were some who agreed with Sumner that ordinarily territorial aggrandizement was to be achieved not through pecuniary contract but through solicitation from those in " preestablished harmony " with us.[34] These fastidious ideals impose such stringent conditions upon expansion as to seem the morality of the anti-expansionist.

However, this anti-imperialism was allied in many cases with an expansionism as ardent as that of the filibusterer. One factor underlying the intensity of expansionism was the same idealism which had given rise to abolitionism. Proud that the " old effete democracy " tolerating slavery had been invigorated by Republican "universal liberty," [35] Americans believed themselves better fitted and more obligated than ever to fulfil the " destiny of spreading the blessings of liberty . . . over the American continents " [36] and eventually over the entire world. But the expansionist impulse came also from a national egoism which had been powerfully stimulated as victory over rebellion made Americans " conscious of . . . power, full of hope and confidence." [37] With remarkable frankness Representative Shellabarger, in his speech on the purchase of Alaska, analyzed this nationalism:

> Our propensities as Saxons, our vanity as Americans, our pride as a great and progressing nation, our love of dominion, our lust of power, our self-glorification, our notions of what a great thing in diameter our country ought to be, and, above all, our ideas that it is as unpatriotic and out of fashion to hold that our future glory is not to be found in owning all the continents and the islands between, all impel us to take this land.[38]

Add to idealism and emotional nationalism various practical interests — strategic, commercial, and political — and there is at hand a potently stimulating mixture.

The fact that anti-imperialism and expansionism each made its urgent claim created the possibility of a paralyzing conflict. Such a conflict could seem unnecessary only by virtue of one assumption. It was expressed in Sumner's theory that America's destiny was " mightier than war " and that " through peace it will have everything." [39] Precisely this saving theory was justified with quasi-scientific as well as metaphysical authority by the anti-imperialistic but radically expansionistic doctrine of political gravitation.

Though recommended by the need to which it answered, this doctrine, like all the other ideas of manifest destiny, depended ultimately for acceptance upon the acquiescence of reason. This acquiescence could more easily be given because the doctrine of gravitation seemed plausible in the light of the contemporary political condition of the continent. To the south abundant disorder seemed to confirm Seward's conception of an inevitable process of " decay of Spanish-American power "; to the north certain disputes between Canada and the mother country appeared to confirm Seward's idea of a process of " general decolonization " on the continent.[40] In some cases these unstable political conditions were associated with the willingness of European governments or factions of American communities to sell or cede their territory to the United States. Viewing such a scene in 1870, the *New York Herald* affirmed that " manifest destiny " was not merely a sentiment but a fact:

> The revolution in Cuba, the insurrection in the Winnipeg country, the application of the people in British Columbia for annexation, the chronic disorders of Mexico, the growing disposition of the Canadians and other British American colonists to be united with us, and the condition of the West Indies generally show that our republican empire must become continental.[41]

The optimism of such observations far exceeded, however, any encouragement afforded by reality. This exaggeration reflected the fact that the doctrines of manifest destiny owe their manifestness less to the tendencies of events than to a priori reasoning. Thus the doctrine of political gravitation posited certain " laws " which were not so much a deduction from objective conditions as preconceptions in the light of which conditions were apprehended. What, then, were the laws which this political Newtonianism implicitly postulated?

Analysis of many of the predictions of the believers in political gravitation reveals first the explicit or implicit assumption of a geographical law. That a geographical consideration underlay the prophecy of Adams is evidenced by his thesis that Cuba was placed in geographical relations with this country by nature.[42] Secretary of State Seward, who frankly told the Spanish Minister that Cuba must ultimately come to us " by means of constant gravitation," had a similar conception.[43] He observed in 1859 that Cuba had been formed by the Mississippi in washing American sand into the Gulf — a geological origin which seemed significant of Cuba's permanent geographical relationship to the United States.[44] Representative Orth, affirming in 1870 that Cuba " must inevitably gravitate toward us," likewise stressed Cuba's geographical position:

> Its proximity to our coast; its geographical position, standing in the very door-way of the Gulf, and thus commanding a very large portion of our commerce; the increasing weakness of the Spanish Government—these, and many other considerations, point most clearly to the ultimate destiny of that rich gem of the Antilles.[45]

But the growth of the idea of proximity since Adams's time resulted in a corresponding enlargement of the geographical range of America's attraction; its operation now seemed to affect not merely Cuba but also the more distant West Indian islands which had become of interest during the Civil War as possible naval bases. The islands of St. Thomas and St. John, declared President Johnson in his message announcing the treaty of purchase with Denmark, could be secured in harmony with the principle of political gravitation. Johnson presented also a much broader claim:

> I agree with our early statesmen that the West Indies naturally gravitate to, and may be expected ultimately to be absorbed by, the continental States, including our own.[46]

In fact no prominent early American statesman seems to have said anything which indicated agreement with Johnson's conception that not merely Cuba but all West Indian islands would gravitate to the continent. It is true, however, that what they said of Cuba involves assumptions which would tend to extend themselves to all " adjacent " islands.

President Johnson did not affirm that the entire West Indies would fall only to the United States. This was left for the expansionists who spoke in the congressional debates on our policy toward the troubled conditions in Santo Domingo. In 1869 Representative Banks, chairman of the Committee on Foreign Affairs, introduced a resolution authorizing the extension of a protectorate over the island of Santo Domingo upon request. In his presentation of this resolution he declared:

> It would be idle for me to say, Mr. Speaker, in view of the history of this country and the opinions of such men as John Quincy Adams and those who acted with him at the beginning of the century, that the time will not come when the Island of San Domingo and the other islands of the Gulf of Mexico will incline to and become a part of the United States.[47]

Representative Butler, whose amendment extended the protection to all the islands of the Antilles, urged that we hold our mouth "ready to catch the plum which is now ripe and ready to fall." Butler also focussed upon the geographical consideration: ". . . they belong to us so far by position and by the laws of nature that it is required for us to interpose our good offices to aid them to come to us and under our laws."[48]

The most far-reaching application of the geographical doctrine was that of Representative Spalding in connection with his amendment declaring the protectorate open to Pacific as well as Atlantic islands. Spalding said with reference to the luscious tropical fruit Hawaii: "The pear is nearly ripe enough to fall, and when it does fall it must fall into the American lap." That the principle of adjacency was determinative here too is shown by the fact that Spalding applied his amendment to all islands which "lie nearer to the coast of the United States than to that of any foreign government."[49] Although Hawaii is not adjacent in an absolute sense, it is indeed closer to the United States than to Europe.

In sum, it seems that two propositions were entertained with respect to islands. The first is that, as Adams expressed it, they are "incapable of self-support." This view was represented by Representative Butler's prophecy that all the island governments of the Caribbean "will crumble to pieces . . . by natural process." [50] It was exemplified also by Representative Spalding's assertion that in Hawaii "the work of disintegration is now rapidly going on." [51] The second proposition concerning islands is that the direction of their gravitation is determined by the adjacency of a large country. Both postulates are stated by Miss E. C. Semple, in her *American History and Its Geographic Conditions*, in the following form:

> Islands are detached areas physically and are detachable areas politically. They tend to fall to the nearest political domain; this is what we may call the politico-geographical law of gravity.[52]

The word "tend" is a loophole that takes care of exceptional cases like England, one of whose patriots proudly defined Europe as a continent lying off the British Isles.

The geographico-political law of gravitation was not limited by expansionists to islands alone. The doctrine concerning islands was part of a broader thesis which posited generally that within a circumference defined by adjacency large territorial bodies exerted an attraction upon smaller ones. In 1846 the *New York Herald* touched on this law when it affirmed: "That law of nature which enforces the union and embodiment of small globules of water with a larger quantity of the element with which they come in contact, is not more sure in its operation than that by which the small territories adjoining the United States will ultimately unite with the central power—and become part and parcel of this republic." [53] Similarly, in 1858 the *United States Democratic Review* described political gravitation as "a natural law of attraction which makes large bodies overcome smaller ones." [54]

The expansionist literature following the Civil War contains numerous instances of the application of this geographical doctrine to continental territory. With reference to Alaska, a retrospective expansionist declared that Russia "was wise enough to know that what was on this side by an irresistible law must come to us . . . not . . . by conquest, but by the law of absorption, attraction, evolution, and gravitation." [55] The observation happened to be correct, as was shown by a subsequently discovered Russian document advising resignation to the American belief in "manifest destiny." [56] Once Alaska had been yielded, it appeared to many that, as Representative Donnelly affirmed, the British dominion between Alaska and and Oregon would "disappear between the upper and the nether mill-stones." [57] W. W. Miller asserted that British Columbia would "drop of its own gravity" as an apple from a tree; [58] Representative Raum merely changed the metaphor to a pear.[59] The *St. Paul Daily Press* declared that the territory was wedded to the United States by "geographical affinities which no human power can sunder, as He has divorced it from Canada by physical barriers which no human power can overcome." [60] The *St. Paul Free Press* went further and affirmed that not only the Northwestern Coast but also Upper and Lower Canada must "gravitate" through the same geographical affinities.[61] Although Seward was "content to wait for the ripened fruit which must fall," [62] Sumner as chairman of the Senate Committee on Foreign Relations sought to obtain Canada immediately through unmerciful hoisting of the Alabama Claims. Representative Donnelly brought the geographical law of gravitation to a form embracing all the continent: "From both North and South the territory and the peoples of the continent gravitate inevitably toward us . . ." [63] The fact that the United States was not always closest to the gravitating countries shows that the principle of propinquity was qualified by the secondary principle of the attraction of size. Thus Miss Semple observes that "the attraction of a larger and stronger country may prove more potent than that of a nearer but smaller land." [64]

So far the doctrine of gravitation seems curiously mechanistic; it explains America's expansion by geographical factors but not by human volition. Yet expansionists like Sumner thought of America as "recognizing always the will of those who are to become our fellow-citizens." [65] They assumed further that other people were ardently "wishing for the time when they can call our flag their own." [66] Such considerations make it evident that geographical propinquity was regarded as the necessary condition of gravitation rather than as its sole cause. The expansionist, seldom as stupid as his hasty rhetoric suggests, explained gravitation not merely by physical factors but also by certain psychic attractions.

What were the factors which seemed to establish a psychic attraction of America for other peoples? One was suggested by Representative Donnelly when he said that gravitating peoples were drawn by "the individual prosperity manifest everywhere through all our broad expanse." [67] One may thus speak of an economico-political law of gravitation. Such a law seemed particularly evident in the case of islands; indeed Adams formulated the doctrine of political gravitation in connection with a reference to the commercial relations rapidly forming between Cuba and the United States. By the late 'sixties other West Indian islands and Hawaii as well had come to be regarded as parts of the American economic system. It was supposed that (to quote from Miss Semple's discussion of the doctrine of gravitation) "an island environment suffers always from the limitation of its size, especially in commerce." [68] In consequence, it seemed, an island seeks to sustain its economic existence by forming close commercial relations with a country on the mainland; Miss Semple gives as example Hawaii's pursuit of an American market for its sugar. The conclusion of the expansionist's economic reasoning is the assumption that islands are attracted politically toward the country drawing most of their trade.

The economico-political law of gravitation was supposed to affect adjacent continental territories as well as islands. "Our population, our wealth, our railroad system, our manufactures, and our agricultural resources are all so expanding," declared Senator Stewart, "that the commercial relations of this country to the surrounding provinces will be such that they must come and go with us." [69] There were more specific predictions. The entire Western Coast, Robert J. Walker believed, "must come to us eventually by a commercial and political gravitation, which is as irresistible as the law of gravitation." [70] The *St. Paul Free Press* extended the same conception to Upper and Lower Canada: "Canada and the lower provinces must gravitate by the resistless force of economic laws and political and geographical affinities, to the same great center, and round out with their annexation the *continental unity* of the American dominion." [71] The Taylor-Banks proposal of 1866 to make an offer for the economic reconstruction of Canada contingent upon annexation met considerable approval from believers in economic gravitation. The *Chicago Tribune* boasted that the economic bait was "a new invention in diplomacy — a new lesson in statecraft — a new mode of conquest." [72]

The neighboring republic to the south, though less interested in economic development, was nevertheless supposed to be also subject to economico-political gravitation. According to Senator Stewart, its people would see that it could never amount to anything materially if not a part of the United States.[73] Seward's expansionistic yet passive attitude toward Mexico was also determined by his "expectation that Mexico would eventually be acquired by the gradual process of Americanization which would result from the emigration of capital and colonists from the United States." [74] We may note in passing that this economic conception of gravitation is implicit in much of the ideology of modern economic imperialism: an example is the hypothesis of the Russian statesman Sazonoff that "geographical position and economic development draw these districts [Chinese regions beyond the Great Wall] more and more towards Russia." [75]

Although touching upon an influential motive, the politico-economic law does not seem an adequate explanation of the ardor for annexation which was attributed to the subjects of political gravitation. It suggests rather a reluctant yielding to the attractions indicated by the Yankeephobe Manuel Ugarte when he wrote: "The 'manifest destiny' of peoples frequently serves to encourage slackness, but it is undeniable that given historical or geographical conditions exercise a strong pressure which may bring a community to an *impasse,* from which it is difficult to find an escape." [76]

But the expansionist's conception of other peoples as ready to "knock loud for entrance into the Home of the Free," [77] reflected his assumption that their inclinations were governed by a spiritual attraction as well as by an economic. The source of the spiritual attraction was that stated by the ancient Chinese admonition to kings: "Possession of virtue attracts the people, the people bring territory . . ."[78] American expansionists doubted neither the preeminent virtue of their country nor the obviousness of this virtue to others. George Boutwell described the attractive power of American virtue by an egoistic comparison pleasing to American pacifists: "Other nations take by force of arms, ours by force of ideas."[79] The words exemplified what might be called the ideologico-political law of gravitation.

The specific idea which was to take other nations by storm was republicanism, the alpha and omega of political virtue to the American mind. This conception was eloquently expressed by Charles Sumner in his *Prophetic Voices Concerning America:*

> . . . the name of Republic will be exalted, until every neighbor, yielding to irresistible attraction, seeks new life in becoming part of the great whole; and the national example will be more puissant than army or navy for the conquest of the world.[80]

In praising the acquisition of Alaska for dismissing one more monarch from the continent, Sumner exalted America's fastidious method of political union above even the pacific *mariage de convenance* traditional in *la haute politique:* "More happy than Austria, who acquired possessions by marriage, we shall acquire them by the attraction of republican institutions."[81] It is uncertain whether Sumner was familiar with the lines in Kant's essay on *Perpetual Peace:*

> For if fortune should so direct, that a people as powerful as enlightened, should constitute itself into a republic (a government which in its nature inclines to a perpetual peace) from that time there would be a centre for this federative association; other states might adhere thereto, in order to guarantee their liberty according to the principles of public right; and this alliance might insensibly be extended.[82]

Stirred similarly by the ideal of a *pax Americana,* Sumner envisaged as its agency of fulfilment the "absorbing Unity" implied by *E pluribus unum.*[83]

The scope most frequently ascribed to the absorbent process was indicated by Sumner's words declaring the Alaskan treaty "a visible step in the occupation of the whole North American continent." John Adams, as Sumner pointed out, had long ago established the tradition of regarding continental dominion as the "manifest destiny" of American republicanism.[84] But whereas Adams had conceived of the fulfilment of this destiny by migratory American pioneers, Sumner and others now supposed that other continental peoples would gravitate toward America by virtue of the influence to which proximity exposed them. Representative Donnelly, predicting the gravitation of peoples from the north and the south, identified this influence not only with economic attraction but "the benignity of our institutions."[85] The gravitation of the neighbors to the north was awaited with peculiar eagerness in view of the fact that monarchical rule over our Anglo-Saxon kinsmen seemed, as the *New York Herald* said, preeminently "irritating to our republican institutions and an obstacle to the realization of the manifest destiny of the American republic."[86] The *Herald* observed also that if Nova Scotia gave up the old loyalty she would "have no bogus throne, but must gravitate towards the United States."[87] Dr. J. Howard Pugh showed a broader geographical view in predicting the day when "Canada and Mexico, and the States of Central America, will join the Federal Union; not by conquest, not by filibustering and piratical expeditions, but by the attractive power of a political system that combines all the freedom of independent states with the strength and solidarity of a consolidated government."[88]

Extension of the ideologico-political law of gravitation to the West Indies was facilitated by Grant's typical belief that such people as Dominicans "are not capable of maintaining themselves" and "yearn" therefore the more strongly for "the protection of our free institutions and laws."[89] Representative Judd, having avowed his belief in manifest destiny, spoke in the Dominican debate as follows:

> I think the influence of our institutions is not to be limited simply to the territory that now belongs to us, but that in the process of time, if our Government remains stable and perpetuated, it is to extend to other lands, and I have no doubt but that influence will, by its own momentum, peaceably and consistently with all our engagements with other nations, bring these islands as well as the territory adjoining us within the embrace of our institutions.[90]

Representative Mullins felt similarly, but believed that the passage of the resolution offering protection to the republics of Santo Domingo was necessary as " a mere expression of the will of the American people, that we sympathize with them." He predicted that " it will be received by them as a sympathetic cord that reaches across from them to us, and will draw them here naturally when they are ripe." [91]

A high estimation of the drawing power of democracy led the expansionist at times to predict the gravitation of countries lying beyond the usually conceived limits of America's attraction. One fanciful prediction was doubtless inspired in part by an Irish imagination if not by solicitude for a Fenian constituency. Representative Robinson's contribution to the curiosities of American expansionism is as follows:

> I have no doubt that the time will come when Ireland will be annexed to this country. I have no more doubt of that than I have that Cuba will be annexed to this country. Both of them will come to us by the natural laws of affinity, by their sympathy with us upon questions of politics and statesmanship. . . . God Almighty, who rules the universe, will give her [England] no peace, until she lets the people of Ireland go; and the natural affinity of Ireland is with the United States.[92]

Seward had already outdone Robinson when in 1861 he spoke of his expanding and civilizing country as destined to meet Russia " in the region where civilization first began " — words which are interpreted by his biographer and others as referring to the annexation of a part of China.[93] The farthest flight of fancy was President Johnson's — or was it Seward's imagination prompting Johnson? — when he said: " . . . the conviction is rapidly gaining ground in the American mind that with the increased facilities for intercommunication between all portions of the earth the principles of free government, as embraced in our Constitution, if faithfully maintained and carried out, would prove of sufficient strength and breadth to comprehend within their sphere and influence the civilized nations of the world." [94] Though such a conviction was doubtless not accompanied by a serious hope of annexing the world, Johnson's words reveal the great faith in democracy which enabled Americans of this period to approach so blithely the most grandiose projects of expansion in the American Hemisphere. A kind of moral gravitation toward the United States was indeed depicted as world-wide. Just as the Hebrew prophet foresaw the nations as flocking to the mountains whence went forth God's law, so Representative Mullins envisaged America as the "new Jerusalem," which would attract "the gathering in of all nations" by its invitation: "Come to us and we will give you protection." [95]

Such superb confidence in America's destiny was needed to sustain humanitarian expansionists like Mullins in the passive policy which was the primary moral implication of the doctrine of gravitation. Mullins could well say that "rather than go into war with these lands and this people" he would "let them alone." For he believed that the people of Santo Domingo "will come to us themselves." [96] Others too affirmed that the United States need do nothing — or at most next to nothing — to accomplish an expansion which was in the trend of natural law. Thus President Johnson said with reference to the West Indies that it was "wise to leave the question of . . . absorption to this process of natural political gravitation." [97] Representative Orth asserted that because "Cuba must inevitably gravitate toward us" it would be poor statesmanship to hasten its fall.[98] Representative Cullom urged patience with respect to the entire program of manifest destiny:

> I believe that we are destined to own and control the whole western continent from Baffin's Bay to the Caribbean Sea. But, sir, we need not be in a hurry. When the fruit is ripe it will fall into our hands.[99]

But the impropriety of hurry seemed no greater than that of not receiving the fruit when it was ripe. The expansionist implication of the doctrine of gravitation was expressed by Representative Mullins in saying that when the peoples of Santo Domingo "come to us as ripe fruit . . . I would not let them lay there after they are ripe and become sour and spoil." [100] This acceptance of ripe fruit was held by the believer in gravitation to be both natural and right. Acceptance seemed natural because of the supposition that, as John Quincy Adams implied, gravitation rests upon relations creating a mutual need of union.

Reception appeared right because of the assumption that the apple would not be stolen but would fall as the gift of heaven. Under such circumstances, to cast it from one's bosom would be an impious denial of refuge. The item of profit in the rationale was its assurance that the apple could be eaten with good conscience. The doctrine of gravitation enabled land-hunger to be untroubled by thoughts of Naboth's vineyard.

But was the factual premise of this amiable moral philosophy of expansion a valid one? Geography, economics, and moral psychology were all used to rationalize the postulate that fruits fall as predictably in the political sphere as in the physical. Yet the "law" of gravitation was not a summarization of past experience but merely a prediction about future experience. It is pertinent, therefore, to see whether the anticipated political fruit actually fell.

In the years when gravitation was most talked about it was least in evidence. Despite all the great hopes of the expansionists, Alaska was the only country acquired between 1865 and 1871. Moreover, Alaska did not come through the will of its few inhabitants but through the Russian Government's desire to sell. The Dominican Republic was the only country to offer itself voluntarily; this offer, however, represented merely the move of a political faction to save itself from threatened overthrow in civil war. Except with respect to small groups of dissatisfied British Columbians and Nova Scotians, all the assertions of the eagerness of other countries for annexation were apparently instances of wishful thinking. Thus the supposedly eager Mexicans were declared by the American Minister Nelson to cherish a "feeling of jealousy and dislike" toward foreigners, including his own countrymen, which was probably "more intense . . . than ever before."[101]

Two opportunities for expansion — the treaty transferring Denmark's islands and that arranging annexation of the Dominican Republic — were deliberately rejected. These rejections contradicted Adams's doctrine that a law of nature prevented America's casting from her bosom the fallen fruit. The cause of the rejections lay in the fact that the expansionists were only a brave minority. The majority were characterized by Seward's sad complaint in 1868 that their attention "sensibly continues to be fastened upon the domestic questions which arose out of the late civil war," and that they refused to dismiss these questions "even so far as to entertain the higher but more remote questions of national extension and aggrandizement." [102] Thus it came about that with the one exception of Alaska, accepted largely through friendship for Russia, the few apples that fell were allowed to bounce back.

According to the expansionists, however, the doctrine of political gravitation was not to be tested except in the broad range of future years. "However the people of these northern provinces may think now," declared Senator Stewart, "the time will come when they will see that their destiny is as a part of ourselves." [103] This faith in gravitation periodically reasserted itself in the course of subsequent decades which saw the steady increase of America's power and self-confidence. Thus, its continental conception of manifest destiny prompted the *New York Herald* to affirm in 1874 that Mexico "gravitates" more and more toward the United States,[104] and led Senator Burnside in 1879 to use the same word with reference to Canada.[105] The rising interest in the Pacific caused Secretary Blaine in 1881 to call attention to the "drift" of Hawaii toward us,[106] and Senator Morgan's committee report of 1894 to allude to the tendency of the island to "gravitate toward political union with this country." [107] But the annexation which shortly followed Representative Gibson's assertion that Hawaii was "gravitating" [108] to us was due, not to nature, but to the revolution of American planters under the protective bayonets provided by an expansionist American Minister.

Shortly afterward the forces of gravitation seemed to shift to the Atlantic. Despite the Teller Amendment, Murat Halstead believed that "Cuba must some time be ours by gravitation" — and thus fulfil its "manifest destiny." [109] Brooks Adams, who interpreted the consolidation and dissolution of nations in terms of Kelvin's physics, wrote in 1899 that not only Cuba but all the West Indies were gravitating to the United States.[110] But the Danish West Indies came less through gravitation than through Secretary Lansing's warning Denmark of the possible necessity of seizure. Acquisition of Denmark's colony encouraged Edwin Slosson to predict as late as 1920 that the European colonies in the Caribbean were in "gravitation towards the United States." [111] While such expectation of voluntary European departure from America is at least as old as Grant,[112] European governments have thus far shown no disposition to relinquish their American colonies even for the settlement of war debts.

Another type of prediction in the ideology of political gravitation referred not to territorial expansion but to the extension of political power or influence. During the Venezuelan crisis of 1895 Senator Turpie affirmed that the guardianship of all the republics of the American continent had come to the United States in part "by the force of political gravitation." [113] Though the Panama Revolution surely did not occur through unaided processes of nature, the *St. Louis Globe-Democrat* asserted that this episode was a species of "political gravitation" which would finally fix forever the suzerainty of the United States over the whole of the Western Hemisphere.[114] Yet the avowed attitude as well as the conduct of Latin Americans has revealed very little inclination to make voluntary offerings to the power of "*El Colosso*."

The accumulating disappointments of the expansionist are not entirely conclusive because he set no time limit for gravitation, agreed with Sumner that "nature does everything slowly and by degrees," [115] and could thus maintain till the end of time that political gravitation toward America is still in process. But even should the expansionist's already ancient prophecies find confirmation in some curious future, he would nevertheless have made correct predictions for reasons entirely wrong. One such reason was the postulate that the process of gravitation in the physical realm must have its analogy in the political sphere. This analogical reasoning, so prevalent in the past and not entirely non-existent even today, involves a failure to realize that different levels of phenomena must be investigated independently and not with presuppositions derived from superficial similarity. The a priori transference of the law of one level of particulars to a level analogous but essentially different is an engaging instance of the use of analogy as a substitute for logic.

Independently of his curious use of analogy, the expansionist seems to have gone astray in his psychological assumptions concerning the attitude of lesser nationalities toward the greater. It is scarcely true that either economic or moral attraction creates great probability of "gravitation" from independence to dependence. The tendency most apt to predominate, if unchecked from without, is "gravitation" from dependence to an independence which when once achieved is treasured as dear life.

Examples of the predominant tendency are offered not only by the revolts of Latin-American peoples against Spain, but also by their adherence to national independence despite the possibility of federation with the United States. It is true that a Salvador editor recently admitted that America's hegemony in the Caribbean "was due to the law of international gravitation, through which a larger nation attracts the smaller ones within the orbit of its influence." [116] But a tendency more typical than a succumbing to economic attraction is reflected in the very words of this editor. For his admission of the force of gravitation prefaced advice that Central American States form a confederacy capable of resisting this gravitation and securing even the withdrawal of the marines from Managua.

With a curious blindness, due in part to the fact that they focussed upon physics rather than national psychology, American expansionists imagined that the nationalism so strong in themselves was weak in others. In reality Latin-American peoples have cherished independence so strongly as to refuse to subordinate it to their material welfare. This fact is exemplified in the words with which a Mexican deputy in 1878 urged the Mexican Congress not to grant a railroad concession to American interests:

> You, the deputies of the States, would you exchange your beautiful and poor liberty of the present for the rich subjection which the railroad could give you? Go and propose to the lion of the desert to exchange his cave of rocks for a golden cage, and the lion of the desert will reply to you with a roar of liberty.[117]

If one considers the matter carefully, however, it becomes evident that the failure of political gravitation in American history cannot be blamed on Latin-American nationalism alone. Not all lions among the nations have roared for the liberty of the desert. In the days when "Imperial Rome displayed a peculiar attractive power" toward aliens, they were drawn to the Empire in such great numbers that it appeared for a time as if tribalism would be superseded in Europe by universalism.[118] Even after the Empire was superseded by modern national states the federative impulse played the important rôle which Fiske's essay on "Manifest Destiny" describes with the enthusiasm of a believer in political gravitation.[119] The expanding federation has not always seemed to hold out slavery but sometimes a manifest destiny of enhanced liberty.

In the Latin-American attitude toward the United States lies the real clue to the cause of the failure of American expansionists. Rippy's studies of Latin-American Yankeephobia make plain the unpleasant fact that until very recently the American flag has figured in Latin America not as the symbol of federative liberty but rather (to quote Manuel Ugarte) as a "symbol of oppression."[120] When Ugarte speaks of "the danger of falling within the sphere of attraction of Anglo-Saxon America,"[121] he does not refer to the danger of voluntarily yielding to true attraction. The attraction is not that of the magnet but of the grapnel. According to the Latin-American Rodó, the genius of the United States is that of "*force in movement*," or, in a word, imperialism.[122] But imperialism did not prove in the end to be genius.

Against the overactivity of imperialism Americans should have been warned by the doctrine of political gravitation, the apparent implication of which was to do nothing at all. But this was precisely what most of the expansionists did not do. Such was the case even when the doctrine of political gravitation was in fashion. To be sure, the purchase of Alaska was proposed to Seward by Russia; save for the over-insistence of Seward and Sumner with their own reluctant Congress, America merely held her lap to receive the falling fruit. But instead of following Johnson's prescription with reference to the West Indies, Seward used much energy in persuading Denmark to sell the possessions which she was originally disposed to retain. Moreover, he departed from his theoretical anti-imperialism when he at first refused to permit a plebiscite to decide the destiny of the Danish West Indies. Seward and others favoring the annexation of the Dominican Republic made two daring attempts to stampede the House into that action. Sumner sought to obtain Canada by raising the Alabama Claims to a level where only cession of territory could have paid them.

The most flagrant instance of deviation from the doctrine of gravitation was the policy of the Grant Administration toward the Dominican Republic. For the sake of a treaty of annexation with the nominal but seriously imperilled government, this Administration kept the faction favorable to annexation in power by despatching a squadron to Dominican waters and threatening Haiti with violence should she attempt to interfere with the existing régime. This fact, together with his belief that the Dominicans did not desire annexation, prompted Sumner to make his famous denunciatory speech charging too luridly that the Dominican policy committed the nation to a "dance of blood." [123] Much fairer was the metaphor of Representative Cox, who said that this policy "reverses political gravitation." [124] Since certain incidents of expansionism reversed this law even when the doctrine of gravitation was most influential, it is not surprising that practice was even more imperialistic in other periods. American expansionists in general, as Senator Hale said in his satirical treatment of the doctrine of gravitation, were like impatient boys who do not wait for the ripe apple to fall but hit it down with a stick.[125]

The unwillingness of the believer in political gravitation to let destiny take care of itself is a curiosity demanding explanation. His impatience was doubtless caused in part by a conscious or unconscious skepticism which lurked beneath the optimism of theory. Despite his theory of inevitability, the expansionist was no fool; he knew that the apple left to ripen might fall to someone else or rot upon the tree. Nor did it seem to him always that abstention from action was the true implication of his theory of gravitation. Instead of asking, "eventually, why now," as did Seward with reference to Mexico,[126] he on some occasions asked, "eventually, why not now," as did Representative Myers with reference to Alaska.[127] The logic of immediate action was indicated by the *New York Herald* when it demanded the immediate annexation of Cuba precisely because annexation was "merely anticipating the necessary march of events." [128] To anticipate the inevitable seems but due cooperativeness with nature, "the helping on of the good time coming" which is better for coming sooner.

The most potent factor in spurring the expansionist to energetic action was perhaps the aggressive element in the spirit of manifest destiny itself. The latent existence of this element even in those professing belief in the doctrine of gravitation is exemplified by a curious inconsistency in the words of Representative Mullins in 1868. Though speaking in one breath of the "ripening" of other nations for the fulfilment of America's territorial destiny, he in the next depicted the United States as "a burning meteor rushing on in space," a part of the movement which in five thousand years would give the Anglo-Saxon race "the whole world." [129] In the same year Representative Maynard spoke still more aggressively of "that spirit of expansion, if you please—of aggression, that . . . will eventually make" this republic "the mistress of the world." [130] Maynard's words were not typical but something of their spirit was perhaps determinative even in those unconscious of such an influence. The spirit of manifest destiny disposed Americans very little to that patient self-possession which was regarded by the Stoics as the true lesson of cosmic processes for men. For energetic ambition seems to be the prerogative of the people appointed to beneficent mastery. In sum, if the phenomena of physics offer any analogy to the ordinary dynamics of national expansion it is less the law of gravitation than the law envisaged by Rousseau:

> Nations have all a kind of centrifugal force by which they act continually against each other, and tend, like the vortices of Descartes, to aggrandize themselves at the expense of their neighbors.[131]

The doctrine of gravitation, a moral protest against this centrifugal force, overcame it only enough to interfere with the efficiency of its action. This doctrine did not overcome imperialism to the extent of substituting a centripetal force. America remained sufficiently imperialistic to inspire "Yankee-phobia," as was admitted by President Andrew Johnson in regretting that his country had caused in other American governments "distrust if not dread."[132] The fundamental cause of the failure of political gravitation was, in short, an obstacle in the expansionist himself — the centrifugal spirit of manifest destiny.

# CHAPTER IX

## INEVITABLE DESTINY

The failure of the Caribbean ambitions of Johnson and Grant was largely due to a national tradition which bade fair to be stronger than manifest destiny. This tradition was recognized even by Grant's Secretary of State when he said in 1869 that "until recently, the acquisition of outlying territory has not been regarded as desirable by us." [1] In the two subsequent decades of internal reconstruction, this disapprobation of distant oversea expansion increased perceptibly. It was responsible for a restrained policy toward Hawaii, the rejection in 1877 of an offer of annexation from Samoa, and the refusal of two Haitian naval harbors in the 'eighties. In rejecting Haiti's offer Secretary of State Frelinghuysen asserted that "the policy of this Government . . . has tended toward avoidance of possessions disconnected from the main continent." [2] Indeed, Cleveland,[3] Blaine,[4] Bayard [5] and other statesmen expressed a similar view. As the century of grandiose expansion drew into its last decade, it appeared that at least in their self-limitation to the continent Americans were checking manifest destiny by free will.

But to the surprise of those expecting national consistency, the year 1893 brought indisputable signs that resistance to the pressure of manifest destiny was decidedly weakening. In that year there was signed a treaty annexing the Hawaiian Islands, two thousand miles removed from the American continent. Though commercially and strategically these islands had always seemed to stand in relations with the United States which were "entirely peculiar," [6] it was evident that on this occasion, in contrast to the time when Marcy had sought annexation, the interest in Hawaii was not exceptional but part of a general program of oversea expansion.[7] In an article entitled "Manifest Destiny" the disturbed Carl Schurz wrote in *Harper's* that there had arisen a new precept of manifest destiny, advocating "the acquisition of such territory, far and near, as may be useful in enlarging our commercial advantages, and in securing to our navy facilities desirable for the operations of a great naval power." [8]

The proposed policy seemed to Schurz and other conservatives to conflict with such important American traditions as democratic government, homogeneity of population, avoidance of large naval expenditures, cautious abstention from embroilments of world politics, and concentration on the upbuilding of a great continental civilization. Schurz professed to believe that the great mass of his countrymen would oppose an ambition sacrificing the best of America's heritage. Yet one element in the propagandist technique of the imperialist gave Schurz concern. It was the summons to oversea expansion with the very catchword which had stood for the idea of continental expansion. "Manifest destiny," of which the Republican platform of 1892 had once more reminded the people,[9] was used by the expansionists of 1893 to "produce the impression" that all opposition to the new movement toward sea power was "a struggle against fate." [10]

President Cleveland's withdrawal of the treaty of annexation seemed to confirm Schurz's view that "the fate of the American people is in their own wisdom and will." [11] Yet it was not five years before the fatalism of the expansionists was encouraged by the appearance of another treaty, supported more widely and vigorously than the first. And in 1898 the American people, annexing Hawaii, "plunged into the sea." Before the close of the century the fortunate tide had carried the long-harbored ship of state past Hawaii to the Philippines, Guam, and Tutuila, and to Porto Rico in the Atlantic. The one-time continental republic had become monarch of seas in two hemispheres.

Though not attributing empire to a tide of fortune, even anti-expansionists were forced to confess that a factor in the defeat of their stubborn opposition was a "strange fatalism." [12] Representative Mitchell affirmed that the people had been convinced in the Hawaiian issue, less by rational argument than by phrases such as "manifest destiny" and "the logic of events." [13] And with respect to the Philippine venture the

*Nation* observed *post factum* that it "would never have been made were it not for the debilitating effect of the manifest destiny idea at a time of sudden excitement and vainglory." [14] So irritated was Morrison Swift at the effect of the idea that he abusively exclaimed: "Never was such a scurvy thing as this Destiny running around the universe loose. Signs should be erected everywhere — Shoot it at sight." [15]

While apparently loose since the beginning of American expansionism, "destiny" had usually possessed a meaning different from that which it assumed in the 'nineties. The traditional idea of destiny had been naïvely expressed by a Yankee expansionist of the 'fifties: "When we Yankees have once set our souls upon a thing, we always have it." [16] But even such mysticism fell short of thoroughgoing fatalism, since it did not assert that Americans must have anything that their souls were set against. Rather did it imply that American expansion, whether because of omnipotent natural growth or political gravitation, could not be resisted by others. In the 'nineties, however, the doctrine of the inevitable meant not merely that American expansion could not be resisted by others but that it could not be resisted by Americans themselves, caught, willing or unwilling, in the toils of an inevitable destiny.

The conception may seem curious in citizens of the land of the free and the home of the strenuous. It has also aroused wonderment in other countries where conscientious objectors to imperialism were told of the futility of their opposition. In his study of British imperialism, marked by the fatalism of a Lord Salisbury, Hobson sought to explain "the Inevitable in Politics" as "a quasi-philosophic superstition invoked to aid and abet our aggressive policy." [17] But this recurrent idea, which has influenced philosophers as well as imperialists, and the scientific Marx no less than the religious Bossuet, is much more than a superstition even if somewhat less than a truth. One can as little understand as "shoot" it at sight.

A fact clear at the outset, however, is that though the imperialist's doctrine of inevitability was distinct from the traditional idea of destiny, the maturation of the former doctrine was assisted by the latter. The doctrine that expansion cannot be resisted by others tends by its own logic to develop into the idea that it cannot be resisted by oneself. Moreover, the pseudo-biological doctrine of natural growth, while interpreted generally as meaning only that resistance to growth was dangerous, was sometimes associated with the idea that the nation could not resist its growth-impulse even if so disposed. Thus Seward, declaring America's commercial preponderance in the Pacific to be manifest destiny, observed that, though it was the habit of Americans to discuss political and commercial questions "with as much caution and anxiety as if we enjoyed always free choice to make, prevent, or control national movements in that direction," it seemed to him sometimes that "our course has been shaped not so much by any self-guiding wisdom of our own, as by a law of progress and development impressed upon us by nature herself." [18]

The necessitarian doctrine was developed by nothing so much as the ideology which had figured in the Hawaiian issue almost from its beginning. Expansionists of the 'nineties avowedly took encouragement from the fact pointed out by Secretary of State Foster in 1893—that annexation had previously been regarded by American statesmen as a "contingent necessity." [19] The first of these statesmen was Secretary of State Marcy who, though in one place referring to the annexation of Hawaii as apparently "inevitable," [20] showed by his more amplified discussion that he really had in mind contingent inevitability. In a despatch to the American Minister to Hawaii in 1854 he thus declared that, though it was not the policy of the United States to accelerate Hawaii's loss of independence, should this loss become unavoidable the United States itself would assume sovereignty over the islands. Marcy, like Secretaries Legaré and Webster before him, believed that "the large American interests there established and the intimate commercial relations existing" made it imperative to "prevent these islands from becoming the appendage of any other foreign power." [21] His view that prevention of such a contingency was a political necessity was tacitly accepted by succeeding American administrations and was explicitly repeated in 1881 by Secretary of State Blaine. Blaine feared that "the gradual and seemingly inevitable decadence and extinction of the native race" might lead to a foreign colonization and domination. Imminence of foreign control would compel the United States to seek "an avowedly American solution."[22] As "key to the dominion of the American Pacific," Hawaii if drifting from its independent position "must belong by the operation of political necessity" to the United States.[23] All these conditional predictions rest upon the assumption that nations will adopt even inherently unappealing measures when they are necessary to the defense of imperilled vital interests. The assumption is psychologically plausible, but its usefulness is diminished by the difficulty of determining when political necessity exists.

It is important to note that prior to the 'nineties no immediate necessity of annexing Hawaii was believed to exist. Though Marcy considered it expedient to take advantage of Hawaii's eagerness for annexation, he was so far from conceiving himself under political necessity that when the negotiated treaty of annexation failed to satisfy him in all particulars he refused to accept it. American statesmen of three succeeding decades did not assume any immediate danger of foreign acquisition of Hawaii. Nor did they consider that America's growing commercial interest in the Pacific was not adequately protected by such measures as the treaties granting the United States commercial and naval privileges in Hawaii and the exclusive use of Samoan Pago Pago as a naval harbor.

It was only three years after the United States had shown itself opposed to expansionist entanglement in the Samoan issue that the doctrine of contingent necessity began to be superseded by that of the immediate necessity of oversea expansion. The first noteworthy evidence of the change appeared in the diplomatic correspondence of John L. Stevens, American Minister to Hawaii. Although he had affirmed in 1890 that destiny rather than diplomacy would take care of America's preponderance in the Pacific,[24] he not long afterward gave a most striking example of the effectiveness of vigorous diplomacy in forwarding national interests. In November of 1892 Stevens wrote to Secretary of State Foster that the existing state and tendency of things could not be continued; it seemed to him " absolutely necessary " that the United States institute either " bold and vigorous measures for annexation," or a protectorate, the former being preferable as more advantageous.[25] Although the foregoing describes an alternative, Stevens suggested determinism when he declared that " destiny and the vast future interests of the United States in the Pacific clearly indicate who at no distant day must be responsible for the government of these islands." [26] In his supporting argument Stevens was inconsistent in speaking in one breath of the early danger of Hawaii's turning to Asia, and in another of the possibility that the Anglophile princess heir-apparent might turn the country toward Great Britain. Two vague dangers, however, seemed better than one in arguing that a situation of political necessity was now at hand.

Was it real apprehension which motivated Stevens or the belief that, as he wrote, the hour " near at hand " was " golden? " [27] Stevens was aware that an American planter group, perturbed over both the injurious McKinley tariff of 1890 and the anti-foreign tendencies of Queen Liliuokalani, were preparing a most auspicious plot. The " golden hour " came in 1893 when they launched the revolution designed to bring Hawaii within the American political system, and incidentally within the scope of its sugar bounty. This comic opera revolution succeeded only because Minister Stevens permitted the landing of American marines, needed much more for the protection of the revolutionists than of American property. But despite his energetic assistance of the revolution, Stevens publicly supported the resultant treaty of annexation by reference to " the logic of irresistible circumstances." [28]

Others too, like the *Philadelphia Inquirer,* greeted the treaty of annexation with the opinion that " the United States cannot block the movement which it had no hand in beginning " but must yield to " the hand of destiny." [29] For Hawaii, as the *New York Press* said, appeared to be imperatively linked to the American commonwealth by the " bonds of commerce and necessity." [30] Political necessity still seemed to arise from the alleged danger of foreign control, which was now apprehended with special reference to Great Britain. President Harrison's message accompanying the treaty declared that one of the great powers might acquire the islands — a contingency which "would not consist with our safety and with the peace of the world." He observed further: "Only two courses are now open; one the establishment of a protectorate by the United States, and the other annexation, full and complete." This admission of an alternative was virtually nullified, however, when Harrison affirmed that annexation was the only course which would "adequately secure the interests of the United States." [31]

One sees now for the first time a fact which will be met again and again in the history of this doctrine of inevitability. It is that the doctrine tends to be invoked in just the circumstances which upon analysis seem to give it least justification. Though it was now alleged that Hawaii was in danger of falling under foreign control, there was adduced no substantial evidence of acquisitive designs by Great Britain or any other power. The danger was now probably less than ever in the past. For whereas previously Hawaii had been under what Harrison called the "effete" [32] monarchy, open to foreign influence, it was now under the rule of former Americans who were vigorously disposed to cultivate intimate relations with their native country. It is further true that the excluded alternative of a protectorate was now no longer subject to the chief objection which Stevens had urged against it — that of assuming responsibility for a bungling régime. The fact that the doctrine of political necessity was applied precisely when the situation in Hawaii took a turn favorable to American interests may mean merely that not the best logic was used. But it is difficult to avoid the inference that the expansionists were fundamentally not interested in the logic of political necessity. The true instigation to expansionism was perhaps less the alleged danger than the belief that, as Stevens wrote, "the Hawaiian pear is now fully ripe, and this is the golden hour for the United States to pluck it." [33]

The prehensile disposition aroused by temptation was thwarted when President Cleveland arrived in office in time to subordinate manifest destiny to his old-fashioned ideas of international morality. However, his denunciation and withdrawal of the treaty did not sear but rather fertilized the expansionism which the Hawaiian issue had brought into sudden growth. Nor did it weaken the faith expressed by the New York *Sun* when it wrote in 1894: "The policy of annexation is the policy of destiny; and destiny always arrives." [34]

The arrival of destiny became more likely when the original conception of political necessity was sharpened by the new consciousness of the need expressed in the potent phrase "sea power." Whereas Hawaiian annexation had at first seemed necessary only as preventive of foreign acquisition, the doctrine of sea power now supplied positive reasons for regarding American possession as imperative. The popularization of this doctrine began in 1890, when there appeared the first essay in the series of writings in which Captain Mahan, the philosophical naval strategist, expounded and largely helped to propagate the cult of naval, commercial, and imperialistic expansion. In his essay entitled "The United States Looking Outward" Mahan made central a thesis of determinism: "Whether they will or no, Americans must now begin to look outward." [35] Looking outward meant to Mahan a recognition of the importance not only of foreign commerce but also of what were more generally overlooked — the ships and the naval power necessary to foreign commerce. The outward view, involving chiefly a view to enlargement of export trade, seemed to Mahan to be enforced on America primarily by the fact that a growing industrial production was for the first time exceeding national needs. But it was not until 1893, the year of his widely read essay on "Hawaii and our Future Sea Power," that Mahan extended the view of his countrymen to the expansionist implication of the doctrine of sea power. Control of the world's great medium of circulation being the chief element of national prosperity, it followed that "as subsidiary to such control, it is imperative to take possession, when it can be done righteously, of such maritime positions as contribute to secure command." [36] This postulate was shown to be particularly applicable to Hawaii, situated on or near the principal trade routes across the Pacific and located so advantageously for the defense of America's coast as to be called "the Gibraltar of the Pacific." [37]

The foregoing considerations form the background of Mahan's conspicuous strain of determinism. This appears first in his assertion that the expansion issue confronting America had arisen through "no premeditated contrivance of our own" but rather through "the cooperation of a series of events which, however dependent step by step upon human action, were not intended to prepare the present crisis." [38] Such events rendered it inevitable that, "whether we wish or no," America make a decision either for expansion or for its unavoidable alternative, retrogression. This much affirmed merely the inevitability of making a choice; other words implied further that psychological determinism governed the nature of the choice. For Mahan asserted that, if the principles of sea power were accepted, "there will be no hesitation about taking the positions . . . whose interests incline them to seek us." [39] Still further, he referred to American expansion as "natural, necessary, irrepressible." [40] Apparently these words express the conception that expansion is irrepressible because necessitated by natural or vital interests.

In the years following Mahan's essay and the discussion of the Hawaiian treaty, it became evident that at least Republicans did not hesitate to accept Mahan's "long view." The *New York Tribune* affirmed in 1893 that the traditional hostility of the United States toward an extension of authority and of territory among adjacent islands must to some extent shortly give way to "the necessities of our increasing commerce." [41] The possession of the Hawaiian Islands, Representative Draper declared without reservation in 1894, was "a commercial and naval necessity." [42] Senator Platt asserted in 1895 his belief that the men who were fighting against the intimate relations of the United States with Hawaii fought against fate, the stars in their courses, and the inevitable westward march of empire.[43] For now that Americans numbered seventy million, they could no longer shut themselves within narrow limits nor lose time in acquiring any territory which became necessary for defense or commercial development.

Yet it was scarcely a decade since Secretary of State Frelinghuysen had affirmed: "The United States have never deemed it needful to their national life to maintain impregnable fortresses along the world's highways of commerce." [44] In 1890 not even the outward-looking Mahan had asserted the indispensability of such fortresses to commercial expansion. In answer to the strategic argument the minority report of the House Committee of Foreign Affairs reasoned as follows:

> The islands are not from a naval or military standpoint necessary to our defense, as was admitted by General Schofield before the committee when he said there was but one harbor on the island which could be fitted up as a point d'appui against us. That harbor we already have.[45]

Pearl Harbor was in fact assigned to the United States for a naval base by a convention which, even if subject to termination by Hawaii, was not likely to be denounced by the existent Hawaiian Government. These considerations seem to confirm an observation in Professor Beard's critical study of the dogmas of naval experts — that "other elements besides the mathematics of fighting units enter into the calculations of experts who participate in the discussion of naval armament." [46]

One non-technical element in expansionism was shown in the doctrine of necessity which next arose. It held that the existent treaty relation between the United States and Hawaii, far from being a ground for letting well enough alone, as anti-expansionists maintained, was the factor which made annexation a destiny. This doctrine was used in connection with the treaty of annexation which the expansionist Republicans promptly negotiated in 1897 after being returned to power by McKinley's victory of 1896. The idea first appeared in Secretary of State Sherman's note informing Japan in 1897 that Hawaiian annexation was "the destined culmination" of "the progressive policies and dependent associations of some seventy years." [47] It was stated more fully in McKinley's message accompanying the submission of the treaty to the Senate:

> Not only is the union of the Hawaiian territory to the United States no new scheme, but it is the inevitable consequence of the relation steadfastly maintained with that mid-Pacific domain for three-quarters

> of a century. Its accomplishment, despite successive denials and postponements, has been merely a question of time. . . . Under such circumstances annexation is not a change. It is a consummation.[48]

The same certainty of the inevitable wedding of intimates appeared also in the Senate report of 1898 advocating ratification:

> Following the natural course of events in the direction of the inevitable union of Hawaii, by peaceable annexation to the United States, all of our relations have grown more intimate each year until the sovereignty of the islands has thus become, in effect, the sovereignty of the United States through these treaties which are founded alone in the mutual interest of the two countries.[49]

Unconsciously the propounders of this thesis of virtual sovereignty admitted a lack of validity in their simultaneous postulation of a commercial and naval necessity. For if the authority of the United States over the islands had become one of sovereignty " in effect," it was presumably capable of meeting all strategic and commercial needs. Thus the case had to rest solely on the thesis that sovereignty in effect must be consummated by sovereignty in law. The proposition is an instance of the error pointed out by Hobson in his discussion of the doctrine of inevitability — the placing of causation entirely outside the sphere of human will. In presenting annexation as a consummation of past events the expansionist was really seeking to obscure the fact that annexation was a momentous change.

However, even the argument of manifest destiny could not overcome the Senate's traditional inability to consummate any treaty when the opposition party is numerous among its membership. But directly afterward the course of events did intervene in a way offering powerful support to the cause of annexation. The " inevitable " outbreak of the Spanish-American War, the despatch of American ships to the Philippines by way of friendly Honolulu, the fall of Manila, the rise of a desire for retention of the Philippines — all these occurrences produced a reaction which Senator Lodge happily noted as he wrote to Roosevelt in June of 1898 that " the whole policy of annexation is growing rapidly under the irresistible pressure of events." [50]

The little resisted pressure of such events added to the armory of theories of inevitability a new argument — the necessity of annexing Hawaii as a war measure. A month after the battle of Manila President McKinley remarked to his Secretary: "We need Hawaii just as much and a great deal more than we did California. It is manifest destiny."[51] The United States needed Hawaii, the *New York Tribune* among many others alleged, because its extended occupation in the Philippines made the possession of Hawaii as a half-way naval station "imperative."[52] The anti-expansionists countered by arguing that Hawaii's extension of friendly facilities to the American fleet showed precisely that sovereignty over the islands was strategically unnecessary. But the expansionists came to contend also that Hawaii was necessary to the permanent retention of the Philippines as a fruit of victory. Thus the *Baltimore American* declared that nothing could stop America's flag from encompassing Hawaii, the stepping-stone to the Philippines and the great trade of the Orient.[53] The *Cincinnati Enquirer,* feeling constrained by manifest destiny even though of Democratic affiliation, wrote as follows in an editorial entitled "Hawaiian Annexation as a War Measure":

> . . . there suddenly comes upon us the necessity for a half-way station to the Philippine Islands. A scheme of empire has come upon the country in spite of our extraordinary conservatism. . . . Opposition to the annexation of the Hawaiian group is merely another fight against destiny.[54]

This argument that the annexation of Hawaii was indispensable to the possession of the Philippines elicited from the anti-expansionists a denial of the necessity of acquiring the Philippines. Curiously enough, a reason alleged for annexing the Philippines was the necessity of an outpost for Hawaii.

The foregoing theories of inevitability fall under a common type, which may be designated as "objective determinism." All postulate that the inevitabilities of national life result primarily from factors outside human will, from external events and resultant circumstances. The theory of objective determinism is dramatically stated by Victor Hugo in his interpretation of the French Revolution:

> It seems the joint work of grand events and grand individualities mingled, but it is in reality the result of events. Events dispense, men suffer. Events dictate, men sign. . . . Desmoulins, Danton, Murat, Grégoire, and Robespierre are mere scribes. The great and mysterious writer of these grand pages has a name—God; and a mask—Destiny. . . . The Revolution is a form of the eternal phenomenon which presses upon us from every quarter, and which we call Necessity.[55]

The same humility before the necessity in events was recorded by Lincoln in the words: "I claim not to have controlled events; I confess plainly that events have controlled me." In the Hawaiian issue this theory of determinism was epitomized by the words of Representative Gibson: "The inexorable logic of events has decreed this annexation." [56]

As described thus far the theory may seem open to the criticism of Hobson: "The only direct efficient forces in history are human motives." [57] Not only nationalist propagandists but even scholars like Sir John Seeley and C. H. Pearson frequently use rhetoric suggesting that circumstances control national action independently of both individual and collective will. But it is improbable that the reflective among them actually believe this far-fetched proposition, which even Americans subscribing to the doctrine of manifest destiny frequently denied. What they probably believe, as was seen, is merely that circumstances force the will itself to choose a direction different from that which it would choose apart from such circumstances. The expansionist's thesis that "necessity is stronger than theory" [58] meant that in any situation dangerous to national welfare the mass of patriots will invariably save the nation rather than the constitution.

Even when stated in its most coherent form, however, the doctrine of inevitability as applied to the Hawaiian issue was open to serious criticism. For anti-expansionist considerations apparently refuted, if not the proposition that annexation had its practical value, at least all the arguments that annexation was a political necessity. In view of this fact alone one may well doubt that a belief in practical necessity could have been the sole or fundamental motive of expansionism. But one's skepticism is the greater because there came a point when numerous expansionists themselves explicitly or implicitly admitted the absence of practical necessity. In the last month of the Hawaiian debate Representative Clark included in his argument for annexation the following confession:

> I am not disposed to think that any statement of reasons following the canons of logic or any showing of the resources and wealth of the islands will have any real weight in deciding American action or the action of Congress as to the annexation of Hawaii.[59]

Such frankness may have been partially prompted by the failure of expansionist canons of logic to refute the anti-expansionist's argument that Hawaiian commerce could be enjoyed to the full without annexation.

However, those who abandoned the doctrine of objective determinism were prepared with an alternative theory of necessity, to which we now turn our attention. Further words of the candid Representative Clark exemplified this new deterministic theory:

> Fear and greed are elementary in mankind. If either, and especially if both, or higher motives than either conspire to make an instinctive impulse of American energy to take Hawaii, we will take it, however the logicians and good reasoners and lovers of precedent be put in despair. The truth is, the premises and predicates of this Hawaiian matter were put into our Aryan blood at the beginning, with the race instinct of migration and its pervading land hunger. . . .
>
> Ralph Waldo Emerson said, 'Hitch your wagon to a star.' When the American flag was made we hitched our national wagon to all the stars, and we have got to go their way. We cannot resist them easily; there is not much American desire to resist.[60]

The fault lies in our stars in the sense that the racial instinct of migration, inherited from the enterprising pioneer of the covered wagon, gives rise to a virtually irresistible land-hunger. This type of theory may for contrast with objective determinism be called "subjective determinism." It affirms that the inevitabilities of national life are produced by subjective factors — instincts, desires, and emotions — which the mass of men cannot refrain from feeling and translating into effective action.

Subjective determinism received frequent enunciation in the months following the victory of Manila Bay; for this victory, by opening up the temptation of empire, aroused in nationalists an expansionist passion of which they could scarcely be unconscious. Other imperialists characterized the fundamental motive of expansionism more or less differently but shared the view of Clark that it was an irrepressible emotional force. Chauncey Depew defined the type of land-hunger more closely in speaking of "a colonial possession desire." "It is in the blood," he declared in an expansionist utterance, "and no power can stop it." [61] According to the editor of the *Overland Monthly,* the completed subjugation of the continent had to be followed by the yearning for new worlds in which to express the colonizing instinct which, "whether our conservative stay-at-homes like it or not . . . is now pushing us out and on . . . to the isles of the sea, — and beyond." [62] But the *Washington Post* believed that a new "yearning to show our strength" was impelling Americans on a path of empire which they "must tread wherever it leads, whatever the sacrifice or peril." [63]

One expansionist in Congress quoted approvingly the still somewhat different explanation of a contemporary writer in the English *Blackwood's Magazine.* Beneath the expansion movement this writer perceived a power at work which no McKinley could control even if bent upon controlling it: "the longing for distinction which no scheme of government could root out from the minds of the people individually." [64] Representative Gibson offered a pluralistic explanation of the determinism which he identified with manifest destiny:

> Wealth, power and glory are the three greatest objects of human ambition. They are the three things for which the Vikings longed two thousands years ago . . . and these are the three things that have prompted their descendants to brave the seas and storm the lands, following the 'star of empire' as westward it took its way; . . . the old Viking spirit is in the land. It is the controlling spirit of our people. It is bound to have its way. 'Manifest destiny' is its platform, its watchword, its faith and its battle-cry; and impelled by this spirit and this principle the people of the United States are even now taking a new departure . . . [65]

Another type of subjective determinism stressed not conscious purpose of any sort but unreflective instinct; the traditional doctrine of natural growth was extended to embrace psychological determinism by means of the conception of an irresistible growth-instinct. Such instinctive determinism was in the minds of those who, like Senator Stewart, affirmed that the Government was estopped from a policy of repression by a "law of growth" which could not be avoided.[66] The popular disposition to believe expansionism inevitable was reinforced by the learned deterministic theories promulgated by many scholars who perhaps desired to rationalize their participation in popular impulse. In an essay entitled the "War as a Suggestion of Manifest Destiny," Dr. H. H. Powers explained the powerful expansionist sentiment by the principle that "the forces that make our destiny come from deep down in the constitution of things and care little for our yea or nea." Expansionism, in other words, expressed a deep-lying instinct of growth which is as imperative in higher social aggregates as in individual species. "There is not a people living," Dr. Powers declared, "which would not, if pressure were removed, populate the earth," and "acquire universal dominion." Such an insatiability seemed to require the explanation that a people "has no sufficient knowledge or voluntary control of its own vital forces to prevent their working out their natural result."[67] The same belief in the predominance of instinct in human behavior was evidenced by Representative Clark when he cited the observation of Brooks Adams: "At the moment of action, the human being almost invariably obeys an instinct, like an animal; it is only after action has ceased does he reflect."[68] Adam Ferguson had affirmed many years before that instinct rather than reason governed the behavior of men in society. But whereas Ferguson viewed social behavior rather cynically, a modern English historian furnished authority for the disposition of the expansionists to idealize irrepressible instinct. Expansionists quoted the tribute paid to instinct by Seeley, the deterministic historian of English expansion: "In a truly living institution the instinct of development is wiser than the utterances of the wisest individual man." Such words supported John Stuart Mill's observation that it was a characteristic prejudice of the nineteenth century to attribute to the unreasoning elements in human nature the infallibility which the eighteenth century ascribed to the reasoning elements.

The view that the wise instinct of the people favored expansion was supplemented by a theory regarding the effect of public opinion upon legislation. A deterministic theory of legislation was used to warn certain legislators, who, not having the wisdom of the people, agreed with Senator Pettigrew that the proposed annexation was a first " step in sin." [69] Confidence in destiny was preserved by a theory which the *Nation* ironically called " democratic fatalism." [70] This fatalism maintained that in a democracy public opinion exercised over the majority of legislators the control of a fate. It was an old theory among a people whose history had so frequently given evidence supporting it. Gouverneur Morris confessed that his belief in the irresistibility of " the lust of dominion " [71] had prevented him from placing territorial aggrandizement under constitutional interdiction. In the impetuous 'fifties Seward declared that " popular passion for territorial aggrandizement is irresistible," [72] and Representative Latham identified the *modus operandi* of manifest destiny with the willingness of leaders to be borne along by public opinion.[73] Captain Mahan affirmed in 1893 that British colonial expansion, which he now commended to his countrymen, had always resulted from " the steady pressure of a national instinct so powerful and so accurate that statesmen of every school, willing or unwilling, have found themselves carried along by a tendency which no individuality can resist or greatly modify." [74]

In 1898 unwilling statesmen were warned by words like those of Murat Halstead: " We shall have Hawaii, of course, if not in one way, in another, and there is nothing in the special pleas of lawyers or the public quirks of other public men, that will prevent our people from having their own way." [75] The commercial and moral impulses of the people, Judge Grosscup observed, are " irresistible forces " which " doctrinairians and statesmen can not, if they would, hold back." [76] Representative Danford defied even a political party to stem the current of events toward annexation.[77] Representative Gibson declared with emphatic repetitiousness:

Manifest destiny says, 'Take them in.' The American people say, 'Take them.' Obedient to the voice of the people, I shall cast my vote to take them in; and to-morrow this House of Representatives will by a good round majority say, 'Take them in.' [78]

Not only the House but the Senate as well said precisely that in voting on the joint resolution of annexation. The fact was perhaps illustrative of the determination of the legislator's vote by the necessity of reelection.

Both objective and subjective determinism were right as to the result, but the two theories presented contradictory reasons for the result. The one generalization held that circumstances appealing to rational self-interest controlled the will; the other generalization held contradictorily that popular passion controlled both the will and circumstances. Each theory was apparently incorrect as generalization because each was used in self-explanation by different expansionists. But the possibility that he may have been right for the wrong reason was lost upon the expansionist in his pride over the fact that his prediction had been verified.

Thus he used the doctrine of inevitability more confidently than before in the ensuing discussion on the Philippines. Indeed, even before the annexation of Hawaii, Secretary of State Day had become convinced that we "could not escape our destiny" on the archipelago.[79] By the time of the armistice with Spain, the talk of destiny was general even among those who were described by Mr. Dooley as not having known six months before whether the Philippines were islands or canned fruit.

The desire for the Philippines seemed to well up from the same tide of nationalist emotionalism which had suggested the theory of subjective determinism in the Hawaiian issue. But perhaps because the moral difficulties of the Philippine issue made expansionists more anxious to avoid personal responsibility, it was the doctrine of objective determinism which first came to the fore in the discussion of the Philippines. President McKinley set the fashion in contradicting Napoleon's dictum that it is policy which makes destiny. Thus his instructions to the peace commissioners disclaimed responsibility for expansionist policy by affirming that "the evolution of events, which no man could control, has brought these problems upon us."

In other words, the fortunes of war brought territory which Americans had "not sought."[80] Yet all this had not been by mere chance; rather, according to McKinley, the Philippines came to the United States "in the province of God"[81] by virtue of "his plans and methods for human progress."[82] A good many others agreed at least with Viscount Bryce that America "drifted into dominion."[83] Thus the Vice-President of the National Geographical Society asserted that "America's progress in territorial development has never been the outcome of ulterior policy; it has always been an expression of manifest destiny."[84] Pietistic expansionists, especially those envisaging missionary opportunities, subscribed also to McKinley's theological dogma. It was paraphrased by Bishop Thoburn as follows:

> . . . such an extraordinary turn of things I did not believe had come by chance, and I am sure it did not come by the deliberate design of the American Government—and so I attribute it to Providence, another name for God.[85]

This theological determinism, an avowed presupposition of George Bancroft in writing American history, tends to crop up in all momentous national issues even though at other times it seems a bit silly or sacrilegious. It has at least the logical merit that it is as little subject to empirical disproof as to proof.

From the point of view of theological determinism, "statesmanship is seeing where almighty God is going and then getting things out of his way."[86] Once more it was supposed that the providential course of events exercised an irresistible coercion upon the human will. But in contrast with the Hawaiian issue, it appeared now that events touched not upon national self-interest, but upon a motive more appropriate for an issue in which God figured — international altruism. A theory which may be called moral determinism was suggested by McKinley in his instructions to the American peace commissioners:

> . . . without any original thought of complete or even partial acquisition, the presence and success of our arms at Manila imposes upon us obligations which we cannot disregard. The march of events rules and overrules human action.[87]

A few weeks later, the advance of McKinley's sense of moral obligation if not of events overrode his original intention to acquire only Luzon. The President's increase of territorial demand to the entire archipelago was justified in Secretary of State Hay's cable to the Peace Commission on the ground that "willing or not, we have the responsibility of duty which we cannot escape." [88] The peace commissioners, while bound primarily by the President's desires, also explained their expansionism in terms of moral determinism. Thus Senator Davis asserted that "whatever we may have desired ourselves, heretofore, destiny has forced upon us responsibilities that we must recognize and accept." [89] Even Senator Gray, who originally asserted that taking the Philippines would sacrifice America's moral position, explained his shortly ensuing change to imperialism by saying that "unquestionable duties had sprung which could not be avoided or evaded by the United States"; for "in this, as in all else, 'man proposes, God disposes.'" [90] Ex-Minister Denby defended both the peace commissioners and Providence in the words:

> Call it destiny, call it the will of God, call it the overruling result of circumstances, call it what you will, it is plain that an overpowering necessity rested on the commissioners who made the treaty to force on Spain the cession of the islands.
>
> There was no other outcome or outlook. Honor forbade that we should turn over to the tender mercies of Spain the insurgents whom we had armed and fed and encouraged in revolt.[91]

When McKinley went before the people to answer his critics, who believed that a different outcome had been quite possible, he summarized the foregoing philosophy in an alliterative epigram: "Duty determines destiny." [92]

But there remained, as the *Nation* pointed out, the further question of "who determines Duty." [93] It appeared to McKinley's critics that he was taking upon himself rather arbitrarily the determination of America's duty and therewith of its destiny. McKinley, however, had a different explanation of the criterion of duty — one which was individually humble even though nationally self-assured. It is supplied by another of his sonorous epigrams: "My countrymen, the currents of destiny flow through the hearts of the people." [94] The *Nation's* editorial "Destiny and Duty" made the irreverent comment that, though this was the only place where the currents of destiny did flow, the hearts of men were bent upon iniquities as well as duties.[95] McKinley, however, meant to say that the moral judgment of the American people as a whole was always right, presumably through divine inspiration. He was repeating, without Fisher Ames's irony, the latter's observation that democrats think the people "a sovereign who can do no wrong," and that the voice of the people has "all the sanctity and all the force of a living divinity." [96]

Perhaps McKinley's inclination to believe the people right in this issue, despite his original uncertainties, was greatly reinforced by his assumption that their expansionism was irresistible — at least by anyone not contemplating political suicide. He implied the theory of democratic fatalism as he asked with reference to the popular currents of destiny: "Who will stop them?" [97] Even Secretary Hay, who once had written verses repudiating oversea expansion, did not attempt to arrest these currents. "No man, no party," he declared later with reference to expansion, "can fight with any chance of final success against a cosmic tendency . . . against the spirit of the age" in a nation "whose object and purposes are the welfare of humanity." [98] However, the purposes of popular sentiment were apparently not determined by expansionist statesmen merely through an objective inquiry into the relative frequency of anti-expansionist and of expansionist utterances. Preponderant public sentiment was assumed to be expansionist because a preconceived theory of religio-ethical determinism required it to be expansionist. Thus Senator Beveridge proclaimed:

> The Republic could not retreat if it would; whatever its destiny, it must proceed. For the American Republic is a part of the movement of a race,—the most masterful race of history,—and race movements are not to be stayed by the hand of man. They are mighty answers to divine commands.[99]

While Providence performs its wonders in mysterious ways, the theory that the American people or their leaders were its reluctant agents who answered to commands implicit in altogether unplanned events — or in the words of President Harding, that the acquisition of the Philippines occurred through "no individual or governmental design" but through "the revolution of the fates" [100] — this metaphysical interpretation of history is open at least in its psychological implications to grave suspicions. What were some of the facts relative to the question of individual design? Although affirming later as President that "the inevitable march of events gave us the control of the Philippine Islands," [101] Roosevelt as Assistant Secretary of the Navy ordered contingently an attack upon them even before the war began. McKinley, who "posed as the victim of destiny," deliberately despatched the expedition to the islands, inquired before the treaty about their economic value, and refused recognition to Aguinaldo's government. At the least, American leaders seemed to meet the course of events somewhat more than half-way. Some hold that they were about as much the marionettes of external events as is the energetic individual who decides upon, plans, and carries out the robbery of a bank.

It is true that probably no expansionist was aware of robbery; it is further true that with respect to some, as Professor Baldwin contemporaneously said, "humanitarian sentiment . . . is the thing that makes expansion inevitable." [102] Yet with respect to the majority it seems improbable that the territory which fitted into Lodge's preconceived "large policy" [103] was retained purely or even primarily because of ethical compulsions. One reason for skepticism is that an informal or formal protectorate could have been reasonably regarded as satisfying amply any moral obligation. The adopted policy, while satisfying the desire for sovereignty, threatened and resulted in such great human devastation that the expansionist's ethico-religious determinism might well appear as the expression of an uneasy conscience. But what casts the gravest doubt upon McKinley's edifying generalization about his supporters is the fact that many of them openly rejected it. Ex-Minister Denby, though at first an exponent of moral determinism, later declared the only question to be the cold practical one of self-interest; if the islands would not benefit us, "set them free tomorrow and let their peoples, if they please, cut each other's throats." [104]

But those impatient with moral imperatives were equipped, fortunately for Filipino throats, with an alternative theory of determinism. It was the familiar argument of commercial necessity which was used by those intent less upon edification than upon stirring the interest of the hard-headed. Commercial necessity no longer, however, seemed to dictate merely the acquisition of naval harbors for the defense and convenience of foreign trade. The principal aim was now to find new trade outlets for a domestic industry which, as Beveridge said, was producing more than the nation could consume and would continue to do so as a result of "the overwhelming productive energy and capacity of the American people." [105] Thus expansionists affirmed (in the words of the *Journal of Commerce*) "the necessity of being ready to defend by force of arms if need be, the right to share on equal terms with all other nations the opportunities of trade which the vast and undeveloped Chinese market affords." [106] This assumption led to the further postulate, stated by R. Van Bergen in his article "Expansion Unavoidable," that if America's interests in China were to be defended, "territorial expansion is a necessity"; only with a near-by base could the arena of international competition be entered on equal terms.[107]

The premise that expansion was essential to vital interest yielded as usual the conclusion that it was inevitable. "Fate has written our policy for us," declared Senator Beveridge, "the trade of the world must and shall be ours." [108] That we could not extricate ourselves from the intricate web of the world's commercial development even if we wished was the widespread view expressed by Representative Kirkpatrick.[109] Ex-Minister Denby affirmed that though America might momentarily turn away from it she could not succeed in escaping her great future, and would thus do better to recognize the certainty of her commercial destiny in good time.[110] The diffusion of this doctrine of determinism must be credited not merely to political leaders and publicists but also to a group of sociologists and other scholars, who played generally an important rôle in leading Americans into the imperialist policy. Thus the influential Benjamin Kidd wrote that, as regards the control of the tropics, "there can be no choice in this matter";[111] the man of the West seemed to him right in holding expansion to be inevitable.[112] From a similar point of view F. H. Giddings affirmed territorial expansion to be "as certain as the advent of spring after winter," an instance of cosmic law against which the contention of our wise men was idle and foolish.[113] The economist Charles Conant described the determinant of our "irresistible tendency to expansion" as "a natural law of economic and race development," that is, an instinctive racial reaction to economic necessity.[114] In the light of economic imperatives Brooks Adams affirmed the unconditional necessity of America's competing for the seat of empire:

> It is in vain that men talk of keeping free from entanglements. Nature is omnipotent; and nations must float with the tide. Whither the exchanges flow, they must follow; and they will follow as long as their vitality endures.[115]

The determinism of all these capitalistic expansionists rested upon the Marxian contention that "economics make destiny," that is, upon the psychological postulate that there is an inevitable impulse in social aggregates to take the direction of economic self-interest.

But the applicability of this theory of economic necessity to the expansion movement is clearer to those maintaining a priori generalizations about human nature than to objective investigators of the historical facts. The failure of most business men and bankers to support even a war painted in glowing colors of economic opportunity has been noted by Professor Pratt.[116] Although the business class eventually accepted appreciatively the fruits of victory, it remains true, as Pratt also points out, that the leading sponsors of commercial expansion were nationalist politicians, naval strategists, and loquacious scholars.[117] How greatly commercial expectations from the Philippines were disappointed has been shown recently in a statistical study by a former member of the United

States Department of Commerce.[118] That these expectations were so much exaggerated as to be linked with a thesis of economic necessity was perhaps not altogether the result of logical error. It was partly the result of the fact that only a thesis of imperious necessity could overcome the serious misgivings about a nationalist ambition fraught with such great political as well as moral perils.

After the nation had become more habituated to these perils the argument of economic necessity ceased to be advanced so urgently, whether because it had already served its purpose or because the mounting costs of rebellion rendered it incongruous. Indeed there were some expansionists who went so far as to admit its invalidity. Thus Representative Bartholdt, in a speech of February, 1900, declared that the expansion issue had been due to no physical necessity; for even at the time there was room in the United States for hundreds of millions more. He denied also that it had been due to moral necessity. The reason for the growing appeal of expansion despite "the undeniable uncertainties of the experiment" was an inner impulse which no laws could down:

> It is the law of nature, the human longing for the change and for the new, the never latent and irresistible force of progress whose mysterious source is nature itself. The western course of the 'star of empire' is one of its most noted manifestations.[119]

The foregoing is typical of the culminating ideology of the Philippine issue as of the Hawaiian — the admission that, after all, the dynamics of the expansion movement lay in "human longing" and thus in a subjective rather than an objective determinism. Charles Kendall Adams declared that the policy of annexation appealed to the people's consciousness of manifest destiny, of an order of nature according to which America should be first in the Pacific.[120] The *Outlook,* denying that destiny came from a passive acceptance of external conditions, identified the manifest destiny of expansionism with "an inward force — the force which has made men of our race discoverers, explorers, settlers, organizers . . . for many centuries." [121] Senator Lodge affirmed that a "law" in America's inner being, imperious even if not entirely irresistible, had impelled the nation toward its manifest destiny of mastery in the Pacific and primacy among the nations.[122] Walter Sulzbach's theory that imperialism represents the senseless pursuit of sheer power was anticipated by Professor Powers in an essay of 1900 on the ethics of expansion:

> To the question, shall we hold aloof, we have yet to hear the most significant answer. *We cannot hold aloof.* The instincts which control . . . masses of men respond to appropriate stimuli with a regularity that suggests little dependence on argument and deliberation. The crisis came and we acted as our impulse dictated and then talked it over afterward. . . . The consciousness of power as naturally expresses itself in self-assertion as the consciousness of weakness does in submission. . . . When the slumbering instincts of race unity and action are aroused, they brush aside the petty barriers of logic and pseudo-obligation without apology or hesitation.[123]

Certainly these admissions of an instinct of self-assertion dispose one to view skeptically the generalizations regarding economic or moral necessity. On the other hand, there has been enough evidence of consideration for " logic and pseudo-obligation " to discredit any psychological generalization overlooking them. The sum of the matter is that the more the monistic theories of determinism accumulate, the more does the motivation of America's imperialism appear complex.

In the perspective of history the necessities determining America's colonial enterprises appeared complex even to that simplifying imperialist, Senator Beveridge. Speaking before the American Academy of Political and Social Science in 1907, he asserted that America's entrance upon colonial administration was " inevitable " for the following reasons:

> Our rapidly-increasing power determined it; our commercial needs determined it; more than either, geography determined it; and, most of all, our duty to the world as one of its civilizing powers determined it.

Senator Beveridge was not content with the facile application of determinism to the past but predicted that " where nature and events shall direct us to go, there we will go." Even greater was the faith of Beveridge that America would not retreat from her present outposts of duty:

> If any one cherishes the delusion that American government will ever be withdrawn from our possessions, let him consult the religious conviction of this Christian people. . . . Let him, above all, consider history and study our racial instinct. No! our flag will not be lowered anywhere. Our duty of administration of orderly government to weaker peoples will not be abandoned.[124]

A little later Lord Curzon supported Beveridge's theory by observing that though most Americans were opposed to imperialism, they were caught in toils from which they could not escape.[125]

But the *Nation* vigorously gainsaid Lord Curzon in an editorial entitled "Imperial Fatalism." "Any vigorous and self-respecting nation," declared this periodical, "ought to regard it as a libel to say of it that it is so hampered by circumstances that it cannot do justice, cannot deal with great problems in accordance with its own fixed principles." [126] Less than a decade later the passage of the Jones Bill, the first formal promise of Philippine independence, indicated that changed circumstance or mood had introduced a confidence in America's ability to deal with problems in accordance with her own principles.

However, the doctrine of the inevitable persisted among those desirous of handling America's relations with Latin America imperialistically. Just about the time of the passage of the Jones Bill, the *Chicago Tribune* was prompted by the purchase of the Nicaraguan canal route to expound a deterministic philosophy of southward extension through establishment of protectorates and other relationships. Although recognizing that the American people no longer liked to call the process manifest destiny or even consciously to will it, the *Tribune* recognized in it "forces deeper than our formal policies, inherent in the character of our people, inevitable while our vitality remains." [127] Not merely such subjective determinism but objective determinism as well marked the ideology of twentieth-century imperialism. Intervention in Nicaragua in 1927 was the occasion of rather numerous expressions of the view stated by the *Kansas City Star* in the words: "The inexorable march of events forces us to accept responsibilities in Nicaragua and through the American tropics. We cannot escape them, try as we will." [128] One element in this theory of objective determinism was the idea of political necessity, exemplified by the *St. Louis Globe-Democrat's* reference to "compulsion of circumstances growing out of self-defense." Another was the concept of moral determinism, illustated by the statement of the same organ that the evolution beginning with assumption of moral responsibilities in the Spanish-American War "must go on, because we could not help it if we would, unless we are to turn back to our past and betray the trust which destiny has placed in our hands." [129]

But the anti-imperialistic policy initiated during the Hoover administration showed that Americans could revolt successfully against previous destiny without any sense of betrayal of trust. The passage of the Philippine independence bills of 1933 and 1934 signified even greater energy in cutting the toils of circumstance. The decision to escape from them seems explicable by two considerations. The first, applicable to some Americans, is that moral obligation came to mean not retention but release of an unwilling subject people. The second, applicable to others, is that the same commercial motive which had helped to entangle us in imperialism now urged cutting loose from a demonstrated source of economic competition.

Whatever its motive, the reversal of policy does not seem to have been influenced by any theory of determinism. On the contrary, Representative Fish spoke words which implicitly repudiated this once so popular nationalist doctrine:

> The Congress of the United States is about to show to the world that we are not an imperialistic nation. Of our own free will and accord we are about to grant that independence to the Philippine people, which we promised them many years ago.[130]

The doctrine of determinism thus passes out simultaneously with the master which it faithfully served — an imperialism determined to have its way with destiny.

In the light of the history of the doctrine its fundamental meaning seems to be revealed less by its internal logic than by the circumstances of its use. The doctrine of inevitability purports to be the justification of what one is reluctant to do. It in fact tends to come into acceptance only when, as René Félix Allendy observes in his *La problème de la destinée,*[131] it is in accord with an at least unconscious current of desire. It is further noteworthy that the doctrine is most used when, as in the case of its imperialistic form, there exist strong objections to the course of destiny because of either expediency or morals. One might almost say with Hobson that "the 'inevitable' is always invoked to defend a *prima facie* bad case."[132] The humorist Josh Billings apparently had this fact in mind when he defined manifest destiny as "the science of going to the devil before one gets there."

Partly because destiny seems the will of God and not the devil, a belief in inevitability does increase the likelihood that any hope will be realized. Necessitarianism either causes abandonment of opposition to the course of events or creates a confidence which increases the individual's ability to control the course of events. It is doubtless in view of this fact that Maurice Maeterlinck observes in his *Wisdom and Destiny* that "it might almost be said that there happens to men only that they desire."[133] Similarly, Allendy writes that, once impressed upon the unconscious, "*l'image-destinée tend activement à sa réalisation.*"[134]

The general validity of the doctrine of inevitability is of course a question independent of the accuracy of specific predictions. In raising this question of validity one can also leave outside discussion the broad philosophical issue of determinism itself. Determinism holds merely that the will lies within the chain of causality, in other words, that whether the individual "decides in the one way or the other, there are certain causes operating within the organism which are responsible for the decision."[135] But the expansionists went beyond determinism to a *non sequitur.* It is, as was shown by their predictions, the dogma that one can know the inevitable before it has happened. This, however, is the dogma of the metaphysician rather than of the empirical scientist. Even prediction projecting the findings of past observation must be of tentative character in that "the long continued association of *a* and *b* gives us a right only to a probable judgment about their further association."[136] But the difficulty of prediction is much greater in the sphere of phenomena which are dependent upon so great a variety of conditions as is the behavior of human groups. For, as the writings of Rickert especially suggest, conditions which have determined past behavior may be peculiar in nature and configuration to a degree which destroys the usefulness of history as a basis for sociological laws.

Admission of the impossibility of certainty in prediction does not, indeed, discredit the concept of probability, which in many cases the expansionists doubtless really had in mind. The use of the phrase "manifest destiny" in a judgment of probability is clearly shown by the paradoxical words of Walt Whitman: "It is impossible to say what the future will bring forth, but 'manifest destiny' certainly points to the speedy annexation of Cuba by the United States."[137] The refutation of this prediction and so many similar ones makes quite manifest the difficulty of forming even judgments of probability with regard to what the future will bring forth.

Some reasons for the difficulty in predicting national behavior have been thrown into sharp relief by the curious data of the foregoing survey. It has shown that the very expansionists who agreed that national behavior was predictable in the light of one dominant motive were in the greatest disagreement about the nature of this motive. At various times or the same time they made pivotal such contrasting motives as deference to external circumstances and determination to mould circumstances, rational strategic interest and emotional impulse toward national glory, international altruism and economic acquisitiveness. *Du choc des opinions jaillit la vérité.* The truth is that fundamental motives are too many, varied, and conflicting to permit foreknowledge of the motive which will actuate the predominant group. But even ability to foretell the victorious motive would not overcome the difficulty offered by another fact which has been demonstrated. It is that the same motive, in accordance with varying interpretations of an issue, impelled different individuals in opposite directions. Both morality and national self-interest impelled some to expansionism, others to anti-expansionism. In consequence the conflict between expansionist and anti-expansionist was at each stage heated and of uncertain outcome.

The sum of the matter was stated by the *Nation,* organ representative of the long and ultimately predominant opposition to what was called manifest destiny:

> But the truth is we know but one thing about destiny—that it is not manifest . . .[138]

# CHAPTER X

## THE WHITE MAN'S BURDEN

The expansionist's belief that a tide of fortune was carrying the nation out to "sea power" had scarcely seemed confirmed by Hawaiian annexation when it was suddenly shattered. Disillusionment came when a *soi-disant* Philippine government met the threatened submersion of its pretension to national independence with unexpected resistance. Shortly after the outbreak of the Philippine insurrection, the anti-imperialistic Bryan could say with malicious humor: "'Destiny' is not as manifest as it was a few weeks ago."[1] What had become painfully manifest was that the fulfilment of expansionist desires could no longer be left to fate but required force—conceived by John Morley as an inevitability of imperialism.

In resorting to imperialist subjugation the expansionists pursued a course which had previously been considered alien to America's humanitarian destiny. To be sure, the principle of consent of the governed had been violated in letter so often that imperialism should have seemed as traditional as philosophical democracy. But such generalizations of nations are formulated with a view not to strict obedience but only to keeping disobedience within reasonable limits. In truth, the principle of consent had never been conspicuously violated by national action to a degree which was in patent conflict with its humanitarian spirit. While it had generally appeared overscrupulous to obtain the registered consent of the governed, it had rarely seemed consistent with the spirit of democracy to override a refusal so sharp and widespread as to require conquest. Until 1899, the year of militaristic imperialism, the American could plausibly repeat the words of Jefferson: "Conquest [is] not in our principles . . ."[2]

However, anti-imperialists shocked at human casualties were wrong in interpreting the conquest of the Philippines as an overriding of principles by mere sadistic ambition. In the complex affairs of state the shedding of blood usually signifies not sadism but merely the fact that, as Bossuet has said, men do otherwise than they intend. Actually, the president called by one anti-expansionist an "insatiable murderer"[3] was one of the most amiable and honorable of men. Even his less amiable supporters were doubtless all honorable men, possessed of that deep-seated conviction of their intention to do right in which Assistant Secretary of State Hill saw the greatness of the American people.[4] A paradoxical fact is, indeed, that the same humanitarian ideal which had once been used to discredit conquest was now employed with equal confidence in its justification.

The central doctrine of imperialism went far beyond Montesquieu's truism that conquest can benefit the conquered. It also benefited the self-esteem of the conqueror by attributing to him a lofty motive which aggressive peoples had not usually claimed before the racially and culturally self-conscious imperialism of the nineteenth century. Like European predecessors in this century, American expansionists conceived force in its various degrees as the means of fulfilling the destined duty of extending civilization to the unappreciative race of color.

As curious as certain marriages of human opposites, this ideological association of humanitarianism and force suggests either of two diverse possibilities as fundamental cause. One possibility is that, in view of a latent element of logical affinity between the two ideas, humanitarianism actually required force as its helpmate. Another is that this association of ideas was intrinsically a *mariage de convenance* which was arranged by nationalist expansionism to give its ambitions quasi-respectable gratification. The meaning of the imperialist ideology will become evident only as assumptions which are more frequently acted upon than carefully analyzed are studied in their historical development.

Despite the anti-imperialist's claim that imperialism was neither the "natural" nor the "necessary" product of American history and traditions,[5] the expansion movement of 1898 emerged after a period of gestation wherein it was subjected to important pre-natal determinants. According to the imperialist of 1899, all previous American history had prepared for the realization of the beneficence of force. He pointed out such outstanding precedents as the domestic limitation of franchise, the disregard of consent in the Louisiana issue, wars of Indian subjugation, and the institution of negro slavery with its presupposition that the relation between races of disparate intelligence calls for humanitarian coercion. But decisive influence cannot be ascribed to precedents which, aside from the fact that no case was precisely analogous to the subjugation of an alien people, were not cited until Americans were already involved in imperialism. John Burgess, expounding in his book of 1890 the humanitarian imperialism familiar to Europe, acknowledged that his own countrymen regarded imperialist policy as one of "unwarrantable interference." [6] Yet the beginning of the 'nineties marked roughly the incipience of the tendency which, little as it was consciously related at first to philosophical imperialism, led most directly to the ideology of 1898. Lying in the popular mood in which ideology often germinates, the seed of imperialism was an inclination toward two emotions akin to the elements of imperialist ideology.

These two emotions, diverse as the olive-branch and the arrow of the American eagle, were humanitarianism and a belligerent spirit of national self-assertion. These were the two components of the new desire for "a vigorous foreign policy," which became widespread as the nation emerged from domestic reconstruction to a keen consciousness of moral and politico-commercial interests beyond its borders. There were some who saw only the second, as obtrusive as the new stress upon warships. The Democratic platform of 1892 spoke of a "tendency to a policy of irritation and bluster"; [7] the conservative Republican, Senator Hale, pointed out a growing "aggressive spirit"; [8] and the liberal Edwin Godkin waxed indignant over the desire to use new-found power "in brutal fashion against any one who comes along." [9] All such strictures, however, overlook the coalescence of bellicose nationalism with humanitarianism, complementary elements of the same will to preeminence.

This coalescence of opposites appeared first in the movement for Hawaiian annexation, conducted forcibly by the revolting ex-American planters but peaceably by the American Government. On the one hand, this movement expressed an aggressive aspiration toward predominant sea power, which was nourished by the jealous feeling that, as Senator Lodge said, the United States "must not fall out of the line of march" as the great nations rapidly absorbed the waste places of the earth.[10] On the other hand, the proposal of this annexation involved an awakening sense of civilizing duty, likened by Captain Mahan to the missionary spirit,[11] and by a Senate committee to paternal love.[12] Shortly after Cleveland withdrew the treaty of annexation, however, he took so belligerent a stand toward Great Britain in the Venezuelan issue that Roosevelt's [13] prescription of a good war seemed more welcome than missionary sentimentality. But Olney's assertion of America's "fiat" as law brought the Monroe Doctrine to the defense of a weak American people whose alleged rights were imperilled. The Venezuelan crisis had scarcely blown over when American sympathy with the Cuban revolt turned bellicosity toward Spain. Within a few years there was the widespread insistence upon war which not even Spain's accession to virtually all American demands could stave off. But the growth of what the *New York Journal* called "aggressive Americanism" [14] was watered by tears over Cuba's exaggerated wrongs at the "cruel" hands of Spain. The Spanish War finally gave Americans the outlet sought throughout previous years of the decade by the convergent streams of humanitarian sentiment and aggressive temper.

The ideology of the Cuban intervention rationalized this convergence by placing humanitarianism and force in association. It made humanitarianism the justification of force that defeated unrighteous force, of force compelling a strong power to release unwilling subjects. McKinley thus based the Cuban intervention upon "the large dictates of humanity" to deliver the Cuban people from oppression.[15] The Omaha *World-Herald* transposed this idea of the war message into the terminology of manifest destiny: "God's most dreaded instrument will, with our arms, be working out a pure intent." [16] Though the intent was that of the knight-errant, it prepared for imperialism by idealizing the sword as humanitarian instrument.

However, the American knight-errant at this time disapproved the use of the sword to annex a weak people. Thus McKinley said of Cuba in his annual message of 1897: "I speak not of forcible annexation, for that can not be thought of. That by our code of morality would be criminal aggression." [17] These words, which later proved a boomerang, conformed to a current political attitude such as was shown by the passage of the Teller Amendment abjuring the annexation of Cuba. The same attitude appeared in the Hawaiian issue even though this ended in annexation. The expansionists took particular pleasure in representing the proposed annexation as a benevolent response to the voluntary request of the Hawaiians — more correctly, their Americanized government — for incorporation. Captain Mahan conceded freely that the blessings of our economy should not be forced upon the unwilling.[18] Senator Hoar saw the annexation as according with America's anti-imperialistic conception of its humanitarian destiny; [19] at the same time McKinley expressed to Senator Hoar a more forcible denunciation of the conquest of Oriental peoples than any voiced by the latter in the Philippine issue.[20]

What caused Americans to stop short of imperialism when their ideology of knight-errantry tended logically toward it? The most obvious reason is that they found it possible to satisfy their desires without imperialism. Another cause, somewhat concealed by the martial talk, was the absence of sufficient iron in the American soul. Again, a source of more conscious restraint was the incompatibility of imperialism with the dominant American "code of morality." These considerations throw into sharper relief the problem of determining the new occasions, emotions, and moral ideas in the strange alchemy which transmuted knight-errantry into imperialism.

The occasion for imperialism arose out of the very war designed to bring a people liberty. This incongruous fact was in accord with the observation of John Quincy Adams that all wars, even wars for liberty, tend to eventuate in imperialism.[21] The trend of the Spanish War toward imperialism began appropriately enough with a magnificent victory of force — Dewey's destruction of the Spanish fleet in Manila Bay. This attack, dictated by the strategy of destroying Spain's naval power, blasted open America's way to an unexpected opportunity. Americans were not long in seeing this opportunity; even before American forces set foot on Philippine soil, incorporation of the islands was " boldly proclaimed in some quarters as the manifest destiny of this country." [22] The expansionist sentiment had become both widespread and clamorous by the time of the armistice. The demand for the Philippines was based legally on the right to indemnity for the war, but rested fundamentally on the imperialistic assumption that a conqueror can put into a treaty of peace whatever he desires.

Long before it was necessary to adopt a policy of force with the Filipinos, expansionism gave emotional preparation for imperialism by virtue of the element which was principally responsible for its intensity. This fundamental element was not an interest in territorial aggrandizement for its own sake; nor was it even the conception of the Philippines as a stepping-stone to the coveted commerce of the Orient. It was apparently — if one may take as criterion the relative emphasis placed upon various incentives by most expansionists themselves — the nationalistic power-impulse which had been gaining strength throughout the decade. This impulse attained full self-consciousness when the spiritual reverberations from Dewey's guns destroyed certain traditional inhibitions as shell-shock may destroy the memories of the past. For Dewey's triumphant guns were heard as the signal summoning America from her politically and morally cautious isolationism to the quarrel-ridden but glorious arena of world politics.

Innumerable voices now called for an assumption of the armed imperial garb which European powers had just made the fashion. Americans saw in entrance upon world power a release from the painful sense of being what Henry Watterson had called " a Pariah among the governments of men " by reason of " squalid Democracy " and " isolation." [23] They envisaged now the kingdom, the power, and the glory — in the secular aspect suggested by Attorney-General Griggs's definition of "Paradise Regained" as "confidence in ourselves."[24] With the exaggerated pride of one suddenly released from a sense of inferiority, Cushman K. Davis, the expansionist chairman of the Senate Committee on Foreign Relations, proclaimed: "The United States has ceased to be the China of the Western Continent. We are alive, thank God, and must not be insulted by any power in this world, great or small."[25] The compensatory self-assertiveness of many is ingenuously described in an editorial of the *Washington Post:*

> A new consciousness seems to have come upon us—the consciousness of strength—and with it a new appetite, the yearning to show our strength. It might be compared with the effect upon the animal creation of the taste of blood.
>
> Ambition, interest, land hunger, pride, the mere joy of fighting, whatever it may be, we are animated by a new sensation. We are face to face with a strange destiny.
>
> The taste of empire is in the mouth of the people even as the taste of blood in the jungle. It means an imperial policy, the Republic, renascent, taking her place with the armed nations.[26]

Yet to this bellicose impulse humanitarian sentiment was a faithful mate from the beginning. So little incongruous did such unions seem to expansionists that Secretary of the Treasury Gage noted unctuously the fact that in America's foreign policy international philanthropy and five per cent would go hand in hand.[27] Nor did it appear at all peculiar to Americans that a philanthropic disposition toward the Filipinos had not arisen during the long suffering of this Oriental people under Spain; for they believed, as McKinley's biographer innocently remarks, that it was not America's duty to interfere until the situation impinged upon its self-interest.[28] As soon as Dewey's victory made the Philippines a prospective prize of war, many immediately felt that, as the *New York Tribune* said, it was "barbarous" either to turn back the Filipinos to their erstwhile oppressors, or, having destroyed the Spanish government, to abandon them to their own folly.[29] This initial sense of protective responsibility led soon to the exalted conviction that it was "the duty and the manifest destiny of the United States to civilize and Christianize"[30] the poor Filipino foundlings, and incidentally to radiate Christian Americanism over the entire benighted Orient. One element in the doubtless sincere expansionist ideal was the enthusiasm of the Protestant church over what one divine called "Manifest Destiny from a Religious Point of View" [31] — the possibility of converting Moros from paganism and others from a "Romanism" considered scarcely less dangerous. Another element was the desire to see the United States conforming to the moral fashion, that is, imitating the great European peoples who had been professing and partially practicing the civilizing mission. But in incongruous association with this imitative morality was the old zeal for the diffusion of that supposedly American product called liberty, which in Lyman Abbott's view could convert orthodox imperialism into "the new imperialism, the imperialism of liberty." [32] Senator Platt of Connecticut wrote to President McKinley of the belief among all classes that "God has placed upon this Government the solemn duty of providing for the people of these islands a government based upon the principle of liberty no matter how many difficulties the problem may present." [33]

Platt scarcely realized the difficulties which the problem in the Philippines was already presenting. Under the circumstances the excited expansionists were perhaps no more fitted to perform delicate international duties without breaking democratic proprieties than is a bull for protecting a china shop. To be sure, the distant scene was marked at first by friendly cooperation between Admiral Dewey and the Filipino insurgent leader, Aguinaldo. The latter, because persuasive American officials told him no more than they thought good for him, apparently believed that "North America, cradle of true liberty, and friendly on that account to the liberty of our people," [34] intended to support Philippine independence as a reward for his solicited military assistance. It is not altogether certain whether Aguinaldo was "honest, sincere, and poor" [35] (as it seemed to Major Bell) or "cunning, ambitious, unscrupulous" [36] (as it seemed to Senator Beveridge). However, either set of characteristics made him a dangerous person for Americans to despatch to a scene of conflicting interests. After

Aguinaldo had effectively rendered his assistance, he and American officials were overtaken by mutual disillusionment. His new republic and all his political pretensions ignored, Aguinaldo protested bitterly against the forcible annexation which now seemed to him designed by the "cold and calculating thoughts of the sons of the North." [37] Thus, although Americans were entertaining the warmest feelings of chivalry toward Aguinaldo's people, the assumption that the latter were grateful beneficiaries was wrong. A *de facto* Philippine government, whose Oriental version of manifest destiny held its people to be "one of the strongest arms of Providence to direct the destinies of humanity," [38] had ideals or ambitions quite at odds with those of the would-be benefactors.

McKinley's demand upon Spain for the cession of its purely nominal sovereignty over the Philippines — a demand which was formally protested by Aguinaldo's government — was the first act of imperialism. The absence of discussion would seem to indicate that not until later was there public awareness of the opposition which gave to McKinley's demand the character of imperialism. But McKinley himself, together with other officials, could scarcely have been ignorant of the opposition, even though he was led to underestimate its extent. That he came to see political expediency in an expansion so widely desired is quite understandable. But there is something of a mystery about his moral psychology — unless one accepts Mr. McKinley's view that it was the result of prayer. He had once said that government rests upon "the free consent of the governed and all of the governed." [39] What could he now say as he demanded a cession in which the inhabitants figured somewhat as serfs sold with the soil?

At the time he said with respect to the embarrassing aspect of the moral problem no more than statesmen usually do — that is, nothing at all. But he spoke rather fulsomely of a humanitarian purpose in the light of which the discussion of theoretic rights may have seemed an academic irrelevance. Thus he implicitly based his demand for Luzon as minimal indemnity upon duty to the very group now leading the movement for independence:

> Without any original thought of complete or even partial acquisition, the presence and success of our arms at Manila imposes upon us obligations which we can not disregard. The march of events rules and overrules human action. Avowing unreservedly the purpose which has animated all our effort, and still solicitous to adhere to it, we can not be unmindful that without any desire or design on our part the war has brought us new duties and responsibilities which we must meet and discharge as becomes a great nation on whose growth and career from the beginning the Ruler of Nations has plainly written the high command and pledge of civilization.
>
> Incidental to our tenure of the Philippines is the commercial opportunity to which American statesmanship can not be indifferent.[40]

Somewhat later came the decisive ethico-religious experience which, as McKinley affirmed in his famous self-revelation before the visiting missionaries, made it plain to him that the only course without practical or moral difficulty was to "educate . . . and uplift and civilize and Christianize" not only the inhabitants of Luzon but those of the entire archipelago.[41] To leave the Filipinos to themselves would be, he affirmed, to invite worse confusion and anarchy than under Spain; moreover, it would expose them to imperialistic powers whose eagerness for every foothold in the then hotly disputed Orient would snatch away unprotected independence at the first pretext. All McKinley's observations, like those of most other expansionists, indicate a belief in what might be called the doctrine of humanitarian necessity. Such a doctrine would imply that the general obligation to respect the right of self-determination is suspended when the allowance of such a right amounts to permitting a suicide.

This doctrine of humanitarian necessity may seem reasonable not merely in the abstract but also in certain of its factual premises respecting this issue. Although Admiral Dewey at first thought the Filipinos better fitted for self-government than were the liberated Cubans, the bulk of the evidence perhaps did support the pessimism which developed in suspicious correlation with expansionism.[42] It was very debatable, in any event, whether without temporary aid this politically inexperienced people, of diverse and partly savage ethnic composition, could manage its own affairs without serious harm to itself. The scarcely edifying documents of the insurgent government suggest that, even if expansionists underestimated Filipino political capacity, certain sentimental anti-expansionists equally overestimated it. Charles Francis Adams could point out, indeed, that American tradition had favored learning self-government by striking out alone; but in this instance a policy of "hands-off" [43] was like giving a child its first chance to swim in water infested by sharks. These considerations are no less valid because national self-interest doubtless contributed to the recognition of their validity.

Nevertheless, McKinley's doctrine of humanitarian necessity contained a flagrant *petitio principii* which suggests that moral logic was confused by self-interest. For it was his assumption that the necessary alternative to abandoning the islands to European sharks was that the United States itself (just as shark-like to the Filipinos) swallow them. What of the protectorate relationship which, as was testified by American officers before the Peace Commission, would have been welcome to Aguinaldo's government? [44] This solution, advocated by most of the anti-expansionists, was dismissed by McKinley as an impracticable course necessitating responsibility without full power.[45] Yet so eminent a political scientist as Ernst Freund advocated it as not merely according with American anti-imperialistic tradition but also as permitting the most flexible and practical policy under American constitutional limitations.[46] That there were difficulties in this as in any other course in the difficult situation is quite true; yet the mode of protection later considered practicable for Cuba was probably the least evil in this issue too. A protectorate would have made possible, under more amicable even if less arbitrary conditions, all the educational, religious, and probably even political uplift. But that a nation should go to so much trouble without compensation seemed perhaps a bit silly, as Generals Merritt and Whittier intimated before the Paris Peace Commission.[47] In any event, a protectorate raised a serious emotional difficulty with respect to the American flag. The difficulty about the flag was suggested by McKinley's rhetorical question: "Who will haul it down?" Surely not the patriotic McKinley, when a not too logical humanitarianism could ascribe to its "protecting folds" indispensability.[48]

The hauling down of the Philippine flag did, however, have an imperialistic aspect which evidently was not altogether pleasant to this erstwhile champion of the principle of consent. For he proceeded to defend his course by obscure doctrines and "masked words" which suggest less a carefully reasoned belief in humanitarian necessity than a need for self-deception. Fundamental among these doctrines was one which, although not propounded by McKinley until the insurrection had compelled abandonment of his philosophical reserve, was doubtless typical of his thinking as he first took the path of imperialism. In his Boston address of February 16, 1899, the charge of disregarding the principle of consent was answered as follows:

> Did we need their consent to perform a great act for humanity? We had it in every aspiration of their minds, in every hope of their hearts.[49]

From this it must strangely follow that the most determined refusal of explicit consent is not a real refusal when consent is implicit in a people's intellectual and spiritual aspirations and hopes. Assuming like Rousseau a rational will capable of paradoxical coexistence with a conflicting actual will, McKinley held that the Filipinos consented to American sovereignty by virtue of their desire for the goods which American sovereignty alone (as it seemed to him) could give them. This doctrine of implicit consent was metaphysical but it served the practical purpose of saving McKinley's face in his violation of the traditional principle of consent.

A practical difficulty, however, lay in the incorrectness of the optimistic assumption which Mr. McKinley revealed to Andrew Carnegie: namely, that the actual opposition among the Filipinos was of slight extent and like the overridden contrariness of children would soon give way to a better will.[50] After Spain ceded the Philippines, opposition so much increased that it became necessary for McKinley to despatch a proclamation warning that dissenters would be "brought within the lawful rule we have assumed, with firmness if need be." This proclamation is another engaging instance of the justification of imperialistic action by speciously democratic philosophy. Thus McKinley declared that though the strong arm of authority must repress disturbances, its fundamental purpose was "to overcome all obstacles to the bestowal of the blessings of good and stable government . . . under the free flag of the United States." Americans came not as "invaders or conquerors" but as friends eager to assure "that full measure of individual rights and liberties which is the heritage of free peoples." [51] The foregoing, like the Schurman Commission's later thesis that "American sovereignty was only another name for the liberty of Filipinos," [52] used the word "liberty" in a sense unusual but presumably conducive to the Filipino's submission. True freedom was apparently not the national liberty which was being withheld but the individual liberty which was being offered. McKinley's imperialist terminology thus presupposed the validity of the anti-nationalistic but utilitarian idea of freedom which had been advocated by Dante in his project for world empire. Although much that is sensible can perhaps be said for it, this sharply limited doctrine of freedom had never been accepted by Americans for themselves. Of course McKinley was not presenting it to Americans but only to a backward people expected to be less pretentious than Americans.

Unfortunately the Filipinos likewise refused to accept it. The proclamation led only to Aguinaldo's angry protest "in the name of God, root and source of all justice . . . against this intrusion of the United States Government in the administration of these islands." [53] With the stiffening and the spread of Filipino opposition, American expansionists could no longer follow McKinley's philosophical method, that is, conceal from the left hand what the right hand was doing. As the Senate took up the ratification of the treaty, the nature and the danger of the right hand's actions were for the first time generally acknowledged. Practically the choice lay between prudent retreat or running into undeniable danger; logically it was necessary either to admit the democratic doctrine of consent of the governed or boldly to break with it.

McKinley to the contrary notwithstanding, the motives of nations are just as human, and therefore at times just as frivolous, as those of their citizens in private experience. Thus the ensuing boldness of the expansionists is perhaps explicable in part by the paradoxical influence of a very homely fear. Described quite simply, it was the fear of the nation's playing the fool. Without any implication that such a phobia is either uncommon or unnatural, this fear of appearing moronic might conveniently be given a coined psychiatric name — "moriaphobia." American "moriaphobia" was the fear that retreat from a handsome opportunity, one such as (it seemed to Whitelaw Reid and others) no European power would miss, would cause America to appear before the world as silly. Thus President McKinley spoke of the danger of becoming the "laughing-stock of the world"; [54] Senator Lodge warned of incurring "humiliation" in the eyes of civilized mankind.[55] What made retreat seem laughable was not merely its aspect of weakness and inconsistency, but perhaps more particularly the fact that retreat was urged chiefly upon the ground of moral principle. Whatever may be said for the influence of their moral ideology, it is also true that no type of fear seems so potent among nationalists as "moral moriaphobia," the fear of playing the fool for merely a moral reason. This fear was now the greater because of Europe's cynicism about America's impetuous self-abnegation in Cuba. So great was ex-Minister Denby's avowed fear of the world's laughter that he urged his fellow countrymen to adopt the entirely non-moral attitude which he ascribed to European diplomats.[56] In general, however, not all national morality but only a particular kind seemed asinine: namely, that unsophisticated morality willing to sacrifice vital and indubitable self-interest because of a moral principle which is not even indubitable. In any conflict between self-interest and a moral principle it seems the part of both practical and moral sophistication to accept wherever ethically possible — and in the complex nature of things it is generally possible — some other moral principle which permits the triumph of self-interest. The man of the world can combine morality and national self-interest more easily than he can find a wife with both virtue and wealth; he may consider himself a fool not to do both.

Thus expansionists resorted to a moral principle which had been used in similar exigencies by all world powers neglectful neither of their moral dignity nor of their self-interest. This was the principle, now for the first time widely asserted by Republicans, that government does not rest upon the consent of all or even of a majority of the governed. It was held to rest, as Senator Platt of Connecticut declared, upon "the consent of some of the governed,"[57] that is, upon the consent of peoples adjudged capable of self-government by civilized powers deeming themselves capable of such adjudication. The Filipinos were alleged by Senator Nelson to be as yet "unfit for self-government, in the sense that we have it," apparently the only sense considered a proper criterion. Unfitness for self-government, thought Senator Nelson, made the granting of independence "the highest cruelty."[58] Though humanitarianism and democracy had once seemed firmly associated, it now appeared to Representative Gibson that the world had moved onward to civilization and Christianity against the consent of the governed. "'Consent of the governed,' indeed!" he exclaimed, with that disdain for technical rights which the humanitarian can so fully feel.[59]

Yet the majority did not like the thought that, as some Edmund Burke might have pointed out, depreciation of the Filipino's freedom was a disparagement of their own traditional ideal. As though to make their peace with America's past, they concealed their imperialism by the obfuscation which may be called the doctrine of trusteeship. The right of self-determination was not being taken away from the Filipinos, this doctrine held, but was merely being held in trust until they were fit to exercise it. Senator Foraker asserted:

> . . . I do not know of anybody, from the President of the United States down to his humblest follower in this matter, who is proposing by force and violence to take and hold those islands for all time to come.[60]

How long before Judgment Day the islands would be released was left uncertain; however, it was proposed, as Senator Nelson said, to give the Filipinos independence "when they are fit for it." [61] Ratification of the treaty, the Republican leader Senator Lodge especially emphasized, would not commit the United States to holding unwilling subjects permanently — a policy which even this tough-minded nationalist professed not to want.[62]

While doubtless no one wanted the Filipinos to be unwilling permanently, there is some question whether Administration supporters really approached the treaty with the idea of later releasing them should they continue to be unwilling. The issue of sincerity was unkindly raised by the anti-expansionists, many of whom, according to Senator Jones,[63] would have been willing to vote for ratification if they had believed that it meant no more than what Administration leaders said. Instead they believed, as did Senator Hale, that there existed a "determination to be content with nothing but permanent annexation." [64] The sincerity of the expansionists was doubted primarily because they were unwilling to accept as an adjunct to ratification any of the numerous resolutions, like Senator Bacon's, that merely renounced the permanent sovereignty which Republican leaders professed not to demand. For this reluctance to pledge ultimate independence there appeared no logical reason — save the truth that, as the Bible says, "it is better that thou shouldst not vow, than that thou shouldst vow and not pay." The allegation that a promise would induce constant agitation for independence seemed trivial in the light of the possibility of insurrection without such a promise. Even the reason offered by the keen Senator Lodge appeared not quite coherent:

> Every one of the resolutions thus far offered on this subject is an expression of distrust in the character, ability, honesty, and wisdom of the American people and an attempt to make us promise to be good and wise and honest in the future . . .
>
> I believe we can be trusted as a people to deal honestly and justly with the islands and their inhabitants thus given to our care.[65]

But why profess the intention to be good, yet be as opposed

as Juliet to oaths? The only answer just to Senator Lodge's political shrewdness seemed to be that there was a method in his incoherence: for the sake of votes he was holding out the hope of ultimate independence to American anti-expansionists but at the same time withholding from the Filipinos anything that might compromise a plan of permanent sovereignty. Because he did not admit at this inconvenient moment the expansionism which he had entertained before and was also to entertain later, Senator Lodge seemed to anti-expansionists to be reprehensibly disingenuous.

But privately Senator Lodge agreed with his friend Roosevelt that the anti-expansionists were "barbarian,"[66] and disingenuousness in dealing with barbarians is not reprehensible. Moreover, though some expansionists knew as well as Senator Lodge what they wanted, many were doubtless disingenuous with themselves. They did not admit to themselves their idea that preservation of America's glory in the present was an impediment even to a promise to haul down the flag in the remote future. In all expansionists there was probably the very human disposition to serve two masters — humanitarian duty and an immovable flag. But in the difficult conduct of international relations is it usually possible to serve two such masters?

The destinies of history seemed eager to give a timely answer. On February 5, the day before the date set for the vote on the treaty, there came the news that the tinder box of the distant islands had flamed into armed hostilities. Judge Blount and others have said without reservation that the passage of the Bacon resolution would have averted them.[67] One preferring to be conservative can say at least that it very possibly may have done so. For although the Filipinos had apparently provoked the first bloodshed, their desire for war had crystallized only as they came to lose the hope of any concession. As late as January, according to General Otis, Aguinaldo's emissaries "begged for some tangible concessions from the United States Government — one which they could present to the people and which might serve to allay the excitement."[68] If the unresponsive McKinley "never dreamed" that the insurgents would reciprocate "our mercy with a Mauser," [69] the fact shows only that his entire approach to imperialism was dream-like in excluding all except wish-fulfilment. According to Tyler Dennett, "the most that can be said in extenuation is that the policy . . . had been adopted in great ignorance of the actual facts in the islands, and in a blissful and exalted assumption that any race ought to regard conquest by the American people as a superlative blessing." [70]

What was the reaction when rifle shots brought awakening from this blissful dream? The first reaction was a widespread indignation which confirmed the adage that "earth has no rage like love to hatred turned." Indignation furnished an additional motive, on the day following the outbreak of the insurrection, for the passage of the treaty, and shortly afterward for the defeat of the Bacon proposal. Former philanthropists raised the cry that (to quote a potpourri of comment) the insurgents who had delivered an "insult" to "the dignity of the government" [71] must be "thoroughly thrashed" [72] until they learned their first duty of "submission to the constituted authority." [73] All this was entirely in accord with the nationalist's code of honor, which demands that the dignity of one's country, like the dignity of one's wife, be defended no matter what the folly which has impaired it. Although the nationalist is for his country "right or wrong," in this instance as in most others there was the additional incentive that he believed it right. For it was undeniable that, as Attorney-General Griggs proclaimed, the United States of America possessed by solemn treaty the only lawful authority over the islands. But had not the British, the anti-expansionists asked, possessed the only lawful authority over the American colonies? This question, unfortunately, implied an unacceptable similarity not only between the despotic British and the Americans of 1898, but also between the intractable Malays and the Americans of 1776. The comparison only increased indignation.

An indignant legalism, however, could scarcely sustain moral assurance for more than the first excited days. For what was at hand seemed to be the first war of subjugation ever waged by a people whose humanitarian tradition had glorified a natural right to liberty. For this anomalous situation a sturdier ideology was needed. But where in America's dominant tradition could such an ideology be found?

The predicament might have been rather serious had not timely assistance arrived from a non-American source. Englishmen eager for a new friend in world politics had once offered the support of their fleet in Manila Bay; now, in the moral crisis developing from the victory of Manila Bay, an English poet despatched the assistance of his sophistication in the ethics of imperialism. It was Rudyard Kipling, whom the exaggerating Godkin not only called "a most pernicious, vulgar person" but blamed for "most of the current jingoism on both sides of the water." [74] Kipling's imperialistic influence on this side of the water came about chiefly through his publication in the February *McClure's Magazine* of a poem which "circled the earth in a day and by repetition became hackneyed within a week." [75] On front pages American newspapers reprinted the heavily edifying lines implicitly exhorting the United States to take up a dark task among dark peoples — "The White Man's Burden."

Incommensurate surely with its technical merit, the extraordinary popularity of this poem is perhaps to be ascribed less to its content than to its name. The title of the poem offered a pleasing substitute for "imperialism," a word from which American imperialists shrank because, as Senator Beveridge pointed out, it had acquired the connotation of "oppression." [76] Kipling provided a balm for burdened souls by an ingenious technique of euphemism which may be named "onomantithesis." This euphemism consists in designating any largely unpleasant thing not by its ordinary name but by the antithesis of the connotation of the ordinary name. Thus imperialism, connoting the burdening of the race of color by military subjugation if not economic exploitation, was called in "onomantithesis" the white man's burden. Similarly the Southern expansionists of 1845 referred to extension of slavery as "extension of the area of freedom," and Stephen Douglas later spoke of the allowance of slavery in the territories as popular sovereignty. With equal obfuscation McKinley named America's colonial plan "benevolent assimilation" [77]—a phrase which, as Senator Chandler assured some of his perturbed colleagues, did not exclude the President's intention to *differentiate* the Filipinos from the citizen body.[78] The method of "onomantithesis" seems to be designed consciously or unconsciously to distract attention from the morally unpleasant element of a reality to a pleasant but perhaps minor element. In the sphere of moral judgments if not of flowers, something malodorous under its ordinary name can be made by "onomantithesis" to smell as sweet as any rose.

Such is the power of names that Kipling's title has caused a frequent misinterpretation of the poem itself. The "little brown brother" idea often attributed to it is as little in Kipling's poem as in the unfraternal ditty of the American soldiers. Without the merriment of the Americans, Kipling also implied in every line that this devilish, childish, foolish, slothful, ungrateful, hateful species "ain't no kin to me." Kipling's depth of disdainful hostility—never has even a poet indicted so fiercely so vast a portion of his human brethren—is understandable only in the light of the excessive trouble which this unsurrendering race had given to his beloved country.

In seeking for the burden-bearer's motive one must first rule out fraternal affection. One might next wonder, in view of the reference to an "end for others sought," whether the burden-bearer's motive is the grim sense of altruistic duty which may take the place of affection in prompting service even for one's enemy. But the assumption that altruism was a primary consideration with Kipling seems at variance with the fact that he did not encourage his burdened hero to work for or expect much improvement in the heathen. Although the burden-bearer was urged to rescue the heathen from sickness, war, and famine, he was not exhorted to cure any of the objectionable personal characteristics which underlay the difficulties. Perhaps Kipling's omission of the true civilizing ideal was due to the fact that he regarded the heathen's personal faults as incurable. Perhaps the explanation is that the civilizing enterprise demands an intimate spiritual and social contact which Kipling thought generally impossible between East and West

— at least until the twain meet before the Seat of Judgment in their one common characteristic of sinfulness. What is clear in any event is Kipling's expectation that the heathen's uncured sloth and folly will ultimately bring even the burden-bearer's limited hopes " to nought." The poem has a pervasive defeatism which, though overlooked by imperialists, prompted the anti-imperialistic Senator Tillman [79] to interpret it not as an invitation to imperialism but as a warning against it. But the view that Kipling would have warned against the burden by a poem repetitiously urging its assumption attributes to him a degree of malice which he could scarcely have possessed — at least in relation to his white fellow men. Kipling did not warn against taking up the burden, but merely against the hope that it would do the heathen much good.

This pessimism, though it might seem to some to make the enterprise senseless, is really the clue to Kipling's presumable sense. For if the heathen cannot be truly helped it is clear that the burden-bearer's aim is the paradoxical one of serving the heathen in order to exalt himself. To be sure, Kipling did not acknowledge the motive to be any selfish interest such as is usually supposed to motivate nations attempting missions of dubious benefit to others. Kipling held the aspiration of such nations to be the growth of the soul: " Have done with childish days." The disciplinary duty to the heathen offers an occasion for attaining moral *manhood,* the goal sought by both savage and civilized romantics in heroisms otherwise pointless. Just as the savage sees tribal manhood as dependent upon endurance in gruesome rites, so Kipling views the manhood of a world power as contingent upon the moral discipline of imperialism. The white man's burden is the heroic deed of force, a deed inherently glorious to the movement of nineteenth-century romanticism represented by figures like Carlyle, D'Annunzio, and Sorel. In sum, the burden must be taken up not because of affection or hope for the nominal beneficiary but because its assumption is the manifest destiny of manly athleticism.

Admitting that their anti-imperialist isolationism belonged to " childish days," American expansionists for the first time permitted a European to patronize them, to teach them an alien wisdom as superior to their own. Previously it had been their joyful conceit to believe with Walt Whitman in the preeminent distinction of their burden of innovative democracy:

Have the elder races halted?
Do they droop and end their lesson, wearied over there beyond the seas?
We take up the task eternal, and the burden and the lesson,
Pioneers, O pioneers! [80]

Doubtless the homespun version of the burden was better than Kipling's as poetry. But it could scarcely serve Americans in a moral difficulty which not only arose from the imitation of a European political fashion but apparently discredited Whitman's prediction that American expansion would always "tenderly regard human life, property and rights." [81] Thus Americans turned for their inspiration to Kipling and his euphemism. However, they largely misinterpreted him and espoused a doctrine of the white man's burden which was neither Kipling's nor Whitman's but a hybrid.

Of course, the expansionists understood that the poem dealt with the motive of "conscience," [82] was intended as "a call and inspiration to duty," [83] and emphasized love of a manly ideal rather than love of the heathen. Responding like Roosevelt to its summons to "the strenuous life," they recognized that "the 'white man's burden' must be borne with the strength of red blood and not with the weakness of a white liver." [84] But they naïvely overlooked Kipling's implication that the only attainable end was the strengthening of their own souls, that "the end for others sought" was merely a pragmatic fiction designed to provide the moral athlete with exercise.

Instead of looking forward as did Kipling to the Filipino's failure, American expansionists continued their traditional identification of destiny with the happy ending. We could not "shift the burden from our shoulders," Representative Mann said, because the plan of Divine Providence demanded that the American flag be held aloft "for the benefit of humanity." [85] The *Salt Lake Tribune* affirmed that the "burden" was particularly beneficial to the "misguided creatures" who needed to have "their eyes bathed enough in blood to cause their visions to be cleared." [86] So beneficent, despite temporary casualties, did the burden seem to Bishop Thoburn that he called it a task which "the providence of God . . . has thrust upon us." [87] The belief was not incompatible with the martial spirit; for it seemed, as the Reverend Dr. Dix was sure, that "some unseen and mysterious power, had been, and is, at work conducting and compelling a certain end, to be accomplished by peaceful methods if possible, but if not peacefully, then by the whole force of the powers of the State." [88] One source of confidence in war was thus the imperialist's mystical conception that force is of "divine origin" [89] in the sense that it is an instrument through which, as Mahan later said, God wills to work.[90] Another source was of course the American's belief in the invariably beneficent destiny of this democracy. President McKinley, who thought "the burden" our moral "opportunity," [91] quoted his poetic Secretary of State: "The free can conquer but to save." Finally, the human cost of conquest seemed justified by the utilitarian principle of the greatest good to the greatest number. If "every red drop, whether from the vein of an American soldier or a misguided Filipino" was "anguish" to McKinley's heart, it was nevertheless his wish and duty to bound his vision by only "the broad range of future years." [92] The regrettable killing of some thousands of Filipinos would make possible inestimable benefits to the bodies and souls of the many more survivors, and to those of their posterity through all futurity. In sum, what Representative Brosius called the "rough surgery" [93] in the burden seemed a means which was as necessary to the good end as is the surgeon's knife to his therapeutic purpose.

But this argument for humanitarian killing seemed to the anti-expansionists to hinge upon a questionable premise: namely, that the war, as not only the Schurman Commission [94] but even a mass-meeting of Chicago clergymen insisted,[95] could be terminated beneficently only by the unconditional surrender of the insurgents. Such an assumption hindered even the early peace negotiations of the well-intentioned Schurman

Commission; for it made the commission unable to grant the armistice which was requested by the discouraged insurgents in order to place submission under legislative consideration. The reasonableness of a demand for unconditional surrender had seemed to Cleveland "not altogether apparent" [96] when Spain insisted upon it to the protraction of Cuban warfare. Though the demand was quite in accord with the general practice of world powers in suppressing insurrections, its necessity to the fulfilment of America's altruistic ideology is not altogether apparent. The imperialist's mating of humanitarianism and force apparently resulted in an illegitimate union — one not blessed by the logic of affinity.

To be sure, the anti-imperialist was probably wrong in attributing his opponent's continuing defense of force to mere "pride of consistency." [97] The difficulty was not that humanitarianism was absent but that the imperialist did not have the surgeon's capacity to decide objectively when force is humane. Though Providence alone can read certainly the hearts of men, it would seem that humanitarian logic was generally subordinate to the self-assertive nationalism expressed in William Allen White's contemporary dogma of "the Anglo-Saxon's manifest destiny to go forth as a world conqueror." [98]

However, the anti-imperialist like the imperialist was interested less in international humanitarianism than in his own nation. Thus one anti-imperialist frankly said: "The serious question for the people of this country to consider is what effect the imperial policy will have upon ourselves if we permit it to be established." [99] These words suggest a problem no less interesting than that of how the ideological union of ill-suited mates came about. It is the problem of the fate of this association of ideas under the influence of the war, the disappointing child to which it gave birth. In what transmutations of character — for ideas no less than human beings are profoundly affected by enduring association — will it result? And which of the two partners will gain the upper hand?

It may be stated *in limine* that the imperialist ideology did change considerably, whether for better or for worse. The first change was in the attitude of Administration supporters toward permanent sovereignty. Insistence upon permanent sovereignty had at first been disavowed — sincerely by some even if insincerely by others. But the very grief experienced in combating the insurrection caused permanent sovereignty to seem more desirable to all as a consolation. Moreover, explicit avowal of the design of permanent sovereignty seemed likely, as Senator Beveridge pointed out, to discourage the insurgents by showing the American mind as made up irretrievably. Thus, on January 5, 1900, Beveridge offered a resolution, framed in collaboration with leading Republicans, declaring that it was the intention of the United States to "retain" the Philippines. The keynote of his supporting speech was that the Philippines "are ours forever."[100] Representative Cannon wanted them still longer — "forever and a day."[101] In March the same Senator Lodge who had declared vaguely for a policy of honest dealing honestly identified such dealing with "the retention of the islands by the United States."[102] Another indication of the new attitude was the assurance in the Republican campaign plank of 1900 that the Filipinos would have "the largest measure of self-government consistent with their welfare and our duties" — a declaration which not only failed to promise independence but was generally interpreted as implying that independence was inconsistent with both the Filipino's welfare and the American's duties.[103]

This change on the issue of permanent sovereignty was apparently the cause of a radical alteration in ideology, capable of automatic adjustment to the self-interest which it usually justifies. It was necessary in the first place to scrap the original view that the Filipinos would eventually be capable of independence. In the place of the former theory that the Filipinos were disqualified for immediate self-government primarily by lack of training, Senator Beveridge set forth a new theory:

> They are not capable of self-government. How could they be? They are not of a self-governing race. They are Orientals, Malays, instructed by Spaniards in the latter's worst estate.[104]

This implication of a racial disqualification for self-government is very distant from the view of Henry Clay that "it is to arraign the dispositions of Providence Himself, to suppose that He has created beings incapable of governing themselves." [105] But without any embarrassment over the arraignment of Providence, expansionists tended rather generally to rate the Filipinos so low that the question whether or when they would be capable of independence became purely academic. Senator Lodge, with all the authority of his presumable historical omniscience, affirmed all human experience to be against the possibility of the Malay's learning democracy.[106] In order to suggest the savagery of the Luzon insurgents, expansionists took to calling them by their ethnic name, "Tagalogs." Against this barbarous-sounding name, the favorable judgment of the eminent ethnologist Ferdinant Blumentritt,[107] and even the optimism of the Schurman Commission, could have little weight.

To deny Tagalogs the possibility of ultimate independence was to repudiate the original philosophy which conceived imperialism as a trusteeship preparing for self-government. And since the moral consciousness of the nationalist abhors a vacuum, Beveridge replaced this ideal with a new one. In a passage which struck his overwrought audience as the height of political eloquence, the most enraptured of all the imperialists stated it thus:

> Mr. President, this question is deeper than any question of party politics; deeper than any question of the isolated policy of our country even; deeper even than any question of constitutional power. It is elemental. It is racial. God has not been preparing the English-speaking and Teutonic peoples for a thousand years for nothing but vain and idle self-contemplation and self-admiration. No! He has made us the master organizers of the world to establish system where chaos reigns. He has given us the spirit of progress to overwhelm the forces of reaction throughout the earth. He has made us adepts in government that we may administer government among savage and senile peoples. Were it not for such a force as this the world would relapse into barbarism and night. And of all our race He has marked the American people as His chosen nation to finally lead in the regeneration of the world.[108]

Here in one of its most turgid expressions is that "imperialism of race" (as Seillière [109] conceives it) which was given its

Teutonic version by Chamberlain and imported to the land of the free by John Burgess. This thesis of racial superiority was eventually to be turned by Hitlerism into an exaltation of one racially "pure" Teutonic people over all others, a transformation which made the entire philosophy irritating to the Englishmen and Americans who had at first delighted in it. Beveridge, unable to foresee that the racial cult would prove a boomerang, used it to affirm the mission of the Teutonic nations among the colored peoples. But his conception of the racial mission is the very antithesis of the previous ideal of leading the tropical people into liberty. Like Kipling he thought of a burden of eternal rule over those who seemed to him as little capable of liberty as the negroes once seemed to their American owners. From the *imperium ac libertas* of the trustee it has come to the *imperium ac justitia* of the master.

The expansion of the idea of *imperium* from temporary to permanent force was prefatory to a still more radical transmutation in the conception of the motive of imperialism. The salient characteristic of the original imperialist ideology was the somewhat unreasonable demand that the sole or primary motive of expansion be "the end for others sought." McKinley held not only that this should be the determining motive but that in fact it was; America's concern, he declared at the outbreak of the revolt, was not for territory, trade, or empire, but for the Philippine people.[110] In this pretension he evidently forgot that he had previously admitted interest in commercial opportunity; yet in truth he had presented economic ambition as merely "incidental." Perhaps his description of national motivation was more true of the American soul as Platonic essence than of the actual consciousness of the ordinary patriot, whose virtues McKinley was led by both the rhetorical conventions of his office and his religious faith in democracy to exaggerate. Yet originally most expansionists did apparently believe that altruism was not only the proper motive but also, as Dr. Schurman said,[111] the actual one; the second belief derived largely from the assumption that the great Republic could not have an improper motive. Without this self-identification with Sir Galahad it would have been difficult to unsheath the sword.

But the sword of chivalry, as that of Sir Launcelot showed, may conquer even the original idealism of its wielder. We need not take too seriously, indeed, the frivolous hostility of the soldier song beginning with "Damn, damn, damn the Filipinos" and ending with "Civilize 'em with a Krag." Yet the soldier, and perhaps even more the lay patriot, finds the altruism of the civilizing mission unexpectedly difficult when it begins to demand love for one's enemy. Altruism was still more sorely strained when the enemy once called by McKinley "a small minority" [112] revealed itself, according to General MacArthur's frank admission, as a preponderant part of the population.[113] Colonel Roosevelt, losing patience in less than six months with such ingrates, went so far as to exclaim that "we cannot fool with anyone who bears arms against our aims and destiny." [114] Altruism was discredited not only by the resistant Filipinos but also by the sentimental anti-imperialists, known to the crudely critical as "copperheads and aunties."

While the impulses of Dr. Jekyll weakened, those of normal national egoism became stronger and more self-conscious. The protraction of martial griefs naturally increased the disposition to think of ultimate compensations not moral in character. Political orators, who in the beginning tended to take profit for granted and to stress service, now found it expedient to reverse the technique. Senator Beveridge almost secularized a religious concept in his speech proving with commercial statistics that America's divine mission of regeneration held "all the profit, all the glory, all the happiness possible to man." [115] But Beveridge had scarcely received the polite rebuke of Senator Hoar for his neglect of morals when the *Washington Post* came out with an editorial which was regarded by moral anti-expansionists as a national scandal. For it affirmed that all the professions of lofty altruism were so much sound and fury, and might as well be superseded by the announcement that we had "annexed these possessions in cold blood and that we intend to utilize them to our own profit and advantage." [116]

Although scarcely typical, this bravado of cynicism was only the exaggeration of a general tendency. Contrary to McKinley's representations, the predominant popular trend established by the war was definitely away from the President's somewhat saintly moral sentimentality.

As the campaign of 1900 drew near with expansion as its paramount issue, the need for a new ideology was more than academic. For the ordinary nationalist, though his philosophy is nearly always somewhat above the plane of his feeling, does not resort to moral ideology in the spirit of conscious hypocrisy. He resorts to it because of a need for self-approbation which is not satisfied when ideology soars too high above his actual feelings. Thus there arose the question whether the original ideology could be so modified as to draw it somewhat farther from the heavens and closer to a now consciously mundane nationalism. The problem was solved with most notable casuistical ingenuity by one whose chief service during the fashion of McKinley's altruism had been skilful politics in behalf of national self-interest. Now that the war had developed tougher souls, his own philosophy could be fully told and could make him chief ideologist of the expansion movement as well as chairman of the Committee on the Philippines. This was Senator Henry Cabot Lodge, one whose austere reserve permitted him little sentimentality except an impassioned devotion to his own countrymen (in the abstract aggregate).

Extracts from two of Senator Lodge's speeches defending the Philippine policy, his Senate speech of March 7 and a later address as chairman of the Republican National Convention, are the self-portrayal of a statesman who granted that international altruism had its place but who was determined to put it in its place. Foreshadowing his strategy relative to the League of Nations, Senator Lodge limited international altruism by a number of "reservations." The first, the cornerstone of Lodge's moral philosophy, was of enviable simplicity and could be stated tersely:

> I conceive my first duty to be always to the American people . . .[117]

Though perhaps not intending to assert the paramountcy of patriotism to all morality—for he could scarcely see the two in conflict — Senator Lodge did imply that his patriotic duty must always take precedence over a conflicting international altruism. Lodge's previous pretension that the Filipinos would be treated fairly meant primarily that they would be treated with fairness to the United States. It thus did not prevent Lodge's rejection both of Philippine independence and of Philippine participation in American tariff benefits. Such concessions conflicted with our "material interests," which, though they were declared by the supersensitive Benjamin Franklin [118] to be inadequate reasons for the shedding of blood, appeared in Lodge's broader view to be "of the highest merit." [119]

The foregoing reservation to international altruism might seem ample for all patriotic caution. But Senator Lodge added a further reservation excluding also all duties which did not benefit national self-interest:

> Whatever duty to others might seem to demand, I should pause long before supporting any policy if there were the slightest suspicion that it was not for the benefit of the people of the United States.[120]

Just how long he would pause at the pitfall of international duty Senator Lodge did not say, but from the public facts of his career one may infer that the duration of the pause was that of his mundane life. For if the American people owe a debt of profound gratitude to Senator Lodge's distinguished career, it is not because he represented their aspirations in international altruism. It is because he did not fail to pour cold water on every representative of these aspirations who left the slightest suspicion that they were not for the benefit of the United States.

Senator Lodge had still not limited sufficiently the international philanthropy which struck him as "somewhat hysterical" [121] in this instance and as mad in Wilson. It is true that the two previous limitations left international altruism free to function nowhere except in conjunction with self-interest. But while admitting that "duty and interest alike" [122] dictated the Philippine policy, Lodge in his speech before the Republican National Convention limited even the altruistic duty keeping this good company:

> We make no hypocritical pretense of being interested in the Philippines solely on account of others. While we regard the welfare of these people as a sacred trust, we regard the welfare of the American people first. . . . We believe in trade expansion.[123]

Although his implication that President McKinley had been hypocritical was doubtless unconscious, Senator Lodge here inverted McKinley's pretense that the welfare of the Filipino was a primary consideration and commercial opportunity incidental. He did so not because McKinley's sentimental expansionism could damage objectively, but apparently because any over-indulgence in altruism might start a bad mental habit.

What do the Lodge reservations to international altruism leave for the heathen's benefit? Lodge's conception of the "sacred trust" apparently resolves itself into the moral principle that the welfare of the heathen is sacred in so far as it is unopposed to, promotive of, and secondary to the welfare of the trustee. The lover of humanity may take this incidental altruism for what it is worth. Senator Lodge thought its worth sufficient to save not only the Filipinos but also "the teeming millions of China," who, as Americans eat their cake of self-interest, would find the crumbs a veritable banquet of commercial and cultural benefits.[124] But in view of all the reservations its value might seem to others, if not purely rhetorical, scarcely any greater pragmatically than that of the altruistic exhortation by John of Salisbury. This monitor of medieval princes placed at the very end of a list of the statesman's duties the following obligation: ". . . very little to foreigners, but still somewhat."

Strange as it may seem after these all but "nullifying" reservations, the crowning element in Lodge's moral philosophy was a doctrine of the "burden." Originally, one may surmise, Senator Lodge probably entertained Montesquieu's belief that "virtue is not a thing that should burden us." But eventually he had to meet the widespread objection that virtue in the allegedly valuable Philippines was proving highly burdensome:

> This, Mr. President, I freely admit. A great nation must have great responsibilities. It is one of the penalties of greatness. But the benefit of responsibilities goes hand in hand with the burdens they bring. The nation which seeks to escape from the burden also loses the benefit . . .[125]

The three reservations to the white man's burden have thus brought it to this quite unhysterical form: The burden should be borne because of its benefit to the burden-bearer. The original doctrine, as formulated by both the pessimistic Kipling and the optimistic McKinley, had held that the burden was to be borne, at least in part, because of temporary or permanent benefit to the heathen. To distinguish this orthodox doctrine stressing " the end for others sought " we shall hereafter call it the Kipling-McKinley doctrine of the white man's burden. Despite an incongruity in associating Senator Lodge with any phrase of a sentimental sound, we may conveniently speak of the new teaching as the Lodge doctrine of the white man's burden.

The Lodge doctrine of the white man's burden, having come to seem to many the more reasonable, doubtless helped to win for the Republicans the election of 1900. But soon thereafter, unfortunately, it became evident that the course of true wisdom never runs smooth. There came into existence an ideological development which threatened to transgress every one of Senator Lodge's cautions and to bring all his hopes to nought.

To understand this perverse development we must look once more at the course of the war to which, with its ebb and flow of fortune, ideology was a means of adjustment. The expansionists had looked for the war to end as soon as a Republican victory signified to the insurgents the repudiation of Bryan's anti-imperialism by the American people. But the Filipinos were apparently deluded by that illogical idea, " conquer we must, for our cause it is just." Thus when Bryan was defeated they refused to abide by the result of the American election. After the election General MacArthur cabled sorrowfully that " expectations based on result of election have not been realized." [126] As an apparently interminable guerilla warfare rolled up its toll of casualties and expense, there was a let-down in exuberance and a rising suspicion that the whole policy had been (in the words of the New York *Evening Post*) " muddle, muddle, toil and trouble." [127] Lodge's doctrine that the burden must be endured for the sake of its ultimate benefits was coming to demand a patience little short of heroic.

The most straining feature of the situation arose out of the very means which the military took to satisfy impatience. After the Republican victory appeared devoid of influence it seemed to army leaders that the Filipinos could be brought "to their senses" only by a policy of greater severity.[128] Concentration, the law of occupied places, and the law of retaliation would henceforth be in order. Not in written orders, but practiced by some on their own initiative, were unnecessary destruction of Philippine property, the painful "water cure" for Filipino patriotism, and even, in the cases of a few soldiers and certainly one high officer, unwarranted ruthlessness in treatment of the exasperating. To be sure, later investigation showed not only that individual cruelties were greatly exaggerated but that the conduct of the army as a whole was not worse and perhaps better than average Occidental behavior in guerilla warfare with Orientals resisting civilization. Moreover, the general logic of the military in this situation was entirely in accord even with the cardinal principle of humanitarian imperialism. Granted that a good end requires a grim means, "then 'twere well it were done quickly." General Wheaton could perhaps wisely say: "The nearer we approach the methods found necessary by the other nations through centuries of experience in dealing with Asiatics, the less the National Treasury will be expended and the fewer graves will be made." [129]

Despite this plausible logic, the stream of tales true and false about the severities of conquest had the American people, just as the censoring General Otis had feared, "by the ears." It was not merely the anti-expansionists who made up the excited chorus of disapproval. Many expansionists as well, reacting with more emotion than logical consistency, contributed to what General Wheaton called "vagaries of . . . public sentiment, which considers war as an affair to be waged for sentimental reasons." [130] Thus the once strongly expansionist *Baltimore News*, learning that the United States was using the same method of concentration (though in relatively humane fashion) which McKinley had condemned when employed by Spain, exclaimed with horror: "And now we have come to it." [131] One of the most curious cases was that of Dr. Jacob Gould Schurman, president of the commission which had submitted the strongest moral defense of the war. After one imprudent visit to a gruesome Philippine battlefield, he had scarcely been restrained by a colleague from sending forthwith an anti-imperialistic cable to the American people.[132] By 1902 his harrowed nerves could be controlled no longer, and he wrote explosively in the *Independent* that the remedy for the continuing casualties was to substitute a government by consent of the Filipinos for government by coercion of the Filipinos.[133] Although most of the imperialists refrained from public confession of error, they could not restrain themselves from a philosophical modification which marks another strange episode in this history of the interaction of imperialist practice and imperialist ideology.

After the tacitly repudiated McKinley had passed from the confusing tumult to his eternal peace, perturbed imperialists did revert from the Lodge to the Kipling-McKinley doctrine of the white man's burden. As Moorfield Storey's account has said: " Power, commerce, and military glory ceased to be invoked as the arguments for the indefinite retention of the Philippines. The administration now defended its Philippine policy on other grounds — namely, philanthropy." [134] It was also noted by Senator Carmack contemporaneously, as a significant concession to public opinion, that " we no longer hear the argument of greed and avarice and the hunger for other men's possessions openly and defiantly proclaimed." [135] But it seems unwarranted for Senator Carmack to attribute hypocrisy; for even the devil would be a saint when sick. In the midst of the atrocity charges, the amiable Taft's felicitous concept of " the little brown brother " could actually strike a sympathetic chord. President Roosevelt, who had certainly been no disciple of McKinley when in 1899 he wished to treat the insurgents " as they deserve," [136] defended the Philippine policy in his speeches of 1901 and 1902 by reference to a philanthropic purpose no less sentimental than McKinley's.[137] Senator Foraker's speech of May 12, 1902, reverted to the humanitarian doctrine of America's " obligations . . . to remain in the Philippines," from which " we will not come away, because we cannot come away . . . unless we write dishonor and poltroonery across the forehead of the American people." [138]

The ideology was the same as McKinley's, but it was enunciated now with unconcealable weariness rather than with its original assurance. Had it not been for "moriaphobia," persistence would have been highly difficult; and if the war had continued much longer it is not impossible that the growing anti-imperialism would have brought the worst spectres of "moriaphobia" to reality. Fortunately for the national dignity, the overstraining affair came to an end before the collapse of the nationalist stubbornness which seemed to Senator Hoar a perverted "sentimentality." [139] The final smoke of battle lifted in the summer of 1902, just about the time when ex-Consul Williams, who once had urged American sovereignty upon Aguinaldo with the expectation of winning his country's gratitude, was confessing publicly that the majority evidently "don't want the burden as it proves to be." [140] The burden remained but it was at last in poise.

Yet we may well consider further the implication of the fact that before the burden was brought into balance Americans had lost the poise of the spirit. Certainly the moral perturbation of both anti-expansionist and expansionist was not in proportion to the significance which the war would have borne in the eyes of any trained and hardened follower of *la haute politique.* Carl Schurz showed a flagrant forgetfulness of the sad content of world history when he called this conventional imposition of legal authority "a blood-guiltiness without parallel in the history of republics." [141] On the other hand, the embarrassed reversion of expansionists to the Kipling-McKinley doctrine evidenced a sentimental perturbation over what, though not a pretty sight, could after all have been dismissed as one of the ordinary and inevitable incidents of a world power's manifest destiny.

One can fully explain the over-reaction of Americans only by the hypothesis that imperialism, at least in its bloodier phases, was contrary to what mystical nationalists call the destinies of national character. To be sure, sharp spurs to America's imperialism had been a shame of America's "provincial" tradition and a desire to imitate the imperialistic glories of Europe. Nevertheless, most American imperialists had been provincial enough to take the humanitarian side of imperialism seriously. Here lay the rub. For martial imperialism requires a certain iron of mind and soul which will steel one against either doubting the necessity of the grim means or flinching from it in mere sentiment. Even the humanitarian imperialist must feel what the British imperialist poet calls " a ruthless obligation on our souls, to be despotic for the world's behoof." [142] But the " iron nerve " which Treitschke idealizes is precisely what the sincere humanitarian finds it difficult to develop. For this reason it might almost be said, as Senator Lodge sagely realized, that imperialism forbids taking humanitarianism too seriously. Americans strained long to hold the white man's burden of cruelty, but on the whole they had taken their humanitarianism somewhat too seriously to maintain this artificial adjustment to the bitter end. By poetic justice the upshot of their yielding to " moriaphobia " was thus an exhibition of moral neuroticism and sentimental weakness which European diplomats, if as hard-boiled as alleged, might well have found a source of scornful amusement.

Ulterior consequences of this strange interlude in American history are still to be seen. As its sad realities were forgotten, the Philippine experience acquired a halo which reflected a light of glory upon partially philanthropic ventures in the benighted lands of North America. The Kipling-McKinley doctrine lived on in the reformist interventionism expressed in Ambassador Page's proposal of the sanitary reformation of Mexico through " conquest for the sole benefit of the conquered." [143] The less idealistic Lodge doctrine survived in the economic imperialism espoused by the *Chicago Tribune* when it declared that, let the humanitarian like or dislike it, Mexico was the next stopping-place in a march of destiny which could not help being imperial because force was the germ of national life — force now of money, now of arms, operating to put the United States in control of everything it needs for its own purposes.[144]

We are here chiefly interested, however, in the sequel of imperialism in the Philippines. Surveying it in brief outline, we discover several further surprises. The first is the fact that the muse of history is not always a grinning goddess. On the occasions when the influence of self-interest upon a nation's moral ideology is relatively slight, she must assume the serious visage which the Greek artist has wrongly pictured as typical. One of these exceptional occasions was offered by the greater period of America's rule in its Oriental dependency.

For the Kipling-McKinley doctrine of the white man's burden was not merely professed but acted upon. Its application was easier after the expansionists had what they wanted. To be sure, the civil government bill of 1902 and subsequent administrative policy did have an absolutist character which reflected the establishment of militarist habit no less than doubt of native capacity for self-government before any but the most distant date. But the very possession of absolute power encouraged in high-minded administrators a sense of the responsibility of using it benevolently. Even after all possible criticism, America's rule was notably meritorious by comparison with the ordinary colonial government which, as students of imperialism largely agree, introduces civilization chiefly in the form of the Western world's institutions of exploitation. American policy gave the slogan, "the Philippines for the Filipinos," an economic and social even if not a political reality.

Yet progress under American rule resulted with amazing rapidity in the development of the very political capacity which a Beveridge had thought never attainable. At the same time, despite Beveridge's predictions of enduring American imperialism, anti-imperialism experienced a resurgence which made it the dominant trend in the Philippine issue. The resurgence was caused in part by responsiveness to the insistent nationalism of the Filipinos, in part by belated recognition that the Philippines were (as Roosevelt said) a source of military weakness.[145] The Jones Bill of 1916 not only liberalized American rule but gave the promise of ultimate independence which an apparently insuperable inhibition had hitherto prevented. Wilson's conception of Americans as "trustees" revived McKinleyism, but with the important addition that the possibility of converting the trust into the trustees' private property was renounced.[146] Thenceforth, despite the ostensibly philanthropic postponements of succeeding presidents, despite the protests of some unphilanthropic expansionists, independence was only a question of time.

But it was America's final offer of release, strange to say, which doubtless brought back to the visage of the historical muse her wonted smile. The motives primarily leading to the adoption of the bill for independence did not permit the burden to be deposited with grace. Among an indifferent people — for the lofty popular emotions trusted by McKinley cannot be very long sustained — a self-interested minority was able to enforce its own method in getting rid of what had come to seem a cause of strategic danger and commercial competition. This group prevented the independence bill from meeting the Filipino's desire for some continuation of the American commercial relationships upon which, after they were forcibly introduced, Philippine economic life had been built. The bill granted no certainty even of partial reciprocity after separation, and imposed for the interim conditions regarded by ex-Secretary Hurley as leading to economic ruin,[147] and by ex-President Hoover as failing to fulfil the "idealism" in which the trust was assumed.[148] The proposal of release was even a kind of imperialism; for as Manuel Quezón said, such an independence bill was an attempt to impose conditions upon the Philippine people.[149] Its rejection by the Philippine Legislature was followed in the Roosevelt administration not by a "new deal" but by legislation repeating the old economic stipulations with the added disadvantage of taxation upon a major Philippine export. Political concessions, however, met in the Philippines a favorable reaction which exemplified the predominance of the nationalistic motive over the economic. Americans in general have shown little disposition to dissuade Filipinos from their prospective indulgence in imprudence.

This haste to drop the burden has been encouraged by a moral assurance as great as that which dictated its assumption. In some cases the assurance was based upon a mistaken conviction that anti-imperialism is under all circumstances a manifestation of altruism. But in a perhaps larger number it rested rather upon the type of idea exemplified by the words of Senator Robinson of Indiana in a speech supporting the Hawes Bill:

> . . . it is a little hard for me to become interested in the argument that we owe the Filipinos a great moral responsibility to stay there and look after them when they constantly order us out. . . .

My judgment is that there will be difficulties of all kinds there almost immediately our sovereignty is completely ended; but that is their responsibility. Our first responsibility is to the American people . . .[150]

This pronouncement, meritorious at least in its candor, is not so far removed from all phases of past imperialist philosophy as one might think. The last sentence, reminiscent even of the language of Lodge, identifies the Lodge doctrine of the white man's burden as the spiritual father of Senator Robinson's idea. It is true, indeed, that the child repudiated his father's action; for Senator Robinson deduced from Lodge's principle of primary responsibility to the American people a conclusion antithetic to Lodge's expansionism. But since the time when Senator Lodge thought the white man's burden a sacred trust rich in dividends for the trustee, its weight had been made painful by Philippine ingratitude and, even more, by absence of the dividends. It was natural that the idea of the burden developed concomitantly to a form from which the concept of the sacred trust is absent. The conclusion of this tragi-comedy of the life of an idea is thus the Robinson doctrine of the white man's burden: When imperialistic responsibility is a burdensome baggage, let the papoose drop.

The statesmen and the poets have departed; their "tumult" and their "shouting" have died. It is not strange, therefore, that the battle in which they engaged us has an aspect largely changed. On the score of self-interest, the wise men of those self-confident times now appear to have judged no less ignorantly than did the ignorant whose passions they shared. On the other hand, there are still, notwithstanding Senator Robinson, those who cherish the spirit of a traditional moral ideal — not that of the excited Beveridge or that of the well-balanced Lodge, but the ideal of the confusedly benevolent McKinley. Yet over this international philanthropy there seems constantly to have hovered a manifest doom — one which threatens even today to bring all hopes to nought.

Was Kipling correct in deriving this doom of failure from "heathen folly"? An indictment of Filipino folly could be drawn, but a true indictment would differ from Kipling's. The folly of the race of color is that it nearly always imbibes whatever is of most dubious value for it from Western civilization. The Indian chose of all things to imbibe the white man's liquor. The Filipino chose a stronger intoxicant, the white man's nationalism. He did so just when Occidental philosophers were beginning to doubt the extroverted Greek's identification of the good life with political activity, just after his native teacher Rizal had counselled primary attention to individual development. But to have his distinctive flag design, his illusion of self-government under native politicians, the Filipino launched a well-nigh hopeless attack upon the bearers of all other gifts than this. And later, amid the undenied benefits of American rule, he took the curious position that he preferred "a government run like hell by Filipinos to one run like heaven by strangers." [151]

Of the folly of Oriental nationalism we nationalists of the Occident speak with poor grace. For the first folly occurs when the white man approaches his burden in a manner which is contrary to his altruistic ideology. Unlike the Christian missionary, who does not find his task too weighty, the nationalist fails to approach the white man's burden with both arms free to lift it. He is not even free to lift it with his strong right arm. In his right arm he holds what is essential to his nation's manifest destiny but not to the heathen's welfare — his national flag, symbol of the purpose of permanent domination. He believes confidently that he can manage the entire cargo. But this flag, as disturbing to any self-respecting heathen as is a toreador's flag to a bull, requires beating his charge *hors de combat* before he can even be lifted. No sooner has the heathen's fractured skull mended than his restiveness in view of the alien flag renews itself. Finally, too much wearied, the white man drops the burden with a crash sufficient to maim or kill. When he blames the catastrophe on "heathen folly" his self-deception is calling the true cause by its antithesis. However, the working of right and left hands at cross-purpose betokens less an intellectual folly than an incoherence in the nationalist's moral sentiment. The altruistic Kipling-McKinley doctrine guides the left arm, but the noble Lodge doctrine the right; the first strives for the heathen's peace, but the second for a national glory cherished more than peace. War or force seems the price which nationalism charges humanitarianism for an alliance according rarely with wise mating.

This spirit of heavily emotional nationalism, a dead weight upon the international ideal and even upon enlightened self-interest, might find in imperialist terminology itself a name which is less harsh than "folly" and more expressive of the nationalist's inevitable pathos. A Kipling who had truly judged his peers with "dear-bought wisdom" would have called self-assertive nationalism the white man's burden.

# CHAPTER XI

## PARAMOUNT INTEREST

America's expansion in 1898 hastened a national decision which in its first aspect seemed to eliminate from the ideal of manifest destiny its inveterate expansionism. It was the resolution to undertake immediately the rupturing of the Central American Isthmus by the construction of a canal, " the greatest liberty man has ever taken with nature." The canal answered to America's need of a water communication between the new Pacific possessions and the Eastern Coast. Since this waterway met simultaneously " the hope of centuries and the wish of peoples," its construction seemed to fulfil also an ideal which colonial imperialism had fostered — America's more active collaboration in the execution of international purposes. Indeed the building of the canal appeared to Senator Morgan and other religious nationalists as nothing less than " the proud mission of our Government and people, under a providence that is as peculiar to them as the founding of the kingdom of the Messiah was to the seed of Abraham." [1] Such observations suggested that the nationalist philosophy which once demanded the Isthmus as America's southern boundary had been sublimated into zeal in behalf of the commercial needs of all nations.

But when the United States entered upon the diplomatic negotiations essential to the canal project, it became evident that even in this issue, calling preeminently for the international mind, expansionism intruded its claim. Though no longer interested in actual sovereignty over countries with Isthmian highways, Americans of the early twentieth century were " expansionist " in the broad sense of the word which includes advocacy of merely substantial sovereignty. They adhered at least to President Hayes's idea of making the canal " virtually a part of the coast line of the United States " [2] through placing it under exclusive American control. Americans thus maintained the proud tradition of manifest destiny by demanding with respect to the canal a paramount right which amounted, as Professor Woolsey contemporaneously declared, to "the substantial possession of sovereignty." [3]

Between international collaboration and expansionism there was the usual sharp conflict. The expansionist attitude conflicted with the desire of other nations, particularly Great Britain, for a neutral canal. The conflict with Great Britain was especially incongruous because the advocates of America's entrance into world politics had looked to that country for partnership. Moreover, Great Britain, keenly desirous of America's friendship after the Spanish War, took the initiative in collaboration by indicating to the McKinley Administration its willingness to make substantial concessions to America's desire for control of the canal. But even the embodiment of these concessions in the first Hay-Pauncefote Treaty did not satisfy the American Senate, whose amendments, as Professor Williams declares, "were practically an elimination of the neutralization policy, and would place the canal in control of the United States with the protection of the route for the use of other powers left entirely to American discretion." [4] Thus nationalist exclusiveness imperilled the fulfilment of international need. Despite the previous enthusiasm for international collaboration, it was found all but impossible to effect what Tyler Dennett has called "the reconciliation of the diverse interests of half a dozen states so that nations could merge their racial pride in a common objective and find glory enough for each in this last gigantic conquest of nature" — a reconciliation which seems "a test of whether man in appropriating civilization had, at the same time, become civilized." [5]

The difficulty arose in large part, however, from the fact that the civilized nationalist usually finds ingenious reasons for expecting most concessions to be made by other countries. Thus America's claim to paramount right was rationalized by a moral method which purported to judge fairly the conflict of international interests but decided it to the marked advantage of one nation. In our accumulating terminology of nationalist morals, the present idea may be called the doctrine of paramount interest. For it was characterized by the conception that competing pretensions to paramount right in the satisfaction of any national interest are subject to adjudication by the formula — paramountcy of right rests properly upon paramountcy of interest.

The doctrine of paramount interest is perhaps the most common weapon of the moral armory of recent expansionism, and is particularly useful in the justification of "spheres of interest." The popularity of the principle is explicable partly by its provision of an ethical affiliate for "national interest," the cliché which, as Charles Beard points out, has in our soberer recent years succeeded "national honor" as the primary rationalization of foreign policy.[6] Let national interest be demonstrated as paramount interest and its pursuit may be attended with all the assurance of the vindication of national honor. For it is a common impression that the determination of paramount interest makes possible the adjudication of conflicts of national interest equitably, simply, and in conformity to the modern utilitarian temper.

Such an impression regarding this moral formula, however, has not yet been tested by a close logical analysis comparable to that received by many less important formulae of moral philosophers. The investigator must inquire first whether the believer in his nation's paramount interest does not underestimate the difficulty in this complicated world of ascertaining national interest itself. But even should this be discoverable there would remain the further problem of determining the relative weight of the competing interest of different nations. Do the typical applications of nationalist ideology indicate any logical standard by which the preponderance of one of various competing interests is determined in all cases? The long history of America's canal diplomacy, in which the doctrine of paramount interest crops up as often as does international conflict, may provide an answer.

An introduction to this history is formed by many foreshadowings, implications, and formulations of the idea in early issues. The doctrine of paramount interest is foreshadowed in the Monroe Doctrine, the spirit of which seemed to Theodore

Roosevelt to tend toward the idea that "our interests in this hemisphere are greater than those of any European power can possibly be." [7] It is implied in an observation of Representative Cambreling in a congressional debate of 1826 on Cuba: "The right of Spain once extinguished, from the nature of our position, and our peculiar and various associations with that Island, our right becomes supreme; it resists the European right of purchase; it is even paramount to the Mexican and Colombian right of war." [8] The doctrine is explicitly stated in Secretary of State Webster's assertion of 1842 about Hawaii: ". . . the United States . . . are more interested in the fate of the islands and of their government than any other nation can be." [9] But despite these and other indications of early familiarity with the idea, the surprising fact remains that the thesis of America's paramount right in an Isthmian canal was for a long time absent from statements of official attitude, as was also the acquisition of special privileges from official policy.

On the contrary, the original position of the American Government explicitly disavowed any claim to paramount right. This disavowal was generally made in the phraseology of altruism but rested on the assumption that exclusive protection was not to America's interest. The earliest official declaration on the subject, Secretary of State Henry Clay's instructions of 1826 to the American delegates to the Panama Congress, averred that a work redounding to the advantage of all America "should be effected by common means and united exertions" and that "the benefits of it ought not to be exclusively appropriated to any one nation, but should be extended to all parts of the globe upon the payment of a just compensation or reasonable tolls." [10] Two decades later President Polk, desiring a communication to America's prospective western possessions, entered with New Granada into a treaty wherein the ceded right of way received America's guarantee of its neutrality. The neutral status was also open to the guarantee of other powers in accordance with the principle stated by Polk as follows:

. . . there does not appear to be any other effectual means of securing to all nations the advantages of this important passage but the guaranty of great commercial powers that the Isthmus shall be neutral territory. The interests of the world at stake are so important that the security of this passage between the two oceans can not be suffered to depend upon the wars and revolutions which may arise among different nations.[11]

In the ensuing Whig administration Secretary of State Clayton, disapproving likewise "an attempt on the part of any one nation to monopolize to itself either the credit due to such an enterprise, or the advantages to be derived from it when effected," [12] wrote the principle of neutrality in its broadest sense into the Clayton-Bulwer Treaty. It forbade both the United States and Great Britain ever to "obtain or maintain for itself any exclusive control" over any Central American Isthmian canal, or "erect or maintain any fortifications commanding the same or in the vicinity thereof." [13] Even the more aggressive Democratic administrations of the 'fifties were marked by Secretary Marcy's disavowal of the desire for exclusive advantages in Panama,[14] and later by Secretary Cass's declaration of American desire for neutral Isthmian routes offering advantages "equally common to all nations." [15] In the unratified treaty of 1867 with Nicaragua the principles of neutrality and collective guarantee of neutrality were recognized by Seward, who said that "this government has no interest . . . different from that of other maritime powers." [16] As late as 1877, Secretary of State Fish sought to effect an adjustment of the Nicaraguan issue on the same principles. Shortly afterward the national canal policy became dominant, but it is noteworthy that the older view persisted among numerous Americans who were apparently both competent and disposed to judge the problem with reference to national interest. Thus Admiral Dewey scouted the idea of fortifying the canal with the effect of making it a prize of war; [17] John Bassett Moore doubted that the advantages from exclusive control in war outweighed the national benefits in America's historic policy of neutralization; [18] and Secretary of State Hay affirmed a collective guarantee of neutrality to be an immense national advantage.[19]

The advantage in a national canal seems at least debatable,

if only because so many eminent Americans denied it. How, then, did the doctrine identifying paramount interest with nationalization come to be asserted so dogmatically? A survey of the circumstances attending the origin and development of this doctrine may indicate as its primary cause the fact that circumstances drew the canal question into the murky sphere of nationalist emotionalism.

The first assertions of paramount interest and right came not from the administration but from critics of the Clayton-Bulwer Treaty. They were made in the 'fifties when expansionists were seized by resentment of the fact that this treaty forbade American expansion in Central America but left Great Britain a former foothold, the boundaries of which came into subsequent dispute. Quite naturally, resentment at British territorial designs developed into umbrage at Great Britain's share in the neutralized canal.

From the very beginning, however, America's case was rationalized in terms of paramount interest. Thus in 1852 a writer in *De Bow's Review* protested that as England was not equally interested in the canal she ought not to claim equal control.[20] In the Senate debate on the Clayton-Bulwer Treaty in the following year, Stephen Douglas made the declaration in which John Bassett Moore sees the beginning of the nationalistic view:

> I would let them all pass freely, as long as they did not abuse the privilege; close it against them, when they did. I insist that the American people occupy a position on this continent which rendered it natural and proper that we should exercise that power.[21]

A few months later a writer in the *United States Review* declared the avoidance of " co-partnery " in the Isthmian ways to be a fair inference from the Monroe Doctrine, now acquiring general recognition.[22] In 1856 the Democratic campaign resolutions likewise associated an affirmation of the Monroe Doctrine with insistence upon " our preponderance " in the adjustment of all questions arising out of the proposed Isthmian highway.[23] The claim to preponderant right thus seems to have been originally an expression of apprehension and jealousy over Great Britain's infringements upon the Monroe Doctrine and the scope of America's manifest destiny. The doctrine of paramount interest and right apparently arose less through an objective calculation of relative equities than through the need of a rather exigent nationalism for moral rationalization.

Although the Civil War put a damper on the aggressive spirit in foreign relations, the triumph of the Union was immediately followed not only by a resurgence of the jealous attitude toward foreign powers but also by a greater confidence in American capacity to enforce its claims. Perhaps this fact largely accounts for the circumstance that Seward's unratified Colombian treaty of 1869 made the first departure from the policy of neutralization. The treaty gave exclusive control of the Isthmian route to the United States and stipulated the right of closing it to the ships of countries at war with the United States or Colombia.

Ten years later the principle which Seward had merely acted upon was for the first time stated officially as national policy. Although Secretary Fish declared for neutralization as late as 1877, events between that year and 1879 make the change comprehensible. In 1878 a private French company, sponsored by the engineer of the Suez Canal, obtained from Colombia a concession which made definite the prospect of a canal owned by European interests. This injury to American pride was followed by another even greater when it appeared that Colombia intended to seek from European powers a guarantee of the neutrality of the proposed canal. American opposition to European private or public interest in a canal developed quickly and received expression in President Hayes's message of March 8, 1880. Hayes affirmed that "the policy of this country is a canal under American control" and asserted "the right and the duty of the United States" to assume the supervision and authority incident to this policy.[24] Secretary of State Blaine wrote to American diplomats a circular letter declaring the proposed European guarantee of neutrality to be an "uncalled for intrusion into a field where the local and general interests of the United States of America must be considered before those of any other power save those of the United States of

Colombia, alone." [25] Encouraged by a congressional resolution proposing the denunciation of the Clayton-Bulwer Treaty, he called upon the British Government for abrogation of this treaty on the novel legal ground that it "impeaches our right and long-established claim to priority on the American continent." [26] The climax of this national self-assertiveness was Secretary Frelinghuysen's negotiation in 1883 of a treaty with Nicaragua which arranged for a canal to be built and controlled by the United States under conditions conflicting with the Clayton-Bulwer Treaty.

It was in the governmental and popular discussions from 1878 to 1884 that America's paramount interest and right in an Isthmian canal were first stated officially as well as widely. The phrase "paramount interest" was brought to the fore by the report of Secretary of State Evarts to President Hayes in March, 1880. Therein he sought to seize the bone of contention by denying that contention existed:

> The paramount interest of the United States in these projects of interoceanic communication across the American Isthmus has seemed quite as indisputable to the European powers as to the States of this continent.[27]

President Hayes's message of the same year further popularized the word and the idea by stating that the relations of the canal to America's power and prosperity as a nation were "matters of paramount concern to the people of the United States." [28] Secretary Blaine's circular letter of 1881 used the idea if not the word in asserting that the interests of European powers in the canal "can never be so vital and supreme as ours." [29] Secretary Frelinghuysen implied the idea in his declaration that America's attitude was no different from what the attitude of the British would be toward a transit from one to another of their territorial possessions.[30]

But it was not possible to advance America's paramount interest when Grover Cleveland refused to recognize either paramountcy or interest, and rejected the Nicaraguan treaty shortly after arriving in the presidency.[31] Cleveland's principle of neutralization, however, prevailed only as long as did Cleveland himself; in the ensuing Harrison administration the national canal policy resumed its favor as a central element of the rising cult of sea power. Senator Morgan's [32] assertion in 1893 that the American people had decided irrevocably for American control seemed confirmed in 1895 when Congress, disregarding the Clayton-Bulwer Treaty, passed a bill giving the United States a controlling voice in the Nicaraguan enterprise of the Maritime Canal Company. Though the Spanish-American War occasioned a friendlier mood toward Great Britain, it induced at the same time an inconsistent impatience to construct and control the canal regardless of what Great Britain might say of her rights in the matter. The strategic lesson taught by the long voyage of the "Oregon," the need for a communication with the new Pacific possessions, and the spirit which felt the canal to be part of "the Book of Fate," [33] combined to make the immediate construction of the canal seem one of the pressing "duties of destiny." [34] McKinley's annual message of 1898 expressed preponderant opinion in calling upon Congress to take action toward a nationally controlled canal. While the Administration contemplated no action internationally precarious, a Congress "bursting with self-confidence" [35] was prepared to apply ex-Secretary Olney's suggestion to "claim paramountcy in things purely American." [36] Its response to McKinley was thus to show a favorable attitude toward the Hepburn bill, which appropriated money for a canal controlled by the United States under conditions directly contrary to its treaty obligations to Great Britain.

Alarmed at the recklessness of Congress, Secretary Hay hastened to conclude with the obliging Lord Pauncefote a treaty which, although providing for America's construction and exclusive regulation of an Isthmian canal, adhered to the neutralization principle of the Clayton-Bulwer Treaty; for it not only incorporated substantially the neutralizing rules of the Suez Canal, but invited adherence to the guarantee of neutrality by any power agreeing to these rules. Hay, however, reckoned without the full ambition of the Senate when he hoped for its recognition of this treaty as the real victory which it seemed to him. Fundamental in the opposition to the treaty, declares Tyler Dennett in his biography of Hay, was a youthful spirit of imperialism.[37] To Hay's consternation the Senate, considering diplomacy to be a taking rather than a give-and-take, amended the treaty; the amendments took for the United States the further exclusive rights of fortifying the canal, closing it to enemy ships in war, and acting as its sole protector. Great Britain, as Lord Lansdowne pointed out in rejecting the amendments, was thereby placed in a position of marked disadvantage.

But the doctrine of paramount interest was brought forth to justify the pretension to exclusive protection no less than the traditional claim to exclusive regulation of the canal. The *St. Louis Globe-Democrat* declared that the United States "has the largest stake in the building of such a waterway." [38] The *Boston Journal* affirmed that "public sentiment in this country insists overwhelmingly that the country which has the paramount interest in it shall control it." [39] To be sure, a minority tried to suggest, as did the *New York Press,* that the true deduction from America's paramount interest was the supreme interest of the United States in neutralization.[40]

Those speaking to such an effect were like voices crying in the wilderness. For their reasoning was shattered as it encountered the impervious emotional nationalism expressed in the words of Representative Stewart:

> If we concede a participation or partnership in this canal to anybody on earth, the radiant glory which has lately settled upon the brow of this nation will fade, and the violet vision of progress, hope and promise that now spreads before us will be lost to our sight.[41]

Together with such turgid prose, poetry like James Jeffrey Roche's verses entitled "Panama" reflected the notions of manifest destiny involved in the demand for exclusive control. Francis Lieber, in his poem of 1847 summoning his countrymen to a noble task, had seen a destiny of sufficient greatness in rending America asunder and uniting the binding sea.[42] But Roche's more pretentious idea of destiny was that "the hand that ope'd the gate shall forever hold the key." He posed the rhetorical question:

Who shall hold that magic key
But the child of destiny,
In whose veins has mingled long
All the best blood of the strong? [43]

The foregoing survey has suggested sufficiently the emotional factors which made the canal issue a matter of national pride, largely determined the claim to exclusive control, and created the need for a doctrine that rationalized the emotion of manifest destiny in terms of paramount interest.

However, the appeal of an idea cannot be entirely understood by looking at the impulses which it rationalizes rather than at its logical content. The idea of "paramount interest" had a coherent meaning which, however much "interest smooths the road to faith," was itself one source of faith. One must now inquire, therefore, as to the logical elements of this firm belief that America's interest in the canal affecting vitally so many nations was paramount.

In a certain sense Captain Mahan spoke truly when he affirmed generally that "nearness" was a "ground for national self-assertion." [44] It is not true, however, that (in the words of a recent American jurist) "mere proximity itself is a vital argument in sustaining the contention of our peculiar interest." [45] Although the greater proximity of the United States to the canal was emphasized throughout the issue, proximity seemed of importance because it allegedly resulted in the fact that certain interests of the proximate nation were affected more vitally than those of the distant. The fundamental problem is thus not the geographical cause of the interests but the interests themselves.

In one of the earliest statements of the doctrine, that of a writer in *De Bow's Review* in 1852, the ground of America's alleged paramount interest in the Canal was held to be a preponderance of commercial interest.[46] In this instance preponderance was asserted in relation to Great Britain alone, but President Hayes later affirmed that "our merely commercial interest in it is greater than that of all other countries." [47] In connection with a similar thesis, the primacy of our commercial interest in the canal was implied by Secretary Blaine to be an obvious consequence of geographical adjacency:

> If the proposed canal were a channel of communication, near to the countries of the Old World, and employed wholly, or almost wholly, by their commerce, it might very properly be urged that the influence of the European powers should be commensurate with their interest. . . . The case, however, is here reversed, and an agreement between the European states to jointly guarantee the neutrality and in effect control the political character of a highway of commerce, remote from them, and near to us, forming substantially a part of our coast-line and promising to become the chief means of transport between our American and Pacific States, would be viewed by this Government with the gravest concern.[48]

Similarly, a House committee report of 1881 declared that "the interest of the United States is greater than that of any other people or government as the proposed transit route would be merely a link in the coastwise trade between the Atlantic and Pacific States of the Union."[49]

But commercial interest was not, unfortunately for simplicity, the only criterion. For as Evarts observed, the completion of the canal would effect, in addition to a commercial revolution, a change in the conditions under which the United States maintained not only its treaty obligations to Panama but its own security. Whereas at present, he pointed out, the Pacific Coast was so situated that railroad connections would always give time to prepare for its defense, "with a canal through the Isthmus the same advantage would be given to a hostile fleet which would be given to friendly commerce; its line of operations and the time in which warlike demonstration could be made would be enormously shortened."[50] This consideration was presented by Minister Maney to the Colombian Government in 1882 when he stated that the canal, "as a means of sudden concentration of large naval forces . . . can contribute to the injury or destruction of American Governments, but not possibly to that of any of Europe." Maney unhesitatingly concluded:

> The security of the two being thus unequal in the matter, their relations to it are of right correspondingly different; for surely the

instinct to self-preservation and self-security, common to all nature, beyond being excusable, is commendable in governments, by reason of their paramount importance.[51]

In the 'nineties Captain Mahan likewise based his claim that America's "interest" was "superior" to Great Britain's on the ground that the canal would bring the Pacific Coast nearer to the great navies of European powers. Hence, he declared, "the bearing of all questions of Isthmian transit upon our national progress, safety, and honor, is more direct and more urgent than upon hers." [52]

An argument related to the preceding grounded America's primacy of interest in the Monroe Doctrine, which itself rests on the principle of self-defense. Whereas a former argument derived preponderant interest from the strategic dangers in the canal itself, the argument based upon the Monroe Doctrine deduced this interest from the alleged tendency of an international guarantee to create European influence in the countries through or adjacent to which the canal would run. Thus Senator Burnside, author of a joint resolution discountenancing European protection of an Isthmian canal, asserted in 1879 that the consequent European control of the destiny of independent American states would be in conflict with the Monroe Doctrine, and "dangerous to the peace and safety of the United States." [53] The same consideration was used by Alfred Williams in his work of 1880, *The Inter-Oceanic Canal and the Monroe Doctrine,* to establish the doctrine of paramount interest in its most radical form. His was the thesis that, because the Monroe Doctrine was based on the paramount consideration of self-preservation, America's interest in the canal was of an exceptional character as compared not only with the interest of any other nation, but also with that of "all other nations," that is, all nations combined.[54]

The discussions from 1900 to 1902 revived all these ideas, in particular the doctrine affirming the canal to be "peculiarly an American canal" because it was "in time of war . . . absolutely essential for our commerce and protection." [55] However, a new argument was suggested by the prospect of building the canal with American funds. It was maintained that the country which paid for the canal was entitled to paramount right by virtue of the very fact that it had the sole financial interest. Representative Ryan thus criticized Great Britain's share in protection under the first Hay-Pauncefote Treaty on the ground that it had not offered to contribute one cent toward the construction of the canal.[56] Those arguing to this effect apparently overlooked the fact that it was precisely the right of construction which the United States had previously been seeking on the ground of paramount interest. Somewhat illogically, as soon as the right was definitively attained it was used as an interest on which to base a further pretension.

To summarize, the thesis of America's paramount interest in the proposed canal meant in the first place that the United States would derive the greatest benefit or injury in accordance with the consummation or frustration of its claims. The pretension to paramountcy appeared in three different forms: in relation to European nations, to all other nations save Colombia, and to any other nation without exception. Two principal grounds supported the claim in all its forms — supremacy of commercial interest and superiority of strategic interest. On the ground that its exceptional interest could not be otherwise protected, the United States claimed the right to the exclusive construction, regulation, and defense of the canal. This pretension did not exclude equality for all nations in peace, but it did give the United States a decided superiority of advantage in war.

Quite aside from any moral criticism, there are logical and factual exceptions which may be taken to the doctrine. Its most obvious weakness lies in the fact that, doubtless because American interest seemed greater by both the commercial and the strategic criteria, we were not told which criterion is more important. In the event that each criterion favored different disputants the method would thus not permit any conclusion concerning paramount interest. This consideration is the more important because international issues ordinarily touch disputants in different interests, the relative weight of which is a matter of difficult decision.

Although America's purely strategic interest was probably

superior at least to that of any European nation, it is not certain that its commercial interest was greater than Great Britain's. This second weakness in the American position was implied by Lord Granville in defending Great Britain's rights under the Clayton-Bulwer Treaty:

> . . . Her Majesty's Government would be wanting in regard to their duty if they failed to point out that Great Britain has large colonial possessions, no less than great commercial interests, which render any means of unobstructed and rapid access from the Atlantic to the North and South Pacific Oceans a matter for her also of the greatest importance.[57]

A statement of the British case even stronger than Lord Granville's was that of Captain Mahan, than whom none was more disposed to argue his own country's rights. Mahan admitted that "from the nature of the occupations which constitute the welfare of her people, as well as from the characteristics of her power, Great Britain seemingly has the larger immediate stake in a prospective interoceanic canal." He maintained, to be sure, that America's interest was still superior for the following reason: "So far as the logical distinction between commercial and political will hold, it may be said that our interest is both commercial and political, that of other states almost wholly commercial." [58] But it is difficult, especially in view of Mahan's own expositions of the relations of commercial to political or strategic interest, to see how the distinction will hold far enough to deny a world power like Great Britain strategic interest in the canal.

Though the ambiguity and elusiveness of the criteria make determinations of paramount interest very difficult, one might grant for the sake of argument that America's sum of interests in the canal was larger than that of any nation except Colombia. This admission throws into sharper relief, however, what is perhaps the most serious difficulty in the American's interpretation of paramount interest. It was his disregard of the likelihood that, even if his country's interest in the canal were paramount to that of any other single nation, it was inferior to the combined interests of international society. There was plausibility in the contention of Lord Granville that "such a canal as the waterway between two great oceans and between all Europe and Eastern Asia is a work which concerns not merely the United States or the American Continent, but the whole civilized world." [59] Even Mahan conceded that, in view of the "great and consequential" interests of foreign states, no settlement could constitute a finality which did not "effect our preponderating influence, and at the same time insure the natural rights of other peoples." [60] The sum total of these interests was great and consequential to a degree which probably exceeded even the largest interests of any single nation.

Between alleged American interest and world interest there existed a potential conflict by virtue of the especial claim which Americans asserted. This fact was denied, indeed, by American statesmen; President Hayes declared that America's exclusive control would be "not only compatible with but promotive of the widest and most permanent advantage to commerce and civilization." [61] But the statesman seldom admits, if indeed he is even able to see, the conflict between his country's interest and world interest. The conflict, however, was evident to Lord Granville, who cited the melancholy effect of competition and imperialism which would ensue from abandonment of the principle of neutralization. Lord Granville could very effectively have added to his own strong arguments the words of an American Secretary of State in the period when nationalization of the canal did not seem nationally advantageous. Cass, protesting against the Belly contract giving the French Government special rights in a Central American canal project, wrote as follows:

> The equality and security of these interoceanic routes constitute a great portion of their value to the world, and all commercial powers are interested in their maintenance. An exclusive right in one of these powers to exercise a permanent armed intervention would give serious cause of dissatisfaction to all the others . . .[62]

Again in 1902 T. S. Woolsey,[63] John Bassett Moore,[64] and other eminent Americans held that the political stability and commercial usefulness of the canal would be better secured by neutralization than by exclusive protection.

An international menace much greater than America's exclusive control, which thus far has in practice proved scarcely harmful, was its policy of not undertaking or countenancing any Isthmian project not meeting its own conditions. In an article in the *North American Review* in 1900, Mayo W. Hazeltine went so far as to declare openly for a contingent obstructiveness:

> We may say at the outset that, if the projected artificial waterway is to be open in time of war to the battleships of a public enemy of the United States, the American people will never suffer the rampart which Nature herself has erected for the protection of our Pacific States to be demolished . . .[65]

The American nationalist's implication that one country's interest and right can outweigh the substantial interest and right of the rest of the world has not seemed reasonable to most moralists. The principle more often accepted is that stated by President Arias of Panama:

> . . . the position of the Panama Canal is one that can not be defined by the mere will of a single nation. The international interests at stake are so many and so important, that it is imperative that . . . account should be taken of this plurality of interests, so that the result achieved should be both equitable and productive of welfare and advancement for mankind.[66]

This view had been espoused by American statesmen themselves when it supported national self-interest. For example, Minister Rush had written in 1825 in connection with the American claim to free navigation of the St. Lawrence:

> The public good is the object of the law of nations, as that of individuals is of municipal law. The interest of a part gives way to the whole; the particular to the general. The former is subordinate; the latter paramount.[67]

Yet in 1900 Congressmen insisted upon controlling a highway of world commerce, as did Representative Ryan, " without considering the . . . desires of . . . any other country." [68] One wonders whether Americans would have taken so nationalistic a stand had they foreseen the moral embarrassment which it was to cause later. At first, indeed, all difficulties seemed to yield to American determination and luck. Despite

Great Britain's initial rejection of the Senate amendments, Hay negotiated and saw ratified a second treaty, which offered the British certain concessions but left America solely privileged to regulate, fortify, and protect the canal. This accomplishment was followed by the Hay-Herran Treaty, in which Colombia agreed to permit the construction of the Panama Canal under conditions meeting America's desire for virtual sovereignty over the Canal Zone. Then just when the nationalist policy seemed on the point of success, a retributory destiny exposed America to the same nationalism with which she herself had obstructed the needs of international society.

Colombia perversely refused to ratify the Hay-Herran Treaty. Her motive, according to American critics, was the desire to receive additional compensation from the United States or the Panama Canal Company — as Roosevelt expressed it, to play the blackmailer.[69] However this may be, the reason which Colombia herself gave, and in all likelihood entertained sincerely, was the fact that the Hay-Herran Treaty, negotiated by Herran without full authorization, infringed upon her sovereignty in the Canal Zone. Though he himself had carried nationalism much farther in the previous phase of the canal issue, Roosevelt at this point would not allow any other people's nationalism to stand in America's way. He prepared a message urging Congress to construct the canal in spite of Colombia's attitude. The necessity of following this aggressive course was obviated by a quirk of events which Representative Hitt attributed to Providence.[70] But it was Roosevelt himself, giving a peculiar interpretation to America's right of intervention under a treaty which guaranteed Colombia's territorial integrity, who used American troops to prevent Colombia from suppressing the revolt on the Isthmus. This intervention, the hasty recognition of the republic at whose birth America had been midwife, and the negotiation of the Hay-Bunau-Varilla Treaty were the events which justified Roosevelt's subsequent boast, "I took the canal zone." [71]

No seizure in the history of American imperialism has provoked more vigorous attack. One may well wonder what enabled Roosevelt to deem his actions "as free from scandal as the public acts of George Washington and Abraham Lincoln." [72] The ironical Lowell's proposition that " our nation's bigger'n their'n an' so its rights air bigger " does not, in all probability, influence American nationalists consciously. Nor was Roosevelt's self-justification the traditional doctrine of paramount interest, which in this case, despite Roosevelt's assertion of America's great interest in the canal, would have favored Colombia. The curious fact is, indeed, that Roosevelt used the doctrine of paramount interest—but in a version antithetic to the traditional.

The new doctrine of paramount interest is revealed in part by the following lines from Roosevelt's special message on the Panama issue:

> . . . I confidently maintain that the recognition of the Republic of Panama was an act justified by the interests of collective civilization. If ever a Government could be said to have received a mandate from civilization to effect an object the accomplishment of which was demanded in the interest of mankind, the United States holds that position with regard to the interoceanic canal.[73]

We see here that Roosevelt was using as moral criterion not national interest but the interest of collective civilization. His inference from this criterion appears in his quotation from one of Secretary of State Cass's despatches relative to the Isthmian canal:

> While the rights of sovereignty of the states occupying this region should always be respected, we shall expect that these rights be exercised in a spirit befitting the occasion and the wants and circumstances that have arisen. Sovereignty has its duties as well as its rights, and none of these local governments, even if administered with more regard to the just demands of other nations than they have been, would be permitted, in a spirit of Eastern isolation, to close the gates of intercourse on the great highways of the world, and justify the act by the pretension that these avenues of trade and travel belong to them, and that they choose to shut them up or, what is almost equivalent, to encumber them with such unjust relations as would prevent their general use.[74]

In other words, the interests of collective civilization, giving the United States a mandate to construct the canal, are paramount to Colombia's sovereignty as exercised in self-interested obstruction of the work. One may also express Roosevelt's conception of the mandate in the words of Professor Hart:

> The essence of this defense is that the United States of America represents a higher kind of human interest than the Latin-American states; and that in case of a clash of interests those of the United States are paramount. . . .
>
> To Roosevelt's mind the question was not that of the interest of a great power against a weak one, but of all other nations against one selfish people—the nation who could not build a canal and would not suffer another to build it.[75]

Roosevelt thus adopted the principle which has been called the right of international eminent domain. This doctrine had been affirmed not only by Cass but also by Representative Cox when he declared in 1858 that "no nation has a right to hold great isthmian highways . . . on this continent, without the desire, will, or power, to use them." [76] Perhaps the principle had been suggested to Roosevelt in part by the article sent to him by Philippe Bunau-Varilla, engineer not only of canals but also of the Panama Revolution, who a few months before that revolution had written in *Le Matin* a remarkable prophecy:

> The property rights of private persons, like those of nations, have a limit, which is the superior law of the necessity of the circulation of the human collectivity. And it is this superior law which President Roosevelt will enforce, and which it will be his next step to enforce.[77]

Though international law recognizes no such principle, even the jurist Elihu Root followed Roosevelt and Bunau-Varilla in affirming, doubtless from the viewpoint of natural or moral law, that "the sovereignty of Colombia over the Isthmus of Panama was qualified and limited by the right of the other civilized nations of the earth to have the canal constructed across the Isthmus and to have it maintained for their free and unobstructed passage." [78] Intense solicitude for the interests of collective civilization was now expressed by many who had formerly been engrossed in nationalism. Representative Grosvenor's internationalism posited "a power greater than the little contemptible spirit of the Colombian Senate . . . that says that in the interest of civilization . . . a canal shall be built." [79] Senator Clarke spoke of "the inevitable march to a manifest destiny " whereby, even through bloody transgressions of international law, the betterment of mankind is effected.[80] The *Brooklyn Eagle* defended Roosevelt's action as the " overthrow of a highwayman on the path of all nations." [81] Similarly the *Atlanta Journal* found America's justification in the fact that Colombia was " needlessly obstructing the world's commerce." [82] The *Denver Republican* related the expropriation of Colombia to the old Western custom of " claim jumping," that is, disregarding land claims which were not made socially productive.[83] One of the most interesting comments of this type was written by Brigadier-General Chittenden some years later, in an article in the *Atlantic Monthly* entitled " Manifest Destiny in America." With reference to the Panama issue he posed the question, " in whom resided the paramount right pertaining to this proposed waterway? " According to General Chittenden the answer could only be, " in the world at large." Like the imperialists of 1903 Chittenden deviated from the traditional doctrine which based manifest destiny upon the paramountcy of American interests as such. In this case, which permitted identification of American interest with the world's, manifest destiny seemed " an assumed natural tendency of events " toward the greatest good of the greatest portion of international society.[84]

All this might be very persuasive had we not learned by now that usually the questionable point about the internationalist's moral syllogism is not its abstract major premise but the correspondence of its minor premise with fact. Roosevelt's minor premise held that his course of action was " the only means by which the end can be achieved." [85] Is it true that Roosevelt's high-handed course in Panama was the only means by which the construction of an Isthmian canal could have been achieved? The answer hinges largely upon the terms of the Spooner Act, which authorized the canal. This Act permitted as an alternative to the Colombian route the passage through Nicaragua. Though longer and more expensive, the latter route had been pronounced practicable by nearly all engineers, was considered preferable by some, and could have been secured without difficulty. Even the Panama route might have been secured ultimately, for Colombia had not opposed the canal project itself, but merely the conditions of a particular treaty. The Hay-Herran Treaty could doubtless have been superseded by a convention which offered Colombia terms better either politically or financially. General Reyes of Colombia thus observed in his protest to Hay that "a state should certainly not obstruct the passage through its territory of a canal which the progress of the age and the needs of humanity have made necessary, but it has the right to impose conditions which shall save its sovereignty and to demand indemnification for the use thereof." [86] It was with these facts in view that Tyler Dennett asserted of Roosevelt's imperialistic course: "The saddest aspect of the episode was that it had all been so unnecessary." [87] But the most frequent error of impetuous nationalism is disregard of the innocuous alternative and unwarranted postulation of political necessity.

Even more striking than its inconsistency with fact is the inconsistency of Roosevelt's moral theory with earlier American ideology upon this issue. Colombia was condemned for asserting what had previously been the implication of America's own policy—the right to the protection of vital national interests even at the possible sacrifice of international interests. In fact America's long unwillingness to permit any save a nationalized canal had probably delayed the Isthmian enterprise much longer than Colombia's course could have done. But the United States had no sooner acquired the right to construct the national canal than the original criterion of paramount interest was superseded by its antithesis. According to the first criterion, paramount interest was that of the nation with greatest need; according to the second, it was that of international society and hence of the nation with the implicit mandate of the world. The first doctrine posited the paramountcy of national to international interest; the second, the superiority of international to national interest. The only thing common to the two interpretations was that each supported the interest of the United States.

Roosevelt's use of international necessity as a cloak for national self-interest drew a penalty. For though his doctrine of the paramountcy of international interest was enunciated for purposes of the moment, it had to figure as the enduring standard for America's own actions in relation to the Panama Canal. Because there had been inadequate moral preparation for the application of this standard, living up to it proved more difficult than even the gigantic task of engineering which America undertook.

The construction of the canal was no sooner completed than American legislators exempted American coastwise shipping from tolls, and thereby violated the principle of commercial equality which was stipulated by both the Hay-Pauncefote Treaty and the doctrine of the paramountcy of international interest. This self-assertive measure was supported not only by a strained legal argument but also by an implicit reversion of many Americans to the doctrine of the paramountcy of America's interest and right in the Canal. President Taft thus declared that "we own the canal" and that "it was our money that built it." [88] Secretary of State Knox's answer to Great Britain's protest against a special concession to Panama contained the observation: "The United States has always asserted the principle that the status of the countries immediately concerned by reason of their political relation to the territory in which the canal was to be constructed was different from that of all other countries." [89] And when Bunau-Varilla told Americans that their country was merely "the trustee of humanity" in Panama, the editor of the New York *Sun* inquired dissentingly, "Who shouldered the expense?" [90]

It was not until President Wilson pointed out not only the moral issue but the fact that the tolls act embarrassed him in "other matters of even greater delicacy and nearer consequence" [91] that its repeal was accomplished. The internationalist doctrine, initiated to Colombia's misfortune by the first President Roosevelt, was ultimately reasserted by the second President Roosevelt just after a friendly visit to Colombia's "sacred" soil. He declared in Panama that because the canal served all nations in peaceful commerce, the United States was "a trustee for all the world in its peaceful maintenance." [92]

The ideal of trusteeship has been applied more easily in commercial regulation of the Canal than in the policies pertaining to the defense of this national interest. The imperialism of these policies, as William E. Dodd observes, could perhaps have been avoided by the neutralization of the Isthmian canal. But the policy of exclusive protection, expected to be a master stroke in America's scheme of national defense, resulted only in creating, as Secretary Hughes said, "new exigencies and new conditions of strategy and defense." [93] In 1905 President Roosevelt called attention to one defensive policy which had to follow from the new exigencies and conditions. It was that of more rigorous maintenance of the Monroe Doctrine in the region of the Caribbean Sea, in which lay the approaches to the Canal.[94] Although stated by Roosevelt in terms of the Monroe Doctrine, America's defensive formula for the Caribbean ultimately became known as a special policy under the designation, "Canal policy." This policy, as Secretary Hughes describes it, forbids to foreign powers "the control of the Panama Canal, or the approaches to it, or the obtaining of any position which would interfere with our right of protection or would menace the freedom of our communications." [95]

This defensive policy was a reversion to a doctrine which had momentarily disappeared. It is the original doctrine of paramount interest, which demands the subordination of the claims of all nations to those of the one most vitally affected. Just as the Monroe Doctrine has been based upon "the paramount interest of the United States in American affairs," [96] so the Canal policy has been founded on what Wallace Thompson calls "the Doctrine of the Special Interest of the United States in the Caribbean Sea." [97] Thus Secretary of State Knox not only told Americans that the zone of the Caribbean was of "paramount interest" to the United States,[98] but also reminded the British that the Caribbean was "a sphere in which this Government is preeminently interested." [99] Again, during the Nicaraguan issue of 1927 President Coolidge asserted America's "special interest" [100] in Nicaragua, and even his critic Senator Borah subscribed to the same thesis.[101]

The rationale of this claim to a special interest in the Caribbean appears in the words of Admiral Chester:

> There is a field, in which the interests of the United States, as far as they relate to the basic principle of the Monroe Doctrine—Self-preservation— are paramount, the protection of which cannot be shared with

any other nation. This district comprises the countries lying contiguous or adjacent to our own, bordering on the Caribbean Sea or the Gulf of Mexico.[102]

More specifically the Canal policy is based upon what George C. Butte calls "the paramount strategic value of the canal to the United States in time of war." [103] Thus the Canal policy like the Monroe Doctrine has been subsumed by American statesmen under the legal doctrine of self-defense. This legal principle of self-defense is itself an assertion of the supremacy of the interest in self-preservation over all else. However, the defensive doctrine of the special interest has been frequently presented without any reference to legal criteria. An example of this is the following citation from the *Chicago Tribune's* editorial of 1916 on the Nicaraguan canal treaty:

> The Caribbean region will be dominated by the United States because it is essential to our security. We built the Canal because we needed it in a special sense not shared by the world, and having built it we know it for our frontier and must make certain that it does not pass into the hands of a rival.[104]

The reference in the foregoing to a "frontier" was not meant literally. But that the conception of a right to "dominate" a region of interest may easily give rise to aspirations of *de jure* sovereignty was shown by the purchase of the Danish West Indies which shortly followed the editorial. Indeed, the application of the doctrine of paramount interest to territorial expansionism had already been demonstrated in the past. Secretary Foster, in connection with the Hawaiian treaty of annexation, spoke in 1893 of "the necessarily paramount rights and interests of the American people there," [105] as did also the *Iowa State Register* in the same year.[106] E. C. Semple placed the significance of America's acquisition of Porto Rico in "the paramount interest of the United States in an interoceanic canal." [107] In 1903 former Consul-General Penfield applied this expansionist doctrine to the canal issue in urging the acquisition of Panama (called by a prominent American diplomat "manifest destiny" as late as 1926).[108] According to Penfield, Panama was "worth comparatively little to Colombia, but of inestimable value to a powerful nation constructing a waterway to unite the Atlantic and Pacific." [109] This type of moral calculus prepared Americans for the occasion when apprehension of Germany's possible acquisition of the Danish West Indies led the United States to acquire this fortress on the path to the Canal. Secretary Lansing adverted implicitly to the doctrine of paramount interest when he wrote in his justification of the Danish treaty that the Caribbean lay within the "peculiar sphere of influence of the United States." [110]

No sooner were the Danish West Indies incorporated than some affirmed that paramount interest made manifest for Americans a much vaster destiny as sovereign of adjacent islands. At the 1917 meeting of the National Conference on Foreign Relations, Professor William R. Shepherd read a paper on the advantage and justification of America's gradual acquisition of all remaining European colonies in the Caribbean Sea. The argument of paramount interest appears with particular clarity in the following:

> Now, just as there are three parties and three sets of interests involved, so there are three circumstances that should determine the attitude of the United States toward the retention by European nations of colonies in and around the Caribbean. The first circumstance is, that we need those areas ourselves; the second is, that the European owners do not; and the third is a natural consequence of the two preceding, namely that the owners ought to turn them over to us for the good of all concerned. . . .
>
> Because of their nearness to the territory of the United States and to the Panama Canal, and because of their remoteness from the territory of their possessors, this country has, and ought to have, a paramount interest in their destiny . . .[111]

This assumption that America's interest in the Caribbean is sufficiently vital to outweigh a large sum of international interests has not as yet been accepted by the European countries in question, interested for sentimental reasons if for none other in retaining their possessions.

But in justifying another phase of American Caribbean policy Americans themselves have implicitly rejected the thesis that national interest can outweigh the sum of international interests. Reference is made to the ideology supporting intervention of the United States in Caribbean countries when there arise disorderly conditions inviting European intervention. The caveat of the Canal policy against intervention by other countries has been based on the hypothesis that in the Caribbean "no one has a stake . . . comparable to ours." [112] This nationalistic doctrine, however, has not ordinarily been used to justify America's interventions; for the nationalistic version does not logically imply the right to subordinate the supremely vital interest of sovereignty to some extrinsic interest of the intervening nation. But the doctrine of paramount interest is like a coat the two sides of which are for different kinds of weather. The side of the doctrine which is adapted to imperialistic interventions is the version holding that the welfare of international society is paramount even to an individual nation's sovereignty.

That America's exercise of police power was essential to the paramount interests of civilization was the implication of Roosevelt's message of 1904 on America's policy of intervention. Secretary Knox viewed the same issue from the standpoint of the paramountcy of the American group of nations to any one American nation:

> Contiguous countries or those approximate by reason of being parts of one of the earth's great geographical subdivisions sustain natural and inevitable relations toward each other, out of which arise certain political correlations to be asserted from time to time as the safety, welfare, and progress of the group as a whole or that of its members may require.[113]

In another address Secretary Knox sounded the same note of internationalism in affirming that "the common interest of nations is being recognized as superior to their special interests," and that "each nation is likely to see itself forced to yield something of its initiative, not to any one nation, but to the community of nations in payment for its share in the 'advance in richness of existence.'" [114] The *New Republic* defended America's "Democratic Intervention" of 1916 in Mexico on the ground that "the right of a nation to rule or riot as it wills is going the way of the right of a private person to do what he wills with his own property." This way seemed forbidden by the principle that "there is no absolute, sovereign nation, immune by natural or divine law from influences originating beyond its own borders." [115] During a dispute with commercially unaccommodating Mexico, President Coolidge implicitly subordinated a nation's domestic laws to "the rights and duties" which had been incorporated in international law "in furtherance of the humanitarian desire for a universal reign of law." [116] William Ledyard Rodgers wrote that, should other measures fail, American intervention in troubled Mexico would be justified by "the democratic principle that the majority has rights over the minority," a principle stated also to the effect that "world interest claims precedence when the impotence of a laggard nation interferes with the good of the greatest number." [117] These observations apparently overlook the fact that Mexico's controversy with this country arose out of her subordination of American property claims to the greatest good of the greatest number of her people.

Has there been a greater consistency in our attitude toward the use of the ubiquitous doctrine of paramount interest by others? At least the relations of the United States with Japan, in connection with the latter country's ambitions to establish spheres of special interest in China, provide official expressions of this attitude. The Lansing-Ishii agreement of 1917 resulted in Secretary Lansing's declaration that "territorial propinquity creates special relations between countries, and, consequently, the Government of the United States recognizes that Japan has special interests in China, particularly in the part to which her possessions are contiguous." [118] This acknowledgment, motivated by various political purposes to which Lansing hoped to secure Japan's adherence in return, would seem to imply the validity of Japan's pretension to such special rights as are claimed by the United States in the region of the Canal. Such at least was Japan's interpretation. And this interpretation of the concept of special interest was recently put to use by a Japanese statesman who maintained with reference to the Manchurian issue that "Japan cannot remain indifferent to any one taking action under any pretext which is prejudicial to the maintenance of law and order in East Asia for which she, if only in view of her geographic position, has the most vital concern." [119] In this statement, as well as in the earlier Lansing doctrine, the conception of paramount right is based upon the paramount interest of a particular nation, happen what may to nations possessing lesser interest.

Recent American statesmen, however, have been by no means disposed to leave unchallenged either Japan's liberal interpretation of the Lansing admission or her independent determination to enforce an Asiatic Monroe Doctrine. Secretary of State Hull, for example, has met Japan's pretensions in contiguous territory with the statement:

> In the opinion of the American people and the American Government, no nation can, without the assent of the other nations concerned, rightfully endeavor to make conclusive its will in situations where there are involved the rights, the obligations and the legitimate interests of other sovereigns.[120]

The foregoing involves more than a legal objection; it implies the version of paramount interest which holds that a large sum of international interests has greater moral weight than the interest even of the nation with greatest individual need. But the effectiveness of the sincerest enunciation of this internationalist principle is lessened by the fact that in the past America has maintained to her own advantage a contrary view, an inconvenient precedent for others.

The ideological history comes to an end before moral illumination has begun. From beginning to end this history has thrown light only on the "heterogeneity, lack of unity, and plurality" which Herbert Kraus calls the earmarks of international morality.[121] What it has not revealed is a uniformly applied criterion of paramount interest. Paramount interest was ascribed on some occasions to the nation with most vital need, but there was not formulated any single method for determining the relative weight of various interests of competing nations. An even more serious difficulty, it became evident, was the ascription of paramount right at other times to the nation whose need, whether or not most vital, best harmonized with the needs of international society; for international welfare formed a different criterion of paramount interest. The divergence of the two criteria was somewhat obscured by the fact that, while putting his stronger foot forward, the American usually maintained that his nation had the better case by both standards. But the nationalist must stand or fall by the foot on which he places his weight. For the two criteria not only represent antithetic philosophies of international relations but tend in practice, whatever the theory, to support pretensions so broad as to be in considerable measure mutually exclusive.

It would be unreasonable not to concede that the difficulty of establishing a single, clear criterion of paramount interest is due in large part to the difficulty of moral judgment itself. It is forced not only to attempt to weigh interests almost imponderable but also, what is even more difficult, to choose between competing values for standards of judgment. The complexity of the matter is increased still further by the fact that both the nationalist and the internationalist doctrines appear in more or less favorable light in accordance with varying degrees of injury or benefit to the nation and to international society.

However, the difficulty of the entire problem is chiefly created by the nationalist himself, in consequence of his failure to adopt the method used ordinarily in individual experience when two cogent moral values conflict. It is compromise, the finding of a course of conduct whereby each of two values, such as self-interest and altruism, is given reasonable satisfaction. The same "obligation to agree to a reasonable compromise"[122] in issues of conflict has been prescribed by Stowell and other jurists for nations. Compromise of all the canal issues was apparently possible through the plan of neutralization embodied in the rejected Hay-Pauncefote Treaty. But the history of America's canal policy confirmed Secretary Hughes's candid observation that "the machinery of international accord works only within the narrow field not closed by divergent ambitions."[123]

Whereas the American nationalist presented the doctrine of paramount interest as the cause of his unwillingness to compromise, it is perhaps truer that the nationalist's aversion to compromise was the fundamental cause of the doctrine of paramount interest. One can perhaps say generally that the great stress upon moral principles in international experience is largely due to the nationalist's unwillingness to apply the moral principles which would forestall conflicts by compromise. In this instance the doctrine of paramount interest provided a splendidly flexible rationalization whereby America's moral triumph in all conflicts was assured. By resorting to one version of the doctrine or another at his convenience, the nationalist had the best of his opponent on either one flank or the other all the time. Such a use of a principle indicates less the frame of mind of the moralist than that of the strategist.

Thus the nationalist, to paraphrase James Harrington, was interested in reason not as it was right or wrong in itself, but as it made for the aggrandizement of his country. But to say further that this attitude represented an engrossment in self-interest is to say what is in part a truism and in part an untruth.

It is a truism that the nationalist's paramount interest, by virtue of something deeper than logic, is his interest in his own country. But this interest itself is reinforced by two moral judgments which even if questionable are doubtless sincere. The first is exemplified by Whitelaw Reid's observation during the Panama crisis that, let the " sentimentalists " say what they will, the statesman as the trustee of his country must " look first to its own interests." [124] The second is the dogma of manifest destiny that advancement of the nation's interest always involves simultaneous advancement of " the interests of collective civilization." Scales which are weighted by such prepossessions are manifestly destined to show paramount interest always on one side.

# CHAPTER XII

## POLITICAL AFFINITY

As though the turn of the century were the turning of a new leaf, the ensuing decade witnessed virtually nothing of the promiscuous expansionism which had been so rife in the preceding half-century. In the latter period America's expansionism directed itself principally upon countries whose populations were dissimilar to the people of the United States in race and all the qualities of " one-hundred-per-cent Americanism." The indiscriminateness of such expansionism seemed to be relieved of vulgarity by the ideal of " benevolent assimilation," an aspiration resting on the assumption that only by becoming similar to Americans could other peoples achieve civilization, virtue, and happiness. The farthest reach of assimilative ambition if not of benevolence was the extension of rule over exotic Malays. These were so different from Americans that Assistant Secretary of the Treasury Vanderlip, unaware that the President would shortly take a contrary view, declared their assimilation to be impossible.[1] After early disappointments, foreseen by Vanderlip but not by McKinley, Americans made a *volte face* which reflected prudence rather than benevolence. They forswore as dangerous the incorporation not merely of overesa heathen but even of adjacent Latin Americans.

The settled condition of the continent made it impossible to revert to the original policy of annexing territories sparsely inhabited. Yet it was not quite true that the romance of manifest destiny had to end for lack of a suitable partner. Throughout the first decade of the twentieth century interest gathered in the one adjacent territory which was not excluded by the prejudice against a heterogeneous population. This was Canada, the American expansionist's earliest love, but one which, in accordance with the usual fate of first loves, had later been subordinated to other attachments.

About the close of the first decade of the new century the interest in Canada rose from a flicker to a high flame. This resurgence of expansionist romanticism occurred in connection with the very practical issue of legislating tariff reciprocity with Canada. Although the President and the Secretary of State declared the issue to be purely economic, the intentions of many were avowedly more serious. Champ Clark, Democratic House leader, caused domestic applause and an international episode when he advocated reciprocity as a step toward the union of the two countries under the Stars and Stripes. Representative Bennet introduced a resolution favoring this union, and a host of Congressmen expressed contemplation, hope, or expectation of annexation as an eventual outcome of reciprocity. Widely prevalent in the United States, according to the *Canadian Annual Review*, were the opinion and spirit which even foreigners had learned to call "Manifest Destiny." [2]

However, the twentieth-century doctrine of manifest destiny was surprisingly different from that which had been the chief article of faith in the past. Despite President Taft's reference to "the dreams of Americans with irresponsible imaginations who like to talk of the starry flag's floating from Panama to the pole," [3] the expansionist imagination showed less irresponsibility than before by floating only toward the north pole. What gave Canada its peculiarly potent attraction was not that it belonged to a continent considered as America's predestined domain. It was rather the fact that of all peoples of the continent Canadians seemed similar to Americans in the basic elements of national character and political life. Thus the doctrine of manifest destiny which rationalized this attraction posited, not the ideal of assimilating unlike peoples, but that of expansion in accordance with political affinity. The destinies of political unions were interpreted in the light of the principle that like does and should attract like.

This assumption that political marriages aim at the mutual happiness of compatible peoples is a departure from the less reasonable but more edifying doctrine of America's past expansionism — that the purpose of political marriages is the superior partner's reforming the lesser partner. But it will be seen that, while the doctrine of political affinity was a deviation from the predominant ideological trend of the past, it was conditioned by the past in a twofold sense. In the first place, this doctrine was a reaction against an earlier thesis in the same way as is the antithesis in an Hegelian dialectical process. In the second place, this antithesis did not emerge suddenly in the twentieth century but was the culmination of an ideological development extending throughout American history. A childhood attraction toward Canada was the beginning of a long-continuing sentiment which grew into something like love as the conception of political affinity was developed by time, growing appreciation, and even unfaithfulness.

Such considerations require a "flash back" from the twentieth century to the eighteenth. Noteworthy at the outset is the fact that the people of Quebec were the first to be invited to join their political fortunes to those of Americans. On the other hand, Americans entertained originally no belief in the affinity of the two peoples in character. The patronizing address of the Continental Congress of 1774 virtually informed the Canadians that "they were neither free nor happy, and if they thought they were they had no business to think so; it must be the result of their deficient education."[4] The Americans deemed it their duty to explain to the Canadians "the transcendent nature of freedom," which was to overcome all differences in language and religion.[5] When most Canadians failed to respond to several such calls to freedom their political ignorance seemed established beyond a doubt. No mitigation could now be found for the Canadian's religious idiosyncrasy, his attachment to "Popery." The prejudices of Americans against such deviations from their own norms were sharpened by awareness of the homogeneity among themselves, cited by the *Federalist* as a ground for firmer union.[6]

Nevertheless, a certain sense of kinship with Canadians was present at the very beginning. It arose in part from consciousness of similarity in political background as well as in present relation to Great Britain. Although in 1775 Americans and Canadians had not been long in the same political unit, the invitation of that year to united resistance averred that Americans considered Canadians as "fellow-sufferers with us."[7] Americans were never to escape the influence of the awareness that, as the Canadian Goldwin Smith said, nothing but the historical accident of a civil war made Americans and Canadians two peoples.[8]

Moreover, even in the beginning Americans felt a greater affinity with the Canadians than with other New World subjects of Great Britain. Although the Revolutionists invited all these British colonies to join their struggle, they picked the Canadians as the one people that might be admitted to the Confederation without special action of the States. Article XI of the Confederation stipulated for Canada this special privilege, the constitutional basis of the military " struggle for the fourteenth colony." Alliance with Britain's largest colony was recommended not only by political expediency but also by a mystic belief that union was ordained by nature. This conception of geographical unity is evidenced in the invitation which the Continental Congress addressed to the Canadians in 1774. " Nature has joined your country to theirs " was the observation which preceded the exhortation that Canadians join their political interests to America's.[9] This idea of geographical unity was suggested in part by the absence of an effective natural boundary between the two countries, an ever-present reminder that Canada was a missing link in " the bright chain of union." As study of the expansionism of the War of 1812 has already shown, geographical relationship was also suggested by interlocking rivers which seemed to form natural outlets to the ocean for American commerce. Geographical relationship was always an element in the later doctrine of political affinity and gave rise in 1888 to the poetic observation of W. H. H. Murray that "never did man see a lovelier evidence of God's design and Nature's unity, than stretches, green as a sleeping sea, from Southern Gulf to the white line of northern snow," with rivers tying " North and South together like threads into whose golden strands new strength is spun continually." [10]

In the first decades of national life Americans dwelt upon external points of unity because they did not feel themselves at one with the Canadians in character and belief. In the War of 1812 the failure of Canadians to welcome General Hull's offer of "the invaluable blessings of . . . Liberty, and their necessary result, individual and general prosperity "[11] suggested that Canadians not merely lacked democratic institutions but were still too ignorant to desire them. For some years after 1815 the American opinion of the Canadians scarcely foreshadowed the future high appreciation of their northern neighbors. The latter, to be sure, heartily reciprocated the uncomplimentary estimate.

The decade of the 'thirties, however, was marked by an event in Canada which induced a greater appreciation in Americans. Reference is made to the Canadian rebellions of 1837-1838, which, though more complex in motivation, were interpreted by Americans as a struggle for democracy. As the imprudent Mackenzie raised the standard of revolt it was felt by American sympathizers that "the slumbering genius of freedom "[12] had at last awakened in this long apathetic people. The adulatory work of E. A. Theller, American participant in the unsuccessful revolts, evidenced the new sympathy which arose from the belief that the Canadians had imbibed the democratic gospel of the United States.[13]

Seven years later, when certain Northerners desired to use Canada as a counterpoise to the suggested extension of southern slave territory, the petitions for the annexation of Canada could play upon this idea of Canadian love of freedom. One to Congress at the time of the Texan issue observed that the acquisition of Canada would introduce into the Union "a highly civilized, intelligent, and liberty-loving people."[14] In 1849 an annexationist movement among dissatisfied groups in Lower Canada developed still more the American expansionist's appreciation of the Canadian's virtues. In reality the annexationists consisted largely of Tories and other individuals interested only in the economic benefits of union. But the expansionist resolutions of the Democratic State Convention of Vermont named "the rising spirit of liberty" as the source of Canadian interest in annexation.[15] Similarly, resolutions of the New York Legislature called in the name of republicanism for the annexation of these people as our "brethren in interest."[16] From the same point of view the editor of the New York *Sun* repeatedly urged annexation as "manifest destiny."[17] Although representative of only an evanescent movement, the Annexation Manifesto of Montreal increased the hold of a notion which the national egoism of Americans had suggested independently. It was the conception that the people of monarchical Canada were at heart so greatly devoted to republicanism as to yearn above all things for membership in America's democracy. Most Canadians were in fact devoted in nearly all periods of their history to British political forms. William Mackenzie, one of the few Canadians who had favored annexation, wrote later somewhat intemperately that "his sojourn in the United States had wrought a disillusionment," had in fact convinced him that "the vaunted liberty of the United States was merely a sham" and inferior to the liberty of the humblest Canadian under the British Constitution.[18]

But the 'forties saw the crystallization among Americans of a non-political conception enhancing the sense of affinity with the Canadians. This was "racial" homogeneity, a value which largely resolved itself into a preference for the Anglo-Saxon stock and a decided aversion to the Spanish-Indian breed of Latin America. To be sure, Jefferson had long before asserted his disapproval of "blot or mixture" [19] in Americans' expanding habitat; similarly, Fisher Ames had expressed his revulsion from the "Gallo-Hispano-Indian omnium gatherum" of Louisianian "adventurers" who seemed to him as little pure in morals as in blood.[20] But it was in the Texan issue of the 'forties that racial homogeneity first received general appreciation. Although many were adventurers and some were not of pure morals, the Texans had at least the merit of being full-blooded Americans. Expansionists, for the first time attracted by a people as well as a land, rejoiced over the fact that this acquisition would be "the easy and natural union of two contiguous nations, both founded by the Anglo-Saxon race." [21] The appeals for annexation often used the simile of Texas as a beautiful bride, garbed for the rite of espousal. Senator Benton went so far as to conclude a summary of points of affinity with the words: "Man and woman were not more formed for union, by the hand of God, than Texas and the United States are formed for union by the hand of nature." [22] Such metaphors exemplify that personifying tendency in national life which may bring into expansionism even some of the emotion of a love affair.

With respect to racial affinity the annexation of Texas gave the one completely harmonious union in American history. But this annexation was also an expression of the sectional purpose which was destined to clash most seriously with the ideal of racial homogeneity. It was the Southerner's aim of adding territory with a view to its suitability for the economic system of slavery rather than to the character of its inhabitants. The Mexican War, the consequence of the annexation of Texas, initiated many Americans into a willingness to incorporate peoples racially "inferior" and in need of "regeneration." Circumstances barely prevented the fulfilment of the ambition to terminate the war by the annexation of all Mexico. Expansionists of the 'fifties believed still more confidently in America's digestive capacity and wished to assimilate all the Spanish-Indian countries between the Rio Grande and the Isthmus of Panama. The fact that America was a melting-pot for immigrants from all lands suggested to many, as to Representative Latham, that America's preeminent talent was the power of "absorbing and assimilating foreign elements," and that this power was "the strongest proof of our historical mission; or, if gentlemen would rather have it, our manifest destiny." It seemed to Latham that under Providence we were "destined to expand by assimilating"; for assimilating meant "elevating those who have been misgoverned and oppressed to the rank of freemen." [23]

But there were others who believed that such palaver about social missions encouraged land-hunger of the most dangerous sort. Many, as has been seen in a previous chapter, regarded Mexico as fruit poisonous to us. "Can we incorporate a people so dissimilar from us in every respect — so little qualified for free and popular government," asked Calhoun in 1848, "without certain destruction to our political institutions?" [24] This apprehension of the political danger of amalgamation with a dissimilar racial stock was combined with an instinctive revulsion from contact on terms of equality with despised aliens. Such a revulsion affected many, for though it is true that all save the Nativists welcomed immigrants, the European immigrants were largely not of the races against whom the American was prejudiced. The southward expansion movement of the 'forties and 'fifties endeared the ideal of racial affinity precisely because it endangered this value. "We want our own Republic and Union," declared the *American Review* in 1848, "with a homogeneous people, men of the same general race . . ." [25] Lest anti-expansionism be idealized unduly, one should note that American anti-expansionism has often been rooted not in morality but in racial exclusiveness. When Calhoun acknowledged that he looked "not to the interests of Mexico, but to those of our own country," he showed that anti-expansionism may have less altruism than expansionism.[26]

It also became evident that the anti-expansionist in one issue may turn into the expansionist in another when the stake is more attractive. The same ideal of racial homogeneity which forbade tropical expansion aroused greater interest in a country with a tolerable racial stock. It was the opponent of southward expansion who first presented Canada as the preeminently natural acquisition, the one political affinity of America. In contrast with the blood of tropical peoples, that of the Canadian appeared not only aristocratic but similar to the American's. Actually there was still a large admixture of French stock in this hybrid people, but Americans were conscious of the rapidly increasing proportion of the Anglo-Saxon element in Canada. Indeed, Americans forgot even their original reserve toward French Canadians in their revulsion from Latin Americans. As an alternative to the annexation of Latin-American peoples, many Whigs proposed the annexation of Canada; for a time it appeared that Canada might be used in the Whig campaign of 1852 as an offset to the Democratic party's exploitation of the popular ambition for Cuba. General Winfield Scott, prospective Whig presidential candidate, in 1849 published a letter advocating the annexation of Canada. "Though opposed to incorporating with us any district densely peopled with the Mexican race," wrote the conqueror of Mexico, "I should be most happy to fraternize with our northern and northeastern neighbors." [27] The Whig party did not declare formally for the annexation of Canada but prominent Whigs in Congress advocated this ambition as preferable to the indiscriminate expansionism of the Democrats. Thus Senators Seward,[28] Hale,[29] and Bell urged the Senate during the Cuban debates of the 'fifties to look northward rather than southward. Bell referred to Canadians as "bone, as it were, of our bone, flesh of our flesh, deriving their origin from the same Anglo-Saxon source." It seemed to him that "Destiny" had ordained the early reunion of the two peoples which were originally one.[30] But in the shortly ensuing Civil War Canada's lack of sympathy for the Union did not greatly encourage this expectation.

The racial issue was renewed after the Civil War when the Dominican Republic and other tropical countries were considered as territorial additions for national rather than sectional reasons. Particularly because America was then "trying the powers of Anglo-Saxon self-governing digestion upon three millions of slaves," it seemed to Whitelaw Reid, later the boldest of the imperialists, over-venturesome to consider "the gastric juices of the body politic equal to the addition of . . . the inferior mixed races of outlying tropical and semi-tropical dependencies." [31] Once again, those opposed to heterogeneous expansion sought to shift attention to Canada. Thus Senator Morrill warned that "indiscriminate and promiscuous" annexation in the tropics would delay union with "our proud and fastidious Anglo-Saxon neighbors." [32] Even some of those not set so strongly against tropical expansion showed their decided preference for the annexation of racially similar peoples. Thus Robert J. Walker, responding to the annexation "feeler" of the Chairman of the Nova Scotia League, assured the Nova Scotian that not all the economic resources of the tropical countries could outweigh the fact that "these people are not, like you, of our kindred race, blood, and language." [33] The *New York Herald* claimed British North America for the United States by "the doctrine of nationalities." [34] Sumner's attempt to obtain Canada as settlement for the Alabama Claims is interpreted by his biographer Pierce as based on a recognition of the tendency of "races of common origin and speech" to gravitate to "oneness and solidarity." [35] Many of such expansionists were probably influenced by the contemporary teachings of Francis Lieber and other political philosophers who made homogeneity of population the central element in American nationality.

The decades following the close of the Civil War were marked by the forging of another link in the chain of political affinity — a conception of affinity with the Canadians in political institutions. The enhancement in the appreciation of Canadian political institutions came about largely in consequence of the formation of the Dominion of Canada in 1867, a disappointment to the expansionist who in the preceding year had introduced a bill permitting the annexation of the British provinces. But the new governmental organization of Canada represented in essential forms an approximation to the democracy which Americans had generously wished to extend to the Canadians. Moreover, its beneficent effects included the marked advance of Canadians in the art of self-government. Observation of the political progress of Canadians developed in Americans an opinion of their neighbors very different from that which they had formerly entertained with respect to the northern monarchists. Previously Americans either questioned the political enlightenment of the Canadians or viewed them with the commiseration due to victims of political oppression. After 1867 they tended increasingly not only to appreciate the merit of Canada's political forms but to regard them as not essentially dissimilar to those of American democracy.

In the 'seventies and 'eighties, decades of little expansionism, Canada was the one land which, in contrast to the tropical territories against which President Cleveland warned, aroused a degree of expansionist interest. In addition to the conceptions of affinity inherited from the past, a sense of institutional affinity now figured as a stimulus of interest. Although in 1879 Senator Burnside asserted that two populations of "common interest" were gravitating toward each other,[36] it was not until 1888 that there were presented congressional resolutions designed to hasten this gravitation. Representative Butterworth's resolution of that year authorized the President to institute negotiations with Great Britain for annexation. Senator Sherman's resolution of the same year, though referring only to improvement of commercial relations, was accompanied by a speech letting the cat out of the bag. Sherman declared union to be "within the womb of destiny" in view of the fact that in institutions and other elements of national life the peoples were so alike that they were essentially "one people." [37] The two resolutions attracted much public notice and encouraged numerous expressions of similar views. The *Cleveland Leader* hailed the prospect of "the peaceful merging into one of two nations allied in business, origin, and habits." [38] W. H. H. Murray, speaking in Boston on "Continental Unity," voiced "the prophecy of Geography, of common blood and language, kindred institutions, like laws, commercial necessities and political institutions that are identical." [39] In January, 1889, Justin S. Morrill, also favoring annexation, wrote in the *Forum* as follows:

> The people of the Dominion are largely of the same English-speaking stock with ourselves. Their jurisprudence and courts are based on similar general principles. They have been practically instructed in a representative form of government, and understand the omnipotence of popular majorities.[40]

In the same year Benjamin F. Butler insisted that "we must look only to the north for that class and condition of men in whose hands we would be most willing to confide the future destiny of our country" and its ideal of "laws enacted by popular intelligence." [41]

The McKinley Tariff Bill of 1890, removing the special advantage which the export trade of Canada with the United States had formerly enjoyed, aroused in certain commercial circles of the northern country an annexation sentiment which encouraged the advocates of annexation in the United States. The New York *Sun* [42] and the *Chicago Herald* [43] thus affirmed annexation to be manifest destiny, the latter emphasizing the slightness of the institutional adjustment required in Canada. In 1894 Representative Van Voorhis formulated manifest destiny in quasi-scientific terms: "That union is decreed by a law that admits of no successful resistance; the people of the two countries and the interests of the two countries are so identical that nothing can keep them apart." [44] Two years later the Republican party, aware that at least most Americans did not desire to keep the countries apart, adopted a platform declaring its hopeful anticipation of the ultimate union of all the English-speaking peoples of the continent through their own free consent.

But the last years of the 'nineties brought temptations of imperial glory which deflected general interest from Canada to ambitions violating in ascending degree the principle of homogeneous population. To be sure, the expansionists alleged, as in the report of the Senate Committee on Foreign Relations in 1898, that the political and commercial predominance of Americans made the islands American in all their traits and habits.[45] But the minority report of the House Committee on Foreign Affairs insisted that Hawaiians were not homogeneous with Americans,[46] and the historian von Holst warned against the introduction of a foreign body unassimilable to American institutions.[47] It was the proposed acquisition of the Philippines which caused the greatest concern to adherents of the principle of affinity in expansion. For in this ambition the imperialists carried out the proposal of Giddings's *Democracy and Empire* to make a deliberate break with the theory of the old empire, that "identity of belief and similarity of practice were essential to the homogeneity without which no society can long hold together." [48] Acquisition of the Philippines threatened to violate every one of the traditional principles of political homogeneity.

Most obviously in peril was the ideal of racial homogeneity. Senator Daniel, calling the diversity of Oriental tribes a "witch's cauldron," expressed his horror in poetry:

> Black spirits and white, red spirits and gray,
> Mingle, mingle, mingle, you that mingle may.[49]

Such mingling, Bryan charged, would also bring into the body politic a people incapable of having a representation in America's democratic government.[50] Champ Clark pointed out that oversea expansion would violate the principle of the natural boundary.[51] Offensive above all to some sensitive souls was departure from the pacific method of homogeneous expansion and the employment of a rape-like imperialism. Many Americans agreed with Manuel Ugarte that imperialism " begins at that point where the combination of homogeneous elements ends, and a sphere of military, political or commercial oppression by extraneous bodies begins." [52] Thus the New York *World* paraphrased this observation when it related the necessity of despotic government in the Philippines to the fact that its inhabitants " do not fit and can not be made to fit into our system." [53]

Their very revulsion from unsuitable acquisitions, described in the metaphors of abnormality, initiated or increased the attachment of many to the annexation of Canada. Even some who were not inclined to expansionism attempted to ward off an allegedly unhealthy impulse by offering Canada as a substitute. Thus Carl Schurz, in his essay of 1893 on " Manifest Destiny," urged that the ideal of manifest destiny be not tarnished by promiscuity but reserved for the well-mated union with the " akin " Canadians which time might unfold.[54] In the same breath with which he condemned the proposed annexation of the Philippines, Representative Hinrichsen urged the annexation of the northern country which lies at our door.[55] Similarly, Champ Clark denied the manifestness of the alleged imperial destiny and proclaimed himself an enthusiastic believer in manifest destiny with respect to the adjacent British possessions, whose people were " of our blood and habituated to institutions similar to ours." [56] But all attempts to deflect attention from the Orient were useless; the fever of colonial imperialism was in the blood, and not even the letting of blood in the war of subjugation prevented the American electorate from giving apparent approval to the Republican policy in the elections of 1900.

However, colonial imperialism had ultimately the beneficent effect which occasionally ensues from the sowing of wild oats. When rebellion and other difficulties of the white man's burden had outlasted impetuous desire, the adventure brought a weariness and disgust which have been largely responsible for America's national virtue in recent decades. It brought also what wild oats are sometimes credited with bringing — an appreciation of the higher values in love. Many former imperialists now turned to thoughts of Canada in the manner of an imprudent lover who discovers ultimately the appeal of a fastidious mating within his own social class. The twentieth-century movement for the annexation of Canada must thus be largely understood in the light of the reaction against the unsatisfying experience in the Philippines. Disillusionment, though influential primarily upon desire, expressed itself also in the shift of ideology from the thesis of the white man's burden to the antithetical doctrine of political affinity.

One of the numerous indications of this nexus between the two antipodal expansionist movements was an article in the *Independent* of 1902, by Oscar F. Williams, who as Consul at Manila had participated in the events leading to the annexation of the Philippines. In this article he confessed his realization that a vast number of our people, perhaps a majority, now "don't want to expand in the Orient . . . don't believe expansion there tends to augment either our national strength or glory." He therefore proposed imaginatively "An Imperial Dicker" whereby Great Britain was to take practically all America's Oriental possessions while the United States was to acquire various British possessions in the Caribbean together with Newfoundland. "This," he observed "is expansion along safe right lines, every critic at home would be disarmed, and all the world admits that Canada will soon float our flag." [57] The last observation was an exaggeration but it did describe the expectation of an increasing number of Americans. Thus in 1903 the Canadian-born Dr. Schurman, avowedly disappointed over the turn of affairs in the Philippines, spoke with pleasure of the likelihood of our annexing his native country.[58] In 1907 Dr. Albert Shaw observed in his *Political Problems of American Development* that the costly and difficult undertaking in the Philippines "has strengthened, rather than weakened, our belief in the old American ideal of a homogeneous republic." The one exception to the contemporary repugnance toward further expansion seemed to him to lie in America's growing willingness to join fortunes with Canada, if, at some future time, the Dominion should so desire.[59]

A second factor in " our growing willingness " to unite with Canadians was the deepened sense of kinship with Great Britain which developed as a result of Great Britain's friendly gestures during the Spanish War, the desire for a partner in world politics, and the early twentieth-century cult of Anglo-Saxon self-appreciation. The expansionists emphasized Canada's affinity to the United States by reference to the virtues which Canadians possessed as members of the British Empire and the Anglo-Saxon race. Dr. Shaw thus adverted in his discussion of annexation to " our ideals of a homogeneous people, using the same language and governing themselves in communities based upon British institutions with the customs and principles of the common law." [60] The *Independent* showed the same conception of democracy as an Anglo-Saxon heritage when it cheerfully admitted, in an editorial urging political as well as social fusion between the two English-speaking peoples of the continent, that it was " by no means clear that our method of government is better than Canada's." [61]

The proposal to annex Canada may seem a curious way of expressing friendliness and admiration for Great Britain. But the apparent inconsistency is largely explained by a sincere even if altogether incorrect assumption of the expansionists: that Great Britain's attitude had not changed since the time when Englishmen in the first flush of enthusiasm over free trade heard sympathetically John Bright's prophecy of a continental American confederation wherein Canada would figure more happily than as a profitless British colony. Many even affirmed, as did John Dos Passos in his book of 1903 on *The Anglo-Saxon Century and the Unification of the English-speaking People,* that the annexation of Canada would remove " the only real obstacle to a complete and sympathetic entente between the Anglo-Saxon peoples." [62] The imaginative Dos Passos envisaged as an incident to annexation the establishment of interchangeable citizenship by Great Britain and the

United States. Andrew Carnegie went farther and saw union of Canadians and Americans — "a common type, indistinguishable one from the other" — as the first step in the political reunification of Great Britain and the United States, "the happy family that should never have known separation." [63] Colonel Higginson, on the other hand, did not think that union of Canada and the United States would take place before the establishment of "some very wide and comprehensive tie which shall bring the whole English-speaking world under some general name." [64] In such observations the expansionism influenced by the doctrine of political affinity comes to its farthest reach. As influential as territorial ambition was the idealistic conception of manifest destiny which held Anglo-Saxon unification to be the best means of effecting "the elevation and enlightenment of mankind." [65] But now the believer in manifest destiny affirmed not the special mission of Anglo-Americans but the mission of Anglo-Saxons and perhaps the Irish. Theological assumptions were usually stated less naïvely than in the past, but there was still a half-belief that, to quote a Canadian exponent of racial manifest destiny, "the Anglo-Saxon-Celtic people headed by John Bull and Brother Jonathan were God's chosen peoples." [66]

However, it is improbable that the American desire for Canada would have become potent or widespread had there not been a more mundane incentive. It was an economic motive, the desire for a marriage of convenience. Even this motive had its characteristic doctrine of affinity — a thesis that natural commercial relationships between the two countries established economic affinity. Although the economic doctrine did not become generally influential until the twentieth century, it had been held by far-sighted individuals long before. Richard Cobden and Charles Sumner found themselves at one when the former wrote to his American friend in 1849: "I agree with you that Nature has decided that *Canada and the United States must become one* for all purposes of intercommunication." [67] Five years later, indeed, they entered a Reciprocity Treaty which, a writer in the *North American Review* and others felt, would "tend to make us one people, and absorb us, irresistibly although insensibly into each other." [68] In 1862 a report of James W. Taylor to the Secretary of the Treasury dwelt glowingly upon the auspiciousness of the geographic relations between the United States and British North America for the economic and perhaps even political unification of "adjacent and homogeneous communities." [69] But the strained relations arising out of Canada's attitude during the Civil War caused the United States to give notice that the trade pact would lapse in 1866. In 1890 the tariff policy of the United States further disassociated the two countries in trade. This policy was greatly regretted by the Canadians, particularly by one like Professor Goldwin Smith who advocated union with the United States. Should anyone scan the geography of the North American continent, he wrote in a work of 1891, "he will see that the continent is an economic whole, and that to run a Customs line athwart it and try to sever its members from each other is to wage a desperate war against nature." [70]

At the beginning of the twentieth century, however, Canada began to experience a prosperity which enabled her to feel less concerned about barriers to her trade with the United States. At the same time the commercial importance of Canada came to seem much greater to Americans for the reasons noted by H. L. Keenleyside:

> The disappearance of the American frontier, the opening of the Canadian West, the rapid reduction of American resources as the result of activities of wasteful and unscrupulous exploiters, the growing American demand for markets and for raw materials, the adoption by the Canadian government of modern advertising methods in their campaign for immigrants—these and other factors tended to increase the importance of Canada in the view of American manufacturers, farmers, and financiers.[71]

Just as the sentiments of individuals fail so often to synchronize, so it was precisely when Canada came into a greater sense of economic self-sufficiency that the doctrine of economic affinity, formerly entertained by Canadians, first took hold on numerous American minds.

Its enunciation in the early years of the century was rather frequently associated with the wishful thought that economic association would certainly or probably lead to political union. A banquet of the Boston Canadian Club in 1902 heard Osborne Howes's prophecy that annexation was "predetermined and inevitable" in view of common interests of trade and general resemblances.[72] Senator Clapp in the same year asserted that the peaceful invasion by American farmers and money pointed to "the manifest destiny" of annexing the Dominion of Canada not through conquest but through assimilation.[73] About the same time Archbishop Ireland mixed romance and economics in declaring: "The hearts across the borders are already beating with love for us and commerce and agriculture are calling for espousals." [74] Early in the following year Representative De Armond introduced into the House a measure looking to the cession of all or part of Canada. The year 1903 witnessed numerous expansionist predictions which, like an editorial article in the *Outlook*, emphasized the "mutual commercial absorption" of the two countries.[75] This trend of thought persisted in subsequent years of the decade. In 1910 a book by Professor Archibald Coolidge [76] advocated annexation, and a work by James J. Hill [77] complete reciprocity, in view of geographico-economic affinities.

Paradoxically, the actual steps toward a closer economic relation were caused not by such appreciations but by a commercial quarrel. The Payne-Aldrich Tariff of 1909, opening up the possibility of imposing maximum tariff duties on Canadian exports in retaliation against Canadian preference to other countries, seemed for a brief time to be the prelude to a tariff war. The tension brought home to many the consideration which Frank B. Tracy had stressed in the *North American Review* in 1903: ". . . contiguously situated peoples of like origin and race grow great only when united; when separated, they become weakened by conflicts, jealousies, and recriminations." [78] While there is no evidence that President Taft and his Administration thought of political union, they did propose to the Canadians — it was the first time that the United States took the initiative — at first free trade and then partial reciprocity, in the hope not merely of ending commercial conflicts but also of making Canada economically (to quote Taft's imprudent words) "only an adjunct of the United States." [79]

The ensuing Reciprocity Bill was viewed even by its non-expansionist adherents in the light of a doctrine of economic affinity which exerted an influence largely independent of specific calculations of profit. Thus Representative McCall, author of the Reciprocity Bill, asserted that the absence of a natural frontier indicated "the plain decrees of nature" that trade should run north and south.[80] President Taft, similarly, spoke of the absurdity of separating Manitoba and Minnesota by as great a distance as Manitoba and Liverpool, when certainly "Providence intended that their separation, socially and commercially, should only be that of their geographical distance."[81] Unaware of the suggestiveness of his argument to the expansionist he based trade reciprocity upon the conception of affinity:

> The identity of interest of two peoples linked together by race, language, political institutions, and geographical proximity offers the foundation.[82]

The issue of reciprocity was the tinder which set into flame the expansionist impulse, inactive recently but still combustible. Americans had been cured of promiscuous expansionism but not of the sentiment for aggrandizing the glory of the Republic through union with a suitable and well-endowed partner. It is true that Governor Osborn of Michigan repudiated economic motives in saying that annexation was "absolutely above an economic consideration."[83] But while some shared this view, most expansionists doubtless felt as did Representative Bennet that "every argument which speaks for commercial arrangements speaks still more loudly for political affiliation."[84]

The expansionist impulse seems to have been fairly widespread, though more evident in congressional than in public or press opinion. While the *New York American* averred that Canada would come when we wanted her,[85] most newspapers maintained silence on annexation out of apparent fear that loquacity might embarrass the economic arrangement which would reduce the price of their paper. It was reported by the *Canadian Annual Review*, however, that there was abundant talk of annexation at the convention of the National Editorial Association in Detroit, well located for a raid of filibusterers.[86] One is perhaps safe in believing that so many Congressmen would not have spoken in favor of annexation if there had not been reason to count on wide public support, even if not the nine-tenths of the people which Champ Clark claimed.[87] The extent of expansionism is not to be determined merely by reference to those who, like Representative Bennet [88] and the *Southern Lumber Journal,*[89] advocated an immediate attempt at annexation. There were more who put their trust in the slow-working laws of economics. The hope of these was that, as Representative Madden said, " if we have closer commercial relations with Canada, some day this relationship may blend the two peoples into one harmonious whole, and . . . the territory lying north of us may become a part of the United States, as it should be." [90] Madden's assumption was the opposite of that which anti-expansionists had entertained as to the effect of the Reciprocity Treaty of 1854.

In the expansionist arguments of the congressional debates, all the criteria of political affinity inherited from the past were sounded individually or in harmonious chord. Four of them were mentioned by Champ Clark, after his notorious declaration that he favored reciprocity because he hoped to see the day " when the American flag will float over every square foot of the British-North American possessions clear to the North Pole." Clark justified this far-reaching hope as follows:

> They are people of our blood. They speak our language. Their institutions are much like ours. They are trained in the difficult art of self-government.[91]

This unusually trustful Representative from Missouri believed also that the same affinity would cause Britons to give away Canada in marriage " joyfully." [92]

The other expansionists used with singular uniformity the same doctrine of political affinity, shown in the following examples which he who runs may read. " These peoples," declared Representative Good, " live under conditions that are in all respects similar, are engaged in the same common pursuits, have a common ancestry, use a common language, have a common religion, and must have a common destiny." [93] Representative Martin observed that he had often expressed his desire for the political union of Canadians and Americans, who "are of kindred blood and have a common history and common ideals." [94] Though opposed for economic reasons to the Reciprocity Bill, Representative Davis trusted that if it did become a law, "a divine Providence . . . may so use this so-called reciprocity treaty, this entering wedge, to further amalgamate these two countries and eventually make them one, with but one flag — the Stars and Stripes." [95] Similarly Representative Hill declared that if instead of the very limited reciprocity there were proposed complete political union between two peoples "with the same hopes and aspirations," not a Representative would oppose it.[96] According to a Canadian paper Representative McCall himself declared that under his Reciprocity Bill "the inevitable day will be more quickly reached when the two countries will be politically one." [97] In a congressional speech McCall spoke of the northern neighbor as "industrially a part of the United States," and urged recognition of "the laws of nature" which ordain reciprocal trade relations.[98] It seemed to Representative Focht that extremely few changes would need to be wrought to make of the two countries one people, and that the ultimate amalgamation and complete assimilation of the great Anglo-Saxon race was inevitable.[99] Representative Madden, in expressing the hope for ultimate annexation that was previously cited, observed that already the two peoples lived along the same lines, spoke the same tongue, and had even the same thoughts.[100] "I cannot think," declared Representative Ferris, "that two countries where the conditions are so nearly identical should longer be separated by any imaginary line." [101] Representative George, like Madden, stressed the similarity of Americans and Canadians in character. With little or no difference between them, they seemed to him to lack nothing to make them one people except the free exchange which exists between State and State.[102] Representative Hobson at least squinted in the direction of annexation. After declaring that the two peoples were more closely bound by ties of blood and of institutions than any two peoples of the world, he affirmed grandiloquently: "Both are marching along parallel paths of destiny, and it was decreed at the foundation of the world that they should march hand in hand."[103] The reciprocity agreement did not go far enough, but it at least began the work of demolishing an unnatural barrier. Representative Prince predicted annexation as a consequence of the inundation of American emigrants, true descendants of the Texans.[104] Senator Townsend, though seeing little hope of annexation, believed none the less that it "would have seemed in the eternal fitness of things" that two countries united by nature should be one politically.[105]

Virtually all the expansionist speakers paid "the magnificent people on the north"[106] compliments which resolved themselves into assertions of their similarity to Americans. Among those tributes, the most interesting was that exemplified by the words of Representative Gillett in arguing that it would be difficult to imagine two countries more alike:

> To be sure, they preserve a monarchy and aristocracy, while we maintain 'a church without a bishop and a State without a king,' but this superficial difference only illustrates the truth of Pope's hackneyed couplet:
>
> 'For forms of government let fools contest;
> Whate'er is best administered is best,'
>
> for in aspiration and enjoyment of personal and political liberty, in deep-rooted hostility to tyranny and persecution, and in legal guaranties against them, it would be hard to detect any difference in the two nations. And it is the spirit of the people and not administration or laws that keeps alive freedom.

This concession that freedom is a matter of spirit rather than of form marks a substantial change of national attitude in a manner not without humor. The ghost of Stephen Douglas, who wished to drive monarchical Britain from the continent, would have flown insulted from the Congress which acquiesced in Gillett's idea that only fools dispute over forms of government. In contradistinction to past expansionists who believed it destiny to extend freedom to Canada, Gillett believed that it was Canada's present possession of freedom which made it possible that at some future date Canadians and Americans would "mutually agree peacefully to unite their fortunes in one government." [107]

The belief that economic union would considerably hasten the day of political union was a contributing factor in the passage of the bill for reciprocity. It seemed to be taken for granted that Canada would also cooperate with manifest destiny. But destiny, as though weary of too long favoritism, had taken to playing tricks on the expansionists. Surprise was great when the Canadian popular election, centering in the issue of economic relations with the United States, registered the Canadian electorate's repudiation of its own Government's program for reciprocity.

One of the most important causes of Canada's rejection of reciprocity was of ironical character. The American expansionism which contributed to the passage of the Reciprocity Bill in the United States had precisely the contrary effect in Canada. The Conservative opponents of reciprocity had collated the indiscretions of American expansionists and converted them into their chief weapon. Despite the insistence of the Liberals that reciprocity was a purely economic issue, the Conservatives sought to convince Canadians that every American hoped deep down in his heart "that Canada will some day be a part of the United States . . . and that reciprocity is the first step in this direction." [108] The Canadian electorate, assuming that they faced a conflict between economic advantage and loyalty to the Empire, rejected the reciprocity which they had sought so eagerly in the past. "The decisive factor in bringing about this abrupt reversal of Canadian policy," writes Professor Dunning, "was the spirit of nationality." [109] Even Sir Wilfrid Laurier, the Liberal sponsor of reciprocity, reminded Americans that Canadians resembled them in the spirit of nationalism too:

> Remember that the blood which flows in our veins is just as good as your own, and if you are a proud people, though we have not your numbers, we are just as proud as you are, and that rather than part with our national existence, we would part with our lives.[110]

The American expansionists were characterized correctly by Representative Harrison when he said that "we Americans are apt to assume that all nations take us at our own valuation of ourselves." [111] Believers in political affinity were as much out of accord with reality as was the Continental Congress when it distributed a philosophical appeal among French Canadians, most of whom could not read.

Even Canada's rejection of reciprocity did not recall all to reality; Champ Clark, for example, avowedly adhered to the prepossessions of manifest destiny.[112] Two years after the defeat of reciprocity, the *Independent* still believed, not only that the two peoples were as one socially, but that political union "may come during the century, for it ought to come." [113] In 1916 Dr. John Allan Wyeth expressed in the same breath a demand for military intervention in Mexico and a belief in the destiny of a peaceful and bloodless conquest of Canada, manifesting the strength of union and brotherhood.[114] So late as 1922 several persistent expansionists introduced congressional resolutions favoring the acquisition of Canadian territories allegedly related to the United States by geographical affinity.[115]

Most other Americans, recognizing the realities, perhaps consoled themselves in the manner suggested by the words of Senator Reed of Missouri in a congressional debate on Canada's status in the League of Nations:

> They are more like us than any other people in the world. . . . They are gallant in war and efficient in the arts of peace; a splendid people; but I refuse to consider the Canadian people, as a whole, the equals of the people of the United States. If they loved liberty as we do, . . . they would not stay under the British flag.[116]

This disparagement of Canadians reflects the fact that the lapse of the expansion issue brought a lessening of the romantic admiration of the year 1911.

As is fortunately the way in love, disappointment was eventually followed by a cooling of desire. The words of President Harding in his Vancouver address of 1923 were not only a repudiation of the political implications of the doctrine of affinity but also a veiled announcement that the Americans no longer desired annexation. Tactfully he advised Canadians as follows:

> Do not encourage any enterprise looking to Canada's annexation of the United States. You are one of the most capable governing peoples of the world, but I entreat you, for your own sakes, to think twice before undertaking management of the territory which lies between the Great Lakes and the Rio Grande. No, let us go our own gaits along parallel roads, you helping us and we helping you.[117]

Considering how seldom Canadians as a whole had ever thought of sharing in the management of American territory, President Harding's entreaty seems to have been superfluous. This is all the more true since Charles Vincent Massey, the first Canadian minister accredited to the United States, affirmed in a public address that the idea of political union now " belongs to the sphere of the antiquarian or the humorist." [118]

The idea belongs to the sphere of the antiquarian, but to relegate it to that of the humorist is rather cruel to the memory of its historic rôle. It represents what was perhaps the most serious as well as the most persistent sentiment in the history of American expansionism. Moreover, except for the interest in Texas the desire for Canada was the only sentiment directed upon a people as well as a land. Since the Texan was admired as an ex-American, the desire for the Canadians as fellow citizens was the only sentiment in which the American expansionist escaped in any great degree from his egocentrism. Since his devotion brought him no luck, the expansionist takes on something of the pathos of one who, though he has had many attachments, has been cheated by fate of his one true love.

Yet if any expansion could plausibly have been called manifest destiny it was the acquisition of this country which seemed destined for America by the logic of all the affinities between the two peoples. Thus the question of the reason for the expansionist's failure becomes rather interesting. It was considered by Senator Townsend in 1911 when he recalled a history which seemed " full of untimely and unsuccessful efforts at union and reciprocity." His explanation was the simple one that " it has been impossible to strike the time and the occasion right." [119] But even granting due weight to the perversity of objective circumstances, it must still seem that the fundamental cause of the failure lay less in the occasion than in the suitor himself.

For the expansionist did not adopt a method proper for his aim. His aim was union with a political affinity through mutual attraction. His method, however, was not that of one striving to render his nation attractive. It was the technique of a blustering Petruchio. If one judges from the irresponsiveness, indeed the revulsion of most Canadians through most of their history, it must seem that this type is successful only in literature. "The people of Ontario do not like their neighbors to the south,"[120] said the *Toronto Globe* in explaining the result of the vote on reciprocity in 1911. The dislike apparently manifested by the vote was explained by the *Canadian Annual Review* in part as follows:

> There was, in a national sense, the . . . complication represented by a sort of subconscious resentment in many Canadian minds as to United States treatment of the Provinces and the Dominion in many and varied matters.[121]

The *Review* followed with an appallingly long list of alleged mistreatments, extending from the invasions of the Revolution to the Alaskan boundary dispute. Doubtless more irritating than any of these was the chronic national pride whose boastings became proverbial over the entire continent. Whether or not a more tactful approach on the part of Americans would have overcome the British Canadian's sense of cultural and economic affinity with Great Britain, or the French Canadian's fear of losing his religious institutions, is of course an unanswerable question. But it is at least true that any chance of winning his political affinity was lost by the American expansionist through his own failing: he didn't know how to woo.

He failed in the technique of wooing because an element in his character made courtship impossible for him. This was his national pride, or to speak of its ideological correlate, the philosophy of manifest destiny itself. Faith in destiny prevented some expansionists from being willing even to attempt courtship. Thus the *Detroit Free Press* asserted in 1892 that the annexation of Canada was manifest destiny but that any effort to hasten the inevitability must be made by the Canadians themselves.[122] Even when considering effort on their own part, most American expansionists tended to contemplate the kind of effort which was incompatible with the doctrine of affinity. Thus an expansionist writer of 1853 in the *United States Review* placed in curious juxtaposition the assertion that the United States expanded " by affinity," and the threat that it would ride over and crush down any foreign power attempting to block its irresistible progress.[123] The belief in manifest destiny did not develop in the American expansionist that touch of humility which in international as in personal relations is required to gain the affection of one's affinity.

To be sure, the expansionist eventually came of spiritual age and took on mellower characteristics. In 1911 he made suit to the Canadian sincerely, ardently, and without condescension. But it was too late for him to efface the bad impressions which had accumulated throughout past relations. His aristocratic neighbor cruelly jilted him. Perhaps it was poetic justice.

# CHAPTER XIII

## SELF-DEFENSE

The purchase of the Danish West Indies in 1917 closed a lengthy chapter of diplomatic history and also the entire epic of territorial manifest destiny as thus far written. Despite the traditional interest in this acquisition, its occurrence during the Wilson administration might well seem somewhat curious. For it was not a year after Wilson's words, "America does not want any additional territory,"[1] that America's domain received another increment and the inconsistency of statesmen another illustration. The greatest inconsistency lay in the method by which the islands were acquired. Although Wilson had declared in his Mobile address of 1913 that the United States would never take another foot of territory by conquest, he approved of an act of diplomatic imperialism—Lansing's compulsion of Denmark's cession of the islands by a contingent threat of seizure.

To be sure, the sole consideration leading the upright Wilson Administration to this course was the maintenance of a principle of national defense. Self-defense was a major motive in the entire history of American expansion: it solely caused America's first acquisition, collaborated subsequently with land-hunger, and brought about the last expansion even though land-hunger had run its course. Self-defense ever seemed its own justification, so righteous as to make self-preservation superior to the ordinary obligations of international law and morals.

But even granting that self-defense is a right, any one not initiated into the mysteries of world politics would scarcely know why self-defense called for the acquisition of tiny, poorly fortified, and relatively distant islands which were possessed by a friendly power and were not in known danger of passing to another. Again and again in American history one experiences the same difficulty in understanding why particular actions and policies were subsumed under the doctrine of self-defense. Indeed a recent jurist, limiting the legal doctrine of necessity to cases in which its application is "essential to the preservation and continuity of the state," [2] has held that in numerous instances America's allegedly self-defensive measures were not in accord with the legal criterion. Whatever be the correct legal view on this question, it seems safe to say that America's policies often diverged from the criterion of self-defense in individual experience, especially from the idea that self-defense implies an immediate threat, generally deliberate.

From such considerations it is not necessary to deduce, as some have done, that America's doctrine of self-defense has been merely a cover for aggression; were this hypothesis correct the United States would have made use of the doctrine to incorporate all of both Americas. But apparently that doctrine does cover conceptions understandable only in the light of the distinctive objective and subjective conditions of national experience. Such an hypothesis, in contrast to the labor-saving assumption that the ideology of self-defense is hypocrisy, suggests with regard to the doctrine in question a laborious historical inquiry. It is the determination and explanation of the many meanings of the doctrine of self-defense in one of its most important though least frequently examined spheres of application — expansion. To pursue this inquiry in American history is to observe an ideological development wherein a doctrine originally moderate grew ever broader until, like a phobia which turns into aggression, it took on manifestations scarcely distinguishable from imperialism.

This long and curious case-history of the idea of self-defense begins with the commencement of American political history. For at the very outset, by virtue of historical circumstances, self-defense and expansionism were placed in inevitable association. Even before the declaration of independence Colonel Arnold wrote to the Continental Congress that "a due regard to our own defense" dictated the invasion of Canada, Britain's potential base of attack.[3] Self-defense meant to expansionists in the first years of independence the defense of the very life of the Confederacy from the repudiated sovereign's armies. Perhaps the mortal danger at the beginning of national life had an effect like that of a "mental trauma" which results in a long-enduring phobia. In any event, it seems that, among all the many instances in which the American declared expansion essential to self-defense, only the first involved a really imminent danger of attack by a foreign foe.

Even the Revolutionists, however, sought in part what later defensive expansionists sought entirely — security for the future. For the sake of this supposed natural right the acquisition of Canada was pursued forcibly by their armies and sought peaceably by Franklin in the diplomatic discussions at the close of the Revolution. It was in the interest of security, as C. J. Ingersoll wrote in his *Recollections*, that early leaders such as Washington, Jefferson, and Hamilton "considered extensive territories as the manifest destiny of the United States." [4] Extensive territory seemed not only a better pledge of safety than the moats and drawbridges of European politics but the means of defense preeminently adapted to America's unique geographical and political conditions.

Even though at times coincident, immediate self-preservation and permanent security are logically distinct goals. Expansion in behalf of security is really defense against a possible and future rather than an actual and immediate danger. But the former is the more frequent spring of national policy, the fundamental axiom of which holds that an ounce of prevention is worth a pound of cure. Security is the central element in the recurrent political concept known as the "vital interest." This is not necessarily the interest of immediate self-preservation but any interest essential to the security of some phase of national life. Thus the development of the doctrine of self-defense is also the evolution of the idea of vital interest through the many forms which its flexibility permits it to assume. The first version of the vital interest was security of the national border from neighbors.

The demand for security of border became more pretentious with the appearance of subsequent dangers, even though these lessened in seriousness. After the precarious American Revolution the first menace which aroused expansionism was the prospective neighborhood of France to the southwest. It raised the issue of security at a point which seemed the key to the West; for the power which possessed New Orleans had control of the river by which the West sent its produce to the sea. The Louisiana issue gave rise to an ideology of self-defense which was in several respects broader than that of the Revolution. First, security meant freedom from the contiguity not of an enemy but of a former ally, feared now merely because of its power. What distinguishes the expansionism of the Louisiana issue even more is the fact that it did not arise as an incident of defensive war but as a protest against a legal territorial transaction of peace. Finally, and most important of all, the preventive method favored by many expansionists amounted to aggression. Washington himself wrote in connection with the Louisiana issue that "offensive operations oftentimes are the surest, if not in some cases the only means of defence." [5] This realistic principle stands in red letters near the head of the nationalist's code of self-defense.

The fortunate cession of Louisiana was at first regarded as what in fact it was, a removal of all immediate serious menace from contiguous territory. Yet the doctrine of security soon renewed its incitements to expansion. A partial explanation of this fact is perhaps that America's geographical detachment, together with her notion of a distinctive mission, had given rise to a feeling of preordained right to *ideal* security. The providential acquisition of Louisiana confirmed this sense of right without providing a security quite ideal. Subsequent American demands for security are not those of a people more exposed to danger than others. They are those of a people which because of being less exposed considers that (in the words of Secretary of State Frelinghuysen) "its natural position entitles it to be relieved" from the ordinary "conflicts" of international life.[6]

In successive issues following the Louisiana Purchase, the expansionist's demand for ideal security expressed itself in various forms. The first appeared in the movement to acquire Florida, which was viewed in relation to the security of the South. Since this territory was held by weak and innocuous Spain, the danger contemplated was only that of its passing from Spain to a stronger European power. The Madison "no-transfer doctrine" and the congressional resolution affirming transfer of Florida to any foreign power to be dangerous to America's "security" [7] were enunciated in 1811 and carried out by the preventive occupation of Florida during the revolt of its inhabitants. Throughout the rather aggressive quest of Florida, the apprehended transfer was not imminent, as in the case of Louisiana, but merely a hypothetical future danger. Nevertheless the prevention of this danger by purchase or conquest was considered America's right.

The issue of security in the expansionist movement of the War of 1812 did rest upon a present menace. It was the danger from Tecumseh's Indians, whose depredations on the Western settlements were incorrectly attributed to the instigation of British agents in Canada. Thus the conquest of Canada seemed to Henry Clay and others to be the one way to "extinguish the torch that lights up savage warfare." [8] But Indian hostility, as contemporary anti-expansionists pointed out, was fundamentally the result of the American policy of pressing aggressively into Indian lands. Despite unconsciousness of the fact, the demand for Canada in behalf of security was tantamount to insistence upon security for the practice of encroachment upon Indian lands.

An even more unusual principle of self-defense was expressed in 1820 by one who opposed the Spanish treaty of 1819 because of its abandonment of the claim to Texas. To be sure, Texas was held by a weak nation and was in no known danger of passing to a stronger. Yet Representative Trimble believed the Rio Grande and the southwestern mountains to be a predestined natural boundary for the following reasons:

> Nations are individuals in relation to each other; and as self-defense is the first law of man, so is national defense the first law of society. The boundaries of States and Kingdoms should be settled with reference to their military defense . . . Every nation should possess the military positions which defend its frontier . . . These barriers are hostages for the peace of nations; and no people can neglect them with impunity, or surrender them with safety.[9]

Yet Spain was expected by Trimble to surrender to the United

States what she regarded as the bulwark of her American empire against the United States. The principle that *all* nations are entitled to strategic positions is apparently qualified in application by an assumption according with the dogma of manifest destiny: namely, that on occasions of conflict the needs of the United States have the greater weight.

While doubtless agreeing with his abstract principles, Americans on the whole did not agree with Trimble that immediate possession of Texas was essential to America's safety. The Spanish treaty of 1819, ceding Florida and territory as far west as the Rockies, seemed to most Americans to give a territorial extension which was strategically ample. After this elimination of the last European rival power from the continent, the question of strategic security against contiguous powers played a declining part in American expansionism. To be sure, the desire for Texas in the 'forties was sharpened by the fear, expressed notably by Andrew Jackson despite his original depreciation of the strategic value of Texas, that this territory was needed to protect America's Southwest from British-Texan attack.[10] The insistence upon the incorporation of all Oregon arose partly from the belief that "no other nation might be allowed to interfere with Oregon consistently with our safety."[11] But in these expansion movements as in subsequent ones, the fear of direct attack was less influential than subtler considerations. Directly after the expansion of 1819 Lincoln could almost have made his later boast that the geographical situation of the United States would prevent Napoleon himself from leading all the armies of Europe to the Ohio River.

Nevertheless, the doctrine of self-defense continued to play a major part in American expansionism. If this fact seems paradoxical it is because one makes the politically naïve mistake of identifying self-defense solely with defense against military attack. Strategic security of border is, indeed, the original and the most urgent vital interest. But when this security has been achieved the conception of the vital interest tends, perhaps even without the nationalist's awareness, to broaden. The question now becomes one of determining what more elaborate interests were held to be vital and why they seemed so.

A second vital interest is one which the Monroe Doctrine, foremost of America's defensive policies, was enunciated in 1823 to safeguard. While security from potential European neighbors was undoubtedly one aim of Monroe, what he specified with reference to European powers was the much broader consideration that "we should consider any attempt on their part to extend their system to any portion of this hemisphere as dangerous to our peace and safety." [12] Europe's political interference and colonization anywhere on the Western Hemisphere were regarded as dangerous to an extrinsic vital interest, the maintenance of an American type of political and economic institution. The importation of European political institutions meant, as Olney said when he posited our "vital interest in the cause of popular self-government," the supersession of friendly republics by countries alien in practices and thus in sympathy.[13] Introduction of European mercantilism involved, as John Quincy Adams explained, exclusion of the United States from free commercial relations on its hemisphere.[14] While Monroe's laying down the law in so broad a sphere was not an international impertinence, as Bismarck charged, it was certainly unconventional in the light of contemporary international law. That Monroe was not trying to be conventional is evident, not only from his failure to refer to international law, but also from his introduction of the concept of a menace to our "happiness," which could embrace anything. To be sure, American statesmen since Olney have emphasized the proposition that the Monroe Doctrine "rests upon the right of self-protection, and that right is recognized by international law." [15] But the important consideration with regard to Monroe is, in any event, that he was concerned with enlarging, beyond the ordinary legal conceptions of his time, the meaning of self-protection.

This enlargement resulted in the fact that, long before the Doctrine itself became an irresistible shibboleth, Americans conceived the defense of North America from Europe's politico-economic system to be an adequate motive for expansion. This expansionist attitude became evident after 1841 when Great Britain and France began intrigues portending the establishment of European control in Texas and California. The expansion movement of the 'forties was fundamentally an attempt to forestall the supposed menace to American interests. One of these, as has been seen, was the interest in keeping North America safe for democracy. Adjacent European influence conflicted with what the historian Ingersoll called "the American continental postulate," namely, that "space and elbow room, with entire freedom from the contamination of European contact, are indispensable for the development of the great republican experiment." [16] Since a previous chapter has considered expressions of this idea in the 'forties, we need only note a few examples of its influence in the subsequent decade. In a speech of 1853 on European encroachments in the southern portion of the continent, Senator Cass attributed to progressive democracy the following defensive principle:

> We do not intend . . . to have this hemisphere ruled by maxims suited neither to its position nor to its interests, and divided into political communities, dependencies of European monarchies, or under their influence, and, therefore, liable to be involved in every war breaking out in the Old World, and thus extending its dangers and its difficulties to the New, and by which means we should be exposed, in all time to come, to have our lines of communication with our Pacific coast interrupted, our *commerce cut in two* . . . and war entailed upon us . . . [17]

The alternative to these catastrophes, Cass observed, was a refusal to be "circumscribed in our expansion." The annexation which seemed most essential to security was that of disorderly Mexico, threatened constantly by European intervention. President Buchanan's message of 1858 urged occupation of two of its northern provinces to prevent violation of America's "established policy"; [18] the expansionistic Minister Forsyth defined this contingency of European triumph as that of "principles, opinions, and purposes" at variance with American interests.[19] The *New York Herald* called with apparent seriousness for the application of the Ostend policy — seizure in the name of self-preservation — not merely to Mexico but to Cuba and Central America as well:

> This would be to them a boon which they would gladly accept, whereas, if we look unconcernedly on while a few selfish European

intriguers endeavor to establish among them a European protectorate and Spanish despotism, we shall only consent to their being immersed in more savage civil wars than they have yet witnessed, and become finally involved ourselves in a general war with the European alliance.[20]

To understand the exaggeration in such fears, one must consider that, as Professor Rippy has said, "manifest destiny was an ever-present force tending . . . to intensify the fear . . . that European powers might intervene in the neighboring republic."[21] Such European projects as existed were in large measure, as the studies of Professor Perkins suggest, an attempt to check the expansionist ambitions of the United States. This impression is given by the words of a French diplomat who wrote to his government in 1853 that, should Americans succeed in their avowed ambition of acquiring Mexico, it would be difficult to arrest their expansion before they were able to "lay down the law to Europe."[22]

A second consideration leading Americans to believe their ambitions defensive rather than aggressive was the supposed menace of adjacent European influence to their economic interests. While groups in all sections felt affected by the economic issue at some point, the principal stress upon the economic menace came from Southerners who feared that British influence would effect so terrible a calamity as abolition of slavery in adjacent countries. The abolition of slavery in Texas would create a refuge for run-away slaves, give the abolition movement in the United States a powerful impetus, and prevent the addition to the South of new territory needed for cotton cultivation by the system of slavery. With all these alleged menaces in mind the Southerner Henry A. Wise wrote in 1843:

So I would say now to England: You shall not interpose at all, to the injury of, or interference with, our institutions in any way whatever; if you do, it shall be at your peril and cost. I will defend my own institutions, at least against your intervention! How? Texas is 'bone of our bone, flesh of our flesh.'[23]

That annexation was a justifiable defense of the South's economic institution was stated also by Secretary of State Calhoun in his correspondence with the British Government. Writing to Pakenham of the British Government's objectionable attitude in regard to slavery, Calhoun declared that the President had felt it an imperious duty to "adopt, in self-defense, the most effectual measures to defeat" the British policy; the treaty of annexation was "the most effectual, if not the only means of guarding against the threatened danger." [24]

In the 'forties the menace to slavery could be met by peaceful annexation. But in the following decade the possibility that Cuba's abolition movement would loosen the hold of slavery on the United States prompted consideration of belligerent self-defense. The preventive measure popular in the South found statement in that frankest of diplomatic documents, the Ostend Manifesto. Should Spain refuse our offer of purchase, and should it be decided that Cuba in the possession of Spain seriously endangered our internal peace and the existence of our Union, then, the Manifesto stated,

> . . . by every law human and divine, we shall be justified in wresting it from Spain, if we possess the power; and this upon the very same principle that would justify an individual in tearing down the burning house of his neighbor, if there were no other means of preventing the flames from destroying his own home.[25]

The principle was that of self-preservation, called elsewhere in the Manifesto "the first law of nature." [26] Here is one of the most unctuous statements of the doctrine that there is a moral and religious sanction for any aggression essential to self-preservation. Moreover, the paradox that aggression is self-defense had in scarcely any previous formulation been expressed in quite such bold and unqualified terms. It is made clear that even the pursuit of domestic policies is considered a justification for aggressive action when such policies endanger the self-preservation of another state.

That many international jurists disapprove this doctrine is due not to their denial of the right of self-preservation but to their belief that the purely domestic policies of one state are not likely to endanger the existence of another. The very authors of the Manifesto admitted that the plea of self-preservation had been misused, though of course not by America. Secretary of State Marcy tacitly admitted its misuse by these Americans when he repudiated their implied "alternative of cession or seizure" as not justified by existent conditions in Cuba.[27] Expansionistic Southerners, who seemed to Senator Hale to have replaced "manifest destiny" by "political necessity,"[28] apparently exaggerated dangers because of extraordinary sensitiveness regarding their peculiar institution. Lincoln ironically conceded to these Southerners that, whatever the expansionist aim, "it is very easy to assert, but much less easy to disprove, that it is necessary for the wants of the country."[29] Lincoln pointed out, however, that the greatest danger to the Union lay not in European abolitionism but in internal dissension over this very institution of slavery. In fact, he was not far from the truth in saying that "this slavery question has been . . . the only one that has ever threatened or menaced a dissolution of the Union."[30]

After the Civil War, however, slavery was no longer a question; similarly, after the collapse of Maximilian's Mexico venture American democracy was never again in serious danger of European attack. From the close of the Civil War to the end of the century a third doctrine of self-defense took the center of the stage in this melodrama of perils. It identified self-defense principally with the acquisition of islands — not merely Cuba, as heretofore, but all those falling under the general principle of adjacency. This geographical broadening of the doctrine of self-defense represented in one phase an extension of the doctrine of the secure border. Whereas it had long been thought that the ocean gave safety, after the Civil War it was believed that a continental power needed adjacent islands as "natural outposts" for the defense of its shores. The change in view was brought about by the advent of steam transportation and the naval lessons of the Civil War. The acquisition of islands as coaling stations and repair-points seemed essential not only for America's own naval use but also for prevention of hostile use by other countries.

The Civil War having revealed the need of a Caribbean base, the administrations of Johnson and Grant were marked by efforts to acquire the two main islands of the Danish West Indies, together with Culebrita and the Dominican Republic. With reference to Danish St. Thomas, President Johnson asserted that " with the possession of such a station by the United States, neither we nor any other American nation need longer apprehend injury or offense from any trans-Atlantic enemy." [31] War-weariness and other factors defeated the program for Caribbean strategic expansion without resulting in any injury to the United States in ensuing years.

The program initiated by Seward was resumed, however, in the 'nineties. The chief instigation to this resumption was the prospect of an Isthmian canal. Captain Mahan asserted, as was previously noted, that in view of the great military import of a canal America should strengthen its control of the adjacent maritime area by securing Caribbean islands whenever they could be acquired " righteously." [32] To carry out this principle Senator Lodge, inclined to consider all expansion righteous, in 1898 introduced a bill providing for the purchase of the Danish West Indies, strategically useful because of their control of the Anageda Passage to the Isthmus. Independently of the canal, however, it seemed important to acquire what Senator Lodge called " outworks," islands essential to the defense of the continental citadel.[33] The most adjacent of such outworks was Cuba, which Senator Baker claimed on the grounds both of self-preservation and of America's manifest destiny. Senator Allen wished to annex all adjacent islands in " due regard to the law of self-preservation." [34] Seeking to give the impression that Caribbean expansion was but a continuation of the defense policy of the past, Representative Newlands declared that geographically the Bahamas and the West Indies belonged to this country as part of its line of defense.[35] But this line was extended to the middle of the Pacific by those who regarded every coaling station within three thousand miles as a possible *point d'appui* for foreign attack. Thus Hawaii, " the only natural outpost to the defences of the Pacific coast," [36] was claimed by Representative Kirkpatrick on the ground of " the highest necessity . . . the law of self-preservation." [37] When Representative Smith declared that the acquisition would lessen the possibilities of future war,[38] he exemplified the truth of Professor Callahan's observation with reference to the history of American expansion: " Although some acquisitions have been made by war the greater number have been obtained under the desire to prevent war." [39]

On the other hand, anti-expansionists wondered at so much inquietude about a nation which was intrinsically powerful, enjoyed the enviable protection of the great seas, and as Representative Clark pointed out, had gotten along for 109 years without "volcanic rocks" in the ocean.[40] Perhaps this skepticism only exemplified the truth of Sir Robert Filmer's observation that "the causes and ends of the greatest politic actions and motions of state dazzle the eyes and exceed the capacities of all men, save only those that are hourly versed in the managing public affairs." But it seems likely that in this instance the statesmen and the naval strategists were themselves laboring under a certain confusion of ideas. For the thesis that islands were essential to defense of coasts appears to have derived its appeal partly from the notion of their necessity to the defense of an interest of quite different character.

This vital interest which islands supposedly protected was in a certain sense extrinsic to America's coasts. Captain Mahan wrote in 1893 that "the word 'defense,' already too narrowly understood, has its application at points far away from our own coast." [41] These words did not mean merely that the defense of extrinsic interests such as trade routes is a necessity of war. Mahan meant also that, irrespective of war, there lie always beyond the sea many of "those essential interests, of those evident dangers, which impose a policy and confer rights." [42] The essential interests were those of commercial expansion, the evident dangers those of commercial competition. Thus Pacific islands were desired not merely for their naval facilities in the defense of carriers of commerce, but also for their provision of markets, raw materials, and bases of political influence in the commercial wars of peace. In sum, islands were the outposts not only of coastal defense but also of the protection of a new vital interest, oversea commerce.

If he had been asked why the aggrandizement of foreign commerce was defense of country the nationalist would have answered that it was economic activity which pumped the life blood through the body politic. But it was only after the Civil

War, wherein began the industrial expansion which superseded the relatively self-subsistent agrarian economy, that there arose the tendency to relate America's economic welfare to foreign rather than domestic trade. The effect of the new viewpoint on expansion appears as early as Seward's statement to the Danish Minister that he desired Denmark's islands for "political and commercial reasons." [43] But it was not until about 1890 that Mahan noted in Americans in general "the turning of the eyes outward, instead of inward only, to seek the welfare of the country." [44] And it was not until the Hawaiian issue of 1893 that expansion of commerce began to seem an imperative reason for expansion of territory. Mahan himself was an influential monitor in his article of 1893 on the bearing of the annexation of Hawaii upon the "commercial and military control of the Pacific." [45] In 1898 the Senate Committee on Foreign Relations declared full ownership of the islands to be "indispensable to the commerce of the United States in respect of its development and safety." [46] In the Philippine issue expansionists became interested in commercial expansion to a degree which probably exceeded Mahan's greatest hopes. The attraction of the islands lay not merely in their intrinsic value but also in their provision of the fulcrum upon which the United States could operate a political lever to secure her share of China's disputed trade. The economist Charles A. Conant summarized the rationale of economic expansionism as follows:

> The United States have actually reached, or are approaching, the economic state where . . . outlets are required outside their own boundaries, in order to prevent business depression, idleness, and suffering at home. Such outlets might be found without the exercise of political and military power, if commercial freedom was the policy of all nations. As such a policy has not been adopted by more than one important power of western Europe, and as the opportunities for the sale of the products of American labor . . . under conditions of equality of opportunity are seriously threatened by the policy of some of these powers, the United States are compelled, by the instinct of self-preservation, to enter, however reluctantly, upon the field of international politics.[47]

One is reminded of Japan's present-day plea of economic necessity: "Now, as the loss of our economic opportunities in China signifies *ipso facto* the loss of our right to exist, the anti-

Japanese movement presents a grave danger to the national existence of Japan." [48] In this day of the release of the Philippines it is difficult to realize that Americans of 1898 sought the Philippines for just as questionable a reason.

The territorial acquisitions of the end of the century might seem to have brought the most far-fetched conception of America's vital needs complete satisfaction. America had achieved strategic security on the continent and in adjacent maritime regions, security of "American" politico-economic institutions in the entire hemisphere, security for the development of oversea commerce. But the Spanish-American War was scarcely a year behind when negotiations for the Danish West Indies were resumed on the ground of a type of defense which seemed as urgent as any of the past.

To understand the further history of self-defensive expansionism it is necessary again to bring into focus the Monroe Doctrine, which served as the source of a new conception of vital interest. Monroe's pronouncement, though it directed attention to the relation between security and distant interests, had not been viewed originally as a permanent determinant of national policy. Polk's restatement of the Doctrine in 1845 was not only the first notable indication of its crystallization as policy, but also the introduction of its broadened version banning Europe's territorial aggrandizement in America by any method. His shortly ensuing reference to the Doctrine in recommending the Yucatan occupation (in his diary he considered annexation) was the first important sign of its coming into relation with expansionism.[49] In the 'fifties, as observations of Ministers Gadsden and Forsyth and of Senator Bell evidence, the Doctrine was invoked with increasing frequency when territorial expansion seemed necessary to forestall European intervention in neighboring countries.[50] By the time of Grant's reference to the Doctrine in urging the annexation of the Dominican Republic,[51] the association of this principle with defensive expansionism had become established. Through most of the nineteenth century, however, the Doctrine was not a primary interest as much as a reinforcement of primary interests; it was invoked only when the stakes were specific interests which would have been defended even had the Monroe Doctrine been non-existent.

But about 1895, just when Lord Salisbury declared to Olney that the dangers envisaged by President Monroe were no longer existent,[52] Olney and his fellow Americans were beginning to regard the Doctrine as a primary consideration, indeed as a sacred and undying oracle of Americanism. It was in the 'nineties, the decade of a new invigoration of American nationalism, that Mahan affirmed: ". . . the precise value of the Monroe Doctrine is understood very loosely by most Americans, but the effect of the familiar phrase has been to develop a national sensitiveness, which is a more frequent cause of war than material interests." [53] The increasing sensitiveness of the expansionists in this respect was reflected in Senator Allen's observation in 1895 that the Monroe Doctrine should have as an essential element the broad principle that "wherever territory is essential to the safety and security of this country we should not only insist that such powers should not acquire additional territory, but we should also insist that this Government shall have the right to such territory by purchase." [54] One motive of the proposal to acquire the Danish West Indies was the fear that the islands were in the market and that Germany might acquire them in violation of the Monroe Doctrine. This apprehension, which apparently was not founded upon fact, was indicated by a Senate committee's statement in 1898 that acquisition of the islands would remove, in view of the Doctrine, "a very probable cause of foreign complications." [55]

After the Spanish War, caused partially by a sense of responsibility under the Doctrine, Monroe's principle did not seem diminished in worth because the vital interests which it had been enunciated to defend were now beyond easy or likely challenge. It was cherished now as the guarding circle about the secure *status quo.* In a speech of 1900 Senator Lodge pointed out that Americans would fight "until their eyelids do no longer wag" for this principle which he, like the Republican platform of 1892, associated with manifest destiny.[56] Such a fusion of the Monroe Doctrine with manifest destiny has been misinterpreted by the foreign writers who account for the Doctrine as a "handmaid"[57] or "emanation"[58] of the dream of manifest destiny. Lodge's assertion that Monroe's policy was manifest destiny signified not the subservience of the former to expansion, but the maturation of the Doctrine as a vital interest in its own right. While it had originally corresponded to what the Talmudist called a fence around the law, the Doctrine came later to be viewed not merely as a fence about vital interests but as something vital in itself. Thus there was a determination to defend the Doctrine whether the issue affected practical interests substantially or not. In this apparent irrationalism there was a certain logic. For the Monroe Doctrine is a generalization which cannot be neglected even in unimportant issues without the possible loss of its usefulness in the important. But nationalist emotion endeared the Doctrine independently of the logic of political expediency.

Such considerations are a necessary preface to the expansion movement following the Spanish-American War. For it was not the need of a Caribbean naval station, the chief motive of Seward, which primarily prompted the renewed quest of Denmark's Caribbean possessions. Porto Rico and Guantanamo, which according to Captain Mahan were more valuable strategically than the Danish St. Thomas, were now in America's possession. St. Thomas had been characterized by Mahan[59] as lacking in fortifications and by Secretary of State Blaine[60] as inferior in strategic utility. While the naval usefulness of St. Thomas was doubtless not ignored, the purely strategic consideration seems never again to have played the leading part.

Apparently the renewal of negotiations for the Danish West Indies was instigated chiefly by the fear of Germany's infraction of the Doctrine. According to the Danish Captain Christmas, Secretary of State Hay expressed anger to him over an alleged attempt of Germany to acquire the islands.[61] Although the testimony of the notorious Christmas may not seem trustworthy, there is abundant other evidence that the supposed German menace was agitating both the American public and Government officials. Such evidence, as Professor Tansill points out, includes a public statement by Representative John Gardner, a veiled reference by Secretary of War Root to fighting for the Doctrine, and the official report of the German Ambassador Schoen on the suspicion of Germany's designs.[62] Most probably Germany was innocent of expansionist designs in North America, but after Secretary Hay arranged for the treaty of purchase of January 24, 1902, press comments reflected the relief over the supposed salvation of the Doctrine. Thus the *New York Times* observed that though the acquisition of Porto Rico had greatly reduced the strategic value of the Danish islands, a justification for their purchase remained in the fact that their possible transfer to some European power menaced the maintenance of the Monroe Doctrine.[63] The *Philadelphia Inquirer* and the *Cincinnati Enquirer* were among the other papers whose comments showed Monroe becoming the patron saint of American expansion.[64]

But after Americans breathed a sigh of relief, the Danish Landesthing turned the tables upon the American Senate by a rejection which followed the precedent set by the latter body in 1867. Secretary of State John Hay and other American statesmen attributed the defeat to German influence, which in fact, as Professor Tansill has recently shown, had nothing to do with it.[65] Numerous American newspapers informed Denmark that at least she would not be permitted to transfer the islands to any European power. The *New York Times* gave a warning which employed the words of the Monroe Doctrine.[66] Some Americans also warned Denmark that eventual acquisition of the islands was manifest destiny in any event. Thus the *New York Herald* spoke of the impossibility of preventing the islands from reaching their "natural destination," a phrase suggestive of the strategic version of the doctrine of the natural boundary.[67]

For approximately thirteen years the evident reluctance of Denmark to dispose of the islands caused a lapse of activity in the matter so far as concerned the State Department itself. In this period, however, there occurred in America's defensive policy a development which was to double the interest in the islands when the question was taken up again. An intensification of strategic and political interest in the Caribbean Sea was brought about by America's actual acquisition of the rights to construct and operate the Panama Canal, a prospective center for the defense of commerce and military communications. President Roosevelt, emphasizing in 1905 the enhanced importance which the Canal gave to the Doctrine, declared that as a "matter of self-defense" it would be necessary to "exercise a close watch over the approaches to this canal" and be "thoroughly alive to our interests in the Caribbean Sea." [68]

The course which Roosevelt subsumed under the Monroe Doctrine came to seem so important as to receive the distinct designation of the Isthmian or Canal policy. This policy was stated by Secretary of State Hughes as follows:

> . . . we have a definite policy of protecting the Panama Canal. We deem it to be essential to our national safety to hold the control of the Canal and we could not yield to any foreign power the maintaining of any position which would interfere with our right adequately to protect the Canal or would menace its approaches or the freedom of our communications. This applies just as well to American powers as to non-American powers.[69]

The Canal policy, as these words show, differs from the Monroe Doctrine because of both a reference to a smaller area and an application to American as well as non-American powers. Thus the Canal policy has been cited, as in the Nicaraguan and Mexican difficulties of 1926-1927, as the justification for American interventions designed to forestall a Latin-American country's acquisition of influence near the Canal.[70] On the other hand, the Canal policy is similar to the Doctrine, as J. Reuben Clark declared, in resting upon the right of national self-defense.[71] Moreover, in this policy as in the Monroe Doctrine a demand for the maintenance of a political *status quo* operates as a generalized pretension irrespective of the intrinsic importance of the specific issue. Like the Monroe Doctrine the Canal policy has at times been justified in the terms of manifest destiny. Wallace Thompson observed that it is grounded in "the facts of life, of policy, and of destiny, perhaps." [72]

The Canal policy added its influence to that of the Monroe Doctrine in creating the most sensitive apprehension of Europe's actions in the Caribbean sphere; so far as European intrusion here was concerned, the two policies coincided. The years following 1902 continued at intervals to witness seizures of suspicion and fear, particularly concerning the intentions of Germany. These fears were nourished less by factual evidence than by the notion that Germany had defeated the treaty of 1902. In June, 1905, the ever-watchful Senator Lodge wrote apprehensively to President Roosevelt of the newspaper rumor that the German Hamburg-American Company was seeking to establish a coaling station at St. Thomas.[73] Seven years later the *New York Times* aroused another scare by its report that Denmark had proposed a lease of St. Thomas to a group of financiers with full powers to sublet.[74] About the same time alarm over an alleged Japanese danger resulted in a new version of the right of self-preservation — the Lodge resolution banning any non-American commercial association from occupying an American strategic area.[75] The episode was marked by one Senator's imaginative proposal to meet the danger by annexing the part of Lower California in question.[76] Expansion is indeed a panacea!

According to his Minister to Denmark, President Wilson himself, little inclined as he was to use expansion as a cure-all, long believed it prudent to acquire the Danish West Indies.[77] Inaction of his Administration was apparently only the necessary consequence of Denmark's continuing reluctance to sell. Shortly before the World War, however, our patience was strained as Secretary Lansing came to believe that Germany was seeking a direct or indirect control of a coaling station in Haiti.[78] After the outbreak of the World War he became convinced that, to quote his words to the Danish Minister, "there was danger that Germany, taking advantage of the upheaval in Europe, might absorb Denmark and that she might do so in order to obtain a legal title to the Danish West Indies, which the German Government coveted for naval uses." [79] One notes that, while the existence of this danger was stated as a certainty, the factual evidence supporting it was not made clear in this statement or any other. Nor does it seem very probable that Germany's preoccupation with the World War permitted it to entertain even secretly the designs upon American territory which its Chancellor denied publicly.[80] Secretary Lansing's fears must be understood in the light of the traditional assumptions regarding German designs, his anticipation of America's entrance into the World War, and the statesman's general principle that in matters of vital interest suspicion is the better part of optimism.

In 1916 Mr. Lansing opened up negotiations with the Danish Minister and came quickly to the point. His manner of avowing America's desire to purchase the Danish West Indies left little room for discussion. He informed the Danish Minister that

> . . . in the event of an evident intention on the part of Germany to take possession of his country or to compel Denmark to cede the islands to her, the United States would be under the necessity of seizing and annexing them, and, though it would be done with the greatest reluctance, it would be necessary to do it in order to avoid a serious dispute with the German Government over the sovereignty of and title to the islands, as we would never permit the group to become German.

Later, Mr. Brun asked in behalf of his Government whether "in case the Danish Government did not agree to a sale of the islands the United States would feel it necessary to take them." Secretary Lansing promptly answered that, although he had not believed such drastic action necessary, he could conceive of circumstances which would compel it. He repeated the circumstances cited in the foregoing and added Denmark's *voluntary* transfer of title to another European power. Two weeks later Mr. Brun, with the grace of the resigned, announced that in view of "the pressure of necessity" his country "would be unable to refuse to consider a proposition for the sale of the islands to the United States." Soon after this, curiously, Secretary Lansing informed President Wilson of the pass reached by the negotiations, and heard from the President an expression of "gratification" that the Secretary of State had been "so frank with the Danish Minister." The frankness, as Lansing himself recognized, brought about the treaty.[81]

In urging its ratification upon the Danish Folkething, Minister Edward Brandes explained that the Monroe Doctrine aroused in Americans a desire to "bind American soil to the United States." He spoke of America's forcible manner of presenting the desire as " a compelling reason to accede to the desire for negotiation, which we had refused two years previous — in such a manner as a little and weak state must accede to the wishes of a large and powerful state when living in a world where justice is abolished or enforced by might, yes, where might not so seldom forms and moulds justice." [82]

However unfavorably Brandes explained American behavior, the thought of moral impropriety was so far from Lansing's mind that he blandly revealed the entire unsuspected episode in the *New York Times Magazine* of 1931. The true explanation is not that of Brandes — that might is seen as moulding justice — but that political necessity is supposed to abrogate ordinary justice in dealing with either the weak or the strong. To be sure, in the very year when the doctrine of political necessity was applied by the United States at Denmark's expense, the American Institute of International Law adopted the principle that self-preservation sanctions no unlawful injury to unoffending states. Whatever jurists may write, most of the statesmen applying the grim doctrine of political necessity do not reckon with the guilt or innocence of a party but merely with objective consequences. From the practical point of view, as Stowell says, " it matters little to the state whether its existence be imperilled through the disregard of its right or through the disregard of some vital interest the protection of which has not been recognized as a matter of general concern as is a right under international law." [83] The basic premise of the doctrine of self-preservation is always that ancient adage, " *Salus publica suprema lex.*" Machiavelli once observed without disapproval that both monarchs and republics break faith and display ingratitude to preserve the state. Jefferson was no Machiavellian, and yet he too wrote that " the law of self-preservation overrules the laws of obligation to others." [84] How little Wilson was disposed to carry self-defense to an unnecessary point is shown by his question whether self-defense required infringing upon Mexico's sovereignty.[85] But Wilson in this instance, doubtless persuading himself that Denmark's injury was much less than what Danes themselves estimated, defended America's vital interest by the very same threat approved in the Ostend Manifesto. It was the perversity of fate that under this anti-imperialistic president America for the first time actually applied the doctrine of political necessity at the expense of a completely innocent state.

Secretary Lansing's report accompanying the treaty merely imparted the information that the convention was " responsive to the conviction of both Governments . . . that the Danish West Indies should belong to the United States." The report contained, in addition to strategic considerations, the following exposition of the political principles underlying this conviction of the United States:

> The Caribbean is within the peculiar sphere of influence of the United States, especially since the completion of the Panama Canal, and the possibility of a change of sovereignty of any of the islands now under foreign jurisdiction is of grave concern to the United States. Moreover, the Monroe Doctrine, a settled national policy of the United States, would have caused this country to look with disfavor upon the transfer of sovereignty of the Danish West Indies to any European nation.[86]

Before the Senate Committee on Foreign Relations, Lansing said more pointedly that it was " desirable to get the islands out of the market to prevent foreign complications." [87] That Senate ratification of the treaty was easy beyond all precedent was perhaps due to the belief that, as Senator Borah asserted, if we had submitted to European acquisition of the islands, " the Monroe Doctrine would have been at an end." [88] Public opinion, though perhaps at first as surprised at this latter-day child of manifest destiny as was the biblical patriarch at his aged wife's deliverance, seemed " to look upon the purchase as one of necessity or expediency; as a means of avoiding any complications with foreign governments through our maintenance of the Monroe Doctrine, and as a necessary incident in our Isthmian Canal policy." [89] The *Philadelphia Evening Ledger* observed that " we are buying something more than a little land in the ocean; we are making it easier to maintain the Monroe Doctrine in the trying days that are coming." [90] The ordinarily anti-expansionist *New Republic* affirmed that since the American people would fight to prevent the establishment of a naval base in the region of the Panama Canal, we were buying "an insurance policy against one specific liability to war." [91]

President Hoover scarcely showed comprehension of the expansionists' logic when he disparaged the purchase of this "effective poorhouse" by declaring that even its strategic utility was very problematical.[92] For the primary consideration in the purchase of the islands was not their strategic utility to the United States or even their strategic menace. Of primary importance was the maintenance of a doctrine of security which had become sacred because, as Senator Lodge once said,

> . . . the instinct of the people recognizes in that doctrine a great principle of national life. Without clinging to it we should be in constant peril, our evolution retarded, our existence menaced. The European power which attempts to establish itself in new possessions in the Americas, whether on a little island or in a continental state, from Patagonia to the Rio Grande, is our enemy.[93]

Thus in 1916 even his reluctance to support the Wilson Administration did not prevent Senator Lodge from publicly stating that "in the interests of peace it is of great importance that these islands should pass into the hands of the United States." [94]

To be sure, pacific expansionism was based not upon a materialized menace to America's peace but upon a lengthy series of assumptions regarding mere contingencies: that Germany *might* entertain or conceive a desire for a Caribbean naval station, decide to conquer Denmark, succeed in such conquest, succeed subsequently in establishing possession of the Danish colonies, engage in hostilities against the United States, and encourage other violations of the Monroe Doctrine which might be injurious to America's vital interests. To characterize the action in this issue as self-defense is evidently to conceive of a self-defense against the possible injury of the possible consequence of the possible action of a possible enemy. While such a formulation may seem a *reductio ad absurdum*, it is in fact only a somewhat strained way of stating a principle in general acceptance — the right of basing defensive policies upon contingencies. As Elihu Root has said, the Monroe Doctrine rests upon the doctrine of international law which affirms "the right of every sovereign state to protect itself by preventing a condition in which it will be too late to protect itself." [95] This doctrine implies as criterion a reasonable likelihood, but in determining political contingencies the line between reasonableness and morbid phobia wavers.

The further one goes in defensive expansionism the greater becomes one's tendency to push the line toward a hysterical apprehensiveness. Thus the acquisition of the Virgin Islands suggested to many Americans a further design of defensive expansion — one which has persisted with a few till the present day — in which the Monroe Doctrine also figured as premise. It was the gradual purchase of all Europe's Caribbean possessions (or their acquisition in settlement of war debts) for America's protective system of outposts. This dream of a comprehensive Caribbean empire did not seem mad or at all unreasonable to various newspapers, publicists, diplomats, professors, and Senators — for example, the *New York Evening Mail*,[96] James C. Bardin,[97] ex-Minister Charles Sherrill,[98] Professor William Shepherd,[99] and notably Senator James A. Reed.[100] It seemed to these and many others that the "logical conclusion" of the Monroe Doctrine was "the eventual exclusion of non-American political power over American soil." [101] Senator Reed, Mr. Bardin, and Dr. Shepherd have referred the expansionist project to the still higher authority of "manifest destiny," defined by Shepherd as "the natural course of things, or whatever the term that may be used to mark the tendency of great powers to round out their defensible frontiers." [102] In the light of history such confidence was perhaps not unnatural. For the manifest destiny of ideas and events had carried far since Monroe, upon negotiating the purchase of Louisiana, wrote that America had attained everything essential to its peace.[103]

A résumé of the interpretations of self-defense in the history of American expansionism resembles almost a progressive madness, and certainly has all the multiplicity and variety of a crazy quilt. The doctrine of self-defense was used to justify actual or proposed expansion of territory or political control in connection with the following alleged dangers: possible attack in the future by the enemy in a present war; possible future quarrels with a powerful neighbor who has replaced a weak one; the possibility that a weak neighbor might not always be able to resist conquest by another power; attack by Indians who resent the seizure of their lands; the contingency that a neighboring power might take advantage of the absence of a defensible natural boundary; injury to America's general prosperity because of European economic power in contiguous countries; injury to the institution of slavery through possible abolition of slavery in a small adjacent island; check of the spread of American democracy through the influence of European absolutism in adjacent countries; a North American people's appeal to a European nation to protect it from marauding Indians; possible political interference by a European nation in a neighboring disorderly republic; possible future attack by a trans-Atlantic country from adjacent Caribbean islands; possible future attack from a Pacific island two thousand miles distant; the possibility of losing a proper share in the commerce of another hemisphere; the possibility that a European power might come into possession of an island in the region of a nationalized isthmian canal; the possibility that an unfriendly American power might acquire influence in the region of the isthmian canal; the possibility that violation of a principle of security in a minor issue might prejudice its maintenance in an important issue; the possibility that Europe's retention of naval bases in this hemisphere violates the spirit of a traditional doctrine affirming that at least Europe's existing possessions would be respected. It is by no means suggested that this list of interpretations of "self-defense" is comprehensive.

That Grotius envisaged so many and such far-reaching implications when he made self-preservation a right of states is not probable. Nor is it probable that many contemporary jurists regardful of international welfare would see in most of the contingencies cited a proper ground for suspension of legal obligations. Strange as it may seem, the right of self-defense was and still is intended by jurists to be the most carefully reasoned, infrequent, and innocuous of legal pleas.

Yet it is untrue that the United States and other nations have played fast and loose with a respectable concept. The concept itself was logically loose to a degree which encouraged casual handling. The idea of self-defense is as little susceptible of strict definition as is the concept of danger. Attempts to circumscribe the right of self-defense have resulted on the one hand in such tautology as the stipulation that its application "should be confined to cases in which the necessity of defending the state actually exists in point of fact." [104] They have resulted on the other hand in adjectives which are as open to varying construction as is the noun itself. An instance is America's insistence in the Carolina case, wherein it was disadvantageous to be a loose constructionist, that Great Britain show a necessity of self-defense, "instant, overwhelming, and leaving no choice of means, and no moment for deliberation." [105] Secretary Kellogg's thesis [106] that individual interpretation of self-defense is an inalienable prerogative of sovereignty could be supplemented by the admission that individual interpretation is an inevitable consequence of the idea of self-defense itself.

This is not to assert the impossibility of distinguishing in specific applications of the doctrine various degrees of reasonableness. Reasonableness is in fact the only thing which can keep its exploitation within bounds. But to formulate a doctrine which is limited only by reasonableness was in effect not to limit it at all. For reasonableness in matters of self-defense is perhaps the last thing which can reasonably be expected in view of present national attitudes — except in so far as nations generally recognize unreasonableness in the defensive policies of all powers other than themselves.

National unreasonableness in "self-defense" is manifested partially in the tendency to exaggeration, which has been particularly clear in the case of a country spared by its detachment and power from most international perils. Exaggeration means on the one hand the identification of the barely possible with the probable or certain, of the remote with the imminent, and of the somewhat injurious with the highly injurious or fatal. It signifies on the other hand the carrying of the concept of self-defense itself beyond the meaning which is ascribed to it in ordinary experience. Thus self-defense is interpreted as defense against not merely actual or imminent attack but also any diminution of security; security is conceived as including the safety of all vital interests; and vital interests are regarded as embracing every interest important to national welfare. These liberties with ideas are not to be ascribed to a deliberate intention of making self-defense equivalent to the satisfaction of national ambition, even though such is their effect. Nor are they to be explained merely by the undeniable dangers of an international life full of interest-conflicts but lacking in effective world agencies for security. The extremism of the nationalist's ideology arises from the assumption that since the dangers of international life are not always calculable by reason, defense should err on the side of madness rather than reasonableness. This instrumental logic rests in turn on a fanatical value — the valuation of the nation's life at infinity.

The unreasonableness of the nationalist's ideology of self-defense lies chiefly in its failure to grant anything like the same importance to the security of other nations. Other nations must fare as badly as the doctrine of political necessity dictates. To be sure, his dislike for facing the unpleasant consequences of his patriotism prompts the nationalist usually to discover reasons for denying any real or serious injury to other peoples. And if asked whether his country's necessity justifies the sacrifice of a vast portion of international society, the nationalist, like the girl in the popular song, probably wouldn't say yes and wouldn't say no; he would probably respond that the extreme improbability of such sacrifice makes consideration of the question morbid. But were the nationalist to carry his doctrine of political necessity to its logical conclusion he would have to answer that his country must live though the heavens fall — on all others.

Even the least subordination of another's rights to national self-defense raises a teasing problem of casuistry. It has not been frequently considered, for the very statement of the problem seems as irreverent as interpolating the throne itself. The philosophical analyst, however, is perhaps permitted as a kind of court jester to raise questions which would be lese-majesty in the man of action. Thus one may finally venture to place in question what is commonly supposed to be unquestionable.

Why is it that, no matter what the cost to another nation or to international society, the right of preserving the nation and all its vital interests is considered morally unquestionable?

The answer of the jurist Hall is that national self-preservation is sanctioned by the same moral principle which authorizes self-preservation by the individual. But the inaccuracy of this explanation is shown by Hall's own statement that individual morality justifies those acts of self-preservation which are "not inconsistent with the nature of a moral being." [107] Whereas the individual as private person attaches to his scheme of self-interest the qualification that it must not conflict with morality, the individual as nationalist associates with his code of morality the joker that it must not conflict with vital self-interest. It is not merely the severely moralistic Kant who has protested against the doctrine that necessity knows no law.[108] All men of honor will meet a Lord Jim's cowardly plea "*Il faut vivre*" with the scornful reply "*Je ne vois pas la nécessité.*" When self-preservation conflicts with a social duty the individual is supposed to set his life at the fee of a pin, indeed to lose his life that he may find it. But the same individual morality appears eccentric when it prompts a Thoreau to demand of the nation: "This people must cease to hold slaves, and to make war on Mexico, though it cost them their existence as a people." [109] Viewed in the light of individual morality the nationalist's subordination of morality to national existence is not merely wrong, it is almost scandalous!

What saves it from being scandalous is in part the fact that the nationalist is bent not upon his individual salvation but on that of a collectivity for which he would sacrifice even himself. Upon the fate of this collectivity, the nationalist believes, hangs humanity itself with all its hopes and all its fears. For the continued life of his nation seems the pledge that "government of the people" or some other humanitarian value "shall not perish from the earth." Such assumptions were expressed by an American imperialist as follows: "Our manifest destiny is the heritage of mankind; then let us neglect no opportunity to strengthen and conserve our proud and responsible position." [110]

Yet it is improbable that the conservation of the nation is motivated fundamentally by social-mindedness. Devotion to the nation's life leads to the regretful but unhesitant sacrifice not only of any number of other nationals but also of fellow citizens. Peoples sacrificing to the grim romanticism of the totalitarian state accept always, and others at least in crises, the mystic idea that the individual citizen's right of self-preservation is zero. A hundred million times zero is not infinity but merely zero.

The dogma that the nation must not die can be explained only by the fact that the state is valued not merely as a means to social goods but as (to quote Treitschke) "in itself . . . a high moral good." The state seems a moral good higher than justice, truth, and honor, all of which at times it sacrifices. It even appears to Treitschke as "the highest community existing in exterior human life," and therefore as one to which "the duty of self-effacement cannot apply." [111]

The true reason of this supreme valuation, toward which all nationalism seems at least unconsciously to tend, is in a sense no reason at all. For if asked the wherefore of this paramount valuation the noblest nationalist might answer in the very words of Shylock: "I can give no reason; nor I will not." Perhaps he will pretend to give a reason but it will amount to Shylock's ignorance of reason. Like the American expansionist the patriot may affirm that the continued life of the nation is a manifest destiny. Manifest destiny corresponds to the ethical ultimate, which, as the American James Wilson long ago suggested, is an inner necessity beyond all reason. It is, then, an inscrutable inner destiny which decrees death for the individual and life for the nation.

While the manifest destiny of national self-preservation has not been questioned, there has finally arisen a question with regard to the best means of assuring the nation's preservation. The greater part of America's history as that of other nations witnessed faith in the defensive measures of integral nationalism, defined by Maurras as "the exclusive pursuit of national policies, the absolute maintenance of national integrity, and the steady increase of national power." [112] But this faith was shaken when the terrifying accumulation of defensive swords resulted in 1914 in Armageddon — a war from which even geographically detached America could not remain aloof without prejudice to its security. It became clear to some that "imagination frames events unknown . . . and what it fears creates."

Since the World War American statesmen have advocated increasingly a new doctrine of national defense, diametrically opposed to that of the past. Thus Norman Davis declared before the Geneva Disarmament Conference that though the claim of a state to safeguard its security is to be recognized, "in the long run this security can best be achieved through a controlled disarmament." He asserted further that "the simplest and most accurate definition of an aggressor is one whose armed forces are found on alien soil in violation of treaties." [113] One would infer from this that the simplest and most accurate definition of the long troublesome concept of self-defense might be phrased with reference to equally objective circumstances. The most pointed of recent American statements concerning the method of self-defense is President Franklin D. Roosevelt's assertion of 1933 that in "concerted action based upon the greatest good of the greatest number" lies the greatest hope of practical results in the "furtherance of durable peace for our generation in every part of the world." [114] Implicit in America's recent internationalism is a belated self-criticism — that self-defensive expansionism is a sword which may cut the hand of its wielder.

# CHAPTER XIV

## INTERNATIONAL POLICE POWER

It is a paradox that the aggrandizement of American empire in the twentieth century has not taken place principally through territorial expansion. This paradox is dissipated, however, by the realization that, as Walter Hines Page once intimated, the acquisition of sovereignty over land is no longer the only or most expedient way to that substantial control which may be called empire. Americans were initiated into more covert methods of imperialism by the very war which marked the virtual culmination of territorial expansionism; for the Cuban intervention of 1898 led not only to satisfying expansion of territory but also, through the Platt Amendment, to expansion of political power. Intervention, acquisition of extensive treaty rights, and the pretension to a sphere of influence have been the devious methods by which American imperialism seemed at one time to tend toward fulfilment almost of the continental dream of manifest destiny.

A paradox not so easily explained is the fact that the perpetrators of these recent deeds of manifest destiny have been the most vigorous disavowers of its spirit. Thus even while American marines fought on Nicaraguan soil Secretary of State Hughes denied before a Pan-American Conference that the United States wished to annex, to govern, or to intervene in any American republic. This country had but a modest desire: "We simply wish peace and order and stability and recognition of honest rights properly acquired so that this hemisphere may not only be the hemisphere of peace but the hemisphere of international justice." [1] Certain anti-imperialists, assuming that things are never as statesmen present them, regard such disavowals as merely the camouflage of the wish for economic domination. But careful students of American imperialism have found reason to believe that the primary desire at least of the Government has in fact been order, favorable to its political interests as well as to its Pan-American ideals.[2]

However, it is undeniable that America's simple wishes for order and other proprieties led to elaborate demands. Even abstractly moderate desiderata may engender a very extensive intervention when entertained with respect to peoples who either are not gifted in orderly self-government or consider it more interesting and virile to conduct elections by bullets than by ballots. For the fulfilment of such wishes requires an imperialist practice as militant as the habits which it is designed to correct. America has thus laid claim to prerogatives of intervention involving more power over Latin-American countries than the legal doctrine of intervention is usually supposed to sanction. At the same time the United States has demanded that European countries should not exercise in the Western Hemisphere even the rights of intervention granted by international law. But the least modest element in American interventionism was its basic moral principle, holding that the United States had the duty as well as the right to exercise in the Western Hemisphere what President Theodore Roosevelt called an "international police power."

It is clear not only that order is as undeniable a value as sunshine, but also that the nation which conceives of itself as an international policeman may, without believing itself imperialistic, be as self-assertive as disturbers of the peace. However, it is not at once clear why international policing has seemed to Americans a power for which they had a warrant, indeed an exclusive warrant. The mystery is the greater because Americans until recently subordinated orderliness in their domestic economy to the same rugged individualism which Latin Americans have preferred to express in politics. Why, in any event, should a nation believe it within its capacity, right, and duty to enforce order in a district as large as a hemisphere — without authorization, restraints of *habeas corpus,* and collaboration?

To answer this question about the policeman's moral psychology requires an approach which combines appreciation with suspicion. It is a question which has been neglected by such participants in the recent argument over American intervention as have used only one of these characteristics. Anti-imperialists have usually been too much engrossed in indicting motives to consider the ideas which made imperialists feel more like policemen than criminals. On the other hand, apologists for our Latin-American policy have ordinarily been too much occupied in establishing the legal and moral justification of intervention to analyze the national egoisms which have made many American interventionists feel more like agents of Providence than ordinary policemen. In consequence, both sides have overlooked a consideration which renders both the moral ideology and the pride of American interventionism more understandable. As what follows seems to suggest, the doctrine of police power is historically and logically a derivative, in large measure, of the philosophy of manifest destiny; this is to say that, despite its elements of reasonableness and modesty, the interventionist principle represents essentially a pretension to special prerogatives by virtue of the special duties involved in the peculiar mission of a nation with preeminent capacities.

To relate the motive of intervention to the ideology of traditional American nationalism seems at first to go counter to salient facts of American history. For this ideology not only sponsored the antinomian conception of " the higher title " but was long almost as much opposed to intervention as is the philosophical anarchist to the policeman. America achieved its independence by a revolution, an assault upon the established political and social order. The Tory Jonathan Boucher did anticipate something of the twentieth-century attitude toward Latin-American disturbances when he called the right of revolution " a damnable doctrine, derived from Lucifer, the father of rebellion." [3] But to rebellious Americans as to Aristotle, revolution was the expression of the desire for equality. Jefferson was so sympathetic to political change as to affirm that once in every twenty years a revolution was a necessary catharsis.[4] It was conservatives especially who approved Washington's proclamation and admonition of neutrality with respect to the political affairs of others. " If there is any one characteristic of the United States which is more marked than any other," wrote Secretary Seward in 1866, "it is that they have from the time of Washington adhered to the principle of non-intervention."[5] The pronouncement which best expressed this principle with reference to Latin America was the Monroe Doctrine. Alluding to the rebelling Spanish-American colonies, regarded by the Holy Alliance as subversive of all decent order, Monroe spoke the classic words: "It is still the true policy of the United States to leave the parties to themselves, in the hope that other powers will pursue the same course."[6]

Yet it was the policy of opposing the imperialism of Europe in America which developed into the doctrine justifying the intervention of the United States in America. This Hegelian development of thesis into antithesis appears less paradoxical when it is remembered that the Monroe Doctrine had in it a latent element of interventionism at the outset. To ban Europe's system from the Western Hemisphere as dangerous to America's "peace and safety" was to attempt a diplomatic intervention in European affairs; that is, the caveat imposed a restriction even upon Europe's legal relations and actions. In curious contrast with later American interventionists, Monroe did not intervene to stop revolutionary disorder but to prevent others from stopping it. Moreover, the Monroe Doctrine was also an intervention in the affairs of American countries, as was pointed out by Representative Smith in 1854 when he said that it "invests us with the right of regulating the relations between the people of this hemisphere and the people of the other."[7] While the Doctrine did not make America "dictator of the earth," it claimed, as Smith's attack on our "pride" charged, privileges in this hemisphere which transgressed the theoretical rights not only of European peoples but also of American.

True, to deprive American peoples of the right to accept European sovereignty was not a serious restriction when they themselves wanted independence. Most people of the United States regarded the Monroe Doctrine as no restriction at all upon Latin Americans, whose "interests" seemed to Jefferson and his compatriots to be "the same" as those of Americans.[8]

Indeed, they believed that in Monroe's dictum the United States, in Webster's words of 1826, had done something useful for "the cause of civil liberty." [9] Implicit in this idea was the assumption that absolutist Europe's control could be nothing but sinister while democratic America's could be nothing but protective.

This very conception of the United States as protector, together with the more selfish aim of preventing European interventions prejudicial to America's peace and safety, was to encourage actual intervention in Latin America. The notion that special love gives special privileges is capable of surprising growth, ending even in chastisement. The first stage in this development was the doctrine that the United States should respond to an American people's appeal for protection whenever assistance was essential to ward off European intervention. The first notable expression of this idea was President Polk's recommendation in 1848 that the United States occupy Yucatan in order to prevent European intervention in this Mexican state. The occupation would have been an infringement upon Mexican sovereignty but it was requested by the people of Yucatan as protection against marauding Indians. From the standpoint of international philanthropy Senator Cass declared: "Providence has placed us, in some measure, at the head of the republics of this continent, and there never has been a better opportunity offered to any nation to fulfill the high duty confided to it than the present . . ." [10] Interventionism as well as expansionism was nourished by the dogma of a manifest destiny to extend and protect democracy in America.

In the subsequent decade Americans showed an enlargement of their sense of providential responsibility by extending interventionist projects to Mexico proper. In 1858 President Buchanan proposed temporary occupation of two of its northern provinces and in the following year military penetration to its interior. During the Mexican civil wars which occasioned these proposals, Americans for the first time became conscious of political disorder as a condition which called for drastic intervention. President Buchanan feared that Mexico's injuries to European interests might cause some European nation to intervene, " and thus force us to intervene at last, under circumstances of increased difficulty, for the maintenance of our established policy." Associated with danger to the Monroe Doctrine, Latin-American disorder was and remained repugnant less because of itself than because of the possibility that it might lead European nations to attempt its suppression. Fear of this possibility caused Americans of the 'fifties to consider military occupation of another country without its express consent; for Mexico did not solicit America's occupation as did Yucatan previously. Nevertheless, the interventionism of the 'fifties was by no means as imperialistic as that of the twentieth century. For President Buchanan's proposal for intervention was based upon the assumption that America, as Mexico's " good neighbor," owed " a helping hand " to the friendly Constitutional party, presumably favorable to an intervention directed against its enemies.[11] America's intrusive hand could seem only helpful to those like Minister Corwin who believed that " the United States are the only safe guardians of the independence and true civilization of this continent." [12] In fact, the sectional difficulties culminating in the Civil War restrained the guardian of the Americas both from its own philanthropic intervention in Mexico and from opposition to Europe's sinister intervention.

However, the three decades following the Civil War witnessed developments which not only revived but strengthened the conception of the United States as the guardian angel of American liberties. In the first place there were such practical efforts in behalf of Latin-American peoples as Seward's diplomatic assistance in terminating Maximilian's empire in Mexico and the diplomatic activity of the Grant régime during the Ten Years War in Cuba. In the same period America's policy of anti-intervention came to crystallization. Intervention for any purpose but the temporary protection of endangered nationals or the preservation of Latin-American independence seemed to Seward and succeeding administrations to be banned by " the respect of the American people for the free sovereignty of the people in every other state." [13] To be sure, one must not exaggerate the influence of liberal sentiments upon the American attitude toward intervention. One must note also the motive of parsimony acknowledged by Secretary of State Frelinghuysen when he declared in 1882 that to intervene in the Americas even for the prevention of war was to " tax our people for the exclusive benefit of foreign nations." [14] In these years there were as yet no large American investments in Latin America to overbalance such hesitation at expense. On the other hand, this period did witness a growing realization of the national interest involved in maintenance of the Monroe Doctrine. Whenever the Monroe Doctrine was at stake Americans associated self-interest with altruism by considering that in this pronouncement their country had proclaimed herself, as Secretary of State Bayard affirmed in 1887, " the protector of this western world, in which she is by far the strongest power, from the intrusion of European sovereignties." [15]

When Great Britain in 1895 pressed against Venezuela claims which seemed to Americans unjust (until they finally came to investigate them), America assumed more fully than ever before the hemispheric " guardianship " which Senator Turpie derived from both America's power and its nobility.[16] President Cleveland's insistence that Great Britain arbitrate its boundary dispute with Venezuela was based nominally upon Monroe's caveat against Europe's territorial encroachment in the Western Hemisphere. Yet it could with considerable reason seem to Senator Sewell that

> . . . the deduction to be drawn from the spirit and the letter of the message is that the mere acquisition of territory is not the cause of the offense, but the real cause is the attempt of a European power to impose upon and oppress a weaker American State or nation.
>
> I can but think that this is a new departure; that it practically means that this Government must assume a protectorate over Mexico, Central America, and all the South American States . . . [17]

A worse departure seemed portended by Olney's declaration that " the United States is practically sovereign on this continent, and its fiat is law upon the subjects to which it confines its interposition." [18] But these words were not as frightful in intent as in sound. They were meant only to deter Great

Britain and other European powers from questioning Monroe's fiat that the territory or independence of American countries be not infringed in any way. They marked an advance over previous policy only in the sense that America's interpositions in behalf of the Monroe Doctrine were no longer confined by doubt of its power to enforce the Doctrine.

This heightened consciousness of interventionist rights under the Monroe Doctrine was a potent determinant of American attitudes toward the Cuban difficulties beginning in 1896. The revolt of the Cubans against Spain was regarded by Americans as the struggle of a liberty-loving and noble American people against a despotic and decadent European monarchy. Spain's attempted suppression of this revolt did not, however, violate the Monroe Doctrine in its original form. It was rather a case for adherence to Monroe's assurance that Europe's existing American possessions would be respected. But almost from the start sentimentalists and demagogues desired intervention to the extent of recognizing Cuban independence and interposing good offices in its behalf. To justify this policy they invoked the spirit if not the letter of the Monroe Doctrine. In a Senate committee's report of 1896, advocating recognition of Cuban independence, the Monroe Doctrine was described as "creating an American law and practice of intervention exclusive of the European within the range of its influence." It was asserted further that, though the American policy was based on the same principle of security as that underlying the European, "so sweeping a right of intervention" as the American "had never been claimed." Its broad scope seemed to give the right "to intervene in favor of communities that plainly displayed their wish and their power to be American." [19] By 1898 this had become the view of the majority of the Senate Committee on Foreign Relations. In its report on the declaration of war it affirmed that, whereas the balance of power was the European principle of intervention, the Monroe Doctrine was the American. This somewhat unusual theory that there can be distinctive national principles of intervention was supported by a citation from Pomeroy to the effect that intervention cannot be regulated by the positive international law but "must be relegated to the domain of those high politics, those principles of expediency, which control the conduct, both domestic and foreign, of nations." [20]

The non-technical populace related intervention not to the Monroe Doctrine but rather, as did McKinley's war message, to "the cause of humanity," which became especially America's concern because "right at our door." [21] However, closer examination of the interventionist ideology reveals that America's humanitarian duty was in part based upon a principle which had been evolved from the Monroe Doctrine — the duty of assisting any American people wishing release from European absolutism and oppression. Thus Representative Cochran declared that he would vote for the fifty-million bill because he regarded it as "premonitory of another forward step in the attainment of manifest destiny . . . dedicating the New World to liberty and republicanism." [22] Representative Norton proclaimed piously that "this country should stand as the realization of His purpose in building up a heritage, erected on the grand foundation principle, the chief corner stone of American institutions, the rights of the people." [23] In supporting the declaration of war Senator Wolcott affirmed that "the war . . . must be fought because it is the manifest destiny of this Republic to stand forever upon the Western Hemisphere a sentinel of liberty." [24]

The ideal of intervention in behalf of liberty had the traditional elements of the dogma of manifest destiny — the notion of America's preeminent moral distinction and that of its representation of Providence by virtue of this distinction. Thus it seemed to the *Columbus Dispatch* that "rarely, if ever, has a nation gone to war with motives so pure and ideals so high as those which actuate the United States today." But this was to be expected, it added, for "never before has so grand a government existed" as this, a government "divinely aided in all that it has done for itself" and "in what it undertakes to do in humanity for others." [25] The *Kansas City Times* affirmed that "no other people could have been commissioned by that power which encourages and stimulates progress in human affairs to do this work." [26] The liberation of Cuba was nothing less than (to quote the *Pittsburg Catholic*) to carry out "the designs of Providence on this continent for the betterment of the race, and the upholding and conserving the rights of the individual MAN." [27]

To be sure, it is not clear that Americans intervened with quite the undiluted altruism which these utterances assumed. The frank President Cleveland emphasized that Americans had a concern with Cuba which was "by no means of a wholly sentimental or philanthropic character." [28] Even the idealizing McKinley pointed out in his war message that this concern arose in large part from Cuba's menace to American life and property.[29] A fact which McKinley of course did not point out was that war answered also to such unphilanthropic motives as rage against Spain, the need for an exciting form of national self-assertion, and the militaristic thesis that "war is healthy to a nation." [30]

Moreover, the judgments of subsequent historians and of well-informed contemporaries alike suggest that, probably in consequence of their less philanthropic impulses, interventionists of 1898 acted with somewhat less than the degree of wisdom which one likes to think is bestowed by Providence upon its agents. A dispassionate historian of the subject writes that "the same ends, peace in Cuba and justice to all people concerned — in themselves good — could have been achieved by peaceful means safer for the wider interests of humanity." [31] So thought America's Minister to Spain, who upon Spain's last-minute accession to virtually all American demands, cabled to McKinley that "with your power of action sufficiently free you will win the fight on your own lines," that is, the attainment of Cuban independence through diplomatic influence.[32] But from the standpoint of political expediency McKinley's action was no longer free when the nation clamored for war. The individual exercise of police power does apparently have the danger of all punitive actions without judicial process, especially those of an impetuous democracy.

The nationalist's assumption of police power is also precarious in that, despite Murat Halstead's assertion of America's "consciousness of manifest destiny," [33] there is no telling how far beyond the original objective the destiny released by force will carry. The objective of the Cuban intervention, to which Cubans seemed to give implicit consent, was the fulfilment of a mission to protect American peoples from European violation of their independence. But this intervention proved to be the prelude to a policy of interference which disregarded the consent of American peoples and infringed upon their sovereignty. By what strange process did interventionism develop from a doctrine of liberation to a doctrine of imperialism?

The first impetus to this development lay in the sequel of the Cuban intervention itself. One course of education in imperialism took place in the distant Philippines, where, by virtue of opportunities and desires arising during a war of liberation, there ensued a war of subjugation. Even though not intervention, suppression of the Philippine revolt helped to establish the ideology of imperialistic intervention by requiring Americans to find reasons for subjugating rather than freeing the under-dog. One reason maintained force to be the necessary instrument of that civilizing and administrative mission to which Senator Beveridge thought Americans specially called by God in consequence of their racial qualities and even their devotion to self-government. This idea, as Sumner Welles points out, was the nucleus of the humanitarian imperialism which later, through its appeal to national vanity, grew "out of all proportions." [34] But the chief contribution of our Oriental imperialistic adventure to interventionism came by way of its development of a concern for civilized peoples, not the uncivilized. As was pointed out by Professor Powers, America's process of expansion represented the use of "coercive consolidation" in "the establishment of universal order." [35] To the imperialist, as Ferdinand Lion has written, "order is the highest value." [36] The reason of this valuation is ironically suggested by Walter Hines Page's comment upon the English: "They have a mania for order, sheer order, order for the sake of order and — of trade." [37] Many Americans had a similar mania when revolt in the Philippines menaced their peaceful enjoyment of the vast Oriental trade which seemed the salvation from their industrial overproduction.

Even before the outbreak of the revolt ex-Minister Denby wrote in favor of a "Doctrine of Intervention" in accordance with which it was America's duty "to intervene in all matters occurring abroad in which it is to our interest to intervene," that is, "our material interest." [38] It was significant that America's first noteworthy intervention occurred at just the time when its foreign investments were beginning to reach a substantial volume; but whereas the economic motive of the Cuban intervention was merely defense of established interests from undue injury, Denby's words mark the transition to a more aggressive interpretation of intervention for trade. However, most other Americans shrank fom Denby's frank national egoism and based the case for intervention on the more edifying ground of world interest. "Disorganization and disorder," wrote Professor Talcott Williams in 1900, "will not be long permitted in a world grown as small as ours." [39] In the same year the *Outlook* affirmed that "either we must take up our share of the responsibilities of keeping the modern world in order, or we must cease to profit by what other nations are doing in this direction." [40] America's participation in the suppression of the Boxer disorders indicated that it would fail neither the world nor its own interests. A prophecy which touched on regions nearer home was made by Charles A. Conant in a work of 1900: "The government of adventurers and financial freebooters is coming to an end in Europe, Africa, and Asia, and it may yet be the mission of the United States to bring it to an end in portions of Latin America." [41]

That Cuba was the first scene of America's performance of this mission in Latin America was another consequence of the intervention of 1898. The war for liberation, undertaken in the anti-imperialistic spirit that passed the Teller Amendment forswearing annexation, could not be terminated without a measure of imperialism. For the Platt Amendment was not only imposed by coercion but provided for prerogatives of coercion which America might exercise in perpetuity. America obtained, together with control over Cuba's sanitation and finances, the right to intervene in Cuba in the event of either foreign menace to Cuba's independence or domestic menace to its order. Police power was thus legalized. America's first intervention for the freedom of an American people eventuated in its first assumption of a semi-protectorate, leaving Cuba nominally free but making it (in the words of Roosevelt) "a part of our international political system." [42]

What had brought about this historical irony? It must be confessed that one factor was our impression of the Cubans themselves, seen at closer range. Their quarrelsomeness with their liberators and each other provoked not only the satire of Mr. Dooley but also disillusionment on the part of former admirers. From an excess of admiration it had come to an excess of depreciation, exemplified by General Young's observation that the insurgents were "absolutely devoid of honor or gratitude" and were "no more capable of self-government than the savages of Africa." [43] Even those who were less harsh in judgment felt that the present capacity of the Cubans for self-government was dubious. The same ideal of order which once dictated war against the ineptly governing Spaniards now seemed to call for restrictive action against the Cubans also. It was clear that strict accordance with the Teller Amendment, renouncing permanent control as well as annexation, would be as dangerous to America's political welfare as would have been the leaving of Cuba in the hands of Spain.

Whereas the altruistic ideology of the interventionists of 1898 placed greatest emphasis upon duty to the Cubans, that of the defenders of the Platt Amendment stressed principally duty to the world. Our obligations to the world at large were derived by Senator Platt from the act of intervention itself — with the more reason because a concert of the great European powers had sought to prevent it.[43a] To abandon Cuba to its own turbulent politicians seemed an imperilment, as the *Boston Journal* said, of "the peace of the world." [44] Under the circumstances Representative Scudder spoke angrily with reference to the obstructive Cuban politicians who sought true independence: "This Republic has done with nonsense." It proposed to accept its responsibilities because "it recognizes alike the dominance of duty and the duty of dominance, wherever it is under contract with mankind to plant civilization, order, pacification, and reasonable liberty." [45]

The difference between liberating and imperialistic interventionism lies evidently in the conception of the source of the policeman's contract. The tendency to conceive the world at large as its beneficiary was developed further by the next intervention of the United States — the first to trespass upon the sovereignty of an independent American state. To be sure, the treaty of 1846 with Colombia authorized the United States to maintain freedom of transit across the Isthmus; but neither reasonable legal inference nor America's own actions from 1846 till 1903 justified the interpretation that this provision authorized the United States to maintain freedom of transit along the Isthmus by preventing the landing or transportation of Colombian troops. Roosevelt was interested in order and not in law, the two being not always inseparable. That Roosevelt conceived himself as exercising a moral police power seems to be indicated by his comparison of America's action to that of a policeman jailing a blackmailer.[46]

According to Roosevelt, " the interests of collective civilization " gave him a warrant for such jailings. The ideology underlying this imposing phrase has been considered in a preceding chapter. It only remains to note the paradox that the comprehensive conception of collective civilization tended to make sharper in the American mind the distinction between Latin-American interests, upon which the altruism of the United States had once concentrated, and those of the commercially progressive powers. For it was the commercial world powers, aside from the United States chiefly European, which formed the great bulk of the collective civilization requiring the canal. Roosevelt did not make bold to identify Colombia with Latin America; yet when he wrote to a friend that he would have treated a " responsible Power " differently he named as examples four European countries.[47] Bunau-Varilla stated openly the invidious distinction which was perhaps in Roosevelt's mind:

> There will be room for a 'Roosevelt Doctrine,' in international law, perfecting and completing the Monroe doctrine. The right of protecting the South American interests against European interference . . . will have to be counterbalanced by the proclamation of the right of protect-

ing the European (and North American interests) against South American interference.[48]

Roosevelt was in fact shortly to formulate a doctrine somewhat like the one suggested — a doctrine which called for America's representation of European interests on a broader scale than had ever before been conceived. Yet strange to say, the conception of Europe as chief beneficiary of intervention was to be presented, not as a counterbalance to the Monroe Doctrine, but as a corollary of it.

This new enlargement of the doctrine of intervention did not, of course, come about merely through philanthropy, but very largely through the increased interest, publicly noted by Roosevelt as early as 1902,[49] in the Caribbean environs of America's prospective Isthmian canal. In the very midst of the Panama crisis of 1903, Whitelaw Reid, in a letter to Representative Gillett, prophesied the "practical protectorate over the Isthmus" which was shortly afterward realized in the treaty with Panama. Reid's simultaneous observation that the Monroe Doctrine would necessitate just such a protectorate over the entire Caribbean presaged the reinterpretation of the Monroe Doctrine with reference to the intervention of Europe in the Caribbean region.[50]

In the Venezuelan issue of 1901-1902 President Roosevelt had at first been willing to allow European countries to "spank" any Latin-American country for misconduct so long as intervention did not threaten seizure of territory.[51] But in the last part of the crisis Roosevelt retreated from this liberal view and insisted — if his own contested account can be trusted — that Germany accept arbitration. While becoming sterner with European powers he adopted a more threatening tone with American countries as well. No independent nation in America, he declared in his annual message of 1902, needed to have the slightest fear of aggression from the United States; but beneath this assurance lurked a threat in the form of the attached provision that it must "maintain order within its own borders and . . . discharge its just obligations to foreigners." [52] In 1904 the Dominican Republic, unable to pay its at least partially just obligations, faced possible intervention of three European powers eager to reimburse themselves from its customs. Such was the situation which led President Roosevelt in his annual message of 1904 to enunciate his famous doctrine of America's exercise of international police power. The passage containing the doctrine speaks softly at the beginning but leads finally to a flourish of the big stick:

> It is not true that the United States feels any land hunger or entertains any projects as regards the other nations of the Western Hemisphere save such as are for their welfare. All that this country desires is to see the neighboring countries stable, orderly, and prosperous. Any country whose people conduct themselves well can count upon our hearty friendship. If a nation shows that it knows how to act with reasonable efficiency and decency in social and political matters, if it keeps order and pays its obligations, it need fear no interference from the United States. Chronic wrongdoing, or an impotence which results in a general loosening of the ties of civilized society, may in America, as elsewhere, ultimately require intervention by some civilized nation, and in the Western Hemisphere the adherence of the United States to the Monroe Doctrine may force the United States, however reluctantly, in flagrant cases of such wrongdoing or impotence, to the exercise of an international police power.[53]

Its declaration of disinterested motive does not prevent Roosevelt's declaration from being one of the most extreme modern affirmations of the right of intervention. The far-reaching character of Roosevelt's interventionism is apparent in three of its features. In the first place, Roosevelt did not limit intervention to legal self-protective measures, but made it coextensive with a "police power" embracing any remedy short of deprivation of independence. In the second place, he did not restrict intervention to legally recognized occasions, but used broad moral criteria which, as one of Roosevelt's contemporary critics pointed out, permit interference with any act or condition disapproved.[54] Roosevelt condemned even something which today is practiced by most of the best peoples and tolerated by the rest — not paying international debts. In the third place, what Roosevelt euphemistically called "international" police power amounted really to exercise of police power by one nation which demanded a monopoly of such power in half the globe. With some justice the *Providence Journal* declared that Roosevelt's doctrine tended toward "an essential suzerainty, latent if not always active, of the United States over all the countries to the south of us." [55]

It is easier to state Roosevelt's stipulations than to analyze their integrating rationale. This is not made plain by the common exposition which stops with describing Roosevelt's principle as a corollary of the Monroe Doctrine. Roosevelt's ideology is actually a complex structure, the foundation of which has nothing to do with Monroe. The basis of the doctrine of police power is a justification of intervention by a civilized state in countries guilty either of doing wrong or of impotently doing nothing. This is the antithesis of Monroe's doctrine that the true policy of both Europe and the United States was to leave revolutionary peoples to themselves. Roosevelt was not disposed by temperament to leave to themselves parties who strongly offended his sensibilities, especially his "passion for law and order." [56] Nor was he so disposed by his education, which included study of law under the imperialistic John Burgess. Doubtless Roosevelt had read Burgess's exposition of the Teutonic nations' manifest destiny:

> Finally, we must conclude, from the manifest mission of the Teutonic nations, that interference in the affairs of populations not wholly barbaric, which have made some progress in state organization, but which manifest incapacity to solve the problem of political civilization with any degree of completeness, is a justifiable policy. No one can question that it is in the interest of the world's civilization that law and order and the true liberty consistent therewith shall reign everywhere upon the globe.[57]

Roosevelt's acceptance of these ideas was already evident in 1899 when he justified America's interference in the affairs of the Filipinos and advocated suppression of their rebellion in the interest of their true liberty.[58] Shortly before he became president Roosevelt spoke words which showed further his virile conception of international altruism:

> Barbarism has, and can have, no place in a civilized world. It is our duty toward the people living in barbarism to see that they are freed from their chains, and we can free them only by destroying barbarism

itself. The missionary, the merchant, and the soldier may each have a part to play in this destruction, and in the consequent uplifting of the people.[59]

Roosevelt only needed to conceive of certain Latin-American peoples as "not wholly civilized" in order to develop this "barbarity" theory, against the dangers of which Grotius himself had warned, into the first thesis of his doctrine of police power.

Somewhat surprisingly, the second thesis in Roosevelt's train of reasoning forbade Europe to exercise in America the very right of intervention which had been justified by the first. Roosevelt's words have seemed to imply that even a European power's temporary occupation of American territory is incompatible with the Monroe Doctrine. This interpretation of the Doctrine is not only false but had previously been rejected by Roosevelt himself. What Roosevelt clearly meant to say was that such an occupation was incompatible with the security of the Doctrine. And in the light of history Roosevelt was reasonable in fearing that temporary occupation of territory might lead by the logic of events to permanent control if not sovereignty. But, through a faith in his own country's superior self-restraint which previous history scarcely justified, Roosevelt overlooked the possibility that permanent control might be the outcome also of American intervention.

For it was Roosevelt's conclusion that the United States had the right and duty of undertaking all the interventions which the iniquity or incompetence of other American peoples justified. This conclusion does not in fact follow from the principles from which Roosevelt explicitly deduced it. It does not follow from "adherence to the Monroe Doctrine," the dominant spirit of which was opposed to intervention whether European or American. It does not follow even from Roosevelt's ban upon intervention by Europe, despite the fact that he wrote to Root that "if we intend to say 'Hands off' to the powers of Europe, sooner or later we must keep order ourselves."[60] The consistent anti-interventionist, somewhat careless of the difficulties of practical statesmanship, would have conceived that saying "Hands off" to Europe imposed the obligation upon the United States also to refrain from intervention. The true moral consideration necessitating Roosevelt's doctrine of America's police power was the fact that he forbade European intervention after starting out with the general assumption that intervention is legitimate and necessary. He was unwilling that the Monroe Doctrine should be used by any American republic "as a shield" to protect it from "the consequences of its own misdeeds against foreign nations."[61] But since he was also unwilling that Europe should punish these misdeeds, the only alternative was that America herself should undertake the duties of the policeman.

By such a rationale Roosevelt deviated from Monroe's conception of America's true policy as one of non-intervention and virtually affirmed that (to jangle Monroe's words) it was now the true policy of the United States to interfere, in the hope that other parties would pursue a different course. Such interference with Latin America had as one purpose, indeed, protection of Latin America from Europe. But Roosevelt also oriented intervention toward the new and heterodox purpose of protecting Europe from Latin America — an aim which on the principles of his moral ideology was more important. Thus the traditional conception of America's manifest destiny as guardian of America was partially eclipsed by the conception of Burgess that America was the representative in the Western Hemisphere of the interests and ideals of Teutonic civilization. The transition from liberating to imperialistic intervention is now complete.

It must be added that Roosevelt's "big stick" was bigger than his actual aggressiveness, that it was flourished more for avoidance than for incitement of action, and that after 1904 his policy in Latin America contained nothing more imperialistic than his helpful supervision of the Dominican Republic's financial affairs and his reluctant intervention in Cuba by treaty right. But despite Roosevelt's repudiation of such a view, certain Americans, as C. F. Dole's article of 1905 pointed out, had been brought to the belief in a "manifest destiny" of our lordship over the Western Hemisphere.[62] And both the practice and the ideology of imperialistic police power were to become still more drastic when some Latin-American peoples adhered to turbulence despite both threats and patience.

The Taft Administration's application of police power included diplomatic pressure in the Dominican Republic's domestic affairs, the despatch of marines with the effect of rescuing a favored Nicaraguan faction, and, most conspicuously, the attempt to place economic functions of Central American countries under American political supervision and financial control. In the judgment of many, such enterprises were prompted exclusively by an economic aggressiveness such as is suggested by the sinister-sounding phrase, "Dollar Diplomacy." It was, indeed, the avowed purpose of the Taft Administration to lend what it pleased to call legitimate support to American economic interests everywhere. But the usual anti-imperialist critic overlooks the likelihood that in the Caribbean its political or defensive interest was primary and to a large extent used economic measures as means. The political motive of America's Caribbean policy was explained by Secretary of State Knox as follows:

> The logic of political geography and of strategy, and now our tremendous national interest created by the Panama Canal, make the safety, the peace, and the prosperity of Central America and the zone of the Caribbean of paramount interest to the Government of the United States. Thus the malady of revolutions and financial collapse is most acute precisely in the region where it is most dangerous to us. It is here that we seek to apply a remedy.[63]

The remedy was the much maligned Dollar Diplomacy, productive only of relatively small direct profits, but more interesting to the Government than to bankers. It was described by President Taft after speaking of the importance of the Monroe Doctrine in the Caribbean region:

> It is therefore essential that the countries within that sphere shall be removed from the jeopardy involved by heavy foreign debt and chaotic national finances and from the ever-present danger of international complications due to disorder at home. Hence the United States has been glad to encourage and support American bankers who were willing to lend a hand to the financial rehabilitation of such countries . . .[64]

While this economic diplomacy was perhaps "international

philanthropy,"[65] it was also a type of imperialism; for it placed under American control such elements of sovereignty as customs control, the pledge for repayment of philanthropy.

Their very effort to escape the practical consequences of their original doctrine that police power is justified *post delictum* led American statesmen to the no less imperialistic doctrine that police power is justified *ante delictum.* The latter doctrine, nevertheless, derives its aspect of validity from the former; the doctrine of preventive police power is a corollary of Roosevelt's corollary to the Monroe Doctrine. Therefore the Taft Administration continued the traditional arguments with respect to the obligations imposed by that doctrine, which, Secretary Knox said in Panama, "Providence" had entrusted to the United States.[66] However, Knox also supported Roosevelt's doctrine of intervention by a consideration which had not before been adduced. Roosevelt said merely that by forbidding European intervention America took on itself the obligation to intervene in Europe's behalf. It was now further alleged that, in the words of Secretary Knox, "we are in the eyes of the world and because of the Monroe Doctrine, held responsible for the order of Central America."[67] Similarly the *Outlook,* in an editorial of 1911 on intervention in disorderly Mexico, affirmed that "it has become more and more clear to the people of Europe . . . that if we are to insist on prohibiting foreign intervention in North and South America, we must insist with equal effectiveness on preventing those social and political disorders which justly call for foreign intervention."[68] This was to say that Europe had acquiesced in America's assumption through the Monroe Doctrine of "a moral protectorate for the Western Hemisphere."[69] It was to say further that Europe had tacitly bestowed upon the United States a mandate to protect its interests in America by intervention. The assumption with regard to the mandate was gratuitous, save with respect to European delegations which were perforce given in particular instances. The protests of Germany and France against exclusion from participation in the Haitian customs control gave evidence in 1914 of European resentment of America's pretensions to monopoly. But the doctrine of the European mandate, pleasing to American pride, became an enduring element in the ideology of police power and brought to its support an added idea of international responsibility.

The doctrine basing police power upon responsibility to Europe had no sooner reached its full logical development than it ceased to be the dominant feature of American interventionism. The idea which next came to the top in this permutation of ideas was a derivative of the original conception that the United States was the protector of Latin America. This shift in premises was apparently occasioned by a development incongruous with it — the arrival of imperialist practice at its greatest height.

Curiously enough, it was not until the administration of the theoretically anti-imperialistic Wilson that the American Government carried police power to the point of imposing upon independent American states military governments which virtually jailed the alleged culprits. Haiti, the Dominican Republic, and Mexico were all the scenes of military incursions which were not only without treaty sanction but were against the protest of native governments. The interventions in Haiti and the Dominican Republic resolved themselves into prolonged military occupations involving unlimited control of both foreign and domestic affairs. Particularly in the Caribbean, where revolutions had usually been conducted with extreme care for Americans, these interventions went far beyond the temporary and limited measures to which jurists ordinarily limit armed interposition during revolutions. Their drastic character arose from the design to "clean up," once and for all, political, social and economic disorder which threatened American lives or property and European respect for, if not acquiescence in, America's pretension to be the policing power of the region between the Rio Grande and Panama. Just when weariness overtook the aggressive spirit of manifest destiny, destiny punished for the over-ambition of the past by producing external conditions which permitted America no rest.

The accompanying interventionist ideology comprised all the doctrines of preceding administrations but its chief thesis was an imperialistic version of the older idea of America's philanthropic mission in relation to Latin America. Wilson developed into imperialistic interventionism the doctrine which he attributed to Monroe — that the United States intended to be Latin America's big brother whether the relationship was desired or not.[70] This fraternal conception of police power arose from the necessity of harmonizing an unprecedented degree of anti-imperialist philosophy with an equally unprecedented degree of imperialistic action. Imperialism can be made tolerable for anti-imperialists only by the presumption of benefits for the coerced. Thus the interventionism of the Wilson Administration was exemplified by official declarations to the effect that the United States sought in the Dominican military occupation the return of the Dominican Republic to " internal order," [71] and had no object in Haiti save " the establishment of a stable and firm government by the Haitian people." [72] The present conception of the policeman's mission portrayed the United States as protector of Latin America not so much from Europe (occupied with the World War) as from itself. In other words, it assumed this particular policeman to be preeminently qualified for uplift work. Wherein did this preeminent qualification seem to lie?

The answers were various. President Wilson's philosophy of humanitarian imperialism combined an humble disclaimer of any overlordship with a proud and inevitably imperialistic philosophy of manifest destiny which held that " America was created to realize " certain moral values of Pan-Americanism.[73] One of these values was mentioned by him in connection with a discussion of the turbulent Mexican situation of 1913:

> We are the friends of constitutional government in America; we are more than its friends, we are its champions; because in no other way can our neighbors, to whom we would wish in every way to make proof of our friendship, work out their own development in peace and liberty.[74]

Another value which America champions was stated by Wilson with curious mingling of anti-imperialism and interventionism:

> America has always stood resolutely and absolutely for the right of every people to determine its own destiny and its own affairs. I am so absolute a disciple of that doctrine that I am ready to do that thing

and observe that principle in dealing with the troubled affairs of our distressed neighbor to the south.[75]

Further moral qualifications for the policeman's task were pointed out by other interventionists. William Bayard Hale, Wilson's personal representative in Mexico, saw "the constitution" of "Our Moral Empire in America" in "the right of Justice, Humanity, and Decency to call to be their champions those who have grown strong under their favor." [76] A writer in the organ of the Navy League declared imperialism to be particularly America's duty because "we are idealists and are therefore bound by establishing protectorates over the weak to protect them from unmoral *Kultur*." [77]

Obviously, however, the policeman's business required in addition to moral qualifications certain capacities of a practical character. To some, as Chester Lloyd Jones observed in a book of 1916, America's actions in the Caribbean were the logical corollary of its supremacy in population and material wealth. Jones himself asserted that "in America, as in all the world, strong nations will lead the weak" and that therefore the United States must fulfil in the Caribbean the rôle made possible by "a position of primacy." [78] Representative Fess laid emphasis upon the quality as well as the quantity of America's population: "This country, with a hundred million people, with the sole purpose to secure the highest welfare of all concerned, is the one policing power to maintain Americanism on this continent." [79] President Wilson adduced another practical consideration in his reference to America's "tacitly conceded obligations as the nearest friend of San Domingo in her relations with the rest of the world." [80] Adjacency dictated similar obligations not only to Mexico, to whom America was "nearest friend," [81] but to all the Latin-American republics of the continent. For it seemed, as Professor Usher wrote, that if any country was to police Latin-American countries "the United States is so situated as to do it at a minimum cost and with maximum effect." [82]

All these considerations, but particularly the notion of America's championship of democracy, help to explain the paradox of President Wilson's imperialism. As Sumner Welles [83] has observed in his discussion of Wilson's Dominican policy, this imperialism had the aim of bringing closer " the development of constitutional liberty in the world." [84] The most radical imperialist in intervention as in expansion is apt to be the one most devoted to liberty. His exalted moral consciousness may destroy conscience itself in the sense that it removes all sense of limitations upon the means of attaining an ideal. Imperialism is even less troubling to the ethical interventionist than to the ethical expansionist, the former being reassured by the assumption that his infringement of sovereignty is but a temporary inconsistency which will eventuate in a greater democracy.

In point of fact the corrective enterprise on the island of Santo Domingo succeeded in everything better than in training for self-government. The authorities responsible for the political education of Haiti " twice dissolved her legislative assembly at the point of the gun, wrote a constitution and forced it upon the Haitian people, and set up on Haitian soil a government contrary to all the principles of political freedom." [85] In the five years when Americans held the Dominican Republic under martial law, " public meetings were forbidden, the press censored, protesters court-martialed," and " every governmental function was taken over by American marines." [86] To be sure, these severities and repressions were due not to design of the Government but to America's lack of preparation for such protectorates, limitations of the military mind in political administration, and the almost inevitable tendencies of militaristic reform itself. Moreover, these later acknowledged and regretted evils were perhaps overbalanced by substantial improvements in the external elements of civilization, such as sanitation, roadbuilding, and security of life. Unfortunately the more self-respecting natives were like Latin Americans in general in appreciating these material benefits less than the purely sentimental satisfactions of independent sovereignty.

The history of the Mexican issue revealed another disheartening contingency which the interventionist failed to take sufficiently into reckoning. He believed that " destiny " (as the Charleston *Courier* said) called to a trespass ending with benefaction and not with land-grabbing.[87] However, developments in national opinion showed that to intervene is to give hostages to a fate which may well be the destiny believed in by the expansionist. The difficulties of establishing continental order by half-way expedients suggested to some that the only practicable consummation of the policeman's intervention lay in giving the offending people a happy life-sentence of confinement within America's own political household.

That the policeman should marry the criminal was a once dominant theory which had declined but never completely died out. Many expansionists of the nineteenth century, particularly of the 'fifties, believed that the disorder of adjacent countries imposed a "Manifest Destiny" of annexation to overcome the nuisance.[88] The view was much less common in the following century but was expressed by various individuals in every instance of Latin-American disorder from the beginning of this century. Discussing Cuban conditions in 1900, Richard Olney expressed the opinion of many when he wrote that no Teller resolution should be allowed to impede "the natural march of events" toward the annexation which alone could give Cuba progress.[89] When Cuba's early relapse into revolutionary disturbances seemed a confirmation of Olney's view, Beveridge asserted similarly that only annexation could fulfil "the task civilization bids us do," and that "in the end destiny will have her way."[90] The outbreak of the tropical malady of revolution in the Dominican Republic in 1904 evoked from the *Baltimore American* the observation that annexation was "the only remedy" and ought to be applied immediately.[91] A few years later Crichfield's *American Supremacy,* chiefly an invective against Latin-American degradation, maintained not only that the United States was "in honor bound to maintain law and order in South America," but that "we may just as well take complete control of several of the countries, and establish decent governments while we are about it."[92]

That the Mexican revolutions aroused more expansionist zeal than did any previous difficulty in the twentieth century is explicable not only by the unusually serious injury to foreign interests but also by the fact that Mexico seemed a choicer morsel than other so-called "porcupines." Thus as early as 1911 Representative Focht, speaking of Americans as "policemen of the Western Hemisphere," asked with reference to Mexico: "Why could we not occupy something that is worth having and where we could be of some great good to humanity?"[93] But the group of expansionists who became most vocal about 1916 generally preferred to give first place to service to humanity. As the United States prepared to intervene, an editorial in the *Independent* urged "No Binding of our Hands" at a time when it was conceivable "that it may become our destiny to extend the borders of the United States to the south — not for our own aggrandizement or profit, but for the sake of the people of those troubled regions, for the sake of the peace and good order of the Western Hemisphere, of which we are in a real sense the rightful guardians, and for the sake of civilization."[94] The *New York American* maintained that establishment of "the free and orderly institutions of American rule" below the Rio Grande was both a duty and the only policy that would not make fools of us.[95] Representative Dies affirmed that he was "not talking about annexing Mexico to gratify any love of conquest" but to establish a government enabling the harrassed people to plant and gather their crops.[96] "Intervention without annexation can only prolong a cruel experiment," was the warning of Dr. Wyeth in his brochure on America's national "destiny" to establish order in Mexico.[97]

That intervention can only pain without curing has also been the medical theory of anti-imperialists, who favor leaving bad enough alone. Dr. Raymond Leslie Buell has declared that it is open to argument whether the partial self-restraint which stops with intervention has benefited Central American peoples. It seems to him that the United States has interfered in their affairs to the extent of protecting its interests but not to that of assuming responsibility for a permanent improvement, such as might have been effected ultimately through valuable experience in complete self-government.[98]

But in the Mexican issue, as in all similar issues of the twentieth century, the expansionist's appeals to assume a responsibility for permanent improvement failed to receive widespread public support, much less to gain the approval of any administration. Why does not the devotee of order seek it through annexation, the method apparently most direct and certain? It would seem that he is deterred not only by a prudent attachment to political homogeneity but also by an at least partial respect for the sovereignty of other peoples. His compromise between these values and his devotion to order explains the partial imperialism of intervention.

Unfortunately, Latin-American peoples were not restrained by this compromise from the greatest hue and cry over the temporary infringement upon their sovereignty. Their own vociferous protests, the politically expedient denunciations by Republicans, and the exposures of the miscarriage of uplift in Haiti and the Dominican Republic combined at the end of Wilson's administration to produce an anti-imperialistic reaction which was comparable to that ensuing upon subjugation of the Filipinos. The attitude of a large section of national opinion suggested that a repetition of such drastically imperialistic interventions was impossible.

But intervention like expansion seems at times to have the inevitability of a destiny — or of long-established national policies which override the disinclination of numerous individuals. President Coolidge's second administration was marked by an intervention in Nicaragua, which had become dependent upon American marines to such an extent that two months after they were withdrawn it relapsed into old revolutionary habits. The assistance of American forces in suppressing the revolution was requested by the government recognized by the United States as legal. But the response to this invitation had an imperialistic look for those who believed with some justification that the nominal government was not legal, but merely a faction favored by the United States for politico-economic reasons.

As though interventionism was losing its self-assurance, the intervention was defended by a type of argument designed to conceal any aspect of imperialism: the United States was now said to have the duty of settling the family quarrels of neighboring countries when the legally recognized disputant requests it to do so. President Coolidge derived this duty from America's sponsorship of the Central American treaties of 1923 in favor of constitutionality. Although the United States was not a party to the convention, its signature at Washington seemed to the President to impose upon the United States " a moral obligation to apply its principles " in order to " prevent revolution and disorder." [99] In his speech before the United States Association, President Coolidge extended the moral obligation of the United States to a scope embracing all recognized governments north of the Panama Canal:

> Toward the Governments of countries which we have recognized this side of the Panama Canal we feel a moral responsibility that does not attach to other nations. We wish them to feel that our recognition is of real value to them and that they can count on such support as we can lawfully give when they are beset with difficulties. We have undertaken to discourage revolutions within that area and to encourage settlement of political differences by the peaceful method of elections.[100]

Such were the considerations which prompted President Coolidge to affirm that " we are not making war on Nicaragua any more than a policeman on the street is making war on passers-by." [101] An admission of belligerent action would indeed have been embarrassing for a president who in his inaugural address had said of his country that " the legions which she sends forth are armed, not with the sword, but with the cross." [102]

The nation's official spokesman had scarcely exaggerated the apparent altruism of some Americans. Upon the despatch of marines to suppress Sandino's revolt, Senator Bingham held that when our neighbors to the south " desire us to help them, as the people of Nicaragua have asked us to do in the present case, it is our duty to do so." [103] The present case appeared to the *Washington Post* to hold out a new opportunity for " the protector of the Western world " — namely, the protection of an American republic against Mexican Communists (supposed to be behind the Nicaraguan troubles) who seemed no less dangerous than oversea imperialists.[104] Representative Eaton explained edifyingly why the United States had to assume such an arduous duty toward Latin-American peoples:

> When they are in trouble and can not solve their troubles by their own resources they have the right to expect that we will listen to their

appeal and do the best we can to help them solve their problems, not for our gain, not for our glory, not because we are militaristic or imperialistic, but because we constitute a brotherhood on these two continents and our Nation is the big brother in the family.[105]

But Representative Fletcher, also believing the rôle of "big brother" to be "in harmony with our Nation's divine destiny," affirmed that in this issue the United States was playing the part of "big bully."[106] This was to take the view that to brother the nominal Nicaraguan government was to bully the Nicaraguan people, most of whom seemed supporters of the party branded as revolutionary. What at least is true is that it is very difficult to tell whether one is acting as brother or bully in such issues. And even if one could identify something so obscure as the rightful constitutional government of a revolutionary Central American country, insistence upon constitutionality tends in Latin America to be in effect an imperialism toward all but the "ins." As H. W. Dodds said contemporaneously before the American Academy of Political and Social Science, President Coolidge's assumption of responsibility for fulfilment of the treaties of 1923 meant declaring to the five republics:

> You must conduct your government in a manner recognized as constitutional under Anglo-Saxon theories of political science. Whether you like these theories or not, we believe them to be the best for you and it is our duty to make you follow them.[107]

At least one interventionist of Congress avowed frankly that the United States was maintaining imperialistic policies — advancing "the imperialism of science and peace and justice." But he quaintly justified this imperialism by a metereologico-theological theory of manifest destiny — that "the weather and the Creator" alike had called this great nation of the temperate zone to police the debilitating tropics.[108]

However, the Nicaraguan policy provoked among Latin Americans generally an unusually vigorous attack which gave evidence of their special resentment of American pretensions to superior status as either agent of Providence or big brother. Largely in consequence, the American ideology of intervention was again subjected to a surprisingly drastic modification. There was a virtual abandonment of the type of reasoning which openly justified America's interventions by reference to the special rights and duties of one people. American statesmen began to subsume American interventions under legal principles applicable to all peoples. Thus at the Havana Conference of 1928, Secretary of State Hughes affirmed that America limited its " interpositions " — as he called America's alleged interventions — to the occasions recognized in international law:

> I am speaking of the occasions where government itself is unable to function for a time because of difficulties which confront it and which it is impossible for it to surmount.
>
> Now it is a principle of international law that in such a case a government is fully justified in taking action—I would call it interposition of a temporary character—for the purpose of protecting the lives and property of its nationals. I could say that that is not intervention. One can read in text books that it is not intervention. . . . Of course the United States cannot forego its right to protect its citizens.[109]

This right of course becomes much broader when interpreted in connection with Coolidge's pretension in the Mexican dispute, that the national's property is everywhere a part of the nation's domain and is therefore not subject to retroactive laws tending to confiscation.

Critics have frequently overlooked, indeed, that all American interventions began under conditions endangering life and property. But though protective action under such circumstances is legally unquestionable, the point at issue, as the *Nation* once wrote, is not the protection of nationals during critical days or weeks.[110] It is rather a policy that ultimately endangers nationals even more than does the absence of marines — drastic and prolonged interference in the affairs of another government against its will. This policy, as a recent writer has observed, " has to do with expedient statecraft rather than with law." [111] The fundamental purpose of such statecraft does not seem to be protection of nationals but rather creation of a *pax Americana* favorable to this country's maintenance of such principles as the Monroe Doctrine and the Canal policy.

Apart from defense of nationals, Hughes has related American interventions to the broader legal principle of self-defense underlying the Canal policy.[112] In the same line of thought is Reuben Clark's memorandum on the Monroe Doctrine, published by the State Department during the Hoover administration. Its primary purpose was to rescue the Monroe Doctrine from the odium into which it had fallen in Latin America because of identification with the Roosevelt doctrine of police power. Clark asserted that the Monroe Doctrine imposed restrictions only upon Europe, and that so far as concerns Latin America "the Doctrine is now, and always has been, not an instrument of violence and oppression, but an unbought, freely bestowed, and wholly effective guaranty of their freedom, independence, and territorial integrity against the imperialistic designs of Europe." But the principal change effected by this definition of the Monroe Doctrine is merely terminological; it saves the good name of Monroe but exposes the sovereignty of Caribbean peoples to intervention under a different name. For the memorandum proceeds to justify America's relations with Cuba, Haiti, and the Dominican Republic "as the expression of a national policy which, like the Doctrine itself, originates in the necessities of security or self-preservation" — that is, the Caribbean policy.[113]

In opposition to this view, B. C. Rodick, in his *The Doctrine of Necessity in International Law,* has maintained that American interventions which merely seek to ward off European intervention in a sphere of interest "are political in their nature and are not to be considered as subject to legal justification and excuse."[114] To be sure, legal concepts such as "self-defense" are so indefinite that they can be applied to almost any intervention without becoming subject to quite certain legal disproof. One can safely say, however, that America's interpretation of the interventionist rights given by self-defense does not appear to conform to the ordinary juristic expositions of intervention for self-defense.

The somewhat far-fetched doctrines of American statesmen need not be attributed to disregard of international law but rather to the "unacknowledged factors" by which Professor Dunn explains many legal decisions in the sphere of intervention.[115] Thus moral ideology, which Roosevelt openly made the justification of his doctrine of police power, has probably been of unconscious influence even upon the American legal interpretation of intervention. One influence was probably the idea of the United States as leader of the hemisphere, protector of Latin America against the non-American world and of the non-American world against Latin America. Another was apparently the conception of the " special interest " of the United States in the Caribbean. Even the metaphysical elements of the dogma of manifest destiny have perhaps exercised unconsciously the effect once exerted consciously by the doctrine of the superiority of divine to positive law.

However, even an unfulfilled intention to base intervention upon purely legal grounds does signify a certain diminution in the hold of the proud conviction of special merits and prerogatives — the conviction of manifest destiny. Recession in theory was shortly followed by recession in policy; for the Hoover Administration proceeded to conduct its Latin-American relations with relative self-restraint and patience. Secretary Stimson, going directly in the face of Coolidge's dictum, announced during the Nicaraguan difficulties of 1931 that protection would be given to life but not necessarily to property. Impartiality to all factions in the Nicaraguan elections of 1928, followed by withdrawal of marines, seemed to disprove the view that the United States would support by all means the faction most favorable to its economic and political interests. This sudden shift to moderation, though doubtless related in part to a growing sentiment of anti-imperialism, was also caused by accumulating evidence that America's philanthropies of intervention had created throughout Latin America an antagonism seriously threatening her commerce. A major dissolvent of American interventionism was thus the realization that " a policeman's lot is not a happy one."

The doctrine of police power which crystallized during the administration of the first President Roosevelt came to dissolution in the administration of the second President Roosevelt. The development was surprising in the light of the part played by Franklin D. Roosevelt as Assistant Secretary of the Navy during the interventions in Haiti and the Dominican Republic. However, it was not surprising in the light of an article by Roosevelt in *Foreign Affairs* in 1928, declaring that "single-handed intervention by us in the internal affairs of other nations must end; with the cooperation of others we shall have more order in this hemisphere and less dislike." [116] President Roosevelt's inaugural declaration in favor of the policy of "the good neighbor" might have meant either the interventionist policy of 1916 or a policy of anti-intervention; for it is an unsettled moral question whether good neighborliness consists in forcible intrusion into a neighbor's family quarrels or leaving them to run to a possibly murderous culmination. But Roosevelt's action in the Cuban crisis of 1933 represented a middle course — that of the neighbor who intervenes not forcibly but within diplomatic limits. It later became still more evident that Roosevelt purposed the difficult and somewhat unusual effort to make good a pre-election declaration in practice. In his speech before the Woodrow Wilson Memorial Foundation on December 28, 1933, Roosevelt's words made the first presidential declaration that "the definite policy of the United States from now on is one opposed to armed intervention." After this, nothing could surprise — not even the relinquishment of the treaty right of intervention in Cuba. Whether one liberal administration can change permanently a policy so deeply rooted in American tradition and temperament remains to be seen.

No criticism of America's past intervention policy could be more pointed than the words of President Roosevelt in his Wilson Foundation speech:

> The maintenance of constitutional government in other nations is not a sacred obligation devolving upon the United States alone. The maintenance of law and orderly processes of government in this hemisphere is the concern of each individual nation within its own borders first of all.
>
> It is only if and when the failure of orderly processes affects the other nations of the continent that it becomes their concern; and the point to stress is that in such an event it becomes the joint concern of a whole continent in which we are all neighbors.[117]

The foregoing view is distinct from the generalized anti-interventionism espoused not merely by Latin-American jurists but also by numerous American anti-imperialists who believe in the absolute inviolability of sovereignty. The earnest individuals who have criticized intervention *per se* are probably not aware of the full implication of their moral theory since they seldom follow it to its logical conclusion. Its conclusion is the political and social anarchism which rejects all coercion, domestic as well as international, beneficent as well as injurious. But even anti-interventionism in its limited connotation represents certain assumptions which, without questioning its moral legitimacy, can be said to be curious. It represents either the as yet unconfirmed assumption that every people is qualified to solve its problems unaided, or a premise still stranger. It may express that fanatical philosophy of laissez-faire which holds that " every nation should be permitted to go to the Devil in its own way." In his interesting historical novel about American filibusterers, *A Manifest Destiny,* Arthur Smith makes one of his characters entertain the paradoxical doctrine of a right of inferior peoples to retrogression.[118] President Roosevelt, on the other hand, takes the more usual viewpoint in denying the right to retrogress to a point destructive of alien interests.

The President's view relative to intervention is different, however, from that of the ordinary imperialist. The latter believes that the maintenance of the world's order is primarily the duty of a few civilized powers, which apparently are not sufficiently occupied in suppressing disorder and crime within their own borders. Roosevelt holds that, though there may come a point when intervention is justified by injury to alien interests, the maintenance of order is primarily the concern of each individual nation with respect to its own domain.

The most noteworthy point in this new doctrine is its attack upon the policy of single-handed intervention which, except for Wilson's consultation with the " A. B. C. Powers " in the Mexican issue, the United States has practiced in the past. In declaring that order in America is no one nation's special duty but the common concern of the continent, President Roosevelt meant to espouse replacement of unilateral intervention by collaboration — if not with the world at large at least with other American nations. The motive of this substitution would appear from Roosevelt's article of 1928 to be his belief that unilateral intervention is not the most effective method of creating either friendliness for the United States or order on this hemisphere. The primary objection to unilateral intervention is the likelihood that it will be used to one nation's advantage; whereas, as the jurist Hall says, it is probable that, by check and balance, "powers with divergent individual interests, acting in common, will prefer the general good to the selfish objects of a particular state." [119] But even the assumption that the United States is exceptional in never abusing intervention would not destroy the force of a second consideration. The remaining difficulty is that single-handed intervention has an aspect of humiliation, painfully obvious to all Latin America despite the most tactful endeavors of American statesmen to conceal it. Humiliation, creating antagonism, precludes the cooperation required for solving the problems leading to disorder. On the other hand, collaborative intervention, or intervention carried out under a collective mandate, is not apprehended as nationalist domination but rather as the interposition of a larger social order.

The foregoing considerations apparently imply that America's traditional doctrine of police power has an internal inconsistency in the sense of a divergence between ideal and method. The ideal of this doctrine is the subordination of national freedom of action to international order and welfare. Its method is the single-handed intervention which permits one nation complete freedom of action. Although the caveat against European intervention helped to save Latin America from European imperialism, a salutary effect did not obviously follow from the rejection of collaboration with other American nations. According to President Franklin D. Roosevelt, America's single-handed interventions were not as efficacious in reducing disorder as would have been the method of American collaboration. A nationalistic policy, then, appears partially to have defeated an internationalist ideology.

The explanation of the adoption of a nationalist policy

should be fairly evident from the study of the circumstances under which this policy developed. The cause was not altogether a failure to recognize the greater consistency of collaborative intervention with the internationalist ideology; for even Theodore Roosevelt, father of the doctrine of police power, admitted the greater desirability of the collaborative method when he no longer had official responsibility for America's policy.[120] The fundamental reason for the inconsistency with internationalist professions is probably the very natural fact that the policy of intervention was practiced primarily for nationalistic reasons. The injuriousness of disorder to international interests was not considered as important as its injury to America's security and economic interests. In pursuing national interests it has seemed expedient not to resort to collaboration but to be reserved in taking counsel and independent in taking action.

But practical interests do not entirely or even primarily explain the matter. For ordinarily the suppression of disorder is a purpose in which the interests of one nation and those of international society converge. Moreover, what is called collaborative intervention usually resolves itself into the delegation of a mandate to the one nation best qualified through resources and interests to undertake intervention. Thus in all likelihood the legitimate interventions of the United States could have been given an international authority merely through the type of consultation which President Roosevelt undertook during the Cuban crisis of 1933.

The chief impediment to America's acceptance of collaborative intervention was probably not national advantage but national pride. This likelihood has been well stated by Professor Parker T. Moon:

> The substitution of Pan-American intervention for United States intervention, and of international financial receiverships for United States financial protectorates, in the region between the equator and the United States, would perhaps keep order there more effectively, and conciliate South America, and therefore aid American trade with South America. But such a substitution will be possible only when public opinion in the United States divests itself of the spirit of domination, discards the 'big stick' along with 'dollar diplomacy' and learns to

treat Latin American nations as associates rather than protégés. The great obstacle is not material interests, but a psychological factor, national pride, and national pride is the mother of imperialism.[121]

The proud spirit of manifest destiny was the mother of the interventionist's conception that America's superior merit as well as strength entitled her to exercise an exclusive police power in the interest both of the world's order and of her own security. And pride goeth, if not before downfall, at least before the partial frustration of many an international ideal. It caused the American interventionist as well as the American expansionist to seek his international "destiny" by the path of nationalism. But to realize its international ideal, intervention apparently must be — in fact as well as in name — an international police power.

# CHAPTER XV

## WORLD LEADERSHIP

Between recent American history and the expansionist's traditional idea of manifest destiny there is not merely a difference but an antithesis. To Benton and other early expansionists it seemed manifest that the American people would always be expansionist, if only because of a land-hunger "founded in their nature" as white men.[1] McKinley, more inclined to interpret destiny in the moral terms of the white man's burden, believed at least that his countrymen would not wish America's beneficent rule to be contracted.[2] But despite the inveteracy of both land-hunger and moral altruism, American history since McKinley's time has been characterized by a rather steady decline of the expansionist temper. This decline did go to the point of a willingness for contraction, represented by release of the Philippines and withdrawal from semi-protectorates. Indeed it went to the depth of an anti-expansionism that forswore all future conquest and even intervention. Thus the antithesis between prophecy and actuality concerns the conception of the god Terminus: the deity whom expansionists saw as eternally progressive is portrayed now as stationary, as the source of an eternal destiny of self-restraint.

The virtual disappearance of the long dominant force of American life might well seem the most surprising phenomenon in a history replete with the unexpected. But in fact this disappearance does not even engage general attention. The memory of past expansionism has met the fate of experiences which the individual cannot happily assimilate: by being pushed out of consciousness it has come to be almost forgotten. The consequence is that the greatest paradox of American history is usually left unpondered and unexplained.

Most of the few statesmen who have taken public note of America's remarkable change either have not explained it or have explained it somewhat naïvely. President Harding's observations about the " inscrutable destiny " in past imperialism gave the impression that cessation of this destiny was also inscrutable.[3] President Wilson referred America's one-time " aggressive purposes and covetous ambitions " not to destiny but to " our thoughtless youth." [4] In this he implied that America went in for expansion as a youth goes in for sin — ignorant of the moral issue. But those who view the question not as anti-imperialistic propagandists but as historical realists will probably be unable to believe either that the American expansionist was aware of sin or that the modern anti-expansionist has been motivated solely by moral considerations. The part of self-interest in causing " the collapse of American imperialism " was recently considered in an article of Professor Pratt [5] — an exception to the general tendency of American historians to devote much more attention to the rise of the spirit of empire than to its less sensational decline.

It is true, indeed, that a moral ideology has been one of the many factors underlying the decline of expansionism. But the moral factor in this decline was not, strange to say, a value which was opposed by the expansionist. On the contrary, it was a moral value which was originated by the expansionist. Such is the sportiveness of history that, just as American expansionism first justified itself by an idea previously used by anti-imperialists, so American anti-expansionism, reversing the trick, converted to its own design a flexible doctrine which developed from expansionism.

The general implication of this theory can be made clearer if one takes the rhetorical liberty of describing the career of ideas in personalizing terms. Indeed, the symbolizing imagination will already have tended to view the various ideas of expansionism as Don Quixotes or Till Eulenspiegels, figures meeting pathetic or comic adventures as they seek their ideal or their fortune, fight duels with their enemies, mate with their affinities, procreate lines of descendants, and lapse eventually into honorable or dishonorable old age. One comes now to a Sophoclean tragedy, grim and morbid. Let us suppose expansionism to be an Amazonian mother, a breeder of children for war. Her children are the many expansionist doctrines that, fulfilling their filial duty and the purpose for which their mother bore them, serve as her knights or statesmen as she pursues her aggressive career of adding to her territorial possessions. Eventually — and thereby hangs the tale — this mighty mother gives birth to one child too many, a child who will prove most unnatural. He is, indeed, his mother's biological masterpiece, endowed with greater intellectual and moral strength than were any of his older brothers. But in the pride of his strength he deserts early his maternal home, pursues his career independently, develops a moral code different from that of his mother, and even ceases to remember her. Eventually some nemesis makes the path of the son cross that of the mother. The son is unsympathetic to his mother and comes into violent quarrel with her. Finally, unaware of whom he attacks, he commits in a passion of moral indignation the terrible crime of Oedipus — the murder of his own parent! Such is the nature of the tragedy with which, it appears, the history of American expansionism comes to its amazing close.

The curtain of this drama rises in that fateful year of 1898 wherein America prepared to reach the height of her expansionist glory — to become the Imperial Republic. As the progeny of the new ambition there entered upon the scene a new moral rationalization. It was, in brief, the doctrine that imperialist expansion was a means to America's assumption of a rôle of thoroughgoing collaboration in pursuing the interests and duties of world politics.

This doctrine, as anti-expansionists abundantly emphasized, conflicted sharply with the dominant American policy and attitude of the past. Rarely in practice, and still more rarely in theory, had Americans repudiated the principle of independent political action (now known under the misnomer of isolationism) which was given its classic formulation by Washington. America's first president, believing that Europe had a different set of primary interests from America's and that America's required time for independent development, declared that "it must be unwise in us to implicate ourselves by artificial ties in the ordinary vicissitudes of her politics or the ordinary combinations and collisions of her friendships or enmities."[6] Jefferson made this doctrine more general by abbreviating it to a warning against "entangling alliances." [7] His somewhat later reference to America's "perfect horror" [8] at anything resembling such alliances evidenced the quick development of isolationism into a dominant emotional phobia, based upon distrust of a different, supposedly more sinister culture and political system.

Expansionism, seemingly a reaching toward the outside world, really was long a major expression of isolationism. Almost from the beginning the American adopted expansion as a means of freeing the United States from the entanglements threatened by European neighborhood. Thus in congratulating Americans upon the Louisiana Purchase Livingston and Monroe wrote as follows:

> We separate ourselves in a great measure from the European world and its concerns, especially its wars and intrigues. We make, in fine, a great stride to real and substantial independence . . . [9]

The expansionist movement of the War of 1812 represented an attempt at a further stride to true independence. Henry Clay's appeals to expel Great Britain from the continent contain the nucleus of his doctrine of 1820 that we must become "real and true Americans," the heads of a system counterbalancing all the "despotism" of Europe.[10] In the 'forties and 'fifties Americans turned to territorial expansion in order to prevent the southern portion of the continent from becoming, as Senator Cass said, the seat of European influence and therefore a possible cause of involvement in every war breaking out in the Old World.[11] The close of the Civil War was followed by the exclusive expansionist's emphasis upon the northern ambitions represented in Sumner's attempt to dismiss monarchy from Alaska and the land of the Canadians. In Sumner as in others it was isolationism which largely prompted the grandiose ambition of making the Republic "nothing less than the North American continent, with its gates on all the surrounding seas." [12]

However, isolationism had not usually urged the expansionist to go farther than the continent and its so-called appendages. And when strategic and commercial ambitions prompted the administrations of Johnson and Grant to suggest a program of expansion in the Caribbean, this program met defeat largely because even expansionists objected to territorial extension which, as Senator Bayard said, destroyed the moorings of Washington's isolationism and embarked America on the "trackless sea of imperialism." [13] In three ensuing decades opportunities of oversea expansion were repeatedly rejected as deviations from the straight and lonely path of the fathers. President Cleveland's message repudiating the Nicaraguan canal treaty [14] and the Hawaiian treaty of annexation [15] spoke of national tradition as proscribing both alliances with foreign states and the acquisition of distant or oversea interests. American entrance into the Samoan condominium in 1889 was a deviation from this line of precedents; yet the most striking feature of the Samoan episode is the fact that isolationism repressed desire to take advantage of the possible opportunity to incorporate any of these distant islands. A few years later Secretary Gresham regretted the troublesome condominium and declared that America's sense of moral obligation had been no reason for departing from its prudent traditions.[16] Just as earlier expansionists believed that "our mission is coextensive with the continent," [17] so Senator Lodge, even when describing his nation's great destiny, was content in 1895 to say that "we must be the leaders in the Western Hemisphere." [18]

Throughout the course of the 'nineties, however, the restraining power of isolationism over American foreign policy visibly weakened. Having noted in 1890 the commercial and strategic needs which were enforcing upon his countrymen the beginning of an "outward view," Captain Mahan wrote during the discussion of the Hawaiian issue in 1893 that "we also shall be entangled in the affairs of the great family of nations and shall have to accept the attendant burdens." [19] Whereas, formerly, Hawaii's membership in America's economic system made it seem the one proper exception to the continental policy, in the expansion movement of 1893 Hawaii seemed to many only the "first-fruit" [20] of a policy entangling us in the commercial even if not the political rivalries of the outside world. A foreshadowing of the transition to a larger political outlook came in the Venezuelan issue of 1895. The boldness of Olney and Cleveland kindled a spark of national pride which let some, like Henry Watterson, feel that the United States was "destined to exercise a controlling influence upon the actions of mankind and to affect the future of the world as the world was never affected, even by the Roman Empire — itself." [21] Although Olney wrote in 1900 that Americans throughout the 'nineties had been fast opening their eyes to the new international position of the United States, he also asserted that "the characteristic of the foreign relations of the United States at the outbreak of the late Spanish War was isolation." [22] Mahan likewise testified to the fact that before this war the vision of expansionists in general "reached not past Hawaii, which also, as touching the United States, they regarded from the point of view of defence rather than as a stepping-stone to any farther influence in the world." [23]

Then suddenly America decisively broke away from traditional moorings, just as its war-ships sailed to activities in another hemisphere. The war was less the cause of the change than its precipitant; the needs of battle, the excitement of the martial spirit, and the opportunities of victory brought to maturation and consciousness interests which had long been developing unconsciously. But it was in the exalted and expansionist mood following Dewey's victory in Manila Bay that American public opinion first gave general acceptance to the view that the "destiny of America" was such that "the United States must henceforth take its place with the other nations of the world." [24] Abandonment of isolation seemed to slough restraints upon commerce, strategic policy, pride, duty, but most important of all, expansion. Richard Olney, contemporary analyst of this abandonment, acknowledged the primacy of the expansionist motive when he wrote: "That relinquishment — the substitution of international fellowship — . . . is to be ascribed . . . above all to that instinct and impulse in the line of national growth and expansion . . ." [25] The line of growth had overreached the continent even before the dream of a continental republic had been fulfilled. Apparently the fundamental cause was neither international fellowship nor objective need, but the appeal to instinct and impulse in the glorious prospect of world empire.

World empire demanded abandonment of isolation but the expansionists preferred to assert that abandonment of isolation demanded world empire. Already in the Hawaiian issue they formulated and came to believe the rationalization that expansion in distant waters was required for the fulfilment of America's international interests and duties. Arguing for annexation from the standpoint of national interest, Representative Gibson scouted the idea that America, with its growing commerce and its need for foreign markets, could continue to live " without much intercourse with foreign nations," as though within Chinese walls.[26] To be sure, anti-expansionists asked why the commerce of Hawaii could not be enjoyed without annexation as previously. But expansionists had another leg to stand on — the duty of international altruism as expounded by Representative Stewart:

> Our country has arisen from lusty youth to vigorous manhood. We must share the responsibilities as well as the blessings of modern civilization. We must participate in the world's destiny. . . . The blessings of our own free republican government should not be selfishly isolated or hugged to our own bosoms alone, but the Stars and Stripes, amid the Pacific and the Atlantic, should salute the dying dynasties of the Eastern World and bid them a cordial welcome and renewed life and a vigorous existence under its starry folds.[27]

It seemed to many that the United States had sufficient scope for altruism in the possibility of enhancing the well-being of impoverished and exploited millions in its own boundaries or in adjacent countries of the continent. But restlessness gave a yearning for new and more interesting scenes. When Hawaii had been annexed the Boston *Transcript* exulted with the sense of a thrilling new career:

> The Rubicon has at last been crossed. The country now enters upon a policy that is entirely new. It has thrown down its former standards, cast aside its old traditions, has extended its first tentacle two thousand miles away, and is growing others for exploitation in southern and eastern seas.[28]

It did come to pass after crossing the Rubicon that the expansionists proposed stretching a second tentacle more than a thousand miles farther — to the Philippine Islands lying at the edge of the most active scene of world politics. The Orient was in fact a locale of international commercial conflict rather than of international collaboration. But numerous expansionists thought as did Charles Conant that "upon this international competition . . . the United States are compelled to enter, whether they wish it or not, by the conditions of their industrial development." [29] Others, preferring loftier aims or rhetoric, identified abandonment of isolation with assumption of international obligations. To pursue isolation, declared Senator Platt of Connecticut, was national selfishness; if we were to "let our light shine" we must "carry it where it can be seen." [30] But it was not merely the enlightenment of the Filipinos which seemed to demand the assumption of the white man's burden. Another typical consideration was that stressed by John R. Proctor in his article "Isolation or Imperialism," namely, that retention of the Philippines was demanded by "the interests of peace" — that is, the necessity of preventing a war of the powers to decide the proper depository of this white man's burden.[31]

America's conception of the territorial expansion essential to the international activities of a world power continued to grow. Even while the Philippine revolt engrossed the national energies General Miles spoke of "other fields to conquer" in the two hemispheres which America's interests seemed to him now to embrace.[32] Governor Theodore Roosevelt, decrying any huddling within our borders, called upon his country to "grasp the points of vantage which will enable us to have our say in deciding the destiny of the oceans of the east and west." [33] Aware "how little such a course is compatible with a policy of isolation," Professor Powers proposed that "the potentially dominant race" occupy every strategic point, military, industrial, and cultural.[34] All these suggestions were rather vague but in addition more concrete objectives called for enterprise or consideration. In 1899 America brought into the national domain Samoan Tutuila, small but significant of a large change in policy. McKinley, believing that "the period of exclusiveness" had given way to "the expansion of our trade," [35] went so far in concern for America's commercial expansion as to permit tentative plans for acquiring a concession and even a coaling station in China.[36]

The steady enlargement of territorial ambition was paralleled by a growth of moral ambition in the conception of America's position among the nations. In the Hawaiian issue expansionists had been modestly content to think of their nation as a collaborator in world politics. But as America prepared to demand the Philippines Senator Davis, chairman of the Committee on Foreign Relations, observed amid grandiloquent rhetorical flourishes that America's paramount power in the Pacific would cause it in the future to "become a leading factor in international politics." [37] This phrase "leading factor" presumably meant approximately what was stated by Reinsch in his *World Politics at the End of the Nineteenth Century* — that America was to play a "leading rôle in international affairs" as "one of the five leading world powers." [38] But after American pride had been inflated by the territorial acquisitions of the Spanish treaty the most exalted patriots were not content to speak of America as less than *the* leading factor, leader of the leaders. Thus in 1900 Senator Lodge was prompted by his "unbounded faith and pride" in his country to summon it to its place "at the head of the nations" — a leadership which would be America's manifest destiny if it followed the laws of its being rather than weak-hearted anti-imperialists.[39] About the same time the nationalistically theologizing Beveridge made his famous proclamation that God had "marked the American people as His chosen nation to finally lead in the regeneration of the world." [40] The immediate task was to regenerate forcibly the Filipinos; but before the clock of the century had struck the half hour America would be "the sought-for arbitrator of the disputes of the nations." [41] With such boasts in view a French writer on American imperialism defined its characteristic ideology as "the pretension to world mastery in order to aid in the development of civilization and the establishment of peace, with scorn for every form contrary to its political or economic interests." [42] If Patouillet had said not "world mastery" but "world leadership" he would have characterized more accurately the aspiration which war and expansion, egoism and idealism, had brought to crystallization.

However, the ideal of world leadership is a sublimation of the Roman aspiration toward world mastery, to which Polybius thought Rome called in consequence of its virtue and wise constitution. It was not until after the rise of modern nationalism that the conception of universal empire became transmuted into that of leadership in a moral empire. This transmutation made the conceit of preeminence more common among nations; for whereas factual mastery must be proven with the sword, the conviction of moral leadership requires only an egoistic or idealistic imagination. Fichte pointed to the German culture-nation as the representative of humanity; Saint-Simon saw France as the bearer of a holy mission to propagate the truths of the new social order; and Lord Roseberry's conception of the British Empire as the preeminent agency of secular reform exemplified the final alliance of the idea of world leadership with imperialism. According to Dostoevsky, himself an imperialist, every great people believes and must believe that in it and it alone lies the salvation of the world, and that it lives to lead all peoples into the milennium. Since only one of many can be right, the probability of correctness in any case is statistically rather small. The sign of divine election, however, has always seemed to be an inner call.

From the beginning of their national history Americans had cherished something like the proud belief stated by John Adams: "Our pure, virtuous, public-spirited, federative republic will last forever, govern the globe, and introduce the perfection of man . . ." [43] But during the greater part of their history Americans, unlike the militant idealists of the French Revolution and the cooperative Mazzini, did not think of leadership as international collaboration. They expected to lead in the manner of the stars with their kindly light — by the passive radiation of their "brilliant example." [44] This radiation was to be assisted by America's continental expansion, making democracy more and more visible until America's moral influence was that of "mistress of the world." [45] But most Americans, like John Adams, felt a dread of European statesmen and would doubtless not have mingled intimately with them until the perfection of man had been achieved. If leadership demands membership in the group this traditional program for world leadership was not only impracticable but logically self-contradictory.

On the other hand, the imperialists of the late 'nineties were at least in theory not averse to international collaboration; their ideology conceived America's fulfilment of distant colonial burdens and its sitting at the council table of the nations as the chief means by which world regeneration would be accomplished. Nevertheless, their therapeutic ointment too had its fly, an attitude bringing their professions of internationalism under suspicion. It was the fact that most of the imperialists who spoke of the give-and-take of world politics appear to have been interested primarily in the taking. Though expansion may sometimes be a taking which creates the possibility of giving, their expansionism had an inordinate, menacing egoism in its ideology and its methods. It bore the earmarks of the nineteenth-century individualism expressed in the pious but unedifying words of Canning, "each nation for itself and God for us all." In the last years of the nineteenth century Americans went so strongly for themselves that other nations, as Lodge proudly and happily noted in Rome,[46] were brought to perturbation. The nationalism which used "international leadership" as its slogan presaged a further expansion which would be as extensive and rapid as rival world powers allowed.

Then suddenly came a phenomenon as strange as would be the pause of an exploded rocket in the middle of its predictable ascent. By 1902, aside from a strategic interest in the Danish West Indies, our "explosive imperialism," as Gertrude Atherton called it, had at least for the time being "subsided."[47] What caused it to subside just when American power seemed greatest?

The answer that the cause was weariness is true but superficial. Previously expansionism always waxed stronger from exercise; it is not likely that weariness now set in without some disillusionment. That there was a specific disillusionment is clear. The expense, the severities, and the casualties in the suppression of the Philippine revolt proved to be more damaging to the cause of imperialism than was all the moral indignation of the anti-imperialists. Forced to question the benefits of "benevolent assimilation" for the parties immediately concerned, many Americans came also to question its value to the professed goal of world leadership. Ex-Secretary of State Olney, who in 1898 had summoned his countrymen to the ideal of international collaboration,[48] in 1900 wrote words which burned acidulously into the theory that international collaboration required colonial imperialism. Without the Philippines, he affirmed, the United States, "in taking its seat at the international council table and joining in the deliberations of civilized states, might have been in an ideal position, combining the height of authority and prestige with complete independence." With the Philippines it was "environed by all the rivalries, jealousies, embarrassments, and perils attaching to every Power now struggling for commercial and political supremacy in the East." [49]

It was while the imperialist's version of world leadership was being discredited that a different one began to come into honor. The new doctrine espoused, not expansion, but the regulative international collaboration to which nations began to have recourse as the imperialistic rivalries at the close of the century brought home the dangers of laissez-faire. As Tyler Dennett observes, Secretary of State John Hay, devoted to international peace and avowedly opposed to isolation, turned in 1899 to an attempt at "stabilization of the existing political order" through promotion of "a concert of the powers." Whereas previously the United States "had been less interested in the *status quo* of European powers than in the spread of republican principles of government," Hay worked for this *status quo* in ways as diverse as the Hague Conference, the diplomacy of the Boxer Rebellion, and the Open Door Notes.[50] The destiny of world events did take at their word the Americans who held that in consequence of expansion "the old continental isolation is gone forever." [51]

It shortly became manifest, however, that international collaboration affected expansionism in an unexpected way. One example of this effect was in American policy concerning China, in whose threatened division the American Government had at first been disposed to demand its share. In 1900 commercial self-interest and a sense of greater international responsibility combined to cause the United States to declare definitively through Hay for the "territorial and administrative entity"[52] of China. About the same time, Hay's interest in an informal entente with Great Britain prompted his efforts to prevent the Republican National Convention from resolving in favor of annexation of Canada. In such episodes of Hay's diplomacy the doctrine of world leadership was twisting toward a direction different from that in which it had started.

This curious but not illogical deflection was caused in part by the discovery that, in the pursuit of a broader self-interest and a larger international ideal, expansionism was an embarrassment to America's demands upon others. It was caused also by the fact that international leadership provided a new and independent interest. Hay's internationalism was, indeed, in advance of that of most of his countrymen. Yet its applauded enterprises were substantially influential in distracting general attention from expansionist ambitions to the flattering spectacle described by Bryan as America's "becoming the supreme moral factor in the world's progress and accepted arbiter of the world's disputes."[53]

Would this once expansionist doctrine of world leadership develop even farther in a direction antipodal to an internationally reckless expansionism? In the year 1902 a then minor prophet gave an answer which is the more interesting in retrospect. Woodrow Wilson, believing that we had come to "full maturity" and that "the day of our isolation" was "past,"[54] affirmed solemnly: "A new age is before us in which, it would seem, we must lead the world."[55]

The early years of the nineteenth century did give rise to a series of international enterprises calling for the subordination of territorial expansionism to world leadership. One was the construction of an isthmian canal which was needed for world commerce as well as for trade of this country. Pointing out that other nations had failed in this purpose, Representative Norton grandiloquently affirmed in 1902 that "the destiny of the United States is to lead the world."[56] The canal was not only "a moral equivalent for war " [57] but also an equivalent for territorial expansion. Another substitute stimulant was Roosevelt's energetic mediation in the Venezuelan issue. When the danger of European intervention seemed past, the *Nation* commended America's mediative diplomacy as " Work for a Real 'World-Power.' " Contrasting this " renowned victory of peace " with the war-breeding imperialism in the Philippines, it declared that the victory " has been won on principles which are a standing refutation of what we have been doing elsewhere for four years past." [58]

Though not admitting self-refutation, Roosevelt in 1903 affirmed America's " great part in the world " to be a decision of fate; moreover, in this manifest destiny he did not make expansion an element.[59] Subsequent years of energetic international activity, affecting world issues from Algeciras to war-ridden Asia, showed America's new international rôle to be at least the decision of Roosevelt. By 1908 Dr. Albert Shaw, repudiating expansionism save with respect to the possible future annexation of Canada, associated America's " destiny " with acceptance of " the responsibility of a great place among the nations." [60] Even the flag-raising Beveridge, rejoicing that Americans had " come to be the dominant factor in the affairs of the human race," could now rhapsodize about America's great destiny without reference to further territorial aggrandizement.[61]

Roosevelt's intervention on the Isthmus and his ensuing enunciation of the doctrine of police power may seem a covert reversion to the expansionist interpretation of America's destiny. But it must be noted in the first place that even interventionism bore the impress not of Roosevelt's original jingoism but rather of the mellower, more internationally oriented imperialism of the *fin de siècle*. Roosevelt thus presented his Panama intervention — whether or not justifiably — as the carrying out of a mandate bestowed by the interests of collective civilization. Similarly, his exposition of the doctrine of police power in 1904 stressed the principle that America's exclusive rôle of policing a hemisphere arose from the duty of representing Europe's interests in backward states. The association of intervention with international responsibility is reflected in the words with which the *Providence Journal* called in 1904 for interference in the disorderly Dominican Republic:

> We cannot shirk this new duty. . . . Our responsibility as a world power, as the dominant and order-preserving nation of the western hemisphere, and our self-interest alike require it.[62]

However imperialistic, America's assumption of the policeman's rôle weaned the American mind further from the type of imperialism demanding extension of territory. The order-preserving power of the Western Hemisphere could enjoy moral authoritativeness only as it guarded against the slightest suspicion of an intention of territorial burglary. Thus from the beginning every warning addressed by Roosevelt to Latin America was accompanied by a disclaimer of territorial ambition; in fact, for annexing troublesome countries like the Dominican Republic Roosevelt had "about the same desire . . . as a gorged boa constrictor might have to swallow a porcupine wrong-end-to." [63] Roosevelt expressed his anti-expansionism more elegantly not only in his message of 1904 on America's police power but also in the following words of a message of 1905: "It can not be too often and too emphatically asserted that the United States has not the slightest desire for territorial aggrandizement at the expense of any of its southern neighbors, and will not treat the Monroe Doctrine as an excuse for such aggrandizement . . ." [64] Assistant Secretary of State Loomis revealed a motive of this self-restraint: ". . . if it be felt and understood that we are not wanton aggressors; that we have no irresistible craving for territorial aggrandizement . . . we cannot fail to become a factor in the international problem on this hemisphere which will continually make for universal prosperity and long years of productive and happy peace." [65] Doubtless the same consideration on the part of the ensuing administration motivated Secretary of State Knox's denial — one soon to become conventional — that America coveted aggrandizement south of the Rio Grande.[66]

But in Taft's administration the imperialistic interpretation of international leadership was still effective to the extent of furnishing the justification for financial imperialism and other activities supporting the principle of constitutionality. President Taft spoke of the "international philanthropy" dictated by America's "larger relation" to the world.[67] Secretary Knox emphasized the principle that each nation must sacrifice something of its sovereignty and initiative to the community of nations.[68] Certain Americans could still find in the principle of leadership a justification even for territorial expansion. Thus in 1911 Representative Focht based his appeal for the annexation of Mexico upon his country's international policing mission; at the same time the incorporation of Canada commended itself to him as an amalgamation of the Anglo-Saxon race which was to "dominate the world." [69]

In truth, even when the rising sense of international relations had militated against expansionism it had done so merely as it offered specific substitute objectives to national self-interest. No commanding national spokesman had as yet promulgated an appealing moral philosophy of anti-expansionism.

The formulation of such a philosophy was left to a president who believed that "interest does not tie nations together" but "sometimes separates them." [70] Upon coming to the presidency, Woodrow Wilson quickly made it known that he discountenanced Dollar Diplomacy. And in the Mobile address an American president for the first time gave to Latin America the promise that the United States would "never again seek one additional foot of territory by conquest." [71]

Wilson's anti-expansionist philosophy developed by stages, and its development reflected the influence of the changing historical context. In its first stage it was a reaction primarily to America's troubled relations with Latin America, fearful of Dollar Diplomacy and police power. Wilson in the first place designed a thesis to destroy the traditional association between extension of democracy and America's expansion. This thesis, for which in his idealizing view America chiefly stood, was that of "the sovereignty of self-governing people." [72] From the view that freedom means "the right of every people to choose their own allegiance," [73] it necessarily followed that "imperialism is absolutely opposed to free government." [74]

So far Wilson's doctrine presents nothing more than the principle of self-determination which had been advocated by anti-expansionists rather sentimentally throughout American history. In itself it is perhaps the weakest of all the arguments against expansion. For to put against all the possible benefits of imperialism merely an academic right of freedom is like attempting to brush away something very solid with a flick of the whisk. But Wilson did not stop with mere anti-imperialism; he replaced the expansionist's method of extending "freedom" with one that seemed to him more useful as well as more democratic.

In place of paternalistic expansionism, Wilson proposed a policy based on another type of kinship — "the relationship of a family of mankind devoted to the development of true constitutional liberty." [75] Even though tact forbade its explicit statement, the rôle of America as leader was implicit in Wilson's presentation of his country's relationship to Latin America. The leadership of the United States in "cooperation between the peoples . . . of America" [76] was primarily to be directed toward renunciation of aggression. Appealing to America to establish the foundations of amity so that no one could doubt them, Wilson proposed that all its states unite in "guaranteeing to each other absolutely political independence and territorial integrity." [77] Here is Hay's conception of the peace-preserving concert of powers transposed from China to America, from the hemisphere where others had paramount interests to that which the United States had once deemed its own special preserve.

This renunciation of aggression upon American states did not, however, prevent either the rather imperialistic diplomacy in acquiring Denmark's Caribbean colony or the military occupation of Haiti and the Dominican Republic. These deviations from theoretical anti-imperialism are not proofs of Wilson's insincerity, but rather of the inadequacy of the theoretical foundation of his anti-expansionism as thus far laid. Wilson was realistically aware that failure to act in any of these instances would invite the danger of European interference in American affairs. Only "an international organization which would seek security for all peoples," [78] observed the *New Republic* upon purchase of the Virgin Islands, could render imperialist measures of self-defense unnecessary.

The full development of the anti-expansionism of both Wilson and his countrymen came through an event which caused them to view the problem of expansion in relation to the world rather than merely to America. This event was the outbreak of the World War, which Americans no less than Mr. Britling tried to think through. The war placed the question of expansion in a new light. Theodore Roosevelt had once said that the expansion of civilized powers was fundamentally the cause of peace.[79] This observation might be very true in so far as expansion puts an end to the petty strife of backward peoples. But consideration of the ambitions underlying the World War now suggested, to the populace as well as the scholarly Veblen, that expansionism is fundamentally a cause of war among civilized peoples themselves. For when not one but each of a host of peoples takes to itself the injunction, "*Tu regere imperio populos*," the consequence is not *pax Romana* but Armageddon.

To be sure, the possibility of action upon these realizations appeared slim when Wilson declared that even impartiality of thought was necessary to "the fixed traditional policy of the United States to stand aloof from the politics of Europe." [80] But Wilson was unable to carry out the prudent advice once given by the Baron von Noltke to John Adams: ". . . have sense enough to see us in Europe cut each other's throats with a philosophical tranquillity." [81] Unfortunately for tranquillity, he soon had to acknowledge: "We are participants, whether we would or not, in the life of the world." [82] From the context in which this admission was made one sees that it was very largely an ideal which made it impossible for Wilson to hold aloof. For the words come from the speech wherein Wilson suggested for the first time that after a just peace America should enter into a league of nations. The basic principles which Wilson ascribed to the proposed league were self-determination, the rights of small nations, freedom of the world from aggression — all antitheses to aggressive expansionism.

Wilson's anti-expansionist objective was presented even more sharply in his later address proposing " that the nations should with one accord adopt the doctrine of President Monroe as the doctrine of the world; that no nation should seek to extend its polity over any other nation or people, but that every people should be left free to determine its own polity." [83] Yet this transmutation of a once isolationist American doctrine into a doctrine of the world represented also the sublimation of territorial expansionism into expansionism of another sort — ambition for the extension of America's moral influence. That the latter is in a sense the more nationalistic is evident from Wilson's observation that " the greatest nation is the nation which penetrates to the heart of its duty and mission among the nations of the world." [84]

The same moral sublimation is observable in Wilson's words announcing America's conclusive demonstration that " her destiny is not divided from the destiny of the world " [85] — her entrance into the World War:

> The world must be made safe for democracy. Its peace must be planted upon the tested foundations of political liberty. We have no selfish ends to serve. We desire no conquest, no dominion. We seek no indemnities for ourselves, no material compensation for the sacrifices we shall freely make. We are but one of the champions of the rights of mankind.[86]

From the traditional conception of America's mission to extend freedom on the continent through expansion, it has finally come, as Walter Hines Page proudly told Englishmen, to the ideal of America's entrance into a " holy crusade to help in its extension in the Old World." [87]

At the conclusion of the war Wilson assumed a position which America had never taken in connection with any previous war: he asked no territorial indemnity. Instead, he sought and obtained the Covenant of a League of Nations the " backbone " of which, Article X, sought to make aggressive aggrandizement forever impossible through stipulating " the renunciation . . . by all the great fighting powers of the world, of the old pretensions of political conquest and territorial aggrandizement." [88] The ideal of America's international leadership, first envisaged by the imperialists of 1898, but later passing through a curious and unexpected development, came with Wilson's championship of the League of Nations to its climax.

When Wilson submitted the treaty containing the Covenant of the League, he displayed the greatest skill in assimilating to traditional American attitudes this radical departure from isolation. After interpreting the expansion of 1898 as in effect an abandonment of provincialism, he reached the climax of his exhortation in words calculated to set long familiar ideals in vibration:

> There can be no question of our ceasing to be a world power. The only question is whether we can refuse the moral leadership that is offered us, whether we shall accept or reject the confidence of the world. . . .
>
> The stage is set, the destiny disclosed. It has come about by no plan of our conceiving, but by the hand of God who led us into this way. We cannot turn back. We can only go forward, with lifted eyes and freshened spirit, to follow the vision. It was of this that we dreamed at our birth. America shall in truth show the way. The light streams upon the path ahead, and nowhere else.[89]

Thus Wilson summoned America to an objective antithetic to expansion by appealing to the pride, the morals, and the metaphysics of expansionism. He presented America's entrance into the League as world leadership; so too O'Sullivan, author of the phrase "manifest destiny," once envisaged a great future in which America would "lead our race." He depicted this leadership as "moral"; so too O'Sullivan once prophesied that America's hemispheric republic would "manifest to mankind the excellence of divine principles." Wilson called America's leadership "destiny," the very word which O'Sullivan had brought into intimate relation with expansion.

The underlying similarity between Wilson's thought-forms and those of expansionism is suggested most dramatically by those words of his annual message of 1920 wherein he again exhorted America to embrace her new international opportunity:

> This is the time of all others when democracy should prove its purity and its spiritual power to prevail. It is surely the manifest destiny of the United States to lead in the attempt to make this spirit prevail.[90]

In these words (the only reference to "manifest destiny" in a presidential message) the reversion to a traditional phrase represents a tribute to its central and still vital implication — America's providential mission of democratic leadership.

The difference between the Wilsonian philosophy of manifest destiny and the old — the profundity of which should not be overlooked because of elements of similarity — lies in the means which Wilson associated with the democratizing mission. He changed the connotation of manifest destiny in a way illustrative of the thesis of Remy de Gourmont in the essay called "The Disassociation of Ideas." [91] Herein, on the basis of associationist psychology, De Gourmont elaborates the conception that the history of thought is composed of episodes in the association and disassociation of ideas. Two ideas enter into association and form a proposition which long passes popularly as a truth. Eventually some independent thinker, both iconoclast and creator, destroys the association. He also, however, places one of its elements in a new association, which in turn enters into social currency as a truth. Similarly Wilson sought from the beginning not only to destroy the old association of the ideas of destiny and expansion but also to replace it with the new association of destiny and moral leadership.

Did this attempt to give currency to a new association of ideas meet with success? Certainly the years of Wilson's influence saw the association between destiny and expansion become tenuous, to such a degree that the once expansionistic Dr. Powers wrote in 1917 that expansion seemed to have reached its limit.[92] It is also true that in the same period the idea of the national destiny came to be conceived more and more in relation to moral leadership. To be sure, grandiloquent propositions like that of Representative Cox in 1916 — that God's voice was calling America to its "high destiny" of weaving a new truth into the warp and woof of the destiny of the world [93] — might be taken as instances of what Richard Olney called posing at leadership. But in the same year a representative of the League to Enforce Peace proposed as America's future foreign policy a "world leadership" which he contrasted with the passivity of isolation.[94] America's popularly approved entrance into the World War soon gave the most convincing evidence that the destiny of leadership signified action. It seems also that in the course of the war Americans acquired still more what Nicholas Murray Butler called "the international mind." [95] And at its conclusion a preponderant public opinion, as Professor Blakeslee and others thought, appeared to favor the League of Nations in principle.[96]

But when the details of its Covenant became known, there arose a hectic and widespread opposition. Leaders in this opposition, curiously enough, were the same Lodge and Beveridge who two decades before urged imperialism as a noble entrance upon international collaboration. The opposition directed itself chiefly against the sanctions of Article X, which threatened to entangle America in the cooperative suppression of imperialism. However, the critics of Wilson were certainly not in disagreement with him as far as concerned their judgment of European imperialism. On the contrary, they believed with Senator Borah that the treaty of peace was objectionable in perpetuating the "sinister and imperialistic" fruits of previous European aggrandizement.[97] Still more objectionable, however, was the alleged possibility that what Senator Reed called "a superworld government" would "dominate the foreign policies" of America; [98] for such domination might not only entangle the United States in European affairs but might even, Beveridge and others feared, prevent it from handling Latin America in its own way.[99] The objection which was presented with the greatest moral gusto was that membership in the League would interfere with true leadership. Thus Senator Lodge argued for his "nullifying" reservations as follows:

> We would not have our country's vigor exhausted or her moral force abated by everlasting meddling and muddling in every quarrel, great and small, which afflicts the world. Our ideal is to make her ever stronger and better and finer because in that way alone, as we believe, can she be of the greatest service to the world's peace and the welfare of mankind.[100]

America's international altruism was thus to rest on the paradox that the best way to help others is to help oneself. That very unfortunate results would ensue were all nations to act upon this principle was not a consideration in Senator Lodge's logic. He expected nations other than America to be cured of their evil egoisms by an American therapeutic which operated chiefly through the masterly inactivity of moral radiation.

If Senator Lodge's moral observations sound less edifying than they were evidently intended to be, it is partly because of one's suspicion that international altruism had very little to do with them. It seems that he and numerous opponents of the League inherited an integral nationalism from a long expansionist history wherein national self-interest was identified with expanded rather than diminished freedom of national action. It was as though there had occurred a reversion, as Senator Williams feared, "to old-time days when we talked about a 'manifest destiny.'"[101] Perhaps it was this unconscious regression to the old concept of destiny which caused Wilson's appeal to "fulfil the destiny of America"[102] — a new destiny — to be disregarded. The Senate's action and apparently also the vote of the "solemn referendum" recorded that "great refusal" which Mazzini identified with unwillingness for fullest international collaboration.

In the immediately ensuing years America retreated still further into what Wilson called "sullen and selfish isolation."[103] As Franklin D. Roosevelt has written, the country "did its best to forget international subjects."[104] President Harding did call to mind a consideration which made this self-engrossment seem well-earned: "We Americans have contributed more to human advancement in a century and a half than all the people of the world in all the history of the world."[105] The international policies of Harding's administration, however, were counted by Franklin D. Roosevelt as lying on "the debit side of the ledger."[106]

Yet even those years of isolationism gave signs that John H. Latané, author of *From Isolation to Leadership,* was perhaps not wrong when he wrote that the verdict of 1920 was not the last word.[107] In the first place, the return to the "normalcy" of isolation did not bring with it a renewal of the expansionism which had been a concomitant of isolation in the past. Secretary Hughes, whether Latin America believed him or not, spoke with general correctness when he said in 1922 that "we do not covet any territory anywhere on God's broad earth." [108] In the second place, America's political interests did lead in at least one case to marked international activity. The Four-Power Treaty of the Washington Naval Conference, allegedly committing America to no "alliance, entanglement, or involvement," [109] actually involved it in an agreement to consult with others in the event of aggression in the Pacific. It was America's opposition to expansionism in the outside world which largely drew it forth by this agreement into the collaborative politics of the world.

The two ensuing administrations, though unsympathetic to early release of the Philippines, showed indifference to further territorial aggrandizement and irresponsiveness even to sporadic suggestions that war debts be exchanged for Caribbean islands. At the same time, opposition to disturbance of international stability led America to a stand even closer to the trenches of the collaborative regulation of international life. President Coolidge's administration was marked in foreign affairs by its espousal of the Kellogg-Briand Pact, fundamentally a defense against the spirit of belligerent expansionism. President Hoover and Secretary Stimson added to the force of this Pact by the so-called non-recognition doctrine, proposing that its signatories refuse to recognize the claims of aggressors to enjoy the fruits of conquest. Together with the enunciation of this doctrine came Secretary Stimson's emphasis upon the consultative implication of the Kellogg Pact, as well as upon more active collaboration with the League of Nations in Far Eastern issues involving apparent aggression.

It was in portions of the boldly innovative administration of Franklin D. Roosevelt, who in 1928 had written in favor of "an active, hearty, and official part in all those proceedings which bear on the general good of mankind," [110] that America's collaboration in behalf of international stability went farthest. Roosevelt's opportunity came when misfortune as well as fortune conspired in his behalf; a people shattered in pride and in the sense of self-sufficiency had an eagerness for the fresh breath of new winds, wheresoever they might blow. President

Roosevelt's circular message proposing a general abstention from sending armed forces across national boundaries was shortly followed by the statement of Norman Davis, asserting America's willingness to consult and even to consider cooperation for the preservation of Europe's peace against aggressors. In the affairs of the Western Hemisphere the President has emphasized a principle which is as much opposed to national tradition as is political help to Europe. This is the replacement of unilateral armed intervention by the program of Pan-American collaboration in meeting problems of disorder.

Such innovations appeared to meet with widespread public approval no less for their anti-expansionism than for their dramatic aspect of leadership. For the people whose history once seemed illustrative of "the inherent desire of man for extension"[111] has become preeminent for its contentment with a policy which, in the words of President Roosevelt, would "seek no conquests and ask only honorable engagements by all peoples to respect the lands and rights of their neighbors."[112]

What is the rationale of this anti-expansionism, stronger than even isolationism? Before answering one must admit that American anti-expansionism is not as deliberate or moralistic as it appears from official formulations; indeed it is in large part merely non-expansionism, an unrationalized lack of interest which followed automatically from the transference of nationalism into less energetic expressions. But inquiry concerning the rationale of American attitude toward expansion is pertinent at least with respect to those, such as statesmen, who approached foreign policy deliberately and encouraged public opinion in its non-expansionism. According to the unsympathetic, American anti-expansionism represents only the recognition by a satiated people that opposition to expansion in the world is now the best means of protecting its accumulated loot and general self-interest. It is quite understandable that peoples deprived of either past or present opportunity for satiation should be too much irritated by America's almost oversevere anti-expansionism to attribute it to any edifying conversion. Their explanation is inadequate not because it is cynical but because it is not shrewdly cynical. It fails to recognize that precisely when self-interest dictates anti-expansionism a sincere international idealism is most apt to be a concurrent motive.

The fundamental premise of America's present attitude toward expansion is exhibited in Secretary Stimson's declaration that "no nation in the world . . . is so deeply interested from the aspect of both its moral and material welfare in the existence of peace" as is the United States.[113] Such an interest in peace is a moral equivalent of America's past zeal for the diffusion of democracy — a philosophy which after the post-war dictatorships seemed neither as likely to become universal nor as essential to the welfare of others as formerly. A selfish factor in this pacifism — one which there is no disposition to deny — is recognition of the importance of world peace to America's own peace and security.

From this zeal for world peace there necessarily arises apprehension of expansionism in the world in general. For it is territorial ambition which primarily, as President Roosevelt implied, "lies back of the threat to world peace." [114] Expansionism is a greater threat to world peace than ever before because nations are today as never before (to quote Secretary Hull) "substantially interrelated and interdependent." [115] One may paraphrase an observation of Secretary Stimson [116] by saying that, in the delicately interwoven fabric of present international relations, expansion anywhere is of concern everywhere. Thus it appears today to be a preponderant belief among virtually all peoples that expansion is generally wrong. The only difficulty lies in the fact that peoples must be divided into two pragmatically different classes: first, those who believe expansion to be generally wrong and do not intend to expand; second, those who believe expansion to be generally wrong and intend to expand because some important principle seems to make it right in their own exceptional case. Unfortunately, the large number of those sensible of exceptions to the general wrongness of expansion endangers the peace of the world as greatly as did the past belief that expansion was generally right.

In contrast to the days when they claimed for themselves a

unique code of natural law, Americans at present not only believe expansion to be generally wrong but do not intend to expand by virtue of any exception. The Kantian principle of acting as one would have all act — the most difficult moral principle for nations to learn — was learned by Americans when they came to interpret their position as one of leadership in the movement to discountenance the perilous exceptions taken by others. It would be not merely an inconsistency but a betrayal of responsibility were America to make exceptions for herself. The claimant to leadership must guard not only against ambition but even, as President Roosevelt has pointed out, against the mere suspicion which would attach to temporary occupation of alien territory.[117] For, as Kirby Page observed during the Coolidge administration, American intervention "inhibits us from any effective protest against the aggression of the other great powers."[118] The leader cannot rebuke others unless he himself is without blame; and the transgressions of the leader become subject to particular blame because they threaten the group principle itself.

The capstone of this anti-expansionist ideology of world leadership is to be seen in a metaphysically phrased dogma which, even in an age of more sober rhetoric, still appears occasionally in the American statesman's solemn announcements of America's international purposes. It is the thesis of a destiny of leadership. This Wilsonian thesis, at first tacitly denied, owed its reassertion at least partly to the fact that the impulse to recapture a satisfying sense of international purposefulness could not be long denied. Ex-Secretary Stimson thus said: "We feel that no nation in the world has been provided by Providence with such a secure position from which to promote the cause of good relations among the nations of the world . . .[118a] It seemed to Secretary Stimson that America "is naturally destined for a leader in the promotion of peace throughout the world."[119] Nor has Secretary Hull, a noteworthy advocate of international collaboration, omitted to voice the same credo: "In my judgment, the destiny of history points to the United States for leadership in the existing grave crisis."[120] The pointing of the compass of history has shifted from America's mission of expansion to leadership in an international stabilization demanding that the long-manifest destiny of continental dominion be left forever unfulfilled.

The ideal of world leadership which was born of expansionism has slain the parent. Only that which had inherited the traits of expansionism — its grandiose egoism, its intemperate ambition, its self-assured idealism — would have had the strength to execute upon the long mighty and aggressive spirit this poetically just retribution.

What in art would be a satisfying ending is in history but a prelude, stirring curiosity about what lies beyond. Eagerness to pierce the veil of the future, as great now as ever in the past, was one factor which gave rise to the predictive method of the philosophy of manifest destiny. Statement of the premises of this method dates back at least as far as Machiavelli, who observed that future events will ever resemble those of preceding times because "they are produced by men who have been, and ever will be, animated by the same passions, and thus they must necessarily have the same results." [121] A figure as recent as Woodrow Wilson expounded the art of interpreting destiny: "There is only one way in which to determine how the future of the United States is going to be projected, and that is by looking back and seeing which way the lines ran which led up to the present moment of power and opportunity." [122] But after the many errors of the users of this method, one cannot feel the old confidence either in its assumption that the lines of the past converge or in its postulate that the future will continue any trend of the past. Though the temptation to reason from the seen to the unseen will always be irresistible to the adventurous intellect, one realizes more and more that the variability of human nature and of outrageous fortune permits at best hypotheses of probability, and frequently enough only confessions of complete uncertainty.

From this point of view it must be confessed that, though relatively to the present a speaking of the "death" of expansionism is metaphorically justifiable, a coroner's dogmatism about the future is a different matter. One would have learned but little from this miraculous history of an impulse with more lives than a cat's were he to feel certain at its end that American expansionism is dead for all eternity, or even for a generation. What one may with warrant believe, however, is that the early revival of expansionism would not be easy. For Americans could revive it only at the expense of hostages which they have given to fate: solemn commitments to the world which could neither in honor nor in prudence be broken.

The question which seems most relevant now is not whether expansionism will be resurrected but whether it will be replaced in the manner that prophetic Wilsonians have described. Will the ideal of world leadership, like those who slay the priest guarding the golden bough and then themselves take on the priesthood, assume in the eyes of Americans the aspect of destiny which attached to expansion before its unnatural death?

Machiavelli has said that it "facilitates a judgment of the future by the past, to observe nations preserve for a long time the same character; ever exhibiting the same disposition to avarice, or bad faith, or to some other special vice or virtue." [123] Whether it was vice or virtue, the expansionist disposition which Americans exhibited so long has perhaps more than anything else "made us what we are," [124] as was said by Wilson himself. But when Wilson held world leadership to be the logical corollary of "the growth of our power," [125] he overlooked the fact that expansion did not develop all the qualities necessary for a rôle demanding restriction of self-assertion and consideration of others. Expansionism developed the conception of self-interest as the steady enhancement of national power. Its instinctive and philosophical egocentrism fostered a type of national morality which generally pointed in the direction of the self-interest sought by integral nationalism. Largely in consequence, the expansionist phase of American history was marked first by the ignoring of international collaboration and second by a perversion of the ideal into a justification for imperialism.

Nor is even the recent past, despite its ideology interpreting world leadership anti-expansionistically, altogether encouraging. Through the first two decades of the twentieth century Americans talked of international leadership more than they acted the rôle; they finally rejected it in 1920 when the opportunity was apparently most promising but called for action. There followed years in which it could with much justice be said by President Butler that America's lack of international policies made it a " dangerous derelict " blocking the channels to international collaboration.[126] Even after America found its course again and ceased to endanger others, its prudence for itself stood in the way of greatest helpfulness to others. A recent presidential pronouncement disavowed the very contemplation of leadership in the Wilsonian sense of initiative within the League; and Senators considered even the World Court identical with the League. The international collaboration which has been offered is only that conforming to Secretary Stimson's formula of " cooperation for peace and justice " within limits permitting " independence of action and . . . flexibility of judgment." [127] A fruitful collaboration is doubtless possible even without complete commitment to the League. But to proffer only a collaboration devoid of all serious commitments may well seem to withhold more than is meet and tend to poverty. To paraphrase President Roosevelt, the way to lead is after all to lead — to encourage group action by preeminent courage in imposing group commitments upon oneself. The inadequacy of anything short of this to the assurance of peace and political stability has been sufficiently evidenced by more than one fiasco of international diplomacy which America's full collaboration might possibly have averted. The difficult question as to what is right or wise need not be answered in order to make with respect to America's foreign policy an internal criticism — that the years of anti-expansionism no less than those of expansionism evidence an inconsistency between ideology and practice. The former centered in the ideal of leadership and the latter was a discouraging example of failure even to accept definitive membership in the group.

From this inconsistency, which is almost the universal relationship between difficult international ideals and practice, it by no means follows that the American's talk of world leadership has been insincere. But when ideology does not fully stamp its implications upon policy it is open to the suspicion of lack of wholeheartedness. Americans have cherished the ideal of world leadership enough for anti-expansionism but not enough for a dangerous or even arduous policy of positive action. In their attitude toward international collaboration many Americans are "divided in their own soul." Still more of them, particularly since the menacing chaos in European affairs has given them a specious justification, are devoted to national self-sufficiency and hostile to all save commercial traffic with the "knaves and fools" outside. The thesis of America's world leadership has been largely used as a pragmatic fiction. It is designed either to convert others to an ideal as yet unaccepted by them or to avoid the painful recognition of the fact that America's actual policy is, relatively to that of others, laggard in international collaboration. Thus Wilson's dogma that America "can only go forward" toward a destiny of leadership is better supported by his faith in Providence than by the empirical study of America's past and present.

However, isolationism as well as internationalism has its uncritical dogmas which it seeks to support by the pseudo-empiricism declaring that "all history shows." An isolationist dogma seems to be implied by Calvin Coolidge's words, "If we have any destiny," it is to be "more and more American."[128] Americanism has been interpreted by Mr. Lothrop Stoddard in a way which prompts him to ask, "Should we not admit frankly that the way to genuine internationalism is barred?"[129] Most of those supporting such a view of destiny assume a deterministic theory of psychology and history: that egoistic motives not only are the sole determinants of national behavior but lead inevitably to a policy of integral nationalism. Historical study of nationalist ideology warns against such dogmatic generalizations — if only because it induces agreement with the observation of John Adams that it is vain if not wicked to hope to understand God's universe completely. Even historical study unusually conducive to cynicism has not, unfortunately for simplicity, supported the generalizations of integral nationalism.

Adam Ferguson's doctrine that "interest and profit furnish the motives by which nations actually determine their organizations and policies" [130] goes counter to the apparent finding that moral ideology, even if seldom a primary motive, must at least give its blessing to the decisions of self-interest. The expansionist may have had the very devil in his blood, but he could not take or enjoy his land without saying grace to a manifest destiny identified with the will of God. The expansionist's piety converged with his self-interest, but this fact does not validate the cynic's doctrine that "interest" is the sole "spring of just and right." When American expansionism flourished, the existence of large areas of backward civilization, of undeveloped economic resources, and of political disorder and oppression, lent plausibility to the American expansionist's thesis that "the spread of empire is . . . most compatible with the establishment of the greatest good to the greatest number." [131] It gave this thesis at least a much stronger basis than the expansionist's usual defective statement of his grounds would suggest. More particularly is this true since the international organization of the world's welfare had not yet become or appeared a practicable alternative to expansionist philanthropy. But as soon as the international benefits of self-restraint and collaboration obviously outweighed those of further imperialist expansion, American expansionism subsided. Expediency alone cannot account for this subsidence; for where expediency demands self-restraint it requires the reinforcing stimulus of principle. It even seems true that a minority replaced expansionism with international collaboration because they, like America's almost successfully idealistic president, believed that "the point in national affairs . . . never lies along the lines of expediency" but always "in the field of principle." [132] Such were those whose hedonism took the form noted by Cicero: "Nothing is more agreeable to nature, more capable of affording true satisfaction, than, in imitation of Hercules, to undertake even the most arduous and painful labors for the benefit and preservation of all nations." [133]

It is perhaps true that, as Madison remarked in the magnificently frank debate on the founding of the Republic, little is to be expected from conscience in large numbers.[134] But the second fallacy of the integral nationalist is his assumption that interest, from which he expects everything, is a bar to the self-restraints of international collaboration. The very cynicism which attributes America's recent anti-expansionism and increase of cooperativeness to interest acknowledges the fortunate fruits of interest. And it is probably true that any progress in the internationalism of American outlook must be credited primarily to the enlightened egoism which sees international collaboration, within certain limits, as the surest instrument of national self-interest. The chief obstacle to further progress in internationalism may lie not in true national interest but in the fact that of two competing conceptions of interest the patriot tends to choose the one which appeals to nationalist emotion rather than to reason.

But it is precisely in the conflict between a false and a true idea of interest that conscience may play a decisive part. It may ally itself with the valid conception of interest; for Jefferson spoke with much truth when he said that "virtue and interest are inseparable." [135] The coincidence of virtue and interest may be attributed to a merciful Providence who does not wish virtue to be too difficult. Little may be expected from social conscience in isolation, if only because of the ease of finding speciously moral reasons for listening to manifest destiny instead. But from conscience in its alliance with interest one may expect much that is fortunate as well as much that is bad; and despite all the frequency of past disappointment hope "springs eternal." One is not without ground for hoping that the moral factor, with its strong emotional appeal, may throw its weight to the more rational and social of two competing ideas of interest and so give to it preponderance. It is the ironical but fortunate system of mutual aid between interest and moral sentiment which after all affords the strongest hope that international leadership may be seen in America's future as interest and therefore as destiny.

At least, it seems a moderately encouraging implication of the history of the doctrine of manifest destiny that the future is open, that it is not closed even by any determinism of self-interest. And once more, just as when Wilson spoke, Americans "have got to choose . . . what kind of future it is going to be for America." [136] Once more, too, the choice is between rejection or acceptance of the leadership which a world in need apparently offers to America almost on America's own terms.

Perhaps this choice of policy involves another in the sphere of ideas: a decision whether the idea of a national destiny, a cosmically important assignment from Providence or "moral necessity," [137] shall be accepted from the past by the present. The idea of a destiny seems to thrive only upon the soil of expansionism, with which, in a sense, such a choice has to do. The expansion in question is the extension of the spirit of the nation in the hope of influencing beneficently a larger social order. Even when expansion was seen as territorial, manifest destiny was defined with reference to our "duties and responsibilities" to "the world." [138] In the light of present American values and contemporary world circumstances, it may seem that an internationally beneficent destiny can lie in only one path. It is the path of active leadership in organizing the rational international life essential to the security of all other humane values.

That the idea of manifest destiny will survive as directive force is, however, by no means manifest. For there is implicit in much of contemporary American thought a by no means unpersuasive opposition which would place upon the idea the inscription, *Requiescat in pace.* It would be admitted that the idea not only nurtured America's expansionism when expansion was advantageous but helped to wean America from expansionism when expansion was no longer an advantage. Yet now that America has apparently found a balance between the will to power and international amity, the idea seems to some to be useful neither to national interest nor to the fulfilment of reasonable obligations. The continuance of this dogmatic, emotional, and pretentious notion would arouse in many the fear that recently prompted an American to write:

> What is dangerous to the world is not that nations should act reasonably, in accordance with their interest, but that they should act

unreasonably, at the dictation of the reforming instinct, or of some megalomaniac dream.[139]

But believers in the idea of manifest destiny — though no longer vocal they may still exist — would maintain that at least in its moral purposiveness the idea of a national destiny is not unreasonable. They would affirm that, since the ultimate standard of reasonableness must in national as in individual life be moral feeling rather than self-interest, there is truth in the doctrine of Mazzini and O'Sullivan — nation is mission. Theirs is the attitude toward destiny and time which was depicted by the American poet of expansionist but humanitarian nationalism in the verses wherein he spoke of democracy as "the destin'd conqueror."[140] It was Walt Whitman's teaching that moral instinct conquers when it fashions the concept of destiny after its own adventurous energy — as something never consummated but always in process, an ever-receding future to be continuously approached in the present.

If the past has bequeathed the fullness of its spirit to the present, America's pursuit of a destiny is not yet ended:

Others take finish, but the Republic is ever constructive and ever keeps vista,<br>
Others adorn the past, but you O days of the present, I adorn you,<br>
O days of the future I believe in you—I isolate myself for your sake,<br>
O America because you build for mankind I build for you,<br>
O well-beloved stone-cutters, I lead them who plan with decision and science,<br>
Lead the present with friendly hand toward the future.

# NOTES *

## Notes to Introduction

[1] Woodrow Wilson, "The Ideals of America," *Atlantic Monthly*, XC (1902), 726.

[2] *Congressional Record*, 63d Cong., 1st sess., p. 5862.

[3] Wilson, *op cit.*, p. 169.

[4] J. A. Hobson, *Imperialism* (New York, 1902), p. 390.

[5] A. Clutton-Brock, "Pooled Self-Esteem," *Atlantic Monthly,* CXXVIII (1921), 721-31.

[6] Albert Shaw, "The Monroe Doctrine and the Evolution of Democracy," *Proceedings of the Academy of Political Science*, VII (1917), 471.

[7] Jesse S. Reeves, *American Diplomacy under Tyler and Polk* (Baltimore, 1907), p. 58.

[8] Charles A. Beard, *The Idea of National Interest: an Analytical Study in American Foreign Policy* (New York, 1934), pp. 388-89.

[9] *Ibid.*, p. 358.

[10] G. Olphe-Galliard, *La morale des nations* (Paris, 1920), p. 78.

[11] William Ernest Hocking, *The Spirit of World Politics, with Special Studies of the Near East* (New York, 1932), p. 492.

[12] Ludwig Gumplowicz, *Allgemeines Staatsrecht* (3d ed.; Innsbruck, 1907), p. 425.

[13] Francis Delaisi, *Political Myths and Economic Realities* (London, 1927), p. 195.

[14] *Works of Fisher Ames*, ed. Seth Ames (Boston, 1854), I, 329.

## Notes to Chapter I

## NATURAL RIGHT

[1] John (Viscount) Morley, *Notes on Politics and History* (New York, 1914), p. 72.

[2] Albert Sorel, *L'Europe et la révolution française* (4th ed.; Paris, 1897), I, 19.

[3] *Mazzini's Letters to an English Family 1855-1860*, ed. E. F. Richards (New York, 1920-1922), II, 169.

[4] *A Letter to the Hon. Henry Clay, on the Annexation of Texas to the United States*, in *The Works of William E. Channing, D. D.* (Boston, 1846), II, 205-06.

---

* The edition cited in the first reference is to be understood in all subsequent citations from the same work, except where another edition is specified.

[5] Arthur O. Lovejoy and George Boas, *Primitivism and Related Ideas in Antiquity* (Baltimore, 1935), chap iii.

[6] Carlton J. H. Hayes, *The Historical Evolution of Modern Nationalism* (New York, 1931), pp. 16 ff.

[7] Sorel, *op. cit.*, I, 39.

[8] Hayes, *op. cit.*, p. 11.

[9] Jean Jacques Rousseau, *The Social Contract*, Library of Liberal Classics ed. (New York, 1893), pp. 13-20.

[10] Paul Henri Thiry (Baron d') Holbach, *La politique naturelle* (London, 1773), II, 195.

[11] Hayes, *op. cit.*, pp. 19-20.

[12] Richard Price, *Observations on the Nature of Civil Liberty* (6th ed.; London, 1776), pp. 32-33, 40-41.

[13] John Cartwright, *American Independence the Interest and Glory of Great Britain* (Philadelphia, 1776), Letters X and XI, pp. 31-39, 107-17.

[14] E. de Vattel, *The Law of Nations; or Principles of the Law of Nature*, 4th Am. ed. from the ed. of Joseph Chitty (Philadelphia, 1835), p. 169.

[15] J. J. Burlamaqui, *The Principles of Politic Law*, tr. Nugent (London, 1752), pp. 231, 233.

[16] *Ideen zur Philosophie der Geschichte der Menschheit*, in *Herder's Sämmtliche Werke*, ed. Bernhard Suphan (Berlin, 1877-1913), XIII, 384.

[17] James Otis, *The Rights of the British Colonies Asserted and Proved* (Boston, 1764), p. 35.

[18] *The Farmer Refuted*, in *The Works of Alexander Hamilton*, ed. J. C. Hamilton (New York, 1850), II, 43.

[19] *Common Sense*, in *The Writings of Thomas Paine*, ed. M. D. Conway (New York, 1894), I, 99.

[20] *The Crisis*, *ibid.*, I, 171.

[21] *The Letters of Richard Henry Lee*, ed. J. C. Ballagh (New York, 1911-1914), I, 128.

[22] *The Works of John Adams*, ed. C. F. Adams (Boston, 1856), I, 230.

[23] Robert Michels, *Der Patriotismus*; *Prolegomena zu seiner soziologischen Analyse* (München, 1929), p. 40.

[24] *The Rising Glory of America*, in *The Poems of Philip Freneau*, ed. F. L. Pattee (Princeton, 1902), I, 49 ff.

[25] *Works of John Adams*, I, 66.

[26] Hezekiah Niles, *Principles and Acts of the Revolution in America* (Baltimore, 1822), p. 63.

[27] *Common Sense*, in *Writings of Thomas Paine*, I, 68.

[28] Claude Halstead Van Tyne, *The American Revolution 1776-1783* (New York, 1905), p. 333.

[29] *Ibid.*

[30] Nathan Fiske, *An Oration Delivered . . . November 14, 1781 . . .* (Boston, n. d.), p. 7.

[31] *Public Good*, in *Writings of Thomas Paine*, II, 35.

[32] John Locke, *Two Treatises on Civil Government* (London, 1884), Bk. II, chap. xvi, 284-94.

[33] Timothy Dwight, "Columbia," reprinted in *A Library of American Literature from the Earliest Settlement to the Present Time*, ed. E. C. Stedman and E. M. Hutchinson (New York, 1891), III, 480.

[34] David Humphreys, *A Poem, on the Happiness of America*, in *A Poem, Addressed to the Armies of the United States of America* (New Haven, 1785), p. 11. (This poem was written during the Revolution.)

[35] Joel Barlow, *The Vision of Columbus* (Hartford, 1787), pp. 250-52. (This poem was in large part composed during the Revolution.)

[36] *A Letter Addressed to the People of Piedmont*, in *The Political Writings of Joel Barlow* (New York, 1796), p. 230.

[37] Samuel Cooper, *A Sermon Preached . . . October 25, 1780* (Boston, 1780), p. 52.

[38] George Bancroft, *History of the United States of America* (New York, 1885), V, 305.

[39] Albert Bushnell Hart, *The Foundations of American Foreign Policy* (New York, 1901), pp. 174-75.

[40] *Warren-Adams Letters*, in *Massachusetts Historical Society Collections*, Vol. 72 (Boston, 1917), I, 208.

[41] Edmund C. Burnett, ed., *Letters of Members of the Continental Congress* (Washington, 1921), III, 476.

[42] Paul Chrisler Phillips, *The West in the Diplomacy of the American Revolution* (Champaign, 1913), p. 178.

[43] *Peace, and the Newfoundland Fisheries*, in *Writings of Thomas Paine*, II, 19.

[44] Jonathan Mayhew, *A Sermon Preach'd . . . May 29th, 1754* (Boston, 1754), p. 37.

[45] *The Writings of Samuel Adams*, ed. H. A. Cushing (New York, 1907), III, 274.

[46] Francis Wharton, ed., *The Revolutionary Diplomatic Correspondence of the United States* (Washington, 1889), II, 667.

[47] Phillips, *op. cit.*, p. 9.

[48] *Common Sense*, in *Writings of Thomas Paine*, I, 116.

[49] Justin H. Smith, *Our Struggles for the Fourteenth Colony: Canada and the American Revolution* (New York, 1907), I, 215.

[50] *Selected Political Essays of James Wilson*, ed. R. G. Adams (New York, 1930), p. 304.

[51] Burnett, *op. cit.*, III, 476.

[52] De Jaucourt, "Conquêt," *Encyclopédie*, ed. Diderot (Paris, 1751-65), IX, 4.

[53] Burnett, *op. cit.*, IV, 185.

[54] *Ibid.*, p. 142.

[55] "The Papers of Charles Thomson, Secretary of the Continental Congress," *Collections of the New York Historical Society, 1878* (New York, 1879), p. 144.

[56] *The Interest of Great Britain Considered with Regard to Her Colonies*, in

*The Writings of Benjamin Franklin*, ed. A. H. Smyth (New York, 1906), IV, 38-40.

[57] *Writings of Benjamin Franklin*, VIII, 472.

[58] Quoted by Charles Sumner, *Prophetic Voices Concerning America* (Boston, 1876), p. 142.

[59] William Edward Hall, *A Treatise on International Law*, ed. A. P. Higgins (8th ed.; Oxford, 1924), pp. 164-71.

[60] *American Museum*, "Address of the Convention of Kentucke, to the United States in Congress Assembled," V (1789), 332.

[61] Barbé Marbois, *The History of Louisiana* (Philadelphia, 1830), p. 216.

[62] *The Writings of Thomas Jefferson*, ed. P. L. Ford (New York, 1895), V, 468.

[63] Thomas Rutherforth, *Institutes of Natural Law* (Cambridge, 1754-56), I, 33.

[64] *Writings of Thomas Jefferson*, VIII, 261.

[65] *The Works of James Madison*, ed. Gaillard Hunt (New York, 1901), II, 121.

[66] *Ibid.*, p. 73.

[67] *Writings of Thomas Jefferson*, V, 217.

[68] *Ibid.*, p. 219.

[69] Cyprian Strong, *A Discourse Delivered . . . July 4th, 1799* (Hartford, 1799), p. 13.

[70] James D. Richardson, ed., *A Compilation of the Messages and Papers of the Presidents, 1789-1897* (New York, 1896-1899), I, 323.

[71] *Writings of Thomas Jefferson*, VIII, 147.

[72] *Ibid.*, p. 145.

[73] *Ibid.*, p. 207.

[74] Gilbert Chinard, *Thomas Jefferson* (Boston, 1929), p. 396.

[75] Gilbert Chinard, ed., *The Correspondence of Jefferson and Du Pont de Nemours* (Baltimore, 1931), p. 51.

[76] *Writings of Thomas Jefferson*, VIII, 145.

[77] Chinard, *Thomas Jefferson*, p. 398.

[78] *Ibid.*

[79] *Annals of Congress*, 7th Cong., 2d sess., col. 84.

[80] *Ibid.*, col. 86.

[81] *Ibid.*, cols. 372-73.

[82] *Ibid.*, col. 183.

[83] *Ibid.*, col. 189.

[84] *The Life and Correspondence of Rufus King*, ed. C. R. King (New York, 1894-1900), IV, 246.

[85] *American State Papers, Foreign Relations*, II, 516.

[86] *New-York Evening Post*, January 28, 1803.

[87] *American Museum*, "Letter from Captain John Sullivan . . . to the Spanish Minister at New York," III (1788), 436.

[88] *New-York Evening Post*, January 10, 1803.

[89] *Writings of Thomas Jefferson*, VIII, 144-45.

[90] Edward Channing, *The Jeffersonian System, 1801-1811* (New York, 1906), p. 88.

[91] James Alexander Robertson, ed., *Louisiana under the Rule of Spain, France, and the United States, 1785-1807* (Cleveland, 1911), II, 125-26.

[92] Talcott Williams, "The Ethical and Political Principles of 'Expansion,'" *Annals* of the American Academy of Political and Social Science, XVI (1900), 232-33.

[93] Richardson, *Messages*, I, 358.

[94] Representative Campbell, *Annals of Cong.*, 8th Cong., 1st sess., col. 1063.

[95] Representative Lyon, *ibid.*, col. 1059.

[96] *Ibid.*, 2d sess., col. 1599.

[97] *Ibid.*, 1st sess., col. 1058.

[98] *Writings of Thomas Jefferson*, VIII, 283.

[99] *Writings of Thomas Paine*, III, 431.

[100] Charles Gayarré, *History of Louisiana* (New Orleans, 1885), IV, 56.

[101] *Writings of Thomas Jefferson*, V, 205.

[102] John W. Burgess, *Political Science and Comparative Constitutional Law* (Boston, 1893), I, 45.

[103] John Neville Figgis, *The Theory of the Divine Right of Kings* (Cambridge, 1896), p. 256.

[104] *Annals of Cong.*, 8th Cong., 1st. sess., col. 1058.

[105] *Ibid.*, col. 1059.

[106] Ellery C. Stowell, *International Law* (New York, 1931), p. 127.

[107] *Le Moniteur Universel*, February 17, 1793, p. 220.

[108] *Writings of Thomas Jefferson*, X, 32.

[109] *The Foederalist*, ed. H. B. Dawson (New York, 1867), I, 57.

[110] *Works of John Adams*, III, 433.

[111] *Adrastea*, in *Herder's Sämmtliche Werke*, XXIII, 214.

[112] *Briefe zur Beförderung der Humanität*, *ibid.*, XVII, 212.

[113] Ezra Stiles, "The United States Elevated to Glory and Honor," in *The Pulpit of the American Revolution*, ed. J. W. Thornton (2d ed.; Boston, 1876), p. 403.

[114] Chinard, *Thomas Jefferson*, p. 428.

[115] *Ibid.*

[116] John Cushing, *A Discourse Delivered . . . July 4, 1796* (Leominster, Mass., 1796), p. 6.

[117] Timothy Dwight, "Good Advice in Bad Verse," in *American History Told by Contemporaries*, ed. A. B. Hart (New York, 1901), III, 203.

[118] Richardson, *Messages*, I, 322.

[119] *Ibid.*, p. 382.

[120] *A Defence of the Constitutions of Government of the United States of America*, in *Works of John Adams*, IV, 293.

[121] Joseph Hopkinson, "Hail Columbia," in *American History Told by Contemporaries*, III, 327.

[122] *New-York Evening Post*, January 27, 1803.

[123] *Southern Quarterly Review*, "The Invasion of Cuba," XXI (1852), 11.

[124] *Brooklyn Citizen*, quoted by *Public Opinion*, XXXIV (1903), 648.

## Notes to Chapter II

## GEOGRAPHICAL PREDESTINATION

[1] *The Writings of James Monroe*, ed. S. M. Hamilton (New York, 1900), IV, 74.

[2] Henry Adams, *History of the United States of America* (New York, 1921), II, 245; III, 22.

[3] Félix (le Chevalier) de Beaujour, *Sketch of the United States of North America*, tr. William Walton (London, 1814), p. 284.

[4] Isaac Joslin Cox, *The West Florida Controversy, 1798-1813* (Baltimore, 1918), p. 668.

[5] Charles J. Ingersoll, *Recollections, Historical, Political, Biographical, and Social* (Philadelphia, 1861), p. 393.

[6] Pliny, *Naturalis Historia*, xxxvi, 1, 2.

[7] Hugo Grotius, *De Jure Belli ac Pacis*, in *The Classics of International Law* (Oxford, 1925), II, 218.

[8] *Ideen*, in *Herder's Sämmtliche Werke*, XIII, 341.

[9] *Paix perpetuelle*, in *The Political Writings of Rousseau*, ed. C. E. Vaughan (Cambridge, 1915), I, 370.

[10] Vicente Folch, *Reflections on Louisiana*, in Robertson, *Louisiana*, II, 331.

[11] De Beaujour, *op. cit.*, pp. xvi, 284.

[12] *Journals of the Continental Congress 1774-1789*, ed. Gaillard Hunt (Washington, 1910), XVIII, 939.

[13] John Bassett Moore, ed., *A Digest of International Law* (Washington, 1906), VI, 465.

[14] Quoted by Frederick Jackson Turner, "The Policy of France toward the Mississippi Valley in the Period of Washington and Adams," *American Historical Review*, X (1905), 276.

[15] *Ibid.*, p. 279.

[16] *American Museum*, III (1788), 437.

[17] *Writings of Thomas Jefferson*, V, 219.

[18] *New-York Evening Post*, December 30, 1802.

[19] *Annals of Cong.*, 7th Cong., 2d sess., col. 150.

[20] *Ibid.*, col. 204.

[21] Burgess, *Political Science and Comparative Constitutional Law*, I, 41.

[22] Quoted by Cox, *op. cit.*, p. 330.

[23] *Am. State Papers, For. Rel.*, II, 626.

[24] *Niles' Weekly Register*, "Cuba and the Floridas," XVII (1820), 305.

[25] *Works of Fisher Ames*, I, 323-24.

[26] Joseph Chandler, *An Oration Delivered . . . on the Fourth of July, 1804* . . (Portland, 1804), p. 11.

[27] *Journal of the Times*, I (1818), 205.

[28] De Beaujour, *op. cit.*, p. 133.

[29] *Annals of Cong.*, 16th Cong., 1st sess., col. 1728.

[30] *Ibid.*, col. 1769.

[31] *Ibid.*, 7th Cong., 2d sess., col. 150.

[32] (Sir) Thomas H. Holdich, *Political Frontiers and Boundary Making* (London, 1916), p. 46.

[33] *Annals of Cong.*, 7th Cong., 2d sess., col. 204.

[34] New Orleans *Gazette*, March 28, 1806, quoted by William F. McCaleb, *The Aaron Burr Conspiracy* (New York, 1903), p. 52.

[35] Quincy Wright, "Territorial Propinquity," *American Journal of International Law*, XII (1918), 520.

[36] Ingersoll, *op. cit.*, p. 21.

[37] Frankfort (Kentucky) *Commentator*, May 28, 1819.

[38] *Political Writings of Joel Barlow*, p. 230.

[39] *Am. State Papers, For. Rel.*, II, 664.

[40] M. F. Lindley, *The Acquisition and Government of Backward Territory in International Law* (New York, 1926), p. 279.

[41] *Am. State Papers, For. Rel.*, II, 664.

[42] Thomas Hart Benton, *Thirty Years' View* (New York, 1854), I, 15.

[43] Robert J. Walker, *Letter . . . Relative to the Annexation of Texas* (Washington, 1844), p. 9.

[44] *Congressional Globe*, 28th Cong., 2d sess., App., p. 270.

[45] Julius W. Pratt, *Expansionists of 1812* (New York, 1925).

[46] D. R. Anderson, "The Insurgents of 1811," *Annual Report of the American Historical Association, 1911*, I, 176.

[47] *Annals of Cong.*, 12th Cong., 1st sess., col. 458.

[48] *Ibid.*, col. 657.

[49] *Boston Patriot*, reprinted in *Republican and Savannah Evening Ledger*, February 25, 1812.

[50] *Annals of Cong.*, 12th Cong., 2d sess., col. 758.

[51] *Writings of Thomas Jefferson*, VIII, 450.

[52] *Annals of Cong.*, 12th Cong., 1st sess., col. 973.

[53] *Ibid.*, col. 995.

[54] Representative Keitt, *Cong. Globe,* 35th Cong., 2d sess., p. 457.

[55] *Annals of Cong.*, 16th Cong., 1st sess., cols. 1762, 1768.

[56] *Cong. Globe*, 28th Cong., 2d sess., p. 86.

[57] Senator Buchanan, *ibid.*, 1st sess., p. 721.

[58] Quoted by J. Fred Rippy, *The United States and Mexico* (New York, 1926), p. 141.

[59] *Cong. Globe*, 40th Cong., 1st sess., p. 603.

[60] *Independent*, "A Scientific Border," LXXIX (1914), 115.

[61] Chandler, *op. cit.*, p. 11.

[62] Thomas J. Green, *Journals of the Texian Expedition against Mier* (New York, 1845), p. 406.

[63] Harry H. Powers, *America among the Nations* (New York, 1921), p. 58.

[64] *Annals of Cong.*, 17th Cong., 2d sess., col. 598.

[65] *Register of Debates in Congress*, 18th Cong., 2d sess., col. 712.

[66] *Annals of Cong.*, 17th Cong., 2d sess., cols. 682-83.

[67] 21st Cong., 2d sess., *Senate Document*, No. 39, p. 19.

[68] Quoted by Ellen Churchill Semple, *American History and Its Geographic Conditions* (Boston, 1903), p. 110.

[69] *Ibid.*, p. 232.

[70] *Cong. Globe*, 28th Cong., 2d sess., App., p. 294.

[71] *Nashville Republican and State Gazette*, reprinted by *St. Louis Beacon*, September 9, 1829.

[72] *Annals of Cong.*, 17th Cong., 2d sess., col. 683.

[73] *Am. State Papers, For. Rel.*, V, 447.

[74] *Ibid.*, p. 554.

[75] *Ibid.*, p. 437.

[76] *Ibid.*, p. 451.

[77] *Ibid.*, IV, 854.

[78] *Memoirs of John Quincy Adams*, ed. C. F. Adams (Philadelphia, 1875), IV, 438-39.

[79] Jonathan Mitchel Sewall, "Epilogue to Cato," in *Library of American Literature*, III, 388.

[80] J. G. M. Ramsey, *The Annals of Tennessee to the End of the Eighteenth Century* (Charleston, 1853), p. 350.

[81] Chandler, *op. cit.*, p. 11.

[82] Nashville *Democratic Clarion and Tennessee Gazette,* April 28, 1812.

[83] Pratt, *op. cit.*, pp. 13-14.

[84] *New York Morning News*, December 27, 1845.

[85] *Common Sense*, in *Writings of Thomas Paine*, I, 89.

[86] Richardson, *Messages*, I, 222.

[87] *The Writings of George Washington*, ed. W. C. Ford (New York, 1891), XI, 204.

[88] *The Foederalist*, No. 11, I, 88.

[89] *The Diary and Letters of Gouverneur Morris*, ed. A. C. Morris (New York, 1888), II, 435.

[90] *Cong. Globe*, 29th Cong., 1st sess., p. 200.

[91] *Am. State Papers, For. Rel.*, IV, 844.

[92] Moore, *Digest*, VI, 552.

[93] George Nathaniel (Lord) Curzon, *Frontiers* (Oxford, 1908), p. 13.

[94] *Annals of Cong.*, 11th Cong., 3d sess., col. 500.

[95] *The Writings of John Quincy Adams*, ed. W. C. Ford (New York, 1917), VII, 372.

[96] *The Everett Letters on Cuba* (Boston, 1897), p. 5.

[97] William R. Manning, ed., *Diplomatic Correspondence of the United States Concerning the Independence of the Latin-American Nations* (New York, 1925), I, 231.

[98] *Writings of James Monroe*, VI, 313.

[99] *Cong. Globe*, 35th Cong., 2d sess., p. 539.

[100] *Am. State Papers, For. Rel.*, V, 446.

[101] Moore, *Digest*, I, 575.

[102] *The Writings of Thomas Jefferson*, Memorial ed. (Washington, 1903), XII, 277.

[103] Representative Levin, *Cong. Globe*, 29th Cong., 1st sess., App., p. 96.

[104] Frank E. Stevens, "Life of Stephen Arnold Douglas," *Journal of the Illinois State Historical Society,* XVI (1923-24), 372.

[105] Washington *Daily Union*, July 21, 1854.

[106] Quoted by Hart, *Foundations of American Foreign Policy*, p. 108.

[107] *Cong. Globe*, 40th Cong., 3d sess., p. 339.

[108] *Boston Herald*, January 31, 1893.

[109] *Cong. Rec.*, 55th Cong., 2d sess., p. 5840.

[110] *Ibid.*, p. 5795.

[111] *New York Tribune*, November 15, 1893.

[112] *Writings of Thomas Jefferson*, Memorial ed., XV, 263.

[113] Charles Denby, "Shall We Keep the Philippines?" *Forum*, XXVI (1898), 281.

[114] *New York Recorder*, quoted by *Public Opinion*, XIV (1893), 467.

[115] E. Kimpen, *Die Ausbreitungspolitik der Vereinigten Staaten von Amerika* (Stuttgart, 1923), p. 298.

[116] *Indianapolis Journal*, September 17, 1898.

[117] *Boston Herald*, December 15, 1898.

[118] *New York Tribune*, quoted by *Public Opinion*, VI (1889), 343.

[119] Whitelaw Reid, *Problems of Expansion* (New York, 1900), p. 239.

[120] *Indianapolis Journal*, September 17, 1898.

[121] James Harrington, *The Commonwealth of Oceana* (London, 1887), p. 14.

[122] *Table Talk*, in *The Complete Works of Samuel Taylor Coleridge*, ed. Shedd (New York, 1854), VI, 446.

[123] George T. Winston to William E. Chandler, January 5, 1899, MS. Chandler Papers, Library of Congress.

[124] Manuel Ugarte, *The Destiny of a Continent*, tr. J. F. Rippy (New York, 1925), pp. 135-36.

[125] George T. Weitzel, "The United States and Central America," *Annals* of the American Academy of Political and Social Science, XXXII (1927), 115.

[126] William R. Shepherd, "The Attitude of the United States toward the Retention by European Nations of Colonies in and around the Caribbean," *Proceedings of the Academy of Political Science*, VII (1917), 394.

[127] Moorfield Storey, "The Caribbean Question," *ibid.*, p. 434.

[128] Moore, *Digest*, VI, 551.

[129] O. D. von Engeln, *Inheriting the Earth; or the Geographical Factor in National Development* (New York, 1922), p. v.

[130] Curzon, *op. cit.*, p. 7.

[131] Semple, *op. cit.*, p. 232.

[132] Representative Trimble, *Annals of Cong.*, 16th Cong., 1st sess., col. 1762.

[133] *Reg. of Debates*, 18th Cong., 2d sess., col. 1825.

[134] Johann Sölch, *Die Auffassung der "natürlichen Grenzen" in der wissenschaftlichen Geographie* (Innsbruck, 1924), p. 10.

[135] *Cong. Globe*, 28th Cong., 2d sess., App., p. 294.

## Notes to Chapter III

## THE DESTINED USE OF THE SOIL

[1] Moore, *Digest*, I, 31.

[2] Ulrich Bonnell Phillips, "Georgia and State Rights," *Annual Report of the American Historical Association, 1901*, II, 53.

[3] *Writings of Thomas Jefferson*, IV, 166.

[4] Representative Cushing, *Cong. Globe*, 24th Cong., 2d sess., App., p. 305.

[5] Carl Schurz, "Present Aspects of the Indian Problem," *North American Review*, CXXXIII (1881), 1.

[6] H. H. Powers, "The Ethics of Expansion," *International Journal of Ethics*, X (1900), 292.

[7] Representative Wayne, *Reg. of Debates*, 21st Cong., 1st sess., p. 1126.

[8] *Cong. Globe*, 27th Cong., 3d sess., App., p. 74.

[9] John Winthrop, *Conclusions for the Plantation in New England*, in *Old South Leaflets* (Boston, 1895), No. 50, pp. 5, 6-7.

[10] Peter Oliver, *The Puritan Commonwealth* (Boston, 1856), pp. 103-04, 102.

[11] John Winthrop, *The History of New England from 1630 to 1649*, ed. James Savage (Boston, 1853), I, 349.

[12] Quoted by James Kent, *Commentaries on American Law* (2d ed.; New York, 1832), III, 387.

[13] James Buchanan, *Sketches of the History, Manners, and Customs of the North American Indians* (New York, 1824), I, 41-42.

[14] *Knickerbocker's History of New York*, in *The Works of Washington Irving* (New York, n. d.), IV, 51-52.

[15] William Hubbard, *A General History of New England* (Cambridge, 1815), p. 210.

[16] *Memoirs of John Quincy Adams*, III, 42.

[17] *United States Magazine*, "Establishment of These United States," I (1779), 161-62. (The author of this unsigned article is probably Hugh Brackenridge, the editor.)

[18] *Narratives of the Perils and Sufferings of Dr. Knight and John Slover* (Cincinnati, 1867), pp. 62-71.

[19] *Autobiography, Writings of Benjamin Franklin*, I, 376.

[20] Vattel, *The Law of Nations*, Bk. I, chap. xviii, as quoted by Representative Wayne, *Reg. of Debates*, 21st Cong., 1st sess., p. 1125.

[21] (Sir) Thomas More, Everyman's ed. (New York, 1910), pp. 60-61.

[22] William Archibald Dunning, *A History of Political Theories from Luther to Montesquieu* (New York, 1916), pp. 17-18.

[23] *The Complete Works of Abraham Lincoln*, ed. J. G. Nicolay and John Hay (New York, 1920), I, 613.

[24] *Memoirs of John Quincy Adams*, III, 27-28.

[25] John P. Kennedy, *Memoirs of the Life of William Wirt* (Philadelphia, 1860), II, 260.

[26] Quoted by John F. Cady, "Western Opinion and the War of 1812," *Ohio Archaeological and Historical Society Publications*, XXXIII (1924), 435-36.

[27] Raymond G. Gettell, *History of Political Thought* (New York, 1924), p. 283.

[28] *Annals of Cong.*, 15th Cong., 2d sess., col. 838.

[29] *Reg. of Debates*, 21st Cong., 1st sess., p. 1078.

[30] *Am. State Papers, Indian Affairs*, I, 13.

[31] 8 Wheaton 603.

[32] Moore, *Digest*, I, 31.

[33] *North American Review*, "Letters on the Eastern States," XI (1820), 94-96.

[34] William C. Dawson, *A Compilation of the Laws of the State of Georgia* (Milledgeville, 1831), Resolut ons—1827, p. 98.

[35] *Journal of the House of Representatives of the State of Georgia, 1830* (Milledgeville, 1830), p. 13.

[36] 21st Cong., 1st sess., *House Committee Reports*, No. 227, p. 7.

[37] *Ibid.*, p. 4.

[38] *Reg. of Debates*, 21st Cong., 1st sess., p. 1083.

[39] Cf. George Lassudrie-Duchêne, *Jean-Jacques Rousseau et le droit des gens* (Paris, 1906), pp. 82 ff.

[40] Kent, *op. cit.*, III, 386.

[41] *Reg. of Debates*, 21st Cong., 1st sess., p. 1125.

[42] *Ibid.*, p. 1103.

[43] *North American Review*, "Removal of the Indians," XXX (1830), 77.

[44] *Reg. of Debates*, 21st Cong., 1st sess., p. 1103.

[45] *Memoirs of John Quincy Adams*, VI, 272.

[46] *Reg. of Debates*, 21st Cong., 1st sess., p. 1066.

[47] *Am. State Papers, Indian Affairs*, II, 463.

[48] *Ibid.*, p. 469.

[49] Kennedy, *op. cit.*, II, 260.

[50] *Memoirs of John Quincy Adams*, III, 27.

[51] Kennedy, *op. cit.*, II, 262.

[52] *Am. State Papers, Indian Affairs*, II, 779.

[53] *Ibid.*, p. 776.

[54] Kennedy, *op. cit.*, II, 250.

[55] 21st Cong., 1st sess., *H. Comm. Rept.*, No. 227, p. 23.

[56] *Am. State Papers, Indian Affairs*, II, 467.

[57] Representative Towns, *Cong. Globe*, 25th Cong., 2d sess., App., p. 366.

[58] *Cong. Globe*, 25th Cong., 2d sess., App., p. 470.

[59] *Am. State Papers, Indian Affairs*, II, 491.

[60] *Reg. of Debates*, 20th Cong., 1st sess., p. 663.

[61] *New Echota Phoenix*, quoted by *Niles' Register*, XXXVI (1829), 40-41.

[62] Grant Foreman, *Indian Removal; the Emigration of the Five Civilized Tribes of Indians* (Norman, 1932).

[63] Jennings C. Wise, *The Red Man in the New World Drama* (Washington, 1931), p. 253.

[64] *Cong. Globe*, 29th Cong., 1st sess., p. 342.

[65] *Niles' Register*, LXXIII (1848), 391.

[66] *New York Herald*, January 30, 1848.

[67] Claude M. Fuess, *The Life of Caleb Cushing* (New York, 1923), II, 225.

[68] *Cong. Globe*, 35th Cong., 2d sess., p. 430.

[69] *United States Democratic Review*, "The Fate of Mexico," XLI (1858), 343.

[70] *United States Review*, "The Message," I (1853), 106.

[71] *New York Herald*, November 30, 1858.

[72] Richardson, *Messages*, V, 567.

[73] Representative Springer, *Cong. Rec.*, 46th Cong., 2d sess., p. 179.

[74] *Ibid.*, p. 4262.

[75] Vattel, *op. cit.*, p. 35.

[76] Burgess, *Political Science and Comparative Constitutional Law*, I, 47.

[77] *Outlook*, LXVII (1901), 132.

[78] Lyman Abbott, *Reminiscences* (Boston, 1915), p. 438.

[79] W. A. Peffer, "A Republic in the Philippines," *North American Review*, CLXVIII (1899), 319.

[80] A. T. Mahan, *The Problem of Asia and Its Effect upon International Policies* (Boston, 1900), p. 98.

[81] Frank A. Vanderlip, "Facts about the Philippines," *Century Magazine*, LVI (1898), 562.

[82] Benjamin Kidd, *The Control of the Tropics* (Boston, 1898), pp. 85-86.

[83] Paul S. Reinsch, *World Politics at the End of the Nineteenth Century* (New York, 1900), p. 11.

[84] Hobson, *Imperialism*, p. 238.

[85] *New Republic*, "Annexation a Suppressed Wish," VII (1916), 210.

[86] Arthur Richard Hinton, "Shall We Annex Northern Mexico?" *Independent*, LXXIX (1914), 125.

[87] *Cong. Rec.*, 65th Cong., 3d sess., p. 1092.

[88] William Ledyard Rodgers, "Can Mexico Maintain Its Isolation?" *Forum*, LXXVII (1927), 888.

[89] Roland G. Usher, *The Challenge of the Future; a Study in American Foreign Policy* (Boston, 1916), p. 301.

[90] John Franklin Carter, *Conquest; America's Painless Imperialism* (New York, 1928), chap. i.

[91] George E. Roberts, "Property Rights and Trade Rivalries as Factors in International Complications," *Proceedings of the Academy of Political Science*, VII (1917), 629, 631.

[92] 71st Cong., 1st sess., *S. Doc.*, No. 1, p. 7.

[93] Baltimore *Evening Sun*, January 27, 1934.

[94] Walter E. Weyl, *American World Policies* (New York, 1917), p. 93.

[95] *Cong. Rec.*, 56th Cong., 1st sess., p. 2629.

[96] George W. Crichfield, *American Supremacy* (New York, 1908), II, 640.

[97] A. T. Mahan, *The Interest of America in Sea Power, Present and Future* (Boston, 1898), p. 167.

[98] H. H. Powers, "Independence or Civilization?" *Atlantic Monthly*, CXXXV (1925), 259.

[99] C. K. Leith, "Exploitation and Progress," *Foreign Affairs*, VI (1927), 131.

[100] Hayes, *The Historical Evolution of Modern Nationalism*, p. 231.

[101] Von Engeln, *Inheriting the Earth*, p. 204.

[102] Leith, *op. cit.*, p. 138.

[103] Vattel, *op. cit.*, p. 100.

[104] Herbert Welsh, "The Ethics of Our Philippine Policy," *International Journal of Ethics*, X (1900), 316.

## Notes to Chapter IV

## EXTENSION OF THE AREA OF FREEDOM

[1] *Works of Fisher Ames*, I, 328.

[2] Representative Johnson, *Annals of Cong.*, 12th Cong., 1st sess., col. 458.

[3] *The Writings of Thomas Jefferson*, ed. H. A. Washington (Philadelphia, 1854), V, 444.

[4] James Schouler, *History of the United States of America* (Washington, 1889), IV, 519.

[5] Ephraim Douglass Adams, *The Power of Ideals in American History* (New Haven, 1926), p. 93.

[6] William Archibald Dunning, *The British Empire and the United States* (New York, 1914), p. 138.

[7] *Cong. Globe*, 28th Cong., 2d sess., App., p. 373.

[8] *Ibid.*, p. 316.

[9] *Ibid.*, p. 371.

[10] Joel Barlow, *An Oration, Delivered . . . July 4, 1787* (Hartford, 1787), p. 20.

[11] *Writings of Thomas Jefferson*, Memorial ed., X, 217.

[12] *Writings of Thomas Jefferson*, IX, 351.

[13] S. E. Morison, ed., *Sources and Documents Illustrating the American Revolution, 1764-1788, and the Formation of the Federal Constitution* (Oxford, 1923), pp. 281-82.

[14] *Writings of Thomas Jefferson*, VIII, 295.

[15] *Works of Fisher Ames*, I, 329.

[16] *Annals of Cong.*, 8th Cong., 1st sess., col. 465.

[17] *Ibid.*, 11th Cong., 3d. sess., col. 542.

[18] *Ibid.*, col. 536.

[19] *Ibid.*, 8th Cong., 1st sess., col. 433.

[20] *Ibid.*, 11th Cong., 3d sess., col. 538.

[21] *Ibid.*, 8th Cong., 1st sess., col. 34.

[22] Quoted by William Cabell Bruce, *John Randolph of Roanoke 1773-1833* (New York, 1922), I, 402.

[23] David Ramsay, *An Oration on the Cession of Louisiana to the United States, Delivered on the 12th May, 1804* . . . (Charleston, 1804), pp. 20-21.

[24] Richardson, *Messages*, I, 379.

[25] *Ibid.*, II, 177.

[26] Edward Everett, *Orations and Speeches on Various Occasions* (2d ed.; Boston, 1850-1868), I, 33.

[27] *Ibid.*, p. 196.

[28] *Ibid.*, p. 210.

[29] *Democratic Review*, "The Canada Question," I (1838), 217.

[30] Richardson, *Messages*, III, 308.

[31] *Democratic Review*, "The Great Nation of Futurity," VI (1839), 427.

[32] *Ibid.*, I (1838), 216-17.

[33] *Reg. of Debates*, 24th Cong., 1st sess., col. 1918.

[34] *North American Review*, "North-Eastern Boundary," XXXIV (1832), 563.

[35] Richardson, *Messages*, III, 307.

[36] Dexter Perkins, *The Monroe Doctrine 1826-1867* (Baltimore, 1933), p. 64.

[37] Richardson, *Messages*, IV, 261.

[38] James Parton, *Life of Andrew Jackson* (New York, 1860), III, 658.

[39] *A Letter of the Hon. Dixon H. Lewis, to His Constituents of the Third Congressional District of Alabama* (n. p., 1844), p. 8.

[40] New Orleans *Jeffersonian Republican*, reprinted in *Richmond Enquirer*, January 7, 1845.

[41] New Orleans *Daily Picayune*, reprinted in *Nashville Union*, March 25, 1845.

[42] Richardson, *Messages*, IV, 398.

[43] *Cong. Globe*, 29th Cong., 1st sess., p. 424.

[44] *Ibid.*, App., p. 229.

[45] *Ibid.*, p. 95.

[46] *Ibid.*, 29th Cong., 1st sess., p. 197.

[47] *American Review*, "California," III (1846), 98.

[48] *The Works of James Buchanan*, ed. J. B. Moore (Philadelphia, 1908-1911), VI, 276.

[49] *New York Herald*, January 6, 1846.

[50] *Cong. Globe*, 28th Cong., 2d sess., App., pp. 161-62.

[51] Julius W. Pratt, "The Origin of 'Manifest Destiny,'" *American Historical Review*, XXXII (1927), 795-98.

[52] *Tri-Weekly Nashville Union*, January 28, 1845.

[53] *Democratic Review*, "Annexation," XVII (1845), 5.

[54] Rippy, *The United States and Mexico*, p. 29.

[55] Walker, *Letter . . . Relative to the Reannexation of Texas*, p. 15.

[56] Dixon H. Lewis to John Calhoun, March 6, 1844, *Correspondence of John C. Calhoun*, ed. J. F. Jameson, *Fourth Annual Report of the Historical Manuscripts Commission, American Historical Association* (Washington, 1900), p. 936.

[57] *Cong. Globe*, 28th Cong., 2d sess., App., p. 233.

[58] *Niles' Register*, LXIV (1843), 285.

[59] *Cong. Globe*, 28th Cong., 2d sess., App., p. 43.

[60] *Ibid.*, p. 178.

[61] *Southern Quarterly Review*, "The Annexation of Texas," VI (1844), 498.

[62] *Cong. Globe*, 28th Cong., 2d sess., App., p. 146.

[63] Representative Sample, *ibid.*, p. 73.

[64] *Writings of Thomas Jefferson*, ed. Washington, VIII, 165.

[65] Carl Russell Fish, *The Rise of the Common Man 1830-1850* (New York, 1929), p. 125.

[66] *Cong. Globe*, 28th Cong., 2d sess., App., p. 178.

[67] Senator Rives, *ibid.*, p. 382.

[68] *New York Morning News*, January 5, 1846.

[69] *Cong. Globe*, 29th Cong., 1st sess., p. 180.

[70] *Ibid.*, 28th Cong., 2d sess., App., p. 43.

[71] *New York Morning News*, January 5, 1846.

[72] Charles T. Porter, *Review of the Mexican War* (Auburn, 1849), pp. 165-66.

[73] Archibald Alison, *The Principles of Population* (Edinburgh, 1840), I, 548.

[74] *Young Hickory Banner*, October 15, 1845.

[75] *Cong. Globe*, 29th Cong., 1st sess., App., p. 277.

[76] *Ibid.*, p. 175.

[77] Representative Hamlin, *ibid.*, 29th Cong., 1st sess., p. 187.

[78] John M. Galt, *The Annexation of Texas*, reprinted in *Political Essays* (n. p., 1852?), p. 5.

[79] Alexis de Tocqueville, *Democracy in America*, tr. Henry Reeve (New York, 1898), I, 557.

[80] *Ibid.*, p. 519.

[81] *New York Morning News*, January 9, 1846.

[82] *Democratic Review*, "The Texas Question," XIV (1844), 429.

[83] *Ibid.*, XVII (1845), 17.

[84] *Writings of Thomas Jefferson*, VIII, 105.

[85] *Cong. Globe*, 28th Cong., 2d sess., App., p. 93.

[86] *Ibid.*, 27th Cong., 3d sess., App., p. 79.

[87] *Ibid.*, 29th Cong., 1st sess., p. 187.

[88] *New York Morning News*, November 15, 1845.

[89] *Ibid.*, January 5, 1846.

[90] Walt Whitman, *Leaves of Grass*, ed. Emory Holloway (New York, 1928), p. 98.

[91] *Democratic Review*, "Retrospective View of the South-American States," II (1838), 99.

[92] *Newark Daily Advertiser*, November 14, 1836, quoted by Justin H. Smith, *The Annexation of Texas* (New York, 1911), p. 66.

[93] *Democratic Review* "Democracy," VII (1840), 228.

[94] Memucan Hunt to John C. Calhoun, October 2, 1844, *Correspondence of John C. Calhoun*, p. 975.

[95] *Cong. Globe*, 28th Cong., 2d sess., App., p. 105.

[96] *Ibid.*

[97] *The Poetical Works of William Cullen Bryant*, Roslyn ed. (New York, 1908), p. 215.

[98] Van Tyne, *The American Revolution*, p. 333.

[99] *Cong. Globe*, 28th Cong., 2d sess., App., p. 178.

[100] "Inaugural Address as Governor of Tennessee, October 15, 1845," *Speeches Congressional and Political, and Other Writings of ex-Governor Aaron V. Brown, of Tennessee* (Nashville, 1854), p. 373.

[101] *Cong. Globe*, 28th Cong., 2d sess., App., p. 227.

[102] *Ibid.*, p. 43.

[103] Representative Stephens, *ibid.*, p. 313.

[104] Representative Haralson, *ibid.*, p. 194.

[105] Representative McClernand, *ibid.*, 29th Cong., 1st sess., p. 984.

[106] *New York Morning News*, February 7, 1845.

[107] *Cong. Globe*, 29th Cong., 1st sess., p. 324.

[108] *Ibid.*, 28th Cong., 1st sess., App., p. 450.

[109] Adams, *op. cit.*, p. 90.

[110] *United States Journal*, October 18, 1845.

[111] Whitman, *op. cit.*, pp. 286, 98.

[112] *The Uncollected Prose and Poetry of Walt Whitman*, ed. Emory Holloway (New York, 1931), I, 159.

[113] *Democratic Review*, "Progress in America," XVIII (1846), 92.

[114] Senator Buchanan, *Cong. Globe*, 28th Cong., 1st sess., p. 380.

[115] Representative Duncan, *ibid.*, 2d sess., App., p. 178.

[116] *New York Morning News*, December 27, 1845.

## Notes to Chapter V

## THE TRUE TITLE

[1] John Holladay Latané, *A History of American Foreign Policy* (New York, 1927), p. 231.

[2] *A Letter to the Hon. Henry Clay on the Annexation of Texas to the United States*, in *Works of William E. Channing, D. D.*, II, 238.

[3] Allen Johnson, *Stephen A. Douglas: a Study in American Politics* (New York, 1908), p. 95.

[4] *Cong. Globe*, 29th Cong., 1st sess., App., p. 99.

[5] Eugene Irving McCormac, *James K. Polk, a Political Biography* (Berkeley, 1922), p. 588.

[6] William Archibald Dunning, *A History of Political Theories, Ancient and Mediaeval* (London, 1902), p. 264.

[7] John Dickinson, "Introduction," *The Statesman's Book of John of Salisbury* (New York, 1927), p. xxviii.

[8] Winthrop, *The History of New England*, II, 352.

[9] *Public Good,* in *Writings of Thomas Paine,* II, 35.

[10] *The Farmer Refuted,* in *Works of Alexander Hamilton,* II, 80.

[11] *Selected Political Essays of James Wilson,* p. 304.

[12] Dickinson, *op. cit.,* p. xxxii.

[13] *Novanglus,* in *Works of John Adams,* IV, 105.

[14] *Ibid.*

[15] Burnett, *Letters of Members of the Continental Congress,* IV, 252.

[16] Ingersoll, *Recollections,* p. 395.

[17] *Annals of Cong.,* 16th Cong., 1st sess., col. 1763.

[18] *Am. State Papers, For. Rel.,* V, 447.

[19] *Ibid.,* V, 451.

[20] 20th Cong., 1st sess., *House Documents,* No. 199, p. 65.

[21] (Sir) Travers Twiss, *The Oregon Question, in Respect to Facts and the Law of Nations* (London, 1846), pp. 312-13.

[22] *The Oregon Question,* in *The Writings of Albert Gallatin,* ed. Henry Adams (Philadelphia, 1879), III, 502.

[23] 25th Cong., 3d sess., *H. Rept.,* No. 101, p. 16.

[24] *Cong. Globe,* 29th Cong., 1st sess., App., p. 26.

[25] *Ibid.*

[26] Robert Greenhow, *Memoir Historical and Political on the Northwest Coast of America and the Adjacent Territories* (Washington, 1840), p. 200.

[27] *Democratic Statesman,* July 5, 1845.

[28] *Cong. Globe,* 29th Cong., 1st sess., App., pp. 26-33.

[29] John George Bourinot, "Canada and the United States: an Historical Retrospect," *Papers of the American Historical Association,* V (1891), 307.

[30] *Writings of Albert Gallatin,* III, 533-34.

[31] *Southern Quarterly Review,* "Oregon and the Oregon Question," VIII (1845), 233-34.

[32] *Illinois State Register,* August 29, 1845.

[33] *New York Morning News,* October 28, 1845.

[34] *Ibid.,* November 15, 1845.

[35] Walter B. Scaife, "The Development of International Law as to Newly Discovered Territory," *Papers of the American Historical Association,* IV (1890), 72-73.

[36] E. de Vattel, *The Law of Nations,* in *The Classics of International Law* ed. (Washington, 1916), III, 85.

[37] 20th Cong., 1st sess., *H. Doc.,* No. 199, p. 63.

[38] *Cong. Globe,* 29th Cong., 1st sess., App., p. 99.

[39] *Ibid.,* 29th Cong., 1st sess., p. 136.

[40] Representative Smith, *ibid.,* App., p. 104.

[41] Representative Goodyear, *ibid.,* p. 110.

[42] Ralph Waldo Emerson, "Politics," in *Essays, Second Series* (Boston, 1903), p. 200.

[43] *Cong. Globe,* 29th Cong., 1st sess., p. 200.

[44] *Ibid.,* p. 207.

[45] *Ibid.,* p. 301.

[46] *Ibid.*, App., p. 95.
[47] *Ibid.*, 29th Cong., 1st sess., pp. 323-24.
[48] *Ibid.*, App., p. 96.
[49] *Ibid.*, 29th Cong., 1st sess., p. 200.
[50] *Ibid.*, App., p. 154.
[51] *Democratic Review*, XVIII (1846), 93.
[52] *Cong. Globe*, 29th Cong., 1st sess., p. 136.
[53] *Ibid.*, pp. 136, 279.
[54] *Ibid.*, App., pp. 209, 211.
[55] *Baltimore American*, quoted by *Niles' Register*, LXX (1846), 31.
[56] *Cong. Globe*, 29th Cong., 1st sess., p. 340.
[57] *Ibid.*, p. 342.
[58] *Ibid.*, App., p. 92.
[59] *Ibid.*, p. 97.
[60] *New York Morning News*, December 27, 1845.
[61] *Baltimore American*, quoted by *Niles' Register*, LXX (1846), 31.
[62] Frederick Sherwood Dunn, *The Protection of Nationals: a Study in the Application of International Law* (Baltimore, 1932), p. 200.
[63] *Cong. Globe*, 29th Cong., 1st sess., App., p. 30.
[64] *Baltimore American*, quoted by *Niles' Register*, LXIX (1846), 408.
[65] *New York Morning News*, June 12, 1846.
[66] Charles Cheney Hyde, *International Law Chiefly as Interpreted and Applied by the United States* (Boston, 1922), I, 5.
[67] Richardson, *Messages*, IV, 441.
[68] Walt Whitman, *The Gathering of the Forces*, ed. Cleveland Rodgers and John Black (New York, 1920), I, 266.
[69] *United States Review*, I (1853), 106.
[70] Senator Pugh, *Cong. Globe*, 35th Cong., 2d sess., p. 937.
[71] Senator Collamer, *ibid.*, p. 1186.
[72] *Ibid.*, p. 299.
[73] Baltimore *Evening Sun*, March 2, 1934.
[74] *Cong. Globe*, 31st Cong., 1st sess., App., p. 265.
[75] *Compilation of Reports of Committee on Foreign Relations, United States Senate, 1789-1901*, VII, 333.
[76] *The Editorials of Henry Watterson*, comp. Arthur Krock (New York, 1923), p. 295.
[77] Senator Allen, *Cong. Rec.*, 55th Cong., 3d sess., p. 1484.
[78] Ernst Freund, "The Control of Dependencies Through Protectorates," *Political Science Quarterly*, XIV (1899), 19.
[79] *Ibid.*
[80] Albert J. Beveridge, *For the Greater Republic, Not for Imperialism; an Address Delivered . . . February 15, 1899* (Philadelphia? 1899?), p. 4.
[81] 56th Cong., 1st sess., *H. Rept.*, No. 351, p. 8.
[82] *Cong. Rec.*, 56th Cong., 1st sess., App., p. 271.
[82a] Henry F. Pringle, *Theodore Roosevelt* (New York, 1931), p. 318.
[83] Theodore Roosevelt, *Thomas Hart Benton* (Boston, 1895), p. 268.
[84] Elihu Root, *Addresses on International Subjects*, ed. R. Bacon and J. B. Scott (Cambridge, 1916), p. 178.

[85] Quoted by Tyler Dennett, *John Hay* (New York, 1933), p. 381.
[86] Joseph Patouillet, *L'impérialisme américain* (Paris, 1904), pp. 46-47.
[87] Arthur O. Lovejoy, "Ethics and International Relations," *Bulletin of the Washington University Association,* April 23, 1904, p. 57.
[88] *New Republic,* "Sovereign Mexico," VII (1916), 134.
[89] Crichfield, *American Supremacy,* II, 628.
[90] *Ibid.,* p. 48.
[91] Herbert Kraus, "La morale internationale," in *Recueil des cours, 1927, Académie de Droit International* (Paris, 1928), I, 437.
[92] *Cong. Rec.,* 58th Cong., 2d sess., p. 1516.
[93] Charles Evans Hughes, *Our Relations to the Nations of the Western Hemisphere* (Princeton, 1928), p. 80.
[94] Powers, *International Journal of Ethics,* X (1900), 296.

## NOTES TO CHAPTER VI

## THE MISSION OF REGENERATION

[1] Moore, *Digest,* I, 431.
[2] Justin H. Smith, *The War with Mexico* (New York, 1919), II, 243.
[3] John Douglas Pitts Fuller, "The Movement for the Acquisition of All Mexico, 1846-1848" (Ph. D. dissertation, Johns Hopkins University, 1932), p. 109.
[4] *Peace with Mexico,* in *Writings of Albert Gallatin,* III, 585.
[5] Richardson, *Messages,* III, 457.
[6] *Works of Fisher Ames,* I, 329.
[7] *Annals of Cong.,* 8th Cong., 1st sess., col. 462.
[8] *Writings of Thomas Paine,* III, 431.
[9] Galt, *The Annexation of Texas,* p. 10.
[10] O. C. Hartley, *An Address Delivered . . . July 4, 1844* (Bedford, 1844), p. 19.
[11] *Cong. Globe,* 28th Cong., 2d sess., App., p. 178.
[12] Frederick Starr, *Mexico and the United States* (Chicago, 1914), pp. 437-38.
[13] Charles Francis Adams, *'Imperialism' and 'The Tracks of Our Forefathers'* (Boston, 1899), p. 17.
[14] Rippy, *The United States and Mexico,* p. 1.
[15] *North American Review,* "Politics of Mexico," XXXI (1830), 112.
[16] *New Orleans Commercial Bulletin,* March 16, 1846.
[17] Quoted in *The War in Texas,* anonymous (Philadelphia, 1837), p. 38.
[18] *Democratic Review,* "Territorial Aggrandizement," XVII (1845), 243.
[19] *Ibid.,* p. 245.
[20] *Ibid.,* p. 246.
[21] *Illinois State Register,* December 27, 1844.
[22] *Missouri Reporter,* quoted by *Illinois State Register,* August 1, 1845.

[23] *Democratic Review,* XVII (1845), 9.

[24] *Hartford Times,* quoted by *Nashville Union,* August 7, 1845.

[25] H. von Holst, *The Constitutional and Political History of the United States,* tr. J. J. Labor and A. B. Mason (Chicago, 1881), III, 272.

[26] *New York Herald,* August 30, 1845.

[27] *Richmond Enquirer*, quoted by Smith, *op. cit.*, I, 126.

[28] Richardson, *Messages*, IV, 442.

[29] 29th Cong., 1st sess., *H. Rept.,* No. 752, p. 52.

[30] *Cong. Globe,* 29th Cong., 1st sess., p. 837.

[31] James Russell Lowell, *The Biglow Papers* (6th ed.; Boston, 1866), pp. 23-24.

[32] Whitman, *The Gathering of the Forces,* I, 240, 242.

[33] *Tri-Weekly Nashville Union,* October 22, 1846.

[34] *Cong. Globe,* 29th Cong., 2d sess., App., p. 191.

[35] *Illinois State Register,* July 10, 1846.

[36] *New York Herald,* July 27, 1846.

[37] "Dow, Jr.," in *Illinois State Register,* July 17, 1846.

[38] *Democratic Review,* "New Territory versus No Territory," XXI (1847), 291.

[39] *Ibid.,* "The War," XX (1847), p. 100.

[40] *American Review,* "The Whigs and the War," VI (1847), 338.

[41] Whitman, *op. cit.*, I, 246-47.

[42] In *Memorial and Petition of Col. J. D. Stevenson of California* (San Francisco, 1886), p. 16 b.

[43] *New Englander,* "The War with Mexico," V (1847), 141-42.

[44] *Illinois State Register,* July 10, 1846.

[45] *Ibid.,* December 12, 1846.

[46] *Cong. Globe,* 29th Cong., 2d sess., p. 148.

[47] *Ibid.,* p. 290.

[48] New York *Weekly Herald,* October 29, 1847.

[49] *Boston Post,* April 5, 1847.

[50] *Democratic Review,* XX (1847), 100.

[51] New York *Sun,* February 10, 1847.

[52] *New York Herald,* May 15, 1847.

[53] F. W. Byrdsall to John C. Calhoun, July 19, 1847, *Correspondence of Calhoun,* p. 1127.

[54] *National Era,* August 19, 1847.

[55] John D. P. Fuller, "The Slavery Question and the Movement to Acquire Mexico, 1846-1848," *Mississippi Valley Historical Review,* XXI (1934), 31-48.

[56] *Richmond Enquirer,* December 2, 1846.

[57] New Orleans *Daily Picayune,* November 27, 28, 1847.

[58] New York *Weekly Herald,* October 29, 1847.

[59] *Ibid.,* November 30, 1847.

[60] *National Whig,* November 10, 1847.

[61] St. Louis *Republican*, quoted by *Illinois State Register*, November 26, 1847.
[62] Quoted by Smith, *The War with Mexico*, II, 243.
[63] New York *Sun*, October 22, 1847.
[64] Washington *Daily Union*, October 14, 1847.
[65] *New York Journal of Commerce*, October 12, 1847.
[66] *Democratic Review*, XX (1847), 100.
[67] *Cong. Globe*, 30th Cong., 1st sess., p. 54.
[68] *The Diary of James K. Polk*, ed. M. M. Quaife (Chicago, 1910), III, 226.
[69] John M. Niles to Martin Van Buren, January 20, 1848, MS. Van Buren Papers, Library of Congress.
[70] *Niles' Register*, LXXIII (1848), 336.
[71] *Cong. Globe*, 30th Cong., 1st sess., App., p. 446.
[72] *New York Herald*, January 30, 1848.
[73] Lowell, *op cit.*, p. 56.
[74] *Cong. Globe*, 30th Cong., 1st sess., p. 321.
[75] *Ibid.*, App., p. 69.
[76] *Niles' Register*, "'Manifest Destiny' Doctrines," LXXIII (1848), 334.
[77] *Ibid.*, p. 392.
[78] *Ibid.*, p. 335.
[79] *Cong. Globe*, 30th Cong., 1st sess., App., p. 87.
[80] *New-York Evening Post*, quoted by Washington *Daily Union*, December 28, 1847.
[81] Quoted in *Cong. Globe*, 30th Cong., 1st sess., App., p. 445.
[82] *Ibid.*, p. 427.
[83] *Ibid.*, p. 87.
[84] *Ibid.*, p. 363.
[85] *Ibid.*, p. 251.
[86] *Niles' Register*, LXXIII (1848), 335.
[87] *Cong. Globe*, 30th Cong., 1st sess., App., p. 128.
[88] *Ibid.*, p. 261.
[89] *National Era*, February 3, 1848.
[90] *Cong. Globe*, 29th Cong., 2d sess., App., p. 191.
[91] *Ibid.*, 30th Cong., 1st sess., App., p. 194.
[92] *Ibid.*, 30th Cong., 1st sess., p. 321.
[93] *Democratic Review*, "Mexico—the Church and Peace," XXI (1847), 101.
[94] *Ibid.*, "The Mexican War," XXII (1848), 120-21.
[95] New Orleans *Daily Picayune*, December 31, 1847.
[96] New York *Sun*, quoted by *National Intelligencer*, November 20, 1847.
[97] *New York Herald*, January 30, 1848.
[98] *Cong. Globe*, 30th Cong., 1st sess., p. 135.
[99] *Niles' Register*, LXXIII (1848), 391.
[100] *Cong. Globe*, 30th Cong., 1st sess., App., p. 379.
[101] Senator Henley, *ibid.*, p. 251.
[102] Senator Breese, *ibid.*, p. 349.
[103] Senator Sevier, *ibid.*, p. 262.

[104] Quoted by Rippy, *op. cit.*, pp. 16-17.

[105] *Cong. Globe,* 30th Cong., 1st sess., App., p. 87.

[106] *Ibid.*, p. 350.

[107] Carl Schurz, "Manifest Destiny," *Harper's New Monthly Magazine,* LXXXVII (1893), 737.

[108] New York *Weekly Herald*, February 25, 1848.

[109] Senator Greene, *Cong. Globe*, 30th Cong., 1st sess., App., p. 344.

[110] *New-York Weekly Evening Post,* March 16, 1848.

[111] *Cong. Globe,* 30th Cong., 1st sess., App., p. 596.

[112] *Ibid.*, p. 604.

[113] *Ibid.*, p. 591.

[114] *Ibid.*, p. 636.

[115] *Washington Union,* Octobeı 7, 1858

[116] *Cong. Globe,* 32d Cong., 2d sess., p. 211.

[117] Thomas K. King, *An Oration Delivered . . . July 4, 1854* (Providence, 1854), p. 13.

[118] *Cong. Globe,* 33d Cong., 1st sess., App., p. 1016.

[119] *United States Democratic Review,* XLI (1858), 342.

[120] *Cong. Globe*, 33d Cong., 1st sess., App., p. 952.

[121] Rippy, *op. cit.*, p. 278.

[122] 44th Cong, 1st sess., *H. Rept.*, No. 343, p. 149.

[123] Adams, *op. cit.*, p. 17.

[124] Mark Sullivan, *Our Times, I, The Turn of the Century* (New York, 1927), pp. 55-56.

[125] Quoted by Edwin M. Borchard, "Common Sense in Foreign Policy," *Journal of International Relations,* XI (1920), 41.

[126] Rippy, *The United States and Mexico,* p. 355.

[127] Beard, *The Idea of National Interest,* p. 388.

[128] *Cong. Rec.*, 65th Cong., 3d sess., p. 1092.

[129] L. S. Rowe, "The Development of Democracy on the American Continent," *American Political Science Review*, XVI (1922), 8.

[130] Henry L. Stimson, *American Policy in Nicaragua* (New York, 1927), p. 101.

[131] *Writings of Albert Gallatin,* III, 586.

[132] Representative Duer, *Cong. Globe,* 30th Cong., 1st sess., p. 347.

[133] Porter, *Review of the Mexican War,* pp. 164-65.

[134] *New York Herald,* January 30, 1848.

[135] Richardson, *Messages,* I, 223.

[136] Huntington Wilson, "The Relation of Government to Foreign Investment," *Annals* of the American Academy of Political and Social Science, LXVIII (1916), 300.

[137] John Emerick Edward Dahlberg-Acton, *The History of Freedom and Other Essays* (London, 1909), p. 290.

[138] Adams, *op. cit.*, p. 16.

[139] In *Memorial and Petition of Col. J. D. Stevenson,* p. 16 b.

## NOTES TO CHAPTER VII

## NATURAL GROWTH

[1] Quoted by James Morton Callahan, *Cuba and International Relations; a Historical Study in American Diplomacy* (Baltimore, 1899), pp. 304-05.

[2] *Cong. Globe,* 33d Cong., 2d sess., App., p. 91.

[3] Grotius, *De Jure Belli ac Pacis,* II, 11, 13.

[4] Gettell, *History of Political Thought,* p. 402.

[5] Francis Lieber, *Political Ethics* (Boston, 1838), I, 193.

[6] Ralph Waldo Emerson, "The Method of Nature," in *Nature; Addresses and Lectures* (Boston, 1903), p. 202.

[7] *Democratic Review,* "Growth of States," XXII (1848), 395.

[8] Quoted by M. E. Curti, "Young America," *American Historical Review,* XXXII (1926), 34.

[9] *New York Morning News,* December 27, 1845.

[10] *Ibid.,* January 5, 1846.

[11] *Cong. Globe,* 29th Cong., 1st sess., p. 141.

[12] Representative Crittenden, *ibid.,* p. 679.

[13] *Ibid.,* App., p. 368.

[14] *Ibid.,* p. 119.

[15] *Democratic Review,* XVIII (1846), 92.

[16] *Ibid.,* XXII (1848), 398.

[17] Quoted by Adams, *The Power of Ideals in American History,* p. 88.

[18] 31st Cong., 2d sess., *S. Ex. Doc.,* No. 9, p. 7.

[19] Representative Marshall, *Cong. Globe,* 32d Cong., 1st sess., App., p. 386.

[20] Richardson, *Messages,* V, 165.

[21] Moore, *Digest,* VI, 465, 469.

[22] Everett, *Orations and Speeches,* I, 48.

[23] Edward Everett, *Stability and Progress. Remarks Made on the 4th of July, 1853, in Faneuil Hall* (Boston, 1853), p. 10.

[24] *Cong. Globe,* 32d Cong., 3d sess., App., p. 289.

[25] J. R. Seeley, *The Expansion of England* (London, 1891), p. 296.

[26] U. S. State Dept., *Correspondence on the Proposed Tripartite Convention Relative to Cuba* (Boston, 1853), p. 53.

[27] Thomas Aquinas, *De Regemine Principum,* Bk. I, chap. ii, as translated by Francis William Coker, *Readings in Political Philosophy* (New York, 1914), p. 133.

[28] Whitman, *Leaves of Grass,* p. 231.

[29] *Imperatoris Justiniani Institutiones,* tr. J. B. Moyle (Oxford, 1883), II, 4.

[30] As described by William M. Urban, *Fundamentals of Ethics* (New York, 1930), p. 97.

[31] *Southern Quarterly Review,* "The Cuban Question," XXV (1854), 468.

[32] *Cong. Globe,* 32d Cong., 3d sess., App., p. 273.

[33] *Ibid.,* 33d Cong., 1st sess., App., p. 949.

[34] *Ibid.*, 32d Cong., 2d sess., App., p. 131.

[35] *Ibid.*, pp. 121, 123.

[36] *Ibid.*, p. 131.

[37] *Ibid.*

[38] *Ibid.*, p. 96.

[39] *Ibid.*, p. 95.

[40] *Ibid.*, 3d sess., p. 262.

[41] Richardson, *Messages*, V, 198.

[42] Washington *Daily Union*, March 27, 1853.

[43] *United States Review*, "The New and the Old World," I (1853), 222.

[44] 35th Cong., 2d sess., *S. Rept.*, No. 351, p. 9.

[45] *De Bow's Review*, "The Late Cuba Expedition," IX (1850), 167.

[46] *National Party Platforms*, comp. Kirk H. Porter (New York, 1924), pp. 31-32.

[47] Caleb Cushing, in *Library of American Literature*, VI, 31, 32.

[48] Fuess, *Life of Caleb Cushing*, II, 225.

[49] *Western Democratic Review*, "The Annexation of Mexico," I (1854), 292.

[50] J. F. H. Claiborne, *Life and Correspondence of John A. Quitman . . . Governor of the State of Mississippi* (New York, 1860), II, 223.

[51] Moore, *Digest*, VI, 469.

[52] 35th Cong., 2d sess., *S. Rept.*, No. 351, p. 1.

[53] 33d Cong., 2d sess., *H. Ex. Doc.*, No. 93, p. 128.

[54] Quoted by John Bach McMaster, *A History of the People of the United States* (New York, 1913), VIII, 339.

[55] Henry Martyn Flint, *Life of Stephen A. Douglas, United States Senator from Illinois* (New York, 1860), p. 186.

[56] *Cong. Globe*, 35th Cong., 2d sess., p. 940.

[57] 35th Cong., 2d sess., *S Rept.*, No. 351, p. 9.

[58] King, *op. cit.*, p. 13.

[59] 35th Cong., 2d sess., *S. Rept.*, No. 351, p. 9.

[60] *Cong. Globe*, 35th Cong., 2d sess., p. 1186.

[61] *United States Democratic Review*, "The Acquisition of Cuba," XLIII (1859), 32.

[62] *New York Herald*, October 11, 1852.

[63] Senator Mallory, *Cong. Globe*, 35th Cong., 2d sess., p. 1331.

[64] Frank Soulé *et al.*, *The Annals of San Francisco* (New York, 1855), p. 476.

[65] Claiborne, *Life of Quitman*, II, 110.

[66] Niccolo Machiavelli, *Discourses on the First Ten Books of Titius Livius*, in *The Historical, Political and Diplomatic Writings of Niccolo Machiavelli*, tr. C. E. Detmold (Boston, 1882), II, 113.

[67] Algernon Sidney, *Discourses Concerning Government* (Philadelphia, 1805), I, 293.

[68] William W. Greenough, *The Conquering Republic. An Oration Delivered . . . July 4, 1849* (Boston, 1849), p. 34.

[69] Moore, *Digest*, VI, 466-67.

[70] Richardson, *Messages*, V, 199.

[71] Washington *Daily Union*, March 27, 1853.

[72] *Ibid.*, December 7, 1853.

[73] *Ibid.*, January 5, 1853.

[74] *Richmond Enquirer*, April 16, 1855.

[75] *United States Review*, "The United States and the United Kingdom," I (1853), 411.

[76] *Ibid.*, "Foreign Policy of the United States in 1825-6," I (1853), 41.

[77] *Cong. Globe*, 33d Cong., 1st sess., App., p. 952.

[78] Ingersoll, *Recollections*, p. 19.

[79] Parke Godwin, *Political Essays* (New York, 1856), p. 169.

[80] *De Bow's Review*, IX (1850), 167.

[81] Representative Thayer, *Cong. Globe*, 35th Cong., 1st sess., p. 228.

[82] *Democratic Review*, "Frank Pierce and Major-General Scott," II (1852), 300.

[83] George Fitzhugh, "Acquisition of Mexico—Filibustering," *De Bow's Review*, XXV (1858), 616.

[84] Richardson, *Messages*, V, 469.

[85] William Walker, *The War in Nicaragua* (Mobile, 1860), pp. 429-30.

[86] A. V. Hofer, "The Central American Question," *De Bow's Review*, XXI (1856), 129.

[87] Quoted by Callahan, *op. cit.*, p. 240.

[88] George Frederick Holmes, "Relations of the Old and the New Worlds," *De Bow's Review*, XX (1856), 529.

[89] Claiborne, *Life of Quitman*, II, 113.

[90] *Cong. Globe*, 35th Cong., 2d sess., p. 430.

[91] *Ibid.*, p. 737.

[92] Dionysius of Halicarnassus, *Antiquitatum romanarum*, i, 5.

[93] Theodor Mommsen, *The History of Rome*, tr. W. P. Dickinson (New York, 1908), V, 3.

[94] Adam H. Müller, *Die Elemente der Staatskunst* (Berlin, 1809), p. 13.

[95] Karl Pearson, *National Life from the Viewpoint of Science* (London, 1905), p. 46.

[96] Charles Kendall Adams, "Colonies and Other Dependencies," *Forum*, XXVII (1899), 46.

[97] H. H. Powers, "The War as a Suggestion of Manifest Destiny," *Annals* of the American Academy of Political and Social Science, XII (1898), 181.

[98] *Cong. Globe*, 34th Cong., 1st sess., App., p. 77.

[99] *Ibid.*, p. 1298.

[100] *United States Review*, "Foreign and Continental Policy of the United States," I (1853), 11.

[101] *Western Democratic Review*, I (1854), 292.

[102] Samuel J. Bayard, *A Sketch of the Life of Commodore Robert F. Stockton* (New York, 1856), App., p. 82.

[103] *New York Herald*, December 14, 1868.

[104] *Cong. Globe*, 32d Cong., 2d sess., App., p. 59.

[105] *Ibid.*

[106] *Ideen*, in *Herder's Sämmtliche Werke*, XIV, 52.

[107] 33d Cong., 2d sess., *H. Ex. Doc.*, No. 93, p. 128.

[108] John S. Thrasher, *A Preliminary Essay on the Purchase of Cuba* (New York, 1859), pp. 9-10.

[109] Moore, *Digest*, VI, 463.

[110] *Correspondence on the Proposed Tripartite Convention*, p. 61.

[111] Representative Levin, *Cong. Globe*, 29th Cong., 1st sess., App., p. 96.

[112] *Ibid.*, 33d Cong., 1st sess., p. 1566.

[113] *Illinois State Register*, June 2, 1853.

[114] *De Bow's Review*, "The Islands of the Pacific: the Hawaiian Cluster," XIII (1852), 457-58.

[115] "Verses on the Prospect of Planting Arts and Learning in America," *The Works of George Berkeley*, ed. A. C. Fraser (Oxford, 1901), IV, 366.

[116] E. L. Magoon, *Westward Empire* (New York, 1856), pp. v-vi.

[117] *Cong. Globe*, 36th Cong., 2d sess., App., p. 74.

[118] Oswald Spengler, *The Decline of the West*, tr. Francis Atkinson (New York, 1928), I, 37, 36.

[119] Rousseau, *Social Contract*, p. 125.

[120] Robert Flint, *The Philosophy of History in Europe* (New York, 1875), p. 573.

[121] *Democratic Review*, "American History," XXIV (1849), 161.

[122] *Cong. Globe*, 29th Cong., 2d sess., App., p. 192.

[123] *Works of George Berkeley*, IV, 366, 365.

[124] *United States Review*, "Brother Jonathan," I (1853), 435.

[125] *United States Democratic Review*, XLI (1858), 337-38.

[126] *Cong. Globe*, 41st Cong., 3d sess., p. 427.

[127] Washington *Star*, quoted by *Public Opinion*, XXII (1897), 773.

[128] *Cong. Rec.*, 55th Cong., 3d sess., p. 110.

[129] Jacques Bardoux, *Essai d'une psychologie de l'Angleterre contemporaine* (Paris, 1906), p. 471.

[130] Albert Heston Coggins, "The Menace of Imperialism," *Arena*, XXIV (1900), 348.

[131] E. V. Long,, *ibid.*, p. 343.

[132] L. A. Coolidge, *An Old-fashioned Senator*: *Orville H. Platt* (New York, 1910), p. 302.

[133] Reid, *Problems of Expansion*, p. 152.

[134] Powers, *Annals* of the American Academy of Political and Social Science, XII (1898), 180-81.

[135] *Cong. Globe*, 32d Cong., 3d sess., App., p. 274.

[136] Seeley, *op. cit.*, p. 56.

[137] Mahan, *The Problem of Asia*, p. 30.

[138] Homer Lea, *The Valor of Ignorance* (New York, 1909), p. 12.

[139] Edward H. Finlay, "The Decadence of Race," *Seven Seas Magazine*, I (1915), 13.

[140] *Independent,* "The Expansion of the United States," LXXXVII (1916), 288.

[141] Quoted by Victor A. Yakhontoff, *Russia and the Soviet Union in the Far East* (New York, 1931), p. 234.

[142] Arthur Dix, *Deutscher Imperialismus* (Leipzig, 1914), p. 5.

[143] Quoted by Luis Anderson, in Alejandro Alvarez, *The Monroe Doctrine* (New York, 1924), p. 233.

[144] Friedrich Meinecke, *Die Idee der Staatsräson in der neueren Geschichte* (München, 1924), pp. 5 ff.

[145] Adolph Hitler, *Mein Kampf* (München, 1933), p. 267.

[146] *Literary Digest*, XC (1926), 16.

[147] Quoted from the *Saturday Review* by Lindley Miller Keasbey, *The Nicaragua Canal and the Monroe Doctrine* (New York, 1896), p. 573.

[148] F. W. Coker, *Organismic Theories of the State*, in *Columbia University Studies in History, Economics and Public Law* (New York, 1910), XXXVIII, No. 2, 195-96.

[149] *The Politics of Aristotle*, tr. Benjamin Jowett (Oxford, 1885), I, 213.

[150] *Cong. Globe*, 35th Cong., 2d sess., p. 1180.

[151] C. Delisle Burns, *The Morality of Nations* (London, 1915), p. 152.

[152] Quoted by Urban, *op. cit.*, p. 112.

[153] Horace, *Sermones*, tr. Creech, i, 3, 113.

## Notes to Chapter VIII

## POLITICAL GRAVITATION

[1] Henry Brooks Adams, "The Session," *North American Review*, CVIII (1869), 639.

[2] Representative Spalding, *Cong. Globe*, 40th Cong., 2d sess., p. 3810.

[3] John Fiske, *American Political Ideas Viewed from the Standpoint of Universal History* (Boston, 1911), pp. 101-02.

[4] Representative Cox, *Cong. Globe*, 41st Cong., 3d sess., p. 408.

[5] Robert J. Walker, *Letter . . . on the Annexation of Nova Scotia and British America* (n. p., 1869), p. 25.

[6] Flint, *The Philosophy of History in Europe*, I, 160-61.

[7] *Democratic Review*, "Social Destiny of Man," VIII (1840), 431 ff.

[8] *Journals of Ralph Waldo Emerson*, ed. E. W. Emerson and W. E. Forbes (Boston, 1912), VIII, 8-9.

[9] *Oeuvres de Mr. Turgot* (Paris, 1808), II, 66.

[10] Sumner, *Prophetic Voices Concerning America*, p. 41.

[11] Carl Becker, *The Declaration of Independence* (New York, 1922), chap. ii.

[12] *Common Sense*, in *Writings of Thomas Paine*, I, 92.

[13] Abbé Raynal, *A Philosophical and Political History of the Settlements and*

*Trade of the Europeans in the East and West Indies*, tr. J. O. Justamond (London, 1783), VII, 474.

[14] *Ibid.*, p. 496.

[15] Seeley, *The Expansion of England*, p. 296.

[16] Thomas Pownall, *A Memorial Addressed to the Sovereigns of Europe* (London, 1780), pp. 4-5.

[17] Quoted by Henry Adams, *History of the United States of America*, III, 85.

[18] Nashville *Clarion*, April 28, 1812.

[19] *Writings of James Monroe*, V, 368.

[20] *Memoirs of John Quincy Adams*, IV, 438-39.

[21] *Writings of John Quincy Adams*, VII, 373.

[22] Quoted by Callahan, *Cuba and International Relations*, p. 140.

[23] *Democratic Review*, XIV (1844), 423.

[24] *Cong. Globe*, 29th Cong., 1st sess., App., p. 96.

[25] Senator Dix, *ibid.*, 30th Cong., 1st sess., App., pp. 181-82.

[26] Halifax (pseud.), *Future Annexations and Their Effects* (n. p., 1849), p. 1.

[27] Edward L. Pierce, *Memoir and Letters of Charles Sumner* (Boston, 1894), III, 42.

[28] *Cong. Globe*, 35th Cong., 2d sess., p. 542.

[29] *Ibid.*, p. 539.

[30] *United States Democratic Review*, "Non-Intervention of Nations," XLII (1858), 100.

[31] Adams, *op. cit.*, IX, 226.

[32] *The Works of William H. Seward*, ed. G. E. Baker (Boston, 1884), III, 409.

[33] O. A. Brownson, *The American Republic: Its Constitution, Tendencies, and Destiny* (New York, 1865), pp. 436-37.

[34] *The Works of Charles Sumner* (Boston, 1876-1883), XI, 233.

[35] *New York Herald*, April 17, 1867.

[36] Robert J. Walker, Washington *Daily Morning Chronicle*, January 28, 1868.

[37] Representative Stevenson, *Cong. Globe*, 41st Cong., 3d sess., p. 409.

[38] *Cong. Globe*, 40th Cong., 2d sess., App., p. 377.

[39] Sumner, *op. cit.*, p. 175.

[40] *Cong. Globe*, 32d Cong., 2d sess., p. 141.

[41] *New York Herald*, January 28, 1870.

[42] *Writings of John Quincy Adams*, VII, 372.

[43] Moore, *Digest*, VI, 456.

[44] *Cong. Globe*, 35th Cong., 2d sess., p. 539.

[45] *Ibid.*, 41st Cong., 2d sess., App. p. 507.

[46] Richardson, *Messages*, VI, 580.

[47] *Cong. Globe*, 40th Cong., 3d sess., p. 318.

[48] *Ibid.*, pp. 333-34.

[49] *Ibid.*, p. 333.

[50] *Ibid.*

[51] *Ibid.*, p. 334.

[52] Semple, *American History and Its Geographic Conditions*, p. 403.
[53] *New York Herald*, September 23, 1846.
[54] *United States Democratic Review*, XLII (1858), 100.
[55] Representative Ermentrout, *Cong. Rec.*, 55th Cong., 2d sess., App., p. 649.
[56] Frank A. Golder, "The Purchase of Alaska," *American Historical Review*, XXV (1920), 416 ff.
[57] *Cong. Globe*, 40th Cong., 2d sess., p. 3660.
[58] 40th Cong., 2d sess., *H. Ex. Doc.*, No. 177, p. 59.
[59] *Cong. Globe*, 40th Cong., 2d sess., p. 3813.
[60] *St. Paul Daily Press*, December 23, 1869, quoted in 41st Cong., 2d sess., *S. Ex. Doc.*, No. 33, p. 44.
[61] *St. Paul Free Press*, *ibid.*, p. 10.
[62] *Cong. Globe*, 32d Cong., 1st sess., App., p. 917.
[63] *Ibid.*, 40th Cong., 2d sess., p. 3660.
[64] Semple, *op. cit.*, p. 403.
[65] *Works of Charles Sumner*, XI, 233.
[66] I. C. Parker, *An Address Delivered . . . July 4, 1871* (St. Joseph, 1871), p. 19.
[67] *Cong. Globe*, 40th Cong., 2d sess., p. 3660.
[68] Semple, *op. cit.*, p. 431.
[69] *Cong. Globe*, 41st Cong., 3d sess., p. 429.
[70] Washington *Daily Morning Chronicle*, January 28, 1868.
[71] *St. Paul Free Press*, *loc. cit.*
[72] *Chicago Tribune*, July 4, 1866.
[73] *Cong. Globe*, 41st Cong., 3d sess., p. 429.
[74] Rippy, *The United States and Mexico*, p. 277.
[75] B. de Siebert and G. A. Schreiner, *Entente Diplomacy and the World* (New York, 1921), p. 38.
[76] Ugarte, *Destiny of a Continent*, p. 34.
[77] George H. Hepworth, *Oration Delivered . . . July 4, 1867* (Boston, 1867), p. 16.
[78] Quoted by Pao Chao Hsieh, *The Government of China, 1644-1911* (Baltimore, 1925), p. 6.
[79] *New York Herald*, December 30, 1869.
[80] Sumner, *op. cit.*, p. 176.
[81] *Works of Charles Sumner*, XI, 233.
[82] Immanuel Kant, *Perpetual Peace*, U. S. Library Association ed. (Los Angeles, 1932), p. 33.
[83] *Works of Charles Sumner*, XI, 223.
[84] *Ibid.*, p. 222.
[85] *Cong. Globe*, 40th Cong., 2d sess., p. 3660.
[86] *New York Herald*, December 14, 1868.
[87] *Ibid.*, February 8, 1868.
[88] J. Howard Pugh, *The Success and Promise of the American Union, an Oration, Delivered . . . July 4th, 1865* (Philadelphia, 1865), pp. 21-22.
[89] Richardson, *Messages*, VII, 61.

[90] *Cong. Globe*, 40th Cong., 3d sess., p. 335.

[91] *Ibid.*

[92] *Ibid.*, p. 336.

[93] Frederic Bancroft, *The Life of William H. Seward* (New York, 1900), II, 472.

[94] Richardson, *Messages*, VI, 689.

[95] *Cong. Globe*, 40th Cong., 3d sess., p. 335.

[96] *Ibid.*

[97] Richardson, *Messages*, VI, 580.

[98] *Cong. Globe*, 41st Cong., 2d sess., App., p. 507.

[99] *Ibid.*, 40th Cong., 2d sess., App., p. 474.

[100] *Ibid.*, 3d sess., p. 335.

[101] Quoted by Rippy, *op. cit.*, pp. 280-81.

[102] 52d Cong., 2d sess., *S. Ex. Doc.*, No. 77, p. 140.

[103] *Cong. Globe*, 41st Cong., 3d sess., p. 427.

[104] *New York Herald*, December 4, 1874.

[105] *Cong. Rec.*, 46th Cong., 2d sess., p. 13.

[106] Moore, *Digest*, I, 489.

[107] *Rept. of Comm. on For. Rel.*, VI, 382.

[108] *Cong. Rec.*, 55th Cong., 2d sess., App., p. 549.

[109] Murat Halstead, *The History of American Expansion and the Story of Our New Possessions* (n. p., 1898), p. 584.

[110] Brooks Adams, "England's Decadence in the West Indies," *Forum*, XXVII (1899), 467.

[111] Edwin E. Slosson, "The Question of the Caribbean," *Independent*, XCIX (1919), 394.

[112] Richardson, *Messages*, VII, 99.

[113] *Cong. Rec.*, 54th Cong., 1st sess., p. 263.

[114] *St. Louis Globe-Democrat*, quoted by *Public Opinion*, XXXV (1903), 644.

[115] *Works of Charles Sumner*, II, 125.

[116] Quoted by Isaac Joslin Cox, *Nicaragua and the United States*, in *World Peace Foundation Pamphlets*, X (1927), 747.

[117] *Foreign Relations of the United States*, 1878, p. 552.

[118] J. Holland Rose, *Nationality in Modern History* (New York, 1916), pp. 4-5.

[119] Fiske, *American Political Ideas*, chap. iii.

[120] J. Fred Rippy, "Literary Yankeephobia in Hispanic America," *Journal of International Relations*, XII (1922), 366.

[121] *Ibid.*, p. 367.

[122] *Ibid.*, p. 356.

[123] *Cong. Globe*, 41st Cong., 3d sess., p. 227.

[124] *Ibid.*, p. 408.

[125] *Ibid.*, 35th Cong., 2d sess., App., p. 161.

[126] *Ibid.*, 32d Cong., 2d sess., App., p. 147.

[127] *Ibid.*, 40th Cong., 2d sess., p. 3662.

[128] *New York Herald,* October 16, 1852.
[129] *Cong. Globe,* 40th Cong., 3d sess., p. 335.
[130] *Ibid.,* 2d sess., App., p. 403.
[131] Rousseau, *The Social Contract,* p. 70.
[132] Richardson, *Messages,* VI, 688.

## Notes to Chapter IX

### INEVITABLE DESTINY

[1] Moore, *Digest,* I, 431.
[2] *Ibid.,* p. 432.
[3] *Ibid.,* p. 433.
[4] *For. Rel.,* 1894, App., II, 1159.
[5] Moore, *Digest,* I, 432-33.
[6] *For. Rel.,* 1894, App., II, 113.
[7] Julius W. Pratt, "The 'Large Policy' of 1898," *Mississippi Valley Historical Review,* XIX (1932), 230.
[8] Schurz, *Harper's New Monthly Magazine,* LXXXVII (1893), 738.
[9] *National Party Platforms,* p. 175.
[10] Schurz, *op. cit.,* p. 737.
[11] *Ibid.,* p. 746.
[12] Representative Fleming, *Cong. Rec.,* 55th Cong., 3d sess., App., p. 87.
[13] *Ibid.,* 2d sess., p. 6188.
[14] *Nation,* "Non-Manifest Destiny," XCI (1910), 464.
[15] Morrison I. Swift, *Imperialism and Liberty* (Los Angeles, 1899), p. 449.
[16] Quoted by Laura A. White, "The United States in the 1850's as Seen by British Consuls," *Mississippi Valley Historical Review,* XIX (1933), 528.
[17] J. A. Hobson, *The Psychology of Jingoism* (London, 1901), p. 79.
[18] *Cong. Globe,* 33d Cong., 1st sess., p. 1566.
[19] *For. Rel.,* 1894, App., II, 5.
[20] *Ibid.,* p. 106.
[21] *Ibid.,* p. 121.
[22] *Ibid.,* p. 169.
[23] *Ibid.,* p. 1160.
[24] John L. Stevens, *American Patriotism: Predominance in the Pacific* (Honolulu? 1890), pp. 11-12.
[25] *For. Rel.,* 1894, App., II, 383.
[26] *Ibid.,* p. 381.
[27] *Ibid.,* p. 402.
[28] John L. Stevens, "A Plea for Annexation," *North American Review,* CLVII (1893), 745.
[29] *Philadelphia Inquirer,* quoted by *Public Opinion,* XIV (1893), 591.
[30] *New York Press, ibid.,* p. 439.
[31] *For. Rel.,* 1894, App., II, 198.

[32] *Ibid.*

[33] *Ibid.*, p. 402.

[34] New York *Sun,* quoted by *Public Opinion,* XVI (1894), 546.

[35] Mahan, *The Interest of America in Sea Power,* p. 21.

[36] *Ibid.*, p. 52.

[37] *Ibid.*, pp. 42 ff.

[38] *Ibid.*, p. 33.

[39] *Ibid.*, pp. 52-53.

[40] *Ibid.*, p. 36.

[41] *New York Tribune,* January 29, 1893.

[42] *Cong. Rec.*, 53d Cong., 2d sess., p. 1849.

[43] *Ibid.*, 3d sess., p. 1829.

[44] Moore, *Digest,* I, 432.

[45] *Cong. Rec.*, 55th Cong., 2d sess., p. 6016.

[46] Charles A. Beard, *The Navy: Defense or Portent?* (New York, 1932), p. 76.

[47] Moore, *Digest,* I, 505.

[48] *Rept. of Comm. on For. Rel.*, VII, 253.

[49] *Ibid.*, p. 194.

[50] *Selections from the Correspondence of Theodore Roosevelt and Henry Cabot Lodge 1884-1918* (New York, 1925), I, 311.

[51] Charles S. Olcott, *The Life of William McKinley* (Boston, 1916), I, 379.

[52] *New York Tribune,* quoted by *Public Opinion,* XXIV (1898), 708.

[53] *Baltimore American,* quoted by *Literary Digest,* XVI (1898), 752.

[54] *Cincinnati Enquirer,* quoted by *Public Opinion,* XXIV (1898), 707.

[55] Victor Hugo, *Ninety-three,* tr. F. L. Benedict (New York, 1874), p. 152.

[56] *Cong. Rec.*, 55th Cong., 2d sess., App., p. 549.

[57] Hobson, *op. cit.*, p. 84.

[58] *Chicago Evening Post,* quoted by *Literary Digest,* XV (1897), 243.

[59] *Cong. Rec.*, 55th Cong., 2d sess., App., p. 508.

[60] *Ibid.*

[61] *Los Angeles Herald,* July 2, 1898.

[62] *Overland Monthly,* XXXI (1898), 177-78.

[63] *Washington Post,* quoted in *Cong. Rec.*, 55th Cong., 2d sess., App., p. 573.

[64] Representative Clark, *ibid.*, p. 511.

[65] *Ibid.*, p. 548.

[66] *Ibid.*, 55th Cong., 2d sess., p. 5748.

[67] Powers, *Annals* of the American Academy of Political and Social Science, XII (1898), 181.

[68] Brooks Adams, *The Law of Civilization and Decay,* as quoted by Representative Clark, *Cong. Rec.*, 55th Cong., 2d sess., App., p. 508.

[69] R. F. Pettigrew, *The Course of Empire, an Official Record* (New York, 1920), p. 75.

[70] *Nation,* "Democratic Fatalism," LXVII (1898), 404.

[71] *Diary and Letters of Gouverneur Morris*, II, 442.

[72] *Works of William H. Seward,* III, 409.

[73] *Cong. Globe,* 33d Cong., 1st sess., App., p. 952.

[74] Mahan, *op. cit.,* pp. 36-37.

[75] *Brooklyn Standard-Union,* quoted by *Public Opinion,* XXIV (1898), 807.

[76] Peter S. Grosscup, *Chicago Tribune,* May 3, 1898.

[77] *Cong. Rec.,* 55th Cong., 2d sess., p. 5916.

[78] *Ibid.,* App., p. 549.

[79] *Correspondence of Roosevelt and Lodge,* I, 313.

[80] *Cong. Rec.,* 55th Cong., 3d sess., p. 2518.

[81] *Speeches and Addresses of William McKinley, from March 1, 1897 to May 30, 1900* (New York, 1900), p. 302.

[82] *Ibid.,* p. 134.

[83] James Bryce, *The American Commonwealth* (New York, 1910), II, 584.

[84] W. J. McGee, "The Growth of the United States," *National Geographic Magazine,* IX (1898), 381.

[85] 57th Cong., 1st sess., *S. Doc.,* No. 331, III, 2677.

[86] Quoted from Dr. Frank W. Gunsaulus by Harry F. Atwood, in *Keep God in American History* (Chicago, 1919).

[87] Moore, *Digest,* I, 527.

[88] *Ibid.,* p. 529.

[89] New York *World,* August 29, 1898.

[90] Quoted by John R. Dos Passos, *A Defense of the McKinley Administration from Attacks of Mr. Carl Schurz and Other Anti-Imperialists* (New York? 1900), pp. 43-44.

[91] Charles Denby, "Why the Treaty Should be Ratified," *Forum,* XXVI (1899), 643.

[92] *Speeches and Addresses of William McKinley,* p. 134.

[93] *Nation,* "'Destiny' and 'Duty,'" LXVII (1898), 307.

[94] *Speeches and Addresses of William McKinley,* p. 131.

[95] *Nation,* LXVII (1898), 307.

[96] *Works of Fisher Ames,* II, 346, 347.

[97] *Speeches and Addresses of William McKinley,* p. 131.

[98] Dennett, *John Hay,* p. 278.

[99] Beveridge, *For the Great Republic, Not for Imperialism,* p. 4.

[100] *Cong. Rec.,* 67th Cong., 2d sess., p. 9336.

[101] Theodore Roosevelt, *California Addresses* (San Francisco, 1903), p. 97.

[102] F. Spencer Baldwin, "Some Gains from Expansion," *Arena,* XXII (1899), 571.

[103] *Correspondence of Roosevelt and Lodge,* I, 300.

[104] Denby, *op. cit.,* p. 647.

[105] Claude G. Bowers, *Beveridge and the Progressive Era* (Cambridge, 1932), p. 71.

[106] *Journal of Commerce and Commercial Bulletin,* quoted by *Literary Digest,* XVII (1898), 242.

[107] R. Van Bergen, "Expansion Unavoidable," *Harper's Weekly,* XLIV (1900), 885.

[108] Bowers, *op. cit.,* p. 69.

[109] *Cong. Rec.*, 55th Cong., 3d sess., App., p. 162.

[110] Charles Denby, "America's Opportunity in Asia," *North American Review*, CLXVI (1898), 36.

[111] Kidd, *The Control of the Tropics*, p. 46.

[112] Benjamin Kidd, "The United States and the Control of the Tropics," *Atlantic Monthly*, LXXXII (1898), 726-27.

[113] Franklin Henry Giddings, *Democracy and Empire* (New York, 1900), p. 270.

[114] Charles A. Conant, *The United States in the Orient* (Boston, 1900), p. 2.

[115] Brooks Adams "The Spanish War and the Equilibrium of the World," *Forum*, XXV (1898), 650.

[116] Pratt, *op. cit.*, pp. 237 ff.

[117] *Ibid.*, pp. 238 ff.

[118] Rufus S. Tucker, "A Balance Sheet of the Philippines," *Harvard Business Review*, VIII (1929), 10 ff.

[119] *Cong. Rec.*, 56th Cong., 1st sess., App., p. 44.

[120] Adams, *Forum*, XXVII (1899), 46.

[121] *Outlook*, "America in the World," LXVI (1900), 150.

[122] *Cong. Rec.*, 56th Cong., 1st sess., p. 2630.

[123] Powers, *International Journal of Ethics*, X (1900), 306.

[124] Albert J. Beveridge, "The Development of a Colonial Policy for the United States," *Annals* of the American Academy of Political and Social Science, XXX (1907), 4, 6.

[125] Quoted by the *Nation*, "Imperial Fatalism," LXXXVI (1908), 4.

[126] *Ibid.*

[127] *Chicago Tribune*, quoted by *Literary Digest*, III (1916), 552.

[128] *Kansas City Star*, *ibid.*, CXII (January 29, 1927), 8.

[129] *St. Louis Globe-Democrat*, *ibid.*

[130] *Cong. Rec.*, 72d Cong., 2d sess., p. 1763.

[131] René Félix Allendy, *La problème de la destinée; étude sur la fatalité intérieure* (Paris, 1927), p. 17.

[132] Hobson, *op. cit.*, p. 80.

[133] Maurice Maeterlinck, *Wisdom and Destiny*, tr. Alfred Sutro (London, 1912), p. 29.

[134] Allendy, *op. cit.*, p. 200.

[135] Edwin R. A. Seligman, *The Economic Interpretation of History* (2d ed.; New York, 1912), p. 92.

[136] Sidney Hook, "Determinism," in *Encyclopaedia of the Social Sciences*, V, 111.

[137] Walt Whitman, *I Sit and Look Out*, ed. Emory Holloway and Vernolian Schwartz (New York, 1932), p. 157.

[138] *Nation*, XCI (1910), 464.

## Notes to Chapter X

### THE WHITE MAN'S BURDEN

[1] William Jennings Bryan, *et al., Republic or Empire? The Philippine Question* (Chicago, 1899), p. 83.

[2] *Writings of Thomas Jefferson,* V, 230.

[3] Swift, *Imperialism and Liberty,* p. 490.

[4] David J. Hill, *Our Place among the Nations; an Address* . . . (Philadelphia, 1901), p. 18.

[5] Representative Kitchin, *Cong. Rec.,* 56th Cong., 1st sess., App., p. 574.

[6] John W. Burgess, *Political Science and Comparative Constitutional Law* (Boston, 1890-91), I, 45.

[7] *National Party Platforms,* p. 163.

[8] Quoted by Walter Millis, *The Martial Spirit* (Boston, 1931), p. 50.

[9] *Life and Letters of Edwin Lawrence Godkin,* ed. Rollo Ogden (New York, 1907), II, 202.

[10] H. C. Lodge, "Our Blundering Foreign Policy," *Forum,* XIX (1895), 17.

[11] Mahan, *The Interest of America in Sea Power,* p. 50.

[12] *Rept. of Comm. on For. Rel.,* VII, 203.

[13] *Correspondence of Roosevelt and Lodge,* I, 205.

[14] *New York Journal,* quoted by *Public Opinion,* XXIV (1898), 484.

[15] *For. Rel.,* 1898, p. 757.

[16] Omaha *World-Herald,* quoted by *Public Opinion,* XXIV (1898), 519.

[17] *For. Rel.,* 1897, p. XV.

[18] Mahan, *op. cit.,* pp. 49-50.

[19] *Cong. Rec.,* 55th Cong., 2d sess., p. 6665.

[20] George F. Hoar, *Autobiography of Seventy Years* (New York, 1903), II, 308.

[21] *Writings of John Quincy Adams,* VII, 201.

[22] Baltimore *Sun,* quoted by *Public Opinion,* XXIV (1898), 772.

[23] *Editorials of Henry Watterson,* p. 269.

[24] Quoted by Swift, *op. cit.,* p. 341.

[25] New York *World,* August 29, 1898.

[26] *Washington Post,* quoted in *Cong. Rec.,* 55th Cong., 2d sess., App., p. 573.

[27] Quoted in *Cong. Rec.,* 57th Cong., 1st sess., p. 6218.

[28] Olcott, *Life of William McKinley,* II, 141.

[29] *New York Tribune,* May 5, 1898.

[30] William H. Davis, "The 'National Duty' Delusion," *Arena,* XXI (1899), 740.

[31] Luther Tracy Townsend, *'Manifest Destiny' from a Religious Point of View* (Baltimore, 1898).

[32] *Outlook,* "The New Monroe Doctrine," LIX (1898), 1006.

[33] Coolidge, *An Old-fashioned Senator,* p. 287.

[34] 55th Cong., 3d sess., *S. Doc.,* No. 62, p. 431.

[35] *Ibid.*, p. 381.

[36] *Cong. Rec.*, 56th Cong., 1st sess., p. 705.

[37] 56th Cong., 1st sess., *S. Doc.*, No. 208, p. 15.

[38] *Ibid.*, p. 95.

[39] Hoar, *op. cit.*, II, 309.

[40] Moore, *Digest*, I, 527.

[41] Olcott, *op. cit.*, II, 111.

[42] 55th Cong., 3d sess., *S. Doc.*, No. 62, pp. 362-677.

[43] Adams, '*Imperialism*' *and* '*The Tracks of Our Forefathers*,' p. 35.

[44] 55th Cong., 3d sess., *S. Doc.*, No. 62, pp. 369, 380, 504.

[45] *For. Rel.*, 1899, pp. L-LI.

[46] Freund, *Political Science Quarterly*, XIV (1899), 37-38.

[47] 55th Cong., 3d sess., *S. Doc.*, No. 62, pp. 369, 504.

[48] *Speeches and Addresses of William McKinley*, p. 161.

[49] *Cong. Rec.*, 55th Cong., 3d sess., p. 2518.

[50] Andrew Carnegie, "The Opportunity of the United States," *North American Review*, CLXXIV (1902), 607.

[51] 56th Cong., 1st sess., *S. Doc.*, No. 208, pp. 82-83.

[52] Jacob Gould Schurman, *Philippine Affairs; a Retrospect and Outlook* (New York, 1902), p. 7.

[53] 56th Cong., 1st sess., *S. Doc.*, No. 208, p. 104.

[54] Quoted by Millis, *op. cit.*, pp. 405-06.

[55] *Cong. Rec.*, 55th Cong., 3d sess., p. 959.

[56] Denby, *Forum*, XXVI (1898), 279, 281.

[57] *Cong. Rec.*, 55th Cong., 3d sess., p. 297.

[58] *Ibid.*, p. 836.

[59] *Ibid.*, App., p. 108.

[60] *Ibid.*, 55th Cong., 3d sess., p. 572.

[61] *Ibid.*, p. 837.

[62] *Ibid.*, p. 959.

[63] James K. Jones to William J. Bryan, January 24, 1899, MS. Bryan Papers, Library of Congress.

[64] *Cong. Rec.*, 57th Cong., 1st sess., p. 5972.

[65] *Ibid.*, 55th Cong., 3d sess., p. 959.

[66] *Correspondence of Roosevelt and Lodge*, I, 389, 400.

[67] James H. Blount, *The American Occupation of the Philippines 1898-1912* (New York, 1912), p. 178.

[68] 56th Cong., 1st sess., *S. Doc.*, No. 208, p. 62.

[69] *Speeches and Addresses of William McKinley*, p. 216.

[70] Tyler Dennett, *Americans in Eastern Asia* (New York, 1922), p. 629.

[71] *Denver Republican*, quoted by *Public Opinion*, XXVI (1899), 195.

[72] *Minneapolis Tribune*, *ibid.*, p. 196.

[73] Senator Allen, *Cong. Rec.*, 55th Cong., 3d sess., p. 1484.

[74] *Life and Letters of Edwin Lawrence Godkin*, II, 30.

[75] Charles Burke Elliott, *The Philippines to the End of the Military Régime* (Indianapolis, 1916), p. 370.

[76] Beveridge, *For the Greater Republic, Not for Imperialism*, pp. 16-17.
[77] 56th Cong., 1st sess., *S. Doc.*, No. 208, p. 83.
[78] *Cong. Rec.*, 55th Cong., 3d sess., p. 923.
[79] *Ibid.*, pp. 1531-32.
[80] Whitman, *Leaves of Grass*, p. 194.
[81] Whitman, *Gathering of the Forces*, I, 33.
[82] *Chicago Journal*, quoted by *Public Opinion*, XXVI (1899), 198.
[83] *Minneapolis Tribune*, *ibid.*
[84] *Troy Times*, *ibid.*, p. 195.
[85] *Cong. Rec.*, 55th Cong., 3d sess., p. 1827.
[86] *Salt Lake Tribune*, quoted by *Literary Digest*, XVIII (1899), 387.
[87] *Cong. Rec.*, 56th Cong., 1st sess., App., p. 430.
[88] Quoted by Coolidge, *op. cit.*, p. 302.
[89] Moritz Julius Bonn, "Imperialism," in *Encyclopaedia of the Social Sciences*, VII, 606.
[90] A. T. Mahan, *Armaments and Arbitration* (New York, 1912), p. 117.
[91] *Public Opinion*, XXVIII (1900), 291.
[92] *Cong. Rec.*, 55th Cong., 3d sess., pp. 2518-19.
[93] *Ibid.*, p. 1695.
[94] *Report of the Philippine Commission to the President, January 31, 1900-December 20, 1900* (Washington, 1900), p. 121.
[95] Quoted by Swift, *op. cit.*, p. 362.
[96] Richardson, *Messages*, IX, 720.
[97] Frederick W. Gookin, *A Liberty Catechism* (Chicago, 1899), p. 17.
[98] *Emporia Gazette*, March 20, 1899.
[99] Gookin, *op. cit.*, p. 18.
[100] *Cong. Rec.*, 56th Cong., 1st sess., p. 704.
[101] Quoted in *Cong. Rec.*, 57th Cong., 1st sess., p. 7453.
[102] *Cong. Rec.*, 56th Cong., 1st sess., p. 2618.
[103] *National Party Platforms*, p. 234.
[104] *Cong. Rec.*, 56th Cong., 1st sess., p. 708.
[105] *Annals of Cong.*, 15th Cong., 1st sess., col. 1483.
[106] *Cong. Rec.*, 56th Cong., 1st sess., p. 2621.
[107] Ferdinand Blumentritt, *The Philippine Islands*, tr. D. J. Doherty (Chicago, 1900), p. 61.
[108] *Cong. Rec.*, 56th Cong., 1st sess., p. 711.
[109] Ernest Seillière, *Introduction à la philosophie de l'impérialisme* (2d ed.; Paris, 1911), pp. 46-53.
[110] *Cong. Rec.*, 55th Cong., 3d sess., p. 2518.
[111] Schurman, *op. cit.*, p. 82.
[112] Quoted by Moorfield Storey, *The Conquest of the Philippines by the United States* (New York, 1927), p. 172.
[113] Philippine Information Society, *Facts about the Filipinos* (Boston, 1901), Vol. I, No. 9, p. 62.
[114] Quoted by Swift, *op. cit.*, p. 99.
[115] *Cong. Rec.*, 56th Cong., 1st sess., p. 711.

[116] *Washington Post,* January 14, 1900.

[117] *Cong. Rec.*, 56th Cong., 1st sess., p. 2627.

[118] *Writings of Benjamin Franklin,* VI, 461.

[119] *Cong. Rec.*, 56th Cong., 1st sess., p. 2627.

[120] *Ibid.*

[121] *Ibid.*, p. 2617.

[122] *Ibid.*, p. 2629.

[123] *Official Proceedings of the Twelfth Republican National Convention . . . 1900* (Philadelphia, 1900), p. 88.

[124] *Cong. Rec.*, 56th Cong., 1st sess., p. 2629.

[125] *Ibid.*, p. 2628.

[126] 56th Cong., 2d sess., *S. Doc.*, No. 135, p. 2.

[127] New York *Evening Post,* quoted by *Public Opinion,* XXX (1901), 132.

[128] Quoted from General Bell by Philippine Information Society, *op. cit.*, Vol. I, No. 10, p. 41.

[129] *Ibid.*, p. 50.

[130] *Ibid.*

[131] *Baltimore News,* quoted by *Public Opinion,* XXIV (1902), 138.

[132] Dean C. Worcester, *The Philippines Past and Present* (New York, 1914), I, 317.

[133] Jacob Gould Schurman, "The Philippines Again," *Independent,* LIV (1902), 1107.

[134] Storey, *op. cit.*, p. 177.

[135] *Cong. Rec.*, 57th Cong., 1st sess., App., p. 353.

[136] Quoted by Swift, *op. cit.*, p. 99.

[137] *Addresses and Presidential Messages of Theodore Roosevelt 1902-1904* (New York, 1904), pp. 157, 316.

[138] *Cong. Rec.*, 57th Cong., 1st sess., p. 5289.

[139] *Ibid.*, p. 5791.

[140] Oscar F. Williams, "An Imperial Dicker," *Independent,* LIV (1902), 903.

[141] *Reminiscences of Carl Schurz* (New York, 1908-09), III, 447.

[142] John Davidson, *Self's the Man: a Tragi-Comedy* (London, 1901), p. 136.

[143] Burton Hendrick, ed., *The Life and Letters of Walter H. Page* (New York, 1922), I, 273.

[144] *Chicago Tribune,* quoted by *Current Opinion,* LXI (1916), 152.

[145] Theodore Roosevelt's statement of January, 1915, quoted by Harry B. Hawes, *Philippine Uncertainty* (New York, 1932), p. 273.

[146] *Cong. Rec.*, 63d Cong., 2d sess., p. 44.

[147] *Hearings before the Committee on Territories and Insular Affairs,* 72d Cong., 1st sess., on S. 3377, pp. 29-30, 41.

[148] 72d Cong., 2d sess., *H. Doc.*, No. 524, p. 2.

[149] *Literary Digest,* "A Perilous Freedom Handed to the Philippines," CXV (January 28, 1933), 5.

[150] *Cong. Rec.*, 72d Cong., 2d sess., p. 1793.

[151] D. R. Williams, *The United States and the Philippines* (New York, 1924). p. 124.

## Notes to Chapter XI

### PARAMOUNT INTEREST

[1] *Cong. Rec.,* 58th Cong., 1st sess., p. 443.

[2] Richardson, *Messages,* VII, 586.

[3] Theodore S. Woolsey, "Suez and Panama—a Parallel," in *Annual Report of the American Historical Association, 1902,* p. 311.

[4] Mary Wilhemine Williams, *Anglo-American Isthmian Diplomacy 1815-1915* (Washington, 1916), p. 304.

[5] Dennett, *John Hay,* p. 364.

[6] Beard, *The Idea of National Interest,* p. v.

[7] *Addresses and Presidential Messages of Theodore Roosevelt,* p. 115.

[8] *Reg. of Debates,* 19th Cong., 1st sess., col. 2437.

[9] Moore, *Digest,* I, 476.

[10] *Ibid.,* III, 2.

[11] *Ibid.,* p. 9.

[12] 47th Cong., 1st sess., *S. Ex. Doc.,* No. 194, p. 57.

[13] Moore, *Digest,* III, 130.

[14] 46th Cong., 2d sess., *S. Ex. Doc.,* No. 112, p. 19.

[15] 47th Cong., 1st. sess., *S. Ex. Doc.,* No. 194, p. 134.

[16] Moore, *Digest,* III, 13.

[17] 56th Cong., 1st sess., *S. Doc.,* No. 268, p. 22.

[18] John Bassett Moore, *The Interoceanic Canal and the Hay-Pauncefote Treaty* (Washington, 1900), p. 26.

[19] Dennett, *op. cit.,* p. 259.

[20] *De Bow's Review,* "Nicaragua and the Proposed Interoceanic Canal," XIII (1852), 246.

[21] *Cong. Globe,* 32d Cong., 3d sess., App., p. 261.

[22] *United States Review,* "Mexico and the Monroe Doctrine," I (1853), 448.

[23] *National Party Platforms,* p. 46.

[24] Richardson, *Messages,* VII, 585-86.

[25] 56th Cong., 1st sess., *S. Doc.,* No. 237, p. 381.

[26] *Ibid.,* p. 386.

[27] 46th Cong., 2d sess., *S. Ex. Doc.,* No. 112, p. 16.

[28] Richardson, *Messages,* VII, 586.

[29] 56th Cong., 1st sess., *S. Doc.,* No. 237, p. 383.

[30] *Ibid.,* No. 161, p. 13.

[31] Richardson, *Messages,* VIII, 327-28.

[32] *Cong. Rec.,* 52d Cong., 2d sess., p. 1526.

[33] Representative Gibson, *ibid.,* 55th Cong., 2d sess., App., p. 549.

[34] Halstead, *The History of American Expansion and the Story of Our New Possessions,* p. 593.

[35] Dennett, *op. cit.,* p. 251.

[36] Richard Olney, "Growth of American Foreign Policy," *Atlantic Monthly,* LXXXV (1900), 298.

[37] Dennett, *op. cit.*, p. 257.

[38] *St. Louis Globe-Democrat,* quoted by *Public Opinion,* XXX (1901), 355.

[39] *Boston Journal, ibid.*, p. 356.

[40] *New York Press, ibid.*, XXVIII (1900), 198.

[41] *Cong. Rec.*, 56th Cong., 1st sess., p. 4946.

[42] Francis Lieber, "The Ship Canal from the Atlantic to the Pacific," *De Bow's Review,* V (1848), 388 ff.

[43] James Jeffrey Roche, "Panama," reprinted in *Poems of American History,* ed. B. E. Stevenson (Boston, 1908), p. 651.

[44] Mahan, *The Interest of America in Sea Power,* p. 46.

[45] Henry G. Hodges, *The Doctrine of Intervention* (Princeton, 1915), p. 190.

[46] *De Bow's Review,* XIII (1852), 246.

[47] Richardson, *Messages,* VII, 586.

[48] 56th Cong., 1st sess., *S. Doc.*, No. 237, p. 382.

[49] 46th Cong., 3d sess., *H. Rept.*, No. 390, p. 8.

[50] 56th Cong., 1st sess., *S. Doc.*, No. 237, p. 472.

[51] *Ibid.*, p. 434.

[52] Mahan, *op. cit.*, p. 84.

[53] *Cong. Rec.*, 46th Cong., 2d sess., p. 13.

[54] Alfred Williams, *The Inter-Oceanic Canal and the Monroe Doctrine* (New York, 1880), p. 112.

[55] Representative Stewart, *Cong. Rec.*, 56th Cong., 1st sess., pp. 4945-46.

[56] *Ibid.*, App., p. 271.

[57] 56th Cong., 1st sess., *S. Doc.*, No. 237, pp. 398-99.

[58] Mahan, *op. cit.*, pp. 84, 83.

[59] 56th Cong., 1st sess., *S. Doc.*, No. 237, p. 399.

[60] Mahan, *op. cit.*, p. 83.

[61] Richardson, *Messages,* VII, 586.

[62] 47th Cong., 1st sess., *S. Ex. Doc.*, No. 194, p. 135.

[63] Woolsey, *op. cit.*, p. 308.

[64] Moore, *op. cit.*, p. 26.

[65] Mayo W. Hazeltine, "The Proposed Hay-Pauncefote Treaty," *North American Review,* CLXX (1900), 357.

[66] Harmodio Arias, *The Panama Canal: a Study in International Law and Diplomacy* (London, 1911), p. 108.

[67] *Am. State Papers, For. Rel.*, V, 571.

[68] *Cong. Rec.*, 56th Cong., 1st sess., App., p. 270.

[69] Theodore Roosevelt, "How the United States Acquired the Right to Dig the Panama Canal," *Outlook*, XCIX (1911), 318.

[70] *Cong. Rec.*, 58th Cong., 2d sess., p. 139.

[71] *New York Times,* March 24, 1911.

[72] Roosevelt, *op. cit.*, p. 314.

[73] *For. Rel.*, 1903, p. 275.

[74] *Ibid.*, p. 260.

[75] Albert Bushnell Hart, *The Monroe Doctrine—an Interpretation* (Boston, 1916), p. 220.

[76] *Cong. Globe,* 35th Cong., 2d sess., p. 430.

[77] Philippe Bunau-Varilla, *Panama—the Creation, Destruction, and Resurrection* (New York, 1914), p. 288.

[78] Root, *Addresses on International Subjects,* p. 181.

[79] *Cong. Rec.,* 58th Cong., 2d sess., p. 1489.

[80] *Ibid.,* p. 1516.

[81] *Brooklyn Eagle,* reprinted in "*I Took the Isthmus*" (New York, 1911), p. 94.

[82] *Atlanta Journal,* quoted by *Literary Digest,* XXVII (1903), 691.

[83] *Denver Republican,* reprinted in "*I Took the Isthmus,*" pp. 85-86.

[84] H. M. Chittenden, "Manifest Destiny in America," *Atlantic Monthly,* CXVII (1916), 55, 48.

[85] Roosevelt, *op. cit.,* p. 318.

[86] Moore, *Digest,* III, 88.

[87] Dennett, *op. cit.,* p. 382.

[88] 62d Cong., 2d sess., *H. Doc.,* No. 343, pp. 11-12.

[89] 63d Cong., 2d sess., *S. Doc.,* No. 474, p. 95.

[90] Bunau-Varilla, *op. cit.,* p. 522.

[91] *Cong. Rec.,* 63d Cong., 2d sess., p. 4313.

[92] Baltimore *Sun,* July 12, 1934.

[93] Charles Evans Hughes, "Observations on the Monroe Doctrine," *American Journal of International Law,* XVII (1923), 620.

[94] *Cong. Rec.,* 59th Cong., 1st sess., p. 97.

[95] Hughes, *op. cit.,* p. 620.

[96] James Morton Callahan, "The Modern Meaning of the Monroe Doctrine," in *Latin America,* ed. G. H. Blakeslee (New York, 1914), p. 168.

[97] Wallace Thompson, "The Doctrine of the 'Special Interest' of the United States in the Region of the Caribbean Sea," *Annals* of the American Academy of Political and Social Science, CXXXII (1927), 153 ff.

[98] *For. Rel.,* 1912, p. 1092.

[99] *Ibid.,* 1913, p. 559.

[100] *Cong. Rec.,* 69th Cong., 2d sess., p. 1326.

[101] *Ibid.,* p. 1555.

[102] Colby N. Chester, "The Present Status of the Monroe Doctrine," *Annals* of the American Academy of Political and Social Science, XIV (1914), 25.

[103] George C. Butte, *Great Britain and the Panama Canal: a Study of the Tolls Question* (n. p., 1913), p. 24.

[104] *Chicago Tribune,* quoted by *Literary Digest,* LII (1916), 552.

[105] *For. Rel.,* 1894, App., II, 5.

[106] *Iowa State Register,* quoted by *Public Opinion,* XIV (1893), 417.

[107] Semple, *American History and Its Geographic Conditions,* p. 409.

[108] Nelson O'Shaughnessy, *New York Times,* December 30, 1926.

[109] Frederick C. Penfield, "Why Not Own the Panama Isthmus?" *North American Review,* CLXXIV (1902), 272.

[110] *For. Rel.,* 1917, p. 694.

[111] Shepherd, *Proceedings of the American Academy of Political Science,* VII (1917), 394.

[112] Chester Lloyd Jones, *Caribbean Interests of the United States* (New York, 1916), p. 351.

[113] *For. Rel.,* 1912, p. 1083.

[114] *American Journal of International Law,* IV (1910), 182, 181.

[115] *New Republic,* "Democratic Intervention," VIII (1916), 207.

[116] *New York Times,* April 26, 1927.

[117] Rodgers, *Forum,* LXXVII (1927), 888.

[118] 67th Cong., 4th sess., *S. Doc.,* No. 348, III, 2721.

[119] Baltimore *Evening Sun,* May 1, 1934.

[120] Baltimore *Sun,* May 1, 1934.

[121] Kraus, *Recueil des cours, 1927, Académie de Droit International,* 1927, I, 436.

[122] Stowell, *International Law,* p. 127.

[123] Charles Evans Hughes, "The Centenary of the Monroe Doctrine," *Annals* of the American Academy of Political and Social Science, CXI, Supp. (1924), 7.

[124] Royal Cortissoz, *The Life of Whitelaw Reid* (New York, 1921), II, 292-93.

## Notes to Chapter XII

### POLITICAL AFFINITY

[1] Vanderlip, *Century Magazine,* LVI (1898), 562.

[2] *Canadian Annual Review of Public Affairs,* 1911, "Reciprocity with the United States," p. 62.

[3] *Cong. Rec.,* 62d Cong., 1st sess., p. 759.

[4] A. G. Bradley, *The Making of Canada* (New York, 1908), p. 67.

[5] *Journals of the Continental Congress,* I, 112.

[6] *The Foederalist,* No. 2, pp. 7-8.

[7] *Journals of the Continental Congress,* II, 68.

[8] Goldwin Smith, *Canada and the Canadian Question* (New York, 1891), p. 267.

[9] *Journals of the Continental Congress,* I, 111.

[10] W. H. H. Murray, *Continental Unity; an Address . . . Delivered . . . December 13, 1888* (2d ed.; Boston, 1888), pp. 7, 6.

[11] William Wood, ed., *Select British Documents of the Canadian War of 1812* (Toronto, 1920), I, 26.

[12] *Rochester Democrat,* quoted by Hugh L. Keenleyside, *Canada and the United States* (New York, 1929), p. 108.

[13] E. A. Theller, *Canada in 1837-1838* (Philadelphia, 1841).

[14] *Cong. Globe,* 28th Cong., 2d sess., App., p. 151.

[15] Keenleyside, *op. cit.,* p. 135.

[16] Cephas D. Allin and George M. Jones, *Annexation, Preferential Trade and Reciprocity* (Toronto, 1912), p. 379.

[17] New York *Sun,* October 25, 1849.

[18] *Toronto Examiner,* January 31, 1850.

[19] *Writings of Thomas Jefferson,* Memorial ed., X, 296.

[20] *Works of Fisher Ames,* I, 329.

[21] Representative Seymour, *Cong. Globe,* 28th Cong., 2d sess., App., p. 212.

[22] *Dollar Globe,* August 29, 1844.

[23] *Cong. Globe,* 33d Cong., 1st sess., App., p. 953.

[24] *Ibid.,* 29th Cong., 2d sess., App., p. 327.

[25] D. D. Barnard, "The Whigs and Their Candidates," *American Review,* VIII (1848), 225.

[26] *Cong. Globe,* 30th Cong., 1st sess., App., p. 52.

[27] *Saratoga Whig,* July 6, 1849.

[28] *Cong. Globe,* 32d Cong., 1st sess., App., p. 917.

[29] *Ibid.,* 2d sess., App., p. 97.

[30] *Ibid.,* pp. 59-60.

[31] Quoted by Carl Schurz, *American Imperialism* (Boston, 1899), p. 13.

[32] *Cong. Globe,* 42d Cong., 1st sess., p. 526.

[33] Walker, *Letter . . . on the Annexation of Nova Scotia and British America,* p. 20.

[34] *New York Herald,* December 14, 1868.

[35] Pierce, *Memoir and Letters of Charles Sumner,* IV, 637.

[36] *Cong. Rec.,* 46th Cong., 2d sess., p. 13.

[37] *Ibid.,* 50th Cong., 1st sess., p. 8671.

[38] *Cleveland Leader,* quoted by *Public Opinion,* VI (1888), 215.

[39] Murray, *op. cit.,* p. 1.

[40] Justin S. Morrill, "Is Union with Canada Desirable?" *Forum,* VI (1889), 464.

[41] Benjamin F. Butler, *Should There Be a Union of the English-speaking Peoples of the Earth? A Dissertation Delivered . . . July 2, 1889* (Boston, 1889), p. 10.

[42] New York *Sun,* quoted by *Public Opinion,* XIV (1892), 224.

[43] *Chicago Herald, ibid.,* p. 349.

[44] *Cong. Rec.,* 53d Cong., 2d sess., p. 1908.

[45] *Rept. of Comm. on For. Rel.,* VII, 205.

[46] *Cong. Rec.,* 55th Cong., 2d sess., p. 6016.

[47] Hermann Eduard von Holst, *The Annexation of Hawaii* (Chicago, 1898), pp. 27-28.

[48] Giddings, *Democracy and Empire,* p. 12.

[49] *Cong. Rec.,* 55th Cong., 3d sess., p. 1430.

[50] Quoted in *Cong. Rec.,* 56th Cong., 1st sess., p. 2620.

[51] *Ibid.,* App., p. 148.

[52] Ugarte, *The Destiny of a Continent,* p. xix.

[53] New York *World,* quoted by *Public Opinion,* XXIV (1898), 806.

[54] Schurz, *Harper's New Monthly Magazine,* LXXXVII (1893), 739.

[55] William H. Hinrichsen, "Territorial Expansion," *Democratic Magazine,* I (1898), 493-94.

[56] *Cong. Rec.*, 55th Cong., 3d sess., App., p. 148.

[57] Williams, *Independent,* LIV (1902), 903, 905.

[58] *Canadian Annual Review*, 1903, p. 390.

[59] Albert Shaw, *Political Problems of American Development* (New York, 1907), pp. 239, 246.

[60] *Ibid.*, p. 233.

[61] *Independent,* "Social and Political Fusion," LXVII (1909), 1394.

[62] John R. Dos Passos, *The Anglo-Saxon Century and the Unification of the English-speaking People* (New York, 1903), p. vii.

[63] Andrew Carnegie, *Drifting Together—Will the United States and Canada Unite?* (New York, 1904), p. 4.

[64] T. W. Higginson, "A Reunited Anglo-Saxondom," *Century Magazine,* LXXII (1906), 474.

[65] Dos Passos, *op. cit.*, p. 234.

[66] W. G. Mackendrick, *The Destiny of Great Britain and the United States* (6th ed., rev.; Boston, 1926), p. 4.

[67] *Works of Charles Sumner,* XIII, 129.

[68] *North American Review,* "The Reciprocity Treaty," LXXIX (1854), 483.

[69] 37th Cong., 2d sess., *H. Ex. Doc.*, No. 146, pp. 84-85.

[70] Smith, *op. cit.*, p. 284.

[71] Keenleyside, *op. cit.*, p. 307.

[72] *Canadian Annual Review*, 1902, p. 185.

[73] *Ibid.*

[74] *Ibid.*, pp. 185-86.

[75] *Outlook*, "The Future of Canada," LXXV (1903), 531.

[76] Archibald Cary Coolidge, *The United States as a World Power* (New York, 1910), pp. 265-66.

[77] James J. Hill, *Highways of Progress* (New York, 1910), pp. 85-101.

[78] Frank B. Tracy, "The Republic and the Dominion," *North American Review,* CLXXVII (1903), 579.

[79] Keenleyside, *op. cit.*, p. 312.

[80] *Cong. Rec.*, 61st Cong., 3d sess., p. 2376.

[81] *Ibid.*, 62d Cong., 1st sess., p. 759.

[82] 61st Cong., 3d sess., *S. Doc.*, No. 787, p. iv.

[83] *Canadian Annual Review*, 1911, p. 66.

[84] *Cong. Rec.*, 61st Cong., 3d sess., App., p. 92.

[85] *New York American*, quoted by Keenleyside, *op. cit.*, p. 316.

[86] *Canadian Annual Review*, 1911, p. 69.

[87] *Ibid.*, p. 63.

[88] Resolution of February 16, 1911, *Cong. Rec.*, 61st Cong., 3d sess., p. 2743.

[89] *Southern Lumber Journal*, quoted by *Canadian Annual Review*, 1911, p. 68.

[90] *Canadian Annual Review*, 1911, p. 65.

[91] *Cong. Rec.*, 61st Cong., 3d sess., p. 2520.

[92] *Ibid.*, p. 2521.

[93] *Ibid.*, App., p. 124.

[94] *Ibid.*, 61st Cong., 3d sess., p. 2457.

[95] *Ibid.*, 62d Cong., 1st sess., p. 490.
[96] *Ibid.*, 61st Cong., 3d sess., p. 2436.
[97] *Regina Standard*, September 15, 1911.
[98] *Cong. Rec.*, 62d Cong., 1st sess., p. 529.
[99] *Ibid.*, p. 948.
[100] *Ibid.*, p. 828.
[101] *Ibid.*, p. 369.
[102] *Ibid.*, p. 373.
[103] *Ibid.*, p. 455.
[104] *Ibid.*, p. 726.
[105] *Ibid.*, p. 2551.
[106] Senator Jones, *ibid.*, p. 3112.
[107] *Ibid.*, p. 390.
[108] Keenleyside, *op. cit.*, p. 318.
[109] Dunning, *The British Empire and the United States*, p. 340.
[110] *Canadian Annual Review*, 1911, p. 85.
[111] *Cong. Rec.*, 61st Cong., 3d sess., p. 2451.
[112] *Canadian Annual Review*, 1911, p. 270.
[113] *Independent*, "National Expansion," LXXV (1913), 654.
[114] John Allan Wyeth, *The Great Republic: the United States of North America* (New York, 1916), p. 3.
[115] *Canadian Annual Review*, 1922, pp. 81-82.
[116] *Cong. Rec.*, 66th Cong., 2d sess., p. 4018.
[117] *Canadian Annual Review*, 1923, p. 84.
[118] *New York Times*, February 24, 1927.
[119] *Cong. Rec.*, 62d Cong., 1st sess., p. 2551.
[120] *Toronto Globe*, September 22, 1911.
[121] *Canadian Annual Review*, 1911, p. 21.
[122] *Detroit Free Press*, quoted by *Public Opinion*, XIV (1892), 224.
[123] *United States Review*, "On the Rumored Occupation of San Domingo by the Emperor of France," I (1853), 179-80.

## Notes to Chapter XIII

### SELF-DEFENSE

[1] *Cong. Rec.*, 64th Cong., 1st sess., p. 9030.
[2] Burleigh Cushing Rodick, *The Doctrine of Necessity in International Law* (New York, 1928), p. 119.
[3] Smith, *Our Struggle for the Fourteenth Colony*, I 237-38.
[4] Ingersoll, *Recollections*, p. 392.
[5] *The Writings of George Washington*, ed. Jared Sparks (Boston, 1858), XI, 443.
[6] 56th Cong., 1st sess., *S. Doc.*, No. 161, p. 10.

[7] Moore, *Digest*, VI, 372.

[8] *Annals of Cong.*, 11th Cong., 1st sess., cols. 579-80.

[9] *Ibid.*, 16th Cong., 1st sess., col. 1763.

[10] Parton, *Life of Andrew Jackson*, III, 659.

[11] Representative Baker, *Cong. Globe*, 29th Cong., 1st sess., p. 136.

[12] Moore, *Digest*, VI, 402.

[13] *Ibid.*, p. 552.

[14] *Ibid.*, p. 417.

[15] Root, *Addresses on International Subjects*, p. 111.

[16] Ingersoll, *op. cit.*, p. 223.

[17] *Cong. Globe*, 32d Cong., 2d sess., App., p. 95.

[18] Richardson, *Messages*, V, 568.

[19] Quoted by James Morton Callahan, *American Foreign Policy in Mexican Relations* (New York, 1932), p. 246.

[20] *New York Herald*, November 23, 1858.

[21] Rippy, *United States and Mexico*, p. 29.

[22] Quoted by Perkins, *The Monroe Doctrine 1826-1867*, p. 329.

[23] *Madisonian*, October 12, 1843.

[24] 28th Cong., 1st sess., *S. Doc.*, No. 341, pp. 50-51.

[25] 33d Cong., 2d sess., *H. Ex. Doc.*, No. 93, p. 131.

[26] *Ibid.*

[27] *Ibid.*, pp. 135-36.

[28] *Cong. Globe*, 35th Cong., 2d sess., p. 543.

[29] *The Works of Abraham Lincoln*, ed. A. B. Lapsley (New York, 1905), IV, 139.

[30] *Ibid.*

[31] Richardson, *Messages*, VI, 580.

[32] Mahan, *The Interest of America in Sea Power*, p. 103.

[33] Lodge, *Forum*, XIX (1895), 16.

[34] *Cong. Rec.*, 54th Cong., 1st sess., p. 37.

[35] *Ibid.*, 55th Cong., 2d sess., p. 5829.

[36] From General Schofield's statement of 1875, in *Rept. of Comm. on For. Rel.*, VII, 274.

[37] *Cong. Rec.*, 55th Cong., 2d sess., App., p. 670.

[38] *Ibid.*, 55th Cong., 2d sess., p. 6007.

[39] James Morton Callahan, *An Introduction to American Expansion Policy* (Morgantown, 1908), p. 26.

[40] *Cong. Rec.*, 55th Cong., 2d sess., p. 5789.

[41] Mahan, *op. cit.*, p. 104.

[42] *Ibid.*, pp. 35-36.

[43] Charles Callan Tansill, *The Purchase of the Danish West Indies* (Baltimore, 1932), p. 26.

[44] Mahan, *op. cit.*, p. 6.

[45] *Ibid.*, p. 47.

[46] *Rept. of Comm. on For. Rel.*, VII, 204.

[47] Conant, *The United States in the Orient*, pp. iii-iv.

[48] Japan, Foreign Office, *The Present Condition of China with Reference to Circumstances Affecting International Relations and the Good Understanding upon Which Peace Depends*, Document A (Tokyo, 1932), p. 74.

[49] Richardson, *Messages*, IV, 399, 582.

[50] Perkins, *op. cit.*, pp. 326-27, 334-35, 233.

[51] Richardson, *Messages*, VII, 100.

[52] Moore, *Digest*, VI, 560.

[53] Mahan, *op. cit.*, p. 21.

[54] *Cong. Rec.*, 54th Cong., 1st sess., p. 37.

[55] *Rept. of Comm. on For. Rel.*, VII, 312.

[56] *Cong. Rec.*, 56th Cong., 1st sess., p. 2629.

[57] Carlos Pereyra, *La Doctrina de Monroe*; *el Destino Manifesto y el Imperialismo* (Mexico, 1908), pp. 56-118.

[58] Quoted from David Mills by *Canadian Annual Review*, 1902, p. 176.

[59] Mahan, *op. cit.*, pp. 298 ff.

[60] Tansill, *op. cit.*, p. 191.

[61] *Ibid.*, pp. 417-18.

[62] *Ibid.*, pp. 418-23.

[63] *New York Times*, January 25, 1902.

[64] *Philadelphia Inquirer* and *Cincinnati Enquirer*, quoted by *New York Herald*, February 10 and 15, 1902.

[65] Tansill, *op. cit.*, chap. vii.

[66] *New York Times*, October 25, 1902.

[67] *New York Herald*, quoted by *Public Opinion*, XXXIII (1902), 552.

[68] *For. Rel.*, 1905, p. xxxiii.

[69] Hughes, *Our Relations to the Nations of the Western Hemisphere*, p. 19.

[70] Coolidge's message of January 10, 1927, *Cong. Rec.*, 69th Cong., 2d sess., pp. 1325-26.

[71] J. Reuben Clark, *Memorandum on the Monroe Doctrine* (Washington, 1930), p. xix.

[72] Thompson, *Annals* of the American Academy of Political and Social Science, CXXXII (1927), 159.

[73] *Correspondence of Roosevelt and Lodge*, II, 135-36.

[74] *New York Times*, February 25, 1912.

[75] *Cong. Rec.*, 62d Cong., 2d sess., p. 9923.

[76] Thomas A. Bailey, "The Lodge Corollary to the Monroe Doctrine," *Political Science Quarterly*, XLVIII (1933), 228.

[77] Maurice Francis Egan, *Recollections of a Happy Life* (New York, 1924), p. 286.

[78] *Cong. Rec.*, 67th Cong., 4th sess., p. 1129.

[79] Robert Lansing, "Drama of the Virgin Islands Purchase," *New York Times Magazine*, July 19, 1931, p. 4.

[80] *New York Times*, August 17, 1916.

[81] Lansing, *loc. cit.*

[82] Tansill, *op. cit.*, pp. 508-09.

[83] Stowell, *International Law*, p. 127.

[84] *Writings of Thomas Jefferson*, VI, 221.

[85] Edgar E. Robinson and Victor J. West, *The Foreign Policy of Woodrow Wilson, 1913-1917* (New York, 1917), p. 337.

[86] *For. Rel.*, 1917, pp. 692-94.

[87] Tansill, *op. cit.*, p. 499.

[88] *Cong. Rec.*, 65th Cong., 3d sess., p. 195.

[89] Eldred E. Jacobsen, "Our New Caribbean Islands," *American Review of Reviews*, LV (1917), 276.

[90] *Philadelphia Evening Ledger*, quoted by *Literary Digest*, "Buying Islands for Defense," LIII (1916), 1697.

[91] *New Republic*, VII (1916), 313.

[92] *Literary Digest*, "Our $25,000,000 'Poorhouse,'" CIX (April 11, 1931), 10.

[93] *Cong. Rec.*, 56th Cong., 1st sess., p. 2629.

[94] *New York Times*, August 5, 1916.

[95] Root, *op. cit.*, p. 111.

[96] *New York Evening Mail*, quoted by *Current Opinion*, LXI (1916), 152.

[97] James C. Bardin, "'Manifest Destiny' in the Caribbean," *Sea Power*, December, 1920, p. 263; January, 1921, p. 305.

[98] Charles H. Sherrill, *Modernizing the Monroe Doctrine* (New York, 1916), p. 179.

[99] Shepherd, *Proceedings of the Academy of Political Science*, VII (1917), 392 ff.

[100] *Cong. Rec.*, 67th Cong., 4th sess., pp. 4101-02.

[101] Shepherd, *op. cit.*, p. 398.

[102] *Ibid.*, p. 393.

[103] *Writings of James Monroe*, IV, 74.

[104] Rodick, *op. cit.*, p. 119.

[105] Moore, *Digest*, II, 412.

[106] James T. Shotwell, *The Pact of Paris, with Historical Commentary*, in *International Conciliation*, October, 1928, No. 243, p. 61.

[107] Hall, *A Treatise on International Law*, p. 322.

[108] Immanuel Kant, *The Philosophy of Law*, tr. W. Hastie (Edinburgh, 1887), pp. 52-53.

[109] "Civil Disobedience," in *The Writings of Henry David Thoreau*, Riverside ed. (Boston, 1884-94), X, 138.

[110] Representative Smith, *Cong. Rec.*, 55th Cong., 2d sess., p. 6007.

[111] Heinrich von Treitschke, *Politics*, tr. Blanche Dugdale and Torben de Bille (New York, 1916), I, 106, 94.

[112] Quoted from Charles Maurras by Hayes, *Historical Evolution of Modern Nationalism*, p. 165.

[113] *New York Times*, May 23, 1933.

[114] *Ibid.*, May 17, 1933.

## Notes to Chapter XIV

### INTERNATIONAL POLICE POWER

[1] *Report of the Delegates of the United States of America to the Sixth International Conference of American States* (Washington, 1928), p. 14.

[2] *Survey of American Foreign Relations, 1929*, prepared by Charles P. Howland (New Haven, 1929), p. 311.

[3] Gettell, *History of Political Thought*, p. 299.

[4] *Writings of Thomas Jefferson*, IV, 467.

[5] 39th Cong., 2d sess., *H. Ex. Doc.*, 1866-67, II, 414.

[6] Moore, *Digest*, VI, 403.

[7] *Cong. Globe*, 33d Cong., 1st sess., App., p. 1016.

[8] *Writings of Thomas Jefferson*, IX, 213.

[9] *Reg. of Debates*, 19th Cong., 1st sess., col. 2269.

[10] *Cong. Globe*, 30th Cong., 1st sess., App., p. 591.

[11] Richardson, *Messages*, V, 568.

[12] 37th Cong., 2d sess., *H. Ex. Doc.*, No. 100, p. 16.

[13] 39th Cong., 1st sess., *H. Ex. Doc.*, No. 73, II, 554.

[14] *For. Rel.*, 1882, p. 57.

[15] 49th Cong., 2d sess., *S. Ex. Doc.*, No. 64, p. 15.

[16] *Cong. Rec.*, 54th Cong., 1st sess., p. 263.

[17] *Ibid.*, p. 787.

[18] Moore, *Digest*, VI, 553.

[19] *Rept. of Comm. on For. Rel.*, VII, 55-56.

[20] *Ibid.*, p. 333.

[21] Moore, *Digest*, VI, 219.

[22] *Cong. Rec.*, 55th Cong., 2d sess., p. 2611.

[23] *Ibid.*, p. 2879.

[24] *Ibid.*, p. 3893.

[25] *Columbus Dispatch*, quoted by *Public Opinion*, XXIV (1898), 520.

[26] *Kansas City Times*, *ibid.*

[27] *Pittsburg Catholic*, *ibid.*, p. 519.

[28] Richardson, *Messages*, IX, 718.

[29] *For. Rel.*, 1898, p. 750.

[30] Representative Warner, *Cong. Rec.*, 55th Cong., 2d sess., p. 2619.

[31] Elbert J. Benton, *International Law and Diplomacy of the Spanish-American War* (Baltimore, 1908), p. 108.

[32] *For. Rel.*, 1898, p. 747.

[33] Halstead, *The History of American Expansion and the Story of Our New Possessions*, p. 29.

[34] Sumner Welles, *Naboth's Vineyard: the Dominican Republic 1844-1924* (New York, 1928), II, 916.

[35] Powers, *International Journal of Ethics*, X (1900), 295.

[36] Ferdinand Lion, *Grosse Politik* (Stuttgart, 1926), p. 137.

[37] Quoted by Ray Stannard Baker, *Woodrow Wilson: Life and Letters* (New York, 1931), IV, 287.

[38] Charles Denby, "The Doctrine of Intervention," *Forum*, XXVI (1898), 392.

[39] Williams, *Annals* of the American Academy of Political and Social Science, XVI (1900), 240.

[40] *Outlook*, LXVI (1900), 151.

[41] Conant, *The United States in the Orient*, p. 114.

[42] *For Rel.*, 1902, p. XX.

[43] Quoted by Millis, *The Martial Spirit*, p. 362.

[43a] Coolidge, *An Old-fashioned Senator*, p. 299.

[44] *Boston Journal*, quoted by *Public Opinion*, XXX (1901), 293.

[45] *Cong. Rec.*, 56th Cong., 2d sess., p. 3371.

[46] Roosevelt, *Outlook*, XCIX (1911), 318.

[47] Quoted by William Roscoe Thayer, *The Life of John Hay* (Boston, 1915), II, 327.

[48] Bunau-Varilla, *Panama*, p. 308.

[49] *Addresses and Presidential Messages of Theodore Roosevelt*, p. 6.

[50] Cortissoz, *The Life of Whitelaw Reid*, II, 292-93.

[51] Pringle, *Theodore Roosevelt*, p. 283.

[52] *Cong. Rec.*, 57th Cong., 2d sess., pp. 9-10.

[53] *Ibid.*, 58th Cong., 3d sess., p. 19.

[54] New York *Evening Post*, quoted by *Public Opinion*, XXXVI (1904), 681.

[55] *Providence Journal*, *ibid.*

[56] Howard C. Hill, *Roosevelt and the Caribbean* (Chicago, 1927), p. 197.

[57] Burgess, *Political Science and Comparative Constitutional Law*, I, 47.

[58] *Public Papers of Theodore Roosevelt, Governor* (Albany, 1899), pp. 304 ff.

[59] Hill, *op. cit.*, p. 207.

[60] Pringle, *op. cit.*, p. 295.

[61] *Cong. Rec.*, 59th Cong., 1st sess., p. 97.

[62] C. F. Dole, "The Right and Wrong of the Monroe Doctrine," *Atlantic Monthly*, XCV (1905), 571-72.

[63] *For. Rel.*, 1912, p. 1092.

[64] *Cong. Rec.*, 62d Cong., 3d sess., p. 9.

[65] Quoted by John Mabry Mathews, *American Foreign Relations; Conduct and Policies* (New York, 1928), pp. 55-56.

[66] *Speeches Incident to the Visit of Philander Chase Knox . . . to the Countries of the Caribbean* (Washington, 1913), p. 15.

[67] *For. Rel.*, 1912, p. 588.

[68] *Outlook*, "The United States and Mexico," XCVII (1911), 621.

[69] *Ibid.*

[70] *Selected Addresses and Public Messages of President Wilson*, ed. A. B. Hart (New York, 1918), p. 264.

[71] *For. Rel.*, 1916, p. 247.

[72] *Ibid.*, 1915, p. 481.

[73] *Cong. Rec.*, 63d Cong., 1st sess., p. 5845.

[74] *Ibid.*, 2d sess., p. 43.

[75] *The New Democracy; Presidential Messages, Addresses, and Other Papers (1913-1917), by Woodrow Wilson*, ed. R. S. Baker and W. E. Dodd (New York, 1926), II, 2.

[76] William B. Hale, "Our Moral Empire in America," *World's Work,* XXVIII (1914), 58.

[77] Edward H. Finlay, "The Decline of the Federal View," *Seven Seas Magazine*, I (November, 1915), 28.

[78] Jones, *Caribbean Interests of the United States*, pp. 341, 351.

[79] *Cong. Rec.*, 63d Cong., 2d sess., p. 8599.

[80] Baker, *op. cit.*, IV, 448.

[81] *Cong. Rec.*, 63d Cong., 1st sess., p. 3804.

[82] Usher, *The Challenge of the Future*, p. 294.

[83] Welles, *op. cit.*, II, 739.

[84] *Cong. Rec.*, 63d Cong., 1st sess., p. 5845.

[85] Henrik Shipstead, "'Dollar Diplomacy' in Latin America," *Current History*, XXVI (1927), 885.

[86] Ernest W. Gruening, "Conquest of Haiti and Santo Domingo," *ibid.*, XI (1922), 895.

[87] Charleston *News and Courier*, quoted by *Literary Digest*, LXII (August 9, 1919), 15.

[88] *Chicago Herald*, March 10, 1860.

[89] Olney, *Atlantic Monthly*, LXXXV (1900), p. 291.

[90] Quoted by Crichfield, *American Supremacy*, II, 561.

[91] *Baltimore American*, quoted by *Public Opinion*, XXXVI (1904), 104.

[92] Crichfield, *op. cit.*, II, 635.

[93] *Cong. Rec.*, 62d Cong., 1st sess., p. 949.

[94] *Independent*, "No Binding of Our Hands," LXXXVII (1916), 4.

[95] *New York American*, quoted by *Literary Digest*, LIII (1916), 2.

[96] *Cong. Rec.*, 63d Cong., 2d sess., App., p. 606.

[97] Weyth, *The Great Republic*, pp. 6-7.

[98] Raymond Leslie Buell, "The United States and Latin America," *Foreign Policy Association Information Service*, III, Spec. Supp., No. IV (1928), 79.

[99] *Cong. Rec.*, 69th Cong., 2d sess., p. 1324.

[100] *New York Times*, April 26, 1927.

[101] *Ibid.*

[102] *Cong. Rec.*, 69th Cong., spec. sess., p. 7.

[103] *New York Times*, January 15, 1928.

[104] *Washington Post*, quoted by *Literary Digest*, XCII (January 29, 1927), 8.

[105] *Cong. Rec.*, 69th Cong., 2d sess., p. 1661.

[106] *Ibid.*, p. 2266.

[107] H. W. Dodds, "The United States and Nicaragua," *Annals* of the American Academy of Political and Social Science, CXXXII (1927), 137.

[108] Senator McLean, *Cong. Rec.*, 69th Cong., 2d sess., p. 2227.

[109] *Reports of the Delegates of the United States of America to the Sixth International Conference of American States*, pp. 14-15.

[110] *Nation*, XCV (1912), 226.

[111] *Survey of American Foreign Relations, 1929*, p. 299.

[112] Hughes, *Our Relations to the Nations of the Western Hemisphere*, pp. 19, 84.

[113] Clark, *Memorandum on the Monroe Doctrine*, pp. xxv, xix.

[114] Rodick, *The Doctrine of Necessity in International Law*, p. 49.

[115] Dunn, *The Protection of Nationals*, chap. vi.

[116] Franklin D. Roosevelt, "Our Foreign Policy," *Foreign Affairs*, VI (1928), 585.

[117] *New York Times*, December 29, 1933.

[118] A. D. H. Smith, *A Manifest Destiny* (New York, 1926), p. 119.

[119] Hall, *A Treatise on International Law*, p. 348.

[120] Theodore Roosevelt, "Chili and the Monroe Doctrine," *Outlook*, CVI (1914), 636.

[121] Parker T. Moon, *Imperialism and World Politics* (New York, 1930), pp. 455-56.

## Notes to Chapter XV

## WORLD LEADERSHIP

[1] *Cong. Globe*, 27th Cong., 3d sess., App., p. 74.

[2] *Speeches and Addresses of William McKinley*, p. 302.

[3] 67th Cong., 2d sess., *S. Doc.*, No. 126, p. 12.

[4] *Current History*, III (1915), 488.

[5] Julius W. Pratt, "The Collapse of American Imperialism," *American Mercury*, XXXIII (1934), 269.

[6] Richardson, *Messages*, I, 222.

[7] *Ibid.*, p. 323.

[8] *Writings of Thomas Jefferson*, VIII, 98.

[9] *Am. State Papers, For. Rel.*, II, 559.

[10] *Annals of Cong.*, 11th Cong., 1st sess., cols. 579 ff.; 16th Cong., 1st sess., col. 2228.

[11] *Cong. Globe*, 32d Cong., 2d sess., p. 95.

[12] *Works of Charles Sumner*, XI, 221-22.

[13] *Cong. Globe*, 41st Cong., 3d sess., p. 194.

[14] Richardson, *Messages*, VIII, 327.

[15] *Ibid.*, IX, 461.

[16] John B. Henderson, Jr., *American Diplomatic Questions* (New York, 1901), p. 208.

[17] Representative Maynard, *Cong. Globe*, 40th Cong., 3d sess., p. 339.

[18] *Cong. Rec.*, 54th Cong., 1st sess., p. 420.

[19] Mahan, *Interest of America in Sea Power*, p. 104.

[20] *Ibid.*, p. 49.

[21] *Editorials of Henry Watterson*, p. 269.

[22] Olney, *Atlantic Monthly*, LXXXV (1900), 289.

[23] Mahan, *The Problem of Asia*, p. 7.

[24] *Public Opinion*, XXIV (1898), 613; *Outlook*, "The New Duties of the New Hour," LIX (1898), 211.

[25] Olney, *op. cit.*, p. 291.

[26] *Cong. Rec.*, 55th Cong., 2d sess., App., p. 546.

[27] *Ibid.*, 55th Cong., 2d sess., p. 5844.

[28] Boston *Transcript*, quoted by *Public Opinion*, XXV (1898), 41.

[29] Conant, *The United States in the Orient*, pp. 159-60.

[30] Coolidge, *An Old-fashioned Senator*, p. 292.

[31] John R. Proctor, "Isolation or Imperialism," *Forum*, XXVI (1898), 25.

[32] Quoted by Swift, *Imperialism and Liberty*, p. 102.

[33] *Public Papers of Theodore Roosevelt, Governor*, p. 298.

[34] Powers, *International Journal of Ethics*, X (1900), 304-05.

[35] 58th Cong., 2d sess., *S. Doc.*, No. 268, p. 9.

[36] John W. Foster, *Diplomatic Memoirs* (Boston, 1909), II, 257.

[37] Quoted by Callahan, *Cuba and International Relations*, p. 493.

[38] Reinsch, *World Politics at the End of the Nineteenth Century*, p. 311.

[39] *Cong. Rec.*, 56th Cong., 1st sess., p. 2630.

[40] *Ibid.*, p. 711.

[41] Bowers, *Beveridge and the Progressive Era*, p. 143.

[42] Patouillet, *L'impérialisme américain*, pp. 47-48.

[43] John Adams to Thomas Jefferson, November 15, 1813, *Writings of Thomas Jefferson*, ed. Washington, VI, 258.

[44] W. J. Sasnett, "The United States—Her Past and Her Future," *De Bow's Review*, XII (1852), 628.

[45] Representative Maynard, *Cong. Globe*, 40th Cong., 2d sess., App., p. 403.

[46] *Correspondence of Roosevelt and Lodge*, I, 400.

[47] Gertrude Atherton, "Denmark and the Treaty," *North American Review*, CLXXV (1902), 501.

[48] Richard Olney, "International Isolation of the United States," *Atlantic Monthly*, LXXXI (1898), 577 ff.

[49] Olney, *Atlantic Monthly*, LXXXV (1900), 296.

[50] Dennett, *John Hay*, pp. 335, 329-32.

[51] Reid, *Problems of Expansion*, p. 114.

[52] *For. Rel.*, 1900, p. 299.

[53] William Jennings Bryan and Mary Baird Bryan, *The Memoirs of William Jennings Bryan* (Chicago, 1925), p. 501.

[54] Wilson, *Atlantic Monthly*, XC (1902), 734.

[55] Baker, *Life and Letters of Woodrow Wilson*, IV, 85.

[56] *Cong. Rec.*, 57th Cong., 1st sess., App., p. 23.

[57] Dennett, *op. cit.*, p. 251.

[58] *Nation*, "Work for a Real 'World-Power,'" LXXVI (1903), 25.

[59] Roosevelt, *California Addresses*, p. 98.

[60] Shaw, *Political Problems of American Development*, p. 249.

[61] Albert Beveridge, *Americans of To-day and To-morrow* (Philadelphia, 1908), p. 9.

[62] *Providence Journal*, quoted by *Public Opinion*, XXXVI (1904), 104.

[63] Pringle, *Theodore Roosevelt*, p. 293.

[64] *For. Rel.*, 1905, p. 334.

[65] Frank B. Loomis, "The Attitude of the United States toward Other American Powers," *Annals* of the American Academy of Political and Social Science, XXVI (1905), 23.

[66] *Speeches Incident to the Visit of Philander Chase Knox . . . to the Countries of the Caribbean*, p. 57.

[67] *Cong. Rec.*, 62d Cong., 3d sess., p. 14.

[68] *American Journal of International Law*, IV (1910), 181.

[69] *Cong. Rec.*, 62d Cong., 1st sess., p. 948.

[70] *Ibid.*, p. 5845.

[71] *Ibid.*

[72] *New York Times*, January 30, 1916.

[73] *Ibid.*, January 7, 1916.

[74] *The Messages and Papers of Woodrow Wilson*, ed. Albert Shaw (New York, 1924), II, 1210.

[75] *Cong. Rec.*, 63d Cong., 1st sess., p. 5845.

[76] Baker, *op. cit.*, IV, 65.

[77] *New York Times*, January 7, 1916.

[78] *New Republic*, VII (1916), 313-14.

[79] Theodore Roosevelt, "Expansion and Peace," *Independent*, LI (1899), 3404.

[80] *Cong. Rec.*, 64th Cong., 1st sess., App., p. 1985.

[81] *Works of John Adams*, VIII, 178.

[82] *Cong. Rec.*, 64th Cong., 1st sess., p. 8854.

[83] *Ibid.*, 2d sess., p. 1743.

[84] Quoted by Denna Frank Fleming, *The United States and the League of Nations, 1918-1920* (New York, 1932), p. 352.

[85] *New York Times*, November 5, 1916.

[86] 65th Cong., 1st sess., *H. Doc.*, No. 1, p. 7.

[87] London *Daily Telegraph*, July 5, 1917.

[88] *Current History*, XII (1920), 28.

[89] *Cong. Rec.*, 66th Cong., 1st sess., p. 2339.

[90] *Ibid.*, 3d sess., p. 25.

[91] Remy de Gourmont, *Decadence and Other Essays on the Culture of Ideas*, tr. W. A. Bradley (New York, 1921), chap. i.

[92] Powers, *America Among the Nations*, p. 112.

[93] *Cong. Rec.*, 64th Cong., 1st sess., App., p. 146.

[94] George Nasmyth, "Isolation or World Leadership? America's Future Foreign Policy," *Annals* of the American Academy of Political and Social Science, LXVI (1916), 22 ff.

[95] Nicholas Murray Butler, "The International Mind: How to Develop it," *Proceedings of the Academy of Political Science*, VII (1917), 208-12.

[96] George H. Blakeslee, *The Recent Foreign Policy of the United States* (New York, 1925), p. 27.

[97] *Cong. Rec.*, 66th Cong., 2d sess., p. 3803.
[98] *Ibid.*, p. 3808.
[99] Fleming, *op. cit.*, pp. 374, 174.
[100] *Cong. Rec.*, 66th Cong., 1st sess., p. 3784.
[101] *Ibid.*, p. 798.
[102] *Ibid.*, p. 5942.
[103] *Selected Literary and Political Papers and Addresses of Woodrow Wilson* (New York, 1926-27), II, 399.
[104] F. D. Roosevelt, *Foreign Affairs*, VI (1928), 577.
[105] Quoted by Paul Scott Mowrer, *Our Foreign Affairs: a Study in National Interest and the New Diplomacy* (New York, 1926), p. 21.
[106] F. D. Roosevelt, *op. cit.*, p. 573.
[107] John Holladay Latané, *From Isolation to Leadership* (New York, 1922), p. 290.
[108] *New York Times*, November 5, 1922.
[109] 67th Cong., 2d sess., *S. Doc.*, No. 126, p. 10.
[110] F. D. Roosevelt, *op. cit.*, p. 581.
[111] *United States Democratic Review*, "American Civilization," XLII (1858), 52.
[112] 73d Cong., *U. S. Statutes at Large*, vol. LXVIII, pt. 2, p. 1717.
[113] *New York Times*, October 27, 1932.
[114] *Ibid.*, December 29, 1933.
[115] *Ibid.*, June 15, 1933.
[116] *Ibid.*, October 27, 1932.
[117] *Ibid.*, December 29, 1933.
[118] Kirby Page, *Dollars and World Peace: a Consideration of Nationalism, Industrialism and Imperialism* (New York, 1927), p. 57.
[118a] *New York Times*, October 27, 1932.
[119] *Ibid.*, October 2, 1932.
[120] *Ibid.*, April 30, 1933.
[121] *Discourses*, in *Writings of Machiavelli*, II, 422.
[122] *Cong. Rec.*, 64th Cong., 1st sess., p. 3308.
[123] *Discourses*, *loc. cit.*
[124] Wilson, *Atlantic Monthly*, XC (1902), 726.
[125] 66th Cong., 1st sess., *S. Doc.*, No. 120, p. 62.
[126] Nicholas Murray Butler, *The Path to Peace* (New York, 1930), p. 60.
[127] *New York Times*, August 9, 1932.
[128] *Cong. Rec.*, 69th Cong., spec. sess., p. 5.
[129] Lothrop Stoddard, *Lonely America* (New York, 1932), p. 297.
[130] William Archibald Dunning, *Political Theories from Rousseau to Spencer* (New York, 1925), p. 68.
[131] *United States Democratic Review*, "Democratic Policy—the Empire," XLII (1858), 362.
[132] *Cong. Rec.*, 64th Cong., 1st sess., p. 3308.
[133] Cicero, *De officiis*, iii, 99 (Chitty tr. of Vattel's quotation).

[134] Max Farrand, ed., *The Records of the Federal Convention of 1787* (New Haven, 1911), I, 135.

[135] *Writings of Thomas Jefferson*, X, 69.

[136] *Cong. Rec.*, 66th Cong., 1st sess., p. 5940.

[137] *United States Democratic Review*, "The Verdict of the People of the United States," XXXVIII (1856), 355.

[138] Senator Cass, *Cong. Globe*, 32d Cong., 2d sess., App., p. 94.

[139] Mowrer, *op. cit.*, p. 49.

[140] Whitman, *Leaves of Grass*, pp. 286, 291.

# INDEX OF NAMES

# INDEX OF SUBJECTS